知の新視界

脱領域的アプローチ

二〇〇三年三月二十五日　第一刷発行

編著者　秋山正幸
発行者　南雲一範
発行所　株式会社南雲堂
　　　　東京都新宿区山吹町三六一　郵便番号一六二-〇八〇一
　　　　電話　（〇三）三二六八-二三八四〔営業〕
　　　　　　　（〇三）三二六八-二三八七〔編集〕
　　　　振替口座　東京〇〇一六〇-四六八六三
　　　　ファクシミリ　（〇三）三二六〇-五四二五
装丁者　木庭貴信（オクターヴ）
印刷所　壮光舎印刷株式会社
製本所　長山製本

落丁・乱丁本は、御面倒ですが小社通販係宛御送付ください。送料当社負担にて御取替えいたします。

IB-280　〈検印廃止〉

©2003 Masayuki Akiyama
ISBN4-523-29280-9 C3098

New Intellectual Prospects
Cross-disciplinary Approaches

Edited with an Introduction
by
Masayuki Akiyama

NAN'UN-DO
TOKYO

CONTENTS

Introduction — 009(742)
Masayuki Akiyama

01

The Fiction of Oe and Gao, — 015(732)
or, Portraying
the Here and the Now
A. Owen Aldridge

02

The Life and Adventures of — 037(714)
***Martin Chuzzlewit*:**
A Tale of Two Cultures
Yiu-nam Leung

03

The Italian Cinderella Type — 053(698)
in the 17th-century Japanese Tales
Chieko Mulhern

04

Speak, Memory! — 071(680)
Edo Netsuke in Their Literary Context
Haruko G. Iwasaki

05

From Proselytization to Assimilation: — 105(646)
New French and German Fictional
Approach to Jesuit China Missions
Adrian Hsia

06
The Underestimated Strength of Cultural Identity
Between Localising and Globalising Tendencies in the European Union

Rien T. Segers

123(628)

07
Comparative Literature: Globalization and Hegemony

John T. Dorsey

155(596)

08
Nightmare Come True: Postmodern Paranoia and Terrorism

Naomi Matsuoka

169(582)

09
Myth in *Black Elk Speaks* and *Aterui*: The Empowering Matrix

Adam Lebowitz

185(566)

10
Baltic Security: A View from Altruism

Toshiyasu Ishiwatari

205(546)

Notes on Contributors   219(532)

II

Introduction

Masayuki Akiyama

New Intellectual Prospects:Cross-disciplinary Approaches is a compilation of essays by the members of The Comparative Culture and Literature Society of Nihon University, my colleagues of the College of International Relations of Nihon University, and other scholars who have generously agreed to contribute to this interdisciplinary publication.

The Comparative Culture and Literature Society was founded in December, 1987, on which occasion I explained its purpose as follows:

> The significance of comparative culture and literature studies lies in the investigation of possibilities and methods for mutual understanding among different cultures. In this sense the foundation of the Comparative Culture and Literature Society of Nihon University is important in the era of information and internationalization. It is the mission of the Society to promote objective studies of different cultures, and, in doing so, to foster peaceful coexistence in the world.

In the fourteen years since the Society's founding, the world has continued to change dramatically, as symbolized by the fall of the Berlin Wall and the end of the Cold War. In *The Clash of Civilizations and the Remaking of World Order*, Samuel Huntington writes as follows:

> In the late 1980s the communist world collapsed, and the Cold War internationl system became history. In the post-Cold War world, the most important distinctions among peoples are not ideological, political, or economic. They are cultural. (21)
>
> In sum, the post-Cold War world is a world of seven or eight major civilizations. Cultural commonalities and differences shape the interests, antagonisms, and associations of states. The most important countries in the world come overwhelmingly from different civilizations. The local conflicts most likely to escalate into broader wars are those between groups and states from different civilizations. The predominant patterns of political and economic developmemt differ from civilization to civilization. The key issues on the international agenda involve differences among civilizations. Power is shifting from the long predominant West to non-Western civilizations. Global politics has become multipolar and multicivilizational. (29)

He continues, "In the clash of civilizations, Europe and America will hang together or hang separately. In the greater clash, the global "*real* clash," between Civilization and barbarism, the world's great civilizations, with their rich accomplishments in religion, art, literature, philosophy, science, technology, morality, and compassion, will also hang together or hang separately. In the emerging era, clashes of civilizations are the greatest threat to world peace, and an international order based on civilizations is the surest safeguard against world war." (321)

010(741)

There have been many critiques of Huntington's thesis, and I myself have reservations about it. Nevertheless it seems especially relevant to some who see at present a clash between Islam and Western Civilization. The terrorist attacks on the World Trade Center, the symbol of the economic power of the U.S., and the Pentagon, the symbol of its military power, on September 11, 2001 shook the world.

It is said that the terrorist groups which support the radical Islamic fundamentalist Osama bin Laden exist in several countries and are trying to construct a global network of violence. Some specialists argue that the terrorist attacks constituted a direct challenge against the U.S., the leading representative of Western Civilization. It is also true, however, that poverty and huge gaps in standards of living have contributed to the rise of terrorism. In such an era, it is important to establish an interdependent international society that includes all races and nations. We must join together in the resolution of worldwide issues such as environmental pollution and poverty as well as in the promotion of free trade and democracy.

As globalization advances, cultures gradually assimilate, but it should not be forgotten that individual cultural identities still exist. It is important for us to promote adequate understanding of other cultures while maintaining our own cultural identities. If we become self-centered, however, we will invite conflicts and aggravate "the clash of civilizations." In *Understanding Different Cultures*, Tamotsu Aoki writes, "It is better not to debate about choosing one alternative: globalization or the clash of civilizations" (136). Each ethnic group has a cultural identity that is passed down, despite changes, and remains deeply rooted. The Japanese view of death, for example, is related to Buddhism and is influenced significantly by the idea of transience, and this, at the bottom of the Japanese heart, has profoundly affected the Japanese view of nature and aesthetics. For this reason, it would be very difficult for outsiders to appreciate the true Japanese spirit without understanding the Japanese view of transience and how intimately Japan's lifestyle is related to nature.

While we must therefore hold up democracy as a universal principle to construct peace, at the same time it is important to understand respective cultural identities, which is the first step toward peaceful coexistence of all ethnic groups. Such understanding requires great patience and effort.

In the 21st century, we need to work not only to understand the conflict between globalization and cultural identities but also to create harmonious relationships. For example, environmental issues need to be dealt with from a global point of view, but we also need to understand the cultural identities of individual ethnic groups. This is why interdisciplinary studies are so important. *New Intellectual Prospects* has been compiled to respond to this call. The articles here concern various academic issues from the past to the present day, and, as a whole, the collection offers a "cross-disciplinary approach."

It is a great pleasure for me to include here essays by A. Owen Aldridge, Professor Emeritus of the University of Illinois, who has long been my teacher and friend. I would like to extend my gratitude to all of the scholars who have responded to my call by writing essays of such high academic quality in their respective fields of study.

It will be a source of great pleasure for me if the innovative ideas expressed in *New Intellectual Prospects* can help lead to peace and coexistence in the present era of confusion and uncertainty.

I would like to thank Mr. Nobuo Hara of Nan'un-do Publishing Company who has closely supported this project and, indeed, made it possible.

Finally, it is a great honor to mention the name of the President of Nihon University, Yukiyasu Sezai, MD, who has enthusiastically encouraged me to conduct research in comparative culture and literature.

Works Cited

Aoki, Tamotsu. *Ibunka Rikai* (Understanding Other Cultures). Tokyo: Iwanami, 2001.

Huntington, Samuel. *The Clash of Civilizations and the Remaking of World Order.* New York: Touchstone, 1997.

The Fiction of Oe and Gao, or, Portraying the Here and the Now

A. Owen Aldridge

It is a commonplace to label the literature of the last few decades of the twentieth century as postmodern, following the example of commentators on architecture and the pictorial arts, who regularly apply the term to esthetic novelty, experimentation and professional independence. In my opinion, however, the term is a meaningless and illogical cliché. "Whatever is, is," to borrow a phrase from Alexander Pope, and everything after the present is the future pure and simple. The adjective post can be applied rationally to events and conditions only when they have appeared after others existing previously, as in post-romantic. An American statesman, Eugene McCarthy, has rejected the term post-modern in the political sense. In his words, modernism has "always indicated the 'now' and could not be 'past,' unless the word was to be fixed as having no future use. There could never be a 'post-modernism.'"[1] The present essay, designed to compare the themes and literary devices used by two recent Nobel Prize Laureates, a Japanese, Oe Kenzaburo, and a Chinese, Gao Xinjian, will focus on presumed departures from literary conventions and rank them under the rubric of the here and the now rather than that of post-modern. In so doing, I shall stress universal elements rather than transitory ones that are associated with artificial chronological boundaries.[2]

Gao in his Nobel acceptance speech specifically rejects the emphasis on chronological novelty, affirming that "an aesthetic based on human emotions does not become outdated even with the perennial changing of fashions in literature and in art." He charges that "literary evaluations that fluctuate like fashions," that is, those that are "premised on what is the latest: that is, whatever is new is good" are reacting to "a mechanism in general market movements" from which the book market is not exempted. "If the writer's esthetic judgment follows market movements it will mean the suicide of literature."

Oe, whose fiction strays considerably further from the traditional than Gao's, does not specifically reject chronologically-based evaluations, but he insists fervently upon an esthetic based solidly on individual human emotions. His Nobel speech, like his fiction, is highly subjective. He even asks to be forgiven for declaring that the "fundamental style of my writing has been to start from my personal matters and then to link it up with society, the state and the world." He also specifically describes himself as "one of the writers who wish to create serious works of literature which disassociate themselves from those novels which are mere reflections of the vast consumer cultures of Tokyo and the subcultures of the world at large."

Both Gao and Oe in their Nobel speeches soberly emphasize their need to express the individual personality, and Oe does this as well in his fiction in a dramatic and sensational manner. The two major themes of Oe's work — almost fixed ideas — are the problems associated with caring for a son, Hikari, who is afflicted with a mental disability, and the dangers of a universal holocaust inherent in nuclear research. In his speech he explains how Hikari remained mute until the age of six when he responded to the chirping of birds by actual words and subsequently, still under the spell of birds, became a musician and composer. He pays tribute to his literary mentor Watanabe Kazuo and to Kawabata Yasunari, an earlier Japanese recipient of the Nobel Prize. In addition to his purely personal revelations, Oe indicates his painful reaction to the ambiguous effects of the modernization of Japan through its contact with the West. Although the nation has retained its traditional Asiatic culture, Western influence on its economy and political structure, he fears, have led to isolation from its neighboring countries, a condition exacerbated by its collapse in the last war. On the positive side, Japan's defeat offered its people a moral "rebirth" based upon the conception of democracy and the renunciation of war embodied in its new constitution. As accompanying these "moral props," Oe adds widespread opposition to the use of nuclear weapons. He deplores a remaining ambiguity, however, in the survival of support for the old constitution together with a burgeoning ambiguity associated with the nation's economic prosperity and environmental precautions. In order to define "a desirable Japanese identity" he adopts from George Orwell the adjective "decent," using it as closely related to "humanist," which he associates with his literary mentor Watanabe. "The brotherhood of world literature" he relates to recent efforts in China and elsewhere in Asia to retain fundamental human freedoms. He adopts from the West, moreover, many of his own literary techniques, unfortunately becoming in the process somewhat neglected by his own countrymen.

On the surface, Gao's ideals and principles seem to be partly opposed to Oe's. He affirms somewhat elliptically that "literature is not concerned with politics but is purely a matter of the intellect together with an observation, a review of what has been experienced, reminiscences and feeling or the portrayal of a state of mind." This sounds more like the style of Proust than that of any contemporary writer including Gao himself. It can perhaps be explained, however, as primarily a protest against the ideologies enforced by a dictatorial political regime such as that existing in China during his entire lifetime. He maintains that "the writer is not a hero acting on orders from the people nor is he worthy of worship as an idol [a sentiment often expressed by Oe as well] and certainly he is not a criminal or enemy of the people... . When the authorities need to manufacture a few enemies to divert other people's attention, writers become sacrifices and worse still writers who have been duped actually think it is a great honour to be sacrificed." Although Gao does not use specific terms such as "decent," "comely," or "humanist," to describe the ideals of literature, he indirectly suggests the same qualities. Literature's "own criteria of merit," he says, is "its esthetic quality." Although estheticism depends upon individual judgments based upon different emotional constituencies, "aesthetic judgments do have universally recognized standards." The power of language allows communication between individuals, even those of different cultures and times. It is through this process of sharing times and places that literature acquires its "eternal spiritual values." Rather than fashionable Western criticism of the past few decades, this strongly resembles Irving Babbitt and the New Humanism of the 1920s.

Gao places content over style in unambiguous terms. "It is a writer's insights in grasping truth that determines the quality of a work and word games or writing techniques cannot serve as subusitutes." He, nevertheless, cites Kafka as a prime example of "spiritual activity" even though the latter's work is noted more for form and structure than intellectual content. Oe does not introduce the topic of structural techniques, although he seems to have experienced considerable delight in featuring shocking and ludic ones in some of his works. No single technique appears in all of his fiction, however, no doubt a deliberate display of versatility.

In my subsequent remarks, I shall limit myself to a single novel by each author. Oe's novel that seems to be the least conventional or most experimental is *Pinchi ranna chosho*, published in 1976, but not translated into English until 1994 as *The Pinch Runner Memorandum*, a title that in itself reveals an unconventional approach. The only one of Gao's two novels so far to be translated into English (*Soul Mountain*, 2000) was published originally in Chinese in Taiwan as *Lingshan*, 1990; in Swedish as *Andarnasberg*, 1992, and in French as *La Montagne de l'ame*, 1995. Although both novels are autobiographical in the sense of casting the author as the primary character and tracing major events in his life, neither one can be classified as belonging completely to the Japanese genre of the I-novel. Generally speaking, the I-novel reveals completely the personality, emotions, motivations, triumphs, and failures of the narrator, who is identified as the author. Rather than the pictorial or historical reality of his surroundings, the perspective of the novel portrays the author's private world. Gao does not even consistently use first person pronouns to refer to his protagonist, a characteristic I shall return to later in my remarks. Both novels, moreover, cover a range of subject matter far exceeding the psychological limits of any individual consciousness, embracing the landscape, political organization, religion, philosophy, social contacts, sex and family relationships. The autobiographical content of these novels consists in revealing the major intellectual occupations of each author, his attitude toward nature and the cosmos along with the political system of his native country. Oe also follows the I-novel in exploring intimate relations with the members of his own family, an area conspicuously absent in Gao. All that we know about his private life is that he is a Chinese male academic of middle age who seeks casual but frequent sex, who finds philosophical and esthetic release in exploring mountain heights, and had earlier been diagnosed with cancer, a minor parallel with the protagonist of *Pinch Runner*. Gao's Nobel Prize speech tells us little more about himself, not even whether he is or ever has been married, or even whether he has any other family connections. Oe, however, in both his Stockholm speech and in his novel goes beyond rudimentary and mundane details to reveal his most profound emotional contacts, especially those with his mentally-handicapped son. In a later work, he suggests that his life has been a "long career of writing about himself for a wide readership." (*A Quiet Life*, p.123) All the events in *Pinch Runner* are associated with a single identifiable protagonist whereas it is not clear whether the protagonist of *Soul Mountain* is an individual or a composite figure. Nor is it clear whether the protagonist is to be identified with the author — a relationship that is constantly clear in *Pinch Runner*.

Whatever elements of novelty or experiment are to be found in either author derive from artifices of rhetoric, those of structure and style, in contrast to the complementary elements drawn from real life activities, those based upon character and plot, which are more universal, depending upon human nature and its intricacies. The latter have been the subject matter of previous world masterpieces. Only cultural, scientific, political and social developments change with the centuries, and these are ordinarily adumbrated in connection with human personality. Oe's title *Pinch Runner Memorandum* does not even remotely suggest his twin topics of personal relations with his handicapped son and his opposition to further development of the A-bomb. The title refers to the strategy in a game of baseball in which a fast runner is substituted for an elderly hitter already on base to complete the run while the fans shout "go-go" in order to increase his speed. The situation, which has nothing to do with actual events in the novel, is intended merely as a metaphor to support the author in his paternal and humanitarian efforts. In a previous novel, *A Personal Matter*, Oe exposes in a fairly conventional style the heartaches of the protagonist over the birth of a son with a cranial deformity, leaving him incapable of speech, and this father's struggle to reach the point of accepting the child with appropriate love and care into his family circle. *The Pinch Runner* takes up the fortunes of the child, Hikari, at the age of 8, when he has gradually developed an incredibly subtle musical talent. In both novels he is also known as *Mori*, which in Japanese means *forest* and in English translation is associated with the Latin *mori*, relating to both death and idiocy.

Pinch Runner opens with the narrator's recollection of a dialogue with a "former nuclear power plant engineer" concerning amateur baseball and his own primitive attempts at pinch running. Memory of the exhortations of his teammates, "Go, Go, Go," had stimulated his later ambitions and attempts to carve a successful career. The narrator and the nuclear physicist come together on the school grounds, where each is calling for his own mentally retarded son, each parent representing the author. Whether instantaneously or almost immediately afterwards, the narrator-protagonist is duplicated, becoming himself and another personality named Mori-father. The latter could, but not necessarily, represent Oe before recognizing his sons's musical potentialities. They engage in a number of subsequent conversations on topics associated with theories of psychology and the education of children with mental disabilities during which the protagonist engages Mori-father to become his "ghost-writer" while he retains his own identity. Oe does not use the word "schizophrenia," but this condition would seem to have some relationship to the situation, the novelty of which derives from the separation of the narrator into two personalities. I shall later comment on the degree of its novelty. Oe used this device of double narrators or "the stratification of a verbal account" in several later novels.[3] In *Pinch Runner*, the ghost writer records the words of the other, the memorandum of the title — "yet filters them through his own consciousness and his own flesh." (34) Along with this process, the narrator "steals" into Mori-father's "secret world," grasping the "essence of his existence," but at the same time he objects to the notion of Mori-father occupying his own world. From this point on, however, the ghost writer predominates. He has a dream in which he and Mori help an old man they call the Patron gain absolute political power in Japan. In explaining the dream to Mori, he suggests that the Patron's power, like Hitler's, came as a result of the Cosmic Will. The ghost-writer breaks in as he continues to do throughout the novel — raising various objections. The father associates the politics of nuclear power with his brain-damaged son, arguing that a chance exposure to radiation in his own past had brought about harmful cells forming in his son's brain. Then in a drawn-out episode resembling hallucination but presented as an actual occurrence, Mori and his father exchange both physical and psychological identities, Mori eventually becoming almost a clone of his father and the latter reverting to the age of 18 physically, but retaining intact his adult memory and psychological personality. Oe describes this process as a switch-over, apparently referring to the metaphor of the pinch runner, involving two beings of different physical attributes working together for a common purpose.

This binary playfulness, first, by the duplication of the narrator as both the I character and an anonymous observer and, second, by the switch-over between father and son, initially seems to be a radical departure from tradition. The foremost of these devices, however, can be found as far back as the eighteenth century in Laurence Sterne's English novel *Tristram Shandy* in which the narrator may be Tristram in his mother's womb or Tristram after he has become an adult of dubious age. It may not be entirely coincidental that in England today, a beverage composed of half beer and half lemonade is familiarly called a "shandy." The Mexican novelist Carlos Fuentes several years after the publication of *Pinch Runner* greatly expanded the treatment of a speaking fetus in his *Cristobal Nonato*, 1987 (in English *Christopher Unborn*, 1989). The device of the switch-over or change in physical identity is even more common in previous literature, a variant of the notion of metamorphosis made famous in the West by Ovid and a host of imitators, including Kafka. In North America, Philip Roth's *The Breast*, 1972, has a male mammary gland as its narrator-protagonist.

As Oe's action continues, the father's physical impediments and blemishes are healed, but he retains his adult memories in the body of an eighteen-year old. This leaves father and son with almost equivalent physical and mental qualities, and they henceforth interact as contemporaries. No corresponding structural transformations exist in Gao — his characters retain a permanent identity just as his chapter divisions retain a more or less standard length. As he observes in his Nobel acceptance speech, the only structural-stylistic idiosyncrasy of his prose is grammatical. "In my fiction I use pronouns instead of the usual characters and also use the pronouns I, you, and he to tell about or to focus on the protagonist. The portrayal of the one character by using different pronouns creates a sense of distance." (7) Accepting that the creation of a sense of distance is a viable technique for fiction, the translator of the English edition of *Soul Mountain* affirms that the author engages in conversations with characters who are "projections of his self" in order "to tell the stories of many different types of people who populate China, but yet who in the final analysis can be found in all cultures and societies." (ix) Other commentators feel that this universality or rather homogeneity detracts from the realism of Gao's characters as opposed to Oe's, despite the grotesque features of some of the latter. The portrayal of characters as abstract or generalized rather than individualistic can obviously not be considered a contemporary or even a recent development, moreover, going back in China as it does at least as far as *Journey to the West* and in Europe to morality plays of the Middle Ages such as *Everyman*. Oe also experiments briefly with the switching of pronouns. The subject *you* in the first paragraph of *The Pinch Runner*, for example, turns into the first person of the second with no commentary of any kind.

Gao traces the invention of pronouns to a period of mere collective consciousness of the two sexes. Apparently agreeing with some linguists that a written language preceded speech, he affirms that "Mankind's earliest concepts are derived from totems, afterwards these came to be linked with sounds to form speech and meanings." (307) Although including a good deal of local anthropology in his novel, Gao makes no pretense of interpreting the human condition. Indeed in the final paragraph of *Soul Mountain*, he admits that he understands nothing of his condition or whereabouts even though pretending that he does. "The fact of the matter is I comprehend nothing. I understand nothing."

Soul Mountain, nevertheless, belongs to the genre of pilgrimage or quest literature such as works about the Holy Grail or "following the gleam" in Europe or *Journey to the West* in China. The protagonist seeks a mountain named Lingshan on the peak of which he hopes to find mystic or supernatural enlightenment. Lingshan is not a real mountain in any country or on any map, but a creation of Gao's imagination, a composite of a number of real and fictional areas. In Chinese "ling" means "spirit" or "soul" and "shan" is "mountain." In his wanderings, the protagonist does not pursue a definite itinerary keyed to any time or space frame, but engages in a series of mental or physical experiences not necessarily taking place in an orderly sequence. The chapters in the book resemble a collection of vignettes which are neither chronological episodes nor flashbacks, but which could stand independently or be arranged in a different order at will. Some of the sites he describes are actual places, but others are unnamed and unidentified. Lingshan is a metaphor for memory, consciousness and aspiration. The mountain as a source of mystical experience is parallel with Thomas Mann's equally imaginary *Magic Mountain*, and the amorphous sensations being sought could be compared to those in Kawabata's *Sound of the Mountain*.

Pinch Runner, in contrast, is not pastoral, but highly urban, most of the action taking place in Tokyo. After the switch-over Mori and the father seem to develop a relationship like that between an older and a younger brother with the father as the 18-year-old. When one of his former girl friends calls on the telephone, he pretends as a joke that he has left on a trip with Mori. He taunts the woman with highly-pornographic and demeaning descriptions of her most recent sexual encounters. Suddenly father and son are attending a demonstration against nuclear power led by the Patron. When fighting breaks out between pro and anti-factions, they support the opposition.

The narrator's involvement in the anti-nuclear movement is partly personal, partly developed from relations with Mori-father's mistress, and partly a reaction to the personality of the Patron, who is somehow linked to America and Korea. At an anti-nuclear demonstration, Mori-father accidentally delivers a devastating blow to the Patron, who is then taken to a hospital. Here the Patron removes a huge bag of money from his clothing, with which he attempts to persuade Mori-father to devote toward continued production of the A-bomb. The climax and denouement follow immediately linked together in a short space. Mori seizes the money bag, escapes from the building pursued by the Patron's bodyguards. While his father shouts "go-go," Mori casts the bag into a ceremonial fire in front of the hospital, following its path with his own body and instantly perishes. This ending is stark and gloomy in contrast to the spirit of levity accompanying the many grotesque, weird and cynical episodes in the body of the novel. The son is a victim and a martyr, the father a grieving survivor. This is a closure without a solution. Happily Mori comes to life again in a subsequent novel, *A Quiet Life*, which presents a harmonious and fulfilled family circle.

Gao's ending has none of Oe's sensationalism, remaining true to his rhetorical strategy of separate chapters without plot or character development. His final chapter to contain elements of narrative recounts a conversation with three visitors, each of whom asks him for a favor. The last chapter of all consists of a Buddhist-like self-dialogue over the concept of knowledge in which he admits that although he knows everything, he actually comprehends nothing, understands nothing. This absolute Pyrrhonism blends with the unrelieved seriousness of the text as a whole.

As I have already indicated, the narrator in both novels is understood to be the author himself, and both texts treat personal affairs as well as his view of the universe. Gao has an entire chapter devoted to what he calls "this strange thing the self." (Chap.26, p.150) Concomitant with his perception of his own identity as constantly changing, he perceives several different personalities during his self-analyses. When regarding his photograph he has varying interpretations of the meaning of his features, and when he regards other people he looks for characteristics belonging to himself, arriving at the conclusion that "the self is in fact the source of mankind's misery." (152) He quotes the Buddhist aphorism that "the myriad phenomena are vanity, the absence of phenomena is also vanity." Gao also cites the Taoist interpretation that in primitive times there was no awareness of individuality or the distinction between "you" or "not you." The concept of "I" derived from the fear of death, and the opposite "you" as "not I" came subsequently. Later a third person "he" was gradually recognized as existing everywhere in large numbers, and then the consciousness of "I" and "you" as separate entities became secondary. In the struggle for survival, the self was gradually forgotten, "churned like a grain of sand into the chaos of the boundless universe." (308) This reduction of the individual has ingredients similar to Oe's identity switching and the ambiguity of figures like the Patron.

Oe's Nobel speech entitled "Japan, the Ambiguous, and Myself," contains much more information about Japan than about himself.

His assertion that his writing style starts with himself is offered almost apologetically, and he keeps other revelations under control. After a few details concerning his childhood and his problems with Hikari, he turns to the political and economic history of Japan during the past half century. He literally asks "What kind of identity as a Japanese should I seek?" (7) Gao, however, devotes himself almost entirely to his personal identity even though he cannot consistently be equated with his narrator. Despite the abstractedness of his title "The Case for Literature," he professes in the body of his speech to speak as an authentic individual, not as the representative of any nation, political party, class or group. He affirms that literature as such is primarily "derived from the feelings of the individual and is the result of feelings." He argues that "talking to oneself is the start of literature" and communication by language is only secondary. "Literature is inherently man's affirmation of the value of his own self" and his "need for self-fulfillment." (p.2) It "transcends national boundaries" and makes "profound revelations about the universality of human nature." (3) Even though the reader may not always sense the intense individualism of *Soul Mountain*, Gao indicates that the work belongs to the type of literature that is purely a matter of personal isolation." "It is the gratification of the intellect together with an observation, a review of what has been experienced, reminiscences and feelings or the portrayal of a state of mind." (p.4) Not everyone admires this type of writing, but it is not likely to be considered as innovative. Nor will another aspect of Gao's individualism, the doctrine that "literature is simply man focusing his gaze on his self and while he does a thread of consciousness which sheds light on this self begins to grow." (p.6) It is a direct consequence of this view that in his own fiction he uses pronouns instead of the names of characters as well as the grammatical case of all pronouns indiscriminately in referring to the protagonist. (p.7)

Oe, to the contrary, develops the sociological more than the psychological aspects of the self, treating the individual as a member of various groups. His relations with Mori, including the metaphor of the switch-over, indicate his profound sense of family ties and obligations, and his opposition to further nuclear development reveals an equivalent recognition of social obligation. He seems at the end of the novel to burlesque the antinomy between self and society, however, by means of an argument between firemen and civilians over whether burning a religious ceremonial bonfire in the midst of Tokyo should be permitted. (233)

Gao seems to override this self-society antinomy by means of his grammatical freedom. He specifically maintains that "the I of the writer can be the writer himself, can be equated to the narrator, or become the characters of a work. As the narrator-subject can also be he and you, it is tripartite." Oe through his ghost writer has a more encompassing tripartite scheme, consisting of "me and you who transcribe my accounts" and a third party, "the unspecified number of readers." (97) Gao's grammatical eccentricity represents his major departure from tradition along with his complete disregard for chronological order. Instead of a series of episodes leading to a climax or a solution, his chapters are completely independent vignettes linked only by the theme of the mountain, its inhabitants, and the mysteries surrounding it. Gao argues that literature may change, but only because of the limitless capacity of expression possessed by language. "There is no substance to flippant announcements of the death of certain genres of literature" such as fiction or the drama. (Nobel speech p.7) "The writer is not the creator of the world neither can he bring it to an end. (Science-fiction writers pay heed!) The writer, however, can certainly make innovative statements either adding to what earlier people have said or else starting where other people stopped." In his novel, Gao compares the writer playing with words to "a child playing with blocks. But blocks can only construct fixed patterns, the possibilities of structures are inherent in the blocks and no matter how they are moved you will not be able to make anything new." (p.351)

The opening chapter of *Soul Mountain* describes a passenger dismounting from a bus in a mountain town in Southern China and becoming acquainted with its inhabitants. The next chapter finds him half way up a mountain in the border area of the Qinghai-Tibetan highlands. He explains that he is trying to escape earlier "contaminated surrouundings" that had tried to convince him that "literature had to be faithful to life, faithful to real life," a reference to the official line during the Communist regime. He argues that this literary doctrine covers only "the manifestations of life" but that real life is composed of more basic substance, presumably referring to nature and its mysteries as treated in transcendental philosophy.

Toward the end of his novel, Gao devotes an entire chapter to a defense of his fictional technique against an imaginary critic who condemns it. (Chap.72) This disgruntled critic charges that the book is not a complete story — merely a collection of episodes not organized into foreshadowing, climax and conclusion. The author maintains, to the contrary, that a story could have parts in any sequence as well as parts that do not need to be completed. When the critic complains about the lack of a protagonist and major characters, the author points to his pronouns; he does not wish to go beyond them to create personalities, not even knowing whether he is a personality himself. When he asks the critic to define fiction as he sees it, the critic seems defeated and snarls, "This is modernist, [notice: not post-modernist!] it's imitating the West but falling short." When the author suggests the alternate view that it is Eastern — and that none of the Chinese writings through the ages have ever had any fixed models, the critic calls him a nihilist and departs in despair. The author then engages in his own speculation on the nature of fiction — its relation to language and rhetoric, to the self, to anthropology, to sex, to life and death, and even to "the worship of idols by atheists." (452-54) All of these motifs are exploited in Gao's text, some of them related to language and the self which we have already touched upon. One of the few elements of fiction not listed by Gao is that of creating an atmosphere, one of the major characterisics of *Soul Mountain*.

Gao's mountain traveler's primary motivation seems to be the assuaging of a spiritual urge, but he also portrays the secular curiosity of anthropology. While visiting a camp of Yi singers, he hears a dirge that leads him to inquire into the funeral ceremonies of the Yi people. He then proceeds to summarize recent research on the connection between the Yi and the Han. In another location he acquires a historic stone axe, but under the influence of liquor leaves it behind when he moves on. (Chap.20) Elsewhere he describes a ceremonial exorcist mask he encounters in a remote museum (Chap.24) and completes a list of other areas where similar museum masks had been gathered. He distinguishes between sex and love in the origins of dragon boat music (228), describes aspects of Taoist ritual from an anthropological perspective (242, 402), and portrays his attitude toward Buddhism at the time when he believed he was suffering from cancer. (71)

Unlike Oe, Gao does not manifest his views of politics or political theory in specific declarations, but weaves into his text occasional references to recent history, for example, to the Cultural Revolution. (10) This is perhaps because of his broader general theme of the mystical mountain. On the subject of sex, however, he is scarcely less inhibited than Oe. He recounts a far larger number of amatory encounters, but does so chiefly through extended conversations between the participants composed of realistic anatomical terms, neither euphemistic nor offensive, rather than references likely to arouse libidinous reactions. He seems to be more interested in the intellectual process of his various feminine companions — mostly pick-ups — than in his own physical enjoyment. Nearly every woman in his narrative is a sex object, but he makes no pretense of masculine superiority. He finds comfort and self-assurance rather than titillation in his encounters. In one of his primitivistic moods, he suggests that so-called civilization "separated sexual impulse from love and created the concepts of status, wealth, religion, ethics, and cultural responsibility." (228) Presumably in reference to ancient beliefs, he recounts his adventure in a mountain village with a girl who turns out to be a shuhuapo, a species of beautiful females resembling ancient Greek sirens, possessing mystical sexual powers. (Chap.12) In a dialogue with three sexual participants instead of the usual pair, a lawyer argues that soliciting for illicit sexual activities is not a criminal offense and that if "having sexual urges is criminal then all human being are guilty." (427, 428)

Oe's treatment of sex is far more blatant and grotesque than Gao's, occasionally bordering on the pornographic. This is one of the characteristics of his ludic style, stemming partly from Rabelais, whom he designates as one of the French humanists studied by his mentor Watanabe. A few examples should suffice. After acquiring his 18-year-old body he has with his former mistress what he calls "the best orgasm" of his life, describing in detail the positions and activities of each of their body parts. (93) Elsewhere he portrays her being forced to masturbate with a Coke bottle. (147) While he is in the care of a hospital masseuse, he gradually shifts their positions in order to engage in oral sex. (139) In a humorous mood, he describes the female sex organ as "the gash gouged by the devil's claw." (125) Although these ludicrous physiological passages are presented in realistic and graphic language, they partake of the grotesque rather than the erotic. Gao's sexual encounters also have little or no erotic content; the language is clinical and the purpose psychological. He has one passage, however, that superficially seems to go beyond Oe in the direction of the weird or grotesque. A Buddhist nun, "a veritable beauty," in the process of bathing, thrusts a pair of scissors into her navel, pulls out her intestines, washes them, winds them around her wrists, then presses them neatly together, restores them to her interior and she is once again whole. (284) This tale might be classified as an example of the grotesque if Gao had not immediately identified it as a Buddhist text that could be used to illustrate a number of theories or doctrines, for example, to teach the "morally superior man that each day he should investigate his own personal conduct, or that human life is suffering, or that suffering in life derives from the self." Even though some readers might characterize this tale as twisted eroticism, it represents nothing new. One of Kawabata's short stories, for example, "Kataude" or "One Arm," concerns a young virgin who removes her limb to bestow it upon an older man, who converses with it while lying in bed.

Although Gao affirms in his Nobel speech that he is an atheist, in his fiction he devotes considerable attention to religion. The same anomaly exists in Oe, who in *A Quiet Life* portrays himself as lecturing on "The Prayers of a Faithless Man," but in *Pinch Runner* devotes a number of pages to what he labels as *matters of the soul*. He refers to Buddhist and Shinto prayers and perceives threads in his meditations connected with Christian symbols such as the Antichrist (74), the Millennium (117), and the Apostle Peter's denial of Christ. (176) Although he seems on the whole to be a convinced materialist, he expresses belief in a force that he describes as the Cosmic Will, presumably based upon recognition of a purpose in life, death, and the cosmos. He associates this force with personal circumstances such as his relations with Mori (112-13, 240-41) and with universal history and social progress. (184, 242-43) In other works he recognizes the appeal of the landscape and other aspects of nature, but *Pinch Runner* is entirely concerned with materialistic urban society.

With Gao the emphasis is just the opposite. Although he professes to be an atheist, he analyzes the experiences of life from the perspective of both religion and transcendental mysticism. At the outset of his novel, he indicates that his attempt to fathom the mysteries of "true life" came as the direct result of the discovery that he had been previously improperly diagnosed with cancer. (12) He does not specifically admit the existence of a human soul, however, until a woman as part of an erotic conversation indicates that she wishes to possess his. No clarification here or elsewhere is given as to whether or not the soul is eternal. When the narrator isolates his own soul, he associates it with his constant seeking to be "self-activated." "The problem is if my soul manifested itself, would I be able to comprehend it? And even if I were able to comprehend it, what would it lead to?" (202) He encounters monks and shamans in nearly every village he passes through, recording prayers and sermons, particularly those of Taoist origin. (294, 402-3) In connection with his theories of the self he wonders whether collective consciousness existed before the recognition of identity. (307) [Oe has similar queries concerning "collective memory," (61) "collective consciousness" and "collective imagination." (141)] The ancient graves and compounds Gao comes upon stimulate his speculations on eternity. "You can't help wondering whether you have another life, that you have retained some memories of a previous existence, or that these places will be your refuge in a future existence." (328) Gao's continued association of primitive philosophy with the landscape creates an atmosphere of mysticism reminiscent equally of Western transcendentalism and Eastern Taoism.

Although the narrative methods of Oe and Gao differ sharply from conventional fiction as well as from each other's, Oe experimenting with fantasy and Gao with mysticism, their objectives are actually quite similar. Both attempt to isolate, if not to solve, the fundamental philosophical problems of humanity from a secular rather than a religious perspective. In their analysis of the cross-currents of self, society, and the cosmos, Oe combines emotional attachment with sardonic humor, Gao, practical hedonism with poetic scepticism. Despite the contrast in their techniques, both revive the traditional values of humanism by resisting the pressures of contemporary economic and political trends that offend human dignity or restrict social justice. Both are essentially dedicated to what Oe designates in his Nobel speech as "a cure and reconciliation of mankind."

Works Cited:

Gao, Xingyian. *Soul Mountain*. Trans. Mabel Lee. New York: Harper-Collins, 2000.

Oe, Kenzaburo. *The Pinch Runner Memorandum*. trans. Michiko N. Wilson and Michael J. Wilson. Armonk, New York: M.E. Sharpe, 1994.

———. *A Quiet Life*. Trans. Kunioki Yanagishita and William Wetherwell. New York: Grove Press, 1990.

Wilson, Michiko N. *Oe Kenzaburo. A Study in Themes and Techniques*. Armonk, New York: M.E. Sharpe, 1986.

Nobel Speeches on the Internet:

Gao, Xinjian, "The Case for Literature."
wysiwyg://102http://www.nobel.se/laureates//2000/presentation-speech.htn
Oe, Kenzaburo, "Japan, the Ambiguous, and Myself."
wysiwyg://98/http://www.nobel.se/literature/laureates/1994/oe-lecture.html

[1] "Musings on Postmodern Politics," in *Humanitas* 8 (1995) 3. For a lengthy discussion of the problems with the concept of postmodernism see Djelal Kadir, "Postmodernism/Post-colonialism" in *World Literature Today* 69 (1995) 17-21.

[2] I am pleased to write about Oe for the reason that I once had the privilege of spending part of an evening in his company at the University of Illinois sometime in the early 1980s. I had been invited to a reception in his honor at the home of the senior professor of Japanese at the university, which Oe attended with a colleague, Masao Miyoshi, from the University of California at Berkeley. I was there in the company of one of our graduate students, who had received her undergraduate training at Nihon University and had later studied with Oe's

colleague at Berkeley. After the reception the four of us moved on to a neighborhood bar, where we engaged in a highly stimulating round of talk. I do not recollect who did most of the talking, but I remember that the most cheerful and witty of all was Oe, who won me over completely by his conviviality and good humor.

[3] Michiko N. Wilson, *The Marginal World of Oe Kenzaburo*. New York: 1986. 20.

02
The Life and Adventures of Martin Chuzzlewit: A Tale of Two Cultures

Yiu-nam Leung

The current trend of treating "imagology in a multicultural setting" parallels the so-called "influence studies" popular in the 1950s and 1960s, those, for example, revealing connections between François Rabelais (1494-1553) and Laurence Sterne (1713-1768), or Johann Wolfgang von Goethe (1749-1832) and Thomas Carlyle (1795-1881). Instead of treating two authors and two languages, however, I intend to show the influence of two separate cultures on a single author, following a newly-accepted method in comparative-literature theory which highlights cultures rather than texts and focuses on separate nationalities rather than on separate languages. Even though I shall not be treating Asian literature or culture, I believe that my methodology may be found applicable to parallel studies of authors from different cultures who use Asian languages in common as their medium of expression.

"Imagology," a term used in literary study, is "broadly defined as the study of national/ethnic/racial/cultural images or stereotypes as they appear in literary contexts. Imagology explicitly includes the study of literary images of other groups (hetero-images) as well as images of one's own group (auto-images)" (Firchow 135). As Firchow further explains, it is "a means of self-discovery, a way of looking at others which is also a way of looking at ourselves. It is also the discovery that only by looking at the other can we really see ourselves. Or that by changing the way we look at others, we can also change ourselves" (142). Imagology is as ancient as the discipline of comparative literature. The present emphasis of imagology in comparative literature studies strongly resembles the vogue for influence studies in the 1950s and 1960s when the works of authors in two separate literatures were brought together for the discernment of resemblances and differences. As part of the prominence of multiculturalism in our times, it has become acceptable to compare cultures as well as individual authors. In the present inquiry I shall analyze two diverse cultures as portrayed in the work of a single author, Charles Dickens (1812-1870). In his novel *The Life and Adventures of Martin Chuzzlewit* (1844),[1] Dickens uses the arts of fiction to show affinities and differences between two separate cultures, carrying on the tradition established in ordinary prose by Voltaire (1694-1778) in *Lettres Anglaises* (1734) and Madame de Staël (1766-1817) in *De L'Allemagne* (1810). Although I am not treating Asian authors, the same methodology could be used to compare diverse cultures in these phonic areas.

Dickens's *The Life and Adventures of Martin Chuzzlewit* is a classic example of multiculturalism in fiction as innovative in its way as Madame de Staël's *De L'Allemagne* in literary criticism. Conventional scholarship has interpreted Dickens's *The Life and Adventures of Martin Chuzzlewit* as a somewhat ferocious assault on American manners and institutions as retaliation against the somewhat unfriendly reception by the Press he received on his first visit to the United States after his advocacy of the need for international copyright laws in his open speech.[2] An alternate reading based primarily upon the images of American and British national culture portrayed throughout the entire novel indicates that the work should be considered not as a satirical attack on America alone, but as a comparison between the United States and the United Kingdom. Dickens found the good and the bad in both political units, not a preponderance of the enviable in one or of the objectional in the other.

In the Preface to the first edition in 1844, Dickens feels called upon to justify his portraiture of one of his most notable villainous characters, Mr. Pecksniff, presented as a representative type and an exponent of consummate hypocrite and egotists in English society. There is no mention whatsoever of America. In a subsequent Preface in 1849 he feels it necessary to vindicate his American scenes against the accusation of some groups in that country that they are "violent exaggerations." The scenes in question reveal the absurdities uttered publicly by members of a political association, printed in the *New York Times*. Dickens admits his intent to subject them to ridicule, but adds that he did not do so in a spirit of animosity and that he would have done the same if a similar "opportunity had arisen" in reference to any part of the British isles. He described the American portion of his book as "in no other respect a caricature than it is an exhibition, for the most part, of the ludicrous side of the American character" (847), that which is most obtrusive and likely to be seen by the foreign traveler. The scene concerning political oratory takes up relatively little space and has almost no effect on the protagonist of the novel.

In the Preface to the "Cheap Edition" (1849), Dickens introduces a paragraph on the problems of literary imagery:

> What is exaggeration to one class of minds and perceptions, is plain truth to another. That which is commonly called a long-sight, perceives in a prospect innumerable features and bearings non-existent to a short-

sighted person. I sometimes ask myself whether there may occasionally be a difference of this kind between some writers and some readers; whether it is always the writer who colours highly, or whether it is now and then the reader whose eye for colour is a little dull? (846)

Dickens records his traveling experience to the United States in his letters to his friends in England, a travelogue, and a novel.[3] His views on America are based mostly upon his observation, experience, and memory. Before traveling to the New World, he, well-informed as he always was, read extensively accounts of America written by Harriet Martineau (1802-1876), Frances Trollope (1780-1863), Captain Frederick Marryat, and others (Metz 78).[4] This six-month tour did cast an everlasting impression on the British author. His craving for visiting America is not without reasons. For Dickens, America symbolizes, among other things, "the goal of liberty and democracy toward which he hoped that English might be tending" and "the flowing promise of a future in which the worn-out snobberies, aristocratic privileges and corruptions of the old world gave way to a better scheme" (Johnson 357). His reaction to America in fact undergoes a series of emotional changes from initial enthusiasm and gradual disappointment to final animosity. His hostility towards the United States, however, was to a certain extent tuned down as the Postscript to the novel (1868) written after his second trip to that country indicates.

The American episodes of *The Life and Adventures of Martin Chuzzlewit*, though occupying one eighth of the total length of the narrative, deserve our attention since they not only constitute the fictional representation of Dickens's impression of the New World but also reflect "in part the technique of alternating irregular sequences of chapters about the characters left in England with chapters about American events" (Monod 34). Originally, Dickens intended to boost up the declining sales of the first few monthly installments of the novel by making Martin travel to the United States. His efforts proved to be in vain. The American interlude contains a rich array of topical satires. One critic neatly summaries them as follows:

> American party names, gouging, dueling and violence, politically inspired criminal accusations, lounging, blunt questions, attitudes to immigrants, American English, moneyed aristocracy, American drinking habits, democratic journalism, smartness, forgery, Broadway, pigs, master-servant relations, spitting and spittoons, stoves, rocking chairs, repudiation of debts, the prevalence of fires in New York City, dining at table d'hote, greedy feeding, the faded beauty of American women, the profusion of meaningless military honours, the pursuit of dollars, the absence of culture and reading habits, American ineptitude for social pleasure and censorship of unpopular ideas. (Metz 80)

In regard to the good and the evil in human behavior, there is a considerable preponderance of evil among the English characters of the novel. Indeed Dickens maintains a balance between the two cultures only by means of an almost imperceptible preference for British social manners. The major difference in exposition concerns the individual versus the general. English characters are presented as deficient in one way or another as individuals, but American culture as a whole is the butt of authorial condemnation. The undoubted reason for this collective rather than individual impression of America is that on his hurried tour Dickens had little opportunity of cultivating personal relationships with his hosts.

In theme the novel is composed of two parts, the English and the American, each of which has its own set of characters who participate only casually, if at all, in the other part. Most caricatures in both parts are typically Dickensian, particularly that of Mr. Pecksniff, who borders on the heinous. There are several noble souls in Part I, particularly Tom Pinch and John Westlock, but there is only one American, Bevan, in Part II who can be considered at all worthy. The young Chuzzlewit is spoiled by selfishness in Part I and sees the light only in Part II through the assistance of his friend, Mark Tapley. Despite its disorganized construction, the novel in structure has three divisions: the first covering chapters 1 to 15, with the action taking place in England; the second covering chapters 16 to 35 with the action in America; and the third covering chapters 36 to 54 with the action once more in England. The novel contains two separate Martin Chuzzlewits, moreover, a grandfather and his grandson, both appearing in the first and third divisions, but only the grandson making the trip to America in the middle section. This is perhaps the reason why he is generally considered to be the protagonist of the work even though he plays a relatively minor role in the two other divisions.

Throughout the novel, Dickens cites or paraphrases a number of literary progenitors, but rarely identifies his sources by name. He, for instance, makes special references to Benjamin Franklin (1706-1790) twice, perhaps because of his eminence as an American man of letters, one citation anonymous and the other with full acknowledgment. The first reference derives from a maxim in Franklin's *Poor Richard's Almanac* (1732), which Dickens describes in a somewhat misleading manner as a "great discovery made by the ancient philosopher, for securing health, riches, and wisdom; the infallibility of which has been for generations verified by the enormous fortunes, constantly amassed by chimney-sweepers and other persons who get up early and go to bed betimes" (V, 83). If the reference is to Poor Richard as a person, it must be considered as patronizing and ironical. If the reference is to the remote past, the maxim has never been traced to a source prior to Franklin. Dickens quotes another passage from Franklin that depends for its effectiveness largely upon Franklin's prestige. Intentionally or not, this citation places both the American luminary and the culture he represents in an unfavorable light. Bevan, the only American in the novel portrayed as a civilized gentleman, refers to journalists as belonging to the class of men in whom Franklin "foresaw our danger and disgrace" (XVI, 276). Bevan affirms "that Franklin, in very severe terms, published his opinion that those who were slandered" by newspaper editors, "having no sufficient remedy in the administration of this country's laws or in the decent and right-minded feeling of its people, were justified in retorting on such public nuisances by means of a stout cudgel" (XVI, 276). It is true that Franklin published a squib setting forth such an opinion, but he did so in highly ironical terms, indicating that his words were not to be taken literally. His purpose was to condemn the lack of libel laws rather than to justify any individual taking the law into his own hands. His irony was not at all, as Dickens suggests, couched in "very severe terms" (XVI, 276). Even the title of Franklin's squib clearly demonstrates his ironical intention: "An Account of the Supremest Court of Judicature in Pennsylvania, viz. The Court of the Press."

Not content with taking Franklin's irony literally, Dickens embellishes his narrative with his own notions of American violence and mob law. One of his characters is "much esteemed for his devotion to rational liberty; for the better propagation whereof he usually carried a brace of revolving pistols in his coat-pocket" along with several other weapons (XXXIII, 520). His efficacious use of these weapons and advocacy of the lynch law were duly chronicled in the newspapers (XIII). He boasts to Martin that he has seen men who have spoken too freely lynched or beaten senseless by his enlightened fellow citizens.

To give a flavor of American journalism, Dickens goes far beyond

Franklin in satirizing the lack of ethics and decorum. A newsboy in New York shouts his wares: "Here's this morning's New York Sewer! ... Here's this morning's New York Stabber! Here's the New York Family Spy! Here's the New York Private Listener! Here's the New York Peeper! Here's the New York Plunderer! Here's the New York Keyhole Reporter! Here's the New York Rowdy Journal!" (XVI, 255) Martin asks one of the editors whether he ever publishes forged letters "purporting to have been written at recent periods by living men" and the editor replies proudly in the affirmative (XVI, 265). He adds with satisfaction that the practice had been invented in the old country, which was to blame for it, not the new country. He probably had in mind another of Benjamin Franklin's bagatelles, "Information to those who would Remove to America," which informs potential immigrants of the hazards likely to be encountered and warns them not to expect an easy time in earning a livelihood there. He cites many Europeans who imagine "that the Inhabitants of North America are rich, capable of rewarding ... all sorts of Ingenuity," and at the same time ignorant of the sciences, making it possible for talented foreigners immediately to find esteem and well-paid employment. They also believe that local governments, anxious for settlers, not only pay transportation expenses, but provide free land and agricultural utensils. "These are all wild Imaginations; and those who go to America with Expectations founded upon them will surely find themselves disappointed." One of the characters Martin encounters before sailing for America has similar notions of its conditions of comfort and equality. His brother had gone there, landing "without a penny to bless himself with" and was warmly welcomed (XIII, 217). "All men are alike in the U-nited [sic] States, an't they? It makes no odds whether a man has a thousand pound, or nothing, there — particularly in New York..." (XIII, 217).

For the average American social and economic mobility meant roughly the same thing, but from Martin's perspective similarities in

American life-styles represented mere standardization, a regrettable condition. Symbolic of this cultural uniformity were the public rooms in a railroad hotel where people of similar mode in "looks, dress, morals, manners, habits, intellects and conversation" are collected together (XXI, 349). "They did the same things; said the same things; judged all subjects by, and reduced all subjects to the same standard." Dickens explains ironically why these people became "the social, cheerful, winning, airy" specimens they were (XXI, 349). A typical example was a Major Pawkins of Pennsylvania. Pawkins, a gentleman characterized by having a large skull, a great mass of yellow forehead, and a heavy eye, is a patriot, a bold speculator, and an orator adept at swindling in commercial dealings. Devoted to public affairs, he always likes to engage in fraudulent business transactions. Having experienced a bad turnover in his business investment, he has nothing to do but is currently supported by his wife who runs a boarding house. Many Americans, moreover, are portrayed as exceedingly lax in their hygienic habits. Every one of the gentlemen aboard a river steamer, for example, "appeared to have had a difference with his laundress, and to have left off washing himself in early youth" (XXXIV, 530).

Despite the many disturbing habits and personal traits of the average standardized American, he reveals extraordinary pride and arrogance, not necessarily in his own abilities and achievements, but in his countrymen as a collective unit. One of the first Americans Martin encounters immediately discourses on his nation as "the Palladium of rational Liberty at home, sir, and the dread of Foreign oppression abroad; ... the Envy of the world, sir, and the leaders of Human Civilization" (XVI, 257). In a subsequent chapter Martin rebukes another patriot for boasting of national institutions associated with bullying and blood-letting. "Are pistols with revolving barrels, sword-sticks, bowie knives, and such things Institutions on which you pride yourselves? Are bloody duels, brutal combats, savage assaults, shooting down and stabbing in the streets, your Institutions! Why I shall hear next that Dishonour and Fraud are among the Institutions of the great republic!" (XXXIV, 534) One of the social-economic institutions prevalent in the United States at that time was that of slavery. Dickens repudiates it as a form of Oppression, visited upon both the white laborer and the black slave. "Steel and iron are of infinitely greater account in this commonwealth, than flesh and blood ... The stars wink upon the bloody stripes [of the American flag]; and Liberty pulls down her cap upon her eyes, and owns Oppression in its vilest aspect for her sister" (XXI, 341). Dickens includes in his narrative one or two references to actual slavery, but most are oblique; for example, when a boastful citizen affirms, "There are no masters here," Martin retorts, "All 'owners,' are they?" (XVI, 267) Dickens may have had an experience, however, similar to that of Martin, whose friend pointed out a wretched creature, who had at the end of a miserable life purchased his own freedom. While young, "he was shot in the leg; gashed in the arm; scored in his live limbs, like crimped fish; beaten out of shape; had his neck galled with an iron collar, and wore iron rings; upon his wrists and ankles" (XVII, 284).

Although slavery may have been the greatest evil Dickens encountered in America, he did not label it as such. He did offer mild praise, however, for what he described as the only American institution superior to its counterpart in the United Kingdom. An American citizen, Bevan, the only one in the book treated as a tolerable gentleman, says about education that his country does "pretty well on that head. ... Still no mighty matter to boast of; for old countries, and despotic countries too, have done as much, if not more, and made less noise about it. We shine out brightly in comparison with England, certainly, but hers is a very extreme case" (XVII, 279).

Dickens harshly epitomizes his ridicule of American patriotism in references to that nation's symbol, "the great American Eagle, which is always airing itself sky-high in purest aether, and never, no never, never, tumbles down with draggled wings into the mud" (XXXIII, 512). Martin's companion says that if he were presenting it pictorially, he would "draw it like a Bat, for its shortsightedness; like a Bantam, for its bragging; like a Magpie, for its honesty; like a Peacock, for its vanity; like an Ostrich for putting its head in the mud, and thinking nobody sees it" (XXXIV, 545). Martin breaks in, however, to add hopefully, "And like a Phoenix, for its power of springing from the ashes of its faults and vices, and soaring up anew into the sky" (XXXIV, 546). Here Dickens emits a glimmer of hope. On the topic of objectionable histrionic patriotism, Dickens treats his own country as no better than America. The villainous arch-hypocrite Pecksniff, for example, implores his listeners to bear with mankind. "It is our duty so to do. Let us be among the Few who do their duty. If, as the poet informs us, England expects every man to do his duty, England is the most sanguine country on the face of the earth..." (XLIII, 667). Actually the saying joining England and duty was the utterance of the naval hero Horatio Nelson, and its only connection with a poet derives from its presence in a biography of Nelson by the poet Robert Southey. Dickens's attributing it to a hypocrite who does not seem certain of its provenance indicates that he intends to expose meretricious patriotism at home. Dickens also points to the emptiness of patriotic language in high places elsewhere in his nation: "among all the six hundred and fifty-eight members in the Commons House of Parliament of the United Kingdom of Great Britain and Ireland, who are strong lovers... of their country; in a passion of that kind (which is not always returned) it is the custom to use as many words as possible, and express nothing whatsoever" (XLIII 673). In another significant parallelism, Dickens satirizes the mispronunciation of standard English in both the United States and Great Britain, each culture in its own way mistreating the language.

He suggests, however, without making a specific assertion that the fault is widespread among Americans although confined to the lower classes in England. Here is an example of American mispronunciation as one country dweller explains animal and insect life.

> "'Fleas?' says I. 'And more,' says he. 'Wampires?' say I. 'And more,' says he. 'What more?' says I. 'Snakes more,' says he; 'rattlesnakes. You're right to a certain extent, stranger, as graze upon a human pretty strong; but don't mind them—they're company. It's snakes,' he says, 'as you'll object to: and whenever you wake and see one in a upright poster on your bed,' he says, 'like a corkscrew with the handle off a sittin on its bottom ring, cut him down, for he means wenom.'"(XXI, 343)

This discourse is no less erratic than the weird and wonderful delivery of Mrs. Gamp, one of Dickens's notable proletarian personalities.

> "Which shows," said Mrs. Gamp, casting up her eyes, "what a little way you've traveled into this wale of life, my dear young creetur... Mrs. Harris through the square and up the steps a turning round by the tobacker shop, 'Oh Sairey, Sairey, little do we know wot lays afore us!' 'Mrs. Harris ma'am,' I says, 'not much, it's true, but more than you suppoge. Our calciations ma'am,' I says, 'respectin wot the number of a family will be, comes most times within one, and oftener, than you would suppoge, exact.' 'Sairey,' says Mrs. Harris, in a awful way, 'Tell me wot is my indiwidge number.' 'No, Mrs. Harris,' I says to her, 'ex-cuge me, if you please. My own,' I says, 'has fallen out of three-pair backs,

and had damp door-steps settled on their lungs, and one was turned up smiling in a bedstead, unbeknown...." (XL, 624-25)

My thesis concerning the binary division of *The Life and Adventures of Martin Chuzzlewit* into American and British segments may perhaps not have been greatly enforced by the foregoing *potpourri* of images, most of which admittedly relate to the United States. My primary evidence, however, is structural, not only in the obvious shifting of the scenario of the novel from the European continent to the American continent and back again, but also in regard to the activities of the range of characters. Each of the segments has an unscrupulous financial scheme bringing disaster upon innocent victims. In America dishonest real estate promoters sell to ignorant buyers, mainly immigrants, worthless land in a remote, desolate, and unproductive swampy area fancifully labeled Eden. In England an almost identical scheme hoodwinks native citizens. Entirely on the basis of an expensive office and a grandiloquent prospectus, a mythical Anglo-Bengalee Disinterested Loan and Life Assurance Company entices innocent investors to purchase worthless shares. Dickens does not excoriate any one of the American promoters individually, but treats them as supporting evidence of the general moral laxity of the nation. He develops two of his English characters, however, into consummate villains, Tigg Montague, the founder of the scheme, and Jonas Chuzzlewit, who becomes a partner, is in turn deprived of his fortune, and finally resorts to murder. The most hilarious and despicable character in the novel, however, is Mr. Pecksniff. He is often considered by critics as "the quintessence of bourgeois respectability" (Steig 61) and as "one of the unquestionable masterpieces of Dickensian characters" (Monod 89). Ironically enough, Mr. Pecksniff, as depicted by Dickens, is "a moral man, a grave man, a man of noble sentiments and speech" whose behavior, desire, and villainy are in every respect contradictory to the positive and favorable epithets (II, 11). He always pretends to exemplify a high standard of morality, but descends to any level of baseness to attain power and influence. Despite his villainous hypocrisy, he fails in all of his evil schemes and falls victim to speculative investment. In the Preface to his first edition, moreover, Dickens felt called upon to justify his harsh treatment of Mr. Pecksniff.

By means of his detailed dissection of the faults of Mr. Pecksniff and other individual characters Dickens exposes his country to reprobation no more flattering than that proceeding from his survey of America. He condemns vice and foolishness as endemic to American culture, but exposes similar or even worse attributes among individuals in England. His images of both cultures are on the whole unprepossessing.

Notes

[1] Charles Dickens, *The Life and Adventures of Martin Chuzzlewit*, 1844, ed. and introd. Margaret Cardwell (London: Oxford UP, 1982). Hereafter all references to the novel are quoted from this edition and parenthetically cited in the text by chapter and page.

[2] A number of scholars have written on this subject. See, for instance, Harry Stone, "Dickens' Use of His American Experiences in *Martin Chuzzlewit*," *PMLA* 72 (1957): 464-78; Ivor Brown, "The American Scene," in *Dickens in His Time* (London: Thomas Nelson, 1963) 215-28; Michael Slater, ed. *Dickens on America and the Americans* (Brighton: Harvester, 1979); Jerome Meckier, "Dickens Discovers America, Dickens Discovers Dickens: The First Visit Reconsidered," *Modern Language Review* 79 (1984): 266-77; Sylvère Monod, "The American Episodes," *Martin Chuzzlewit* (London: George Allen, 1985) 33-54; Sidney P. Moss and Carolyn J. Moss, "The American Chapters of *Martin Chuzzlewit*," *American Episodes Involving Charles Dickens* (New York: The Whitston, 1999) 28-52; Nancy Metz, "The Life and Adventures of Martin Chuzzlewit: Or, America Revised," in *Dickens, Europe and the New Worlds*, ed. Anny Sadrin (Great Britain:

Macmillan, 1999) 77-89.

[3] Madeline House, Graham Storey et al., *The Pilgrim Edition of the Letters of Charles Dickens*, 13 vols. (Oxford: Clarendon, 1969) vol. 2 (1840-1841), vol. 3 (1842-1842), and vol. 4 (1844-1846); John Forster, *Life of Charles Dickens* (London: Chapman and Hall, 1874); Charles Dickens, *American Notes for General Circulation*, ed. John S. Whiteley and Arnold Goldman (New York: Penguins, 1972); Dickens, *The Life and Adventures of Martin Chuzzlewit*.

[4] Information is drawn from Metz's article entitled "The Life and Adventures of Martin Chuzzlewit: Or, America Revisited." See Frances Trollope, *Domestic Manners of the Americans* (New York: Dodd, Mead & Com., 1927); Captain Frederick Marryat, *Diary in America with Remarks on Its Institutions* (New York: D. Appleton & Co., 1839); and Harriet Martineau, *Society in America*. Metz also points out that it is highly possible that Dickens was familiarized with works of Frances Tocqueville, Franz Lieber, Captain Thomas Hamilton and Basil Hall, and other guidebooks (78).

Works Cited

Dickens, Charles. *The Life and Adventures of Martin Chuzzlewit*. 1844. Ed. and introd. Margaret Cardwell. London: Oxford UP, 1982.

Firchow, Peter. "The Nature and Uses of Imagology." *Toward a Theory of Comparative Literature: Selected Papers Presented in the Division of Theory of Literature at the XIth International Comparative Literature Congress*. 3 Volumes. Ed. Mario J. Valdes. New York: Peter Lang, 1990. 3: 135-42.

Johnson, Edgar. "The New World." *Charles Dickens: His Tragedy and Triumph*. 2 Volumes. Boston: Little Brown, 1952. 1: 377-449.

Metz, Nancy. "The Life and Adventures of Martin Chuzzlewit: Or, America Revisited." *Dickens, Europe and the New Worlds*. Ed. Anny Sadrin. Great Britain: Macmillan, 1999. 77-89.

Monod, Sylvère. *Martin Chuzzlewit*. London: George Allen, 1985.

Steig, Michael. *Dickens and Phiz*. Bloomington: Indian UP, 1978.

The Italian Cinderella Type in the 17th-century Japanese Tales

Chieko Mulhern

Most people know what Cinderella is — the well-known rags-to-riches success story featuring a persecuted stepdaughter aided by a fairy Godmother and identified by a shoe. But this is just one type of Cinderella made famous by Charles Perrault in 1697. In a larger number of Cinderella tales, Heroine is neither a poor girl nor even a stepdaughter, and Shoe and Fairy are never mentioned.

In 1892, Marian Roalfe Cox compiled a decisive collection of 341 variants entitled *Cinderella*. She classified the tales into three types according to what she considered "differentiating" incidents. Type A is the Cinderella as most of us know it, with ill-treated heroine and recognition by means of shoe. This type represents 39% of Cox's book, and the same ratio is observed in a 1951 collection of an equal number of additional variants entitled *Cinderella Cycle* by Anna Birgitta Rooth. Tales lacking some or all of Cox's differentiating incidents are put into "the Indeterminate" group, which amounts to another 30%. The most significant to my study is this indeterminate 30%, which falls into B and C types. The B type is called "Catskin" and features a heroine fleeing from her father who wants to marry her. The C type is "Cap o'Rushes", which includes the King Lear judgment ("Who loves the father most?") and a Cordelia-like outcast heroine. Cox's B and C types are grouped together by the modern folklore type index as AT510B.

A survey of the Cox variants in regard to geographical distribution reveals some interesting points. First of all, the Italian cycle alone accounts for a whopping 24.3% of the entire collection, which covers Europe, India, Africa, South America, and a bit of Asia. So Cinderella seems a dominant and popular fairy tale in the Christian-disseminated cultural sphere. Even more significant is the curious tendency of the Italian cycle to gravitate noticeably away from the Cinderella variant, with the shoe incident, and to lean heavily toward the AT510B type involving father and outcast heroine in flight.

The Cinderella Cycle in the Otogizoshi Genre

What I call the Japanese Cinderella cycle belongs to the same 510B type. Japanese folklore collections list many variants under this type, but they are fragmentary undated oral tales transcribed in modern times. Each of three folk variants contains only some of the Cinderella motifs. My definition of the Japanese Cinderella cycle is more specific: a group of literary tales that are extant in print, fully equipped with a complete plot, and follow a prescribed sequence of Cinderella motifs and incidents. The only group that fits this definition is found in a medieval short story genre known as *otogizoshi*. The otogizoshi Cinderella cycle consists of four related but distinct tales which have no traceable predecessors or progeny in indigenous literature.

My own previous article, "Cinderella and the Jesuits," in *Monumenta Nipponica* (Winter, 1979), presented a hypothesis based on analysis of these tales and on a comparative study of the Western Cinderella cycle. The salient points of the article that pertain directly to the discussion in this paper are as follows:

1) The Japanese tales show an overwhelming affinity to the Italian Type 510B.

2) The Western influence is traced to the Japanese-speaking Italian Jesuits and Japanese Christian writers active in Japan during the heyday of the Kirishitan Press around the year 1600. The most plausible candidates include Father Organtino and Japanese Brother Toin Vicente.

3) Their primary motive in writing the Cinderella tales based on the Italian type was for proselytizing through the glorification of exemplary Japanese converts.

4) The tales contain internal evidence pinpointing possible models, all of whom were aristocratic Japanese Christians involved in sensational political incidents affecting the welfare and very existence of the Christian church in Japan.

5) The initial inspiration for the adoption of Cinderella motif-complexes was the tragic, romantic life and spectacular death of Lady Hosokawa Tama Gracia.

In this paper, I intend to discuss some of the key motifs in these tales, namely, the yamauba and her robe, and Kannon and her bowl-shaped headcover. My focus will be on three issues. First, I will propose some interpretations of these motifs, whose origins have not been convincingly argued by Japanese scholars. Second, I will consider whether the possible Kirishitan authorship can adequately explain the sudden emergence of these peculiar motifs. And lastly, I will examine contemporary sources to see whether the Jesuits had the specific information necessary for developing such motifs.

The longest and the most literary tale in the Japanese Cinderella cycle is *Hanayo no hime* (Princess Flora). Its story line closely parallels the legend of Lady Gracia. It was apparently written soon after her death in 1600. The best-known of the four tales is *Hachikazuki* (The Bowl-bearer) published in the Otogibunko edition of the 1660s but probably written around 1608. The most likely model is a man, Tsutsui Sadatsugu (1562-1615), the lord of Iga who was eventually sentenced to death for refusing to renounce his Christian faith. He is believed to have been married to Hosokawa Gracia's sister. *Hachikazuki* has a less-known but more important and earlier version preserved by the Mikanagi family, which I call Mikanagi-bon. Thinly disguised names of characters identify the primary model as Kiyohara Kojiju Maria, whose father was the first known convert among the court nobles. Maria is the devout Christian companion who performed the baptism of Gracia. The briefest tale is *Ubakawa* (The Bark Gown), written around 1608. Characters' names indicate the blue-blooded Kyogoku family members as models, with one of the earliest Christian converts as the father-in-law and the very last known convert of the daimyo class as the prince charming.

These four Japanese tales share crucial motif-complexes with the Italian cycle: noble heroine called *hime* (princess) loses mother and is cast out or flees from home; wandering ends at a nobleman's mansion, where heroine performs menial tasks in disguise; discovery by son of the master is followed by happy marriage. Both Italian and Japanese cycles lack certain motifs which are prevalent in non-Italian type tales, such as Enslavement of heroine by stepmother, Encounter at the ball, and the shoe test. In place of these familiar motifs, Japanese and Italian tales emphasize heroine's Flight, Disguise, and Aid.

Catskin and Cap o'Rushes Motifs Adopted

As indicated by Cox's designations for Type B and C as Catskin and Cap o'Rushes, the Italian 510B tales show a distinct preference for disguise, particularly in the form of plant covering or skin. Disguise occurs in 65% of Italian tales, while the figure for the rest of the world is a mere 19%. As for the means of disguise, the Italian cycle features wooden covering in 52% of the instances and old-woman skin in 13%, whereas the other countries favor animal skin in 72% of the cases over the meager 17% wooden covering and a single instance of old-woman skin. In Italian tales, the old-woman skin is literally the skin of heroine's dead mother, or the skin bought off the corpse of an old woman.

The Aid motif is also an Italian characteristic. Aid occurrs in 65% of Italian variants vs. 27% for the others. Of those Aid incidents, 33% involve old woman and 30% supernatural creatures in the Italian cases, while the other regions have 17% old woman, 20% supernatural, and various other choices. In the Japanese cycle, *Ubakawa's* heroine is protected by a bark gown which is a type of wooden covering, or can be considered an old-woman (*uba*) skin (*kawa*). Hachikazuki's bowl adhered to her head is clearly a wooden covering. And Hanayo wears a gown given by an old woman. Aid in the four tales is Kannon and/or yamauba. In short, the Japanese cycle shows close affinity to the Italian cycle in the choice of Disguise and Aid motifs.

In *Hanayo no hime*, it is yamauba who provides supernatural aid, a means of disguise, and an omniscient counsel to guide the heroine to safety and happiness. A number of theories have been proposed to explain this essential motif of the old woman of the mountain. The pioneering folklorist Yanagita Kunio has speculated that nomadic aborigines had been driven into remote areas by the alien Japanese to become mountain inhabitants, particularly in the high peaks around Mt. Fuji. That particular locale happens to be the setting of *Hanayo no hime*. According to Origuchi Shinobu, mountain dwellers were plains people who had entered into service of the mountain deity: yamauba was originally a priestess chosen to serve the mountain god and eventually even takes the role of his wife, or assumes the status of mountain goddess herself. Origuchi believed that in olden days, young women who were appointed priestesses customarily resided deep in the mountains; most of them lived to be old or perhaps wizened women and the word yamauba came to mean "aged woman of the mountain."

Yamauba (Mountain Clone) Provides Aid and Disguise

However, the old woman in *Hanayo no hime* (called uba during the cave incident and yamauba in the heroine's recollections) looks nothing like a Japanese woman, however aged or wizened. She is described as a creature with a tray-like face (square rather than predominant Japanese oval or oblong), deep-set bulging eyes, a wide mouth, a pointed beak-like hooked nose, a gigantic head, and curly red hair. This does not fit the description of Hannya, the demon woman, either. But a look at what is known as *namban-e* (Southern Barbarian paintings) of the Muromachi period would confirm the striking resemblance of her appearance to the pictorial representation of the Southern Barbarians (Westerners).

When Hanayo encounters a yamauba in the cave, she is asked to pick lice out of the old woman's hair. In an Italian tale called "Marion de Bosch" (Cox 247), the heroine picks lice and nits from the hair of an old woman who is actually the Madonna in disguise. In *Kojiki* (Japan's oldest history compiled in 712), too, Okuninushi delouses the storm-god Susanoo as a courtship task. Thus "delousing" is a folklore commonplace both in the West and Japan. But where did the otogizoshi authors get the idea of "hornlike" wens growing on the scalp of Hanayo's yamauba? Louis Frois has an illuminating entry in reference to Japanese religious beliefs in his letter of February 20, 1565: "Those who belong to another sect by the name of *enki* (or *zenki* — good ogre) are said to ... have small hornlike protuberances on their head and dwell in ghastly mountains.... They believe that if they climb a tall peak and wait in great faith for a certain period of time, an ogre called Amida will pass before the devotees or manifest himself on another mountain." Hanayo's cave incident is obviously a combination of the delousing motif from the Italian sources and the endemic religious myth as understood by the Jesuits.

Hanayo no hime has another parallel in the Italian cycle. In "The Three Daughters of the King" (Cox 313), the youngest daughter stumbles into the house of an ogre and is helped by an ogress who hides her from the ogre husband. But an interesting change is detected in *Hanayo no hime*. The Italian tale's ogre is named Uorco, derived from the ancient god of the lower world. Upon returning home, he exclaims, "What a smell of Christians!", signaling that the ogre and ogress represent a pagan religion in the Christian age. The ogre husband of Hanayo's yamauba, on the other hand, exclaims, "What a smell of living flesh!" Since Hanayo's setting is undoubtedly the Japan of non-Christian religions, the ogre may very well stand for Christianity in contrast to the Buddhist heroine. Despite his eyes flashing lightning, the ogre is in fact a benevolent benign creature who looks after the old woman, takes her explanation on faith, and goes away laughing. This ogre and the yamauba have been generally associated with agricultural religion on the grounds that they live in the vicinity of Mt. Fuji and she is in possession of sacred rice. But they are presented as eaters of raw meat. No scholar has ever explained how the meat-eating pair can be construed as a Shinto god and his priestess wife, while Shinto abhors contamination through contact with the dead above all else.

Moreover, the ogre in *Hanayo no hime* cannot possibly be an indigenous god served by the yamauba, for it is unthinkable for a Japanese male deity to cut firelogs and stack them for his priestess to make fire in his honor. It would be more reasonable to assume that both are in service of some deity, obliquely associated with Mt. Fuji in this case. Though the ogre is called "my husband", the yamauba seems to be a wife in name only, for the narrative dwells on the fact that the ogre comes during daylight hours instead of cohabiting with her; and in more realistic terms, she is "much too old even to be human". In short, the ogre and the yamauba are celibate but capable of love ("he loved me deeply"); they are not Shinto but sacerdotal in their capacity, and alien in their appearance and habits. The three grains of rice that would ward off hunger for sixty days (reminiscent of the Miracle of the Three Loaves) need not be an agricultural symbol but an apt substitute, for example, for the three life-sustaining liquor drops featured in another Italian tale, Cox 200, which also shows common elements including the delousing motif. In this tale, the heroine's old nurse plays a crucial role in providing the liquor, hiding her in a magic wardrobe, and rescuing her when she is buried alive. Amazingly enough, Hanayo's old nurse is also told by a fortune-teller that her lost princess will be found in the spring, even though she is now buried under arrowroot leaves. The sequence of motifs in Hanayo corresponds to the Italian tale closely enough to rule out the possibility of a mere coincidence.

Sacred Sites During Heroine Flight

The cave in which the yamauba tends the fire also has a religious connotation. A single most popular medieval *soshi* (short story booklet) is believed to have been one called *Fuji no Hitoana soshi* (the Human Cave of Fuji): by order of Shogun Minamoto no Yoritomo, warrior Nitta Shiro ventures into the cave, whereby a Bodhisattva gives him a tour of Paradise and Hell, illustrating the karmic law of cause and effect. Yet the terrifying implication of the cave is such that Shiro's failure to keep the vow of silence (until his thirtieth year when he must make public the Soshi in which the Bodhisattva depicted Paradise and Hell) leads to the instant loss of his own life and that of Yoritomo, who forced him to break the taboo. This tale itself may be related to the classical motif of a journey into the lower world (such as in the *Odyssey*, the *Aeneid*, and *Kojiki*), but apparently, this extremely popular soshi did not escape the attention of the Jesuits in Japan. After mentioning Yoritomo's famous hunt for wild animals in the foot field of Fuji and pilgrimage prevalent in the area,

Joãn Rodrigues (1561?-1634) reports: "There is a long cave running into one side of the mountain and nobody knows where it ends; it is called Fuji-hito-ana and they say that inside there are temples and altars with statues."

To reach the cave, Hanayo wades through a field of bamboo grass. Some scholars relate this motif to the mountain people in the Fuji area who are said to be fond of eating bamboo leaves. Hanayo, however, makes no reference to eating bamboo leaves. One remarkable episode collected in modern times by Mita Gensho in his *Kirishitan Densho* (Christian Legends, 1975) sheds a new light on the matter: Hearing of the legend of *kurusu-jo* (site of the cross) that had come down through generations at a Christian hamlet in Mt. Ashitaka next to Mt. Fuji, August L.Billing, the pastor of Hamamatsu Church, went looking for the site some time during the Meiji period. After going through a field of bamboo grass, much like Hanayo, Billing saw with his own eyes a cross carved into the rock wall. He tried later to bring other people and show it, but was never able to find the place again. Quite possibly the hamlet was one of those Christian villages that originally sprouted in Suruga Province, while its ruling lord Tokugawa Ieyasu was still amenable toward the Jesuits. Then throughout the prohibition period, it must have survived as one of the "hidden" Christian enclaves thanks to their topographical advantage. The yamauba's cave in *Hanayo no hime* could very well be a Christian habitat.

In what ways, then, is the yamauba related to Christianity? In general agreement with folklorists, modern scholar Odaka Keisuke offers a latest theory relating her to the mountain women who are said to have worn clothes made of woven strips of tree bark. But nowhere is Hanayo's disguise called ubakawa or described as of wooden material. Such misconception is a result of somewhat arbitrary lumping together of the two tales *Ubakawa* and *Hanayo no hime* as the ubakawa type in absence of any definite theory as to their origins. The yamauba says to Hanayo, "I let you have the robe (*kinu*) I have just taken off in the summer heat. Please put on this *ubaginu*." In the extant text that uses virtually no *dakuten* (the diacritical mark for sonants) this word generally accepted as *ubaginu* (old-woman robe) is written *uwakinu*, which literally means upper garment or robe. If the reading *uba* is based on no more compelling reason than that the robe comes from an old woman (the word for which can be read only as uba even without a dakuten), it could just as well be *uwa*. Similarly, the title of the tale *Ubakawa* is written *uwakawa* (outer layer of the skin), which is far more precise and descriptive of the robe made of tree bark (outer skin of wood). Rodrigues's Japanese-Portuguese Dictionary does mention the word and reading of "uwakawa" as meaning "robe."

Ubakawa (Old Woman Skin) and the Catholic Cleric Cassock

The next question is what kind of a robe would turn a girl in her teens into an old woman. Both Hanayo and Ubakawa girl are accepted as old ladies while wearing the robe. Bernardino de Avila Giron, a Spanish trader who stayed in Japan in 1594-98 and 1607-19, provides a helpful insight. In his observation on Japanese women's custom of wearing cloaks outdoors to hide their heads and faces, he remarks: "This garment is made of fine linen according to age and social rank. If the robe is for a young woman, it is normally left white with some light and dark blues.... If it is for a girl of five to twelve years of age, then some red is allowed; but if it is for an old woman it must have large stitching and dark blues or blacks. A maidservant does not wear such a robe, unless she is an old woman or a deserving favorite or a wet nurse." Women's fashion of pulling a kimono robe over the head and letting it flow loose down the back is called *kinukazuki*, a common sight in Muromachi paintings. Thus a robe worn this way covering the glossy black hair and young face would obscure a girl's noble identity, beauty, and age.

If for some reason, a young girl is wearing a dark blue or black robe in the *kinukazuki* fashion, she would surely be taken for an old woman by the rule of age distinction by color scheme. If a girl needs to survive as a servant while hiding her noble identity, her best choice is to masquerade as an old woman entitled to wear a robe. *Kinukazuki*, however, has at least two drawbacks in its use in the Cinderella tales: it is an outdoor fashion; and it is not suitable for menial work, especially if this heroine is to retain the old woman disguise at all times, for she must hold the robe with her hands to keep it from slipping off. Where could the author have found a robe ample enough to cover a girl from head to toe, functional enough to impede no body movement, and subdued enough in color to designate her as an old woman? The answer is again in the contemporary art works, more precisely the Southern Barbarian paintings, in which the most conspicuous figures are tall Westerners clad in flowing robes of dark colors. The priest's cassock in particular would be ideal with its deep hood concealing the face, a sash binding at the waist, and long sleeves covering the hands. Ubakawa's disguise suggests a dark-brown robe resembling tree bark color, while Hanayo's may be black.

Supposing Hanayo's disguise is of Western origin, whom does the yamauba represent, and how did Hanayo's real-life model Hosokawa Gracia gain access to Westerners? Gracia herself made a furtive visit to the church only once in her life, when she pleaded with Gregorio de Cespedes to grant her baptism and conversed with Japanese Brother Cosme, before she was whisked away by the retainers. Quite possibly, this experience is reflected in the cave incident: the Japanese Brother may be the old woman who "used to be human (heathen)" but is now in service of God alongside a loving alien, the Father Cespedes, who only met Gracia briefly and refused to comply with a precipitous request for baptism by an unidentified noble lady. And the spiritual food provided by Cosme's lecture on Christianity did sustain Gracia until she found true happiness as a Christian. Incidentally, Aid in the Italian cycle appears all but exclusively as old woman, unlike other countries where old man occurs frequently. And Christian nuns were unknown in Muromachi Japan. So the changing of gender in the case of Cosme can be considered a folklore necessity for a Japanese variant.

Bodhisattva Kannon in Multiple Manifestations

Heroine disguise in the Japanese cycle is associated with convincing validity to Kannon, who is believed to function in an endless variety of earthly manifestations (disguises) to save souls. But this observation in no way contradicts the hypothesis that in Japanizing the Christian tradition, the authors made an inevitable and wise choice of Kannon as the Buddhist counterpart of the Madonna; or that Kannon was later substituted as a code name for the Madonna during the long prohibition period. Actually statuettes known as "Maria Kannon" were being smuggled in from China or carved out by hidden Japanese Christian artists at the risk of death. Hase Temple Kannon, who manifests herself to the parents pleading for a baby and actually bestows the bowl and box on them in the Mikanagi-bon *Hachikazuki*, appears "in the form of a beautiful lady," while the other Hachikazuki variants dispensed with the manifestation scene altogether. Creation of this incident in the Mikanagi-bon suggests an attempt to play down the pagan form of Hase Kannon, who is a six-armed *Nyoirin* Kannon. This is consistent with the fastidiously repeated mention of "Sho Kannon" (of normal human form) in *Hanayo no hime*. *Ubakawa* does not designate the type of Jimoku Temple's Kannon, perhaps because it was a famous Sho Kannon. Of course, as a fairy tale essential, they could not have found a better choice than Kannon for the surrogate mother to a virtually orphaned girl.

My hypothesis that the yamauba stands for a Christian cleric and her gift is a cassock can at least provide one explanation as to why the otogizoshi illustrators missed such a prime opportunity to demonstrate their imagination and artistic skill in rendering this key motif into a visual image. Generally speaking, to be fair, the extant otogizoshi illustrations are often not contemporaneous with the text and show many instances of anachronistic errors and discrepancies from the story. Hanayo is depicted in the extant text as dressed in the Heian court lady fashion with voluminous layers of bulky kimono robes even during her flight and menial period, though she is supposed to have been stripped of her original apparel by the abductor. The yamauba is growing two distinct horns over her forehead, when there are supposed to be over a dozen hornlike wens on her scalp. In the Nara-ehon *Ubakawa*, the disguise is a dark robe of thick but soft material, and the heroine's uncovered hair is shown as entirely grey — something not mentioned in the text.

Magic Adhesion of a Cornucopia

When it comes to Hachikazuki's bowl, painters seem to have been at a loss as to what shape it should take. The bowls in most versions are so shallow and wide, all but a large flat hat that would submerge the girl's face completely in the river even if the bowl itself remained above water. This is contrary to the story line, for she is supposed to be prevented from drowning by the bowl which keeps her face above the river water. Moreover, it would take a feat defying imagination to sleep with the bowl covering one's head all the way down to the shoulder, as the Mikanagi-bon specifies. And in all versions, the heroine consummates the nuptial vow before the bowl falls off to yield treasures. The Mikanagi-bon, which seems the oldest of the variants, has all its illustrations cut out, leaving no hint as to what the bowl looked like. All this confusion may be attributable to a plausible cause that initial pictures were deliberately destroyed or obscured at some time during the persecution period for fear of detection, because the disguises were of Christian or foreign origin. Hachikazuki's bowl was at least conceivable in terms of mundane Japanese utensil, and that may explain why *Hachikazuki* was the only story of this cycle that diffused the most in its own time.

The bowl is a gift by Hase Kannon. The heroine's mother on her death bed places it over the girl's head as had been stipulated by Kannon. Magic adhesion results in the heroine's nickname the Bowl-bearer, and the disfigurement invites the stepmother's dislike of her. The treatment of this particular motif has mystified scholars. In the otogibunko *Hachikazuki*, the prince charming called Saisho spies a new bath attendant and says, "I have never seen a more charming woman." Comparing her looks to flowers, floral essence, and famous Chinese beauties, he wishes, "If only I could remove her bowl to see her as clearly as a full moon." Ikeda Yasaburo, an authority on stepchildren tales, points out that the author seems to have momentarily forgotten the difference between the magically adhered bowl and an *ubakawa* which can be taken on and off at will. Citing the author's failure to clarify the reason for Saisho's falling in love with a girl whose face is hidden by the large bowl-hat, Ikeda speculates that the bowl was a later motif injected into a conventional love story. For similar reasons, Ichiko Teiji considers the bowl symbolic of a taboo, the purpose of which is to hide the heroine's beauty and protect her chastity. But then, why does Hachikazuki consummate the connubial pledge with the bowl still adhered to her head? According to Origuchi Shinobu, the bowl as a cornucopia is associated with the god of water in Japanese folklore pictured as an aquatic animal (*kappa*) equipped with an inverted dish on his head under which treasures are believed to be hidden; hence, Hachikazuki is an ancient priestess assigned with the duty of assisting in ablution. This theory still falls short of explaining why Hachikazuki must suffer derision and abuse because of the bowl, and why she as a priestess can lose her virginity and get rewarded with happy marriage instead of being punished.

In Muromachi Japan, the bowl worn over the head was not an unusual sight by any means. Muromachi picture scrolls abound in examples of *kinukazuki* under a deep *ichimegasa* (large-brimmed wooden hat), which can only be described as the *hachikazuki* fashion. So what makes Hachikazuki a monstrosity is not the bowl-hat itself but the magic adhesion of a head cover which is a motif peculiar to Japan. Being a fairy tale love story, the Japanese tale is naturally told from a child's point of view, and as such the bowl is subjectively conceived as a disfiguring, abnormal factor that causes the child enough shame to drive her to a suicide attempt, or to develop a persecution complex. The 510B type of tales deal with the concept of sin and guilt from the child's viewpoint, as I discussed in another article, "Cinderella as a Pubertal Girl's Fantasy," published in *Southern Folklore Quarterly* in 1980. In this context, the disguise or a head cover is an answer to her need to hide her real self or her face from prying eyes, but ironically it serves as a sign of her guilt to brand her in effect.

Wooden Bowl-Hat Symbolizing Sin and Shame

It is no surprise, then, to find in the Mikanagi-bon a passage associating the heroine's suffering with a sense of disgrace: "How wretched I feel thus displaying my disgrace to suffer derision from many people." The word *haji* (shame, disgrace) written without a dakuten appears, of course, as *hachi*, exactly the same as the word for "bowl".

Actually, the bowl is not the primary cause for the persecution of the Mikanagi heroine. The stepmother at first hates her for her withdrawn unsociable attitude, and people of Kyoto are kind enough to feed her and clothe her instead of laughing at her. Even the father-in-law orders her thrown into the Yodo River because of her seemingly low social status, and not because of the bowl. It is only the heroine who is despondent over her abnormal appearance and her reduced circumstances. Her father ponders, "I have loved you no less than myself. I am resigned to the anguish of parting with my loved ones as the inevitable human lot, but still, what sins have I committed for which you must be afflicted with such an unheard of deformity?" Combined with certain incidents in the model Kiyohara Maria's life, the bowl seems to symbolize a Christian concept of sin.

Maria was a devout Christian of impeccable reputation known for charitable activities. Why then make her wear a bowl symbolizing sin and shame? When she was accorded the honor of performing Lady Gracia's baptism, Maria made a vow of chastity at the church in the presence of a priest and cut her hair short as a sign of sincerity. Despite this vow duly witnessed and recorded by the Western Jesuits, Maria eventually married a high-ranking vassal of Hosokawa Tadaoki at her feudal lord's command. A curious coincidence is found in a common belief that Maria was compared to St. Cecilia in her time. What aspect of this legendary saint of the second- or third-century Italy could have inspired such a comparison? The most extraordinary part of the legend of the patrician Cecilia is that she died a virgin martyr despite her marriage. Forced by her father into marrying a pagan noble, she succeeded not only in securing his promise to respect her virginity but also in converting him; both were eventually martyred and buried in Rome. Cecilia, therefore, was one noble Christian woman who had managed to keep her religious vow while obeying an irrevocable secular command. So it is possible that Hachikazuki modelled after Kiyohara Maria known as Cecilia wears the bowl symbolizing the Original Sin of all Christians and also the shame of her breached vow. After she is purified by the ablution in the river, she is reunited with her princely lover and accepted as his bride. Then the bowl releases her and rewards her with exotic treasures, a list of which actually resembles the Jesuit gifts to Oda Nobunaga and other influential warrior lords and nobles recorded in history.

The Jesuit Versions of Japanese Saints' Lives

Did the Jesuits have the inclination to write fairy tales? And more importantly, did the Jesuits of the sixteenth century know the Cinderella tale type? The answer to both questions is a definite yes.

The oldest variant in Cox's collection is a romantic version of a folktale belonging to the 510B type, printed by Straparola in his *Tredici Piacevoli Notti*. This book was published in 1550, so the Italian Jesuits stationed in Japan had access not only to folktales with Cinderella motifs already popular in Europe but also to a literary version well before 1600, the presumed date of *Hanayo no hime*.

The Jesuit Christian Press active in Japan in 1590-1614 did publish the still extant Japanese translation of Aesop's fables (in 1593) as well as originally written short stories in Japanese, from which Joãn Rodrigues quotes passages in his *Arte da Lingoa de Iapam* (1604-1608).

The priest who had most contact with the presumed models and the possible Japanese authors was Organtino Gnecchi-Soldi (1530-1609). Back in Italy, he had been actively involved with the Madonna Association, the primary objective of which was moral edification and education of the young.

The use of fairy tales and plays in church sermons in medieval Europe was quite extensive and well documented. Royal courts in the 16th-century Europe, moreover, were known for the literary vogue and keen appetite for travelogs and fairy tales for adult entertainment. Jesuits were some of the most widely travelled people, and possessed both the privilege of access to court circles and literary talents in weaving sophisticated tales.

It would have been natural for them, while stationed in Japan, to entertain the local nobility and proselytize at the same time with literary tales created by means of combining the Italian Cinderella type and the saints' lives format.

REFERENCES

Bettelheim, Bruno. *The Uses of Enchantment*. New York: Alfred A Knopf. 1976.
Cooper, Michael, ed. *They Came to Japan*. London: Thames and Hudson. 1965.
Cox, Marian Roalfe. *Cinderella*. Nendeln, Liechtenstein; Kraus Reprint. 1892, reprinted in 1967.
Dundess, Alan, ed. *Cinderella: A Folklore Casebook*. New York: Garland, 1982.
Ikeda Hiroko. "A Type and Motif Index of Japanese Folk-Literature." *FF Communications No. 209*. Helsinki: Suomalainen Tiedeakatemia, 1971.
Mita Gensho. *Kirishitan Densho* (Kirishitan tradition). Tokyo: Hobunkan, 1975.
Mulhern, Chieko. "Cinderella and the Jesuits," *Monumenta Nipponica* 34, 1979, 409-447.
Mulhern, Chieko. "Japanese Cinderella as the Pubertal Girl's Fantasy," *Southern Folklore Quarterly* 44, 1980, 203-214.
Mulhern, Chieko. "Analysis of Cinderella Motifs, Italian and Japanese," *Asian Folklore Studies* 44, 1985, 1-37.
Murakami Naojiro, transl. *Yasokaishi Nihon Tshushin* (Japanese correspondence of the Jesuits). Tokyo: Yushodo. 1966.
Rodriguez, Joãn. *Arte da lingoa de Iapan*. Nagasaki, 1604-1608.
Rooth, Anna Birgitta. *The Cinderella Cycle*. Lund Gleerup. 1951.
Yokoyama Shigeru and Matsumoto Takanobu, editors. *Muromachijidai Monogatarishu III* (Collection of tales from the Muromachi period). Tokyo: Kadokawa Shoten, 1962.

04

Speak, Memory!
Edo Netsuke in Their Literary Context

Haruko G. Iwasaki

What in a fine piece of netsuke so intrigues and frustrates many of its viewers? The answer may well lie in its silence, the eloquent silence that emanates from the piece. The physicality of this "real thing" alone, poised on one's palm, can attest to the wit of the man who designed it, the skill of the artisan who carved it, and the centuries of loving use that mellowed its patina. Unfortunately, the netsuke provides us with no texts and few other means through which to articulate its rich history. It was a toggle, after all, an item too casual to deserve a properly marked box or formal documentation. About one-third of extant netsuke bear no signature. Subsequent netsuke fever in the West further deepened this anonymity. Severed from the inro, tobacco pouches, and other items with which they once formed a set, and repeatedly sold from one country to another, even superb pieces have grown tantalizingly mute.

How can we awaken the netsuke's memories? One effective way would be to reconstruct the cultural environs in which this unique art was created and appreciated. The restorative efforts have already begun, in the broadening basis of netsuke studies. Collectors and dealers have already made a prodigious amount of information available on the physical attributes, signatures, and general knowledge of folklore and legends most popularly used in netsuke. Academic interest also seems to be stirring. In an article published in the Spring 1997 issue of this journal, Professor Kendall Brown of State University at Long Beach, California, lamented art historians' general neglect of this subject and exhorted them to join forces with the lay researchers.

As another academic studying the related field of Edo literature, I discovered from my recent encounter with netsuke a whole range of interrelated issues between this art and popular literature — and more broadly, the whole popular culture — in the late Edo period. The discovery led me to a series of conjectures. The sophisticated urbanites who wrote, illustrated, and read the witty popular fiction in the Edo period probably overlapped with the elegant men-about-town who designed, purchased, and enjoyed the most elaborate pieces of netsuke. And, if this is the case, the texts of this fiction might provide netsuke studies with the very kind of information netsuke themselves cannot supply. In short, the knowledge gathered from popular literature may well help netsuke break through their silence.

Illustrated humorous fiction (kibyoshi) seems most promising for comparison with netsuke.

The genre of popular literature that seems most promising for this comparison is *kibyoshi*, or "yellow-cover booklets." This illustrated humorous fiction evolved in the 1770s from the format of children's story books, but its wholly adult contents portrayed the contemporary society in the shogun's capital, Edo (today's Tokyo). The light-hearted parody met the taste of the urban readers and quickly became a major genre of popular literature. Over two thousand titles appeared in nearly three decades of prosperity, until its suppression toward the end of the eighteenth century.

In this article I will explore one example of the themes popularly shared by netsuke and kibyoshi. It is the age-old interest Japanese held in mutable identities among men, beasts, and even inanimate things. During the Edo period, the idea of many selves lurking in one being so appealed to the Japanese imagination that a host of themes developed around this preoccupation. Topics as varied as magical transformation, deceptive surfaces, and ambiguous fusion of opposites all seem to have derived from this enduring interest. What underlies these manifestations, perhaps, is an unwillingness of the people of the time to wholly believe that one identity is the permanent state of being.

1. A tanuki at the moment of transformation.

2. Falling asleep, a tanuki reveals his true self.

Netsuke of Foxes, Tanuki, and Demons with Masks

The netsuke collection exhibited in the Santa Barbara Museum of Art contained a conspicuously large group of images that relate to the issue of multiple identities. One group deals with animals with transformative power, typically a *tanuki* or a fox, animals that populate folklore and children's stories. Netsuke's treatment of these magically endowed animals ranges from simple to complex. **Figure 1**[1] catches a clever tanuki, at the very moment of turning into human form. Another tanuki, in **Figure 2**,[2] has managed to turn into a priest, but reveals his tanuki face while falling asleep. Even more clever is the fox, whose wide repertory of transformations has enriched centuries of theatrical productions and literature. The foxes in **Figures 3**[3] and **4**[4] are both taken from the medieval *Kyogen* drama *Tsurigitsune* (The Snared Fox), but with a different twist. **Figure 3** simply shows the crafty fox in priestly garb setting out to trick humans, while the image in **Figures** 4a-b presents the amazingly complex configuration of the hunter and the hunted within the exacting confines of a tag's antler. One side of this netsuke (**4a**) shows the fox hiding under the priest's robe; on the opposite side (**4b**), the burly hunter kneels, intent upon ambush.

3. A fox, as a holy man.

The combined image in this netsuke is full of subtly ambiguous details. The two opponents' bodies are smoothly fused by the shared backs; the strange beckoning gesture of the hunter seems more suitable to the sly fox; and the soft curve of the hunter's furry chaps (*mukabaki*) surely evokes the image of a fox tail. When all these details are put together, this double-image netsuke seems to suggest an uneasy

4a-b. The hunter and hunted, fused.

5. An oni hiding behind Shoki's mask.

074(677)

New Intellectual Prospects

6. An oni struggles with an Okame mask.

possibility: the aggressor and the victim may actually be two inseparable parts of one being.

In another group of netsuke, the same issue of changing identities is variously explored by using masks, each again with a different twist. **Figure 5**,[5] for example, shows the demon, *oni*, peering cautiously from behind the mask of his much-feared oppressor, Shoki. The message we first sense is mildly satirical: evil is trying to hide behind the surface of good. But the humor in the cowardly look of the demon also adds finer nuances to the total effect. For one, it humanizes the demon, once feared as a ferocious supernatural power. Humor also softens or even compromises the satire, since the humanized demon is more likely to attract our compassion to his all too human deception.

In the similarly masked oni in **Figure 6**,[6] humor intensifies at the expense of the demon. Bumbling and perhaps drunk, the demon seems to be struggling with the mask of the moonfaced female Okame (also known as Otafuku), which clings upside down around his head. The dynamic of the two opposites is again evident between the male oni and the female mask, but exactly what is happening between the befuddled oni and the leering Okame remains unclear, until we find some parallel texts elsewhere.

Netsuke of Mask Clusters

Another variant of the mask theme in netsuke is a mask cluster, an assortment of masks presented as a composite. Extremely elaborate pieces, such as the one shown in **Figure 7**,[7] make us wonder what may have motivated artists to attempt such a demanding task. First to be considered is the power of tradition. Japanese literature and arts

7. An elaborate mask cluster.

had long loved to enumerate a series of items that belong to the same category.[8] In the Edo period, this technique of listing (indicated by the suffix *zukushi*) spread to many other fields. In this context, the composite of masks can be considered a *men-zukushi*, a natural application of this technique to the netsuke format.

Technical challenges must also have provided incentive to the artists. As is known among netsuke specialists, the artisans of netsuke included carvers of *Noh* and other masks. For these professionals, the enormous difficulty of carving a miniature cluster of distinctly featured masks — and the profit such a piece would garner — may have seemed irresistible.

The last and most intriguing factor we must consider is the issue of identity. Strung together as one netsuke, these many faces may again hint at the multiple manifestations of all human and non-human existences. In support of this view, we only need to consider the essential function of Noh masks. Each mask of course helps the actor transform himself into a young woman, a happy old man, etc. But, even more importantly, it enables him to perform the climactic scene of Noh, where the main character transforms himself into another identity. A fisherman may reveal himself to be the ghost of a warrior, while an old man turns out to be a local deity, and so on. These changes, which form the core of Noh drama, reflect the Buddhist belief in the infinite chain of transmutations among all beings in the universe. With the coming of the modern Meiji period in 1868, however, clustered masks show an interesting development. I will return to this topic at the end of this article.

Multiple Selves in Noh, Kabuki, and Literature

The theme of multiple selves and metamorphosis was by no means limited to the world of netsuke. As we have noted, transformation was the central theme in the medieval art of the Noh theater. During the Edo period, the theme continued to grow in popularity and eventually spread into a wide range of popular culture by the end of the period, including *Kabuki* plays, *ukiyo* prints, and various genres of entertainment.

In the Kabuki theater, for example, most of the famous plays exploit the dual or multiple identities of the central characters. The great Kabuki play popularly known as *Sukeroku* is a typical case. The leading character, Sukeroku, first appears as a townsman hero of contemporary Edo. But at the climactic moment, he suddenly declares that *jitsu wa* (actually) his true identity is Soga Goro, the hero of a medieval vendetta.

In another famous Kabuki play, *Yoshitsune Senbonzakura* (Yoshitsune's One Thousand Cherry Trees), the most dramatic scene features a retainer of General Yoshitsune revealing his true identity as an orphaned fox. The ever-heightening interest in transformation led some actors of the late Edo period to develop the spectacular type of Kabuki dance called *shichihenge* (seven transformations). In this dizzying number, the lead actor dances through seven transformations, performing complete changes of hair, costume, and make-up, all on stage.

In the field of literature, there were certain genres that particularly welcomed the theme of dual and multiple identity. Obviously, realistic genres rarely treated it, but genres that featured the fantastic and parody thrived on the idea of transformation or characters with more than one identity. As noted above, kibyoshi seems most promising of these genres for comparative studies with netsuke. One reason is the large number of stories in this genre that feature various transforming characters. This is by no means a coincidence. Kibyoshi inherited this stock theme from the two related genres, children's stories and Kabuki. In fact, the majority of kibyoshi tales are parodies of fairy tales or Kabuki plays.

The other advantage of kibyoshi is its hybrid format, borrowed from the story books for children. Since illustrations dominate all pages of kibyoshi, its images can be easily compared to the three-dimensional visual art, netsuke. Familiar images of fairy tales — from the mischievous tanuki, sly foxes, powerful oni in his tiger-skin shorts, to such imaginary animals as *kappa* and *tengu*, along with a few immortals from China — all wreak havoc in the typical kibyoshi scenes, set in pleasure quarters and theaters. Below, I will discuss obvious examples of thematic parallel between kibyoshi and netsuke.

Foxes and Demons in Kibyoshi

A 1780 kibyoshi by a minor writer, Iba Kasho, *Cleverly Transformed, the Dandy Fox* (Sate mo baketari, kitsune no tsujin) provides a fairly straightforward example of kibyoshi that parodies the old fairy tales of foxes. This story of a prodigal son duly follows the kibyoshi formula, but the roles of the spoiled young man and his well-established family are completely recast with a similarly situated clan of foxes.

Visual and textual details work together to enhance humor. Let us look at the eloquent details in the opening scene (**Figure 8**),[9] which shows the elegant interior of a townsman's house. The concerned parents are discussing with the cunning clerk their son's misconduct. Father is nervously puffing at his pipe, while mother laments with her hand on her aching heart. Their clothes, postures, language, and the interior all evoke the

8. A fox family, worried over their prodigal son.

image of a wealthy conservative family caught in a domestic crisis. But a small detail turns the whole sad scene into a comedy: the furry faces and tails of the characters.

Tails continue to act as the identity markers. In the following scene in the pleasure quarters (**Figure 9**),[10] the young master and the clerk appear transformed into patrons. Dressed in the latest Edo fashion, they look every inch dandies, except for their tails peaking from their jackets. Back at home in **Figure 10**,[11] the treacherous clerk is now trying to seduce the master's daughter. Here, the well-combed tail of the young lady serves as the object of male desire, as alluring as a maiden's soft breast. To underscore the comic parallel, the maiden sternly commands, "Unhand me, young man!"

9. Fashionably dressed, but tails showing.

Simple as it is, this kibyoshi of the fox shares some important features with the fox or tanuki in the netsuke form. Most evident is the friendly, teasing attitude with which humans deal with these mischievous animals. The other notable point is the obvious centrality of townsmen's culture to that of samurai. The fox family in kibyoshi aspires to the elegant life-style of Edo merchants. Few tanuki or fox in

10. "Unhand me, young man!" the lady commands.

netsuke transform themselves into samurai.

Another magic creature as popular in the kibyoshi as in the netsuke is the burly demon, or oni. Most kibyoshi tales of oni are taken from *Momotaro*, the adventure tale of the boy born from a peach. When he grows up, Momotaro sails to Demon Island and, with the help of dog, monkey, and pheasant, subdues the indigenous clan of oni, and returns home with a pile of treasures and the chief demon in chains.

Among many kibyoshi that parody Momotaro, the most interesting for our comparative study is its comic sequel, *The Latter-Day Tale of Momotaro* (Momotaro gojitsu-banashi), 1777. Written by a major samurai author, Hoseido Kisanji, this work not only focuses on the theme of transformation but also treats oni's involvement with the Otafuku-type of female.

This sequel begins from Momotaro's return, but shifts its focus to the captive demon's new life in Japan. The old-fashioned material from the original Momotaro story is comically twisted to fit into contemporary urban scenes, for under the fairy tale of Momotaro lurks the formulaic plot of kibyoshi: initiation of a naïve youth into the fashionable lifestyle of Edo. In this version, the oni of course fills the role of the uninitiated, while the civilized human, Momotaro, acts as his teacher. The focus is the remarkable process of the savage from Demon Island turning into a meek townsman and successfully assimilating into the bourgeois society of Edo.

The pleasures of kibyoshi lie in the clever details, where the incongruous mix of the old and the new are visually and verbally presented. Let us see **Figure 11**,[12] for example, where Momotaro helps his captive's makeover. The master shaves the oni's pate, cuts off his horns, and carefully hides the stubs under the hair. The oni's tiger-skin boxers are to be coverd with a stylish set of kimono, and his name is changed to a more townsman-like "Onishichi." He then sells his horns to an apothecary as a rare imported medicine. The windfall profit of twenty gold pieces he receives qualifies Onishichi now as a full member of the increasingly capitalistic Edo society.

These happy changes create turmoil in Momotaro's household, however. The amorous chambermaid Ofuku is smitten by Onishichi's "big, exotic eyes" and aggressively tries to seduce the naïve youth. But the odd pair is caught in the act by Monkey. **Figure 12**[13] shows the bare-breasted Ofuku (drawn as Otafuku) in a love rampage, Onishichi in flight, and the jealous Monkey crying "Foul!" The two are promptly kicked out of Momotaro's household; but not to worry. Using the capital that the oni's horns have yielded, the enterprising Onishichi and Ofuku open a popular tobacco shop named "The Islanders" (**Figure 13**).[14]

11. Momotaro helps with the oni's makeover.

Details of this kibyoshi variously help our interpretation of the demon in netsuke, because of the clear parallel Onishichi bears to the netsuke versions — specially to the one wearing the mask of Otafuku (**Figure 6**). One similarity is found in the attitudes the Japanese of this period had toward demons. In earlier times, demons were feared as supernatural beings, but here we see that both demons in kibyoshi and netsuke are de-demonized and humanized through the same humorous approach. This suggests that the increasingly secular atmosphere of the late Edo period was seeping into the realms of kibyoshi and netsuke alike.

12. Amorous Ofuku and sheepish Onishichi.   13. Onishichi and Ofuku open a tobacco shop.

    Another important similarity concerns Oni's relationship to females. Both demons are entangled with the same homely type of women, known as Otafuku. In the case of netsuke, the precise relationship of the oni to the woman seemed ambiguous. But thanks to the existence of this closely paralleled kibyoshi, we can now use its well-articulated sexual dynamic to clarify the ambiguity in the netsuke piece. It now seems reasonable to conclude that the overly sexed Okame is the aggressor, whose clinging passion drives even herculean Oni into flight.

    The existence of such a parallel has a further implication. It hints that "oni chased by the lascivious Otafuku" may well have been a joke circulating in Edo society at the time. We then wonder what sort of man would have worn the netsuke with such a motif. He must surely have enjoyed its slightly risqué humor and its high recognition value among his friends. Could he also have found in the oni's image something of his own relationship? In that case, the oni could have been his self-mocking caricature.

The tobacco business occupies a prominent position in kibyoshi. The *Latter-Day Tale* contains yet another illuminating detail that adds to our knowledge of netsuke's social and cultural context. It is the prominent position the tobacco shop occupies in this kibyoshi. The main part of the story recounts how Onishichi acquires all the fashionable attributes of contemporary society. Then, toward the end, masterless and jobless, Onishichi goes ahead and opens a tobacco shop. Why does he choose the tobacco business out of all possible careers open to ambitious townsmen like himself?

The history of tobacco in Japan provides the answer. By the late eighteenth century, tobacco had made a great inroad into the lives of the Japanese. As regionally grown tobacco increased in kind and the wider range of flavors became available through cutting and blending, the smoking population and the tobacco business soared. The image of smoking as an elegant habit was further enhanced in the pleasure quarters: courtesans lit and passed their pipes to customers as part of a highly ritualized communication.

As a result of all these developments, retailing tobacco and designing and selling the pipes, pouches, netsuke, and other paraphernalia became a particularly attractive career for sophisticated townsmen. Many writers, illustrators, and performers of popular entertainments took much interest in the tobacco culture, and some actually ran tobacco shops themselves. In fact, the best known of these dealers of tobacco and tobacco culture was the greatest kibyoshi writer, Santo Kyoden.

All this information helps to explain Onishichi's choice. The tobacco shop was the most effective way to show how completely this oni has assimilated himself into the newest lifestyle in Edo. All this also accounts for the publication of several kibyoshi on tobacco in the 1770s and 1780s. Some of them cheerfully promoted new tobacco shops, while others presented personified battles between the popular blends of tobacco. Now we know why this topic was so favored. The tobacco business was not only a hot topic; it was also a business that closely related to the very lives of the authors and friends of popular literature.

Such a connection between kibyoshi and tobacco also helps to explain why the lightly twisted humor characteristic of the kibyoshi genre was so widely shared by the netsuke. As a toggle, netsuke was an indispensable part of a smoking set; and as such, it formed an integral part of the growing tobacco cult, which also involved the core readers and writers of kibyoshi.

Human Transformation in Kibyoshi

The topic of transformation in kibyoshi was by no means limited to the tales of the supernatural or animals in kibyoshi. Many stories of human characters, especially those that derived from Kabuki plays, also exploited the multiple, transforming identities. The two works below, both written and illustrated by the aforementioned writer-artist-tobacconist Santo Kyoden, show the amazing range of variants he developed on this theme.

The Hand-Drummers in Duet: A Contemporary Period Play (Jidai-sewa, nitcho tsuzumi, 1788) parodies the legend of the tenth-century usurper, Taira no Masakado, who reportedly had six other identical selves invisible to the eyes. The historical Masakado was killed in a battle by the famous warrior Fujiwara no Hidesato. In the light-hearted world of kibyoshi, however, the deadly battles are replaced by the comic contests of domestic skills between the two warriors. In the first match (**Figure 14**),[15] the two warriors compete in speed-slicing daikon radishes. Masakado predictably mobilizes his six invisible selves to dish out seven servings of salad. But Hidesato

14. Two warriors compete in a vegetable-slicing match.

scores an easy win. His secret weapon is a kitchen gadget he happened to pick up on his way, the "Magic Eight-Man Slicer." Growing frustrated, Masakado (plus his sextuplet selves) then performs the Kabuki style seven transformations sequence all at once on stage (**Figure 15**).[16] But Hidesato wins this match, too, by his acrobatic performance on eight musical instruments. Now desperate, Masakado reveals all his six clones to intimidate his foe. "A bumper crop of Masakados!" jeers the unimpressed Hidesato and, in return, offers a "magic device" that makes his own multiple identities visible. **Figure 16**[17] shows the images the terrified Masakado sees through this ominous device, a prism from Europe. Eight identical Hidesatos are puffing on eight identical tobacco pipes.

In the final battle scene, Hidesato's military victory contains an intriguing visual detail. The text narrates that when Hidesato cuts off the rebel's head, "strangely enough, Masakado's seven souls leaped out of his body into the sky." But how can the artist visually represent the invisible souls of a man's multiple identities? The picture in **Figure 17**[18] shows the ingenious kibyoshi technique

15. Seven Masakados dance the Seven-changes Dance all at once.

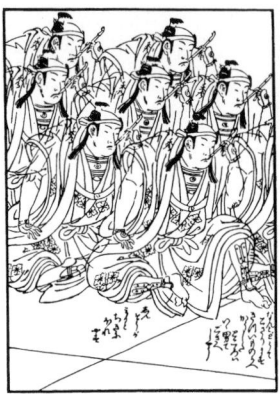

16. A prismatic view of Hidesato, multiplied by eight.

17. Masakado's seven souls fleeing his body.

Kyoden and others before him have developed. On the left, Hidesato is holding Masakado's severed head; on the right sits the headless body of the General. Blood gushing from his neck ejects into the air seven circles, each of which contains the Chinese character *kokoro* (soul). This method of representing the soul attracted attention of fellow writers and artists. In time, many variant images appeared to represent various abstract aspects of the multiple identities.

18. A woman and a man fused in one body.

In the *Silver Pipe, Spliced* (Sogitsugi gingiseru), published in the same year (1788), Kyoden gives another twist to the theme of identity, again evoking a curious parallel in the netsuke genre. In contrast to Masakado, who multiplies his own self, the protagonists of this kibyoshi are the two people fused in one body (**Figure 18**).[19] One male and one female with conflicting interests, the Siamese twins are the fusion of opposites. They fight viciously but, being caught in one body, neither side can win.

The air of hostile stalemate that permeates this kibyoshi is curiously close to the stale mood that enwraps the fox-and-hunter netsuke (**Figure** 4). The twins are as frustrated as the hunter, who can never catch the fox, and as desperate as the fox, who can never flee from the hunter. But unlike the hunter and the fox, stuck in the ambiguous fusion forever, Kyoden's twins find a wondrous solution in modern technology. A doctor specializing in European medicine surgically removes the male head and transplants it to the body of an executed convict.

Multiple Selves of Kibyoshi Writers

As the examples above indicate, many people of the Edo period were deeply preoccupied with the question of multiple selves. The writers and artists of popular literature of the time avidly exploited in their fictions this pervasive interest in multiple selves. But their engagement with this theme went far beyond their fictions. Many took a step further and actually constructed multiple selves in their own lives.

> ... many people of the Edo period were deeply preoccupied with the question of multiple selves.

Construction of many selves was far more than a whim of a frivolous writer or artist. There is no doubt that this practice began as fun, but it often proved to be highly beneficial to his artistic and social lives. By the late eighteenth century, the use of separate identities became a profitable, as well as a fashionable, routine among the artists, writers, and performers of popular culture. Many writers of kibyoshi fiction even featured their own "alter egos" as the characters of their stories.

Works and lives of these writers suggest the social, political, and economic factors that contributed to this trend. Under the rigid hierarchical system of the Tokugawa government, everyone in society was born to, and supposed to stay in, one of the three classes of samurai, peasants, or townsmen. Crossing the class lines was severely restricted, especially between the samurai and commoners. Despite this political rule, however, social and economic reality continued to shift and change through the two and one-half centuries of the Edo period. As the Tokugawa regime passed its mid-point in the eighteenth century, the growth of the commoner's economic power and the relative impoverishment of the samurai class combined to erode the rigid class lines of the feudal system.

The leveling process was especially notable between the samurai and the prosperous townsmen. Samurai as a whole clung to their status, but many of them were forced to seek the merchants' capital just to remain solvent. Townsmen remained stuck at the bottom of the feudal scheme, but many with means had successfully attained the level of cultural sophistication equal to that of the upper-class samurai.

It was obviously no accident that just around this time — past mid-eighteenth century — a new form of cultural interaction began to take place among the lively groups of samurai and those of townsmen. What initiated this largely spontaneous movement was their common desire to develop the new culture that reflected their age. The locus of this movement was the shogun's military capital, Edo, where contacts between samurai and townsmen were the closest.

Samurai and townsmen, creative urbanites of Edo, gradually came together, and they began to produce witty and ironic works dealing with the increasingly bourgeois world they had to share. The movement, which began in a genre of comic verse in samurais' uptown, soon spread to the prose literature, and then to the visual and performing arts in the merchant-centered downtown.

What facilitated this unprecedented merging of classes most was the construction of artistic personae, independent of one's primary, feudal identity. The participants met in frequent parties and outings, not as samurai or tradesmen or artisans but as comic poets, fiction writers, ukiyo artists, actors, singers, and various kinds of entertainers. Once they had established their identities as talented citizens of Edo, all were free to address each other almost as equals.

A few unwritten rules seem to have evolved to protect this newly found freedom. All guests suspended their primary identities at the door. They switched to their artistic pseudonyms, equalized their language, and sometimes slipped on costumes. Most parties had literary themes on which each guest composed, depicted, or performed in the genre of choice. Eating, drinking, and merriment brightened all these festivities. Once the party was over, though, the guests all returned to their normal worlds, where rigid hierarchy again separated them.

As such parties became popular throughout the town of Edo, the use of multiple identities spread to the farther reaches of society. Many writers and artists found this practice so congenial that they developed more and more aliases for each area of their playful activities. They slipped these names on and off, as though the names had been masks to flip on and off.

Let us look at a few examples. The leading kibyoshi writer we have already met was most widely known as Santo Kyoden, but he had an equally important identity as a talented ukiyo artist, Kitao Masanobu. In his primary capacity as a townsman, though, he was merely Denzo of the Kyoya, a small tobacco shop downtown. A more complex example is the baffling case of Hoseido Kisanji, the reporter of Oni's makeover. In the realm of popular culture alone, he held a dizzying array of roles: a versatile poet, a publicist for the Yoshiwara Pleasure Quarters, a connoisseur of kabuki, and so on. For each of these activities and genres, Kisanji invented several names, and treated each as an independent personality.

Even more startling than Kisanji's numerous literary personae is his primary identity. In the world of samurai, Hirazawa Heikaku served the powerful daimyo Satake as his deputy (rusuiyaku) — a top-ranking post in the lord's Edo residence. The deputy's duty was collecting sensitive information from other domains, often through bribery, espionage, and other devious means. Given the nature of Heikaku's work, we can safely assume that Deputy Hirazawa Heikaku fully exploited the extensive connections he had cultivated in the world of popular culture as Hoseido Kisanji and under many other guises.

090(661)

Censorship and Lying Low

Alas, good things never seem to last forever. This relatively free world of urban writers and artists began to crumble with the death of the indifferent tenth shogun, Ieharu, in 1786, and the fall of the permissive Grand Chamberlain soon after. In the late 1780s, the new regent, Matsudaira Sadanobu, launched the broadly suppressive Kansei Reforms. The goal of the zealous regent was to tighten Confucian class structure and reaffirm the samurai's leadership. In the course of this increasingly harsh suppression, the vibrant popular culture, from Kabuki to humorous literature, came under heavy attack, and the freewheeling world of the popular culture ground to a halt.

Ironically, the most interesting works on multiple identities were produced in response to the turbulent beginning of this suppression. We find a particularly illuminating case in Hoseido Kisanji's *The Household Monsters of Kisanjin* (Kisanjin ie no bakemono), published in the New Year of 1787. In this curiously self-reflexive work, the samurai author Hoseido Kisanji casts his own personae as the main characters. (I will italicize *Kisanji*, a character, to distinguish him from the writer Kisanji.) **Figure 19**[20] shows the over-the-hill kibyoshi writer *Kisanji* dozing off in his den. In his dream (indicated by the balloon), *Kisanji* is trying to get some advice from his three visitors, whom he calls his "soul-mates." He had promised to write a kibyoshi for the New Year, but now, nearing the end of summer, he has not written one line. None of his cronies can offer any fresh ideas, since all these friends are also the author Hoseido Kisanji's other literary personae. Wearily (and still in his dream), *Kisanji* starts to write another monster story, a stock theme in kibyoshi. He smears a page in black "to show the darkness of the soul," but, more truthfully, to procrastinate writing.

The uninspiring story about Kisanji's dream drags on all the way to the final page, when Kisanji reaches a stunning conclusion. **Figure**

19. Writer Kisanji dreams of himself consulting with his other literary personae.

20[21] shows a man, labeled as Kisanji, squarely facing the reader. In the accompanying text, he explains the self-insight he has just acquired. All his recent troubles were nothing but a long confusing dream, induced by allowing his soul to leave his body and float around. But now that he is finally awake, he knows exactly what he should do. "In order never to let it happen to me," exclaims the character, "I will now swallow my soul!"

Visual clues in the illustration even more crucially affect our interpretation of this ending. The man posed to swallow his vagrant soul (the character *kokoro*, in a circle) is identified as *Kisanji* by the characters on his vest. But his image has distinctly changed from the earlier, slovenly image of the kibyoshi hack writer. If this is not *Kisanji*, then who is he? We find the answer implied in his dignified square face, his formal costume, and the long sword he proudly wears. All suggest that this square-jawed image represents the prominent samurai bureaucrat Hirazawa Heikaku — the author Kisanji's primary identity.

This scene also hints at the vaguely defensive position Kisanji seems to be taking about his activities in the popular culture, and especially his use of many personae. But the exact reasons why Kisanji wrote this strangely defensive piece are not clear from this work alone.

Documents introduced by a Japanese specialist on Kisanji shed new light on this question.²² The records of the Satake House that Inoue Takaaki unearthed reveal the daily activities of its Edo deputy, Hirazawa Heikaku, in the crucial years preceding the Kansei Reforms. As the documents show, the death of the shogun in the late summer of 1786 threw Heikaku into a frenzy of action. As the Satake domain's chief diplomat and information officer, Heikaku had to gather information vital to his domain's future. He met with deputies of other domains, paid frequent visits to key officials of Edo Castle, delivered gifts, and filled out reports, while the reformer Matsudaira Sadanobu was poised to seize power in the following year. And in these self-same months of tumult, Heikaku's literary alter ego, Kisanji, was scribbling away the draft of this kibyoshi.

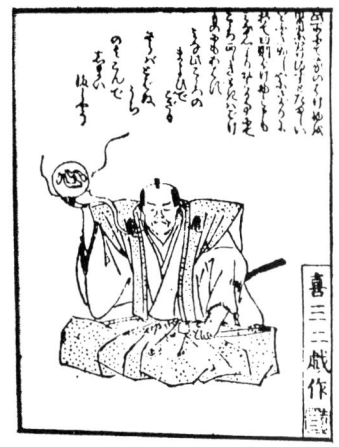

20. Kisanji, posed to swallow his vagrant soul.

By collating the lives of these two "selves," we gain more insight into *The Household Monsters*. While Kisanji was preparing this work, the able diplomat Heikaku probably began to sense Sadanobu's impending rise to power and his resolve to stop the erosion of the class distinction. If the reformer really meant business, he was bound to disfavor samurai who, under pseudonyms, enjoyed the cultural activities of commoners.

Seen in this light, this kibyoshi can be interpreted as a signal that Kisanji/Heikaku was sending to his samurai world. His signal is still tentative, because Sadanobu has not yet secured power or made his intent public. As though to anticipate Sadanobu's next move, however, Kisanji put the question of multiple selves on the kibyoshi agenda. The strange ending of this tale is most likely to contain his very tentative message: "OK, I will clean up my act — only if push comes to shove."

Sadanobu did rise to power and he did mean business. The reform he then launched proved to be far more extensive and serious than Kisanji or any other playful writers seemed to have expected. In a few years, major samurai writers of kibyoshi and other popular literature were all silenced, including Kisanji. Commoners were exhorted to return to their place and mind the didactic teachings of the newly popular Shingaku (teaching of the mind), which emphasized contentment with one's lot.

The townsman writer Santo Kyoden barely survived the reforms and continued his brilliant career in popular literature, even though he had to embrace didacticism for survival. *Quickly Dyed in Moral Teaching* (Shingaku hayazomegusa), published in 1790, is a surprisingly successful example of such a compromise. Here, Kyoden again addresses the issue of the split selves, but deflects censor by ingeniously tying it to the teaching of Shingaku.

While his earlier story of General Masakado dealt with multiplying selves, and *The Silver Pipe, Spliced* featured a male and a female fused in one body, Kyoden, in *Quickly Dyed in Moral Teaching*, traces what we might call the "moral growth" of one unremarkable young man, Ritaro. If this topic sounds unpromising, the plot below will confirm the doubt.

When Ritaro is born as the heir to a loving bourgeois family, the Heavenly King wards off evil and allows him to grow up with all goodness. But one day, when Ritaro is napping, the evil elements gain control and turn the youth into a prodigal, then a criminal.

Fortunately, Ritaro meets a teacher of Shingaku, who guides him back to the rightful path.

What turned this morality tale into a kibyoshi best-seller was the brilliant visual strategies Kyoden deployed in rendering Ritaro's moral conflicts. Most important, Kyoden separated the conflicts from the youth, and turned them into two external forces fighting over him.

21. The Heavenly King (with halo) sends "Good" to the newborn, while restraining "Evil."

In the illustrations (beginning with Ritaro's birth scene in **Figure 21**[23]), these forces were personified into quasi-human agents of Good and Evil. Their faces reflect their abstract identities: they are just circles, respectively marked with the Chinese characters "Good" and "Evil." Many readers would have smiled in recognition: these faces had derived from the technique that Kyoden and Kisanji had used to represent the abstract entity, "Soul."

Their body language further deepens meaning and enhances humor. In **Figure 22**,[24] Ritaro's moral turmoil is represented literally by the tug of war between Evil and Good. Evil's group, which outnumbers single Good, easily wins, and Ritaro decides to stay another night in the brothel. In **Figure 23**,[25] the victorious Evils, dancing wildly at Ritaro's party — one waving a fan — contain another visual message: they clearly refer to the raucous "jesters" (taikomochi), who often danced at such parties. These amusing figures of "Good" and "Evil" lived on beyond the Edo period and continued to turn up in caricatures, comics, and netsuke way into the modern Meiji period.

22. Ritaro being pulled by "Evils," who outnumber the lone "Good."

23. "Evils" dance victoriously as Ritaro carries on in the pleasure quarters.

The Old and the New in the Meiji Period

The Meiji Restoration of 1868 brought enormous changes to the lives of the Japanese. Their impact was especially serious on such traditional arts as ukiyo prints and the netsuke. In the once popular theme of multiple identity, subtle but fundamental changes seem to have taken place. Let us see the interesting case of the ukiyo artist Kobayashi Kiyochika. As the last bearer of Edo ukiyoe tradition, he continued to produce the haunting images of multiple identities. The image in **Figure 24**,[26] dated around 1878, is a fusion of three famous geisha, representing the cities of Tokyo, Osaka, and Kyoto.

At the same time, they evoke the three lovely elements of nature — snow, moon, and blossoms. The technique of fusion and the layering of meanings are all legacies of the Edo period.

But the new series of sketches Kiyochika produced in 1884 reveals an important change (**Figure 25**).[27] The title of the series, "One Person, Six Faces," suggests another exercise in multiple identities, but the six faces we see here are realistic sketches of the six facial expressions of a single individual. The titular "Man with a Hat" has many moods but only one identity.

This development in Kiyochika seems to be subtly paralleled by a strange netsuke of clustered masks, produced around the same period (**Figure 26**).[28] While the earlier composites portray multifarious manifestations of human existence, this modern cluster seems more like a psychological study of one person's face in distress. The emotions range through fury, terror, and despair, but all these variously distorted faces seem to belong to someone, or anyone, with no clear identity. In this sense, the mask cluster breaks from the traditional practice, in the same way as Kiyochika's Man with a Hat moved away from the faces of three

24. The faces of three geisha fused into one.

25. Six facial expressions of one individual.

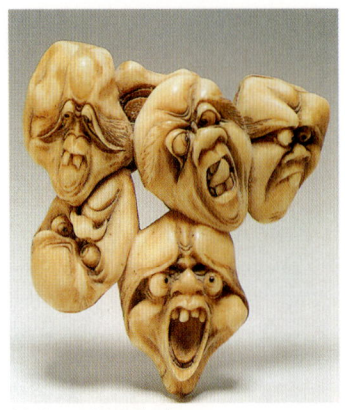

26. A netsuke study of distress, in cluster.

geisha fused into one.

But some artists of the Meiji period tenaciously held onto the old Edo tradition. Kiyochika, in fact, remained such an artist for most of his career. In the field of netsuke, the maverick carver of stag antler, Ozaki Kokusai, presents another interesting example of a traditionalist in Meiji. He chose his themes mostly from the Edo period and applied a bold innovative approach to creating brilliant works.

The design of one striking work of Kokusai can be traced back to Kyoden's work on multiple selves, which in turn had derived from other kibyoshi. Note the dancing *obihasami* in **Figure 27**,[29] which graces the cover of Eskenazi's catalogue. Knowledgeable readers would immediately recognize its link to the "Good/Evil" images Kyoden had developed a century earlier. In particular, Kokusai seems to have relied on the images traceable to the party scene where "Evil" agents dance like party clowns (**Figure 23**).

Some artists of the Meiji period tenaciously held onto the old Edo tradition.

Well-informed viewers would also admire Kokusai's uncanny ability to find the right topic and adapt it to his own purpose. One reason he chose this particular image of "Good" for his netsuke must have been its skinny body. The lanky, naked figures of "Good" fit perfectly the shape of his favorite material, stag antler. But the netsuke is trying to tell us more by way of a few discrepancies with Kyoden's version. The most obvious thing is the identities of these figures. The dancing figures in the kibyoshi party scene are all marked "Evil," whereas the netsuke image here is clearly marked "Good." Another difference is in the fan. In the kibyoshi, the fan held by the dancer in the center is blank, but that of the netsuke has the word *oiri*, "a full house," written on it. And thirdly, the toes of the netsuke figures turn into swirls, in contrast to the normal feet of the dancing guys. What is Kokusai telling us by these details?

> ...this octopus may well be Kokusai's self-portrait, in caricature.

The answer is found in the recent *INSJ* article "Red Robe Kokusai," which uncovered Kokusai's little known background.³⁰ According to the author, Yoichi Shimatani, this netsuke artist was equally popular as "jester" (*taikomochi*) — a professional entertainer hired to brighten party scenes and outings to sumo or kabuki. Kokusai's trademarks were his bright red jacket, a fan with which to cheer the full house and, most strikingly, his huge, bald head, not unlike that of an octopus. Now we can make a good guess at the messages Kokusai worked into this netsuke. The curled up toes of this figure and the large circle that defines his head probably allude to an octopus. Then, combined with the "Full House" fan and the clowning gesture, this octopus may well be Kokusai's self-caricature.

This interpretation draws additional support from another obihasami by Kokusai, the two views of which appear in Shimatani's article (**Figure 28**).³¹ Most viewers would only see that this netsuke is an octopus. But those who are familiar with Kokusai's background would readily recognize, from the fan and the cards in the octopus' arms, that the octopus is Kokusai's own image in caricature. Now that we know the octopus' identity, we can try comparing it with the netsuke of "Good" to confirm the latter's identity. Immediately

27. Kokusai's netsuke of "Good."

28. A dancing octopus—Kokusai's self-caricature.

obvious is the lean body shape the two figures share. They also share the jester's profession, implied in their fans and dancing pose. And, most importantly, their spherical heads and their curling toes are virtually identical. This observation further affirms our view that Kokusai's netsuke figure "Good" connotes the artist's self-caricature, while it asserts the long tradition of Edo culture, reaching back to Kyoden times.

As this preliminary study suggests, the more we can examine netsuke in their cultural context, the better able we are to sift through their acquired layers of meaning and discover the richness of their original connotation. For such a context, I have here concentrated on popular literature, but the net can be cast much more widely, and researchers can find themselves very profitably considering the Noh and Kabuki theaters, the demimonde of the licensed quarters, the ever-changing interaction between social classes, and even the vicissitudes of politics. For the time and the place of the netsuke were dynamic, and the art of netsuke, as was the case with probably all Japanese art, was not only pursued for its own sake, but also for the ends of personal expression in the hurry-scurry of real life.

Notes

1. Matthew Welch and Sharen Chappell, *Netsuke: The Japanese Art of Miniature Carving*, catalogue by The Minneapolis Institute of Arts (Pentagon Publishing, 1999), #122, P.89.
2. Welch/Chappell, *Netsuke* #167, p.115.
3. Welch/Chappell, *Netsuke* #121, p.89.
4. Welch/Chappell, *Netsuke* #69, p.59.
5. Welch/Chappell, *Netsuke* #54, p.52.
6. Welch/Chappell, *Netsuke* #103, p.80.
7. welch/Chappell, *Netsuke* #163, p.113.
8. In a tenth century court lady's musings, *The Pillow Book*, for example, the author took delight in listing such items as "Adorable things" or "Annoying things."
9. Iba Kasho, "Sate mo baketari, kitsune no tsujin." *Edo no parodei ehon*, zokukan 1, ed. Koike Masatane, et al. (Shakai Sisosha, 1984), 131.
10. Iba Kasho, *Sate mo baketari*, 132-133.
11. Iba Kasho, *Sate mo baketari*, 144.
12. Hoseido Kisanji, "Momotaro gonichibanashi." *Edo no parodei ehon*, vol. 1, ed. Koike Masatane, et al. (Shakai Shisosha, 1980), 68.
13. Kisanji, *Momotaro*, 72.
14. Kisanji, *Momotaro*, 75.
15. Santo Kyoden, "Jidai-sewa nicho tsuzumi." *Nihon koten bungaku zenshu*, vol.46, *Kibyoshi, Senryu, Kyoka*, Hamada Giichiro, ed. (Tokyo: Shogakukan, 1971), 151.
16. Santo Kyoden, *Jidai-sewa*, 152.
17. Santo Kyoden, *Jidai-sewa*, 155.
18. Santo Kyoden, *Jidai-sewa*, 157.
19. Santo Kyoden, "Sogitsugi gingiseru."
20. Hoseido Kisanji, "Kisanjin ie no bakemono." *Edo no parodei ehon*, vol.2, ed. Koike Masatane, et al. (Shakai Shisosha, 1981), 189.
21. Kisanji, *Kisanjin ie no bakemono*, 214.
22. Inoue Takaaki, "Tenmei 8 nen no Kisanji." *Edo bungaku kenkyu*, ed. Jinbo Kazuya (Shintensha, 1993), 295-309.
23. Santo Kyoden, "Shingaku hayazomegusa." *Nihon koten bungaku taikei*, 59, Kibyoshi sharebon shu, Mizuno Minoru, ed. (Iwanami, 1958), 201.
24. Kyoden, *Shingaku*, 209.
25. Kyoden, *Shingaku*, 207.
26. Henry D. Smith II and Susan Tai, *Kiyochika: Artist of Meiji Japan* (Santa Barbara Museum of Art, 1988), 59.
27. Smith, *Kiyochika*, 62.

[28] Welch/Chappell, *Netsuke*, #211, 142. The approximate date given is late 19th century.
[29] Shimatani Yoichi, "Ozaki Koyo no 'kakushichichi.'" *Geijitsu shincho*, May 2000, p.108. The image of this obihasami graces the cover of Eskenazi's catalogue along with four other Kokusai pieces.
[30] "Red Robe Kokusai" was published in two parts in the *INS Journal*, vol.19, No.2 (Summer 1999) and vol.20, No.3 (Fall 2000).
[31] *INSJ*, Vol.20, No.3 (Fall 2000).

Works Cited

Hoseido Kisanji. "Kisanjin ie no bakemono." *Edo no parodei ehon*, vol.2. Ed. Koike Masatane, et al. Tokyo: Shakai Shisosha, 1981. Original edition at the Kaga Bunko.

———. "Momotaro gonichibanashi." *Edo no parodei ehon*, vol.1. Ed. Koike Masatane, et al. Tokyo: Shakai Shisosha, 1980. Original edition at the Kaga Bunko.

Iba Kasho. "Sate mo baketari, kitsune no tsujin." *Edo no parodei ehon*, zokukan 1. Ed. Koike Masatane, et al. Shakai Shisosha, 1984. Original edition at the Diet Library.

Inoue Takaaki. "Tenmei hachinen no Kisanji." *Edo bungaku kenkyu*. Ed. Jinbo Kazuya. Tokyo: Shintensha, 1993.

Santo Kyoden. "Jidai-sewa nicho tsuzumi." *Nihon koten bungaku zenshu*, vol.46, *Kibyoshi*, *Senryu*, *Kyoka*. Ed. Hamada Giichiro. Tokyo: Shogakukan, 1971. Original edition at the Kaga Bunko.

Santo Kyoden. "Shingaku hayazomegusa." *Nihon koten bungaku taikei*, 59, *Kibyoshi sharebon shu*. Ed. Mizuno Minoru. Iwanami, 1958. Original edition at the Kaga Bunko.

Shimatani Yoichi. "Ozaki Koyo no 'kakushi-chichi.'" *Geijutsu shincho*. May 2000.

———. "Red Robe Kokusai." *International Netsuke Society Journal* 19/2 (Summer 1999) and 20/3 (Fall 2000).

Smith, Henry D. II and Susan Tai. *Kiyochika: Artist of Meiji Japan*. Santa Barbara Museum of Art, 1988.

Welch, Matthew and Sharen Chappell. *Netsuke: The Japanese Art of Miniature Carving*. Catalogue by The Minneapolis Institute of Arts. Pentagon Publishing, 1999.

Acknowledgments

We are grateful to the following Tokyo publishers for granting permission to reproduce illustrations from the various kibyoshi publications cited within this article: SHAKAI SHISOSHA • SHOGAKUKAN • IWANAMI SHOTEN

We also extend our thanks to publishers of the netsuke illustrations: MINNEAPOLIS INSTITUTE OF ARTS–PENTAGON PUBLISHING • ESKENAZI, LTD., LONDON • SANTA BARBARA MUSEUM OF ART

We would like to express our gratitude to the International Netsuke Society for granting permission to use Haruko G. Iwasaki's article entitled "Speak, Memory! Edo Netsuke in Their Literary Context" in *International Netsuke Society Journal*, Volume 21, Number 4, Winter 2001.

05
From Proselytization to Assimilation: New French and German Fictional Approach to Jesuit China Missions

Adrian Hsia

Generally speaking, self-centeredness is a necessary means for survival for individuals and groups. No culture could have developed without a fundamental line between us and the others. Such differentiation led to conflicts and the expansion of one culture (and nation) at the expense of others. The siege, conquest, and destruction of Troy is a typical example. Genocide is not a modern invention. Closer to our own times, the Enlightenment is celebrated as the triumph of reason and humanitarianism; however, its economical foundation was based on conquest, colonization, enslavement, genocide, and trade, including in slaves and opium. This is the Yin and Yang of culture. In the last millennium, there were three monolithic cultures: Christianity, Islam, and the Celestial Empire. The first two share the characteristics that they are both theistic and were developed from the Mosaic religion. Between the root and its branches there is, however, a fundamental difference. Judaism is self-restricting in expansion; it can basically only be expanded biologically. The other two, being offshoots, discarded tribal limitations and became universal. Early Christianity was spread by word of mouth. When it became the state religion of the Roman Empire, things began to change. The Crusades, both those external and internal, and the Inquisition bore witness to the militancy of Christianity, not to mention the religious wars such as the Thirty Years' War in the 17th century. In the Age of Discovery, the Bible and the sword worked hand in hand. The Americas were won this way. However, when Portugal found its way to Asia, it managed only to establish colonies in parts of the Indian subcontinent and Malacca; the colossal Chinese Empire and even Japan were beyond its military reach. Both in the Americas and in South Asia, colonization and conversion went hand in hand. The Inquisition, for instance, was in full force in Goa. Only Japanese converts were won by genuine missionary efforts; Francis Xavier serves as an example.

Before the first steps of accommodation were introduced by Alexander Valignano in 1578, being converted meant total surrender of one's cultural identity, because everything non-European was considered heathen. Not only did one receive a baptismal name, but also a new, usually Portuguese, family name. The father of Zheng Chenggong, for example, had a complete Portuguese identity which he later gave up. In all, a convert in a colony had to become an imitation European as much as possible. He remained, of course, a second class citizen, only better than his pagan brothers. Before Valignano had the inspired idea, there was no single missionary, in Macau or elsewhere, who bothered to learn Chinese, a heathen tongue. Even Francis Xavier, when he tried to enter China, had a Chinese interpreter with him. The only problem was that this interpreter, who had received his Christian education in Goa, was so Europeanized that his Chinese became inadequate for the purpose. When Valignano decided on the new course, his first task was to recruit a Jesuit who was willing to learn Chinese. None of those who were already in Macau, ten in number, volunteered. From among the new arrivals in Goa, Michele Ruggieri was sent and arrived in Macau in July, 1579. This was the concrete beginning of accommodation. Ruggieri was joined later by Mateo Ricci shortly after the latter's ordination in Goa. Valignano was serious in his decision. Not only did he find money from the Portuguese community (when there was none owing to the loss of a ship) to finance the China Mission, he also permitted the two Jesuits to shave their heads and beards and to enter China dressed or disguised as Buddhist bonzes. For years, these two Jesuits went about in their disguise until Ricci had learned enough of the language and culture to recognize the futility of this effort. Henceforth he (Ruggierri had since returned to Europe) transformed himself into a Confucian scholar. The rest of the story is well known.

Accommodation was a serious concession to reality. China could not be conquered even though Spanish Manila (Portugal was ruled by the Spanish crown at that time) did have plans to do so and petitioned the Spanish court for permission and support. This was roughly at the time when Ricci was in Chaoqing. But a decision was never made, and the Spanish Armada was defeated in 1588. This made all military ventures on a large scale an impossibility. Thus proselytization could not be aided by prior colonization; accommodation became the only possibility. The Buddhist disguise of the Jesuits shows that Valignano was at least as determined as Francis Xavier to accomplish the goal of converting the Chinese. Given the disgust the Christians felt for idolatry, transforming himself from the disguise of a Buddhist monk — an idolator! — into a Confucian scholar must have been a great relief for Ricci. If the Jesuits were willing to disguise themselves as Buddhists, it would be even less difficult to deal with Confucianism on the religious side. They persuaded themselves that Confucianism was originally theistic. To do this has a cultural connotation. It means almost to accept the Chinese and their culture as equal. In the journals of Mateo Ricci and works of other Jesuits, we usually experience a sympathetic, at times even laudatory description of Chinese achievements. Only when the three indigenous religions of China are touched, do we witness the change of the tone to ridicule and condemnation. Nevertheless, accommodation means acquiescence to a large degree, comparable to a Christian convert in a colony. The goal of Christianizing China, of course, was never given up. That the decision of accommodation was locally made, i.e. in China, sowed the seeds for future strife, because Eurocentrism was growing stronger in the following centuries. When the initial enthusiasm created by Jesuit propaganda in Europe cooled down and the anti-Jesuit propaganda, especially of the mendicant orders, spread, Eurocentrism could no longer tolerate accommodation. In a novel written by Rudolf Gasser, a Capuchin Monk from Switzerland, titled *Historia von Philologo*,[1] published about a century after the establishment of the Jesuit China Mission, the protagonist resorted to the sword and kidnapping to Christianize China. That was before the first semi-official condemnation of Jesuit accommodation pronounced by the Faculty of Theology of the Sorbonne University in 1700. Seventy-three years later, the Jesuit order was dissolved and China was looked upon as a mummy shrouded in silk.[2] At the end of the 19th century, China reacted violently to the European presence on Chinese soil, and the Western powers collectively punished China. It took another century for the two novels which this paper intends to discuss to be written and published. In them, we notice that the Eurocentrism has changed. Even though both novels deal with missionaries in China, the subject matter, however, is not proselytization, not even accommodation, but assimilation of the European missionaries.

The first novel, titled *Der Maler von Peking* (*The Painter of Peking*), was published in 1993.[3] The author, Tilman Spengler, has a Ph.D. in Chinese History; this fact makes his novel particularly interesting. *The Painter* is his second novel, following *Lenins Hirn* (*Lenin's Brain*)[4]. In 1999, another novel, titled *Die Stirn, die Augen und die Nase* (*The*

Brow, the Eyes, and the Nose) appeared. It deals with post-Mao China. 2001 has already seen the publication of two more books, one novel, *Meine Gesellschaft-Kursbuch eines Unfertigen* (*My Society-Schedule of an Unaccomplished Person*) and a non-fiction book (*Moskau-Berlin. Stereogramme*), both published by the Berlin Verlag. In addition to being a journalist and writer, Spengler is also a film-maker. His written works including essays, stories, and novels, are well received and have been translated into 15 languages so far, including English and French. He was named the 15th City Scribe of Mainz in 1998, an honour which includes occupying a wing in the Gutenberg Museum for one year and a cash prize of DM 24,000. Even the uncrowned king of the German literary scene, Marcel Reich-Ranicki, had words of recognition for Spengler's talent. Of his literary works, *The Painter* was the most historically remote, being situated in the first half of the 18th century. Historicity makes reception difficult. Chinese readers and Sinologists[5] would question the authenticity of the historical China delineated in the novel. In doing so, they underrate its satirical tone. On the other hand, the general reader, not versed in historical China and the Jesuit Mission, may not fully appreciate the historical side. In our analysis we shall try to do justice to both.

Being a historical satire, the characters depicted in *The Painter in Peking* are atypical. On the Chinese side, we have four major characters: Lu, an art dealer who forges paintings; Yang, his friend, a dismissed Mandarin who now tries in any way possible to earn a living; Mi Lan, the dealer's daughter, who is a wild young woman; and finally, her dismissed house tutor. On the Jesuit side, we have, among others, the hero, the painter Lazzo; the Provincial who instructs Lazzo to convert the Chinese emperor with his art; a novice who wants to make Confucius a Christian prophet; and another Jesuit who, after living in China for 20 years, comes to the conclusion that the best way to convert the Chinese is to destroy all rhubarb fields in China so that they would suffer from constipation like Europeans; as a result they could learn to think and feel like Christians.

From the very beginning, the world of the Europeans on both continents is openly described through the eyes of Lazzo as a first-person account. The reader experiences with the hero his childhood, the development of his artistic talent, and his joining the Church to further his art. Then the Church calls him to serve in the China Mission. Upon arrival in China, he is summoned to the Father Provincial. There we hear a discussion on the central perspective[6] in painting. Europe faults China for not knowing the one-point perspective in the arts. Chinese paintings are considered flat because of the lack of this perspective. According to the Provincial, Chinese painting allows too many different perspectives. This liberal attitude results in polytheism. It is Lazzo's secret mission to teach the Chinese Emperor the advantages of the central perspective. Once the monarch appreciates that only one perspective is correct, he would then be led to God, the centre, concludes the Father Provincial. The other remedy is, as we have already seen, to make Chinese suffer from constipation. Thus, the fundamental ironic nature of the novel becomes apparent: the religious aspect of the centred perspective is intentionally trivialized. One theory seems now as serious and potent as the other.

The description of the Chinese world is sheathed in mystery. The narrator pretends to be an observer. The novel begins with a scene which rivals Jin Yong's wuxia-novels. A group of beggars in rags sit outside the city during a sand storm for days on end, waiting. With the winds howling, the city gate opens and a small caravan, consisting of two horses, three sedan-chairs, and five camels, exits. The gate is immediately closed behind them. Pretending to be begging for alms, these beggars take out their knives and kill both men and animals. The latter they dissect and distribute among the beggars. Much later, we learn that the murdered are princes and princesses and one foreign painter.⁷ Including this last mentioned, the novel mentions three European painters; the two others are the fictitious Lazzo and his idol, the historical Giuseppe Castiglione. This painter at the court of Qian Long is often mentioned in the novel as a model painter as well as a model Jesuit. Lazzo, towards the end of the novel, will become an excellent painter, but he betrays the China Mission.

After the massacre, Peking seems to be flooded by cheap camel meat and horse tongues,⁸ as well as, among other things, European paintings. The art forger and dealer has acquired one. He is fascinated and disturbed by the linear perspective of the painting and becomes obsessed with it. Gradually it is revealed that the secret Society of Double Swords was involved in the murders. It seems that this Society had chosen Mi Lan as its virgin queen. The reason why father and daughter have become involved with the Society was never revealed. A partial enlightenment is offered by the dealer's best friend, the dismissed mandarin Yang, who is now more associated with the twilight world.⁹ He informs the art dealer Lu that his house has been under observation by the secret society because of the position of his daughter. Furthermore, it is also revealed that the Society seeks to overthrow the emperor and drive out the aliens, because in their perception, the emperor has fetched the foreigners to destroy the Chinese culture. Yang, styled a Confucian scholar, has learned that the Society of Double Swords has found the mystic virgin elsewhere; therefore Lu's family, both father and daughter, are spared further hassle. A pause is thus introduced in the Chinese plot.

In the meantime, Lazzo is in Peking, and the Superior of the Mission moves heaven and earth to introduce him to the emperor. At the audience, the emperor puts his art to the test by asking him to draw portraits of the Jesuit fathers. These please him, and Lazzo is then employed as painter in the Royal Academy, while the portraits are handed over to the police to check on the movement of the

Jesuits. This is further proof that irony, not historicity and authenticity, is the concern of Spengler. The author also makes fun of the Western perception that Chinese painting lacks the one-point perspective, because China, represented by the emperor, considers this European perspective vulgar. Therefore, the emperor asks Lazzo how this perspective is employed to indicate space and time in a painting. The painter jokingly answers if one bends down and looks backwards between one's legs, one will be able to perceive things, although upside down, in the right perspective. The emperor considers it a joke. He gives Lazzo three days to show how he can paint standing on his head. Frantically, Lazzo seeks help to accomplish this. Finally, the only advice comes from the Chinese servants of the Mission. Accordingly, Lazzo practises some Chinese martial arts techniques day and night. When the moment of truth comes, he is able to paint upside down before the emperor. This episode ends the discussion of central perspective and Lazzo's attempt to convert the emperor through European painting. He now learns Chinese brush techniques.[10] Unexpectedly, but predictably, he is invited to dinner at Lu's house. Mi Lan, against all Chinese etiquette, is present. In him she has found the ultimate alien being whom she has been craving for. Lazzo satisfies her longing for everything non-traditional and different. These two unusual persons become lovers. However, gradually, Lazzo realises that the Society of Double Swords, for its own purpose, is the mastermind of their encounter and love affair. The secret is now in the open. This leads inexplicably to the elimination of Lu, Mi Lan's father and the forger and art dealer, who is, we learn later, a renegade member of the Society. During the funeral service, his body disappears from the coffin. This leads to a police investigation and eventually to the break up of the Society. In the meantime, Mi Lan becomes the ward of Lu's best friend, the unconventional Confucian scholar. To keep her out of harm's way, he sends her to her ancestral village until things settle. Years later, the thread of the plot is picked up again. Lazzo, a celebrated court painter and the favourite of the emperor by now, has already left the Mission, and his visits there have become rarer from year to year. Admonitions diplomatically applied by the Superior are of no avail. Rosaries and images of the holy Virgin Mary also fail to bring Lazzo back to the Mission. He now paints without the tyranny of the central perspective, but with a perspective of feeling which has been refined by Chinese art. It is not European realism anymore. However, anyone expecting a happy end will be disappointed. Even though Yang tries to arrange a marriage between Mi Lan and Lazzo, the end of the novel indicates this will come to nothing. The stumbling block is the fact that Mi Lan has not changed. She continues to rebel against the Chinese tradition. She would be ready to marry a real Italian, but not a sinisized one. The novel terminates with her cutting up her wedding dress. Thus ends the depiction of two unusual persons.

Lazzo is produced by Eurocentrism, with the central perspective as its essence. Monotheism is supposed to do away with polytheism represented by the multiple perspective, or the lack of any perspective. In the end, Lazzo is drawn to the opposite. He learns, however, that China does have a centre, even though its uniformity is not achieved through religion, but secularly. In the words of the Chinese emperor in the novel, the queue, decreed by the Manchus, is the emblem of Chinese uniformity. Both monoliths are convinced of their own righteousness. Ironically, each cultural system has produced its specific rebel. Lazzo is drawn to the multiplicity represented by Chinese painting and, consequently, to Chinese culture, while Mi Lan is attracted to Europe without its religious aspects, as Lazzo is perceived only as an expressive and spontaneous Italian painter, not as a missionary, by Mi Lan and her family. The reader is presented with two centristic and imperfect societies. Each has its own rebel. An easy solution is not offered, because marriage would destroy the imbalance. At the end of the novel, the reader is left with an uncertainty. Neither religious centrality nor political uniformity is acceptable for independent spirits, and individuals will remain individuals, no matter from which monolith they originate.

Tilman Spengler's novel has a historical setting in the 18th century. The year of the massacre of the caravan is given as 1724. About this time, Lazzo's idol Giuseppe Castiglione is supposed to be dead. In the novel, it is the world of the fictional hero. In real history, Castiglione did not die until 1768. During his life in China, he mostly served the historical emperor Qian Long who reigned from 1736 to 1796. These dates show that the historicity of the novel is really only a farce. Since the protagonists are anti-traditionalists rebelling against the dictates of centrality and uniformity, labelling them inauthentic does not do the novel justice, even though some details do seem to be objectionable and certain episodes are simply incredible. Through the ironic tone which is carried consequently throughout the novel, the novelist Spengler seems to be ridiculing centralization, in religion as well as in politics. The historical setting is employed to expose this phenomenon in both cultures, so it seems.

In contrast, Jacques Baudouin's novel, *Le Mandarin blanc*, is, in the author's own words, a free interpretation of the life of Teodorico Pedrini.[11] The popularity of this novel can be attested by its pocket book edition and translation into German and Italian. Those who are familiar with the music of the 18th century and the Rites Controversy will know Pedrini, for he was a celebrated composer/musician and the papal emissary to China. As court musician he served three Qing emperors. Reading the novel is like witnessing the dramatic development of the Rites Controversy in Beijing. In this paper, we deal only with the second part of the novel describing Pedrini's life in China. This involves, of course, the Jesuit China Mission in Peking. The reader encounters such prominent personalities as Bouvet, Parennin, and Castiglione. In the novel, the Jesuits (except the latecomer Castiglione), especially the Portuguese, appear as villains who seek the destruction of their enemy Pedrini. Even Bouvet appears as an intriguer and liar. As a matter of fact, Parennin is the only Jesuit in the novel who seems not to have taken an active part in seeking the ruin of the protagonist. Historically, as well as in the novel, this French Jesuit succeeded in converting Prince Surniama to Christianity, thus making the latter the most celebrated Chinese martyr. His faith and his martyrdom were dramatized across Europe in Jesuit colleges in the 18th century.[12] We also learn of the execution of the Portuguese Jesuit Morao who belonged to the party persuading Kang Xi to name his ninth son as his successor. After Yong Zheng ascended the throne, he first exiled Morao and then had a dagger, a silk cord, and poison sent to the Portuguese. The latter, of course, refused to commit suicide. After having waited for three days, his executioners "sandbagged" him to death.[13] Strangely, he was not hailed as a martyr.

Teodorico Pedrini was sent by Pope Clement XI as his personal emissary to the Chinese court. He departed for China in 1702, but because he kept missing connecting boats everywhere, it took him seven years to reach China. He lived for years in Peru, a station on his way to China, and openly took a mistress or concubine. However, his faith won over his love and lust. He finally continued his journey to China. Throughout the novel, especially in the second part dealing with his China years, he is depicted as a passionate man, a faithful Lazarist loyal to the Pope, and a dedicated musician. This trinity has a unity, i.e. his humanity, because he is, above all, himself, creating his own destiny. Consequently, we are facing a novel firstly of a European who has exotic adventures in South America and China, secondly a novel of a Lazarist who is sent by the Pope to convert the Chinese emperor and to check on the Jesuits in China, and thirdly a novel of love and passion. In addition, his Chinese concubine bears him a son who, after the death of his mother in an earthquake, works at the side of his father. Pedrini's personal destiny makes him an adept of the *Daodejing*, and the founder of Xi Tang, the west church, which was built with the blessing of Emperor Yong Zheng. After the closing down of Bei Tang, the north church of the Jesuits, it becomes the refuge of all Chinese Christians. In his final years, he reconciles with the Jesuits through Castiglione, because he is now assimilated by the Chinese spirit. Jesuit accommodation becomes perfectly acceptable. Even his sermons are a mixture of the *Daodejing* and the Bible.

Pedrini's entry into China was adventurous in the true sense of the word. In the last leg of his journey to China, in Manila, he was disguised as the captain of the ship which took him to Macau. As a matter of fact, he really navigated the ship, resulting, as Mateo Ripa, who was a passenger on board, tells us,[14] in near catastrophe two or three times. The historical Ripa also corroborated that Pedrini went ashore in the same disguise to pay his first visit to Charles de Tournon, who was under house arrest in Macau. After he was consecrated Cardinal, de Tournon wrote to Kang Xi, offering the services of the new arrivals, altogether six Lazarists. In real life, but not in the novel, Ripa was quite unhappy to be sent to China as a painter, because he did not consider himself one. Ripa lived in China for thirteen years and returned to Europe to found the famous Chinese College in Naples which, for example, supplied interpreters for Lord Macartney's embassy to China towards the end of the 18th century. As long as he was in China, Ripa was Pedrini's closest associate and only friend. And he became the best engraver in Beijing. After Ripa left China for Europe with five young Chinese to found his College, Pedrini was entirely on his own.

Of all famous missionaries, most were mathematicians and astronomers; however, Castiglione had attained fame through his painting and Pedrini through his music. The duty of the latter was to tune the European instruments in Kang Xi's possession. However, after the emperor heard his music, Pedrini was appointed court musician and thus became a mandarin of second degree. The Jesuits watched this development with unease and jealousy. They considered the Lazarists spies of the Pope who were in China to discredit their achievements. Altercations did arise, and every time Kang Xi took the side of the Jesuits because he considered them very important as astronomers and engineers of the empire, while Pedrini was only his personal musician. As such, Kang Xi ordered Pedrini to teach music to some of his sons, including the later Yong Zheng emperor, who became and remained Pedrini's benefactor.

In the novel, the influence of the Jesuits at Kang Xi's court seems to be immense. As early as 1713, one year after his arrival in Beijing, a letter from the pope written in the year 1709 arrived, condemning the insertion of Chinese rites in Christian religious services. Obviously the Jesuits did not tell Kang Xi the full truth regarding the Rites Controversy. Called to a private audience, Pedrini explained to the emperor that the pope did not object to paying homage to the ancestor tablets as such, but only during Christian services. To his great joy, Kang Xi agreed with the pope's position. He was asked to draft an answer without the knowledge of the Jesuits and give it to the emperor's confidant, Wang Tao Aloa, and Muscovites were to forward this letter to Rome. This draft, however, found its way to the Jesuits, who came to confront Pedrini with it. In this instance, he learnt that the Jesuits in China were as powerful as their counterparts in Europe. This experience, however, introduced him to Wang Tao Aloa, one of the two most important men in his life in China. The other person was the fourth son of Kang Xi who succeeded him to the throne. The prince and Pedrini not only practised and discussed music, but also theological matters. This friendship with the 4th prince sowed the seed for his subsequent founding of Xi Tang, the West Church.

Another proof of Kang Xi's favour towards Pedrini is the

following incident. Soon after a European concert performed by the royal princes, Pedrini fell seriously ill. Ripa feared that the Jesuits had poisoned him and went to the emperor for help. Kang Xi had him moved to Wang Tao Aloa's residence and cared for there. His personal physicians were to cure Pedrini. There he met Wang's daughter, Yao Niang, and they became fond of each other, even though Pedrini was about her father's age. At Wang's residence, Pedrini was also initiated into the esoteric of the *Daodejing*. Both factors were to determine the course of his later life. Kang Xi was informed of the love affair, and he arranged for a house for Pedrini. With the emperor's secret blessing, Yao Niang became Pedrini's concubine. From that time on, he, 48 years old, began to lead a double life as a priest and a lover. The friendship with the father continued; from him he learned about qi, which was to become a tenet of his Sino-Christianity.

Soon it came to the last confrontation and altercation with the Jesuits. A new papal delegation arrived, led by Ambroise de Mezzabarba, Patriarch of Alexandria. Kang Xi received him on December 31, 1720. Pedrini was the official interpreter. Kang Xi was so enraged by Rome's position that he accused Pedrini of having incited Rome to condemn Chinese rites. After severe corporal punishment, he was cast into an imperial prison. However, Wang Tao Aloa managed to visit him and brought him a copy of the *Daodejing*. Ten days later, Pedrini was transferred to Bei Tang to be guarded by French Jesuits. During his confinement, he read Lao Zi's booklet intensely. Through the intervention of the 4th prince he was set free. However, the Jesuits were stronger and had him arrested again within a few days. During his short period of freedom, he had fathered a son who was born during his second confinement. Because he had found fulfilment as a father, his bitterness towards the Jesuits increasingly diminished. Parennin, during their first discourse after Pedrini's miseries, opined that their positions were irreconcilable because the Jesuits had become Chinese while Pedrini remained Roman. Little did Parennin know that Pedrini too had undergone the same metamorphosis. Kang Xi died and his successor, Emperor Yong Zheng, the former 4th prince, ordered Pedrini's immediate release. Pedrini's first act was to baptise his son — Pedrini was then 52 years old. The new emperor received him kindly and ordered him to pursue his private life. Xi Tang, the West Church, was built and later, when it was destroyed in an earthquake, rebuilt with Yong Zheng's silver.

When Qian Long ascended the throne, he summoned the two foreign artists in his empire, Castiglione and Pedrini, to his presence and rewarded them for their services to Kang Xi and Yong Zheng, presenting each artist with the signal honour of a peacock feather with one eye which they could wear on their hats. However, the practice of Christianity remained forbidden as under his predecessor; Xi Tang was an exception. It was permitted to continue its religious activities and remained the only legitimate place of worship for the Christians in China. Pedrini, who suffered so much because he opposed the Jesuit position of Chinese rites, had become a practitioner of similar rites long before. His Christian services were so Chinese that Wang Tao Aloa once thought he was witnessing a Daoist service instead of a mass. Now the musician Pedrini proposed to the painter Castiglione that the opposing factions should join forces. Since both he and the Jesuits had become Chinese, the Christianity they would continue to proselytize would not be European anymore. Thus the novel ends.

It is remarkable that in the last decade, a German and a French novel using China as a background should choose to depict missionaries who opted for assimilation instead of proselytization. On second thought, perhaps it is not remarkable at all. To an increasingly diminishing degree, Europe considers itself to be the centre of the world. Thus it is easier for European intellectuals to regard China's past in a non-Eurocentric way. Of course, one should not rewrite history, but one can come to terms with it and one can wish the history to be different. Consequently, one writes fiction. A German writer who is a trained Sinologist creates a Jesuit painter. He is sent to China to convert the Chinese emperor with his art and its central perspective. However, he acquires a new perspective and the Chinese way of painting, which seems to be less restricted and more spiritual. As an artist, the new way is more to his liking. Consequently, he turns his back on what he now perceives as fundamentalism. His transformation is counterbalanced by the heroine who seems to have a much stronger character. She is wild and her feet are unbound so that her strides are not hampered. She is attracted to things which are foreign or alien, including people. She does not want the Italian, who is ready to become entirely Chinese, to assimilate. Both forces are in full play; in contrast, fundamentalism, such as secret societies which wish to drive out foreigners and a church which wishes to impose its beliefs and customs on a different people, were subdued one way or other. In an intriguing way, the French novel on Pedrini is comparable, even though it is a more traditional historical novel. Nevertheless, the form of fiction has been chosen, the past has been fictionalized. It is not the historical truth which counts despite the fact it is full of historical details. Pedrini is a passionate man; as such his nature is stronger than his will or vow of chastity. He loves as a man, and he is also a loving father. As a musician, he knows his music is superior in technique and virtuosity, but he learns a lesson in the meaning of music from Kang Xi. Even though the Chinese music is, technically speaking, crude, yet it seeks to harmonize heaven, earth, and men. As a Lazarist, Pedrini opposes the Jesuit position vehemently. Then he learns about the *Daodejing*, which opens up new perspectives for him. The historical and the fictional Jesuits accommodated to Confucian rites, and Pedrini reconciles European and Chinese music and their respective instruments, and he adopts Daoist metaphysics. Both he and the Jesuits do not wish to transplant Roman Catholic culture and customs wholesale to China and impose them on the Chinese. Instead, they become Chinese themselves in order to preach in a congenial way to the people. Even though the novel ends here, we know their way was not the historical way. Historically, accommodation in one way or another other did not influence the decision-making body. Catholicism did not become Chinese as Buddhism did. But history teaches a lesson. Consequently, a historical novel is born. Departing from cultural self-centeredness is an undeniable sign of maturity.

Notes

[1] The novel has three volumes of approximately 2000 pages and was published in the years 1686-88. For more details and a discussion of the novel, see Adrian Hsia, *Chinesia*, "The European Construction of China in the Literature of the 17th and 18th Centuries." Tubingen: Niemeyer, 1998, p.45ff.

[2] Johann Gottfried Herder (1744-1803) wrote this in *Ideen zur Philosophie der Gesichte der Menschheit*, 1784-91. For a discussion on this, see Adrian Hsia, *Chinesia*, p.118ff.

[3] I am, however, quoting from the pocket book edition, Reinbeck: Rowohlt Taschenbuch Verlag, 1995.

[4] The German original was published by Rowohlt Verlag in Hamburg in 1991. The English translation was published by Farrar, Straus, & Geroux in 1993.

[5] Rudolf Wagner, Chair of Sinology at the University of Heidelberg, a co-frere of Spengler, in a book review published in *The Spiegel*, no. 46 of November. 11, 1993, pp.263-265, criticized rather severely along this line. A Chinese student of mine who wrote a paper on the novel also finds certain manners of Chinese characters un-Chinese.

[6] This term seems to be Spengler's invention to emphasize the theological point. Usually it is called the linear or one-point perspective.

[7] There is no explanation why they are targeted.

[8] How much meat can five camels and two horses produce? This would seem to be a neglect of a minor detail. There are others.

9. This detail is also hard to accept.
10. I am grateful to Richard Lynn, University of Toronto, who helped me to grasp the importance of perspective in the arts.
11. The novel was first published in 1999. I am using a pocket book edition published in 2001 by the same publisher Jean-Claude Lattes in Paris. The French original of the quotation above is in "Remerciements" on p.373.
12. For a discussion on the dramatization of Prince Surniama, see the chapter on "The Transformation of Jesuitical Fiction to Jesuit College Drama. A Preliminary Survey," in Adrian Hsia, *Chinesia*, pp.55-74.
13. Sandbagging" was considered a mild form of execution as it leaves the body intact. A heavy sandbag is put on the chest of the prisoner so that he cannot breath and suffocates.
14. See Mateo Ripa, *Memoirs of Father Ripa, during Thirteen Years' Residence at the Court of Peking in the Services of the Emperor of China*. Selected by Fortunado Prandl. London: John Murray, 1846, pp. 31f.

The Underestimated Strength of Cultural Identity
Between Localising and Globalising Tendencies in the European Union

Rien T. Segers

1. Introduction
A nursery rhyme for scholars and students

At the annual meetings of the World Bank and the International Monetary Fund in Washington in September 1999, Wole Soyinka, the Nigerian writer and Nobel laureate, said: 'Culture is a matrix of infinite possibilities and choices [...] from which we can extract arguments and strategies for the degradation or enoblement of our species, for its enslavement or liberation, for the suppression of its productive potential or its enchantment, for the stagnation of social existence or its renewal.'

Soyinka's quotation will function as a background against which I would like to introduce the concept of cultural identity. I think there are at least two reasons for devoting a paper to questions concerning cultural identity.

The first reason can be found in the immense popularity of the concept of cultural identity itself. The scholarly, journalistic and popular press is filled with references to the field of cultural identity and its related themes, national and corporate identity. You often feel that you are encountering a huge container concept, which has lost its specific semantics due to the abundant use of that very concept. Scholarship's task is to look at the specificity of semantics, especially if it concerns such an important social concept. That's exactly what I am trying to achieve here: looking for the lost semantics of the concept of cultural identity and framing it within its natural context.

The second reason is concerned with demonstrating the validity of the concept of cultural identity. I strongly believe that insight into cultural identity will result in a deeper insight into the European integration process, when viewed from a contemporary social perspective.

Let us focus briefly on a simple but intriguing nursery rhyme:

The Germans live in Germany, the Romans live in Rome, the Turkeys live in Turkey; but the English live at home.

We could ask a number of questions here. For instance:
-which nation invented this nursery rhyme?
-when was it invented?
-to what extent is it justified?

It is the last question which will be the specific focus of this paper. In other words, the focus will be on the question of what situation the cultures and nations of the EU in particular find themselves in today. Should this situation be characterised by the concept 'localisation' or by the concept of 'globalisation'? Is it correct to define 'localisation' — as some do — as a predominantly nineteenth-century concept and 'globalisation' as a predominantly late twentieth-century concept?

These are simple questions but with complicated answers. I shall explain and deconstruct the current Great Millennium Myth, which implies a belief that the structure of contemporary society or even 'the world' can only be characterised by the concept of globalisation,

globalisation as a mythical construction of post-industrial European society.

There is a caveat here: my talk denotes a specific set of Western assumptions concerning concepts such as culture, nation and cultural identity. I shall mainly concentrate on cultural identity here, since this concept is not only *en vogue* in many scholarly circles around the globe, but also because to a great extent this concept determines other concepts which are of crucial importance to the discourse of our time: globalisation, localisation, multiculturalism, ethnicity, nation state, ideology, etc. Insight into cultural identity implies at the same time a partial insight into all the tricky container concepts I have just mentioned.

My guiding principle is the systemic theory of culture (Even-Zohar, Luhmann, Maturana, Varela; for a bibliography see, e.g. Tötösy de Zepetnek, 1992; for a recent critical analysis see Sevönen, 2001). This theory considers culture as a system consisting of a number of subsystems, such as economic, educational, religious, technological and artistic subsystems. Each subsystem is based on all activities as performed by participants, people active within that subsystem. This means that a systemic approach is interested in all the 'actions', in all the 'activities' as performed by the participants within a particular subsystem.

2. How to recognise a culture when you see one? An attempt at a definition

Before its anthropological incarnation, 'culture' predominantly meant refinement. The nineteenth-century humanist Matthew Arnold, for instance, considered culture as a study of perfection, an inward condition of the mind and spirit. He regarded cultured people as drawing ever nearer to 'the beautiful' and 'the graceful'. Culture in his view was the best that has been thought and said. This conception of culture still remains very much *en vogue* today.

Cultural anthropologists have reworked this accepted concept of culture to apply it not only to a learned and sophisticated few, but to *all* human beings. As Clifford Geertz notes: 'Culture [...] is not just an ornament of human existence, but [...] an essential condition for it [...]. There is no such a thing as a human nature independent of culture.' This implies that as human beings we are *all* cultured. 'Culture' in this sense has become a value-free concept as opposed to the value-laden Arnoldian concept.

The question whether this concept of 'culture' is needed seems to be justified, since there are so many other words seemingly describing more or less the same anthropological concept, such as a set of norms, value system, behaviour pattern, rituals and traditions. The organisational psychologist Edgar H. Schein (1992: 10-11) correctly answers this question as follows. Unlike all the other words just mentioned, the concept of culture adds two relevant critical notions.

First of all there is the implication of structural stability in a community or group of people. Cultural elements are elements that are not only shared but are also stable and 'deep', which means less conscious, less tangible and less visible. Cultural elements also bind together into a coherent whole; they reveal a certain pattern at a deeper, invisible level.

Secondly, 'culture' denotes the accumulated shared learning of a given group, covering behavioural, emotional and cognitive elements of the group's members' total psychological functioning. Schein (1992: 10) correctly observes: 'For shared learning to occur, there must be a history of shared experience, which in turn implies some stability of members in the group.'

The implication behind the above points of departure is the constructive nature of culture. Culture is not a set of innate or ontological characteristics which have a static nature, but rather a set containing a great number of actions performed by those who participate in that (sub)culture. These actions are performed on the basis of more or less conventional schemes.

My understanding of 'culture' is influenced by Geert Hofstede's (1994:5) ideas about it. I subscribe to his view because his definition unites three important elements: the decisive value of culture, the importance of cultural relativism and the constructed character of culture.

Hofstede (1994:5) distinguishes two meanings of the word culture. There is culture one, which refers to civilisation, a refinement of the mind which can be found in education, art and literature. This is not a description of culture I would like to refer to. I shall select Hofstede's culture two which '[...] deals with much more fundamental human processes than culture one; it deals with the things that hurt. Culture (two) is always a collective phenomenon, because it is at least partly shared with people who live or lived within the same social environment, which is where it was learned. It is *the collective programming of the mind which distinguishes the members of one group or category of people from another.*'

According to Hofstede, culture is learned, not inherited. It derives from your social environment, not from your genes. He distinguishes culture from human nature based on the following reasoning: as a human being you can feel fear, anger, love, joy, sadness, etc. All these feelings are part of human nature. However, the way these feelings are expressed is modified by culture. Culture is the software of the mind. It is also distinguished from the personality of an individual. The latter is described as a unique personal set of mental programmes he/she does not share with any other human being. Hofstede's description of 'personality' is somewhat naive, but his concept of culture is extremely useful.

An example of this is the Lewinsky affair in the US, or perhaps we should say the Clinton affair. In many cultures, no wife, children or even an entire nation wants the husband, father or political leader to engage in adultery, perjury, or bribery. It doesn't fit the image you construct of a husband, a father, or a president. Even the supposition of adultery, perjury or bribery gives rise to the same human feelings of anger, sadness and disgust in many cultures. It would result in the same headlines in the media and in the same criticism from the media in most cultures, since this is the level of human nature: violation of confidence, a central human value in most cultures. But the way those feelings of violation of confidence are expressed is culturally bound, is dependent on 'the programming of the mind' in that particular culture.

The programming of the Dutch political mind in this respect would be such that a Dutch political leader in a similar position to Mr. Clinton would have resigned immediately on his or her own initiative, not necessarily out of respect for the people of the country or for his or her relatives, but out of fear of the Dutch House of Representatives. It would mean the definitive end of a political career. After a year of silence the fallen Dutch leader would become Chairman of the Association of Cheesemakers or Tulip Growers and he would be out of public sight forever. The programming of the Dutch mind is still heavily Calvinist.

The programming of the Japanese political mind is completely different. A Japanese political leader in similar circumstances would step down immediately out of shame, since he would think that he had lost face. At the press conference he would bow very deeply, apologise and take all responsibility, even for things he cannot be held responsible for. Recently, a new phenomenon has been added to this traditional programme: the leader must weep and cry. After a year of silence, the Japanese political leader re-enters politics through the back door of the Lower House, where he can direct his faction again and significantly influence Japanese politics as if nothing has happened. The programming of the Japanese mind is heavily based on the Japanese version of Buddhism.

Hofstede has a systemic (*in sensu* Niklas Luhmann) conception of culture. He doesn't see 'culture' as a vast unspecified domain, but rather as an entity consisting of different levels, which are interrelated. At the same time, a person always belongs to a number of the following levels, or indicators of identity, for instance: a national level according to one's country; a regional/ethnic/religious/linguistic affiliation; a gender level; a generation level; a social class level; an organisational or corporate level for those who are employed. The implication is that it is impossible to speak about 'the' identity of a person or of a group; it may vary according to circumstances.

Hofstede undertook a large-scale intercultural research project which revealed the following five dimensions, on the basis of which cultures can be classified:

1. Social inequality, including the relationship with authority;
2. The relationship between the individual and the group;
3. Concepts of masculinity and femininity; the social implications of having been born as a boy or a girl;
4. Ways of dealing with uncertainty, relating to the control of aggression and the expression of emotions;
5. A long-term orientation in life versus a short-term orientation.

Hofstede's conception of culture has a number of advantages. In his conception, culture is an ever-changing entity not a static one; culture is learned not inherited; there are no criteria on the basis of which culture A is 'intrinsically' better than culture B (with exceptions such as a culture that deliberately and seriously violates human rights); 'culture' is a mental construction rather than the innate property of a certain community. This implies that Hofstede's view of culture is more useful with respect to its application in actual research than many other definitions of culture, which base themselves on ontological or essentialist conceptions.

3. What is cultural identity: just another container concept?

A weak aspect of Hofstede's book, however, is that the very concept of cultural identity is not used. This concept, however, is needed to discuss questions whenever two cultures come into contact with each other or — on an academic level — are compared with each other. A key question such as 'How can the distinctiveness or the specificity of this culture be determined?' is in fact a question concerning the *cultural identity* of a particular community. The extent to which a certain culture can be said to have distinctive *and* common traits can only be determined on a comparative basis. As the American sociologists Jepperson and Swidler (1994: 368) recently stated: 'The essential strategy for making the invisible visible is *of course* comparative research. And that is exactly why disciplines which have a comparative basis should take the lead in research in this domain.' [my italics]

Giving a description of cultural identity is clearly linked to other important concepts such as ethnicity, nation and nation-state. I take here the guidelines given by Adrian Hastings to define those terms. Hastings (1997: 3) considers ethnicity to be a group of people with a shared cultural identity and spoken language. He correctly considers ethnicity to be the major distinctive element in a pre-national society, but ethnicity — he adds — 'may survive as a strong subdivision with a loyalty of its own within established nations.'

Hastings (1997: 3) defines a nation as follows: 'A nation is a far more self-conscious community than an ethnicity. Formed from one or more ethnicities, and normally identified by a literature of its own, it possesses or claims the right to political identity and autonomy as a people, together with the control of specific territory, comparable to that of biblical Israel and of other independent entities in a world thought of as one of nation-states.'

This clears the way to a description of a nation-state: '[...] a state which identifies itself in terms of one specific nation whose people are not seen simply as "subjects" of the sovereign but as a horizontally bonded society to whom the state in a sense belongs. There is thus an identity of character between state and people. [...] In [the state], ideally, there is a basic equivalence between the borders and character of the political unit upon the one hand and a self-conscious cultural community on the other. In most cases this is a dream as much as a reality. Most nation-states in fact include groups of people who do not belong to its core culture or feel themselves to be part of a nation so defined. Nevertheless almost all modern states act on the bland assumption that they are nation-states.' (Hastings 1997: 3)

Books discussing the cultural identity of a particular nation or nation-state often refer to certain 'special features', 'characteristics' and 'traits' of that nation-state or its people. Often these observations are principally based on impressions, introspections, myths and — not to forget — jokes rather than on factual evidence or empirical research. Obviously, I do not want to deny, for instance, that the thousands of jokes concerning national and cultural stereotypes may highlight particular aspects of the cultural identity of a particular community or nation, but they are just indicators and no more than that.

Consider for instance the following two jokes. The first originated in New York, the second in Tokyo.

In a New York hotel, an American and Japanese engineer meet for the first time and introduce themselves to each other. Obviously the American goes first: 'Hello, my name is John, John Smith. Nice to meet you. I am an electrical engineer and — by the way — at the moment I am working for Kodak.' After two minutes of silence the Japanese says: 'Hello, I am Toyota and my name is nobody.' This joke may serve as an indicator of the American self-image as individualistic, self-confident and successful. The joke also implicitly constructs an image in which Japanese professionals are not individuals, and are neither self-confident nor successful.

Obviously, the Japanese in their turn have a pagoda full of jokes about Americans, such as this one. An American and a Japanese meet each other on a safari trip in Kruger Park. They take a walk together, somewhat outside the safe tourist path. All of a sudden they are confronted by a hungry-looking lion. The American immediately starts running and running. But the Japanese does not move and carefully opens his black leather briefcase in order to take out a pair of running shoes. Looking back at the Japanese the American starts shouting: 'Come on! Run for your life! Leave those running shoes behind; you don't have a chance anyhow to run faster than the lion does.' The Japanese thinks, waits a bit and says politely: 'The one I have to outrun is not the lion, but you.' This joke may serve as an indicator of the Japanese self-image as smart, civilised and competitive, whereas the American is seen as impulsive, thoughtless and pushy.

These jokes not only demonstrate the well-known fact handed down to us by social psychology that the image of a neighbouring people is constructed as a negative counterpart of one's own image, on the basis of which the ingroup people can identify themselves more easily with their own self-image (Fink 1991: 453). But the jokes should also show that the construction of cultural identity involves at least two parts: the ingroup and the outgroup, the perception of oneself and the perception of the other ('Selbstwahrnehmung' and 'Fremdwahrnehmung'). The Japanese looks at the American from a Japanese perspective, and vice versa.

In our times, it is of great importance to have an adequate, well-balanced insight into the cultural identity of a particular nation. A distorted view can significantly hamper good understanding and adequate communication with citizens of that nation. Very often political conflicts and wars find their deep origin in distorted visions of one's own and the foreign identity.

In his latest collection of essays, Ernest Gellner (1994: 45) asks for serious attention to be paid to cultural identity: '[It] is not a delusion, excogitated by muddled romantics, disseminated by irresponsible extremists, and used by egotistical privileged classes to befuddle the masses, and to hide their true interests from them. Its appeal is rooted in the real conditions of modern life, and cannot be conjured away, either by sheer good will and the preaching of a spirit of universal brotherhood, or by the incarceration of the extremists. We have to understand those roots, and live with their fruits, whether we like them or not.'

Much scholarly research and journalistic writing about 'cultural identity' takes as its point of departure well-established stereotypes, which sometimes do not exceed the level of the type of jokes mentioned above. These writings are normally based on an ontological belief in the specificity of a certain community. What alternative can we offer which would make it possible to overcome the old essentialist approach to identity and to by-pass the new extreme relativism which says that identity escapes every attempt at definition?

In order to understand the roots of cultural identity we need to understand the semantics of this very concept. Here, we don't have to go through the work of Sigmund Freud, George Herbert Mead, Erik Erikson, Talcott Parsons, Jurgen Habermas and others to come up with a well-grounded description of identity. William Bloom (1990: 53) offers an elegant summary of current thinking concluding that '[...] identification is an inherent and unconscious behavioural imperative in all individuals. Individuals actively seek to identify in order to achieve psychological security, and they actively seek to maintain, protect and bolster identity in order to maintain and enhance this psychological security which is a sine qua non of personality stability and emotional well-being. This imperative works from infancy through adulthood and old age. Moreover, identifications can be shared, with the result that individuals who share the same identification will tend to act in concert in order to protect or enhance their shared identity.'

These are beautiful words with which one can easily agree. But the problem arises when we try to describe somebody's personal identity or the cultural identity of a particular people. Talking about personal and cultural identity can be tricky, especially if wishful thinking, stereotypes and a strong belief in the overstressed uniqueness of a particular person or country are the only guidelines.

For the concept of 'cultural identity', this implies that the cultural identity of a particular group or people is only partly determined by their national identity. Cultural identity is a broader concept than national identity. In this respect I subscribe to E.J. Hobsbawm (1990:182) who emphasises that belonging to a particular state 'is only one way in which people describe their identity among many others which they use for this purpose, as occasion demands.' Whether it is justified to conclude on the basis of that argument that the power of nationalism is receding around the globe, as Hobsbawm does, is another matter and seems to be wishful thinking. The struggle between localisation and nationalisation on the one hand and globalisation on the other is not yet decided. Based on recent political developments in some parts of the world, however, on the wars, fighting and severe discussions which are going on, my forecast would differ from that of Hobsbawm. I shall return to this point in the next section.

Often, cultural identity is seen as a range of characteristics which are unique for a particular culture and 'innate' to a specific people. The Japanese scholarly tradition of *Nihonjinron* (studies about Japaneseness) is a typical example of this approach (for a critical survey see e.g. Dale 1986, Yoshino 1992 and Segers 1996). But in other cultures, too, many examples of this type of thinking can be found, and in many cases not only practised long ago but even nowadays, and not only primarily in the periphery of scholarship either.

Another view suggests that cultural identity has a structuralist character, where a particular culture is seen as consisting of a set of characteristics which are all related to each other, more or less independently of the people who produce that culture.

The alternative for the conception of 'identity' as a set of unique or structural characteristics is the idea of identity as a *construction*. Within such a constructive framework, the cultural identity of a particular nation or of a certain ethnic group within that nation can be attached to three factors: (1) the statistics concerning that nation or group at a given time in history, (2) the programming of the mind within a particular community on the basis of which the cultural identity by the ingroup is being constructed, (3) and the way in which people from outside conduct a process of selection, interpretation and evaluation concerning the specificity of the ingroup: in other words, the outside image of the cultural identity of a foreign nation or group. The relationship between these three elements is a dynamic one. Ideally, the (scholarly) construction of identity should be based on all three actors. (For a more extensive explanation see Segers, 1992.)

What are statistics with respect to cultural identity? They are 'facts', figures which can be found in statistical handbooks concerning a particular country or ethnic group and which determine to a great extent the programming of the mind of a given society, and vice versa. For instance: they list the total number of citizens of a country, the size of the country, the gross national product, average income, percentage of unemployment, the number of museums, the number of books produced, etc.

Since we do not have direct access to the way in which peoples' minds are programmed, we have to resort to visible indicators thereof. We have to look at the style of conduct and communication in a particular community, to use Gellner's (1983:92) more pragmatically oriented definition of culture. This style of conduct and the communication of the citizens of a state or the members of a particular ethnic group is their visible cultural identity. This visible cultural identity can be suppressed or thematized by opinion leaders (individuals and institutions) within that particular community. It is impossible to talk about cultural identity without taking into consideration which spokesmen/women are defining it and along which lines this happens.

The third element of the identity triangle consists of the constructions made by people, usually opinion leaders or important institutions from outside, concerning the conduct and communication of the people inside.

It would be somewhat misleading to think that the idea of considering national or cultural identity as a construction originated in systems theory (from Ludwig von Bertalanffy to Niklas Luhmann). Scholars working outside this domain have arrived at more or less the same conclusion. An interesting example is Benedict Anderson (1983:15), who coined the term 'imagined community'. In an attempt to define the concept of 'nation', he states: '[...] it is an imagined political community — and imagined as both inherently limited and sovereign. It is imagined because the members of even the smallest nation will never know most of their fellow-members, meet them, or even hear of them, yet in the minds of each lives the image of their communion.' I am not saying that Anderson's 'imagination' is equivalent to Luhmann's 'construction'. The similarity is to be sought in the emphasis on the mental processing of a particular object.

To consider cultural identity as a construction means that it is a mental conception which may vary according to the constructor, the time and place of construction. This implies that it is impossible to speak about 'the' cultural identity of a community. In theory there are as many cultural identities of a given community as there are times, places and people that construct those identities. This should not prevent scholars, however, from the necessary task of describing and systematising the common characteristics based on those several existing identities. Moreover, in reality we are usually confronted with only one dominant construction of the cultural identity of a particular country.

The most recent development concerning the concept of cultural identity has been the addition of the prefix 'post' as an attempt to resolve the paradox between globalisation and nationalisation. The term 'postnational identity' is coined in a book by Dewandre and Lenoble (1994). It implies the paradox between the necessity of the construction of one political European identity based on the development of the European Union as against the promotion of the cultural distinctiveness of the several European nations and regions. One political identity versus many distinctive cultural identities, all living under the same roof of a house called postnational identity. This concept of postnational identity seems rather utopian, prompted by wishful thinking 'from Brussels with love'. (For more extensive criticism see Picht, 1994; for an extensive discussion on European cultural identity see the essays in Segers and Viehoff, 1999b.)

There is, however, yet another caveat to be considered, one which in particular applies to cross-cultural or comparative studies concerning cultural identity. Richard Handler (1994: 27) has formulated the following reasonable objection in this respect: 'Identity has become a salient scholarly and cultural construct in mid-twentieth century, particularly in social-scientific scholarship in the United States. Its prominence in that context, however, does not mean that the concept can be applied unthinkingly to other places and times.'

Western notions of collective identity are grounded in individualist metaphors. Attributes of boundedness, continuity, uniqueness, and homogeneity which are ascribed to human beings are ascribed to social groups as well. This leads Handler (1994: 33) to the following conclusion: 'Thus it seems to me that if other cultures imagine personhood and human activity in terms other than those we use, we should not expect them to rely on Western individualistic assumptions in describing social collectivities.'

Clifford Geertz (1980: 24-25) tells an anecdote which reveals a completely different approach to boundaries and the essence of a community. It concerns the Balinese state, where the rulers did not compete for boundaries (territory) but for the allegiance of men: 'The Dutch, who wanted [...] to get the boundary between two petty princedoms straight once and for all, called in the princes concerned and asked them where indeed the borders lay. Both agreed that the border of princedom A lay at the farthest point from which a man could still see the swamps, and the border of princedom B lay at the point from which a man could still see the sea. Had they, then, never fought over the land between, from which one could see neither swamp nor sea? "Mijnheer", one of the old princes, replied, "We had much better reason to fight with one another than these shabby hills." '

4. Cultural identity squeezed by globalisation?
Concerning the vitality of the local: the cultural turn

The scholarly focus on cultural identity is confronted with two serious objections. First of all, there is the fear that research into the specificity of a particular culture invokes nationalistic tendencies. Research into cultural identity could reinforce 'old-fashioned nationalism', based on the fact that it could result in determining the 'unique' characteristics of a certain community or people.

I am not so sure whether this objection is justified. The outcome of a research project is strongly dependent on the status of the research methodology employed. If the methodology is based on an ontological understanding of the innate characteristics of a particular culture, the research results will reveal the full colours of this metaphysical basis. However, if the methodology is based on the idea that cultural identity should be defined by the triangle characteristics explained above, then the danger of stressing the innate uniqueness of a culture is absent. In addition, the fact that we consider cultural identity to be a construction rather than a 'given' adds to the rejection of the imminent danger involved.

A second objection which is levelled against the concept of cultural identity concerns the idea that the current globalisation tendency in the world will destroy most parts of the specificity of a particular 'local' culture. It's the famous adage concerning the big unknown world becoming a small familiar village. From a superficial point of view, the village theory looks good and it has strong advocates, starting with its guru Marshall McLuhan. But let us take a more refined look at the globalisation problem.

If we examine the interrelations between cultures now, at the beginning of a new millennium, we can perceive two contradictory but strong tendencies: '[...] on the one hand, there is the search for cultural authenticity, the return to origins, the need to preserve minor languages, pride in particularisms, admiration for cultural self-sufficiency and maintenance of national traditions; on the other hand, we find the spread of a uniform world culture, the emergence of supranational myths and the adoption of similar lifestyles in widely different settings. Modern technological societies have generated a transnational, composite, mass culture with its own language whose linguistic imprint is already universally evident.' (OECD, 1989: 16).

This paradox between localisation and globalisation can be found in many parts of the world and in many different ways. Concerning European unification, for example, Philip Schlesinger (1994: 325) has aptly described this paradox as follows: 'On the one hand, the difficult search for a transcendent unity by the EC — one which must recognise component differences — throws the nation-state into question from above, arguably contributing to crises of national identity. The political and economic developments in the integration process, however, are out of phase with the cultural: what European identity *might be* still remains an open question. On the other hand, the ethno-nationalist awakenings in the former communist bloc and current developments within western Europe — whether neo-nationalist separatisms or racist nationalisms — tend to reaffirm the principle of the nation-state as a locus of identity and of political control.'

Schlesinger correctly points a finger at the ultimate paradox of the last decade of the 20th century: the clash between the indigenous, inner culture of a particular community on the one hand and the global outer culture of a certain constructed *ensemble* of a number of communities. On a programmatic level, this paradox goes under different catchwords and slogans, including: localisation or nationalisation versus globalisation, 'small is beautiful' versus 'big is necessary and inevitable', individual responsibility versus centralist efficiency, etc. On a pragmatic level, these slogans relate to conflicts at several distinctive levels: between an individual and his or her direct working environment (say a university department), between a department and a new faculty structure, between the faculty and the development of a new government system, between a national government and the regulations of the European Union, etc.

The paradox between localisation and globalisation has appeared under a great number of different labels. William Butler Yeats, long ago, said that our world is caught between the two eternities of race and soul. Race: reflecting the tribal past, and soul: anticipating the cosmopolitan future.

Closer to our time, Benjamin Barber, in a well-known book (2000: 21) has labelled both sides of this paradox Jihad and

McWorld, respectively.

The Jihad trend, named after the Islamic fundamentalist movement, stands for extreme localisation: the Balkanisation of nation states in which culture is pitted against culture, people against people, tribe against tribe. It's a movement against interdependence, against integrated markets and against modernity and against modern globalised technological developments.

On the other side, McWorld, according to Barber, paints the future in shimmering pastels, 'a busy portrait of onrushing economic, technological and ecological forces that demand integration and uniformity and that mesmerise peoples everywhere with fast music, fast computers, and fast food — MTV, Macintosh and McDonalds — pressing nations into one homogeneous global theme park, one McWorld tied together by communications, information, entertainment, and commerce.' (Barber, 2000: 31) Barber notices that the Jihad tendency pursues a bloody politics of identity, while McWorld strives for a bloodless economics of profit.

With regard to the latter movement (McWorld), Barber sums up in a black observation: 'Music, video, theatre, books and theme parks — the new churches of a commercial civilisation in which malls are the public squares and suburbs the neighbourless neighbourhoods — are all constructed as image exports creating a common world taste around common logos, advertising slogans, stars, songs, brand names, jingles and trademarks. Hard power yields to soft, while ideology is transmuted into a kind of videology that works through sound bites and film clips. Videology is fuzzier and less dogmatic than traditional political ideology; it may as a consequence be far more successful in instilling the novel values required for global markets to succeed.' (Barber, 2000: 25)

It is clear that Barber holds an extremely negative view of a future in which localisation and globalisation will go hand in hand and reinforce each other constantly. But is it all that dark? Need it be all that pessimistic? Let us first consider what is really understood by globalisation, this fashionable container concept.

Arjun Appadurai (1990: 6-7) has suggested that globalisation consists of five dimensions, five cultural flows which cross each other at various levels in many parts of the world. 'Firstly, there are *ethnoscapes* produced by flows of people: tourists, immigrants, refugees, exiles and guest workers. Secondly, there are *technoscapes*, the machinery and plant flows produced by multinational and national corporations and government agencies. Thirdly, there are *finanscapes*, produced by the rapid flows of money in the currency stock exchanges. Fourthly, there are *mediascapes*, the repertoires of images and information, the flows which are produced and distributed by newspapers, magazines, television and film. Fifthly, there are *ideoscapes*, linked to flows of images which are associated with state or counterstate movement ideologies which are comprised of elements of the Western Enlightenment world-view — images of democracy, freedom, welfare, rights, etc.'

It is tempting to speculate on the question: What will be the strongest force in the near future, localisation or globalisation, Jihad or McWorld? Obviously, the question is too tricky to be answered in a couple of pages. In any case, both tendencies with their completely opposite aims exist in the same place and at the same time. It is difficult, however, as has been tried in a number of publications, to come up with convincing arguments implying that the globalisation tendency will be a much stronger force than the localisation tendency in the near future.

The well-known Japanese economist and consultant Kenichi Ohmae could be mentioned as a representative of the globalisation movement. His recent book *The End of the Nation State: The Rise of Regional Economies* became a 'global' academic bestseller. In this book Ohmae advocates the theory that nation states have already lost their role as — in his words — 'meaningful units of participation in the global economy of today's borderless world.' What are his arguments for his theory? He comes up with four reasons, which I shall give in his own words (Ohmae, 2000: 207-208):

'First of all, the uncomfortable truth is that, in terms of the global economy, nation states have become little more than bit actors. They may originally have been, in their mercantilist phase, independent, powerfully efficient engines of wealth creation. More recently, however, as the downward-ratcheting logic of electoral politics has placed a death grip on their economies, they have become — first and foremost — remarkably inefficient engines of wealth distribution.

Secondly, and more to the point, the nation state is increasingly a nostalgic fiction. It makes even less sense today, for example, than it did a few years ago to speak of Italy or Russia or China as a single economic unit. Each is a motley combination of territories with vastly different needs and vastly different abilities to contribute.

Third, when you look closely at the goods and services now produced and traded around the world, as well as the companies responsible for them, it is no easy matter to attach to them an accurate national label. Is an automobile sold under an American marque really a US product when a large percentage of its components comes from abroad?

Finally, when economic activity aggressively wears a national label these days, that tag is usually present neither for the sake of accuracy nor out of concern for the economic well-being of individual consumers. It is there primarily as a mini-flag of cheap nationalism — that is, as a jingoistic celebration of nationhood that places far more value on emotion-grabbing symbols than on real, concrete improvements in quality of life.'

Another example frequently used to prove the supremacy of globalisation is what has come to be called Americanisation. Many scholars and journalists go so far as to suggest that those two concepts are synonymous. But by Americanisation is meant the spreading of American culture (or what is regarded as such) into all corners of the world: Hollywood films, American TV soaps, American bestsellers, American cars, Americanised food, etc.

There are two main problems with substituting globalisation with Americanisation. First of all, you could question the extent to which the elements just mentioned really are representative of the culture of the USA. It is altogether possible that in constructing these art forms, parts of the value system and some of the artistic norms of the so-called non-American global periphery were seriously involved. As far as I know, no serious research has yet tackled these or similarly structured questions.

Secondly, it should be stated that the reception of these so-called American cultural products might be different according to the specificity of the receiving culture. Important conventions which make up that specificity structure the direction and the depth of Americanisation. I would venture the hypothesis that Americanisation has been carried out differently in every member state of the EU.

Ralf Dahrendorg (1994) may be introduced as a representative of the localisation theory. After his fine analysis of the future of the nation state, he remarks: 'Auf absehbare Zeit wird der Nationalstaat der Rahmen individueller Rechte und die Aktionseinheit der internationalen Beziehungen bleiben. Das gilt auch in und fur Europa. Der Nationalstaat wird hier und da angenagt und angekratzt, bleibt aber in seinem Kern durch neuere Entwicklungen unberührt. Er ist auch der Raum, in dem Menschen Zugehorigkeitsgefühle empfinden konnen. Einstweilen haben wir noch nichts besseres erfunden als den heterogenen Nationalstaat.' To phrase this in other well-known German words: 'Europa ist ein Kopfgeburt und die Regionen sprechen das Herz an.'

Thus, localisation and globalisation are two sides of the same coin. On the one hand we can observe that 'nationalism is back today with a vengeance all over the world' (Radhakrishnan 1992: 83), from Canada to India, from the former USSR to Iraq, from Japan to Turkey. For the time being, I am one of those who believe that nationalisation or localisation will dominate globalisation, at least for the foreseeable future, and not only outside western Europe as some critics want us to believe, but also to a considerable extent in the countries that belong to the key group members of the EU. In this context Helmut Dubiel (1994: 896) points at new forms of German nationalism: 'sei es des inszenierten Lobs des Vaterlandes, der wahlkampfstrategischen Instrumentalisierung nationaler Ressentiments und des besoffenen Rufs "Deutschland den Deutschen".' But similar tendencies are alive and well in many other countries of the EU.

On the other hand, we can see the severe impact of the five cultural flows of globalisation. Globalisation will persist as an extremely strong tendency and its strength may even increase. But in the decades to come the nationalisation tendency will be able to adopt and adapt many global trends. Globalisation will be nationalised to a great extent.

Let me add here that the threat to the nation, to nationalisation or localisation, doesn't primarily consist of globalisation tendencies, but rather the threat comes also from within the nation itself. We could think here of several well-known ruptures, such as in Canada, Belgium, Spain, or in former countries such as the USSR, Czechoslovakia and Yugoslavia, and in a way, we could add paradoxically the unification of Germany, where the following joke could be heard shortly after the unification: an East German says to a

West German: 'We are one people now!' The West German replies: 'We too!'

Understanding the complicated paradox contained within localisation versus globalisation is an object that is highly interesting and rewarding for a number of scholarly disciplines. Understanding this paradox, however, can only be achieved through the central concept of cultural identity. This very concept represents the ultimate reason for the serious conflicts between the smaller community and the larger constructed ensemble or between two or more smaller communities.

When applying the concept of cultural identity, another fallacy should be deconstructed — the old opposition between the West and the Rest. This opposition is in many cases the hidden, invisible basis upon which many theories are being based. This fallacy of cultural imperialism considers — consciously or not — the West (which often just means: the USA) to be the centre and 'the rest' to be the periphery. Localising movements are performed in the periphery, globalising trends are realised in the Centre, such as the Newconomy and successful and appealing TV programmes.

In order to avoid cultural imperialism, the simplistic centre-periphery oppositional geography should be replaced by a more realistic model of regions. Sinclair et al. (2000: 301) presents a more realistic scenario: that of creolisation. 'Instead of the image of "the West" at the centre dominating the peripheral "Third World" with an outward flow of cultural products, we see the world as divided into a number of regions which each have their own internal dynamics as well as their global ties. Although primarily based on geographic realities, these regions are also defined by common cultural, linguistic, and historical connections which transcend physical space. Such a dynamic, regionalist view of the world helps us to analyse in a more nuanced way the intricate and multi-directional flows of television across the globe.'

We could now ask why there is this focus on culture and cultural identity? In a moment of unsophisticated generalisation, you could say that half the Library of Congress consists of books which more or less deal with this very topic. But there are at least two reasons that make it necessary to concentrate systematically on these topics and to reinterpret them according to ever-changing social circumstances. The scholarly reason is — as we have seen — that 'culture' is still too often conceived of as an ontological concept, which directly leads to unjustified claims of superiority, dominance and ultimately atrocious wars. These wars and other evil developments immediately lose their raison d'etre and their justification if culture is seen within a systemic and constructivist context.

The second reason is based on the socio-political relevance of the concept of culture around the turn of the millennium. A recent book by Samuel P. Huntington (1997), an academic bestseller in the USA since 11 September 2001, convincingly argues for the central role cultures play now and will play in the next decades. His general thesis is that the communist world collapsed in the late 1980's, which meant the end of the Cold War, the end of a world divided by ideological, political and/or economic principles.

Obviously, the end of the Cold War doesn't mean either eternal or temporary peace, as some utopian voices said right after the fall of the Iron Curtain in 1989. Another distinction quickly arose: the cultural distinction. This implies '[...]that culture and cultural identities, which at the broadest level are civilisational identities, are shaping the patterns of cohesion, disintegration, and conflict in the post-Cold War world. [...] The most important groupings of states are no longer the three blocs of the Cold War but rather the world's [...] major civilisations.' (Huntington, 1997: 20-21)

Huntington distinguishes nine different cultures: Western, Latin American, African, Islamic, Sinic, Hindu, Orthodox, Buddhist and

Japanese. We can, of course, disagree with Huntington about the number of civilisations he distinguishes or about his definition of each civilisation. This boils down to questions such as why is Japan recognised as a distinct civilisation and Korea is not? Is it justifiable to define 'African civilisation' as sub-Saharan including the country of South Africa? Regarding this question, Huntington sums up some of the problems himself: 'The north of the African continent and its east coast belong to Islamic civilisation. Historically, Ethiopia constituted a civilisation of its own. Elsewhere European imperialism and settlements brought elements of Western civilisation. In South Africa Dutch, French, and then English settlers created a multifragmented European culture. Most significantly, European imperialism brought Christianity to most of the continent south of the Sahara. Throughout Africa tribal identities are pervasive and intense, but Africans are also increasingly developing a sense of African identity, and conceivably sub-Saharan Africa could cohere into a distinct civilisation, with South Africa possibly being its core state.' (p.47)

Whatever the justification for the number and specificity of the several civilisations may be, the message is clear: the most important distinctions between peoples are no longer ideological, political or economic, but cultural. To quote Huntington once more: 'In this new world the most pervasive, important, and dangerous conflicts will not be between social classes, rich and poor, or other economically defined groups, but between peoples belonging to different cultural entities.' (p.28) And Vaclev Havel (1994) stated along the same lines: 'Cultural conflicts are increasing and are more dangerous today than at any time in history.'

5. Conclusion: the 'Cultural Turn'

Looking at the contemporary world, be it a region, a nation-state or an ethnic group within that nation, implies looking at a complicated wrestling game between globalisation and localisation. In order to understand the fact that in many cases localisation will be the winner, we should pay attention to a neglected force: the importance of the cultural factor which is like a home crowd, always in favour of the local wrestler. Whereas the globalisation tendency is a force which is mainly driven by technological and economic flows in one form or another, the localisation tendency is based on cultural identity. In many cultures globalising tendencies are being localised to a certain degree, as we have seen above. To what extent? That depends on the strength of a particular cultural identity.

The fact that cultural identity is the decisive factor in constructing the specificity of a certain society could be called the 'Cultural Turn'. This means, among other things, that contemporary political and social developments, and also economic and technological developments, whether they have a global or rather a local nature, can only be understood via the concept of cultural identity as it has been defined above. Without an interest in and an understanding of the major differences and the striking similarities between cultures, no adequate construction can be made of modern civilisations or of groups of people within those civilisations.

In most parts of today's world, cultural borders no longer coincide with national borders; cultural diversity within one nation-state is more the rule than the exception. To give just one example, until the late nineteen-sixties, The Netherlands was a state with hardly any ethnic diversity, a rather homogeneous state despite its international history, like many others in Western Europe at that time. On 1 January 1991, the four largest cities in the country (Amsterdam, Rotterdam, The Hague and Utrecht) had a total population of almost two million. Of those two million people, more than 400,000 (21%) were people of non-Dutch descent (i.e. mainly Turks, Moroccans and people of Surinam and Netherlands Antilles ethnic origin) (source: OECD 1992: 71).

All over the world, a growing number of severe political and ethnic conflicts have arisen, originating in an imbalance in the relationships between the three cultural factors in the triangle, as explained above. The nature of this imbalance may vary from place to place: it may be a wrong, one-sided selection of the material statistics, an inadequate and too strong self-image or a distorted look at the foreign partner. The nature of the imbalance may be different, but the result is always the same: cultural relativism gives way to cultural absolutism.

It goes without saying that the current political situation in many parts of the world implies that the study of culture and of cultural identity has become an important item for scholarship. Issues related to culture and cultural identity seem to be and will stay the issues of the coming decades of the new millennium. The 'Cultural Turn' will continue to bare its teeth. In one of its many reports, now more than fifteen years ago, the OECD (1987: 43) wrote: 'Awareness of an ethnic or regional identity, or of a minority status, can be hidden for many decades by the myth of national unity and identity, of ethnic homogeneity, of mass culture or planetary culture. It can also be hidden by an analysis in terms of social groups or the evocation of proletarian internationalism. Today, ethnic or racial claims, nationalist or regionalist movements, and movements for independence or autonomy, have broken up communities which were merely a facade.' This process of breaking up seemingly homogeneous communities and the consequent struggle for identity will undoubtedly continue for a number of years in many parts of the world. To study this process from a cultural point of view offers as many challenges as possibilities for cultural studies in the years to come.

I have been trying to demonstrate in this article that the 'English' in the following English nursery rhyme:

'The Germans live in Germany, the Romans live in Rome, the Turkeys live in Turkey; but the English live at home.'

can be substituted by any other nation or any ethnic group living in a particular nation. As Hofstede (1994: 235) has observed: 'Everybody looks at the world from behind the windows of a cultural home and everybody prefers to act as if people from other countries have something special about them (a national character) but home is normal. Unfortunately, there is no normal position in cultural matters. This is an uncomfortable message, as uncomfortable as Galileo Galilei's claim in the seventeenth century that the Earth is not the centre of the Universe.'

To conclude with a variation on Hobsbawm (1990: 183): the owl of Minerva which brings wisdom flies out at dusk. It is a good sign that it is now circling around cultural identity.

Bibliography

Anderson, Benedict. *Imagined Communities. Reflections on the Origin and Spread of Nationalism*. London: Verso, 1983.

Appadurai, Arjun 'Disjuncture and Difference in the Global Cultural Economy.': Featherstone, 295-310, 1990.

Barber, Benjamin 'Jihad vs. McWorld.': Lechner and Boli, 21-26, 2000.

Bloom, William. *Personal Identity, National Identity and International Relations*. Cambridge, etc.: Cambridge U.P, 1990.

Dahrendorf, Ralf. 'Die Zukunft des Nationalstaates.': *Merkur. Zeitschrift fur Europaisches Denken* 48, no. 9/10, 751- 761, 1994.

Dale, Peter. *The Myth of Japanese Uniqueness*. London: Croom Helm, 1986.

Dewandre, Nicole and Jacques Lenoble (eds.). *Projekt Europa. Postnationale Identität: Grundlage für eine europaische Demokratie?* Berlin: Schelzky & Jeep, 1994.

Dubiel, Helmut. 'Über moralische Souveränität, Erinnerung und Nation.': *Merkur. Deutsche Zeitschrift für Europäisches Denken* 48, no. 9/10, 884-897, 1994.

Featherstone, Mike (ed.). *Global Culture. Nationalism, Globalization and Modernity*. London, etc.: Sage, 1990.

Fink, Gonthier-Louis. 'Das Bild des Nachbarvolkes im Spiegel der deutschen und der französischen Hochaufklarung (1750-1789).' Giesen, 453-492, 1991.

Geertz, Clifford. *Negara: The Theatre State in Nineteenth-Century Bali*. Princeton: Princeton UP, 1980.

Gellner, Ernest. *Nations and Nationalism*. Oxford: Blackwell, 1983.

────── *Encounters with Nationalism*. Oxford: Blackwell, 1994.

Giesen, Bernhard. *Nationale und kulturelle Identität. Studien zur Entwicklung des kollektiven Bewusstseins in der Neuzeit*. Frankfurt/M: Suhrkamp, 1991.

Handler, Richard. 'Is 'Identity' a Useful Cross-Cultural Concept?', John R. Gillis, *Commemorations. The Politics of National Identity*. Princeton, N.J.: Princeton UP 1994. 27-40.

Hastings, Adrian. *The Construction of Nationhood. Ethnicity, Religion and Nationalism*. Cambridge: Cambridge UP, 1997.

Havel, Vaclev. 'The New Measure of Man', *New York Times*, 8 July, 1994.

Hobsbawm, E.J. *Nations and Nationalism Since 1780. Programme, Myth, Reality*. Cambridge, etc.: Cambridge UP, 1990.

Hofstede, Geert. *Cultures and Organizations*. Hammersmith, London: Harper Collins, 1994; first publ. in 1991.

Huntington, Samuel P. *The Clash of Civilizations and the Remaking of World Order*. New York, N. Y.: Touchstone, 1997.

Hutchinson, John and Anthony D. Smith (eds.). *Nationalism*. Oxford, New York: Oxford UP, 1994.

Jepperson, Ronald L. and Ann Swidler. 'What Properties of Culture Should We Measure?': *Poetics* 22, 359-371, 1994.

Lechner, Frank J. and John Boli (eds.). *The Globalization Reader*. Malden, Mass. and Oxford: Blackwell, 2000.

Luhmann, Niklas. *Soziale Systeme. Grundriss einer allgemeinen Theorie*. Frankfurt/M: Suhrkamp, 1988.

OECD. *Multicultural Education*. Paris: Organisation for Economic Co-operation and Development; Centre for Educational Research and Innovation, 1987.

OECD. *One School, Many Cultures*. Paris: Organisation for Economic Co-operation and Development; Centre for Educational Research and Innovation, 1989.

OECD. *Trends in International Migration*. Paris: Organisation for Economic Co-operation and Development; Centre for Educational Research and Innovation, 1992.

Ohmae, Kenichi. *The End of the Nation State. The Rise of Regional Economics*. New York: Free Press, 1995.

Parker, Andrew, Mary Ruso, Doris Sommer and Patricia Yaeger. *Nationalisms and*

Sexualities. New York and London: Routledge, 1992.
Picht, Robert. 'Europa – aber was versteht man darunter? Aufforderung zur Überprüfung der Denkmuster.' *Merkur. Deutsche Zeitschrift fur europäisches Denken* 48, no. 9/10, 1994. 850-866.
Radakrishnan, R. 'Nationalism, Gender, and the Narrative of Identity', Parker et al., 1992. 77- 95.
Rusch, Gebhard. 'Zur Systemtheorie und Phänomenologie von Literatur. Eine holistische Perspektive.' *SPIEL. Siegener Periodikum zur Internationalen Empirischen Literaturwissenschaft* 10, 1991. 305-339.
Schein, Edgar H. *Organizational Culture and Leadership.* San Francisco: Jossey-Bass, 2nd printing, 1992.
Schlesinger, Philip. 'Europeanness: A New Cultural Battlefield?' Hutchinson and Smith, 1994. 316-325; first publ. in 1992.
Segers, Rien T. 'Research into Cultural Identity: A New Empirical Object. The Case of Japanese 'Uniqueness' Between East and West.' *SPIEL.* Siegener *Periodikum zur Internationalen Empirischen Literaturwissenschaft* 11, 1992. 149- 162.
────── 'Japanese Cultural Identity and Reading Behavior.' *The Japan Foundation Newsletter* 22, no.1, 1994. 15-20.
────── *Sleutelboek Japan.* Amsterdam: Balans, 1996.
Segers, Rien T. and Reinhold Viehoff. 'Die Konstruktion Europas. Überlegungen zum Problem der Kultur in Europa', in Segers and Viehoff 1999, 9-49.
────── (eds.). *Kultur Identität Europa. Über die Schwierigkeiten und Möglichkeiten einer Konstruktion.* Frankfurt/M: Suhrkamp, 1999.
Sevänen, Erkki. 'Art as an Autopoietic Sub-System of Modern Society.' *Theory, Culture & Society* 18, no.1, 2001. 75-103.
Sinclair, John, Elizabeth Jacka and Stuart Cunningham. 'Peripheral Vision.' *Lechner and Boli*, 301-306.
Tötösy de Zepetnek, Steven. 'Systemic Approaches to Literature: An Introduction with Selected Bibliographies.' *Canadian Review of Comparative Literature/Revue Canadienne de Littérature Comparée*, 19, 1992. 21-93.
Yoshino, Kosaku. *Cultural Nationalism in Contemporary Japan. A Sociological Enquiry.* London, New York: Routledge, 1992.

Comparative Literature: Globalization and Hegemony

John T. Dorsey

Two opposing discourses have surfaced in regard to the development of comparative literary studies: globalization and hegemony. It seems to me that the two develop in tandem, for as the discourse of globalization develops, so does a discourse of suspicion and fear of hegemony. In comparative literature, the concept of globalization is often embraced as evidence of harmony between academic studies and world tendencies in politics, economics, technology, and communications. And for academic comparatists in particular, such signs of rapprochement with reality are welcome indeed. Still, there seems to be some confusion as to whether globalization has already occurred and we merely have to recognize and to adapt to it or whether it is the natural and inevitable wave of the future. Others, however, question the nature of this inevitability, and to them globalization appears to be less a natural phenomenon than a political and economic conspiracy of hegemonic domination that must be exposed and challenged at every occasion. For example, Edward Said notes in passing that "ironically, as we shall see, the study of 'comparative literature' originated in the period of high

European imperialism and is irrecusably linked to it" (43). The spin is in the adverb — who would want to be irrecusably linked to anything? Chastened and willing to reconsider, reform, and rehabilitate, in this essay I would like to survey the field of battle, as it were, and discuss a few models of conceptual strategies for a productive dialectic of discourses.

There are various definitions of globalization, and we all remember enthusiasms for other terms such as internationalization. Still, it is the term of the moment, and it seems that everyone is talking about it. I am not being cynical; rather, I expect that there is more than a grain of truth in this term, especially as it applies to comparative literature. What does it mean? One view is that there is a tendency for the world to become one unit; another is that we tend to view the world in this manner. Some say that the globalization process is not a new phenomenon but actually began some five hundred years ago with the discovery of the "New World" and with the Renaissance. The circumnavigation of the globe was a key symbol, and it was echoed in the "eighty days'" journey of the 19th century and in the eighty-some minutes' orbit of the astronauts in the 20th century. Some say that we can date the perception of globalization to the first magnificent pictures of the globe taken from a space capsule headed to the moon some thirty years ago. To others, this view merely reflects Eurocentrism — the view that significant events in Western Europe are significant for people around the world. Indeed, this literally external view of the globe, which was broadcast around the world, is seen by many as a view from America, signaling the ascendancy of American cultural hegemony, along with cable news and the Internet.

Let us not anticipate but return to the discourse of globalization at hand, according to which it has become evident to "everyone" that for all our alleged differences, we inhabit the same world and should not be surprised to discover that we participate in a global culture.

Roland Robertson notes the global discourse about global culture: "As is well known, there has recently been considerable expansion of the rhetoric of globality, globalization, internationalization, and so on. In fact there appears to have crystallized across the world a relatively autonomous mode of discourse concerning such themes. Put another way, 'globe talk' — the discourse of globality — has become relatively autonomous, although its contents and the interests that sustain them vary considerably from society to society and also *within* societies" (88). From a more materialistic point of view there are those who define globalization primarily if not entirely in economic terms, for example, as the full development of a world market system, the apotheosis of capitalism. A similar case has been made for global communication, including travel, telecommunications, and the Internet. Others point to the migration of millions of people in this century, to the unification of Europe, to the search for international law and international government. In comparative literature, we have made a great stride from studying the literary balance of trade among Western European and American literatures to East-West comparative literature, then on to a kind of literature "without frontiers" in the realm of theory, that branch of literary studies that so soon declared its independence of mere literature. On closer examination, there is clearly a presumption of universality in even the most self-referential, self-doubting, self-problematizing of these theories. E. San Juan, Jr., for example, notes in *Hegemony and Strategies of Transgression*, "Reception aesthetics and reader-response protocols are not innocent ventures; both are motivated by the exploitive interests not of interpretive communities but of the institutions that reproduce normality, the status quo, quotidian business; hence the need not only for critical-realist 'reflection' but also a semiotics and pragmatics of distanciation" (69). In a broader context, Edward Said notes in *Culture and Imperialism*, "Without significant exception the universalizing discourses of modern Europe and the United States assume the silence, willing or otherwise, of the non-European world. There is incorporation; there is inclusion; there is direct rule; there is coercion. But there is only infrequently an acknowledgement that the colonized people should be heard from and their ideas known" (50). The discourse of globalization includes all of these concepts and more, but I believe that it concerns a real process, a significant development in the real world and in the academic world of comparative literature.

But inasmuch as the discourse of globalization is a way of perceiving and describing phenomena, there are serious concerns in regard to the question of *who* does or perceives *what*. This is always a problem with nominalized verbs used as buzzwords, and globalization underwent several predictable grammatical transformations on its way to becoming a widespread, not to say global, concept. The noun "globe" and the adjective "global" lead us to the verb "globalize," which in turn is nominalized as globalization. We note in passing that of course we are dealing with an English term of Latin roots, which itself might raise Eurocentric concerns. The term "internationalization" underwent similar transformations from the root word "nation." But with these nominalized verbs, the question remains open concerning *who* is doing *what* to whom. *Who* or *what* is being globalized? *Who* is globalizing or internationalizing what? Obviously it does not make much sense to say that the globe or even the earth is becoming globalized. This process of nominalization is a means of avoiding the direct expression of subjects and objects. In a sense, it makes the phenomenon seem natural, something that could be perceived objectively. However, is the formation and regular use of such words accidental, ingenuous, dishonest, or insidious? Or is it just a matter of fuzzy thinking? Turning once again to the field of comparative literature, can we say that literature is being globalized? Are authors being globalized? Is literature merely one more commodity in the world market? Should we propose something like a World Trade Organization to observe, monitor, and perhaps even control the flows, movements, and tendencies of literary contacts? Again, there are those who will ask, *who* precisely is globalizing literature? What purpose lies behind such an endeavor? Such questions concerning subjects and objects lead us to the discourse of hegemony.

Hegemony can be simply defined as "preponderant influence or authority, especially of one nation over others." Etymologically it points to leadership, and historically it has been applied to various spheres of influence in various civilizations. However, what seems to be leadership to the leaders will most likely seem to be domination to the dominated. It was not only Sparta that took exception to the so-called "leadership" of Athens. In *Culture and Imperialism*, Edward Said writes, "Most professional humanists as a result are unable to make the connection between the prolonged and sordid cruelty of practices such as slavery, colonialist and racial oppression, and imperial subjection on the one hand, and the poetry, fiction, philosophy of the society that engages in these practices on the other" (xiii-xiv). And indeed the discourse of hegemony is composed of increasingly negative terms, ranging from undue or excessive influence, to control, to manipulation, and on to domination. The discourse of hegemony thus develops as a critique of the discourse of globalization, as a challenge to it, indeed, as a replacement for it.

Of the two questions mentioned above concerning *who* does or sees *what*, the discourse of hegemony generally focuses on the first, the subject, the doer or viewer, we might say. Traditionally, the accusing finger has been raised at Europe, using the familiar variations, Eurocentric, Eurocentrism, but recently it has more often been pointed at the United States. For example, Frederic Buell writes in *National Culture and the New Global System*, "American hegemony in the postwar period, resting on the advocacy, dissemination, and manipulation of the ideal of national self-determination, thus globalized, in the neocolonial world system, the American Janus face I have referred to previously. Stavrianos calls it 'anti-colonial imperialism,' a new form of domination that sought, in the words of Anthony Eden, to make 'former colonial territories, once free of their masters . . . politically and economically dependent on the United States'" (151). To some, the influence of Western, European, or American culture is merely a cover for nefarious economic, political, and military power. To others it is a weapon in the arsenal of those who seek hegemony in the sense of cultural, political, and economic domination of the world. Bertolt Brecht once said something to the effect that "When someone mentions culture, I reach for my knife" (i.e., to defend myself). And if we take into account the selective praise of national culture in fascism in general and Nazism in particular, we can understand how culture can be perceived as dangerous, indeed as a weapon. The lessons from Edward Said's *Orientalism* can clearly be applied to the development and spread of American culture, but we should take into account that it is most likely that American music, film, and television, rather than literary works per se, wield such power, even in America.

The discourse of hegemony is of course applied not only to literature but also to literary studies, including comparative literature, and here we face one more question, problem, or crisis of comparative literature. Looking back at the history of our discipline, we might conclude that such controversy is its only common point — it may be the only thing all comparatists agree about. Has the discipline been quite as idealistic as it claimed to be at first? That is, did it really transcend national borders, political boundaries to consider literature in a supranational, egalitarian way? Or has it in fact served to suppress or silence large realms of literature, subordinating some forms to others? A few years ago, when the American novelist Saul Bellow conversationally challenged some partisan of multiculturalism to show him the "Proust" of Africa, he was strongly criticized, but how often has comparative literature made similar gaffes? And how innocent were they?

In comparative studies, the battle lines between the discourses of globalization and hegemony are thus sharply drawn. On the one hand, there are those who proudly maintain that globalization has from the beginning been the aim and purpose of comparative literary studies, with Goethe's phrase *Weltliteratur* still appearing here and there as an example of globalization *avant la lettre*, despite cautions to the effect that Goethe had something quite different in mind. The traditional humanistic argument is that literature is *one* because mankind is *one*, and overcoming the artificial barriers of language, culture, and politics is a means of exerting influence from the microcosm of humanistic studies to the macrocosm of international relations. According to this humanistic view, globalization in comparative literature would thus be a forerunner of and guiding light to globalization in the mundane world of economics and politics, as we emerge from a world divided by the ideologies of colonialism and cold war geopolitics.

The key word in this view of comparative literature is "transcend," for globalization is posited as distinct from internationalization. For example, in *Undoing Culture*, Mike Featherstone writes, "The very notion that we can undertake a comparative analysis based upon homogeneous national cultures, consensual traditions or 'organic' ethnic communities is being challenged and redefined" (10). Thus, in comparative literature, we are out of the business of crossing borders or frontiers, checking passports or certificates of national origin, or balancing cultural trade accounts. In the discourse of globalization, it is taken for granted that while literary works are written in different languages, in different places on the globe, such distinctions need not be the focus or the *raison d'être* of our study. And yet it is precisely such distinctions that have for so long been a part of the definition of comparative literary studies. From this point of view, the recognition of globalization does not necessarily mean the end of difference or distinction, but points to networks of relationships among literary texts, readers, and writers.

In contrast to this relatively rosy view of the globalization of culture, many view the relationship between the little world of literature and the precincts of power in quite a different manner. The discourse of hegemony describes the flow of influence in quite the opposite direction, that is, from the world of economic and military might to the outposts of art and academics, where writers and scholars, the foot soldiers of capitalism, colonialism, and cultural domination, pursue their "civilizing," "humanistic" functions, not unlike the missionaries of yore who spread the true faith with merchants and soldiers at their back. For most academics, as noted by Said above, it is very difficult to imagine themselves as agents of Western capitalism or imperialism, especially considering our salaries, but it is a historical fact that those who believe in something humanistic or transcendent are generally available at lower prices.

The critique of globalization thus busies itself with unmasking the traditional, humanistic discourse of globalization as a cover or even a direct support for conquest and domination, a continuance of the hegemonic extension of power and influence, or at least a justification of it, through other means. The alleged "harmony" observed between globalization in literary studies and international relations is accordingly depicted in a sinister manner as at best an unwitting alliance and at worst a united front of masters against the mastered. Accordingly, the last thirty years have seen a plethora of criticism on criticism, rather than on literature. And a great deal of that meta-criticism has been aimed at revealing and denouncing the subtext of white, male, Western, Christian, Eurocentric hegemony in the microcosm of the university and the "global" macrocosm.

Postcolonial theory, according to Leela Gandhi, is devoted to "a postnational reading of the colonial encounter by focusing on the global amalgam of cultures and identities consolidated by imperialism. To this end, it deploys a variety of conceptual terms and categories of analysis which examine the mutual contagion and subtle intimacies between colonizer and colonized" (129). And even the extremely popular pursuit of pure literary theory beyond contact with literature or most readers, let alone reality, has been seen as little more than feigned protests of ignorance and impotence by those who should know and should act on that knowledge. They are compared to the millions of silent collaborators who did not take notice of the more egregious atrocities of the twentieth century as they were occurring.

However, even when the discourse of hegemony does not focus on political or economic domination, it often includes an openly nationalistic fear of cultural domination or of the so-called "homogenization" of culture through which the local culture disappears. This variation on the discourse of hegemony focuses on an opposition of the local and the global, and the global always seems to threaten the existence of the local, so that such affirmative sounding words as extension, transcendence, and unification in the discourse of globalization appear as encroachment, intrusion, and homogenization in the discourse of hegemony. For example, in *Postcolonial Theory*, Leela Gandhi notes some sign of progress along these lines in the self-critical, meta-criticism mentioned above: "In contrast, poststructuralist and postmodernist anti-humanists maintain that any universal or normative postulation of rational unanimity is totalitarian and hostile to the challenges of otherness and difference" (27). And Takayuki Yokota-Murakami, in his critical study of the methodological and ideological "problematics" of comparing such "common" themes as "love" in "East" and "West," concludes, "If, however, American comparative literature has been an attempt to subsume the cultures of the world under the pretext of humanistic values into the Western civilization, a similar politics is found in the disciplines of comparative literature of Eastern countries too," and he points to the emphasis on East-East (Japan-Korea, Japan-China, etc.) comparative study of literature in Japan, which he claims "displays a political intention of subsuming Asian powers as opponents to the Western influence, with Japan as a center," concealing "a colonial ambition which Japan failed to achieved half a century ago" (186).

As mentioned previously, the target of such criticism has most often been Western culture or more specifically, European culture. The word "Eurocentrism" and its derivatives have been used to affirm the continuity between imperialism, colonialism, and culture. However, increasingly the target has shifted to the growing hegemony of American culture. It has been said, for example, that people are writing American novels, that is, American-style novels, all over the world. To put this remark in context, we should note that many observers of world culture have noted with dismay that people are making American films, designing American clothes, and preparing American food all over the world. Characteristically enough, Americans themselves have expressed much of this dismay and regret. American culture in particular is thus seen as a multinational phenomenon modeled on the myth of the multi-national corporations, the result being the elimination of the local, the indigenous. If, as Harold Bloom has called it, there is a diachronic anxiety of influence between writers of one generation and their predecessors, in the discourse of hegemony, there is a synchronic anxiety of influence between local cultures and European and/or American culture.

Various models have been proposed for creating an arena for the interaction of these apparently discordant discourses in comparative literature. The task at hand is to create a conceptual space to allow a dialectic to develop so that we may better understand the object of these two discourses and its implications for comparative literary studies. First of all, there is the eighteenth-century model of the encyclopedia: the open-ended inclusion of information on various subjects arranged in alphabetical order rather than in some historical, hierarchical, or theoretical framework. We need not posit the existence of an actual multi-volume compendium here. Let us rather think of the model in terms of a Platonic ideal. If the encyclopedia model for comparative literature can be freed from its Eurocentric, Enlightenment roots, including something as rudimentary as Western alphabetical order (歌舞伎 [kabuki] doesn't really start with a "k"), it would allow multiple writers and readers to interact in non-linear, non-hierarchical conceptual space. An encyclopedia is an open-ended enterprise in which information can be added, updated, expanded, and corrected. Needless to say, attention must be paid to keep the enterprise open-ended; otherwise, we will face the same charges of privileging and silencing, of dominating rather than contributing. Even in the narrow context of literary reference works in multi-cultural America, there are vituperative arguments among academics, editors, publishers, and readers concerning inclusion/exclusion and the relative length of individual entries. And there is always the question of whether "information" or "knowledge" can be objective in a global sense — in other words, can it really be free of the culture that produces it? There are many who do not believe in culture-unbound truths. But one attractive feature of this model is the underlying presumption that in principle everything can be explained to everyone, and this presumption is based on another — the universality of reason and to some extent of the scientific method. In an age in which we are predisposed to question any universals, there is good reason for us to reject the idea that reason and science are "Western." In a sense, I think that this model has been with us in comparative literature from the beginning, and even now most would agree that the goal of comparative literature is to add to something like a storehouse of knowledge.

Another model is the museum, a place for the preservation and display of representative works of art from all world cultures. Here the emphasis is more on preservation and presentation than on analysis and interpretation. As in the case of the encyclopedia model, we are not talking about an actual building along the lines of the Tower of Babel. We are concerned even more here with conceptual space, for works of literature are, of course, not physical objects made of ink and paper and strictly speaking do not exist in space like paintings or statues. A library is the proper place for the storage of books as physical objects, or others may argue that the proper image is that of a shopping market filled with literary commodities, available thanks to the world market system and Internet sales. In a physical museum, that is, a building, there is literally much space for contention concerning inclusion and space allotted, but here in our conceptual museum, no quarter should be given to such proprietary claims. Accordingly, the model of a museum of literature must free itself from the image of ages of acquisition/plunder in the interest of art. Comparative literature in the form of world literature would, according to this view, be like a museum neatly organized and arranged, at any visit, but infinitely open to expansion and rearrangement.

A third model is the Internet, and the corresponding images of our work as comparatists is the opening of gateways or the development of interfaces between independent systems of knowledge and information, again allowing rather than determining paths of interaction. As everyone knows, there is no center to the Internet, no headquarters, and no boundaries. Although the English language has dominated so much of the Internet since its beginnings, this is changing rapidly because of the integration of various languages, the development of high speed translation, and the growing use of non-verbal, audiovisual media. Even the "digital divide" that allegedly separates rich and poor seems to be narrowing on a daily basis as Internet access is increasingly separated from ownership of expensive equipment and knowledge of arcane cyber matters. Our job as comparatists would then be to open windows, if that is not a trademark, doors, and gateways, or perhaps merely to remove obstacles to the understanding of literature as a global phenomenon. Frederick Buell speaks of a time of "global interconnectedness, not the global fiction of local autonomy" (63). And of course, one of the fundamental networks is the literary work itself, or as Ihab Hassan, who recently described himself a "wandering scholar" and "an itinerant lecturer," has described the matter, "literature is the site where the local and the global, the concrete and the universal imaginatively transact the enigma of the human" (66). Will the Internet be the best model for comparative literature? It is a decentered world, fragmentary and yet in a sense at any moment complete. And it is growing prodigiously as we use it. Unlike the development of other networks such as trade routes, railroads, and telephone systems, the Internet develops in surprising, unpredictable, and self-renewing ways. As a network of networks, the Internet may well be the most appropriate model for globalization in comparative literature without hegemony — multiple, non-linear, decentered interrelations of literary works.

Works Cited and Reference Works:

Bassnett, Susan. *Comparative Literature: A Critical Introduction.* Oxford: Blackwell, · 1993.
Bernheimer, Charles, ed. *Comparative Literature in the Age of Multiculturalism.* Baltimore and London: The Johns Hopkins UP, 1995.
Buell, Frederick. *National Culture and the New Global System.* Baltimore: Johns Hopkins UP, 1994.
Featherstone, Mike. *Undoing Culture: Globalization, Postmodernism and Identity.*

London: Sage Publications, 1995.
Femia, Joseph V. *Gramsci's Political Thought: Hegemony, Consciousness, and the Revolutionary Process.* Oxford: Clarendon / Oxford UP, 1981.
Fontana, Benedetto. *Hegemony & Power: On the Relation between Gramsci and Machiavelli.* Minneapolis: U of Minnesota P, 1993.
Golding, Peter and Phil Harris, eds. *Beyond Cultural Imperialism: Globalization, Communication & the New International Order.* London: Sage, 1997.
Hassan, Ihab. "Globalism and Its Discontents: Notes of a Wandering Scholar" in *Profession* 1999. New York: The Modern Language Society of America.
Jameson, Fredric and Masao Miyoshi, ed. *The Cultures of Globalization.* Durham and London: Duke UP, 1998.
King, Anthony D., ed. *Culture, Globalization and the World-System: Contemporary Conditions for the Representation of Identity.* Minneapolis: U of Minnesota P, 1997.
Koelb, Clayton and Susan Noakes, eds. *The Comparative Perspective on Literature: Approaches to Theory and Practice.* Ithaca: Cornell UP, 1988.
Moses, Michael Valdez. *The Novel and the Globalization of Culture.* New York and Oxford: Oxford UP, 1995.
Peyser, Thomas. *Utopia & Cosmopolis: Globalization in the Era of American Literary Realists.* Durham and London: Duke UP, 1998.
Said, Edward W. *Culture and Imperialism.* New York: Vintage, 1994.
———. *Orientalism.* Harmondsworth: Penguin, 1985. (Original: Routledge & Kegan Paul, 1978.)
San Juan, Jr., E. *Hegemony and Strategies of Transgression: Essays in Cultural Studies and Comparative Literature.* Albany: State University of New York Press, 1995.
Valdes, Mario J., Daniel Javitch, and A. Owen Aldridge, eds. *Comparative Literary History as Discourse: In Honor of Anna Balakian.* Bern: Peter Lang, 1992.
Yokota-Murakami, Takayuki. *Don Juan East/West: On the Problematics of Comparative Literature.* Albany: State U of New York P, 1998.

Nightmare Come True: Postmodern Paranoia and Terrorism

Naomi Matsuoka

Contemporary fiction and films, especially American works, have repeatedly fictionalized conspiracies and terrorism and depicted their aftermaths, the images of which are very often the destruction of New York and other American cities and even the end of the world. After the terrorist attacks in Washington D.C. and New York on September 11, 2001, it may be said that these works predicted the disaster; on the other hand, it seems that people's anxieties reflected in these works may have worked to realize the disaster. In other words, it seems that the anxieties of our time depicted in contemporary fiction seem to have finally erupted into reality. From this perspective, it is worth re-reading some works of postmodern fiction, for they not only convey the anxieties of our time but also help us to recognize alternative realities and cope with them in this postmodern era. In this essay, I would like to discuss novels by Thomas Pynchon, Oe Kenzaburo, and Murakami Haruki as examples of such works.

In the introduction to *Postmodern American Fiction*, Thomas Pynchon is defined as a conspiracy writer: "[w]ith *The Crying of Lot*

49 and *Gravity's Rainbow* (1973), Thomas Pynchon presciently introduced conspiracy into the novel, both as a subject and as a model for how a novel could communicate meaning to its reader" (xiii). Indeed, in *The Crying of Lot 49*, Pynchon depicted the postwar American psyche, people's anxiety about conspiracy and the paranoia caused by it, warning us of the near-insanity of the human condition far ahead of time. Kihara Yoshihiko notes that the scene of the two hijacked airplanes crashing into the World Trade Center buildings calls to mind the closing image of *Gravity's Rainbow*, in which one ICBM approaches the top of a movie theater in downtown Los Angeles, supposedly run by a Nixon-like figure. He states also that the ICBM could be the developed form of the V rocket that the survivors of the African Herero tribe assembled from the war rubble to build their own rocket. This interpretation would support Noam Chomsky, who argues that the September 11 terrorist attack was the first counterattack of the colonized on the colonizer on its land in our history. It seems that we have been neither keen enough to understand Pynchon's message nor tough enough to face reality. The situation parallels that of Kafka's depiction of the anxiety of his time, more than twenty years before the Holocaust.

World War II traumatized many societies and peoples, and the United States is not an exception. People tend to think that such great destruction, including the Holocaust and the atomic bombings of Hiroshima and Nagasaki, could not be a coincidence but rather must have been plotted and realized by some sinister force. People became suspicious of everything and came to look for plots and conspiracies everywhere. With the beginning of the Cold War, many Americans became paranoid and excessively self-defensive about the Soviet threat, and some drove themselves into the social hysteria of McCarthyism in the 1950s. The nuclear arms race escalated to the point at which some planned to produce a cobalt bomb that could split the earth and they seriously discussed, following the nuclear deterrence theory, developing something like a Doomsday Machine to destroy the entire world. This shows how excessive defensiveness could result in self-destruction, and yet even now the US government seems to be determined to complete the National Missile Defense System despite strong objections from the international community. In the 1960s the assassinations of John and Robert Kennedy, Martin Luther King Jr., and Malcolm X, also inspired people to suspect conspiracies behind them. With the Vietnam War and the Watergate Scandal in the 1970s, the American people were further convinced that there were many things they were not told and that their lives were being manipulated by the military, the corporations, the President, the government, the FBI, the CIA, and so forth. In the 1980s, President Reagan called the Soviet Union "the Evil Empire," referring to the popular movie series *Star Wars* by George Lucas.

In recent years, cult groups and secret societies are also conspicuous. They fear attacks by the federal government and arm themselves heavily in self-defense to the point where they become a danger in society. The Branch Davidians is one such group. Their headquarters was surrounded by the FBI in Waco, Texas in 1994 and destroyed by explosion and fire, killing numerous followers, including women and children. Paranoid militia groups, who also fear attacks from the federal government, have recently become united closely by the Internet and are heavily armed to prepare for the attacks from outside. Timothy mcVeigh, a Gulf War veteran, said to be a militia member, destroyed the Oklahoma City Federal Building in 1995, believing that many FBI agents were working in the building. His motive was retribution for the FBI's attack on the Branch Davidians. Among many others, Ruby Ridge, the UNA Bomber, and Heaven's Gate cult group may be remembered. These people are so fearful of sinister conspiracies that they attack their supposed enemies before they are attacked or kill themselves in order to escape. And now Osama bin Ladin and Al Qaeda, the alleged mastermind and the network of the terrorism of September 11, are determined to attack the United States because they have been threatened by American hegemony.

In America, nowadays, not only "conspiracy" but also "conspiracist" and "conspiracism" are commonly used in both academic and journalistic writing, and, as Sam Roberts reflects, the concept has been fascinating American people for some time. In return, their love and fear of conspiracy has been fed by many best-selling fictions by writers like Tom Clancy as well as by Hollywood movies, which are often based on these fictions. (Minzesheimer) On September 11, these fictional nightmares became reality.

Although popular fiction and Hollywood movies depict terrorist attacks and disasters, the world and the United States are saved at the end by the heroic acts of one man or a small group of people. Pynchon's fiction, however, focuses on the anxieties imbedded in contemporary society and suggests that we must live with them. In *The Crying of Lot 49*, Pynchon develops the theme of conspiracy around the search for and revelation of the secret society Tristero by the protagonist Oedipa Maas. In the novel, there are three overlapping conspiracies concerning: 1) Tristero, an alternate postal or communications system; 2) Oedipa Maas, a character who pursues the truth about her fictional world; and 3) the text which ensnares the readers into playing a game which they must learn as they play. Does Tristero exist? Does it control Oedipa? Does it create or deliver or subvert itself? The whole conspiracy concerning Tristero is actually a never-ending digression which appears suddenly, just as Oedipa sets out on her suddenly imposed duty of sorting out the details of her former lover's inheritance. Beneath the surface success story of this American millionaire are various links to the Tristero postal network, which traces its roots to a revolt against the totalitarian monopoly of the official postal system both in Europe and then later in America. This secret but paradoxically omnipresent network is a reflection of a desire to resist the monopoly of truth.

The text of the novel contains various "documentary facts," obviously fabricated, which entice rather than enlighten us. The Tristero system, for example, is acknowledged by "the Protestant noble William of Orange" in the latter half of the sixteenth century. It survived the turmoil of European history for the next two hundred years, surfacing every once in a while whenever a ruler became overly oppressive in a region. Then, it is said, most of the members of the Tristero system fled to America in the 1850s, and since then it has continued to exist as an underground postal system in America, reflecting the desire of Americans to protect their idealistic pursuit of the rights to life, liberty, and the pursuit of happiness. In this sense, Oedipa's investigation of the Tristero system turns out to be a rediscovery of the American spirit. And although neither she nor the reader ever know whether the Tristero system exists or not, we do learn of the possibility of such an alternative to the official control of communication, whether it be in cyberspace or in the novels secretly sent to market by a writer who has kept his whereabouts and even his physical appearance a mystery, which only recently seems to be on the verge of full discovery.

Oedipa's quest to settle the affairs of Pierce Inverarity leads her, by way of the Tristero mysteries, to attempt to sort out her own affairs, which remain indeterminate as long as she searches for something she fears — the overriding truth that will put everything in this proper and fixed place. In other words, she fears the discovery of a plot to the novel she inhabits. This paradoxical process can be described as paranoia, but it is playful as well. The open ending of this novel, in which the revelation of Tristero is forever suspended before our eyes, suggests that it is better to be aware of one's paranoia, of one's complicity in plotting reality as well as in creating enemies.

The Crying of Lot 49, as a whole, conspires against its readers as much as it conspires with them in their search for meaning or for the equally comfortable conclusion that there is no meaning. Along the way, Pynchon subverts various strategies of interpretation and investigation such as decoding, conducting research, and systematically explaining texts. Through the process, readers become aware that they routinely fabricate stories and give them meanings just as a novelist writes fiction. As Oedipa comes to understand, we project the world. The novel thus frees us from the paranoid standoff of "us" against "them, the enemy."

The fictional world of Oe Kenzaburo as well has been hovering around some secret evil from World War II, some unresolved problem, some unacknowledged guilt and secret identification with the excesses of the war. Oe was about ten years old when the war ended, old enough to see and experience both the reality of the Japanese war and of the American Occupation. He has deeply ambivalent feelings about the war: for although many have considered him liberal and even left-wing, he has confronted the right-wing extremist in himself.

As in *The Crying of Lot 49*, conspiracy is a central theme in *Man'en Gan'nen no Futtoboru*: first, there are the literal conspiracies of revolt in the past with parallels in the present; second, the suspicions of the main character; and third, the plot of the novel often seems a plot or conspiracy in which the readers find themselves caught up, as they try to play the history game but become suspicious or simply confused as the rules seem to change in the process of the game. Also, as in *The Crying of Lot 49*, there is a quest here, an obligation or duty that is somehow imposed on the main characters Mitsusaburo and Takashi when they return to a village on Shikoku Island because they want to put an end to their present troubles and search for a new life. Both brothers become entangled in the family history that reached a climax in the farmers' revolt of 1860 and its aftermath in 1870.

While the younger brother actively engages himself in the present day social problems of his village in emulation of his ancestor, the elder brother Mitsusaburo tries to find out just what happened and what it might mean.

Takashi organizes the village youths by playing football and eventually leads them in a final game to a riot against the only supermarket store in the village, which Takashi believes has destroyed the self-sufficient village economy through its monopoly of the distribution system. He models the riot on the farmers' revolt in 1860, which was led by his ancestor, the younger brother of his great-grandfather, the village chief. Idealizing the farmers' revolt and identifying himself with its leader, Takashi romanticizes his football riot, which fails, leading him to commit suicide.

Meanwhile, Mitsusaburo is rather cynical about Takashi's efforts and increasingly disillusioned with what he finds out from the historical records about the farmers' riot of 1860 and its leader. He attempts to reconstruct the historical truth by sifting through historical documents and village legends. In the process, he concludes that the revolt was insignificant and its leader a coward. This, of course, parallels his feelings about his brother's activities in the village, so his objectivity is undercut.

After Takashi's suicide, however, he discovers some old documents in the cellar of the storehouse of their residence, and he is forced to revise his conclusions about the farmers' revolt, his brother's social activities, and his own perspicacity. He learns that the leader of the farmers' revolt had confined himself for the rest of his life in the cellar as a form of self-punishment. However, he did emerge once in 1870 to lead a successful revolt, only to return to his self-imposed imprisonment until he died. Mitsusaburo, humbled by his discoveries, renews his faith in human dignity.

It has been observed that the dates 1860 and 1870 correspond to important events that happened in 1960 and were approaching in

1970 in Japan — the riots against the renewal of the US-Japan Security Treaty. The novel was written in 1967, at a time when many Japanese looked back at the failure of the widespread riots in 1960 against the treaty and looked forward to the possibility of a united resistance in 1970. Both of these treaties were based on "security" arrangements imposed on the Japanese after World War II, so here the football riots in the 1960s in the novel and the basically historical farmers' revolt in the nineteenth century should be seen in terms of the pattern of suppression and revolt in the relations between America and Japan since World War II. After September 11, however, the voice of revolt has been generally subdued, and the Japanese Government was able, with little resistance, to pass a new law allowing the "self-defense" army to be deployed to support American military activities.

Just as Japanese have avoided their main problems — their responsibility in World War II and their relations with the United States since then — Oe's main character heads for Shikoku at the beginning of the novel in order to avoid the main problems in his life. He has lost the sight of one eye in an accident, his first child was born with a serious brain defect, and his close friend went insane and killed himself in a bizarre, humiliating manner. Moreover, his wife has retreated into alcoholism, fearing that he will also kill himself. Unable to understand why these things have happened to him, he grows paranoid, believing that some power is at work, trying to destroy him. In particular, the suicide of his friend obsesses him. Although his friend was not political, he happened to be caught in a clash between the police and demonstrators against the US-Japan Security Treaty in June 1960. He was struck on the head by a policeman, and since then he suffered from a mental disorder. In an insane asylum, he protested against an oppressive caretaker and was forced to leave. He went back home and killed himself in a humiliating manner.

Perhaps this obsession with the apparently absurd demise of his friend leads Mitsusaburo to criticize his brother's involvement in local grievances and to minimize the farmers' revolt and its leader. Eventually, he realizes that whether you are political or not, you can be the victim of the dominant power in society or worse, its tool. In order to live a dignified life, you must live with that awareness, no matter how terrifying it might be, and you must oppose oppression even if it means death. With this realization, he is able to stop escaping and merely observing, and he resumes his life with this awareness, free from paranoia.

Other than *Man'en Gan'nen no Futtoboru* (1967), Oe has written many works dealing with the theme of revolt and terrorism from the point of view of rebels and terrorists. One of his earlier works, *Seventeen*, for example, portrays the seventeen-year-old right wing boy who in 1960 assassinated Asanuma Inejiro, the leader of the anti-US-Japan Security Treaty movement and the chairman of the Japan Socialist Party in 1960. Oe reveals a very personal sexual obsession of the assassin beneath the nationalistic cause. *Memushiri Kouchi* (1968) is about a group of young boys who create an independent community in a mountain village after the villagers abandon them in the turmoil of war and epidemic. With *Kozui wa Waga Tamashii ni Oyobi*, Oe is said to have predicted the Asama Villa Incident in 1972, the standoff between the young members of the Japan Red Army and the police. *Dojidai Gemu* (1979) is about the history of a mountain village in Shikoku that managed to win independence from the Meiji Government, even going to war with the national army, and that maintained itself during World War II by giving false birth reports to the national government. The history is retold in other works, suggesting another, alternative course of modern Japan. In *Moeagaru Midori no Ki* and *Chugaeri*, Oe deals with the rise and fall of a cult group that resembles the Aum Supreme group. The former novel more or less predicted the disasters caused by the Aum group, although in the world of fiction, the religious leader sacrifices himself to prevent calamity.

With these fictional works Oe presents another, alternative Japan, different from the Japan that rushed toward modernization and Westernization, competed with the Western nations in expansion and colonization of other parts of Asia, was defeated unconditionally, and then enjoyed economic prosperity in pseudo-independence. The repeated revolts and acts of terrorism in his fiction are meant to be simulation games and lessons for the readers to reflect upon the possibility of another reality.

Often described as postmodern and Pynchonesque, particularly in regard to the exploration of hidden networks of conspiracy, Murakami Haruki's fiction has reflected similar aspects of contemporary Japanese society. In particular, from *A Wild Sheep Chase* (1982), through *Hardboiled Wonderland and The End of the World* (1985), to the recent *The Wind-up Bird Chronicle*, Murakami has revealed an underground world of modern Japan in which sinister forces are at work to control the society: "the powerful underground kingdom" ruled by the mysterious sheep, the dark and dangerous underground world just beneath Tokyo inhabited by malicious creatures called INKlings, and the wells connecting Setagaya, Tokyo, in the 1980s to the Manchuria-Mongolia border in the 1930s. After the publication of *The Wind-up Bird Chronicle*, we see Murakami's sinister force taking a clearer shape: the evil and its driving force are embedded in the course of Japanese modernization from colonialism, fascism, to late capitalism. Wataya Noboru in *The Wind-up Bird Chronicle* is the most up-to-date incarnation of such a force, a brilliant economist who is to become a technocrat-type statesman ambitious to rule Japan, most likely directing Japan to the course of violence it once took. Murakami's protagonist, an ordinary man, is forced to descend into the underworld, sometimes via Hokkaido, sometimes through subway exits and dried-up wells, to fight such an evil power. His only motivation is his love of an ordinary life, as symbolized mostly by his wife, and his urge to regain it.

As Murakami states, in his fictional works the underground has been associated not only with social evil, that is, the evil mind of each period in modern Japanese history, but also with the heart of darkness of individuals. And also, it is a place to which the protagonist must descend in order to find the truth and then return to a more or less normal life. In *The Wind-up Bird Chronicle*, he is after the truth about the Japanese war with China. He takes us on a trip to the past in order to face the violence and cruelty of the war and shows us how ordinary people could be caught up in the situation and commit acts of violence and cruelty themselves. Several scenes, such as the executions of a Japanese intelligence officer and Chinese rebels and the killing of animals in the zoo in Changchun (then the new capital of Manchuria) in China at the end of the war, evoke historical atrocities during the war and reveal human cruelty in an extreme situation. Murakami probes the modern-time universal theme of the inner horror and insanity of human beings, which breaks out in the form of violence and cruelty in the extreme situation of colonization, in one form of encountering an unknown culture, in which one system loses its self-control.

In the afterward to *Underground*, "Blind Nightmare: Where Are We Japanese Going?" Murakami explains that "the place called 'underground,' has been an important motif in my novels." He also explains the title *Underground* as "the shadowy area of our inner self which we consciously and unconsciously avoid and eliminate from the phase of reality." Then, he associates the darkness of the individual human mind with the real space and the darkness of society, saying, "the darkness just beneath our feet, that is, the literal underground from which this unprecedented terrorism broke out in the form of a nightmare, and which revealed at the same time the contradiction and weakness our social system has contained deep inside."

The Aum Shinrikyo group seems to be the realization of the "underground" Murakami has developed in his fictional world. When he wrote his first work of non-fiction *Underground*, I think that Murakami expected to see a similar situation with Asahara Shoko and the Aum Shinrikyo members when they opted for mass murder and terrorism, that is, that they had blundered across some forbidden border, had been thoroughly corrupted by their own purity of intention. In this context, it is troubling to find that Murakami often has his characters resort to acts of violence in order to combat evil — precisely what at least some of the Aum Shinrikyo followers may have thought they were doing. For example, the protagonist in *A Wild Sheep Chase* blows up a summerhouse in order to destroy the evil sheep and its agent completely, and Okada Toru, the protagonist of *The Wind-up Bird Chronicle*, clubs his evil enemy Wataya Noboru with a baseball bat in order to rescue his wife from the hellish darkness in which she is confined by his power. And yet, Murakami emphasizes at the end of the afterword to Part I of *Underground*, that his message is never to let such violence erupt and destroy society.

In reality, however, he saw that violence erupts repeatedly. At the beginning of *A Wild Sheep Chase* there is a scene in which the protagonist and his girl friend watch the TV news about Mishima Yukio's attempt at a coup on November 25, 1970. We also remember that Murakami belongs to the so-called Zenkyoto generation, the generation of the student movement at the end of the 1960s. The most radical group of the generation organized the Japanese Red Army in order to provoke a simultaneous world revolution, and actually carried out a series of destructive, anti-social incidents both in Japan and abroad. Murakami was a student at the end of the 1960s and shared a deep sympathy with the idea of social reform, and although he did not advocate such violent acts, he was profoundly disillusioned when the movement subsided and many students went back to school, resetting their course and adjusting themselves to fit to the coming rise of the Japanese economy of the 1970s and 80s. And this time in the Aum sarin gas attack, he sees that the evil spirit is freed to carry out violence.

What the interviews in *Underground* convey to us, on the other hand, is that conformity is pervasive in Japan, that people obey the rules and orders, so they can stay in the mainstream system. Murakami showed this by linking the Nomonhan Incident, a failed invasion of Mongolia in 1939, with Japan in the 1980s in his fiction. The interviews with the Aum followers reveal their unworldliness, and their stories are in a way more interesting than those of the victims. They are different enough from others to leave the mainstream, and yet they have not created their own stories. Instead they embrace the paranoid stories of their leader Asahara Shoko. After all, Murakami's fiction provides us with far better and far more insightful stories to understand modern Japan.

But such warnings and foreshadowings are not limited to the world of postmodern literary works. Best-seller novels by writers like Tom Clancy (minzesheimer) and Hollywood movies such as *Executive Decision* or *Air Force One* are surprisingly similar to the September 11 terrorist attacks on America. They explore the plots of terrorist attacks on the United States. The terrorists, whether Arabs or Russians, hijack airplanes in order to achieve their religious or political aims. On the other hand, Hollywood-made science-fiction movies such as *The Planet of Apes (I, II)*, *Independence Day*, *Men in Black*, *Armageddon*, *Matrix*, *AI*, and so forth, have repeatedly depicted the end of the world and very often showed the destruction of New York. In these films the world has been or is about to be destroyed by some sinister force: extraterrestrial life, computer systems, or natural phenomena like meteorites.

Indeed, it is noteworthy that the end of the world is often depicted by images of the destruction of New York: falling skyscrapers, shattered pieces of the Statue of Liberty half buried in the ground or mostly under water, and such. Rather than Washington D.C., New York has been not only the symbol of the United States but also the symbol of Western civilization in its development of humanism, science, and technology. The repeated depiction of the destruction of New York thus reflects people's anticipation and fear that New York will not go on forever, that this human challenge will come to an end. Like the Tower of Babel, the buildings on Manhattan Island are entirely artificial constructions of human desire and technology, displaying the challenge of mankind, and in the 20th century it finally reached the point at which it had actually gone far beyond human control. Consequently, when the terrorists attacked the twin towers with hijacked airplanes and when all the TV screens showed the towers crumbling down, many of us felt a strange familiarity — we had seen it many times before in movies and we had been harboring the vision in our minds, although the incident was unprecedented. This is why some of us, in front of our TV sets, could not help but think that it was just like watching a disaster movie. Our collective nightmare became real last September.

Bibliography

Chomsky, Noam. *9-11*. New York: Seven Stories Press. 2001.
Geyn, Paula, et al. *Postmodern American Fiction*. New York: Norton, 1998.
Hite, Molly. *Ideas of Order in the Novels of Thomas Pynchon*. Columbus: Ohio State University, 1983.
Kihara, Yoshihiko. "Pynchon, Zizek, dojitahatsu tero." *Eigo Seinen*. Jan. 2001. No. 1835.
McGuigan, Jim. *Modernity and Postmodern Culture*. Buckingham: Open UP, 1999.
Minzesheimer, Bob. "Novelists Find New Reality after 9/11." *USA Today*. January 17, 2002

Murakami, Haruki. *Andaguraundo.* Tokyo: Kodan-sha, 1997.
———. *Hitsuji o meguru boken.* Tokyo: Kodan-sha, 1982.
———. *Kami no kodomo-tachi wa mina odoru.* Tokyo: Shincho-sha, 2000.
———. *Nejimaki dori kuronikuru.* Tokyo: Shincho-sha, 1995.
———. *Sekai no owari to hadoboirudo wandarando.* Tokyo: Shincho-sha, 1997.
———. *Yakusoku sareta basho de: underground 2.* Tokyo: Bungei shunju, 1998.
Murakami, Mutsuko. "The Storyteller: 'I wanted to know what happened.'" Asiaweek. http://www.cnn.com/ASIANOW/asiaweek/97/1003/feat5.html Oct. 3, 1997.
Oe, Kenzaburo. *Chu gaeri.* Tokyo: Kodan-sha, 1999.
———. *Dojidai gemu.* Tokyo: Shincho-sha, 1979.
———. *Kozui wa waga tamashii ni oyobi.* Tokyo: Shincho-sha, 1973.
———. *Man'en gan'nen no futtoboru.* Tokyo: Kodan-sha, 1967.
———. *Me mushiri, ko uchi.* Tokyo: Kodan-sha, 1968.
———. *Moeagaru midori no ki.* Tokyo: Shincho-sha, 1995.
Pynchon, Thomas. *Gravity's Rainbow.* Harmondsworth: Penguin, 1987.
———. *The Crying of Lot 49.* New York: Harper and Row, 1986.
———. *V.* New York: Harper & Row, 1990.
Roberts, Sam. "Americans Love a Conspiracy, but Why?" *The New York Times.* December 18, 2001.
Weisenburger, Steven. *Gravity's Rainbow Companion: Sources and Contexts for Pynchon's Novel.* Athens: U of Georgia P, 1988.

Myth in *Black Elk Speaks* and *Aterui*: The Empowering Matrix

Adam Lebowitz

> Sometimes dreams are wiser than waking
> Black Elk in *Black Elk Speaks*

It is by no means a "story" unique to any one country or region: Communities of aboriginal groups come under the authority of a central administration that comes to dictate the historical narratives of the countries. However, there are occasions when in contradistinction to the dominating victors' voices, narratives of the defeated survive to tell a quite different story that continues to have social relevance and resonance several decades or even centuries after the actual occurrence of the factual events in question. *Black Elk Speaks*, the story of a Native American Sioux medicine man active in the nineteenth century, and *Aterui*, the tale of a northeastern Japanese tribal chieftain killed in the ninth century, are two such narratives. Interestingly, key plot features in the two narratives show marked similarities: Contact with an invading foreign power committed to economic and territorial hegemony; initial victory; followed by defeat; "death"; and "return".

Beyond the bones of structural parallels, however, lies a deeper point of comparison in the thematic heart of the narratives, namely the mythopoeic viewpoints that are their raison-d'etre. For Black Elk and Guantei Yusa[1] there is truth implied in the mythic consciousness of their cultural group, and it frames their interpretation of history. Despite their formalistic disparities — *Black Elk Speaks* is an autobiographical memoir from direct personal experience, and *Aterui* is a solo theater piece recreated from historical records and folk tales — the texts can be compared thematically due to analogous epistemological intentions to explain present circumstances according to particular mythic realities. Thereby, the mythic realities function as entities of empowerment in the midst of cultural alienation and destruction, and contribute to their present-day resonance.

The experience of face-to-face confrontation with historical "turning points" initially compels the title characters to recite their plight. With historicity being such a conspicuous and primary foundation of these texts, quantitative understanding of the circumstances surrounding their creation is a prerequisite for analysis of the mythopoeic vision applied to the narrative voice.

Textual Historical Backgrounds

Black Elk's Sioux tribe was one of a number of nomadic Plains Indians tribes inhabiting a wide expanse in the middle of the North American continent extending between Canada and Texas, and from the Rocky Mountains to the Missouri and Mississippi Rivers. Horses had been introduced by the Spanish in the sixteenth century and the Sioux were skilled bison hunters. The bison provided not only food, but also materials for clothing, shelter, tools and implements, weaponry, and fuel.[2]

It would not be misleading to say that the fortune of the Plains Indian tribes was suddenly changed by gold. With the discovery of the Mother Lode in California in 1848, Comstock Lode in Nevada in 1859, and other sites in Colorado, prospectors from the eastern US "travelling across the plains soon insisted that the US Government must keep the trails clear of aggressive Indians even though these trails, and the routes followed later by the railroads, cut across the Indians' best hunting country and threatened to destroy their traditional way of life by breaking up the herds of buffalo on which they depended." (Selby 199). A settlement with the Cheyenne and Arapaho negotiated by the US Government in 1865 following the brutal Sand Creek Massacre[3] south of Denver offered a temporary solution, recognizing hunting rights east of the Rocky Mountains.

The opportunity for future conflict was created with the development of the Bozeman Trail in 1865 to goldfields in Montana discovered by General George Custer. The trail cut directly through buffalo hunting ground sacred to the Plains tribes, and federal authorities proved unwilling to enforce the treaty and suppress movement along the trail as the US Treasury was in need of gold bouillon following the Civil War. The construction of the new Fort Phil Kearny caused already soured relations to worsen, culminating in the Fetterman Fight[4] where Black Elk's father participated and broke his leg. Additional skirmishes continued the following year until the army negotiated a treaty with chief Red Cloud, abandoning the Bozeman Trail and granting the Sioux land claims for "as long as grass should grow and water flow" (*Speaks* 18).

Black Elk's historical memory began at age three with his father's injury from the "Battle of the Hundred Slain", the Sioux term for the Fetterman Fight. Despite coinciding with a period of uncompromising US expansionist policies into the Southwest frontier and Native American territory, his childhood by his own admission was peaceful, with little contact with Wasichus (White People). With the Red Cloud treaty the Sioux were free to hunt and food was plentiful despite the construction of the Union Pacific Railway —

the "iron road" — across southern Wyoming. Although the timing of his birth anticipated greater contact with Wasichu people and culture, the culture Black Elk experiences in his youth was exclusively tribal, having "never seen a Wasichu" (*Speaks* 8).

When Black Elk was ten years old he saw Wasichus for the first time while his family was camping near a US Army fort outpost in South Dakota. The next year brought further incursion into Sioux territory by the Wasichus spurred on by discoveries of gold by General Custer in the Black Hills of South Dakota, an area of geographical and spiritual importance for the Plains tribes. Black Elk's family decided to join his cousin the great warrior Crazy Horse, who launched a campaign against Wasichu intrusion culminating in Custer's defeat at Little Big Horn. Such victories, however, were made redundant by the sheer volume of soldiers and settlers; Crazy Horse and Black Elk, their band greatly reduced by fighting and starvation, surrendered in May 1876, the Black Hills and surrounding territory having been "sold" to the US government the previous winter. By 1883 the Wasichus had hunted the bison into extinction[5] and confined Black Elk's people to a sedentary life in "boxes" on the Pine Ridge reservation. While touring the US and Europe in Buffalo Bill's Wild West Show, Black Elk's sense of alienation in the Wasichu world intensified: "... I was like a man who had never had a vision. I felt dead and my people seemed lost and I thought I might never find them again" (*Speaks* 217).

Living under conditions of near desperation, many Sioux began to find cause for hope in the messianic Ghost Dance movement. Black Elk joined in the summer of 1890 and while dancing envisioned a "sacred shirt" design impervious to bullets. In reaction, three thousand US troops were sent to the Badlands in South Dakota to force the tribes to return to reservation life, resulting in the massacre at Wounded Knee Creek, which Black Elk observed from a distance. In a small skirmish following he was badly wounded, and surrendered for the final time in January, 1891. "The Ghost Dance was the Indian's last hope. Accommodation had failed. Retreat had failed. War had failed. And now Wounded Knee made it plain that religion had failed. No choice remained but to submit to the dictates of the government" (Utley 410).

Black Elk Speaks is first-person experience; in contrast, the key to understanding the relation of myth to history in *Aterui* is to approach the work as a discourse between past historical and present events, the former a metaphor for the latter. Text and performance are based on the experiences of author Guantei and his family in the fishing communities on the northern tip of Honshu Island, the Shimokita Peninsula. His choice as subject matter of a ninth-century chieftain addresses a specific need: "As there is a necessity to illuminate the past, the past must be spoken of, and the future predicted from there" (*Aterui* 26).

Historical study can provide an understanding of the cultural and environmental problems facing Shimokita at present. In 1981 the Construction Ministry announced the planned construction of a berthing station for nuclear-fueled vessels on the beachfront in and around Guantei's hometown. Despite cash settlements and assurances that the construction of breakwaters would not disrupt the movements of water currents, the policy dictated from Tokyo without prior notification of the local population was met with great resistance. Protest slogans such as "Don't kill the Sea!" demonstrated the concern residents had with the effect of development on the natural environment, demonstrating that the bond with the sea went beyond the economic, and endangerment of the economy was seen as endangerment of identity.[6] To "illuminate" this current conflict in Japan Guantei reproduces a narrative from a period of intense warfare over 1000 years ago and through the eyes of Aterui the resistance leader. The outcome of the conflict was the containment of the whole of Honshu Island under centralized authority.

Upon coming to the throne in 781, the fiftieth Emperor of Japan had two political aims: 1) to move the capital of the Yamato court from Nara to Heian, present-day Kyoto, and 2) to extend the existing Northeastern boundaries of the country through the long-desired "Azuma" (east) territory today encompassing the Kanto and Tohoku regions of Japan. Companies of soldiers were dispatched to the area in 790, and engagements continued with the Isawa (modern-day I-wate Prefecture) Azuma aboriginals until Aterui's death in 802.[7] Thematically *Aterui* functions as social criticism by pointing to similarities between hegemonic policies of the Heian court and present-day developmental policies planned and enacted by federal authority in Tokyo. The Heian policies targeted for eradication a foreign culture for economic and "civilizing" reasons; similarly, "development" policy negatively affects the livelihood of the Shimokita fishing industry primarily consisting of small-scale independents.

The aboriginal tribe of Tohoku, the Emishi, differed ethnically and culturally from the Yamato. The Yamato grew rice and worshipped an emperor; in contrast, the Emishi hunted and foraged in the forests, raised horses, and were animistic.[8] Written Chinese ideographs in Yamato court records can act as "signs" indicating Yamato attitudes towards the Emishi, thereby making the analysis of the course of Yamato-Emishi relations from period documents very much an etymological task. Historian Takahashi Tomio, in his research into ideograph assignment, contends Yamato nomenclature concerning northern people reveals attitudes that were initially conciliatory but later formatively derogatory, the latter occurring around the turn of the second century when predatory designs were first made towards the territory. At this time, in place of the neutral "hairy people" ideograph read as "Emishi" formerly used, was a new one whose alternative meaning was "savage". Takahashi also calls attention to an alternate reading in the latter assignation meaning "countryside" affirming a dichotomy between the rural life of the savages and the civilized city of the Yamato.[9] A court record entry is indicative, and could have been taken from the diary of a US Army frontier officer seventeen centuries later:

> The Azuma Emishi possess a strong and violent consciousness and are fierce fighters. They do not stay long in any one place nor have they leaders. They are covetous of their borders and steal what they can. They have wicked mountain gods and lecherous field ones. They obstruct progress on our roads and make life difficult and uncomfortable for everybody... They live in holes in the winter and hives in the summer. They wear fur and drink blood, are of questionable ancestry, and can fly like birds in the mountains and run like beasts in the grass... When attacked they hide in the grass and when pushed enter the mountains.[10]

The play opens not with the actual narrative, but with the onstage presence of a miko, a female shaman from the folk tradition of northern Japan.[11] In slightly comic fashion Yuasa as the miko asks the audience with whom they would like her to establish contact. Acting also as a member of the audience, Yuasa asks the miko to find Aterui.

> Audience: He was a hunter-gatherer. The Yamato who attacked were rice-cultivating. That his people were probably more peaceful than the Yamato is something that is a recent archaeological discovery.
> Miko: Wow, I'm learning a lot today.
> Audience: (...) He was brought to Kyoto with the promise that he wouldn't be killed, but he was hanged. There is the

>   legend that his head then flew back to his hometown
>   afterward.
> Miko: That's some power.
>
> (*Aterui* 55)

The miko successfully contacts Aterui's spirit, assuming the warrior's person and his family as he tells his story. Reacting angrily to the negative portrayal of the Emishi in written records, he tells his wife that he felt forced into warfare to protect ancestral lands. His wife soothes him: "You were mad as the devil at the Yamato, but I know in truth you don't like battle. There is not one Isawa who does" (*Aterui* 74). The actions of the Yamato, however, initiate conflict as they besiege the natural landscape through cutting and digging. For the Isawa this is unacceptable, and even sacrilegious: "If we continue to allow these people to do as they please, the trees will disappear. They are turning the earth inside out. We have got to stop them, or else our god Hitakami will die" (*Aterui* 77). The Yamato are condemned for using nature wastefully, cutting trees, pulling grass, driving out foxes and deer; they also engage in a war of attrition, burning houses and killing children.

In the end Aterui decides to compromise and travel to the capital for negotiations. In its early stages the Isawa Emishi had won some early battles due to superior horsemanship and a knowledge of the terrain; the manpower supply of the Yamato, however, seemed almost unlimited and Aterui does not want to see any more deaths of his own tribe's people. Over his wife's protests he departs knowing that he will be killed — as a spirit from the world of the dead he already knows his fate and can tell his story from first-person omniscience outside of historical time — and urges his family to take refuge even further north.

Some broad conceptual comparisons can be made concerning

background similarities between the two stories. The narratives occur during periods of intense social instability in which the narrator's ethnic group — Black Elk's Sioux and Aterui's Emishi — are considered a minority with an undeveloped culture and attacked by a centralized authority intent on territorial expansion; in addition, the narrator is a leader in the forefront of the conflict who attempts to defend but is ultimately defeated. In addition, they are defeated not necessarily by superior skill (although the technology of weaponry played a major part in the campaigns against the Sioux) but due to unceasing volume of settlers. "In 1890, 8.5 million settlers occupied the Indian's former hunting grounds, where in 1866 there had been less than 2 million." (Utley 410). In addition, violation of the natural environment contributes to capitulation.

For Takahashi this time of violent ethnic interaction means the end of one era in Japan and the beginning of another with its own individual cultural implications:

> We can consider the second year of the Gangyo emperor (878), the year that initiates the chaos of the period (Gangyo-ran), as the ending point of the Ebisu (Emishi) problem as it existed in the old era together with the starting point of the middle era dominated by feudal ethics. Militarism and creation: it was the intersecting point between the two eras. It was not only the end of the old era in Tohoku (Northeast Japan); the Ebisu (Emishi) war as a force that united two entities was the epilogue of the old era in Japan. From the late 860's to the early 880's the background and setting are laid which trigger the rise of feudal, which is the prologue for the middle era.[12]

Sweeping generalities on this scale might arouse contention; nonetheless, it does point to one historian's understanding of the time close to when Aterui was active as a "turning point" in the whole of the Japanese historical narrative. To draw a parallel with Black Elk's historical time frame, similar sentiments were echoed by a US government census taker: "Whether coincidentally or not, in this very year of 1890 the statisticians of the Census Bureau discovered that they could no longer trace a distinct frontier of settlement on the map of the United States" (Utley 410).

We can see additional points of comparison in life and death activity when human action is contextualized in myth: Both experience a form of death in a foreign land, and then return through "flight" to their home. Additionally, shortly before final surrender Black Elk and Aterui envision a pre-invasion paradise. For Black Elk it is part of his Ghost Dance vision: "... I could see a beautiful land where many, many people were camping in a great circle... Everywhere there were drying racks full of meat. The air was clear and beautiful with a living light that was everywhere" (*Speaks* 242). In Aterui's story it is a dream: "I was a child playing in the midst of butterflies that were flying madly around flowers... The sunlight was shining bright, and the forest surrounding was dark and silent" (*Aterui* 114). After their dreams they make their last important decisions while experiencing full social freedom: Black Elk decides to throw in his lot with the Ghost Dancers, and Aterui in negotiations with the Yamato court at Heian.

The Matrix of Myth

Considering mythic modalities as they exist in the texts is another important point of comparison. A primary part of the thematic substance of these texts insofar as they provide answers to the historical questions outlined above is the veracity the creators place in certain mythic matrices. These matrices in turn are sources of thought and wisdom beyond simple observation and experience, and their existences in the texts are another important point of comparison. I choose the term "matrix" as it appears in two definitions of myth that I believe are pertinent to this analysis.

For Native American (Pueblo/Sioux) writer Paula Gunn Allen myth is "psychospiritual ordering of nonordinary knowledge," "a sense of reality that includes all human capacities," and "a kind of story that allows a holistic image to pervade and shape consciousness, thus providing a coherent and empowering matrix for action and relationship."[13] The metier of the myth receives a slightly different treatment in John B.Vickery's consideration — a "religiosocial matrix... from which literature emerges as an endlessly self-complicating phenomenon"[14] — but despite the notional difference in function ("psychospiritual" vs. "religiosocial") both terms suggest an immediate, close and substantive relationship can exist between the complex reality of the matrix and the historical material constructs of "ordinary reality".[15]

The issues surrounding the interrelationship between mythopoeic and historical viewpoint are complex for the reader. If as Hans-Georg Gadamer suggests the reader's understanding of text is demarcated by time and cultural limitations,[16] and in particular if myth is understood to mean "lie",[17] then the texts might seem to be wanting in thematic value. Discounting the popular assignation of falsity applied towards myth, I want to compare the mythopoeic view in these texts as emblematic of "empowerment", to use Allen's expression.

For Allen myth in Native American culture is shared "vision", literally something that is seen by one and shared with the community (Allen 116). Visitation to a metaphysical world where existential truths are palpably seen and explained is an important part of Black Elk's story. His first experience is at age seven (chapter 3 "The Great Vision"): Lying comatose in his parent's teepee for twelve days his spirit — defined by Allen as "mythic character" (Allen 111) — was led to the realm of the "Six Grandfathers" of the Sioux nation. Meeting with them in a teepee-shaped cloud, he received instruction concerning implements that will give him healing power as a medicine man, including the potent and multicolored "herb of understanding". The white goose will symbolize his prowess as a warrior.

After proving his will through various trials, he is sent back to the temporal world. Thereafter, the medicine man credited with curing him mentioned to his parents that their son is "sitting in a sacred manner" emanating light (*Speaks* 49). The child Black Elk was sure he had been on a journey, but unaware and unsure of the power conferred to him; what he must do then according to Allen is "... take this vision and its powers to his people and use both on their behalf. In no other way can such a vision become actual or positive. Without this sharing of what is conferred on one for the benefit of the many, the vision itself will turn on the visionary, making him ill or even killing him" (Allen 111). Eight years passed before he confessed to a tribal medicine man what he had learned, and only then when fears of animals crying "It is time!" drove him to the brink of insanity. The medicine man wisely declared that he must reconstruct his vision in ceremonial form "as closely as may be done of the nonordinary in this material plane," (Allen 114) recounted in chapter fourteen, "The Horse Dance".

To recreate his "mythic character" Black Elk's body was painted in design as per the vision, red with black and white stripes at the joints. The exact setting was reproduced with six elders playing the Grandfathers sitting inside a rainbow-door teepee. Horses representing the four directions were assembled as they appeared in the vision. In the course of re-enactment the behavior of the horses was consistent with the vision as they "raised their voices, long and loud; all the other horses in the village neighed, and those out grazing in the valley and on the hill slopes..." (*Speaks* 169). Furthermore, so accurate was the reconstruction in ceremony that it "was like a shadow cast upon the earth from yonder vision in the heavens, so bright it was and clear. I knew the real was yonder and the darkened dream of it was here" (*Speaks* 169). Additional attestation came from the spirit world as "the thunder beings were glad and had come in a great crowd to see the dance"; dark clouds threatened storms, but only brought a sprinkling of rain (*Speaks* 170-1). After the ceremony concluded Black Elk entered the teepee and around the image of "the nation's hoop" drawn with red and black roads "were the prints of tiny pony hoofs as though the spirit horses had been dancing while we danced" (*Speaks* 174-5). Later, he discovered the healing herb growing in form exactly such as he had seen in his vision, and became fully able to apply his healing power directly to the service of his people as a medicine man (*Speaks* 197).

Although deterioration of the Sioux political and social situation prevented Black Elk from becoming a great leader, he was aided by visions later in life. While his body lay comatose for three days while travelling in Paris, he felt his spirit rising high in the air, over "the big water" of the Atlantic, back to his own country where from aerial view he viewed his parents' teepee. Later, after his return to Pine Ridge, his mother confesses she saw his cloud-based visitation in a dream (*Speaks* 224-9). Finally, although "lesser visions" enhanced his experience during the Ghost Dance, his primary one warned him of potential disaster at Wounded Knee (*Speaks* 249-50). In the aftermath, imitating a white goose protected him as he battled in close conflict with the Wasichus, and he received his potentially fatal wound only after "waking up" and ceasing to think on his vision (*Speaks* 266).

Myth in *Aterui* requires a slightly different reading than in *Speaks*; the Aterui character and story as myth is for Guantei Yuasa metaphoric rather than visionary,[18] but no less palpable nor informative. While extrapolating the historical Aterui from Yamato historical annals — the *Shoku-Nihongi* — it is important to remember they are in fact the only written records available, as the Isawa Emishi created none. When taken as historiography they must be read metatextually considering the nature of background intent.

The *Shoku-Nihongi* is fourth in a series of historical annals beginning with the *Kojiki*, an origin narrative starting from literally "the opening of heaven"[19] followed by an explanation of filiation between divinities and the temporal ruling imperial family. Obayashi Tairyo in his analysis, while neither outright accepting nor rejecting this genealogical notion, does contribute the supposition of causality through suggesting the *Kojiki* acts primarily as a religio-political paradigm legitimizing authority.[20] Therefore, events, even while recorded as fact, were reconciled with the extraordinary mythic matrix.

It might appear to be tenuous "guilt by association" to anoint the documented *Aterui* with notional mythic status due to Aterui's appearance in the *Shoku-Nihongi*. As difficult as it is to pre-suppose the intent of the creators of the document (Obayashi's causality notwithstanding), other recorded events concomitant with Aterui's detention suggest that the court scribes were looking up for reactions from the heavens just as they were looking down on the chieftain's body hanging from the gallows.[21] Furthermore this tension between the mythical and historical Aterui contributes to the story's theme, and therefore its power as theater. Augmenting Aterui's mythic character are folk stories from Iwate of his head returning through flight following execution.[22]

By placing the Aterui story from the myth-based annals in a historical context, that is, presenting the actions of the past as consistent with the present and thus proving a historical pattern, the Aterui story becomes historicized. The specific circumstances surrounding past and present, story and text are different, but with the matrix of myth Guantei is able to find congruence, compressing historical time into a clear pattern and positively identifying historical currents that have contributed to his alienation. In other words, by mythologizing the past the historical movements of the present become all the more clear.

Conclusion: Comparing Legendary Narratives[23]

In their contribution to a collection of essays entitled *Comparative Literature In the Age Of Multiculturalism*, Ed Ahearn and Arnold Weinstein write:

> (The) geopolitical activities, conflicts, and dilemmas of our time require a citizenry that has learned something about the history, aspirations, and complex realities of other peoples, and the study of literature and other arts is a privileged entry into these matters (because it) illuminates the artistic and cultural patterns of sameness and difference which exist both within and between societies, and it thereby gives us precious contrastive portraits of societies' values and beliefs...[24]

If the desired result is heightened understanding of foreign culture, the comparative methodology applied to narratives concerning decisive historical moments — that is, how they are experienced and perceptually formatted by and into "complex realities" — should bear especially fruitful results. However, as a prerequisite to such analysis we must be prepared to recognize as valid phenomena that underscore "complex realities". This is always a challenge due to the distraction of the hermeneutic filter through which the reader views the texts according to personal cultural and historical viewpoints.

With a nod to cognitive and structural anthropological paradigms, Richard Waswo finds myth, history, and perception intimately and inextricably linked. He writes: "As the languages we speak determine how we know the world, so the stories those languages tell determine how we act in it. Such determination is not produced on the venerable model of mimesis as the individual's imitation of timeless moral exempla. It is rather a determination of our consciousness, a control of perception. The process is collective, cognitive, and historically contingent."[25] The "collective, cognitive" aspect is fundamental to both stories: Black Elk shares his vision through ceremony, and Guantei has Aterui come to the stage to publicly elucidate his vision of history. Indeed, these mythical stories ensconced in literature continue their existence as "self-complicating phenomena": *Speaks* has become a "North American bible" for young Native Americans of all tribes, and Aterui's hero-status continues to grow as well.[26]

Black Elk Speaks and *Aterui* are two first-person narratives under strikingly similar historical circumstances in which the title characters articulate personal experience in confluence with the matrix. Their stories re-articulating personal experiences become transformed into legendary narratives with the speakers understanding their place within the "multidimensionality" (Allen 147) of mythic time and thus their responsibilities within historical time. Perhaps more importantly, their narratives stand in teleological counterpoint to the victors' historiographies, the oversouls of which are the actions of the political institutions in Washington, D.C. and Heian. In both narratives myth plays an important role, for it is the centrality of myth that permits the narrator of the first-person accounts to perceive the decisive historical moment via their own cultural viewpoint. In both instances, although not necessarily leading to victory, myth allows the narrator to maintain identity in the midst of being subsumed in the world of the victor.

Notes

[1] The texts for this study are: John G. Neihardt, *Black Elk Speaks: Being the Life Story of a Holy Man of the Oglala Sioux* (Lincoln and London: University of Nebraska Press, 1988). Guantei Yusa, *Aterui* (Tokyo: Jizen-shoku Tsushin-sha, 1994). For purposes of this analysis Black Elk and Guantei will be considered the "creators" of their stories, although the question of "authorship" is a complex issue. *Speaks* is an oral transcription: Black Elk's 1930 spoken words were translated from Sioux to English by his son Ben, and transcribed into shorthand by the poet John G. Neihardt's daughter Enid. Neihardt then annotated and published the text in 1932. The author's credit "as told to John G. Neihardt" was later changed to "as told through" at his request. Guantei Yusa is the nom de plume and stage name of Matsuhashi Yuzo.

[2] John Selby, *The Conquest of the American West* (London: George Allen and Unwin Ltd, 1975) 199-200.

[3] An attack led by Colonel John Chivington on a Cheyenne camp, inhabited mostly by women and children, despite the surrender of chief Black Kettle waving a white flag under an American flag given to him by the Commissioner of Indian Affairs. The attack was later investigated by a Congressional committee. *Conquest* 207; David E. Stannard, *American Holocaust* (Oxford UP, 1992) 131-4.

[4] On a footnote to page 7 John G. Neihardt writes, "The Fetterman Fight, commonly described as a 'massacre,' in which Captain Fetterman and 81 men were wiped out on Peno Creek near Fort Phil Kearney, December 21, 1866". Selby's title for chapter 9 of *Conquest* is "The Fetterman Massacre", although he describes the incident as a battle between armed soldiers; despite the similar use of the appellation "massacre" there appears to be little congruence with Sand Creek (see note 3).

[5] Efforts to eliminate the wild bison herds as a means of subjugating the Plains Indians were part of deliberate and concerted US Army policy. See Robert M. Utley, *Frontier Regulars* (New York: Macmillan, 1972) 412-3, n.20.

[6] A discussion of the sea-related folk culture in the region lies outside this discussion, but in a preface to the printed text of the play Guantei describes his father's New Year's ceremonies involving prayers offered for the health of the fish (35-6). Guantei describes in greater detail dynamics of resistance to the oceanfront development in his autobiography, *Jinsei-tojo. Tabi-tojo* (Tokyo: Shizen Shokutsu Shinsha, 1997).

[7] Engagements with Emishi on the Japan Sea side continued through the rest of the century.

[8] The re-envisioning of pre-modern Japan as a multicultural and multi-ethnic space

has been recently burgeoning in Japanese academia based on archaeological discovery; see Suzuki Kimio, *Jomonjin no Seikatsu to Bunka* (Tokyo: Kondansha, 1988), Donald Denoon, et al, eds, *Multicultural Japan: Palaeolithic to Postmodern* (Cambridge U: 1996), and my own analysis of the trend as historiographical paradigm in "Japanese Newspaper Journalism on Recent Archeological Discoveries: The Ethno-Historical Narrative Reconsidered," *Studies in International Relations: Intercultural Relations* 20: 1 (Nihon U International Relations Research Center, 7/99): 81-98. To my knowledge there has as yet been nothing written concerning the impact of the paradigm on literary criticism in Japan, although I believe it is an implication that warrants further study.

[9] Quoted in Egami Namio, Umehara Kyo, and Ueyama Junpei, *Ainu to Godai Nihon: Shimuposhiumu* (Tokyo: Shogakkan, 1982) 22-35. The ideographs were altered from 毛人 to 蝦夷. Concomitant with Yamato terminology denoting savagery and rural backwardness to the Emishi was changed ideographs for the Yamato country: 日本国 replaced 倭の国. This new name incorporated the first character of 日高見国 — referring to a certain area of Azuma — and implies the Yamato court desired to "unite" the Emishi region with Yamato territory. See Takahashi Tomio, *Godai Ezo wo Kangaeru* (Tokyo: Yoshikawa Hirofumi Kan, 1991) 3.

[10] Maruyama Rimpei, ed. *Teihon Nihonshoki*; 3 vols. (Tokyo: Kodansha, 1966) 1:161.

[11] For a complete discussion of the ahistorical world of shamanic possession, see Mircea Eliade, *Shamanism: Archaic Techniques of Ecstacy* (Princeton U: Bollingen Foundation, 1964), and Hori Ichiro, *Folk Religion in Japan: Continuity and Change* (Chicago and London: U of Chicago P, 1968). For the definitive analysis of a theater movement concerned with the materialist historical implications of ahistorical consciousness, see David G. Goodman, *Japanese Drama and Culture in the 1960s: The Return of the Gods* (Armonk, NY and London: ME Sharpe, Inc, 1988). I believe Guantei's work is a legacy of the movement.

[12] Takahashi 290. What I have translated as "the middle era dominated by feudal ethics" is chuseibumonkeirekishi（中世武門型歴史）.

[13] Paula Gunn Allen, *The Sacred Hoop: Recovering the Feminine in American Indian Traditions* (Boston: Beacon Press, 1992) 104-5.

[14] John B. Vickery, "Literature and Myth," *Literary Criticism and Myth*, ed. Robert A. Segal (New York and London: Garland Publishing, 1996) 288, vol.4 of Robert A. Segal, gen. ed., *Theories of Myth: From Ancient Israel and Greece to Freud, Jung, Campbell and Levi-Strauss*.

[15] Allen 104 quoting Carlos Castaneda.

[16] Terry Eagleton, *Literary Theory* (Oxford: Basil Blackwell, 1983) 71.

[17] Allen begins chapter six "Something Sacred Going on Out There: Myth and Vision in American Indian Literature" in *The Sacred Hoop* with a discussion of this problem, quoting for example the definition for "myth" in the Oxford English Dictionary: "a wholly fictitious story" (105).
[18] Guantei does not reject visionary experience, and recounts a visitation from his mother following her death in *Jinsei-tojo. Tabi-tojo* 21.
[19] Tenchi-kaibyaku（天地開闢）.
[20] Obayashi Tairyo, "Shinwaron", in Asao Naohiro, et al., eds., *Nihon Tsushi* (Tokyo: Iwanami Shoten, 1993), 1:299-300.
[21] I refer specifically to the July 12, 802 entry two days following Aterui's arrival in the capital: "A wolf ran down Crimson Sparrow Boulevard (the main street) and was caught." Kataju Katsuhiko, in an essay postscript to the play's text, believes this unusual event was interpreted as augury, implying momentousness to the Emishi leader's incarceration (149).
[22] Interestingly, ethnologist Oka Masao notes there is a dual-structure to the religious paradigm as illustrated in the annals; at times it is vertical, at others horizontal. Divinities move from heaven to earth, hence vertically; ambiguous visitors such as spirits from the dead and strangers (marebito) move horizontally. Oka was above all a comparative methodologist; when examining parallel structure of Japanese mythic narratives and those of other regions, horizontality, he found, was a key feature of myth from hunter-gatherer culture. As a narrative motif it is consistent with a significant feature of the Aterui record: The horizontal movement of his head upon decapitation reaffirms his identity as an Emishi, a hunter-gatherer outside the pale of Yamato culture (see Obayashi 301). A poetic reworking of the floating-head folk story is in Aizawa Shiro, "Ura no Bunka" (Tokyo: Jiji Tsushin-sha, 1976) 8-9.
[23] Legendary stories represent "transition from myth to history... (including) the history of heroes and the histories of ancestors..." that are "unfolding in a time lying between the time of origins and that of recent events." (Paul Ricoeur, "Myth: Myth and History," in Mircea Eliade, ed., *The Encyclopedia of Religion* (New York: Macmillan, 1987) 10: 273.
[24] Ed Ahearn and Arnold Weinstein, "The Function of Criticism at the Present Time: The Promise of Comparative Literature", *Comparative Literature in The Age of Multiculturalism*, ed. Charles Bernheimer (Baltimore and London: Johns Hopkins UP, 1995) 78-81.
[24] "The History that Literature Makes." *New Literary History* 19 (Spring 1988) 541-64.
[26] From Vine Deloria, Jr.'s "Introduction" to *Speaks* (xiii). Attesting to Aterui's

growing popularity is a tablet to his name recently erected in Kiyomizu Temple in Kyoto.

Mizusawa City in Iwate has been promoting the history surrounding Aterui as a tourist attraction, and there are currently 36 titles in the public library, including two animations for children. The establishment of an "Earth-Friendly Aterui Town" promotional committee (Chikyu ni Yasashii Aterui-no-Sato Suishin Kyogikai) also suggests that Aterui has come to be seen as an ur-ecologist by the local community.

Baltic Security: A View from Altruism

Toshiyasu Ishiwatari

1. Introduction

Unfortunately, the Baltic states are not yet so well known in Japan. We cannot find many descriptions of the Baltic states in the current year's edition of Japan's Diplomatic Blue Paper. However, we Japanese know that these countries have an ancient and rich heritage and culture. The Baltics "restored their independence" after the fall of the Soviet Union. So we tend to think that they should not now be going through such a tragic experience.

Taking the title of "Baltic Security" into consideration, and seeing that I am neither from the Baltic countries nor from any other European country, I feel I have the responsibility of showing how Japan looks at the Baltic region, especially in the context of Japanese-Russian-European relations, and of putting forward some new ideas or views on Baltic security. I will do so in the last three parts of this paper.

2. Bsltic Security and Efforts for "Threat Elimination"

Security Environment

The end of the Cold War has led to an improvement in the level of security in the world, especially in Europe. It has reduced international tensions. The preoccupation of all the European countries with promoting economic development has encouraged them to accelerate cooperative commercial relations with their neighbouring countries. This has also contributed to a reduction of international tensions.

Keeping Baltic security in mind, I would like to look at the international political and military changes that have taken place since the Cold War. The following are of vital importance for the security of the Baltic countries: First, there is the fact that the United States remains the only superpower. Second, NATO, one of the two military alliances of the Cold War era, is no longer the same military alliance it used to be. NATO today is seeking a new function, and only NATO is equipped to provide crisis-solving functions. Third, the military threat from the East has diminished. Fourth, the then concept of security, which was one-dimensional and mostly concerned with military aspects, is no longer prevalent. Fifth, the two neutral nearby countries, Finland and Sweden, have now become members of the EU. Now the EU shares her borders with Russia. NATO is expanding eastward. Russia objects to NATO's eastward expansion.

Analysis of Threats

"Security" and "threat" are two sides of the same coin. We could discuss different threats and different concepts of security, as the words have different connotations. Due to changes in international systems since the Cold War, the concept of security has changed drastically: from common security to comprehensive security and then to cooperative security.

Needless to say, in the discussion on Baltic security, relations between the Baltic countries and Russia are a key issue. It is true that the military threat from Russia has now diminished. The disintegration of the Soviet Union has weakened the military power of its successors, and the Baltic countries no longer feel, at least officially, a direct military threat from Russia.

However, I still think that there is psychological pressure or, I dare to say, a psychological threat from Russia to the security and stability of the Baltics. Moreover, even though Russia does not seem to pose any serious military threat, conflicts could still occur somewhere in Russia. And no one can surely say that such conflicts would not affect the status quo of the Baltic countries. In the worst case, flames spreading from such conflicts might seriously affect the Baltic countries.

We may also foresee totally different types of threat: The first is the threat to national identity, which could mostly be caused by illegal immigration and refugees coming from the East. National identity could be threatened for another reason. In Estonia Russians comprise nearly 30% of all the population. The figure is 34% in Latvia and 10% in Lithuania. One could not exclude a situation where Russia would intervene in the domestic affairs of the Baltic countries. Such an intervention would occur either on the pretext of Russians being unjustly treated in the Baltic countries or if the Russian government tried to direct her people's attention away from its own internal economic instability to the outside. This is a common trick of politics not only in Russia, but also in other countries.

The second threat is one which is concerned with territorial integrity.

Fear of "Grey Zoning"

In 1997 a U.S.-Russia summit was held in Helsinki. Prior to the summit, EU foreign ministers met in Holland to discuss EU enlargement and its relationship to the enlargement of NATO. Contrary to the EU officials, U.S. representatives were pushing for a solid link between NATO and EU enlargement, hoping such a solid link would calm down the Baltic countries' fears that they would become a sort of "grey zone".

The Helsinki Summit, however, left the Baltic issue unchanged. The two leaders discussed enlarging NATO, the reduction of armaments, and economic relations. For the Baltic countries, the most important issue was without doubt NATO's enlargement eastward. In the summit, the U.S. President did not mention the Baltic countries specifically. The Baltic countries knew that they would not become NATO members in the first round. This is what is meant by the Baltic countries' "grey zoning". Taking all these things into consideration, there is the need to make sure of Baltics security both within the larger European context and within the regional context.

Set-up of Security Networks

Should the Baltic countries stay as they are? The answer is negative. In my view, the best security for the Baltic countries is membership in the EU followed by admission to NATO, or vice versa.

In any case the admission of the Baltic countries to NATO, whenever it may happen, would meet with opposition from Russia. Therefore, we have to make an enviroment where Russia also feels itself to be in a "safety zone". That is to say that Russia must be integrated into a safety zone made by NATO or by other effective measures and instruments. In this respect the Baltic countries and Russia could be said to be in almost the same situation.

The difference is, however, that Russia's fear of being hemmed in by NATO lacks real possibilities, whereas the Baltic countries' fear of

Russia is backed by fifty years of illegal occupation by the Soviet Union.

Now the question is how to create a situation where both the Baltic countries and Russia would no longer feel any fear. In my view the question should not be posed in the form of "either-or". Many measures could be conceivable to create a "safety zone" for the Baltic countries and Russia. The measures must be manifold. There are many international cooperative systems around the Baltic countries and Russia that include them both. In any case the underlying idea of creating such a situation must be cooperative security strengthened by preventive diplomacy.

Regarding cooperative security we are able to think about two things: namely, "stabilizing factors" and "means of security". As to the stabilizing factors, the OSCE is the only pan-European framework which both Russia and all other countries, including the Baltic countries, are in agreement upon. The OSCE is also a common forum for future arms control in Europe. Its roll will be made more important by strengthening the linkage with the UN.

The newborn EAPC, which replaced the former NACC, would be expected to become a constructive element of vital importance in security cooperation together with PFP. The latter especially has a confidence-building effect on the participants. The EU also would be an important cooperative framework for the Baltic countries, when they one day become members.

As a means of security backed by military guarantee, NATO occupies the most important position for European stability. This applies also to the Baltic countries. The Founding Act on Mutual Cooperation and Security between NATO and Russia, commonly called the NATO-Russia Agreement (a framework agreement), establishes a permanent NATO-Russia Council, in which NATO and Russia will discuss such issues as arms control, peace-keeping and terrorism, etc.

The agreement does not give Russia any veto, but only a voice. And Russian President Boris Yeltsin recently warned that Russia would "rethink" its relations with NATO if the ex-Soviet Republics were invited to join NATO. Russia still views NATO's enlargement eastward as extremely dangerous for her. There is a long way to go before the Baltics can join NATO.

I think CBSS is a good tool for promoting mutual understanding concerning security in the Baltic region. When CBSS was established, it was agreed that security matters such as high politics should not be covered. However, there are many relevant security matters of low politics which could be addressed. To strengthen cooperation within the framework of CBSS is of vital importance for the countries concerned, even though the Council will not be able to offer any power-oriented security guarantees.

3. Japan's Foreign Policy Towards the Baltic States

Increasing Interest in the Baltics

While the U.S. and the EU have been the most common focus of international politics in Japan, recent controversies in the Baltic states over NATO enlargement and Russia's objection to it have turned the attention of many Japanese researchers of international relations to the Baltic states. I do dare to presume that Baltic area studies will in the not-so-distant future become a subject of interest at least in Japanese scholarly circles specializing in international politics.

Even though Japan's Diplomatic Blue Paper does not give even a brief description of Japan's foreign policy towards the Baltic states, the Second Section of the European and Oceanic Affairs Bureau of Japan's Ministry of Foreign Affairs, which is in charge of Baltic affairs as well as those of other European countries, several years ago published its Occasional Papers, with six pages each concerning the three Baltic states.

According to these papers and oral information offered by some diplomats of the Section, Japan's basic foreign policy towards the Baltics could be to make a contribution to their economic development, and to enlarge and deepen cultural exchanges between the Baltics and Japan.

Japan has embassies in Estonia and Lithuania, and the Japan Information Center in Latvia. In the field of financial support, in 1992 a $20 million Export Bank credit loan was provided to Estonia, $35 million to Latvia and $45 million to Lithuania.

Japan has not forgotten to promote trade with the Baltic countries. Our most recent trade balances with the Baltics have always been in the red.

Of special note are different types of invitational activities, including the invitation of opinion leaders, parliamentarians, school teachers, and doctors who helped take care of the victims of Chernobyl. These activities are, without doubt, extremely important because they have laid the foundations for grass-roots cooperation between both peoples.

Shortage of Specialists in Baltic Area Studies

At the present stage of affairs, however, there seems to be little, if any, discussion on Baltic security issues in Japanese diplomatic circles: only positive argumentation about what Japan should do beyond the above-mentioned. Unfortunately, security matters in the narrow and strict sense which are concerned exclusively with the Baltic states have not yet become an important subject of interest in Japan's Ministry of Foreign Affairs.

However, is there really any security issue which exclusively concerns the Baltics? Various circumstances are involved in today's security matters. Issues of Baltic security are not exclusively limited to the Baltic states' concerns. Baltic security has different dimensions woven together like a spider's web, and if anything happened in the Baltic region, it would spill over into other countries or regions.

In my view, there seem to be two possible reasons why Japan would neither bring the Baltic states into focus nor take more initiative in cooperating with them.

The first reason is related to the organization of the Japanese Foreign Ministry. Japan is short of specialists in the Baltic region at the Foreign Ministry's Head Office in Tokyo. The said Section itself has only two diplomats who take care of both the Nordic and the Baltic countries. They are in charge of eight countries.

Prevalent Transatlantic Viewpoint

The second reason is a factual one, but also somewhat a psychological one. In Japan's foreign policy its relationship with the U.S. takes precedence over all others. There is nothing wrong with that. This is why Japan often tends to see European issues, save EU issues, through an American point of view. We see what happens in Europe — especially in her periphery, as are the Baltic states — across the two oceans, the Pacific and the Atlantic, with the U.S. between them. Thus, Japan sees the Baltic region from a transatlantic angle. We look at the Baltic region taking an eastward view across more than two-thirds of the earth. Japan's way of thinking on Baltic security is filtered more or less through the transatlantic American point of view.

4. The Baltic States in the Prism of Japanese-Russian-European Relations

Need for a Trans-Eurasian Viewpoint

However, we could look at the Baltic countries from a different point of view, that is to say, from a trans-eurasian or a trans-arctic point of view. Looking at the Baltic states from a westward direction, they are not so far away from Japan. They are in fact only one country removed from us.

Moreover, there are many similarities of geographical situation between us. Our common neighbour is Russia, a vast Eurasian country. The Baltic countries share their boundaries with Russia, and Japan has only the small Sea of Japan separating us from the far eastern part of Russia. The Baltic states Latvia and Estonia have had border disputes with Russia. Japan is still having territorial disputes with Russia over the Kurils. Roughly speaking, both the Baltics and Japan are symmetrically in almost the same situation. Thinking about the Baltics in this way, their security issues could not be looked upon as another's.

The Baltics' Importance for the Future European Security Space

Europe today is trying to expand her security space or area mainly via NATO and the EU. European security would be strengthened by this more reinforced transatlantic relationship. If the Baltic states could be included in this area, a new Atlantic community, consisting of a security space as well as a possible marketplace, would come into reality. So the Baltics hold, without doubt, the key to a future Atlantic community.

An important question in this context is what Russia's reaction will be when her neighbouring Baltic countries move closer to NATO and the EU. We should know the answer this year. Unfortunately, "The Primakov Doctrine" is still prevalent in Russia. Now the problem is this: What can Japan do to contribute to the security of the Baltic states?

5. A New Way of Thinking: "Altruistic Security"

The Concept of "Altruistic Security"

Ideally, military power would not enjoy priority in security policy. The top priority should be to produce a situation in which nearby countries are convinced that they will never feel any actual or psychological threat from any other countries. This could be accomplished by reducing national military forces, stopping the arms trade, and by stepping up cooperative activities in the OSCE, EAPC, and CBSS systems.

The most important thing for the Baltic countries seems to be to aid each other and to cooperate with nearby countries in different spheres not only at the state level but also at the local or municipal level.

Security based on this new non-military concept could be said to take a longer step forward than cooperative security; thus, it might be called "altruistic security". We can summarize the main goal of this security concept as follows: to provide benefits, through different forms of aid and cooperation, to nearby interested countries in order to stabilize their situation and gain their confidence and trust, thereby securing oneself against hostile attitudes or threats. An old Japanese axiom says that "It is in your own interest to help others". A similar sentiment is found in an old Icelandic proverb. This thinking also applies to today's international society. And we must recognize that today's security issues are mostly societal, and not concerned with military dimensions.

Psychological Security Guarantee

Certainly one might argue that this way of thinking is too naive and even unrealistic. Some may also object that I have not proposed any security guarantees to be offered by any interested nearby countries to the country that would put the idea into practice. This is true. However, I am viewing the situation from a rather different angle and speaking of another kind of security, which would be based on a non-military concept, not on traditional ones.

Is there any security guarantee at all? Yes, there is. The security guarantee in this context is somewhat psychological. It is a sort of common feeling of friendship or partnership, firmly rooted in the benefitted country. The Baltic states and nearby countries can also ensure their future national security in this way.

6. Conclusion: Applicability of "Altruistic Security" for the Baltic Region

Spillover Effects of Russo-Japanese Regional Cooperation

Now the question is how Japan could contribute to Baltic security, based on the two above-mentioned assumptions that Japan needs to see the Baltics, which are geographically only one country removed from us, from a trans-eurasian (and a trans-arctic) point of view, and that the concept of altruistic security in a broader sense could have its applicability in the Baltic region.

There are, in my view, two ways of making contributions. The first is to strengthen Russo-Japanese cooperation in the most eastern part of Eurasian Russia. There are still many uncertain elements in understanding the internal affairs of Russia. And territorial disputes over the Kurils remain unsolved.

However, Japanese-Russian relations are now considerably good, especially since in 1993 Japan decided to discontinue application of the "Principle of Politico-Economic Non-Separation". It is now an opportune time to promote all imaginable kinds of regional cooperation in order to develop this underdeveloped region of Russia. Such cooperation would, even though indirectly, bring forth good spillover effects to the European part of Russia near the Baltics. These spillover effects would include a softened Russian attitude towards the Baltic states' access to Western Europe.

Benefits of a Trans-Arctic Sea Route

The second contribution is to activate economic ties between the Baltic states and Japan. This could be done by a trans-arctic route of commerce. The Arctic countries — Scandinavia, the U.S., Canada, Russia, and Japan — are now investigating the most favorable possibility. This sea route, which goes from Murmansk along Russia's shore through the Bering Strait to the Pacific Ocean, would facilitate not only trade between the Baltics and Japan, but it would also give Russia the possibility of developing her infrastructures.

I know that there are pros and cons to the above-mentioned argumentation. However, it seems to me inevitable that we accept the concept of altruistic security in this new century because we have to live interdependently on this minor planet.

References

Answald, Sven. *EU Enlargement and the Baltic States*, 2000.
Haukkala, Hiski & Medvedev, Sergei (eds.). *The EU Common Strategy on Russia: Learning the Grammar of the CFSP*, 2001.
Heikka, Henrikki. "Decentred Subjectivity and the Logic of Anarchy." *Theoretical Reflections on the Russian-Western Security Dilemma*, 1999.
Ishiwatari, Toshiyasu: "A new concept of security and the role of altruistic regional cooperation for the Nordic countries." *Visions of European Security*, 370-379, 1996.
Jopp, Mathias & Arnswald, Sven (eds.). *The European Union and the Baltic States: Visions and Strategies for the Baltic Sea Region*, 1998.
Kruzich, Joseph P. and Faraeus, Anna (eds.). *2nd Annual Stockholm Conference on Baltic Security and Cooperation*, 1997.
Lassinanti, Gunnar. *Toward a Broader Security Concept in Northern Europe: Security in the European North — from "Hard" to "Soft"* (eds. Heininen, Lassi & Lassinantti, Gunnar), 101-123, 1999.
Lejins, Atis and Ozolina, Zaneta (eds.). *Small States in a Turbulent Environment: The Baltic Perspective*, 1997.

Medvedev, Sergei. *Russia's Future: Implications for the EU, the North and the Baltic Region*, 2000.

Moshes, Arkady. *Overcoming Unfriendly Stability: Russian-Latvian Relations at the End of the 1990s*, 1999.

Nordberg, Erkki. *The Baltic Republics: A Strategy Survey*, 1994.

Ojanen, Hanna, together with Herolf, Gunnilla & Lindahl, Rutger. *Non-Alignment and European Security Policy: Ambiguity at Work*, 2000.

Trenin, Dmitri & van Ham, Peter. *Russia and the United States in Northern European Security*, 2000.

Visuri, Pekka. *Russia, the Baltic Sea and Finnish Defence: Northern Dimensions*, 45-57, 1999.

Notes on Contributors

MASAYUKI AKIYAMA is Professor Emeritus and Standing Trustee for International Affairs and Graduate Schools at Nihon University. He received his doctoral degree in international relations and his Ph.D. in English language and literature. He has collaborated with A. Owen Aldridge at the University of Illinois and Nihon University as well as at various international conferences. He has published *Henry James: His World, His Thought, His Art; Henry James's International Novels: Encounter and Conflict with Different Cultures; The World of Henry James: America, Europe and the East; A Study of Narrative Techniques: Comparative Approaches to Works of Henry James and Selected Japanese Authors.*

A. OWEN ALDRIDGE, former president of the American Comparative Literature Association, founder of the journal *Comparative Literature Studies*, and Professor Emeritus at the University of Illinois, has during the past thirty years collaborated extensively with Professor Masayuki Akiyama, especially in editing the special biennial Nihon number of *Comparative Literature Studies*. He has taught and lectured on the Mishima campus on three occasions and published two books containing his lectures in Japanese translation. His most recent book is *The Dragon and the Eagle: The Presence of China in the American Enlightenment*, 1993.

YIU-NAM LEUNG received his Ph.D. in comparative literature in 1987 with A.O. Aldridge as his dissertation director. Since 1978 he has been Associate Professor of Foreign Languages and Literature at National Tsing Hua University. In 1996, he received a Mackay Canadian Studies Grant for research at the University of Alberta. In 2002, he was awarded a sabbatical leave and a grant to conduct research on Chinese Canadian women novelists at the University of British Columbia, Vancouver, Canada. His research interests include English and American fiction, comparative literature, and Asian North American fiction. He has published articles on Bildungsroman, Lao She, and Émile Zola. He has recently been elected President of the English Teachers' Association of Taiwan.

CHIEKO MULHERN earned her B.A. in English Literature from Brooklyn College, and her M.A. and Ph.D. in Japanology from Columbia University. She was Professor of Comparative Literature at Princeton University, and then at the University of Illinois until taking early retirement. Back in Japan, she is writing and lecturing on gender studies. Her publications in the US include *Heroic With Grace: Legendary Women of Japan*, 1992; *Japanese Women Writers: A Bio-critical Source Book*, 1994; and a translation of Arai Shinya's novel, *Shoshaman: A Tale of Corporate Japan*, 1991 [selected as one of the digital texts of the Translational English Corpus by the University of Manchester Institute of Science and Technology in 2002]. Her latest book published in Japan is *Tsumatachi no Howaitohausu* (*The White House Wives*), 1999.

HARUKO G. IWASAKI is Associate Professor of Japanese Literature at the University of California, Santa Barbara. She received her M.A. in English literature from Brooklyn College and her Ph.D. in Japanese Literature from Harvard University. Articles and books she has produced on Edo popular culture focus on the interactions between texts and images and group activities of writers and artists in the later Edo period.

ADRIAN HSIA received his doctoral degree from Freie Universität Berlin, Germany. He is Professor of German at McGill University, Montréal, Canada, and Honorary Professor of Chinese at the University of Hong Kong. He has been Research Fellow and Visiting Professor in Europe, North America, and Asia on many occasions. Up to date, he has published over 20 books and 80 articles on aspects of European and East Asian literature and culture in several languages; of these many are cross-cultural. He has lectured extensively on three continents and is general editor of the monograph series *Euro-Sinica*.

RIEN T. SEGERS received his M.A. and Ph.D. from the University of Utrecht in the Netherlands. He completed the graduate work for his Ph.D. thesis at the universities of Stanford and Yale in the USA. For an extensive period of time he was a visiting professor at several universities in Canada, Finland, Germany, Japan, South Africa and the United States. He has written some 100 publications in six languages. Among his recent books are a book on Japan (*Sleutelboek Japan*, Amsterdam 1996) and a book on the cultural aspects of the European Union (together with Reinhold Viehoff, *Kultur, Identitaet, Europa*, Frankfurt 1999). Rien T. Segers is currently Professor of Organizational Culture at the Faculty of Management and Organization and the Faculty of Arts at the University of Groningen in the Netherlands. He is also Executive Director of the Center for Japanese Studies and is directing a Program in European Culture at the same university.

JOHN T. DORSEY is Professor of English and American literature at Rikkyo University in Tokyo. He received his B.A. in comparative literature from Fordham University and his M.A. and Ph.D. in comparative literature from the University of Illinois. He has published various articles on contemporary American, Japanese, and European drama and fiction.

NAOMI MATSUOKA is Professor of English and comparative literature at the College of International Relations of Nihon University. She received her B.A. from the English Department of Tsuda College in Tokyo and her M.A. in Asian Studies from the University of Illinois. She has published various articles on contemporary fiction in Japan and America.

ADAM LEBOWITZ received his M.A. from the University of Illinois, and teaches language and literature at Nihon University. He has also written an article on Japanese ethnology entitled "Japanese Newspaper Reporting on Archeological Discovery: The Ethnohistorical Record Reconsidered" for *Studies on International Relations*, and has conducted research on Yokohama-area natural food businesses. His essay on the writer Inoue Yasushi appeared in a commemorative volume.

TOSHIYASU ISHIWATARI is Professor of College of International Relations at Nihon University. He received his doctoral degree in international relations from Nihon University. He is Director of Hite Research Foundation (London). He has published *A Study of the Nordic Cooperation*; *Minorities in the Norden*; *Sexual Rights and Human Existence*; *Legal Structure of Sami Right*.

脱領域的なアプローチを必要としているところを実感しての取り組みです。各論文の多くは方法上の工夫と領域上の脱領域的な試みがなされていて、新しい学問研究の視界が開かれているかと思います。二十一世紀の学問研究の一つの可能性に向かっての、あるいはそのフレームワークを考える上での、気概の発露の場ともなっているはずです。書名を『知の新視界─脱領域的アプローチ─』とした理由です。これは秋山先生ご自身による命名です。

最後になりましたが、ご多忙のなかご寄稿下さいました各位のご芳情に対しまして重ねて感謝申し上げます。はやばやと原稿をいただきながら諸般の事情で刊行が遅れましたことをお詫びいたします。秋山先生におかれましては、愈々お元気にご活躍され、後進をお導き下さるよう願ってやみません。本書の刊行にさいして、いろいろとお世話下さった南雲堂の原信雄氏に厚く御礼申し上げます。

平成十五年一月二十日

　　　『知の新視界─脱領域的アプローチ』刊行委員会

　　　　　佐藤三武朗
　　　　　石渡　利康
　　　　　大泉　光一
　　　　　藤澤　　全
　　　　　田中　徳一

リッジ博士、梁耀南博士、リーン・T・セーヘルス博士、アドリアン・ヒシア博士、ハルコ・G・イワキ博士、国内では、亀井俊介博士、川本皓嗣博士、ムルハーン千栄子博士、ジョン・ドーシィ博士、榎本義子教授、それに日本大学比較文化比較文学会の富田仁教授、長谷川勉教授、安藤重和教授、諸坂成利助教授、及び日本大学国際関係学部の多数の先生方から、続々と玉稿を頂戴いたしました。その数は、日本語論文二十五編、英語論文十編、合計三十五編であります。ご執筆を賜りましたことに対しまして謹んで御礼申し上げます。

私どもといたしましては、趣旨に賛同して下さるならば学問分野を限定せず、とにかく自在のテーマで存分にお書きいただいて、集まった論文をみてから適宜の構成を図ろう、ということで出発しました。秋山先生が内外にわたって広範な人脈をおもちですので、これを勘案するに、そのほうが古稀を記念するにふさわしいと考えたからです。お蔭様で比較文化、比較文学、政治・経済・法律・国際社会などといった具合に学問分野が広がり、かつ交差し合うところもあって、文字どおりバラエティに富むものとなっております。

そこで構成に当ってはテーマや領域等で括ることをせず、単に言語種で振り分け、日本語論文は一括のうえできるだけ順序よく配列し、英語論文の方も同様に扱って、前者は縦組みで巻頭から、後者は横組みで巻末から順次収めるかたちをとりました。また論文の表記面にも留意をはらい、注や参考文献等の書き方を調整した場合を除き、あとは当該執筆者の文体を尊重し、かつ全体のバランスと統一性の確保につとめました。ご寄稿下さった先生方には、併せてご自分の簡単なプロフィルを書き添えていただき、「執筆者紹介」欄にまとめてそれを収めました。

本書は、先にふれたように広範囲にまたがる論文集です。新たなる自覚とコンセプトのもと、いよよ

あとがき

　本書は、秋山正幸先生の古稀記念論集です。先生は一九三〇年のお生まれですから、ちょうど二十一世紀の幕が上がったときに古稀を迎えられました。今日、杜甫の言葉にあるような「人生七十古来稀」ということではありませんが、永年同じ職場にあっての先達として、この機会に御自身の編著となるような記念論文集を作って差し上げたいとの声が起こり、私どもが音頭をとるかたちで本書の刊行を計画、先生からはご快諾をいただいて、さっそくご縁をなしておられる方々へとお声をかけさせていただいたわけであります。

　このような次第ですが、みなさまことに温かくお力添え下さいまして、海外からは、A・O・オルド

脱領域的アプローチ

New Intellectual Prospects
Cross-disciplinary Approaches

知の新視界

Edited with an Introduction by
Masayuki Akiyama

秋山正幸 編著

Koji Kawamoto
Shunsuke Kamei
Hitoshi Tomita
Masayuki Akiyama
Saburo Sato
Matoshi Fujisawa
Shigetoshi Morosaka
Yoshiko Enomoto
Shigekazu Ando
Tsutomu Hasegawa
Tokuichi Tanaka
Kenji Munakata
Miyako Hada
Yoko Matsui
Andreas H. Baumann
Junko Umemoto
Masako Sato
Humihiro Odakiri
Ayako Takahashi
Akira Takahashi
Koichi Oizumi
Tsukasa Oda
Toshimitsu Maeda
Toru Kobayashi
Masanori Yoshida
A. Owen Aldridge
Yiu-nam Leung
Chieko Mulhern
Haruko G. Iwasaki
Adrian Hsia
Rien T. Segers
John T. Dorsey
Naomi Matsuoka
Adam Lebowitz
Toshiyasu Ishiwatari

NAN'UN-DO TOKYO
南雲堂

はじめに

秋山正幸

本書は、日本大学比較文化・比較文学会の会員、日本大学国際関係学部において親交の深かった先生方、および『知の新視界』という学際的な著書刊行の趣旨に賛同して下さった国内外の研究者によって書かれたものである。

一九八七年十二月に、日本大学比較文化・比較文学会が創立された。その時、私は学会創立の目的について次のように述べたのであった。

「世界の諸地域で紛争が発生し、この地球上は政治的に不安定な状態が続いている。そして、国際化時代をむかえた今日、世界の多くの国々が貿易摩擦や文化摩擦を経験しているのが実状である。今や世界中の

人々は、好むと好まざるとにかかわらず、何らかの形で異文化に対応して生きていかなければならない時代をむかえていると言える。それ故に、国家間において政治紛争や貿易摩擦が発生している現状において、このような問題を解決していくためには、異文化の相互理解が必要となる。ここに比較文化研究の重要性が存在するのである。つまり、異なる文化、社会を比較研究し、その相違点を明らかにすると共に、それぞれの文化、社会に内蔵されている普遍的なものも明らかにする必要がある。このような異質文化・社会の比較研究こそ、わが学会が今後取り組まなければならない使命であると考える。このような異質文化の比較研究は、幅広い学問分野にかかわる諸問題を内包しているために、学際的研究にたよらざるを得ない。過去から現在へのプロセスを考究し、現在から未来を展望するダイナミックな、組織的な学際的研究を推進していくことが大切である。

さて、文化とは何をさすのか。われわれは従来の専門的学問分野にとらわれず、文化の概念をもっと広範囲に考えてもよいのではないか。文化現象とは人間生活の総称であり、したがって、学問分野は、文化の概念を倫理、哲学、文学、芸術、宗教などに限定せず、法律、政治、社会、経済の諸概念をも含むものとしてとらえたいのである。また、学際的研究の必要性が叫ばれている今日、文学についてももっと幅広く考えてもよいのではないか。つまり、詩や小説や演劇のような伝統的なジャンルだけではなく、歴史や哲学書のような観念的散文をも包含して考えなければならないと思うのである。

ところで、文化、文学の比較研究の重要性はどこにあるのであろうか。われわれは異なる国々の文化や文学を比較考察し、まず、社会的、政治的、経済的、風土的な面と、普遍的人間性の面から、その類似性や非類似性を解明し、異文化の相互理解の可能性と方法を探ることが重要である。その意味において、国際化時代、情報化時代と言われている今日、日本大学比較文化・比較文学会の設立の意味はきわめて大き

い。この学会の設立は、日本人がこれから国際人として活躍する上において、大きな役割を果たすことになるであろう。

自分の国の文化の研究は勿論のこと、異文化についても偏見をもたずに、客観的に研究していくことがわが学会の使命であるが、われわれの学問研究が現代の国際化時代において、異質文化の相互理解、ひいては全人類の平和的共存のために一翼を担うことができれば幸いである。

学会はこのような目標をたてて、毎年、研究発表会、シンポジウム、学術講演会を行ってきた。平成十年十二月五日に開催された学会創立十周年記念大会においては、日本大学総長瀬在幸安先生からご挨拶をいただいた。その折に、瀬在先生は自己の体験に基づいて「紙の比較文化」について、貴重な含蓄のある話をされ、この大会に華を添えて下さった。ここに改めて先生に感謝の意を表するものである。この大会においては、テルアビブ大学のジヴァ・ベン゠ドーラート教授によって、「月と芋とノスタルジア――ヨーロッパ、イスラエル、日本における秋の文化的機能」と題する記念講演が行われた。題名からも読み取れるように、この講演は異文化の特質を比較考察したものであり、学会の趣旨にかなったきわめて興味深いものであった。この大会にジヴァ・ベン゠ドーラート教授を招聘していただき、その上、講演の内容を精密に通訳して下さった川本皓嗣先生に衷心よりお礼申し上げたい。

学会の創立後十四年の月日がたった。その間、世界はめまぐるしく変転し、ベルリンの壁の崩壊に象徴されるように、冷戦構造は終焉をむかえるに至ったのである。サミュエル・ハンチントンは「文明の衝突」と題する論文の中で、「冷戦の終結とともに、国際政治は西欧という枠組みを越えた広がりをみせ、問題の中枢は西欧文明対非西欧文明という構図によって規定されるようになった」と論述している。そして彼は『文明の衝突と二十一世紀の日本』の中において、「冷戦時代の世界は主としてイデオロギーにも

とづいて分けられていた。自由民主主義の国家、共産主義国家、そして独裁主義による第三世界の国々である。出現しつつある世界において、国々の主な違いは、イデオロギーや経済、あるいは政治ではない。それは文化の違いであり、そして国々を文化的に類別するものが文明である」と述べ、さらに彼は「現在、国家をグループ分けする場合に最も重要なのは、冷戦時代の三つのブロックではなく、むしろ七つ（中国、日本、インド、イスラム、西欧、東方正教会、ラテンアメリカ）あるいは八つ（上記にアフリカ文明を加える）を数える世界の主要文明である。この新しい世界において、地域の政治は民族中心の政治に、また世界政治は文明を中心とする政治になる。超大国同志の抗争にとってかわって、文明の衝突が起こるのだ」と主張している。

ハンチントンの分析に対して、国内外の多くの識者から賛否両論の意見が出ていることは周知の事実である。反対論者は、文明や文化が異なっていても共存している集団があり、また宗教が異なっていても共存している人々がいるのであるから、国際的紛争や内戦を単に「文明の衝突」という構図で定式化するのは誤りではないかと説く。確かに文明や文化が異なっていても、政治的、経済的に共存関係が保たれている民族集団が多々存在する。その意味で、文明圏を七つまたは八つに分け、「文明の衝突」論を展開するハンチントンの論理はあまりにも図式化されすぎているとも言える。異文化間の共存関係は、政治的、経済的に密接に絡み合って均衡を保っているということを考えると、「文明の衝突」論の反対者の意見もうなずけるところがある。しかし、特に現在のイスラム文明と西欧キリスト教文明の衝突を見る限りでは、ハンチントンの「文明の衝突」論は傾聴に値するものがある。

二〇〇一年九月十一日、アメリカの強力な経済力を象徴するニューヨークの世界貿易センタービルや巨大なアメリカの軍事力を象徴するペンタゴン等を襲った同時多発テロは、全世界を震撼させた。このテロ

事件後、ハンチントンは、同年九月二十九日の読売新聞で「世界の危機——日本の責任」と題する記事の中で「冷戦後の社会では、イデオロギーの果たす役割はほとんどなくなり、代わって文化、宗教、民族などがより重要な役割を果たすようになっている。中でもイスラム教世界では、イスラムに対する宗教意識が極めて大規模に復活した」と述べ、自分の言説を強調している。

過激なイスラム原理主義者のウサマ・ビンラーデンに同調するテロ集団は、数か国に存在すると言われている。彼らは国と国との関係を越えて、グローバルな規模で、暴力のネットワークを構築しようとしているのである。識者は、今回のテロは、過激思想に取り憑かれたイスラム原理主義による、西欧キリスト教文明圏の代表超大国アメリカへの挑戦であると述べている。貧困や生活環境の格差がテロを惹起する要因となっていることも事実であろう。このような時代であるからこそ、今は世界主義的な相互依存の社会を作り上げることが大切である。そのためには、自由貿易化や自由民主主義化を進めていくための世界共通のルールづくりをしていくと同時に、全世界共通の環境汚染の対策や、貧困の問題解決に、相互依存の精神で取り組まなければならない。

二〇〇二年は、東京や多くの地域で桜の花が早く咲いた。一、二月が暖かかったため観測史上最速の開花となった。日本には桜の種類は三百種以上あると言われている。その中でも成長が早く、美しい花を咲かせるので最も親しまれているのがソメイヨシノである。桜の国日本で、ソメイヨシノを代表とする桜花が爛漫と咲く時期が早まったと言って喜んでばかりいられない。地球のリズムが狂ってきたのではないかと思うと不気味な感じがする。地球温暖化が原因かもしれない。そうだとすると問題は深刻だ。大気中の二酸化炭素濃度の上昇率が高まってきているという。過去百年間で地球の平均気温は摂氏〇・六度上昇したと報告されている。何らかの対策をたてないと、二十一世紀中にはさらに一・四度から五・八度くらい

はじめに

まで上昇するだろうという予測がなされている。恐ろしい予測だ。気象庁気候情報課の予報官は十数年から数十年周期で寒くなったり、暖かくなったりすることがあり、この数か月の高温傾向を地球温暖化と結びつけることはできない、と言っている。しかし、安心はできない。これからは、石油に頼らない新しいエネルギー政策が求められる時代である。

現在、グローバリゼーションが進行する中で、それぞれの文化に画一化現象が多々見られるようになったことは事実であるが、しかし、依然として潜在的にそれぞれの文化的なアイデンティティーが存在することも忘れてはならない。われわれは自文化のアイデンティティーを主体的に保持しながら、異文化の理解につとめることが大切である。自文化中心主義に陥ると、文化間、文明間の相違による紛争が起き、いわゆる「文明の衝突」という対立の構図が発生する恐れがある。

青木保氏は「グローバリゼーションと、文明、文化の衝突論と、どちらに与するべきだというような二者択一の議論にしない方がいい」と言っている。この見解はけだし慧眼である。グローバリゼーションと文化的アイデンティティーの関係を論ずる場合、どちらかに重点をおくべきだという二者択一の議論を進めていくと、国際関係の本質を見誤る危険性がある。どのような民族にも文化的アイデンティティーが存在し、それは受け継がれ、時代と共になんらかの変化はあるにしても、いつまでも根強く残るものなのである。例えば、日本人の死生観は仏教とかかわりをもつ無常観の影響を強く受けており、この無常という感覚は心に深く染み込んで、日本人の自然観や美意識にも影響を及ぼしていると思われる。この無常観は日本文化のアイデンティティーの底流となっていると言えよう。したがって、日本人の無常観や自然と深いかかわりをもった生活態度を念頭におかないと、外国人が日本人の心を理解することは困難であろう。現在、日本人は民主主義の政治体制の下で生活しているが、日本における各種の祭りや年中行事を

はじめに

考察すれば分かるように、日本人には昔から永続的に脈々と受け継がれてきた神仏への帰依の心情が依然として存在しているということを付言しておきたいのである。

平和を構築するためには、世界主義的なルールで民主主義を堅持しなければならないということはすでに述べたが、それと並行して、偏見にとらわれずに、各異なる文化のアイデンティティーを理解することが大切である。この異文化理解こそが各民族の平共的共存の第一歩となる。

二十一世紀においては、グローバリゼーションと文化的アイデンティティーの間を埋めてゆき、さらに調和させてゆく作業が重要である。環境問題を考えてみよう。この問題はグローバルな見地から解決していかなければならないが、民族文化のアイデンティティーを理解していけない。民族文化のアイデンティティーを解決するどころか、むしろ暗礁に乗り上げてしまう。それ故に、グローバリゼーションと文化的アイデンティティーの間を埋めてゆく学際的、複視眼的研究が二十一世紀に求められる重要なテーマとなってきているのである。このような意図で刊行されたのが本書である。本書は過去から現代に至るまでの学問上の諸問題を取り扱っており、研究内容は多岐にわたり、「脱領域的アプローチ」と言えるものである。

本書刊行にあたり、学問研究および学会活動において、ご指導下さったイリノイ大学名誉教授、A・オーエン・オールドリッジ先生から玉稿をいただいたことはこの上もない喜びである。私事にわたって恐縮だが、亀井俊介先生のご推薦により、編著者はオールドリッジ先生の指導のもとで比較文学の研究をする機会を得たのであった。ここに永い間ご指導とご厚誼を賜ったオールドリッジ先生と亀井先生に厚くお礼申し上げる。

この度は、さらに、学問的交流の深い国内外の学識豊かな多くの学究から、おのおのの本領を十分に発

揮された密度の高い貴重な論文を寄せていただき、深甚なる敬意を表する次第である。本書が現代の混迷と不透明な時代において、世界民族の平和的共存のための、知的創造の役割を果たすことができれば幸甚である。

最後に本書の出版の企画立案に尽力された『知の新視界―脱領域的アプローチ』刊行委員会の佐藤三武朗先生、石渡利康先生、大泉光一先生、藤沢全先生、田中徳一先生に心から感謝の意を捧げる。また、本書の出版の趣旨を理解され、親身になってお世話して下さった南雲堂の原信雄氏に謝意を表したい。

[注]
1 サミュエル・ハンチントン「文明の衝突」("The Clash of Civilizations")（中央公論、一九九三年）八月号、三五〇頁。
2 サミュエル・ハンチントン、鈴木主税訳『文明の衝突と二十一世紀の日本』（集英社、二〇〇〇年）二十一頁。
3 同書、九六頁。
4 青木保『異文化理解』（岩波書店、二〇〇一年）一三六頁。

知の新視界——脱領域的アプローチ　目次

I

■ はじめに　秋山正幸　001

01 日本における日本文化研究と外国文化研究　川本皓嗣　023

02 永井荷風訳「死のよろこび」を読む　亀井俊介　037

03 オースマン計画の波動
　　――銀座煉瓦街の比較文化史的考察　富田仁　055

04 蘆花の『不如帰』とジェイムズの『鳩の翼』の比較考察
生活文化の視点から
秋山正幸
081

05 島崎藤村『破戒』から学ぶ
文学的意匠として「遺伝」をどう読むか
佐藤三武朗
099

06 ツルゲーネフと石川啄木
その比較研究
藤澤全
117

07 虎の書跡
ボルヘスと中島敦
諸坂成利
141

08 河野多恵子と『嵐が丘』
人間存在の不思議
榎本義子
163

09 『嵐が丘』を如何に読み替え、如何に書き換えるか
Heathcliffの「悔しさ」を動機として
安藤重和　185

10 「魔女の厨」のメタモルフォーゼを巡る独と伊
長谷川勉　197

11 ブレヒトにおける回り舞台と旅の使用法
田中徳一　213

12 アフリカン・アメリカン・エクゾティシズム
一九二〇年代パリの黒人表象への一考察
宗形賢二　233

13 アメリカ社会におけるジャポニズム小説
オノト・ワタンナを中心に
羽田美也子　259

14 『ドラ・ソーン』と日本の家庭小説
松井洋子 … 279

15 ブラントとゲルトナーの旅行日記の比較
A・H・バウマン … 293

16 文化受容の証人、ラフカディオ・ハーン
―中国の作品の語り直しを中心に
梅本順子 … 315

17 カール・フローレンツとの関係から見たラフカディオ・ハーン
佐藤マサ子 … 337

18 中国白話翻訳小説管見
―『通俗大明女仙伝』をめぐって
小田切文洋 … 359

19 場所、華厳思想、道元
高橋綾子 ... 375

20 津軽作家 今官一
その文学的生涯
高橋章 ... 397

21 二十一世紀における国際テロリズムの脅威管理
脅威評価の方法論について
大泉光一 ... 417

22 許容紛争と訴訟能力を欠く者の上訴
小田司 ... 429

23 二十一世紀社会における「国際政治経済秩序」の理念と構想
「戦争と平和論」を踏まえて
前田利光 ... 455

24 自由貿易主義の理論的根拠
古典派の貿易思想を中心として
小林 通 ……471

25 国際結婚にみる異文化の交流と実践（2）
三島市に生きるフィリピン女性家族の事例から
吉田正紀 ……491

執筆者紹介 ……523

あとがき 佐藤三武朗・石渡利康・大泉光一・藤沢 全・田中徳一 ……527

II

Introduction
Masayuki Akiyama

01 The Fiction of Oe and Gao, or, Portraying the Here and the Now
A. Owen Aldridge

02 *The Life and Adventures of Martin Chuzzlewit*: A Tale of Two Cultures
Yiu-nam Leung

03 The Italian Cinderella Type in the 17th-century Japanese Tales
Chieko Mulhern

04
Speak, Memory!
Edo Netsuke in Their Literary Context
Haruko G. Iwasaki

05
From Proselytization to Assimilation:
New French and German Fictional Approach to
Jesuit China Missions
Adrian Hsia

06
The Underestimated Strength of
Cultural Identity
Between Localising and Globalising Tendencies in the European Union
Rien T. Segers

07
Comparative Literature:
Globalization and Hegemony
John T. Dorsey

08
**Nightmare Come True:
Postmodern Paranoia and Terrorism**

Naomi Matsuoka

169(582)

09
**Myth in *Black Elk Speaks* and *Aterui*:
The Empowering Matrix**

Adam Lebowitz

185(566)

10
**Baltic Security:
A View from Altruism**

Toshiyasu Ishiwatari

205(546)

Notes on Contributors

219(532)

知の新視界——脱領域的アプローチ

I

01 日本における日本文化研究と外国文化研究

川本皓嗣

　日本における「日本文化研究」と「外国文化研究」を同時にまとめて考察せよという、思いがけない、そしてきわめて刺激的な課題を与えられて、あらためて思い当たり、再認識させられることがいくつかある。せっかくの機会なので、なかでも年来もっとも重大だと感じてきた問題に、正面から取り組んでみたい。ただし、視野をできるだけ広くとったため、議論が大ざっぱになる点はお許し願いたい。
　自国文化の研究と外国文化の研究は、正反対の方向を向いているように見えて、実はたがいによく似ている。というよりも、もともと同じ時代の同じ要求から生まれ、発展してきたものに過ぎない。両者の根は一つであり、それらを支えるイデオロギーもまた一つである。両者への強い関心を促したのは、ごく大

まかに言って、フランス革命以後のナショナリズムの高まりであり、ロマン主義的な民族・国家意識の尖鋭化である。欧米でこの動きがにわかに強まったのは、十八世紀の末から十九世紀にかけて、それが本格的な学問領域として制度化されたのは、十九世紀末から二十世紀初めにかけてのことである。そしてこの大波は、ヨーロッパ帝国主義の脅威によって近代化を迫られた東アジアにも、ただちに及んできた。

もちろんそれ以前にも、東洋や西洋のさまざまな国や地域で、自文化の研究や異文化の研究が、さまざまな形でさかんに行われていたのはいうまでもない。とはいえ、おおよそ十九世紀より以前には、文化に関する本格的な学問、ひろくその存在意義を認められた系統的な学問、いわゆる「古典研究」の形をとっていた。例えば西洋では、それはルネッサンス以来の古代ギリシャ・ラテン文化の研究であり、われわれに身近な東アジアでは、古代中国の文化——先秦時代からほぼ宋代あたりまでの古典文化の研究であった。むろん朝鮮や日本の住民にとって、中国の古典文化は当然「外国文化」であるには違いないが、その研究に従事する人々、いわゆる儒学者たちには、自分が外国の文化を扱っているという意識は、きわめて薄かったように思われる。当時の感覚では、先進的で普遍的な中国文明は、すべての人類がよく学び、よく摂取すべきすぐれた手本であり、規範だったのであって、それが異質な外来の文化として感じられた形跡は、ほとんど見られない。

もっとも、そうした一般的傾向に反するように見える事例もないわけではない。例えば日本の平安時代の中ごろから、それまでの漢風全盛時代に対する反動として、和歌その他、日本固有の文化とその研究が重んじられたことや、江戸時代後期、やはり朱子学の圧倒的な支配力への反動として、本居宣長らの「国学」がさかんになったことである。とはいえ、そのどちらの時代でも、公的に権威を認められた正統的な文化の学問と教養が漢学であったことは、紛れもない事実である。漢詩・漢文は教養ある男の世界、かな

文字は「女子供」の世界というのが、近代以前の通り相場だった。しかも、和歌は濃厚な「やまと歌」意識に支えられていたとはいえ、実はそのテーマや発想の上で、漢詩の影響を深くこうむっていたし、また宣長らの国学も、その学問的方法論そのものを、朱子学に負っていた。

一方、西洋で漢文に当たるものは、教養人の普遍共通語としてのラテン語である。それゆえ、ときには東アジアの漢字文化圏が、ヨーロッパのラテン語文化圏に比せられることがある。とはいえ、ラテン語を解するヨーロッパ知識人の数は、漢文の場合にずっと限られていた上に、その権威もはるかに低かったといってよい。なぜなら東アジアでは、それぞれに発音や読み方が異なるとはいえ、国際的な外交・政治・通商・文化などの交流の場では、もっぱら漢文が幅を利かせ、各国の俗語（「古典語」に対するいわゆる vernacular）——中国語、朝鮮語、日本語など（あるいはむしろ、それらのさまざまな方言）をじかに用いてのやりとりが、きわめて少なかった。それに対して、ヨーロッパではすでに中世から、俗語としてのイタリア語やフランス語、スペイン語やポルトガル語、英語やドイツ語などによる相互交流がさかんに行われていたからである。

東アジアにおける漢文の権威を示すめざましい証拠の一つは、「翻訳」の極端な乏しさである。ヨーロッパではルネッサンス以来、ギリシャ・ラテン語の古典の俗語訳が続々と出版された。例えば古代ローマの大政治家・弁論家・哲学者のキケロ（Marcus Tullius Cicero）（前一〇六‐四三）の著作は、早くから根強い研究の伝統を生み、膨大な分量の注解が試みられていたが、すでに中世後期の十三世紀から、彼の修辞学書（一部は偽書）などが、次々にフランス語やイタリア語その他の俗語に翻訳され始める。ルネッサンス期に入ると、その傾向はますます強まったが、その波及のしかたは各国の文化状況に応じてかなりずれがあり、ドーヴァー海峡を隔てた文化的後進国のイギリスで、初めてキケロの修辞学が英語に翻案され

たのは、十六世紀前半のことである（高田一九九九：六二一六五を参照）。その後イギリスでも、ノース（Sir Thomas North）による『プルターク英雄伝』（一五七九、実はフランス語訳からの重訳）やチャップマン（George Chapman）によるホメロスの叙事詩『イリアス』 Iliad（一六一一）と『オデュッセイア』 Odyssey（一六一四-一五）など、すぐれた英語訳が現われた。

そして、古典中の古典としての聖書の翻訳も忘れてはならない。周知のように、キリスト教聖書の完全な俗語訳は、マルティン・ルター（Martin Luther）のドイツ語訳（一五三四）に始まる。これは、当時もっともひろく流布してそれ自体が「一般向け・俗語版」 Vulgata と呼ばれていた、聖ヒエロニムス（Eusebius Hieronymus）によるラテン語訳（四〇四ごろ）からの重訳ではなく、旧約は古代ヘブライ語、新約は古代ギリシャ語原典から直接訳されたものである。英語では、やはり原典から旧約の一部と新約を訳したティンダル（William Tyndale）のテクスト（一五二五-三一）を土台として、一六一一年にいわゆる『欽定訳聖書』 Authorized Version が出た（船戸一九六九：一八-五〇を参照）。フランスその他、ラテン系、カトリック系の国々ではかなり事情が異なるが、こうして聖書を俗語・自国語に訳して、誰にも読めるものにしようという努力は、早くも中世から始まっていた。

ところが近代以前の東アジアでは、例えば四書五経や左国史漢、あるいは漢詩などの俗語訳がほとんど現われなかった、というよりも、誰もその必要を感じなかったらしい。しかもこれは、中国の周辺諸国に限ったことではなく、「古典」の本家である中国の内部でも、事情は同じことである。漢文による「経典」の圧倒的支配のもとで、各時代に流通していたはずの俗語や各種方言ははなはだしく軽視され、漢文の古典を俗語に訳することなどは、まったく問題にならなかったばかりでなく、俗語による創作（たとえば小説や芝居や講談）でさえ、知識人のまじめな関心の対象とはならなかった。つねづね強大な隣国、中国の

脅威のもとにあった朝鮮でも、ほぼ同様の事態が長く続いたのは言うまでもない。

西洋の聖書に当たるもの、例えば仏教の経典についても、やはりその通りである。東アジアでは近代に至るまで、サンスクリットの原典から翻訳された漢訳仏典が唯一の聖典とされた。もちろん僧侶の学習のためには訓読その他、さまざまな補助手段が用いられたとはいえ、公式の読経の場では、つねに漢文の音読という形が用いられた。ここには漢語を解さない一般信者への宗教的配慮はいっさいなく、むしろ漢語のもつオーラによって信者を威圧しようという意図さえ感じられる──ちょうど昔の漢方医がむずかしい漢語を、あるいは近代の医者がドイツ語の医学用語を振り回して、患者を煙に巻いたように。

だがそれでは、俗語への翻訳や俗語での文化交流がさかんだった西洋では、東アジアとは違って古典文化以外についての学問、例えば各地の俗語による文学や演劇の研究もさかんだったかといえば、決してそうではない。諸学問が大いに興隆したルネッサンス以後のヨーロッパでも、文化に関するれっきとした学問として認められたのは、やはり「古典学」──古代ギリシャ・ローマの古典文化を扱う「文献学」だけである。すぐ隣のドイツの文化をさえ本格的に研究しようという文学を学問的に扱おうというイタリア人もいなかった。ましてかなり識字率が低かったとはいえ、教養人なら誰でも簡単に読み、理解することのできる自国の文化や俗語文学を、学校でまじめに研究・教育することなどは、まったく想像の外だった。

ヨーロッパで自国の文化に焦点が当てられ、自国独自の文化の伝統が強く自覚され始めるのは、フランス革命以後のことである。議論を複雑にしないために、話を文学だけに限ると、十八世紀末から十九世紀前半ごろまでに、それまでの古典主義（あるいは擬古典主義）に代わって、ロマン主義が時代の主潮としてヨーロッパを席巻した。ロマン主義は、普遍的な理性に対する個人的な感情を重視し、良識や知恵よ

りも個性と独創性を重んじる。ここで初めて、古代ギリシャ語・ラテン語に対して自国ないし地元の俗語そのものと、俗語による文学作品を尊ぶ機運が生まれ、その流れの源を遠い過去にまで求めるという傾向が強まった。そして、ときには相当の無理や歪曲を冒してまで、はるか昔から連綿と続くという「民族精神」が語られた。グリム兄弟による画期的な『ドイツ文法』Die deutsche Grammatik（一八一九―三七）の作成（兄ヤーコプによる）、『ドイツ語辞書』Deutsches Wörterbuch の編纂（兄弟の死後、代々受け継がれて、第二次大戦後にようやく完成を見た）、ドイツ民話やドイツ神話などの収集・編纂は、その典型的な表われである。

もっともそれ以前にも、古代ギリシャ・ローマの古典語・古典文学に対して、ヨーロッパ各地の俗語・俗語文学固有の価値を主張する動きがなかったわけではない。例えばダンテの『俗語論』De vulgari eloquentia（ほぼ一三〇三年ごろ執筆が開始された）は、イタリア各地の方言を検討しつつ、イタリア語独自の美と力を解き明かして、ラテン語偏重の慣習を打ち破ろうとしたものであり、詞書を交えたダンテの叙情詩集『新生』Vita nuova（一二九四）や、叙事詩『神曲』Divina commedia（一三二一）などは、その主張を立証するイタリア語の傑作である。また十六世紀のフランスでは、デュ・ベレ（Joachim du Bellay）が『フランス語の擁護と顕揚』Défense et Illustration de la langue française（一五四九）で、フランス語の卓抜な表現力を説いて、いわゆるプレイアッド派の仲間たちとともに、古典古代の詩に匹敵する美しいフランス語詩を書いたし、さらに十七世紀後半のフランスでは、古代と近代のどちらの文学が優れているかという点をめぐって、激しい「新旧論争」La Querelle des Anciens et des Modernes が繰り広げられた。そうした趨勢がヨーロッパ全土で一気に表面化したのが、十九世紀の初めだったと見ることもできるだろう。俗語と俗語文学の顕揚は、政治上・文化上のナショナリズムとともに、今日まで全世界に強大な

影響を及ぼし続けている、フランス革命とロマン主義の遺産である。

だが、学問的な研究・教育の面に目を向けると、自国語にせよ外国語にせよヨーロッパ各国の俗語による文学が大学の講座で系統的に扱われるようになってからのこと、意外に最近のことである。イギリスでもフランスでも、高等教育の場で自国や近隣諸国の文学が正式に取り上げられ、それまで圧倒的な主流を占めていたギリシャ・ローマ文献学と肩を並べるようになったのは、せいぜい十九世紀の末から二十世紀の初めにかけての頃に過ぎない。そして興味深いことに、英文学ではイギリスよりもフランスの方が先手を取っている。ドゥエー大学（のちのリール大学）とパリ大学で英語英文学の講師担当講座が開かれたのは一八八一年、そしてパリ大学で英文学の講座が創設されたのは一八九三年、一九〇二年のことである。一方、オックスフォード大学に英文学の初代担当教授が任命されたのは一八九三年、一九〇二年のことである。一方、オックスフォード大学では一八九六年）、そしてはじめて英文学教授が任命されたのは一九〇四年（ケンブリッジでは一八一二年）になってからである（島田一九九五：四六二-八九、島田一九九五：四一-四八、一六〇、二三八-三九、三三八など、川本一九九五：三九五-九六を参照）。

ここでとくに注目したいのは、自国語文学研究と外国語文学研究の間の壁を打ち破ろうとする比較文学もまた、ほぼ同時期に制度化されていることである。周知のように、その先鞭をつけたのはフランスで、まず一八九六年にリヨン大学、次いで一九一〇年にはパリ大学に比較文学講座が設けられた。したがって、自国の俗語文学研究、外国の俗語文学研究、そしてそれらの間の交流や類似・対比を論じる比較文学の研究は、いずれも同じ状況のもとに始められ、同じ要請にしたがって進められたと見ることができる。すでに述べたように、その大きな源流はロマン主義にあるが、より直接的なきっかけは、当時の時代情勢にある。十九世紀の後半を過ぎてから、商工業の大規模な発展にともなって、フランスでは教育体制の

近代化・実用化への要請が高まった。そして、一八七〇年から翌年にかけての対プロシャ戦争での敗北が、にわかにこの動きに輪をかけた。ドイツという強大なライバルの出現が、フランス人の中華意識に揺さぶりをかけ、すぐ隣に住む「他者」を理解し、たがいの交流をよりスムーズにする必要を感じさせた。そこで英語やドイツ語など近代俗語の教育制度が、高等学校や大学のレベルでいち早く整えられたのである。もっとも、そのめざすところはもっぱら実用教育にあったが、ごく一部のすぐれた見識の持ち主たちが、よその国民を知るためには、何よりもその国の文化、ことに文学の理解が欠かせないことを自覚し、進んでその研究や教育の道を切り開いていったというのが実情である。

他を知ることは、自己を知ることでもある。外国語文学とほぼ同時に自国語文学の研究が開始されたのは、ごく自然な成り行きである。そして、十九世紀末からだんだん濃厚になっていく第一次世界大戦への危機感も手伝って、文学を通じて諸国間の相互理解や誤解、交流や影響関係を明らかにする学問として比較文学の研究体制が整備されたのである。

日本の急激な近代化が始まった一八六八年以後、こうしたヨーロッパの大きな潮流が、ほぼ同時進行的に押し寄せたのはいうまでもない。もっとも、比較文学が本格的に移入され、確立されたのは、ずっと後の第二次世界大戦後のことだが、ヨーロッパの各国語文学、ことにイギリス、ドイツ、フランス文学の研究は、ほぼ同時に始まり、並行して推進されてきた。先に触れたように、その意味で、自国語文学研究と外国語文学研究の根は一つであり、その文学についての概念も研究領域の設定も、また研究のテーマも方法論も、おおむね西洋から直輸入されたものだと言ってよい。

例えば、従来の学問観では、「文」の中核をなすのは中国の経典とその解釈であり、国内の産物でも、

やはり漢文による著作が最上位を占めていたのに対して、近代以後は、もっぱら俗語、すなわち日本語の作品だけを重視するという形で、文学史がまるごと書き直された。というよりも、自国語による作品だけを自国固有のものとして容認するという前提のもとに、はじめて「国文学史」なるものが想定され、それを新たに生み出す努力が重ねられたのである。『万葉集』や『源氏物語』や『平家物語』それ句や近松門左衛門の浄瑠璃芝居の価値が、にわかに上がり、奈良・平安朝の漢詩や鎌倉・室町時代の五山文学、そして江戸時代の儒学研究や漢詩文などは、あらかた抹消された。

しかもその際、「文学」の概念自体が西洋からの借り物であったために、もうひとつの重大な価値転換が起こったことに注目する必要がある。というのは、以前は漢学的な価値観にしたがって、倫理思想や政治思想の書、さらには漢文による史論や詩歌が重視されたのに対して、西洋では意外にも「小説」や「演劇」が重んじられていることが分かったため、それまでは「女子供」や大衆の慰み物として軽視されてきたジャンルが、突然株を上げることになったのである。源氏しかり、近松しかり、それだけではなく、当時はすでに忘れ去られていた俗語作品の山の中から、日本の「小説」として世界に誇りうるものを改めて発掘するという作業さえ、熱心に行われた。淡島寒月による井原西鶴の「小説」の「発見」と、幸田露伴や尾崎紅葉によるその喧伝（淡島二〇〇一［一九二七］を参照）は、そうした見直しのもっともめざましい一例にすぎない。

近代日本の自国文学と外国文学の研究は、このように十九世紀から二十世紀初めにかけての西洋文学研究の圧倒的な影響のもとで始まり、今日に至っている。どちらもその学問上の枠組みや手続きを西洋に負っていることは、すでに述べたとおりだが、ごく大ざっぱに見て、いわゆる「国文学」研究は、当初に学んだ十九世紀的な文献学的・実証主義的な方法論をいまも頑強に固守しているのに対し、外国文学研究の

方は、その時その時に西洋で主流を占めているテーマや方法を、夢中で追いかけているという違いが見られる。

だが一見はすっかり西洋化したように見えるその反面、実は前近代の漢学の伝統が、国文学と外国文学研究のどちらにも根強く残っていることに気づいている人は、あまり多くないように思われる。というのは、まず、どちらにも事大主義が明らかに認められることである。漢学の場合、聖なるものとして中心に位置していたのは中国の古典であり、学問の目的は、さまざまな註釈にしたがってその聖典を「正しく」理解することにあった。つまり、周辺の位置から「本家」の学問にどれだけ近づくことができるか、どれだけ中心に肉薄することができるかが、学問的価値の尺度となった。風土や文化が違うために生じる日本的な誤解や曲解が極度に警戒され、そうした中心追従意識からの脱却がもくろまれている（ただし、近世の荻生徂徠らの儒学や、その後の漢詩では、例えば漢詩でいえば、「和臭」が軽蔑されたことを忘れるほどに、向こうの人間になりきることが理想とされたのである。むろんこれは、本家に生まれ育たない限り、けっして到達することのできない「逃げ水」であり、また学問の上では、永久に「本場」の研究に追いつくことも、対等の立場に立つこともできないことを意味する。「正確な理解」という、それはそれで立派な根拠のある目標が強調されすぎた結果、日本人として何のために外国文学を学ぶのか、また日本人として外国文学研究にどのような貢献を果たしうるのかという肝心な点が、軽んじられたので

そしてある意味で、近代日本の外国文学研究は、その「本家」を中国からヨーロッパないし欧米に移し変えたものに過ぎない。そこでもやはり、日本人であることの限界を越えて、イギリスやフランスの文化的伝統や価値観をできる限り忠実に体得することが、正統的なやり方だと見なされた。つまり極言すれば、日本人であることを忘れるほどに、向こうの人間になりきることが理想とされたのである。むろんこれは、本家に生まれ育たない限り、けっして到達することのできない「逃げ水」であり、また学問の上では、永久に「本場」の研究に追いつくことも、対等の立場に立つこともできないことを意味する。「正確な理解」という、それはそれで立派な根拠のある目標が強調されすぎた結果、日本人として何のために外国文学を学ぶのか、また日本人として外国文学研究にどのような貢献を果たしうるのかという肝心な点が、軽んじられたので

ある。

一方、国文学では、中心と周辺の位置がくるりと入れ替わる。日本の文学であるからには、本家は日本であり、その研究においては日本人の学者が絶対的な権威をもっている。テクストの理解や評価についても、調査や分析の方法においても、正当な判断を下すことができるのは日本人だけであり、外国人の研究の価値は、その成果をどれだけ忠実に吸収し、反映できるかどうかにかかっている。だから、例えばアメリカやヨーロッパで行われているような日本文学研究——国文学の伝統では思いも寄らない角度や問題意識による研究は、日本文学の栄光に寄与するという一点を除けば、わざわざ考慮に入れるには当たらない。こうした独善的な本家意識は、前近代の漢学者が中国に対して抱いていた、そして近代の外国文学研究者が欧米に対して抱いている崇敬の念を、そのまま裏返したものにすぎない。

そして、漢学による負の遺産が目に付くもう一つの重大な点は、今日も歴然と認められる俗語による交流の欠如である。さきに見たように、ヨーロッパとは異なって、東アジア諸国間では、聖なる言語としての漢文ばかりが幅を利かせ、それぞれの俗語によるじかの交流は、きわめて乏しかった。むろん一つには、漢文という便利な共通語があるお陰で、筆談の不自由ささえ我慢すれば、知識人のあいだではいつ誰とでも対話を交わすことができたため、その分だけ俗語習得の必要がうすかったせいもある。だがもっと重要な原因は、おそらく他にある。すなわち、前近代の東アジア文化の中心はもちろん中国、なかでも古代から唐・宋あたりまでの古典にあり、周辺の諸国は（中国内部の周辺をも含めて）その中心を仰ぎ見ることに心を奪われて、すぐ近くの隣人たちに関心をもち、交流を深めようという余裕がほとんどなかったのではないか。それはちょうど近代以後、欧米以外のすべての国が、中心としての欧米を仰ぎ見て、聖なる言語としての西洋言語を学ぶに忙しいために、より身近な近隣の諸国に目を向けて、親しく交際する余裕がな

かったのと同様である。

日本で外国語といえば、まず欧米の言語を指し、外国文学といえば、ほぼ欧米の文学を指すという状態が、つい数十年前まで続いていた。日本の近代化以後、自国文学や外国文学の研究に比べて、比較文学研究の移入が大幅に遅れたのも、やはり同じ原因からだろう。ルネッサンス以後のヨーロッパの場合、イタリアからフランスへ、それからイギリスやドイツへといった文化的中心の移動や、軍事的・産業的・通商的な中心の変動はあっても、諸国は基本的に対等で競合的ないし横並びの関係にあった。ところが東アジアでは、近代以前は中国だけを頂点にいただく上下関係、近代以後は欧米を頂点とする上下関係が支配的だったため、近隣諸国やその言語・文学に対する関心が薄く、したがって「比較」という視点の生まれようがなかったのである。その結果、東アジアでは、すぐ隣どうしの韓国語、中国語、日本語の三つを自由に操ることのできる人間さえ、ごく少数しかいないという異様な事態が生じている。

とはいえ今日では、中心としての欧米文化の威光にもようやく翳りが見え始めている。東アジアにおける今後の自国文学・外国文学研究に望まれることは、第一には、前近代的な事大主義を捨てて、西洋ばかりに範を求めることなく、東アジア独自の立場、自国固有の立場を自覚し、みずからの主体的な関心と判断による研究を強化すること、それと同時に、自国文化に対する行き過ぎた特権意識をなくして、外からの視線を謙虚に受け入れることだろう。そして第二には、たがいに隣国の言語、聖なる言語ではない各国の俗語を学びあい、俗語の文学を楽しみあうことによって、東アジア独自の比較文学研究を軌道に乗せることではないだろうか。

[注]

1 本論文は、二〇〇一年十月二十日に韓国天安外国語大学で開かれた秋季韓国日本学協会国際学術大会「東アジアにおける自国文化研究と外国文化研究の問題点とその克服方案」で行った基調講演に手を加えたものである。

[参照文献]

淡島寒月「明治十年前後」、同好史談会編『漫談明治初年』批評社、二〇〇一年［一九二七］、三七一~七九頁。

川本皓嗣「島田謹二先生とフランス派英文学研究」、島田一九九五、三九三~四〇一頁。

島田謹二『近代比較文学——日本における西洋文学定着の具体的研究』光文社、一九五六年。『フランス派英文学研究 上巻 アレクサンドル・ベルジャムの英語文献学・オーギュスト・アンジェリエの英詩の解明』、平川祐弘・川本皓嗣編、南雲堂、一九九五年。

高田康成『キケロ』、岩波新書、一九九九年。

船戸英夫「英語聖書の歴史」、寺沢芳雄・船戸英夫・早乙女忠・都留信夫『英語の聖書』冨山房、一九六九年、一~七九頁。

02 永井荷風訳「死のよろこび」を読む

亀井俊介

死のよろこび

蝸牛（かたつむり）匍（は）ひまはる粘（ねば）りて濕（しめ）りし土（つち）の上（うへ）に
底（そこ）いと深（ふか）き穴（あな）をうがたん。泰然（たいぜん）として、
われ其處（そこ）に老（お）いさらぼひし骨（ほね）を横（よこ）たへ、
水底（みなそこ）に鱶（ふか）の沈（しづ）む如（ごと）忘却（ぼうきゃく）の淵（ふち）に眠（ねむ）るべう。

シヤアル・ボオドレヱル

われ遺書(ゐしよ)を厭(いた)み、墳墓(ふんぼ)をにくむ。
死(し)して徒(いたづ)らに人(ひと)の涙(なみだ)を請(こ)はんより、
生(い)きながらにして吾(われ)蜜(むしろ)鴉(からす)をまねぎ、
汚(けが)れたる脊髄(せきずる)の端々(はしばし)をついばましめん。

おお蛆蟲(うじむし)よ。眼(め)なく耳(みみ)なき暗黒(あんこく)の友(とも)、
君(きみ)が爲(ため)に腐敗(ふはい)の子(こ)、放蕩(はうたう)の哲学者(てつがくしや)、
よろこべる無頼(ぶらい)の死人(しにん)は来(きた)る。

わが亡骸(なきがら)にためらふ事(こと)なく食入(くひい)りて、
死(し)の中(うち)に死(し)し、魂(たましひう)失(う)せし古(ふる)びし肉(にく)に、
蛆蟲(うじむし)よわれに問(と)へ。猶(なほ)も悩(なや)みのありやなしやと。

Le Mort joyeux

Dans une terre grasse et pleine d'escargots
Je veux creuser moi-même une fosse profonde,
Où je puisse à loisir étaler mes vieux os

Charles Buadelaire

Et dormir dans l'oubli comme un requin dans l'onde.

Je hais les testaments et je hais les tombeaux;
Plutôt que d'implorer une larme du monde,
Vivant, j'aimerais mieux inviter les corbeaux
À saigner tous les bouts de ma carcasse immonde.

Ô vers! noirs compagnons sans oreille et sans yeux,
Voyez venir à vous un mort libre et joyeux;
Philosophes viveurs, fis de la pourriture.

À travers ma ruine allez donc sans remords,
Et dites-moi s'il est encor quelque torture
Pour ce vieux corps sans âme et mort parmi les morts.

　日本近代詩の歴史に燦然と輝く永井荷風訳詩集『珊瑚集』の巻頭を飾って、皮肉でまた悲痛な題をもつこの詩は、はじめ明治四十二年五月の『読売新聞』に、同じくボードレールの『悪の華』から訳した「憂悶」「暗黒」の二篇とともに発表された。訳者、三十一歳の時である。

ところで、この詩の原作をボードレールが『議会通信』(Le Messager de l'assemblée) にはじめて発表したのも、一九五一年四月、やはり作者三十一歳の時であった（いずれも数え年）。これは一つの偶然にすぎない。しかし私はこの偶然に、両者の心の結びつきの一端がうかがわれるような気がする。荷風の「死のよろこび」は、後に『珊瑚集』を形成すべくぞくぞくと新聞雑誌に発表され出した多くの訳詞のうちでもほとんど最初期のもので、その意味でいわば意欲にあふれたものといえた。同様にして原詩は、それまですでに何篇かの習作を発表してはいたがむしろ美術評論家として活動していたボードレールが、はじめて真に詩人としての決意と希望をもって一挙に十一篇を発表した中の一篇であって、いわば『悪の華』（一八五七年）誕生の第一歩を印す作品ともいえた。この詩に関する限り、原作者と訳者は似た立場に立っていたのである。

永井荷風は、もちろんこの翻訳を手がける前からボードレールの詩に親しんでいた。随筆「書かでもの記」（大正七年）によると、上田敏が明治三十三年六月の『太陽』増刊号に寄せた「十九世紀文芸史」を読んで、はじめて「ボオドレェルが詩集悪の花のいかなるものか」を知ったという。荷風はさらに続けて、「かくてわれはいかにして佛蘭西語を学び佛蘭西の地を踏まんとの心を起した」とも述べている。ただし彼は当時まだゾラやモーパッサンらの自然主義小説に傾倒しており、すぐに詩に打ち込んでいったには思われない。荷風が実際にボードレールの詩に親しみ出したのは、明治三十六年の渡米後、それも散文的なアメリカ生活に疲れ、その機械的な文明に嫌悪を感じ、文明の道徳の外なる世界、愛欲と詩的美の世界に救いを見出すようになっていった明治三十八、九年以降のことではあるまいか。その有様を、『あめりか物語』（明治四十一年）にうかがってみよう。「落葉」（明治三十九年十月脱稿）の章は、ニューヨークのセントラル・パ

ークでの秋の感慨を語って、ヴェルレーヌの「秋の歌」を引用し、さらに「産業国」アメリカの「実業主義」への反感をあらわした後、「夢、酔、幻、これが吾等の生命である」といった思いを述べ、ボードレールの次の句で結んでいる――「酔ふ、これが唯一の問題である。……もし『時』と云ふものゝ痛しい奴隷になるまいとすれば、絶ゆる間なく酔って居ねばならない……」

「ちやいなたうんの記」(脱稿日不明)は、この悪名高い「悪徳堕落の淵」の、とくに陰惨な裏町の情景を描きながら、「醜と云ひ悪と云はるゝものが、花や詩よりも更に美しく且つ神秘らしく思はれて来る」といって、「私はチャイナタウンを愛する。チャイナタウンは、『悪の花』の詩材の宝庫である」と締めくくっている。

もう一篇、「夜あるき」(明治四十年四月脱稿)は、やはりニューヨークの夜の巷を歩き、「夜の魂」というべき娼婦に誘われて「屍の屍に添ひて横たはる」如くともに眠るまでを綴ったものだが、全篇に「デカダンス派の父なるボードレール」的世界を、『悪の華』からの多数の引用を織りまぜて展開している。

荷風は明治四十年夏、ようやくあこがれのフランスに渡り、リヨンやパリに約十ヵ月滞在した後、帰国の途についた。この間にも、もちろん、ボードレールを熱心に読んでいた。『ふらんす物語』(明治四十二年)には、ボードレールからの引用や、彼への言及、あるいは彼の言葉に依拠した表現が随所でなされている。たとえば「霧の夜」は、霧深い大晦日の夜にリヨンの裏街を孤独にさまよう記事だが、「自分は夜と云ひ、霧と云ひ、猫と云ひ、悪臭と云ひ、名も知れぬこの裏道の光景が作出す暗澹たる調和に魅せられて、覚えず知らず、巴里の陋巷を歩みも遅くボードレールが詩に悩みつゝ行く時のやうな心持になつた」と述べている。

『珊瑚集』は大正二年四月、籾山書店から上梓された時、十三人のフランス詩人の作品三十八篇の翻訳を

収めていた。そのうち、荷風流の表記をすると、シャアル・ボオドレエル（七篇）、ポオル・ヴェルレエン（七篇）、アンリ・ド・レニェ（十篇）の翻訳で、ほぼ三分の二を占める。ただし、典雅で幽婉なレニエの詩に親しみ出したのは、フランスでの生活になれた明治四十年の末以降だと思われる。まずはボードレールとヴェルレーヌの作品の翻訳に打ち込んだが、それはこの二人が十九世紀後半の衆目の認める代表的な詩人であったことに加えて、彼らの感情、ボードレールについていえばそのデカダンスの生き方にともなう「暗澹たる調和」の美的感情に強くひきつけられたから違いない。帰国後間もない明治四十二年三月、荷風はまずヴェルレーヌの訳詩を発表し始め、ついで五月から、先に述べたようにボードレールの訳詩を世に出すことになったのである。その翻訳には、訳者自身の思いのたけがこもっていた。

しかも大事なことは、荷風がこういう原詩の世界にのめりこんで、その再現を志しただけでなく、そのために日本語の表現と真向から取り組んだことである。彼は後年、「当時わたくしが好んで此事に従ったのは西詩の餘香をわが文壇に移し伝へやうよりも、寧この事によって、わたくしは自家の感情と文辞とを洗練せしむる助けになさうと思ったのである」（「訳詩について」）と述べている。この姿勢があって、彼は表現上のさまざまな工夫をこらし、日本近代詩に新しい自由な調べを導入することもしたといえそうだ。

前置きはこれくらいにして、訳詩そのものを読みたい。だがその前に、原詩の内容にちょっとふれておくのも無駄ではあるまい。

"Le Mort joyeux"というこの詩の題は『悪の花』初版に収めた時につけられたものであって、はじめ『議会通信』に発表した時は"Spleen"（憂悶）という題であった。そして、同時に発表された他の十篇と

ともに、"Les Limbes"（冥府）という総題をつけられていた。これらの題が内容と密接な関係をもっていることはいうまでもない。

いったい「冥府」とは何であろうか。キリスト教神学によると、それは天國、練獄、地獄の外にある第四の場所であり、洗礼を受けずに死んだ幼児や善行の異教徒たちが死後に行くべき所であった。いわばそれは混沌の世界であって、そこには神も悪魔もなく、それにつらなるところの法悦も罪苦もない。そこを支配するのはたぶん倦怠のみであろう。彼はかなり前から"Les Limbes"という言葉を自分の詩集の題として暖めていた。（「冥府」という日本語は「冥土」と同じく仏教的な死後の世界をあらわす言葉であって、"Les Limbes"の内容を正しく伝えるわけではないが、ともかく「暗い世界」を意味するから、苦しまぎれの訳語として受けとめておきたい。）

"Spleen"（憂悶）というのは、この「冥府」における生の有様をあらわす言葉として、ボードレールが探し出してきたものにほかならない。「冥府」詩篇の中には"Spleen"と題する詩が三篇もある。いずれも暗鬱で麻痺的な死のうたである。ボードレールはこのほかにも同じ題の詩を数篇書いた（『珊瑚集』で「死のよろこび」の次に訳されている「憂悶」はそのうちの一篇である）。そして、彼は『悪の華』に"Spleen et Idéal"のセクションを設けて詩集の第一におき、また『悪の華』と並ぶ彼の代表作の散文詩集に Spleen de Paris という題をつけた。Spleen はボードレールにとって最も重要な観念の一つであった。

Spleen とは、もとは、ギリシャ語に由来して脾臓の意味だという。だが古代人によれば脾臓は憂鬱な気分の生まれる所であったので、後に憂鬱という意味で用いられるようになった。この一種エキゾチックな外来語は、フランス・ロマン派の文学者たちの間で流行したらしい。しかしボードレールにとっては、

これは単なる気分を示す言葉ではなかった。彼の生の全体を表現すべき言葉であったようだ。「ボードレールのSpleenは悲しみでも絶望でも倦怠でもない。そういう精神状態に通ずるところはある。……Spleenとは、諦めも希望もともに失った、一種の動かざる荒々しい力である」とロベール・ヴィヴィエは述べている。つまりボードレールのSpleenとは、冥府に沈淪する詩人のもだえの表現だといえる。

さて、はじめ"Spleen"と題されたわれわれの詩は、『悪の華』初版に収められた時に、"Le Mort joyeux"と改題された。荷風はこれを「死のよろこび」と訳したが、正しくは「よろこべる死人」という意味である。荷風は詩の中ではそのように訳しているから、この題は誤訳ではなく、内容全体の意味をとってわざとこう訳したのであろう。

ともあれこれは、「死」を「よろこび」と結びつけて、皮肉な気分を含む題である。しかしこれは単なる逆説の表現ではなかったと思われる。詩人は冥府に沈淪してもだえるのであるが、そういう自分を「よろこべる死人」ととらえた。つまり自分のSpleen感情を積極的に受けとめ、「死」を「よろこび」に転化しようとしているのだ。

ボードレールが冥府を魂の故郷としながら、その世界からの脱出を思い、絶えず神への祈願、天国への飛翔の願いを抱いていたことは、つとに研究者たちの指摘するところである。そういう解釈の当否はそれこそ研究者たちにゆだねなければならないけれども、彼が自分の詩で死や虚無への讃美を「よろこんで」懸命にうたうことにそれ自体の中に、冥府における存在を突き抜けて生への飛躍を実現したいという意欲を読み取ることは、不可能ではないだろう。つまり徹底的に堕ちることへの思いは、現状への挑戦であり、新しい価値の創造へとつながる——ともいえるのだ。詩人は、当然、その思いをうたうことによって、そ

ういう創造をなそうとする。その際、厳格な詩の形が、創造行為を引き締めることになる。

このように見てくる時、詩の形式がいかに重要な問題であるかはいうまでもない。"Le Mort joyeux"は一見して明らかなようにソネット形式である。そして各行は厳密に十二音綴（アレクサンドラン）から成り、荘重な響きをもつ。また韻は abab / abab / ccd / ede と、イタリアン・ソネット形式を独自に用いながら、見事に整って緩みがない。この形式の厳密さはいやでも内用の暗澹さと緊張関係を生み出さずにはいないだろう。そしてその緊張関係が、この詩の精神性をたかめているといえそうだ。

では、永井荷風はこの詩をいかに訳しているか。ようやく詩訳そのものの検討に入りたい。順を追って見ていくことにしよう。

第一聯

　蝸牛（かたつむり）匍（は）ひまはる粘（ねば）りて濕（しめ）りし土の上に
　底（そこ）いと深（ふか）き穴（あな）をうがたん。泰然（たいぜん）として、
　われ其處（そこ）に老いさらぼひし骨（ほね）を横（よこた）へ、
　水底（みなそこ）に鱶（ふか）の沈（しづ）む如忘却（ごとわすれ）の淵（ふち）に眠（ねむ）るべう。

まず訳詩のいかにもねばねばした口調に注目したい。それはもちろんこの詩の内容から生まれてくるのであるが、音の構成もまたそれを助けているようだ。この詩の音数を数えてみると、原詩の厳正な壮重さとは違って、だいたい五音七音という日本語では伝統的に最も心地よい口調をもとにしながらも、五七調

や七五調も出てくれば、五五調、七七調も出てくる。時には六音や八音も入っている。さらに音と意味との結びつき工合で各行を見ると、十、十四/十四、七/五、十四/十三、十二、の音構成に分かれ、厳正というよりはむしろ自由な混成の響きをもっている。これをたとえば薄田泣菫がソネットにおいて試みた八六調とか、あるいは蒲原有明が試みたいわゆる独絃哀歌調、さらにもっと具体的には、有明が訳したボードレールの詩「猫」（Les Chats）——これはいま検討している詩と並んでもと『議会通信』に発表されたもの——の五七五七調などと比べることによっても、この訳詩の一見不統一な息の長い破調の意味するところが浮き出てくるであろう。つまり、この調子がこの訳詩に憂悶の情を深める重要な要素となっているのではあるまいか、と思うのである。

いったいに永井荷風はボードレールのカトリック的宗教心、あるいは彼の詩のもつ精神性にはほとんど注意を払っていなかったとよくいわれる。そのことについては私は判断を保留するけれども、荷風がボードレールについて「神の栄え霊魂の不滅を歌ひ得ざる詩人」といっていたことは事実だ。ただ、「罪と暗黒の美」に沈溺した詩人の苦悩については、彼は深い理解と共感を示していた。そのことは、まず『珊瑚集』に訳したボードレールの詩七篇の選択の仕方にあらわれている。「秋の歌」の風土感、無常感と、「月の悲しみ」の官能的な美しさとを除けば、残りの五篇はいずれも「死に対する恐ろしい幻覚」をうたったものであるのだ。だがさらに、荷風のボードレールの受けとめ方の特色は、いま分析してみたような訳詩の沈鬱な音調そのものにあらわれていると私は思うのである。もちろんそれは、折から詩形の再編成期にあった日本の詩壇の状況によるところも大きいであろうけれども。

次に荷風の訳語はどうか。grasse 一字を「粘りて濡りし」とし、pleine d'escargots を「蝸牛匍ひま はる」、dans l'oubli を『読売新聞』の初出では「忘却の底に」として後に『珊瑚集』で「忘却の淵に」とす

るなど、原語にとらわれないで自由に、しかも見事に原詩の内容を再現している。ただし第二行で、「底いと深き穴」(つまり墓穴) を自分自身で (moi-même) うがとうと原詩ではいっているが、訳語にはその語は出ていない。とくにそうことわらなくても、その趣は訳詩に出ているからよいのかもしれない。それとは逆に、訳詩第二行の「泰然として」(原詩では第三行 à loisir) は、初出では訳していなかったのを改訳の時に生かしたものである。このようにして、荷風はかなりの程度まで自由に訳しているが、言葉は厳しく取捨しているのであった。この言葉は、詩人の精神態度を説明する表現として省くことのできないものであった。

第二聯

われ遺書(ゐしょ)を厭(いと)み、墳墓(ふんぼ)をにくむ。
死して徒(いたづら)に人(ひと)の涙(なみだ)を請(こ)はんより、
生(い)きながらにして吾(われ)蜜(むし)ろ鴉(からす)をまねぎ、
汚(け)れたる脊髄(せきずる)の端(はし)々(じし)をついばましめん。

ここでも、五音や七音にまじって八音、十音、十二音などが大きな位置を占めていることに注目しておきたい。そしてこういう比較的息が長く構成された言葉の意味の重さをここでもふたたび計っておこう。
さて、この聯では、第一聯が行動でもってうたい上げたのに対して、詩人の感情が真正面にうち出される。遺書を厭み、墳墓をにくみ、人の涙を請うより鴉に脊髄の端々をついばましめようというのは、世俗

的なものの峻拒であると同時に、自己の完全な消滅への願望である。生ける人の中に思い出や同情として残ってもいけないのである。

この聯の第四行は、初出では、

　汚れし吾が骨の端々をついばまじめん。

とあったが、この「吾が」はどうしても必要な語ではないし、「骨」よりは「脊髄」の方が（carcasseという原語からは少し遠ざかるとしても）ぞっとする恐怖感が生じ、迫真力が増すような気がする。荷風は「腐肉」の中でもこのcarcasseという言葉に「脊髄」の訳語を用い、「憂悶」の中では別の言葉に「脳髄」という訳語を当てている。自然主義以後、こういう解剖学的な言葉は一部の詩人にあくどく用いられるようになってきたとはいえ、荷風のこの恐れげもなくしかも適切な訳語の使用は、やはり注目に価するのではなかろうか。そして迫真性という点では、荷風の訳は原詩にいささかも劣らないのである。

　　　　第三聯

　　おお蛆蟲よ。眼なく耳なき暗黒の友、
　　君が爲めに腐敗の子、放蕩の哲学者、
　　よろこべる無頼の死人は来る。

今や詩人は墓穴の中に身を横たえてあたりを見まわす。と、すでに蛆虫が近寄ってきている。そこで彼は「眼なく耳なき暗黒の友」とそれに呼びかける。蛆虫はボードレールのよく使うイマージュであった。たとえば別の"Spleen"と題する詩では、「われは月に呪われし墳墓なり。長き蛆そこに悔恨の如くはいまわり、わがいつくしき極みの亡骸を食い荒らす」とうたっている。こういう自己をいためつくすような精神的戦慄の創造こそ、暗い倦怠の支配する冥府からの脱出の第一歩であった（かもしれない）のだが、荷風はそれをどう理解していたであろうか。

訳詞はここでも五七調をはずれた破調が目立つが、もう繰り返すことはやめようと思う。それよりも、ここでは、荷風が大きな誤訳をしていることに注目しておきたい。というのは複数形であって、原詩で「蛆虫」(vers) に対し「腐敗の子、放蕩の哲学者」(Philosophes viveurs, fils de la pourriture) というのは複数形であって、原詩で「蛆虫」(vers) に対して呼びかけた言葉であるのに、荷風はそれを「よろこべる無頼の死人」(un mort libre et joyeux) という自分を指す句と同格にとっているのだ。これは単に文法的な誤りにすぎないかもしれない。だがすでに蛆虫のもつ意味の重要さに気づいているわれわれは、「腐敗の子、放蕩の哲学者」というその形容も冥府の住人の形容として大切にしなければならない。原詩では、「腐敗の子、放蕩の哲学者」たる蛆虫が、たとえば「悔恨」識に関係するのではあるまいか。荷風がこれを自分の形容に受けとったことは、彼の自己認のごとく、詩人の肉体と精神に食い入ってくる——そこに冥府からの脱出のきっかけがあるかもしれない。だが荷風はすでにその「腐敗」「放蕩」だからこそ詩人は「よろこんで」それを迎え入れるのであろう。の人間になりきって、いわば冥府の存在であることに陶酔しているようにも見うけられるのである。

第四聯

わが亡骸にためらふ事なく食入りて
死の中に死し、魂失せし古びし肉に、
蛆蟲よわれに問へ。猶も悩みのありやなしやと。

詩は今や結末に到って、一見、凄絶な虚無の讃美となる。蛆虫という冥府の住人にはげしく呼びかけることによって、ボードレールは死から生への転機をつかもうとしていたかもしれぬ。しかし訳詩はそんなこととは無関係に、虚無への陶酔を盛り上げているようだ。

ここでも、誤訳とまではいえないだろうが問題になりうる句がある。原詩の結びの言葉 mort parmi les morts が、訳詩では「死の中に死し」となっているのだ。正しくは「死者たちの中で死んでいる」の意味である。つまり原詩では、詩人はほかの死者たちと違って自己の状況を強く自覚しているのに対し、訳詩では死の度合が強められて、ほかの者との対比の上での自己の存在の自覚が稀薄になっているともいえそうなのである。

だが、それはともかくとして、訳詩における死の果ての「悩み」の忘却への思いの表現はまことに力強い。「蛆虫よわれに問へ」という句が、その問いの内容を示す句の間に挿入されているので、一読して意味がとりにくくなっている。しかしあえてそうしたために、この節の格調はいちじるしくたかまっている。

またロベール゠ブノワ・シェリクスは原詩に於ける or 音の使用が聯を追って多くなるところから死 (mort) の叫びのたかまりを説いているが、日本語ではもちろんその再現は不可能だ。しかし最後の行の「猶も悩みのありやなしやと」の na 音の効果などは、ある程度それに近づいたものといえるかもしれない。

こうしてこの詩（原詩）は、平然と完全な忘却の眠りにつくべく自ら深い穴を掘ることからうたい出して、あたりに這い寄る蛆虫にわが亡骸を、さらにはわが精神の内までをも食いつくすことを呼びかけて終る。「猶も悩みのありやなしや」とわれに問えと昂然としていうのは、一見、その虚無の中では自分に悩みのなくなることをうたうかのごとくであるが、ボードレールとしては、じつは逆に悩みのいかにしても振り切りえないことの自覚がめっての表現らしい。しかもそれを詩にうたい上げることに、冥府からの飛躍の意志が秘められていたかもしれないことは、すでに繰り返し述べてきたところだ。

荷風の訳詩にこのような冥府脱出の精神が見られないと断定することは難しい。原詩と訳詩との相違を強調しすぎることの誤りであることは、いうまでもない。ただ荷風の訳詩から私が感じるのは、高度に緊張した精神の営みよりも、むしろ「憂悶」の情への深い共鳴である。あるいはその表現としての「罪と暗黒の美」への耽溺である。私はそれを訳詩の響きと言葉に即して追跡してみたかった。そして彼が生み出した、五音と七音を基調としながらもねばねばと心に迫る自由な口調を愛するのである。この詩風が後の詩人たちにどのような影響を与えたかは、稿を改めて追跡したいところだ。

なお、荷風がこの詩の「最もむき出しのレアリスム」（シエリクス）の世界を恐れず、むしろ愛したことは、一口に耽美派といわれる彼の別の一面を知る手がかりにもなると思うが、ここでは論じえない。ただ、彼のボードレールに対する帰依はそんなに長く続かず、その後レニエなどにとって代わられたにもかかわらず、この「憂悶」の世界が彼の中で生き残っていったことだけは、ひとことふれておきたい。昭和十八年に編まれた『偏奇館吟草』で、それがはっきりとイマージュの連関をもって表現されているのである。たとえば「からす」という詩の、

からす。
地獄の鳥。
汝飢ゑなば泥海の
干潟あさりて
くされしものを啄め。

と一致するし、「蟲」（大正二年、父を失った頃の作）の、

わが父のしゝむらに食い入りし
耳もなく目もなく縱蟲のわが身よ

は、「死のよろこび」の「おお蛆蟲よ。眼なく耳なき暗黒の友」と同じイマージュである。そして「拷問」のうたい出し、

人の世は牢屋なり。

というのは、「死のよろこび」と同時に訳された「憂悶」の中の「この世はさながらに土の牢屋か」と同じである。

[付記]

この小文は一九六四年頃に書いたと思う。私は大学に職を得て間もなくで、東大比較文学会の機関誌『比較文学研究』の編集に従事していた。『珊瑚集』研究特集号を出すことになり、私は場合によっては埋め草記事にもと思って、これを書いたのだった。しかし秀れた原稿が十分に集まったので、きっぱり引っ込め、以後四十年近く篋底に秘めてきた。先頃、佐々木昭夫教授の東北大学退官記念論文集『日本近代文学と西欧——比較文学の諸相』(一九九七年)に寄稿した「永井荷風訳『九月の果樹園』を読む」も、同じようにして成ったものである。いまこの小文を取り出して読み直すと、内容・表現ともにまことに稚い。ただ、翻訳作品をこうして彼我の言葉の一つ一つに即して検討することに打ち込んでいた自分に、なつかしさは禁じえない。比較文学について長年語り合ってきた秋山正幸教授の古希記念論文集に、若書きの恥をしのんでこの小文を寄せることを思い立ったのも、ひとえに教授との歳月に対するなつかしさによる。若干の補筆をし、措辞を改めはしたけれども、なお残る幾多の不備を教授ならびに読者がご海容下されば幸いである。

03 オースマン計画の波動

銀座煉瓦街の比較文化史的考察

富田 仁

　江戸時代、明暦三年一月十八日（一六五七年）の明暦の大火を含めて約九十件の火災に見舞われている。このように火災に頻繁に見舞われてきた江戸の人びとであるが、必ずしも火災に手をこまねいていたわけではなく、それなりの防災対策を講じてきたにもかかわらず、木造建築の密集する大都会ではそれも十分な効果をあげることができなかった。

　明治五年二月二六日（一八七二年）、午後三時頃、和田倉門内の兵部省添屋敷（元会津藩邸）から出火してたちまちにして銀座方面に燃えひろがっていった。今日残されている「壬申正院御用留」によると、焼失町四十二丁、焼失家屋四八七九戸、官員など邸宅四十三か所、諸官省十三か所、諸藩邸跡六か所、寺

院五八寺、死者八名、罹災者一万九八七二名という大規模な火災であった。

ところで、この火災に際しての鎮火後の対策はきわめて素早いものがあった。焼け跡には本建築はしないように触れが出され、道路拡幅を含む道路改正を内定し、煉瓦家屋建設を行うことを知らせ、工部省がただちに測量を着手し、復興道路の絵図面が完成されたのである。

じつは銀座の大火の翌日、みずから罹災者であった東京府知事由利公正は太政官のもとに赴き、焼跡をすべて煉瓦建築するという計画を申し立てたが、井上馨も大隈邸で話し合ったところ由利公正は反対したけれど火災を防ぐためには家屋を煉瓦石造りにしようということになったと語り伝えられている。

銀座煉瓦街建設には紆余曲折の過程があったが、新しい近代的な都市を造ろうとしたとき、それまでにはなかった街を構想することを余儀なくされたとしても当然であった。明治七年六月刊行の服部誠一『東京新繁昌記』に銀座の表通りの情景が描かれている。その中で服部誠一は「路上亦遍く煉瓦を敷き、砥より平かに席清し。全街燦然、一点の塵無く、況んや犬尿をや。石室は則ち英京倫敦を模し、街道は則ち仏京の巴黎に擬す、亦何んと波涛を越え其国都に到るを用ゐん」と記しているが、ここで注目されるのはイギリスのロンドンとフランスのパリをモデルにして近代都市を建設しようとしたことである。

このようにして銀座煉瓦街はつくられることとなったわけであるが、当時の日本人としては、実際に外国の地に赴いて近代都市の実際を見た人びとはまだ限られていた時代であり、銀座煉瓦街の出現はきわめて大きな驚きであったにちがいない。明治十一年に刊行された由利兼次郎編『東京自慢（名所手続）』をひもとくとき、銀座煉瓦街のショックがいかばかりのものかを知ることができないだろうか。

「煉瓦或ハ石ヲ以テ西洋風ニ家屋ヲ築キ道ノ中央ヲ馬車道トシ、両側ニ数種ノ花木ヲ植エ人道ノ界ヲナシ、人道ヲニ煉瓦石ヲ以テシ、各商社ハ軒ヲ並ヘテ実ニ清潔美麗ナルコト耳目ヲ驚カスノ極点ニシテ自然異域

に入ルノ念ヲ勃発セシム。夜ハ瓦斯燈ヲ以テ尚ホ昼ノ如ク、人民ノ往復頗ル盛ニシテ昼夜跡ヲ絶ツノ間ナク、実ニ東京第一ノ街巷ナリ」

『東京自慢』に描かれている光景は当時の人びとにはまさに近代都市こそこれだったという感動をあたえたにちがいない。ヨーロッパの街路、建物、街路をモデルとしたといわれる銀座煉瓦街を見てきた者はきわめて少なかったことを考えると、銀座煉瓦街の完成はすこぶる大きなカルチャーショックをあたえたことだろう。

銀座煉瓦街建設間もなく西欧回覧の旅に出かけた岩倉使節団の一行はロンドン、パリに赴いたが、そこでは当然近代建築の家屋と街路を見ることとなった。たとえば明治七年七月十四日（一八七二年八月十七日）の岩倉使節団のパリ到着の様子を紹介しておきたい。

「六時ニ巴黎府ノデイスト駅ニ達シ、馬車ニテ巴黎府ノ市街ヲ走リ、皜皜タル層閣、街ヲ挟ミテ聳ヘ、路ミナ石ヲ甃シ、樹ヲウエ、気燈ヲ点ス、日輪正ニ上リ、名都ノ風景自ラ目ヲ麗ワシ、店店に綺羅ヲ陳ネ、旗亭ニ遊客ノ群ル、府人ノ気風マタ英京ト趣キヲ異ニス、既ニシテ『シャンゼルゼー』ノ広衢ヲ馳、『アレチリヨン』門前ナル館ニ著セル」（久米邦武編『米欧回覧実記』第三巻　岩波書店）

パリの市街の詳細な描写が当時の人びとにどのように映ったのだろうか。銀座煉瓦街が出現した時代とパリの市街とき興味をひかれるものがある。

さて、銀座大火災後、その復興計画が討議されたが、その折当然のことのように不燃建築の問題が持ち上った。そこで当然ヨーロッパのような近代的都市構想も取り沙汰されたが、然るべきモデルの都市としてロンドン、パリが浮上してきた。都市計画の根幹には道路の道幅の問題があるで、早速外国都市の道幅を太政官に問い合わせた。

「私が外国都市の道幅を問合わせたら、紐育は二十四間程で、倫敦は二十五間、華盛頓も矢張り二十四間であった。そんな所からあの銀座大通りを二十五間にしてその他の中小路を十二間と八間位とかにしたら宜しからうと言ふた。するとその時分は今と違って二十五間といふ様な広い道程は何処にもないので、皆が笑ってそんなに道幅を拡げてもその必要がないといふ論が盛んで中々行はれんから、それは要りますどうしても、天子が都を奠きめてそこに御住居になれば他国の天子が参朝した時にどうなさると云ったところが、そんな事は今からあて嵌ておく訳にもゆくまいといふ事で、段々協議して十二間にしろといふ事になりました。」（『由利公正伝』）

銀座煉瓦街建設が由利公正または井上馨のいずれによって発案されたのか、さまざまの説があるが、はっきりしないところがある。いずれにせよ、銀座の街を拡げるという話となり、火事を防ぐためには家屋を煉瓦石にしようということになり、ここに煉瓦街建設が動き出したのである。井上馨は国家的、由利公正は東京府政の立場で煉瓦街の問題に対処したのであった。

じつは都市計画の構想はなにも銀座大火直後に起きたわけではなく、江戸時代にも防火的な構造で江戸の街並を災禍の被害から守ろうとする動きがあったことを知らなくてはならない。それは寛政年間に書かれた本多利明（一六三五─一七〇〇）の著作『経済秘策』によるものである。本多利明は天文・数学・物産学に長じ、とりわけ北地経営に才能をみせた人物であるが、その著書『経済秘策』の中で利明は先進的な防災策を論じており、きわめて注目されている。

「火災トハ、江戸ノ儀ハ日本第一最第一ノ都会ノ儀ナレバ火ニモ憂ナク水ニモ苦ミナク、永久不朽ノ石家造リニアリテ万民安堵ノ内ナケレバ、王城ノ地ニ相応ゼズ、然ルニ江戸四里四方ニ焼ケ安キ木ノ家居ヲ建テ並ベ其体余リニ手薄ナリ。毎年四季内旱リ続キ乾燥ナル事ハ毎度ニテ大地モ枯レ、汗水モ絶ル程ノ災天

ナル時、万一大風吹キ起リ砂石モ飛バスル節、フト過チニテ風上前後左右ノ端々処々ヨリ失火アラバ、忽チニ大火トナリ、残ラズ焼失スベシ。小風小火ノ内ニ人力ヲ以テ消留モ安カルベケドモ、大風大火トナラバ人力モ鎮ムベキニ非ズ、此ノ如キ大災害ハ木家作ヨリ出来セリ。故ニ欧羅巴洲都会ノ地ハ貴賤万民皆石家造リノ住居ナレバ稀ニ火災アリモモ、内造作ノ本品ヲ焼失スルノミナラバ、隣家モ知ラザル程ノ事ナリ。欧羅巴洲トモモ国初ヨリノ石家作ニテモアルマジ、度々ノ火災ニ遇ヒ懲々シテ石家作制度建立セシナルベシ。御府内草創以後明暦ノ大火ト明和ノ大火ノ外、大層ノ失火ナキガ故ニ人情惰弱ニシテ恐ルベキヲ恐レズ、且又制度教示ノナキガ故ナリ。当時治平二百有余年ノ内、仏閣、宮殿、伽藍、庶民贄託、殊ニ大造ニ建並ル跡ヨリ或ハ火災ニ焼払ヒ、或ハ修理建間ナク、故ニ此手近キ山々ハ皆伐尽シ、次第ニ深山ニ臨ミ、昔ハ人倫絶タルモ、今ハハヤ残ル所ナク終ルニ柱トナルベキ樹木伐絶ベシ。火災ホド人力ヲ破ル費ヘハナシ。国政ハ人力ヲ扶ケ費ヲ省キ庶人ノ欲スル所ニ随テ建立セサレバ永久ニ伝ヘ保ツルコト能ハザルモノナレバ、人情ヲトルヲ主トセリ。今既ニ備前国中ニ大小ノ橋々皆石橋ナリ。熊沢氏ノ手蹟ニテモアルカ、石ヲ以テ木材ニ換ル意石家作ノ萌ナリ。是等ヲ賞美スレバ漸ヶト伝移シテ石家モ終ニ行ハルベシ。俗吏ノ思フ所ヲ察スルニ、石家作リハ能モヤルベケレドモ、入用大造リニシテ容易ニ出来ベキニ非ズト言フベシ。庶人ナラバ左モアルベケレドモ、国君王侯ノ通用金銀ハ、宝貨トシテ秘蔵スベキニ非ズ、通用スルヲ以テ宝貨ナレバ惜ム可キニ非ズ。」

本多利明はすでにヨーロッパの都市では貴賤万民すべて石家造りの住居であり、火災で類焼を免がれる生活を送っているという知識をもっていたわけで、やがて日本にも不燃建造物を普及させていこうとする動きの到来を予告していたとしても当然のことだろう。

パリでも十八世紀では一七三七年十月二十七日に会計院の火事、一七三七年八月一日と、十二月三十日

の市立病院の火事などが最大の火災であり、多くの人びとの生命を失なわせた大事件であったことも、都市計画の動きへの一つの原因となった。十九世紀末、フランスに大規模な都市計画の動きがみられる一つの原因になったものと考えられる。パリ大改造である。じつは一八五二年末のクーデタで皇帝になったナポレオン三世は新任のセーヌ県知事ジョルジュ・オースマン Georges Houssman を呼びつけて、皇帝みずから作成した整備計画を見せた。パリの道路を工事の優先順位に色分けした彩色の計画図である。

もっとも、この計画図はパリ・コミューンの折にパリの市役所で焼失してしまって残念なことに原図は残されていないが、プロシア政府が万国博覧会のときにもらったものが残されており、今日その内容を知ることができる。ただし、実際に施工されたものと最初に提示されたものと同じだったのか違っていたのかは不明であるといわれている。

オースマン以前にもパリの整備事業を行なってきた者はいた。市街地の開発を奨励したシャブロルなどもそのひとりであるが、今日のラファイエット La Fajette 通りが貫通したのもその名残りである。ちなみに、パリにいまも多く残っているパッサージュ・クーヴェール Pasage couvert（屋根つき通りぬけ通商店街）は通りと通りを結ぶある種のアーケードの商店街であり、十八世紀末から十九世紀前半にかけて建設された鉄とガラスの建築である。王政復古時代に多くつくられたものであるが、それまで少なかった歩道が増えたのもオースマン計画のそのような動きの表われであったのである。なお、左岸ではパッサージュはほとんどいまはなくなっている。中庭を囲むショッピングセンターに改造されてパリ一番の盛り場となった。パッサージュの元祖はパレ・ロワイヤル Palais Royal で、ブルボン王朝の傍系のオルレアン家の居城をあらため一九三四年にフィリック・オルレアン。中庭を囲み、ショッピングセンター一番の盛り場である。

パリの大改造の多角的側面を眺めてみることにする。パリの東部のヴァンセンヌ Vincennes から広い道路クール・ド・ヴァンセンヌに入ったトローヌ（今日のナシヨン Nation）広場は王政時代からパリの東の玄関と考えられていたが、ナポレオン三世はここに帝政の戦勝を記念する凱旋門を建て、これを「東のエトワール広場」とし、西と東の対称性をあたえようと考えていた。もっとも、これは実現されなかったが拡大された新しい市域の貫通道路の交差点には大きな広場、すなわち、エトワール Etoile、サン・トーギュスタン Sainte-Augustain、アルマ Alma、バスティーユ Bastile、ロトーヌ、シャトー・ドー Château d'eau（今日のレピュブリック Republique）、オペラ Opera などがそれである。

新しい道路が貫通したことでパリの道路の幅は一八五二年の十二メートルから一八六〇年の二十四メートルに倍増し、広い歩道が一般的になり、車道の幅との割合が都市の美観を考えて慎重に定められたが、一九五〇年代に自動車の混雑軽減のために車道化された。

オースマンの時代では辻馬車だけでも四千台もあり、小型馬車会社が独占的に経営していたが、馬糞とワラクズの公害を起こしていた。一八二八年には乗合馬車が営業し、一八五四年にはパリ地区の全路線を独占するまでになった。

一八五三年にはパリに地下鉄をつくろうとする動きが起きたが、パリ市、セーヌ県、馬車乗合総合会社などの対立のために実現はできなかった。パリでは鉄道は地方と連絡していても市内の交通には役立たなかった。わずかにサン・ラザール Saint-Lazare 駅からオートゥユ Auteuitle まで鉄道で通勤できるだけであった。

ナポレオン三世がロンドンにならってスクェアをパリにつくりたいというので、オースマンは緑地を整備した。今日のレピュビリック広場のような緑地広場である。湿気が多いと不衛生になるというような反

03 ― オースマン計画の波動 ―― 銀座煉瓦街の比較文化史的考察

対の声があったが、それにもめげず、オースマンは幅二十メートル以上の道路に街路樹を植えることとしたのである。

オースマンは必ずしもナポレオンの命令を受けないで、自分の考えで二百キロも離れた場所の湧き水を大工事の末にひっぱってくるというようなことをしてパリの整備を行なっていった。オースマンの計画はナポレオンの命令によるものであったけれど、その計画になかったものもあったことを見落してはならない。たとえばサン・ジェルマン Saint-Germain 大通りがそれである。もっとも、その代りに大学関係者や左岸の要請を受けてソルボンヌ Sorbonne の北側を植物園方向に向うリュ・デ・ゼコール Rue des Ecol（学校通り）の計画があった。この通りの西側はサン・ミシェル Saint-Michel の大通りで終わっており、幹線の役割を果たすことはない。

オースマンはこの通りの北側にシェリ橋からコンコルドル Concorde 橋まで、左岸を東西に横断するサン・ジェルマン大通りを提案し、右岸の中心地を囲むグラン・ブールヴァールに繋がり、パリ中心部の環状道路を完成させることにする。これはルイ十四世の時代にとりこわされたパリを囲む城壁が一七八四年から八九年にかけて建設されて環状並木通りとなったのである。なお、グラン・ブールヴァール Grand Bourvard は北側に大きく膨らみ、右岸の中心部を抱き込んでいるけれど、サン・ジェルマン大通りは膨らみが少なくなっており、セーヌ河から大きく離ないので、どうしてこの路線が選ばれたのかはっきりした理由はわからないという。

ちなみに、ナポレオン三世はサン・ジェルマン大通りの計画については乗気ではなかったけれど、まず東からサン・ミシェル大通りまでの一キロを一八五五年に着工して、つぎに反対側のコンコルド橋からべルシャックリッヌ通りの四百五十メートルを一八六七年のパリ万国博を控えたどさくさの中に着工して、

翌年にはその先が少しのびるが中間の一・五キロは放置し、両側の完成部分を挟まれて不便待つこととしたのである。この部分の完成はオースマン辞任のあとの一八七六年のことであるが、サン・ジェルマン寺院から西の七百五〇メートルは古い道路の片側の拡幅だけで簡単に事業ができるように道路の位置はきめられていたのである。

ところで、オースマンが道路工事に着工しとときにはいつも二つ以上の目的を以って計画をたてていた。つまり、いくつかの目的を同時に狙っているという含みをもっていたことを見落してはならないのである。オースマンの都市改造計画というのは原則的にはいわば都市機能混合の原則にぴったり合っているといわれている。その意味ではパリの町は機能混合的であって、屠殺場などのようなものだけを都市の中心から追い出した。

オースマンは建築形態の原則は町に厳格に押しつけたけれど、そこに入る機能については従来の考え方を尊重して混在を認め、必要な公共施設、とくに兵舎などは公共の力で設置したところはそれなりに注目されてよいが、それではこのようにオースマン化されたパリの街とはどのようなものだったのだろうか。

一般的にいえば、オースマン化されたパリの建物は一階に商店か業者が入るのが普通であり、ルイ十四世時代からあるカフェで、今日みられるようなカフェのテラスが一般化してきたけれども、そのようなカフェが社会接触、日常的な情報交換の場としてフランス文化の基盤となっていったのである。

パリでは仕事場と住居が混在し、金持も貧乏人もごっちゃになって混じり合って住んでいたが、やがて不動産取得能力によって次第に上下階の住みわけができるようになり、さらにエレヴェーターの普及とともに上階に移動するようになるまでそれが進んでいったのである。つまり、一階と中二階は商店と事務所、二、三階は金持の住居、屋根裏部屋は使用人のそれという区分が行なわれることとなってい

ったのである。

新設の同じ一階でも貧富の区分はある。金持の住居は裏側の階段にも通じていて、そこは勝手口である。使用人と顔を合わせず部屋が移動できるという便利さがある。街裏の不動産価値も裏になるにつれて上ったり、下ったりするために、昔から住んでいた場所に住めなくなったり、周辺に出ていかなくなったりする貧民も少なくなり、やがて「オースマン化」にパリの東西の不均衡を強めるという現象が起きたのである。つまり、パリ周辺において馬蹄形状に貧民を囲ませたのである。

ところで、このオースマン計画の立役者は一八〇九年にパリのフォーブル・デュ・ルール Foubourg、現在のフォーブル・サン・トノレ五十五番地に生まれた生粋のパリッ子である。オースマンが手がけた大通りとしては凱旋門からブローニュの森を下っていくフォッシュ Madelaine Fauche 大通り、マルゼブル Marherbe 広場とマドレーヌ寺院を結ぶマルゼベ大通り、オペラ座とルーヴル美術館を直結してオペラ座通り、左岸のサン・ミシェルからシテ Cite 島を越えてまっすぐ貫ぬいたサン・ミシェル大通り、セバストポル Sebastopal 大通り、ストラスブール Strasbourg 大通りと続く大通り、共和国広場 Place Republique を経て、東駅、北駅の前を通ってモンマルトル Monmartre の方に伸びてゆくマジャンタ Magenta 大通り、ナション広場と共和国広場を結ぶヴォルテール Voltaire 大通りがつくられたのである。

オースマンは広く、かつまっすぐな大通りをたくみに駅、病院、公共施設、広場などと結びつけていったが、そこには馬車、自転車、さらには自動車も行きかうようになっていったのであるが、その結果、大通りはきわめて重要な役割を果たし、その時代の文化を如実に反映していったのである。オペラ座周辺のキャプシーヌ Capcinueies 大通り、イタリヤン Italien 大通りからモンマル大通りの近辺あたりはいわゆ

るグラン・ブールヴァールという大通りであった。パリの街並みを見ていくうえで通用するほどにパリを代表するだけで通用するほどにパリを代表する大通りであった。パリの街並みを見ていく上で注目しなくてはならないのは広場である。というのは広場に囲まれている都市、それがパリなのであるからである。そもそもヨーロッパの都市は広場を囲んで形成されているといわれている。普通は大聖堂と市庁舎が広場の両側に建てられたので、都市の心臓であり、人びとが集い合う中心部の役割を果たしていたのである。

パリでもっとも親しまれている広場はルイ十五世がつくったコンコルド広場であるが、これはそれまでの広場とは違って、周囲を建物に囲まれることなく開放的な広場につくりあげていった。パリが近代的都市に改造されたのはナポレオン三世が実権を掌握して、オースマンにパリ改造と整備を委ねようになったときからのことである。オースマンの道路計画は前述の通りである。そしてパリの右岸と左岸が結びつき、効率よい道路線をつくりあげ、近代都市として不可欠な道路の拡張、公園の新設、上下水道の整備を行なったのである。ちなみに公衆便所は一八三〇年に初めてパリに設けられた。オースマンは多くの建物を壊わして表通りに面して一階は商店、二階以上を住宅とする四、五階建の建造物を並ばせるという近代都市の発想を具現させていったのである。一八五九年制定の建築条例にみられるように幅二十メートル以上の道路に面して建つ建築物ではその高さと道路幅が等しくなくてはならないという規制が課せられることとなったのである。

パリはそれまで市壁（いわゆる徴税請負人の壁）外にあった十二の自治区がパリ市内に編入されることになって、今日のパリ市の輪郭ができあがっていった。人口も百八十万人までに膨れ上がった。そんなオースマンが市街の改造できわめて顕著な大通りとして、古い運河にふたをつけてつくったシャルル・ルノアール Charler Renoir 大通りがある。広い並木通りは手前の広場はバスティーユ Bastile であり、フランス

革命の発端の地として知られ、リヴォリ通りの終点でもある。オースマンが手がけた道路で一番高く評価されているのはオペラ通りであるが、これは当初はナポレオン通りと呼ばれていた。オペラ座広場にはグランドホテルがつくられ、リヴォリ通りとともにパリの中心をなすこととなった。一八三五年、コンコルド広場にマカズム舗装、今日のアスファルト道路が出現した。

パリの街路を眺めていくときにはやはり前述した〈パッサージュ・クーヴェール〉を見落してはならない。これは一七九一年にサン・ドニ通りにつくられた〈屋根つき通りぬけ〉商店街のことであるが、一階に商店、二階以上はアパルトマンとなっている建物である。半世紀のちのギャラリー・デュ・エメルス・エ・ド・ランドリは今日の百貨店に近いものになっているが、一八〇〇年中頃のグラン・コルベール正面の中二階までが板ガラスで覆われていて、開放的な印象がアピールされている。なお、中央ホールをガラス張りにするというやりかたはヴィル・ド・パリやヴィル・ド・フランスに見ることができた。この頃にはパッサージュという形式のアーケードの左右に個人商店が各所に登場してきたが、そこにはカフェ、衣料品店、レストランなどが並んでいたので、さながら小さな百貨店と言ってよかった。

一八〇八年にはリヴォリ通りとサン・トノレ通りを結ぶパッサージュ・ドゥロルム、一八一一年にはパレ・ロワイヤル Palais Royal 近くのパッサージュ・モンテスキュー Passage Montesquieu、一八二二年にはパッサージュ・オペラ Passage Opera がつくられた。とりわけ、一八二八年から一八三〇年にかけてはきわめつきのギャラルー・ドレルアンが完成されたが、これらの商店街は鉄とガラスという新しい素材を応用した過渡期的産物であっても、複合的な多目的性、つまり現代の大衆の要求を意識したものとして注目されるのである。

オースマンに先だって七月王朝の知事ランビュトーはガス灯を導入したパリに固定した公共の照明が設

けられたのは一六六七年、ルイ十四世によって千七百個のランテルヌ灯の街灯設置を命じたときのことで、パリから危険な夜を追放しようとしたのである。ガス灯は劇場やパッサージュなど広々とした室内空間に限られた。ちなみにそれまでは車道の中央に流れていた排水溝への側溝への変更、街路樹の増大などの改善を行なうということもあったが、オースマンの時代に完成されるレ・アール（中央市場）の整備がランビュトーによって始められた。その名残りとしてランビュトー通りがあるが、当時としては驚くほどに広い道路で、幅は十三メートルであり、レ・アール Les Halles から東北に向って通され、鉄道もこの時期に開通を破壊してつくられたのである。これはオースマン化の先駆として注目されるが、鉄道もこの時期に開通することになった。オースマンはサン・ラザール駅に入る鉄道をマドレーヌ寺院まで敷いてこの寺院を駅として使おうとしていた話もあったという。

パリは周知のようにセーヌ河に深くかかわって発達してきた街である。ケルト系のパリジ族がセーヌ河を上り下りしているときに手頃の中洲をみつけてそこに住みついたときに始まったといわれている。そこはルテテチアと名づけられているが、もともとは水に囲まれた住いというほどの意味をもったという。パリ市庁の紋章に示されているように、パリはセーヌ河とその水上交易が生み出した都市であった。シテ島には市庁舎とノートルダム寺院という二つの主要な建物がセーヌ河の両岸に配置されているが、セーヌ河の水は上下水道ともに用いられていた。パリよりの下流の集中排水のための大下水道工事が行なわれた。注目されることはパリの地番もきめており、河筋と平行する道路は東が起点となって、西に向って地番が大きくなっていく。道路の右側が偶数、左側が奇数番地である。ちなみに、パリの建物には琺瑯の青地に白い数字が入った地番の標識がつくられたが、これは王政復古時代の知事シャブロルのパリ整備事業によるものであり、この時期になって歩道がたくさんつくられた。

オースマン計画の波動として思い起こされてくるのは銀座煉瓦街である。明治五年の銀座大火直後の復興対策には見るものが少なくなかった。前述のように近代的不燃性建築物の建造こそ焦眉の急務であり、復興計画が東京府知事由利公正たちによって討議されることになったわけで、その折は外国の都市の道路幅も問題になり、銀座煉瓦街の構想ではとりわけそれが大きく取り上げられることとなったのである。

じつはオースマン計画においても道路はきわめて重要であり、ナポレオン三世がみずから作成した整備計画図でもパリの道路は工事順に色分けしつくられていたことからもうかがえる。いずれにせよ、道路の整備はきわめて重要視されていたのである。

道路の整備とともに歩道のそれも忘れてはならないが、車道の幅の割合も都市の美観と深くかかわることとなる。やがて自動車の混雑軽減化の問題に車道化が起きるに至った。

銀座煉瓦街建設の時点ではまだこれというほどの交通事情がみられなかったが、オースマンの時代では辻馬車だけでも四千台あり、小型馬車の公害は眼にあまるものがあったようである。

銀座煉瓦街建設に際して当時来日していたお傭い外国人の専門家の意見を徴取したが、その記録は今日、東京都公文書館、早稲田大学図書館などに所蔵されている。その内容は街区を整えて道路を拡幅すること、建築法規を制定することと建築物の不燃化を訴えているである。

たとえばルイ・フローラン Lui Flaurent は銀座煉瓦街の根本方針として道路の拡張こそ防火の根幹であることを強調しているのである。人道車道を設けて中央だけに車を通して左右の道にはその通行を禁じて人間だけを通行させて、市街建築の統一を図るという計画がみられるが、まさにパリなど欧米諸都市にみられる街路の姿がそこに見てとれるのである。

銀座煉瓦街には馬車道が設けられて両側には花樹を植え、人道の境として煉瓦石が敷かれ、夜は瓦斯燈

でまるで昼のように街路を照らした。銀座煉瓦街の表通りには街路樹には桜、楓、松が植えられたが、とりわけ桜は日本人には親しみ深い植物とみなされていたようである。もっとも、当初銀座通りを象徴する植物として柳が広く植えられたことは知られている。なお、一八七四年に来日したインリー・フォールズ（一八四三一一九三〇）は銀座通りの両側には松、アカシヤ、梅が植えられていたことを伝えているので、明治二十年前後にすべて柳に代ったのである。

街路樹が必ずしも桜、楓、松の三種類ではなかったことを知らなくてはならない。ちなみに、明治二十一年の市区改正施行で京橋から銀座五丁目まで煉瓦舗装は撤去されてコンクリート平板舗装になった。

銀座の風物詩としてガス灯が点火されたり、アーク灯もともされるようになると、銀座の夜は不夜城のように煌々と輝いて、文明開化の訪れに酔い痴らされるのであった。

銀座煉瓦街がつくられたとき、どのような人びとが購入したのか、きわめて興味深いことである。完成されたところから順次に払い下げられていったのだが、その価格は結構高く、一度に全額支払いすることができる者は少なく、一五〇か月賦ということとなった。それでも煉瓦家屋を購入できたのは裕福な者だったものとみられる。したがって、大火前に銀座に住んでいた人の大半は銀座を去っていったとみられる。この現象は前述のようなパリのオースマン化現象を想起させるものであり、昔から住んでいた場所に住めなくなった貧民が出てくることととなったのである。

銀座煉瓦街の払下げは一等、二等、三頭家屋の順に行なわれていったが、空屋も結構多かったし、途中で売却されるケースも少なくなかった。政府としては統一ある景観を維持してそれに合わない建物は認めないという立場をとったので、完成した建物は払下げ希望者は少なく、空屋のままに建築工事を続行した

が、未着手地域もほぼ明治十年初頭には完成した。

銀座煉瓦街建設は総工費約八十五万円という巨費を投じて進められたのであるが、これは当時の国家予算の二七万分の一強に当たるものであった。帝都・東京を不燃都市にしようとする防災事業に端を発したとはいえ、明治政府の条約改正のための欧化政策によるものであったことはいうまでもない。

銀座煉瓦街はたしかに文明都市として国家が建造した日本最初の欧化道路の街であり、統一された市街の形成されたのである。外国人の設計で二階建総煉瓦の街が大火災を契機として出現したわけであるが、仔細に見ていくとき「オースマン計画」に通ずるものを見出さないわけにはいかない。オースマンが手がけた工事としては道路工事が顕著である。オペラ通りがその一つであるが、それは東京の場合銀座通りであり、のちに「銀ブラ」として人びとを楽しませた散歩道の発祥の地がそこに生まれたのである。

銀座にはアスファルト舗装道路がのちにつくられるが、パリにもアカズム舗装、すなわち今日のアスファルト道路がつくられたのである。

銀座通りには多数の商店が軒を並べたが、銀座大通りは連屋、つまり長屋形式としてすべて一等家屋とし、表には連柱を建て、一間ないし四尺五寸の歩廊、すなわちアーケードをつくった。横町は二等家屋、裏通りは三等家屋とし、一階の表には円柱が立ち並び、その上はバルコニーになっていて、窓はフランス式で外開きになっていたと云われている。ちなみに、築地ホテルは内開きだったが、このホテル館よりは一歩進んだホテルとしてこの形式を取り入れたのである。

銀座煉瓦街は全区すべて連屋二階建の同一様式であるということは、外国人が賞讃したほど外国風化し

た統一ある街区をつくりあげていたことを示すものとして興味深い。銀座通りといえば並木通りであるが、パリには四列の並木をもつシャール・ルノアール Charles Renoir 通りがつくられている。穴の中に根をおろしていく新式の植樹機が用いられたようである。ちなみに、パリに初めて並木が植えられたのは一六八三年と伝えられている。また、ブールヴァールが一般の人びとの歩く道になったのは十八世紀になってのことである。

いずれにせよ、パリといえば、まっすぐの大きな道路がきわめて機能的におたがいに結びつけられて新しい動脈をつくりあげていったことを知らなくてはならない。その点、時代の文化をつねに反映していくこととなり、あたかも大通りを歩いていくといつしかさまざまな情報が伝えられてくる街、銀座にどこか通じてくるようになっていったのである。

自転車、自動車、乗合馬車、さらには地下鉄、バスなどの交通手段の発達がパリと同様に銀座にも大きな変革をもたらすこととなる。いつまでも大通りをのんびりと散策することは許されなくなったのは交通渋滞に悩む大都会の宿命なのであろうか。

銀座煉瓦街のアーケード列柱の基準的寸法や街区の大きさなどを参考にして今日、立面図が作成されているが、きわめて資料が少ないために推測の域をまぬかれない部分があったという。銀座煉瓦街は当初純西洋風に建物はつくられたのであるが、次第に日本一の繁華街に成長していったことで さまざまな要素が取り加えられていった。明治初期に建設された煉瓦建造物はすべて敷地の所有と関係なしに同じ柱間をもって連屋が建てられていた。そのために連屋の一軒ずつの建物と敷地所有関係のずれがみられることがあり、ときには一軒の建物が二人の所有者にまたがって建てられることも少なくなかったという。

パリでは同じ階を複数の住宅が共有するということはかなり後年のことであり、建物は階段ごとに一つの単位、所有区分であり、共通の立面で統一されたような建物にしても、独立した屋根がその区分を示しているのである。一六〇七年の王令で木造建築が禁止されたが、十九世紀になり、木の代りに鉄と煉瓦が使われるまではパリの建物の床は木造だった。

アーケードのついた街区として有名なのはアンリ四世のヴォージェ Voges 広場と革命期のコロマ Colonne 通りがあるが、これらはパリのリヴォリ通りの設計に大きな影響をあたえたものとして忘れてはならない。パレ・ロワイヤルは大革命前、ルイ・フィリップ・ドルレアン Lui Philippe d'Orléan が複合建築物として整備したパリでももっとも賑わった場所であった。とりわけ広い中庭を囲む一階のアーケード街はレストラン、カフェ、宝石店、洋服などの一流店が軒を並べており、階上は大部分が高級アパルトマンであったが、やがてグラン・ブール大通りの賑わいが始まると、パレ・ロワイヤルの繁栄は下火になってくる。リヴォリ Rivoli 通りが計画された時代がパレ・ロワイヤル最盛期であったのである。

リヴォリ通りで一番活気があり、雰囲気があるのはテュイルリー Tuileries 庭園に面した部分である。今日も沢山の商店、土産物が並んでいるが、大衆が自由に通れるアーケードはパリでもきわめて大切な役割を果たしている。その意味では「パリ大改造」計画の重要な部分となっていたのである。オースマンがリヴォリ通りの貫通に精力的に取り組んだのもそのためであったことはうなずけよう。ガラス屋根つきの中庭をもつ大きなルーヴル・ホテル Hôtel Louvre がわずか一年の工期で完成したというのも、そのあたりの事情を反映しているのだろう。

リヴォリ通りに沿った連結棟でテュイルリ、ルーヴル両宮殿の北側を繋ぎ、ナポレオン三世の銅像をその広場のまん中に置いたが、その工事は突貫工事で進められ、夜間には電気のアーク灯が使用された。ち

なみに、日本では明治十五年に銀座・大倉組の前で二千灯のアーク灯が藤岡市助によってともされたところで、今日、パリを代表する大通りといえばシャンゼリゼ Champs-Élysées であるが、当初は金持ちの御用達の馬具屋ぐらいが店を開いていたにすぎなかった。いわば地域サーヴィスの食料品店、たとえばレストランなどにすぎなかったが、やがて自動車メーカーがウインドーを開くようになるし、香水店、カバン店、新聞社などが建ち並び、商業ビル、カフェ、映画館が人びとを魅きつける街づくりに貢献していったのである。もっとも、その反面では、オースマン化の効果は貧民の大半をパリに追い出すというマイナス現象を生んでいたということを知らなくてはならない。

パリの発展の軌跡ということを考えるとき、たしかにオースマン計画における道路網の発達は無視できないが、一八三七年に開通したサン・ジェルマン線の鉄道を忘れることはできない。鉄道と並んで駅舎の偉容はパリの人びとの眼に大きな驚きをあたえたようで、モネ Monet はサン・ラザール駅を七点描いている。

鉄道の駅舎は近代のパリの重要な出発点であり、ホテルとレストランが完備していた。リヨン Lion 駅には一九〇一年開店したレストラン、トラン・ブルー Train Bleu のアール・ヌーヴォー調のインテリアが有名であるが、旅の楽しみを覚えた市民階級の姿が思い出されるものがある。

パリにオースマンによって新しい街並みがつくられていったが、その大通りにはあちこちにカフェから生み出されることとなった。カフェはたんなるコーヒーを飲むためだけの場所ではない。ときにはさまざまな話題を語らい、芸術・思想を談じ合い、音楽に耳を傾けるという場である。もっとも、カフェではときには啓蒙思想が確立され、フランス革命へと育っていったという経緯もあり、日本のカフェとはきわめて異なった歴史をもっているのである。

日本の場合、銀座にも明治四十四年三月、松山省三によってカフェ・パウリスタ Café Paulista が開かれている。名づけ親は小山内薫で、常連客は森鷗外、永井荷風、島村抱月、北原白秋などで、コーヒー一杯十銭、カクテル二十五銭であった。大正十一年、震災で銀座に移転したが、これは文学的サロンであり、パリのカフェとは必ずしも同じではなかった。昭和二〇年三月まで営業。カフェではないが、銀座には資生堂パーラーも開店し、銀ブラ族の憩の場を提供することとなる。ある意味ではパリのプロムナードが銀座に移動、反映してきたように思われて興味深いものがある。

ところで、銀座大通にはパリのような河岸はない。銀座とは、煉瓦街が誕生した区画、つまり堀割に囲まれた北は京橋川、西は外堀川、南は汐留川、東は三原橋を流れる三十間堀に囲まれた範囲を指す区域である。京橋川、外堀川、汐留川、三十間堀などの川に接しているとはいえ、セーヌ河とはまったく別の河川が銀座に流れていたわけではない。したがって、銀座はパリのような街並みが始めから構成されていたわけではない。むしろ整然とした形態の街であり、区画整理されている。明治二年、新両替町一〜四丁目が銀座一〜四丁目に町名変更されるというようにして編入、統合も行なわれていき、銀座一丁目から八丁目、さらには銀座西一丁目から八丁目まで統合されていったのである。

銀座の町名の由来もさまざまで、工事の埋立ての大名の国名、開発者名、職人たちの職種から採ったものもあるというふうだが、やがて銀座、西銀座に統合・整理して今日に至っている。パリの場合、街路は一般に「ブールヴァール」、「アヴニュー」、「リュ」の三種類がある。ブールヴァルは取り壊された城壁の跡につくられた環状の大通りであり、「グラン・ブールヴァール」はその典型である。アヴニューは記念建造物につながるまっすぐな大通りがそれで、シャン・ゼリゼ大通りが有名である。

銀座大通はガス灯の列のために長くまっすぐに遠方まで見通されたが、路地裏は薄暗かったという。夜

になると、表通りを除いては暗く、婦女子はほとんど外出しなかったという。銀座通りは両側に整然と建物が並んでいるために柳など街路樹がガス灯の影を映すこともあったようである。

銀座通には、パリの街路にはみられない「廊下的街路」（リュ・コリドール Rue Corridor）と呼ばれ、軒線より上の屋根の形、道路の境界から突出してよい廂や跳ね出し部分を規制するものとなるものがある。銀座煉瓦街建設にはオースマン計画の模倣があることは新しい道路貫通一つを取りあげてもわかることである。大きな建物をつくるには多量の石材が必要である。テュイルリ宮殿を建てたために右岸の石切り場はすでに底をついていたので左岸の石を使わなくてはならなくなった。そのためにテュイルリからセーヌ河の対岸まで渡し船が開かれたが、渡し船の場所から石切場にまっすぐの道がつくられた。今日も残っているリュ・デュ・バック Rue du bac（渡し船通り）である。

セーヌ河左岸の城壁外に一五七二年後に堀がつくられたが、それが市街地の拡大を止める上ではまったく効果がなく、修道院がつぎつぎに建てられていった。三十間堀は当初銀座一丁目のところで鉤の手に曲っていたが、煉瓦街建設に当たってそれをまっすぐにするすげ替えを行なったために堀の開削、埋めたてを行なったというような工事を余儀なくされたこともあったのである。

銀座煉瓦街には前述のように並木道が設けられたが、パリのテュイルリの大通りにも楡の木を二重に植えた並木通がつくられて「テュイルリー通り」と名づけられ、これがのちに「シャンゼリゼ」（一七〇九年以後）と呼ばれた。

オースマン計画では道路の建設には大きな力を注ぎこんだが、銀座煉瓦街建設でもお偉い外国人のウォートルスは道路の等級に合わせて煉瓦家屋も三等級にわけ、十五間幅の一等道路には三階建て一等家屋、八間幅の二等道路には二階建て二等家屋、三間幅の三等道路には平屋建て三等家屋を建てることとしたと

いうが、建物はなるべく連屋形式、つまり長屋とし、表に列柱を建て、一間ないし四尺五寸の表廊（アーケード）をつくった。

銀座煉瓦街は突然の大火がもたらした不燃都市建設から生まれた事業に起因するものであり、まったく予測しないことが重なり合ってつくり出された「事件」であったといえよう。もともとは焦土と化した場所に新しく不燃建造物として煉瓦街を建造しようとしたわけであり、なにをモデルにするのかもわからず試行錯誤ときに発足した銀座煉瓦街であった。大火の瓦礫の処理も大きな仕事であり、その苦労はいかばかりであったことだろう。そんなことに思い悩んでいる暇もなく、着々と工事を進めてき、銀座表通りが竣工していった。当初、一階には列柱が並び、二階にはバルコニーがつくられ、整然と同じ様式の街並みが並んでいる。それが列柱部分と店に取りこみ、思い思い改造に改造を行なっていったので、次第に元来同じ様式の街並みが別の建物のように見えてきたといわれている。結局、西洋風の煉瓦家屋は日本人には容易に親しむことができなかったが、煉瓦家屋の列柱部分の引込みはあくまでも庇地、つまり公道ではなく、私有地であったために自由に使ってもあたりまえという思いがあったようである。裏通りは嫌応いなしに汚なくなってきたので、次第に粗末な板囲いをしたりしたこともあり、円柱と円柱の間に粗末な店も現れると始末だった。そんなわけで、新しく窓を切りひらかれたり、模様替えすることを東京府で禁ずる達しを出し、条約改正を行なうという本来の目的を果たすために必要な街並みの整然さに立ち向っていったのである。

銀座煉瓦街が誕生したあと、明治四年末に米欧回覧の旅に出た岩倉使節団の人びとが帰国してきた。また欧米に留学していた者たちも帰国し始めたが、それらの中には銀座に家を持って活躍する人たちも少なくなかった。彼らは欧米の地に足を踏み入れてきた眼で煉瓦街の繁華ぶりを見たわけで、その評判はそれ

なりに興味深いものがある。概していえば、評判は悪くなかった。銀座煉瓦街はまさしく「東京第一ノ街巷ナリ」（由利兼次郎編『東京自慢』）に取りあげられるに足る都会であり、街路であったのである。パリのオペラ通りやシャンゼリゼにも劣らない大通りであった。その大通りにガス灯が点灯するや、文明開化が到来したことを実感したことだろう。

結局、銀座煉瓦街の原型は欧米の不燃建築に由来しているが、そのことはすでに明治七年六月刊行の服部誠一『新東京繁昌記』の文章に看取されることでもある。「石室は則ち英京の倫敦を模し、街道は則ち仏京の巴黎に擬す」というようにモデルはロンドンであり、パリであることがあきらかにされていたのである。洋風建築であり、煉瓦を積み、壁四方に囲むけれど、柱は使わないという建築法であるという新しさは当時の日本人の眼をどれほど驚かせたことだろうか。とりわけ煉瓦工事による建造物は文明開化の象徴として人びとの関心をひいたことだろう。

銀座煉瓦街の特徴は文字通り赤煉瓦の舗道であるが、銀座通りは最初の馬車道と人道の分離が有名である。加えて人道が赤煉瓦で舗装されているところがきわめてユニークである。そこにはパリの石畳を思わせるものがある。

今日、銀座ブラする人びとはあまり多くないだろう。というより「銀ブラ」という言葉さえ死語となっている。だが、銀座四丁目の街角に建っている服部時計店の大時計台は銀座を象徴するモニュメントとして多くの人びとの眼に映っていることだろう。もっとも、服部時計店の時計台は昭和七年に登場したのである。

銀座煉瓦街建設の時代には「八官町の大時計」と呼ばれた四角形の時計が明治九年四月に小村伝次郎時計店の屋上に設置されて評判になった。「新橋八景」の一つである。ちなみに、銀座四丁目の京屋時計店銀座支店に古時計塔があったが、大正二年に建物取壊しのためにいまはない。

---

03 ― オースマン計画の波動――銀座煉瓦街の比較文化史的考察

なお、のちのシャルル五世が宮殿の四角い塔に大時計をつくらせたが、これがパリでつくられた大時計の最初のものである。

銀座四丁目西側街並みの立面図が工学院大学建築科初田研究室の骨折で作成されている。柱間を同じくした連屋の家屋が建物と敷地の所有関係にずれがみられることがわかる。いずれにせよ、このような立面図を含めて、銀座の時の姿を偲ぶには写真などを手がかりにするほかないが、これはパリについても同様である。

パリの場合、オースマン計画によって整備されていった街並がきちんと次第に顔を覗かせていくとき、そこにフランスの文化と歴史の重みを感じさせてくれるのを知らなくてはならない。たとえば、パリ改造計画が進行していったとき、ノートルダム Notre-Dame 寺院の容姿が浮かび上ってくるのである。オースマン計画の一環として一八五八年にはシャトレ広場が拡張され、周辺の建物とともに取り壊され、その跡地に二つの劇場が建てられることとなった。今日のシャトレ劇場とテアトル・ド・ラ・ヴィル（市民劇場）Théâtre de la Ville である。古さと新しさが共存する街、パリがオースマン計画によって大きくクローズ・アップされてきたのである。

そういえば、日本では街路に個人名をつけることは少ないが、パリの場合、芸術家、科学者、探検家、政治家など多岐にわたっている。外国人の名も珍しくない。街を歩いていると、いたるところに有名人の名を見出す。その意味では退屈することのない街であり、それもまたパリである。

銀座の場合、町名はあっても、街路名はきわめて無味であり、記号化されたものであり、面白さはない。その点、パリの街路は楽しい。みゆき通りなどは例外である。

最後に、オースマン計画の真の狙いは、オースマンがみずから語っているというように、狭い道路を広

げて移動とバリケードを設営の防止をはかったことにあったという単純なものであったとは考えられない。オースマンがパリの改造にあたって行なったのはロンドンにならって道路の改修に着手したのであるが、それはパリの美化と浄化であり、その結果として公園がつくられ、下水渠が整えられ、広い直線道路が設けられ、古い老朽化した建物が建て替えられるというような思い切った断行が行なわれたのである。

このオースマンのパリ改造に対しては必ずしも賛成する人びとがいたばかりかいたわけではない。パリの下町の情緒をこわしたともいうような非難もあったが、たしかにパリの都市の近代化にもましてその美を損なっただけでなく市民生活を機能化するものではなかったという批判を受けることとなっている。

十八世紀のフランスは都市も田舎も臭かった。とくにパリの悪臭は頂点に達していた。その最大の悪臭源は排泄物であり、その処理のために道路には下水溝を設けたが、その整備は十九世紀末のことであった。オースマン計画は不衛生と犯罪の駆逐、この二つの大きな目的のために企てられたことでもあった。一八三二年のコレラの大流行が大きなひきがねとなったが、加えて七月王政下の度重なる争議と移動もその計画に拍車をかける大きな力となってたのである。まっすぐな大きな道路は移動の阻止には有効であり、為政者にはきわめて効果的なことであったのである。

オースマン計画にはパリ行政上の目的もあったわけであるが、環境整備もまた見落としてはならないものの一つであった。その意味では銀座煉瓦街建設は不慮の火災によってもたらされた都市計画に起因する成果であったわけであり、両者を同一視することはできない。つまり、異質の現象としてどれを捉えなくてはならないことを認めなくてはならないようである。あえていえば、似て非なる都市計画発想の理念がその根元に横たわっていたようである。パリの場合、それぞれの都市の長い歴史に基く民衆の生活から生

まれてきたさまざまな現象が今日なおも続いているのである。パリにはパリなりに、また、銀座なりに都市としてのユニークな文化も人情も育くまれてきているのである。

オースマン計画は決してオースマンだけが計画したわけではない。きわめて必然性を帯びてナポレオン三世に命ぜられて始動した一大イヴェントであった。その点では銀座煉瓦街とはいささか動機を異にして行なわれた事業であった。もちろん、銀座煉瓦街建設には不平等条約の改正という外交、政治上の切迫詰った目的もあり、近代国家の体裁を整えるには首都・東京を不燃都市とすることもまた焦眉の課題にもなっていたのである。

オースマン計画と銀座煉瓦街建設とは直接関係はないが、両者を対比して都市構造論に一瞥を加えることとも比較文化研究に多少なり寄与することとはならないだろうか。

（二〇〇一年十二月二十五日稿）

[参考文献]

宇田英男 『誰がパリをつくったのか』 朝日新聞社（朝日選書）、一九九四年。

『一〇〇年前のパリ 一』マール社編集部編、一九九六年。

『一〇〇年前のパリ 二』マール社編集部編、一九九六年。

『銀座の街並展──世紀をこえる銀座の活力』銀座の街並展実行委員会、二〇〇〇年。

宝木範義 『パリ物語』新潮社（新潮社選書）、一九八四年。

石井洋二郎 『パリ──都市の記憶を探る』筑摩書房（ちくま新書）、一九九七年。

野口孝一 『銀座物語──煉瓦街を探訪する』中央公論社（中公新書）、一九九七年。

鹿島茂 『パリ時間旅行』筑摩書房、一九九三年。

メシエ著 原宏編訳 『一八世紀パリ生活誌』上・下 岩波書店（文庫本）、一九八九年六月／一九八九年。

04

蘆花の『不如帰』とジェイムズの『鳩の翼』の比較考察

生活文化の視点から

秋山正幸

　徳冨蘆花の『不如帰』は明治三十一年（一八九八）から翌年まで国民新聞に掲載され、一般大衆に深く感動を与え、劇や映画にもなった小説である。

　明治三十年八月、蘆花は当時高級別荘地であった逗子の柳屋という旅館に滞在していた。丁度、同じ時期に、陸軍軍人の未亡人福家(ふけ)安子が子供を連れて同じ旅館に逗留した。蘆花の妻愛子はその未亡人と話をする機会が多くなり、やがて両家は親しく付き合うようになった。

　蘆花は福家未亡人から身の上ばなしを聞く機会を得た。安子は四国の香川県の生まれで、同郷の福家家の若い陸軍軍人に嫁ぎ、六人の子供をもうけた。夫は大山巌中将（のちに大将、元帥）に目を掛けられ、

中佐に昇進し、日清戦争の折には大山大将と共に出征するが、戦病死する。話題が大山大将一家のことに移り、大将の娘信子の悲しい運命の話に終始した。信子は大将の先妻の長女で、十七歳の春に青年官吏三島弥太郎の妻になった。夫はアメリカに留学し、修士の学位を取得して帰国し、二十七歳の時に信子と結婚したのである。信子は結婚後間もなく肺結核に罹り、離婚させられたのであった。彼女は大山家に引き取られ、療養生活を送ったが、薬石の効なく、二十歳にも充たぬ短い生涯を閉じたのである。

蘆花は福家夫人から大山信子の悲しい身の上ばなしを聞き、この話を参考にして、『不如帰』を書いたと思われる。その時に、さらにこの話に、女性なるが故に傷心の果てに悲しく死んでいく物語、ワシントン・アーヴィング（Washington Irving, 1783-1859）の短編「ブロークン・ハート」（"The Broken Heart"）のイメージをも重ね合わせていたと考えられるのである。蘆花がアーヴィングの「ブロークン・ハート」の影響を受けているということについては、中野好夫氏も指摘しているところである。蘆花は「ブロークン・ハート」を読んだ感想を『蘆花全集』第十九巻に収められている「偶感偶想」の中の〈アーヴィング氏の「ブロークン・ハート」を読んで〉と題するエッセイの中で、

　婦人の心は悲哀の庫なり、苦痛の家なり。漏れ敢て其哀を告げず、然れ共其心中に深く隠れたる悲哀の念は恰も薔薇花中の小蟲の如く、其淡紅の両頬を噛み去るなり。漏れ更に其苦を云はず、然れ共其苦辛の情は、猶月前の雲の如く、其星の如き一双の明眸を曇らしむるなり。落ちて開くは薔薇なり。此人生の花、人生の月に到ては吁再び見る能はざるを亦明かなるは月なり。吁雲去て亦明かなるは月なり。古往今來六千年、幾何の紅顔か能く其の顰まざる眉を墓中に齎し得たる。一度愛情の海に破船しては終に浮ぶ瀬もなく、空しく身を永遠の淵に投じたるもの夫れ幾何ぞや。幾十

年の心盡しも一朝水泡に屬し、胸に悲惨の歴史を封じて、之を墓中にまで伴ひたる者夫れ幾何ぞや。郎が身は無定河邊の骨となりて、宵々の夢は泣いて邊城の月に漂泊ふもの夫れ幾何ぞや。愛消え寵衰へて玉階の良夜に牽牛織女を羨む者それ幾何ぞや。影も殘さぬ大空は、戀しき人の記念に眺め（大空は戀しき人の記念かは、物思ふ毎に眺めけるらむ）番離れぬ鴛鴦は契りも深きためしに引かれ……

人生婦人の身となる勿れ。百年の苦樂は他人に依る、と樂天の言果して然る耶。抑も亦非なる耶。呼紅顔は薄命の形、苦勞は女人の影、爾が悲哀萬斛の泉、之を斟で輿に泣く者は夫れ誰ぞ。

と彼の女性に對する同情の気持を述べている。「ブロークン・ハート」はある少女の悲しい物語である。その少女はあるアイルランド独立運動の青年闘士を熱愛する。しかし、青年は捕らえられて処刑される。少女は傷心の果てに憔悴して死亡する。アーヴィングは「ブロークン・ハート」の冒頭の一節で次のように書いている。

打ちあけて言えば、わたしはそのような恋わずらいが男性にとって致命的になることさえあると信ずるのだ。しかし、わたしは人が失恋して心が傷つき、命を絶つことさえあると信ずるのだ。ただ多くの美しい女性が、若くして力が萎え、そのためにあの世に旅立たなければならなくなるとかく信ずるのである。（六一頁）

蘆花は「ブロークン・ハート」を読んで「人生婦人の身となる勿れ」と感想を書いているが、この言葉

は、結婚後間もなく肺結核となって離婚させられた大山大将の長女信子の境遇にも符合するものである。蘆花は『ブロークン・ハート』を読み、女性の弱い立場を知り、それに加えて、信子という女性が、明治時代の日本の封建的家族制度下において、いかに悲しい運命にあったかを痛感し、肺結核におかされて、傷心の果てに死んでいった彼女の姿を小説に形象化したかったのだと思う。その思いが『不如帰』という作品となって結晶したと言えよう。

『不如帰』の中の女主人公浪子は、名声を博する片岡中将の長女である。浪子が結婚した相手は男爵海軍少尉川島武男である。武男の父通武は病死し、彼の母のお慶は五十三歳で、リューマチの痛みに時々襲われる以外は元気である。

この作品のプロットはそれほど複雑なものではない。浪子と武男は貴族院議員加藤俊明子爵夫妻の媒酌によって結婚したのであった。加藤子爵夫人は片岡中将の先妻の姉である。

この物語の冒頭の一節では、上州の伊香保温泉に滞在中の武男と新妻浪子の仕合わせな場景が流麗な文語体で描写されている。その後間もなく情況が一転する。武男の母は、浪子が当時不治の病とされていた肺結核に罹っていることを知ると、出征中の武男の了解もえないで、浪子を離婚させてしまう。浪子は実家の敷地内に建てられた離家に住むことになる。

明治時代には、肺結核は伝染病と考えられていたただけではなく、遺伝による病気であると恐られていたのである。一八八二年にドイツの細菌学者ロベルト・コッホ（Robert Koch, 一八四三－一九一〇）は、肺病は結核菌によって感染されることを立証したのであるが、当時の日本ではそのような西洋医学の知識を十分に持っておらず、世間には肺結核の遺伝説が根強く広まっていたのである。それ故に、長男の妻が肺結核に罹ると、その家族に危機をもたらすことになる。長男が家督を相続し、その長子が跡継ぎになる

のが当時の家族制度の特徴であった。したがって、長男の嫁が不治の病に罹れば、当然跡継ぎを生むことができず、新妻が離婚させられるか、彼女の死後後妻を迎える場合が多かった。

封建的な家族制度の下では、長男が家督を相続し、長子を跡継ぎにすることが最も重要なことであり、夫婦相互の愛情はその下位におかれていた。浪子と武男は当時の封建的家族制度の犠牲になり、離婚させられたと言える。この小説は浪子、武男、片岡中将、姪の幾等の善人のグループと、千々岩、山木、姑川島お慶等の悪人グループに分けられて対比して描かれており、愛すべき善人たちと、憎むべき悪人たちの二つのグループに類別されている点を考えると、通俗小説的な要素があることは否めない。しかし、この小説には、近代文学史上重要な問題が含まれていることも事実である。というのは、この明治時代において、女性が蔑視されている日本の封建的家族制度に対する女主人公の悲痛な抵抗の姿が描かれていると言えるからである。浪子の臨終の時の描写を考察してみよう。

ほのかなる笑は浪子の唇に上りしが、たちまち色なき頬のあたり紅（くれない）をさし来たり、胸は波うち、燃ゆばかり熱き涙はらはらと苦しき息つき、

「ああつらい！つらい！もう――生まれはしませんよ。――あああ！」

眉（まゆ）あつめ胸をおさえて、浪子は身をもだえつ。急に医を呼びつつ赤酒を含ませんとする加藤夫人の手にすがりて半ば起き上がり、生命（いのち）を縮むるせきとともに、肺を絞って一盞（さん）の紅血を吐きつ。

浪子は口を閉じ、目を閉じ、影は次第にその面（おもて）をおおわんとす。中将はさらに進みて、昏々（こんこん）として臥床（とこ）の上に倒れぬ。（二一六頁）

「浪、何も言いのこす事はないか。――しっかりせい」

なつかしき声に呼びかえされて、わずかに開ける目は加藤子爵夫人に注ぎつ。夫人は浪子の手を執り、
「浪さん、何もわたしがうけ合った。安心して、母さんの所においで」
かすかなる微咲の唇に上ると見れば、見る見る瞼は閉じて、眠るがごとく息絶えぬ。
さし入る月は蒼白き面を照らして、微咲はなお唇に浮かべり。されど浪子は永く眠れるなり。

（二一八頁）

浪子は封建的家族制度によって虐げられていたが故に、臨終の床で悶え苦しみながら、「もう——もう婦人何ぞに——生まれはしませんよ」と叫んだのである。この小説で、蘆花は、女性が長男に嫁ぎ、不治の病に罹った時に、どのような苦しみに遭遇するかを日本の家庭生活の実情と関連させながら描いているのである。

浪子は八歳の時に母を失い、父は士の家系の女性を後妻に迎えた。彼女は英国に留学し、男まさりの上に西洋風の価値観を身につけていた。父は冗談半分に副官の難波に「なあ難波君、学問の出来る細君は持つものじゃごわはん、いやさんざんな目にあわされますぞ」（十四頁）と言ったことがある。明治時代の女性は家事に従事し、夫に従順であることが求められた。浪子は継母に従順であるようにつとめるのであるが、実母の生活様式を踏襲しがちであった。それ故に、浪子は継母に「本当に彼女はちっともさっぱりした所がない、いやに執念な人だよ」（十六頁）とののしられる始末であった。作者は「浪子は実に日陰の花なりけり」（十六頁）と描写している。このような生活環境の中で育った浪子を、浪子本人はもとより、父中将も、継母も、伯母も、幾も安堵の胸をなでおろが川島武男と結婚した時には、

浪子と武男の伊香保滞在は二人の結婚生活において幸福の絶頂の時期であった。蘆花は二人の仕合わせな日々を伊香保の風光明媚な自然環境を背景にして鮮明に描くことに成功している。

武男と結婚した浪子は、束の間の幸福な結婚生活を送ったにすぎなかった。彼女は肺結核におかされ、出征から帰った武男は、浪子が思いもよらず離婚させられている事情を知り、母に抵抗するのだが、当時の日本の生活文化の伝統的仕来りを打破することはできなかった。浪子と武男の愛は純愛であった。武男は浪子への思い出の中に生きていくことになったのである。

次に人間の愛情、欲望、徳性、生と死という観点からジェイムズの『鳩の翼』(*The Wings of the Dove*, 1902) についてこの小説を考察したいと思う。ジェイムズは作品の序文の中で「人生を楽しむ豊かな能力を自覚しながら、若くして不治の病に犯され、この世界に魅惑されながら間もなく死ななければならない人という着想」(五頁) でこの小説を書いたと述べている。この小説の若い人とはミリー・サール (Milly Theale) である。ミリー・サールと関係する人物として、ケイト・クロイ (Kate Croy)、マートン・デンシャー (Merton Densher)、モード・ラウダー夫人 (Mrs. Maud Lowder)、ストリンガム夫人 (Mrs. Stringham) やマーク卿 (Lord Mark) などが登場する。ミリーとストリンガム夫人はアメリカ人であるが、その他の人物はイギリス人である。

美しい英国女性ケイトは経済的にはあまり裕福ではない新聞記者デンシャーとひそかに婚約する。ケイトの父や姉や伯母は、ケイトが金持ちの人と結婚することを望む。それ故に、二人の結婚は暗礁に乗り上げてしまう。思案の末、ケイトは、デンシャーが、巨万の富をもっているが不治の病でやがて死ぬ運命に

あるミリーと結婚するように仕向ける。ケイトはミリーの死後、デンシャーとミリーの莫大な遺産を手に入れたいと考えたのである。なぜ、ケイトはそのような策略を考えたのであろうか。それは伯母や姉の差し金だったのである。姉はケイトに「私たちすべてのものの立場を考えれば、あなたは自分をむだに投げ捨ててしまう権利はありません」（I、三十六頁）と言い、さらに「あなたはお金持ちにならなければなりません。あなたをお金持ちにさせなければなりません」と強く主張する。（I、三十九頁）ケイトは、母の死後父が経済的に困窮生活を続け、さらに姉も貧乏で苦しんでいる様子を自分の眼で見てきているので、彼女は伯母の助力で金持ちと結婚したいという気持になったのである。F・O・マシーセン (F.O. Matthiessen) は『ヘンリー・ジェイムズ——円熟期の研究』(*Henry James : The Major Phase*, 1944) の中で「この作品に生き生きとした美しさを与えているのは、女主人公ミリー・シールであり、彼女は肺結核のために二十四歳で死んだ従妹ミニー・テンプルに捧げる作者の賛歌として描かれている」と述べている。この言葉から、ミリーは、ジェイムズが青春時代に思いを寄せていたミニー・テンプルの霊をこの小説の中で形象化しようとしたものであることが分かる。『鳩の翼』にはミニー・テンプルというモデルがあり、『不如帰』にも信子というモデルがあり、『不如帰』にも共通性があることが理解できる。両小説のテーマが不治の病と純愛と死であるということを考えると、奇しくも両小説には共通性があることが理解できる。一方『鳩の翼』の中においては、『不如帰』の中では日本の封建社会と低く弱い女性の地位が描写され、一方『鳩の翼』の中においては、ケイトとデンシャーの考え方の違いを考察することが重要である。『鳩の翼』においては、ケイトとデンシャーの考え方の違いを考察することが重要である。「デンシャーがケイトには富への欲望と策略と裏切りの様相が描かれているという点である。「デンシャーがケイトにとって豊かで神秘的で強力な存在に思えたのは彼の精神面であった」（I、五十一五十一頁）とジェイムズが述べているように、デンシャーは高邁な精神をもっていた。彼が精神的に豊かな資質をも

た青年に成長したのは、高邁な精神と豊かな知性をもった父と、優れた美的感覚をもった母のもとで育てられたからである。デンシャーは金銭には無関心であった。一介のジャーナリストである彼には十分な財力がなかった。そのことが、彼がケイトとの愛情を築いてゆく上で大きな障害となってゆくのである。

先ずこの小説は、ヴィクトリア朝を時代背景にしていることを考慮に入れなければならない。ミシェル・フーコー（Michel Foucault）は『知への意志』（La volonté de savoir, 1976）の中で、ヴィクトリア朝の社会状況について次のように語っている。

人は言う、長いこと私たちはヴィクトリア朝の体制に耐えてきたし、今日なおそれを受け入れているとと。女王様のあの淑女ぶった顔は、我らの控え目でおし黙った、偽善的な性 (セクシュアリティ) 現象の紋章の一部に他ならない。

十七世紀の初頭には、まだある種の率直さが通用していた、と人は説く。現実の行動において秘密めかそうとすることはほとんどなかった。言葉で言うことを極端に避けるとか、その事柄自体も殊更に上辺を繕って行われるとかいうことはなかった。人々は許されざることとある種の寛容な親しさの関係を保っていた。卑俗なもの、猥褻なもの、淫らなものの基準は、十九世紀のそれに比べればずっと緩やかだった。直接的な仕草、恥かしいとも思わぬ言説、はっきり目に見える侵犯行為、あけすけに体も見せ、簡単に結合させる。ませた子供たちが走りまわっても、大人たちは大笑いするだけで、誰も照れたり恥かしがったりしない。つまり誰の身体も、いわば孔雀が羽根を拡げるように大手を振って歩いていた。

この白日の光に続いて、たちまち黄昏が訪れ、ついにヴィクトリア朝ブルジョワジーの単調極

まりない夜に到り着く。(七-八頁)

ヴィクトリア女王時代には、フーコーの指摘の通り、「女王様のあの淑女ぶった顔」に象徴されるように、ヴィクトリア朝的禁欲の思想が色濃く浸透していたと言えるであろう。このような抑圧の時代だったからこそ、かえって市民の中には富の力によって、ブルジョワジーの仲間に入ることに憧れをもっていた人も多かったと思われる。イギリスは上流階級と下層階級が判然と分かれていると言える。ラウダー夫人は上流階級に昇りつめたが、ケイトやデンシャーは上流階級には手の届かないところで生活していたのであった。ケイトの父や姉は、ラウダー夫人の力を借り、ケイトが自分の美貌を生かして大富豪と結婚し、上流階級の仲間入りをすることを望んだのである。ケイト自身も家族や親戚の希望を実現すべく思案をめぐらすのであった。ケイトにとって、家族や親戚の夢を現実のものにするためには、金持ちと結婚することが前提条件となるのである。ケイトの婚約者デンシャーは、ケイトを上流階級に押しあげてくれるような経済的な力はなかった。そのような事情があったので、ケイトはデンシャーと婚約をしていたことを秘密にしておいたのである。そのような時期に、巨万の富をもったミリーが、自分が恋い焦がれているデンシャーに会いたい一心で、アメリカからイギリスにやってきたのであった。読者はこの経緯を知る時に、小説のこの部分に破壊的要素が内在していることを実感する。『鳩の翼』の第五部において、ミリーがマッチャムの園遊会に招待された時に、彼女がブロンツィーノの肖像画を鑑賞する光景が描写されている。その場面はミリーの内部世界を知る上できわめて重要であるので引用しよう。

その若い女性の肖像は指先にいたるまでまったく見事に描かれており、華麗な衣裳を身につけ

ミリーはその肖像画を見た時に、「私はこれより決してよくはならないでしょう」（I、二二一頁）と言って、涙を流した。この言葉はミリーの内面世界をよく表わしていると言えよう。彼女は死の到来を自覚しているからこそ、ヨーロッパにおける束の間の滞在期間中に自分の命をかけた恋を実現したかったのである。

第七部において、小説の場面はロンドンからヴェニスに移る。デンシャーは、ケイトの提案通りに、ミリーに会いに、ヴェニスの宮殿パラッツオ・レポレルリを訪れる。ミリーは彼の訪問を歓迎する。彼女は人生の終焉を迎えるにあたり、「生きる以上に最高のものはありません」（II、一五五頁）と言って、残り少ない人生において光り輝く最高の恋を成就しようとしていたのである。ジェイムズは、ミリーの魅力をデンシャーの視点から次のように描写している。

それに、なによりも意外で、これこそ紳士として彼が即座に認めざるを得なかったのは、思い

ていた。顔色はほとんど鉛色と言ってもよかったが、悲しみをたたえていながらも目鼻だちが整った美しい容貌で、豊かな髪は後ろへ高く巻き上げられており、それは時代と共に色あせる前には、ミリー自身の家系との類似性を感じさせたに違いない。いずれにしても、話題のこの婦人は、かすかにミケランジェロ風の角ばった体形、古い時代の人の眼差し、豊かな唇、長い首筋、由緒ある宝石類、錦織りの色あせた赤い衣服など、非常に高貴な女性であったが——ただ喜悦の表情は浮かべていなかった（中略）そして彼女は、死んで、死んで、死んでいた。（I、二二〇-二二一頁）

がけなく魅力的な彼女の印象だった。気の毒な顔色の悪いミリーが壮麗な由緒ある宮殿の女あるじとなった時、その印象にはえも言われず彼の心に訴えるものがあり、彼女の心のこもったもてなしがあらゆる条件に助けられて一層魅惑的なものになった時、彼は到底それを拒むことができなかった。

宮殿の女あるじとしてのミリーの姿には、一種の雄弁というか権威というか似つかわしさというか、彼の形容を絶した美しさがあって、彼は意外の感に打たれざるを得なかった。彼の歓迎ぶり、率直さ、優しさ、哀しさ、明るさなど、彼が時々言葉に窮して彼女の思いがけない詩情と呼んだ魅力は、美しい宮殿を背景に一段と深まっていた。彼が見る人の眼に彼女の魅力を深めた。彼女に接する時、彼は、古風で憂鬱な音楽の途切れがちで定かならぬ微かな調べが、幻聴のようにためらいがちな楽の音を奏で、途絶え、そしてまた震えながら高まるのが聞こえるような印象を受けた。（Ⅱ、四一五頁、青木次生訳）

ミリーは自分が愛するデンシャーに情熱的な愛の炎を燃やし続ける。デンシャーは次第にミリーの魅力に引きつけられてゆく。デンシャーがレポレルリ宮殿に訪れる前に、ケイトとデンシャーは、デンシャーがミリーの宮殿を訪れる条件として一種の儀式を行う。この儀式はベニスの彼の下宿で執り行われた。デンシャーはケイトの愛情の証拠を得るために、ケイトとの性愛を求め、一方ケイトはデンシャーから多額の富を得る条件として性愛を求める。

ここでヴィクトリア朝にいたる二世紀間の性的抑圧の現状について考察しておく必要がある。フーコー

は『知への意志』の中で次のように語っている。

セクシュアリティ現象の歴史が増大する抑圧の年代記として読まれるべきだというこの長い二世紀、それからら我々は自由になっているのだろうか。ほとんどなっていない、と今なお人は言う。多少はフロイトのおかげでなったかも知れぬ。（中略）人は説く、もし古典期以来、抑圧が権力と知と性現象との間の結びつきの根底的なあり方だとしたら、そこから自由になるには相当な代償を払わねばなるまいと。だからこそ必要になるのではないか、法に対する侵犯も、禁忌の解除も、言葉の突然の侵入も、現実の中における快楽の復権も、つまり権力のメカニズムの内部で一つの新しい関係構造がそっくりそのまま、政治的条件の下にある<ruby>関係構造<rt>エコノミー</rt></ruby>がそっくりそのまま、政治的条件の下にあるからだ。（中略）

性の近代的抑圧についての言説は、まだよく保っている。おそらく保ちがいいのは、言うに易しいからである。深刻な歴史的・政治的な保証がそれを守っている。数百年にわたる大っぴらな自由な表現の後に、抑圧の時代を十七世紀に出現させることで、人はうまい具合にそれを資本主義の発展と合致させることができる。抑圧の時代はブルジョア的秩序と一体をなすというのだ。

（十一―十二頁）

フーコーが指摘しているように、イギリスのヴィクトリア朝の体制下では、性に対する抑圧が厳しく、結婚外の性愛は禁忌であった。

ケイトとゲンシャーは、婚約しているとは言え、まだ教会の祭壇の下で神との契約を誓った結婚の儀式

を執り行っていなかったのである。それ故に、二人は、策略を目的とする性愛の儀式を行うにあたっては、イギリスよりもベニスの彼の下宿のほうが差し障りのない格好の場所であると思ったのである。ケイトはデンシャーに次のように言う。

「ミリーはあなたを求めているのです。たとえそれが嘘だとわかっていても、あなたが彼女に与えることができるものを彼女は受け入れたであろうし、そのことを喜ばれたでしょう。あなたが憐れみから嘘をつき、彼女があなたにお会いし、あなたが嘘をついていると感じたでしょうが――それはすべてあなたの思いやりのある気持から出たことですから――彼女はあなたに感謝し、あなたを祝福し、ますますあなたに愛着を感じたことでしょう。と申しますのも、ねえ、それがあなたの強みです――彼女があなたを熱情をもって愛していることが。」（Ⅱ、三二七頁）

ミリーがデンシャーに強い愛情をもっていたわけであるから、ケイトとデンシャーが婚約していたことをミリーに話すべきではないと、ケイトはデンシャーに強く言う。しかし、マーク卿はデンシャーがケイトとひそかに婚約しているという極秘の情報を入手していて、そのことをミリーに告げてしまう。この情報によってミリーは生きる気力を失ったかに思われた。ミリーはデンシャーが心の奥底ではミリーを愛しているということを悟っていたのであった。一方、ケイトは、ミリーの死後デンシャーがミリーの遺産を相続し、彼がケイトと約束通り結婚することを望む。しかし、ミリーとデンシャーがお互いに深く愛し合うようになった時に、ケイトの計画は裏目に出る。ミリーを愛してしまったデンシャーは、ミリーが死んでも、ケイトと結婚する道を選ばなかったのである。こ

の小説の中で、ジェイムズは、ミリーのデンシャーへの純愛と、ケイトの富への欲望とを対照的に描き出すことに成功している。ケイトにとっては富のない愛情はあり得なかったのであり、ミリーとデンシャーにとっては、二人の純愛は富にまさるゆたかな精神的充実であったのである。

『鳩の翼』において、デンシャーは、ミリーがケイトよりも感受性のゆたかな賢い女性であることを感じとったのである。それ故に、ケイトの陰謀の目的であるミリーの富を受け取ることを拒絶することによって、デンシャーはついにミリーとの愛の思い出の中に生きてゆこうと決心する。ケイトとの愛を拒絶することによって、彼は自分の過ちを償おうとしたのである。ジェイムズの高邁な徳性がミリーの生活意識に反映されていると言える。したがって、この小説の主題は、デンシャーとケイトの価値観に対して、ミリーがどのような影響を及ぼしていったかというその変遷過程に力点をおいていると言えよう。

『鳩の翼』という題名は、『旧約聖書』の「詩編」第五十五編と第六十八編に由来している。「詩編」全体の中心思想は、絶えざる悩みがあっても、常に神に祈りの歌をうたい、「喜びの声をあげる」よう心がけることが大事であり、神は公平と義を守るが、それは神が「いつくしみ」深いからである、という内容である。ミリーは「悪しき人」に出会い、たえず悩みがあっても、生きることに「喜びの声をあげ」、自分に苦しみを与えたデンシャーやケイトに対しても「いつくしみ」の心をもって接するのである。「詩編」の中心思想は、ミリーの精神構造と共通するものがある。

徳冨蘆花の『不如帰』の女主人公浪子は肺結核という不治の病に罹り、強制的に離婚させられ、若くして死亡する。浪子は夫によって離婚させられたのではなく、封建的家庭の代表である母によって離婚させられたのであった。このような行動様式は日本の明治時代における生活文化の封建的な慣習から惹起されたのであった。

たものである。

一方、ヘンリー・ジェイムズの『鳩の翼』においては、ミリー・シールは財産目当ての結婚をしようとする人の目標となる女性であった。デンシャーは心ならずも、ケイトの差し金で、財産目当てでミリーに近づこうとした。皮肉にもデンシャーはミリーが恋い焦がれている男性であった。デンシャーはケイトの婚約者であったけれども、彼は罪の意識を持ちながらもミリーに近づいていくことになった。ケイトとデンシャーが婚約をしていることを知らなかったミリーと結婚することをよろこんで受け入れることになる。しかし、ミリーと結婚することを望んだマーク卿は、すでに述べたように、ケイトとデンシャーの婚約の事実を知ったミリーは、デンシャーがケイトの訪問をよろこんで受け入れることを知って、そのことをミリーに密告してしまう。ミリーとデンシャーの愛は純愛であった。なぜならば、ミリーは、デンシャーがケイトと婚約していたにもかかわらず、彼の不実な行動を許すのである。ミリーは一時は大きな衝撃を受けるが、結局はデンシャーを深く愛し、彼の不実な行動を許すのである。なぜならば、ミリーは、デンシャーがケイトと婚約していたにもかかわらず、彼の不実な行動を許すのである。ミリーは一時は大きな衝撃を受けるが、結局はデンシャーを深く愛し、彼の不心の底ではミリーを愛していることを知っていたからである。ミリーとデンシャーの愛は純愛であった。

一方、『不如帰』の中の浪子と武男は強制的に離婚させられたが、伊香保の場面でも分かる通り、二人の愛は純愛であった。ミリーと浪子の病気は二人に死をもたらしたが、人間は窮境の底にあった時に、初めて純粋な愛に目覚めるものであり得たのである。西洋でも東洋でも、人間は窮境の底にあった時に、初めて純粋な愛に目覚めるものであると言っても過言ではないであろう。ミリーと浪子がその何よりの証拠である。

不治の病におかされているミリーのやさしさが、デンシャーを純愛に導く情況は美しくも悲しい。ミリーの情熱は悲劇的な結果に終わったが、彼女の神秘的な輝きは、人の心に不滅の光を残す。ミリーはジェイムズの「四度の出会い」（"Four Meetings", 一八七七）の女主人公キャロライン・スペンサー（Caroline Spencer）の系列に属する人物である。彼女は自己を犠牲にして、他人の幸福に貢献しようとした女性で

ある。彼女は道徳的に清純なピューリタンと言える。寛容でかつ高邁な徳性を備えたミリーも、わが身を他人の幸福に貢献しようとした女性であり、彼女の内奥にはピューリタニズムの精神が脈打っていることがわかる。ミリーは、高邁なピューリタンの徳性をもって生きた当時のアメリカ女性のアイデンティティを示す人物であると言えよう。浪子と武男の純愛も美しく悲しい。しかし、浪子を最後まで守れなかった武男の不甲斐なさは、当時の中央集権国家としての日本の軍国主義的風潮下における日本男性の行動規範の限界を示すものである。武男は当時の封建的な家族制度の中に生きる日本人のアイデンティティを如実に示す人物と言えよう。

[注]

1 「偶感偶想——十二、アーヴィング氏の「ブロークンハート」を読んで」『蘆花全集第十九巻』(新潮社内蘆花全集刊行会、一九二九年) 一五三—一五四頁。

2 福田眞人『結核の文化史——近代日本における病のイメージ』(名古屋大学出版会、一九九五年) 八、二三、一四一、一五九頁参照。

3 F.O. Matthiessen, *Henry James: The Major Phase* (New York: Oxford UP, 1944) 34.

[引証文献]

Irving, Washington. "The Broken Heart". *The Sketch-Book of Geoffrey Crayon Gent.* Oxford: Oxford UP, 1996.

アーヴィング、ワシントン、吉田甲子郎訳『傷心』『スケッチ・ブック』新潮文庫、一九五七年。

James, Henry. *The Wings of the Dove*, I, II. New York: Charles Scribner's Sons, 1937.

ジェイムズ、ヘンリー、青木次生訳『鳩の翼』工藤好美監修 中村真一郎序『ヘンリー・ジェイムズ作品集三』国書刊行会、一九八三年。

徳冨蘆花『不如帰』岩波文庫、一九九九年。

フーコー、ミシェル、渡辺守章訳『性の歴史』第一巻『知への意志』新潮社、一九八六年。

[参考文献]

秋山正幸『ヘンリー・ジェイムズの国際小説研究――異文化の遭遇と相剋――』南雲堂、一九九三年。

中野好夫『蘆花徳冨健次郎』第一部、筑摩書房、一九七二年。

島崎藤村『破戒』から学ぶ

文学的意匠として「遺伝」をどう読むか

佐藤三武朗

ここで言う「遺伝」とは、生物学的な遺伝についてではない。本論で扱うのは、主人公が自己の内面を追求する過程で直面する暗黒の性質、あるいは自我追求の果てに暴露される宿命的な資質、あるいは性癖についてである。端的には、主人公の運命を支配する「血」の呪いであると考えて差し支えない。

西洋文学においては、すでにギリシャ神話が血の問題を扱っている。神話を題材としたアイソキュロス、ソフォクレス、エウリピデスの作品には、そうした傾向が顕著である。とりわけ、ソフォクレスの『オイディプス王』は赤裸々な形で、主人公が血の問題に直面する。注の一に挙げたように、アンティゴネとイスメネの二人の子供を前にして言うオイディプスのセリフは、運命劇としてのみ片づけられない、人間の

本性に潜む悲劇的一面に触れている。

ギリシャ神話や聖書の影響を多く受けて成立する西洋文学は、その根元的なテーマにおいて、近代あるいは現代の人間が直面し、苦悩し、呻吟する問題を我々の前に披瀝する。シェイクスピアの代表作である『リア王』『ハムレット』においても、その傾向が顕著である。リアが長女ゴネリル、次女リーガンに、またハムレットが母ガートルードに見出したように、リアにおいては父が子の中に、ハムレットにおいては子が母の中に、血の汚れを見出している。親子という絶対的な血縁関係の中で、登場人物は自己に潜む「罪」の深さに慟哭することとなる。

日本文学では同種のテーマがどのように扱われているだろうか。

主人公が人間の真実や実体を云々する際に、逆説的な形で自己の一切を否定し去ってしまう程の破壊的な「血の呪い」こそ、実に島崎藤村の『破戒』で扱われるモチーフであり、メイン・テーマである。日本の近代小説において、『破戒』ほどに直接的に、また赤裸々に「遺伝」的な要素を作品化した傑作を、私は他に知らない。

『破戒』の一つの特徴は、血の問題がたえず繰り返されることである。生々しい血の嗅いがただよっていると言っても過言ではないくらいである。復讐劇や戦争小説ならまだしも、この種の小説にしては珍しいと言える。藤村は何故これほどまでして血を小説にとり入れ、テーマとの関わりに意識的、もしくは無意識的に気を配ったのであろうか。『破戒』以後の作品で繰り返し扱われているように、藤村自身が家系にまつわる血の呪い、つまり父の狂気や、自分自身の愛欲の悩み、又は血の騒ぎのために苦しんだことは事実である。ここでは、「血」がこの小説でどう扱われているかを、小説的な意味での血のイメージとその象徴に焦点を当てて考察することにする。その際、扱う人物を住職、丑松と父、お志保、敬之進、蓮太郎

知の新視界

に限り、さらに血を次の四種―血統、血縁、愛欲、流血―に分けて解釈し、実体を明らかにしていきたい。

まず、丑松と父についてであるが、丑松の苦悩と憂うつのすべてはその素性という逃れられない運命に呻吟するところから生まれている。素性が暴露すれば、教職を追われるばかりか、二度と社会的存在として機能出来るか否かわからない。そんな新平民というレッテルをはり、生理的心理的嫌悪のすべてを向けている。世間は丑松個人の資質を無視して新平民という社会的レッテルをはり、生理的心理的嫌悪のすべてを向けている。世間は丑松個人の資質を無視して新平民という社会的レッテルをはり、平民を違う血を持った人間と見る誤った観念に根ざしている。《その血統は古の武士の落人から伝ったもの、貧苦こそすれ、罪悪の為に穢れたやうな家族ではない》（一の三）と父は丑松に語り伝えた。彼等の偏見は、新世間は、その血統を理由に差別と屈辱を与えることをやめない。

丑松もまた初めのうちは自己の宿命を恐れ恥じるがあまり卑屈となり、自己の素性に対してばかりか、同じ新平民仲間に対しても同情と慈愛の目を向けることはできないでいる。彼自身、《種族》《人種》という言葉で、他と自分を区別しさえしている。丑松は仙太と組んでのテニス試合にむきになり、自らの激情を発散しようとするのだが、相手の文平チームとのゲームを、《人種と人種》（五の四）の競争と見ている。教員でありながら、文平は蓮太郎に関して《彼様な下等人種から碌なものの生まれよう筈が無いさ》（十八の五）と、侮辱の言葉を吐いている。科学者の銀之助はもっと客観的な人権区分を表明する。《僕だっていくらも新平民を見た。あの皮膚の色からして、普通の人間とは違って居らあね。そりゃあ、もう、新平民か新平民で無いかは容貌で解る。それに君、社会から度外にされて居るもんだから、性質が非常に僻んで居るさ。まあ、新平民の中から男らしい毅然とした青年などその産れやうが無い。どうして彼様な手合が学問といふ方面に頭を擡げられるものか》（十八の二）。

合理主義者であり、学問的には向上心の強い銀之助ですら、丑松を前にして、これほど誤謬に充ちた偏

見を暴露している。飯山の住民のすべては血統という区別の下に非科学的な根拠によって、新平民に対して軽蔑の顔色を見せている。おのれの本質も本性も見つめることなく、身分差別の誤謬に内在する社会不条理にも悪にも気づかず、不当な偏見による不正義を重ねている姿がここに見られる。自己矛盾に気づかない人間の愚かさは、人を教育する側にある校長や文平を初めとした飯山教育界の堕落と腐敗にも窺える。

丑松は自らの血統を意識し、そのために苦悩し始めて以来、自然の性質をすりへらすだけであった。彼が父の戒の逆説を解けずに自らその矛盾に足をとられて行く時、《子の胸に流れ伝はる親の其血潮》（七の六）は子の表情を苦悩にゆがめることはあっても、明るくすることは全くない。血統という定義による人間性無視に苦しんだのは丑松だけではない。父の苦しみはそれ以上であったろうし、その祖先に至っても同様であった。

この場合、血統という言葉は人間の歴史のページを彩る社会不正義と悪の口実として使われて来たことになる。またぬぐい去ることの出来ない身分という十字架を担って生まれた被差別民にとって、これは原罪的な共通の血の呪いである。一方、この小説では教育者の口を通じて謬見が主張されている。無智と無神経、腐敗と堕落という許し難い罪を永久に罪とも意識することなく、悪の増殖に努める人物群が配置されているので、人間の原罪的傾向は両方の意味を含んだ普遍的疾患として浮彫にされている。丑松の内部にあった自己矛盾の原因としての血統の悩みは、彼が遂に告白を敢行し、さらにお志保が世間的身分の差を取り除くと同時に消滅する。しかし蓮太郎は血統の矛盾を未解決のまま残して、その生涯を終える。

丑松はこうした蓮太郎の未解決の部分、つまり蓮太郎の葛藤を受け継ぐ形で存在の矛盾を解決する訳である。蓮太郎は自分が新平民であることを懺悔こそすれ、血統や差別の問題については解決の道を示してはいない。彼は多くの正直な男女がその素性の故に社会から見捨てられて行く光景を紹介するのだが、

《無智と零落》とを活きた画のように描出しているに過ぎない。一体これはどうした訳か。彼は自らを《同族》（一の四）と見、それを認めこそすれ、それに対する世間の謬見や不正義を批判している形跡はない。彼は《朝空を望むやうな新しい生涯に入る迄》を、嗚咽の声をあげるようにして記録しているだけである。

丑松と違って、蓮太郎は血統に根ざす自己矛盾から生まれる苦悩を掘りさげている訳ではない。彼は新平民であること自体を罪と認めており、それを懺悔することによって社会から許された。人間の血統は果たして懺悔に価する罪なのか。ここに丑松の告白の本質と蓮太郎の懺悔の本質の違いが出てくる。蓮太郎は自分の血統の素性を懺悔し、その贖罪的効能によって罪を許容され、普通人と同じく社会的生活を営む権利を与えられた。

丑松は自己の血統を意識して、苦悩する。閉鎖的となり、彼自身も他の人々に謬見を信じざるを得ないままに、それに悩まされることとなる。彼は血統という言葉そのものの絶対性を信じて疑わない世の人々の持つ社会的偏見と差別という外因と、自らの血統を呪うという自己蔑視と自己崩壊という内因との板ばさみの中で、出口を見出しえない日々を送る。

血統の問題はお志保にとっても悲劇の原因として作用する。丑松の自己闘争に対置する形で、被差別民ではないお志保も、士族の家名とその繁栄の残光にすがって生きている敬之進には、血統意識が強く働いている。士族という身分への執着、家名の誇り等を含めて、敬之進を支えるものは血統についての彼の偏見と自負である。《我輩の家と言ふのはね、もと飯山の藩士で、少年の時分から君侯のお側に勤めて、それから江戸表へ丁度御維新に成る迄》。……見たまへ、千曲川の岸にある城跡を。彼の名残の石垣が君等の目にはどう見えるね》（四の四）。

敬之進には栄華の夢から目を醒まして、現実を直視することはできない。零落した事実は認めても、血統の誇りは捨てるどころかそれに執着し、時勢の変遷をうらむだけで、絶対に自己の零落の原因に目を向けようとはしない。教員という現職さえ自分にふさわしい仕事として取り組むに足らずとしか思えない。

《実際、我輩なぞは教育をして居るとは思はなかったね。羽織袴で、唯月給を貫ふ為に、働いて居るとしか思はなかった》（四の四）。

血統の誇りが完全に敬之進を崩壊させていると言える。しかし、こうした父親の血を引くお志保が、自分の家名や士族の血について自慢するところを、この小説中に見つけることはできない。逆にお志保は血統の犠牲と言えるほどである。例えば、お志保が《父親さんや母親さんの血統が奈何で御座ませうと、それは瀬川さんの知ったことぢゃ御座ますまい》と言う時、これは彼女自身の血統にも適応できる。この時、彼女が士族の誇りに自滅した父親のことを考えているとしたら、人一倍血統というものに対して深い感慨があって当然である。

お志保は人間の価値判断の基準は血統ではなく、個人の資質におくべきことを身をもって学びとっている。

お志保の悲劇は丑松に並行する副筋ドラマとしての役割以上に重要な意味を持つ。つまり藤村の意図は、血統はその社会的評価の如何とは無関係に、一つの伝統的観念として個人が押しつぶし崩壊させる力を持つことを示すところにあったと見てもよい。丑松がやがて新平民の血統そのものに劣等価値が内在するのではないと気付くまでの過程に於て、お志保の境遇は伏線としても働いているわけだ。

さらに彼女の気性には信州北部の女性の血を見ることができる。銀之助はお志保の芯の強い性格を見て、

《烈しい気候を相手に克く働く信州北部の女は、いづれも剛健な、快活な気性に富むのである。苦痛に堪え得ることは天性に近いと言ってもよい》（二十二の三）と感想を述べている。信州が丑松にとって、母

104

知の新視界

胎のように包容性を備えた心の故郷であることはすでに述べたが、信州女であるお志保も同じ気性を与えられていると見ることが出来る。

次に、住職の本性に潜む血についてである。ここでは血と病気の問題に焦点をしぼり、血の呪いについて考察してみよう。住職の妻は愛欲という本能の活動を病気として簡単に片づけている。住職についてばかりか、敬之進の自堕落と「敗残な」性質をも、彼女は《持った病》（三の四）としている。夫の愛欲の本能も敬之進の酒好きも、もはや手の打ちようのない病気と彼女には映っている。また貧困の中で子供が多すぎるにもかかわらず、《夫婦喧嘩をした為に子供が出来たりする》と身の不運を嘆く敬之進も、理性が愛欲の本能に負けたケースである。

住職と敬之進は、愛欲の本能に身をまかせた人間の典型と言える。「破戒」ではまさに血の呪いとも呼ぶべきこの愛欲の本能は、常に社会や家庭の争いの原因となり、時にはその犠牲者を悲惨のどん底に突き落とす。蓮太郎の死、ひいては丑松の素性の暴露や高柳の失脚などの直接原因が、高柳の結婚であったことも、この点で重要になる。自らの《病気》を抑えようともしない人間の本性の暗い部分を住職の妻は夫の内に見て、それを《狂気》とも呼んでいるが、実際それは理性や良識では如何ともし難い悪魔的な力を備えたもので、原罪とでも名づけるしか仕方のない形で扱われている。血の呪いの解決は丑松とお志保が自我確立に成功するか否かにかかっている。ここでは自我確立、又は自己認識のみがこの原罪を克服する手段として構想されているからである。

次には、「破戒」の中で最も強烈なイメージとも言える《流血》の象徴的意味を考察する。まず丑松の父の死とその原因となった牛について述べよう。父親の死は、《老の為でもなく、病の為でも無かった。まあ、言はば、職業の為に突然な最後を遂げたのであった。》（七の四）父は牛の性質を十分に心得、家畜

を愛する心は天性に近く、その老練さは人々の認めるところであった。その彼が預った種牛に突き殺されるという予想外な事故で死ぬのである。丑松の叔父の話では、多くの牝牛の群の中へ一頭の種牛を放った際、その性質が激変し、野生の本性に戻って行方知れずになってしまった。父親はそれを心配して、山から山へ捜して歩いた。ある日、予定の時刻になっても帰らないのを心配した手伝いの男たちが出かけてみると、父親はうめき倒れていた。すでに手当のしようもない程の傷で、無惨にも彼はその夜に息を引き取ったのである。

ここで、興味深いのは、父親は牛に殺されることを本望とし、牛を憎むどころか、次のように遺言している点である。《俺も牧夫だから、牛の為に倒れるのは本望だ。今となっては他に何にも言ふことはねぇ。唯気にかかるのは丑松のこと。俺が今日迄の苦労は、皆な彼奴の為を思ふから。日頃俺は彼奴に堅く言聞かせて置いたことがある。何卒丑松が帰って来たら、忘れるな、と一言左様言ってお呉れ》(七の四)。父う父親の声には「牛」と「丑」がダブルイメージとなり、親が子の犠牲になることを歓んでいる姿が象徴的に描写されている。それ故、父の戒は丑松の頭上に重くのしかかり、父の死後も丑松は父を畏れるようになる。丑松は父によって生きなければならない。その意味で、父の死は、肉体の死ではあっても精神の死とはならず、丑松の中に父は生き続けることとなる。

父の死を象徴的にしているのが、父を殺した種牛の屠殺とその状況である。種牛は屠牛場へ送られる。そこには他に二頭の牡牛も、罪人が牢獄の内に押し籠められ、生命の終りを待つかのように最期の時を待

っている。丑松は種牛への憎しみを抱く代わりに、いたましい父の最期、牧場の草の上に流れた血潮を堪えがたい気持で思い浮かべる。他の二頭が生きながらえる価値もない程にやせて、みすぼらしいのに比べると、種牛は《体格も大きく、骨組もたくましく、黒毛艶々として美しい雑種》（十の三）であり。持主の話によれば、《是に勝る血統のものは一頭も無い。父牛は亜米利加産、母牛は斯々》（十の三）で、名牛としての資格は十分に有していた。他の二頭が、屠殺されるのを予感して悪あがきするのに比べ、種牛はおちつきすまし、悲しい鳴き声ももらさずに、死地へ赴いて行く。この潔い臨終の光景は見る者に哀憐の情を催させ、丑松も少なからず胸をうたれる。
　父親の死はその男らしさで、種牛の死はその潔さで感銘を与えている。父は自ら牛の角にかかって倒れることを本望とし、苦労のすべてが丑松のためであったことを告げている。獣である種牛さえも死地に引かれて行く時は、冷静に悠容としていた。しかし丑松は自己の運命におびえ、社会から見捨てられることを恐れ、進むべき道を見失い、卑怯にも社会の不条理と悪とに妥協し、大切な日々を悶々として無為に過ごして来た。
　父の血は牛の角を赤く濡らした。そして今は屠殺された種牛の血が、割かれた咽喉から板敷へ流れ落ち、膏と血の臭気が屠牛場に満ち溢れている。丑松の父の死と種牛の屠殺の状況は血の印象で満たされる。丑松と父とを結ぶ血統とも住職に見た情欲の血とも違って、ここにおける血は「死」と関係する。この血は死の象徴である。しかし、ここにおける死は勇ましく、男らしい。今の丑松に欠けているものである。その点で、血は死の象徴であると同時に、生をも象徴する。つまり一人の人間の死によって、他者が生への態度を学び、生への姿勢をとり戻した時、流血は生者のためにささげられる犠牲の尊い血、身代りの血とも言える。それを丑松は蓮太郎の死によっても学ぶ。

蓮太郎は病をおして市村弁護士の選挙応援の演説を飯山で行なう。蓮太郎は幾度か血を吐いた。終って演壇を下りる頃には、手に持った帕子が紅く染ったとのことである》（二十の二）。蓮太郎は演技をした訳ではなく、生命を賭して演説を行なったのである。人々は蓮太郎の演説の内容に深い感銘をうけると同時に、全生命を賭して演説をしたその勇気と情熱に心をうごかされた。丑松自身も蓮太郎の演説の様子を聞き、その《大胆な、とは言へ男性らしい行動》（二十の二）に驚く。正に蓮太郎は潔い男らしい姿勢で、生命を賭して人々の心に訴えかけたのである。血は、病む蓮太郎にとって避けられない死の象徴である。

しかし、ここでは血は単なる象徴にとどまらず、具象的なウェイトを与えられている。対立候補の高柳の秘密を暴露した蓮太郎は高柳の復讐に出合う。彼は帰宅途中、《石か何かで烈しく撃たれ》て死ぬ。ただでさえ病弱な身に、ましてや疲労困憊した体に、衝撃に耐える力はなかった。血は雪の上を流れていた。

しかし、ここで蓮太郎の「生」は丑松に受け継がれる。社会に捨てられることを恐れ、憂うつと倦怠の中で、自己矛盾の中から一歩も出られなかった丑松は血の中から、つまり蓮太郎の死から男らしい行動と勇気、すなわち生の情熱を学ぶ。蓮太郎の死は丑松に生の力を覚醒させたのである。生の象徴としての血がここにある。

藤村は、以上のように、血の象徴を種々に使用している。人間の体内に流れる避けがたい遺伝的なものとしてのみではなく、住職に見るような性質、人間の業の形象として、血の騒ぎを人間の本性の暗部と見ている。敬之進のように、士族の出という誉れ高い血統の誇りだけを支えとして生きている場合もあれば、丑松と父親のように、その血統のため、社会的偏見と差別に苦しむ場合もある。血統それ自体が人間に悪用される時、差別や偏見、逆に高慢を生む場合が多く、人間性蔑視の方向にむかう。血統は人間一個の本

質と価値に全く関わりなく、社会的謬見をもたらす。

藤村は血の象徴を生と死に関係させ、実に大胆な小説手法を試みている。父の死、種牛の死、そして蓮太郎の死に見る血と死のイメージは暗いものではない。それは、死の象徴としての血の暗さではなく、常に丑松の内部意識に照射する形で、生の象徴へ結びつけられているからにほかならない。この時、父の死も蓮太郎の死も、さらには種牛の死さえ、生の終焉としての死ではない。肉体は滅びても、その男らしい精神は丑松の内部に蘇生する。つまり父も蓮太郎も丑松によって生きるのである。ここにこの象徴の仕掛けの大きなエネルギーがある。

被差別の対象として血統を設定したことにより、この小説は象徴手法を有効に使うことができた。明治の一般的常識を反映して、藤村も新平民を血統の異なる人種とみている以上、三つの父長的存在がいずれも流血の死を遂げることのこの種族的意味を考察してみなければならない。もし新平民の悲惨がその血の呪いに運命づけられているとすれば、解放または自我の尊厳確立のためには、その血を消滅させることもひとつの方法として考えられる。「お頭」である父の死によって、種族の呪われた血の系図はひとまず断裁されたことになる。丑松の出自に関しては、《橋を渡ると向町になる――叔父の話によりますと、あそこは全町同じ苗字を名乗っているということでしたっけ。その苗字が、確か瀬川でしたっけ》（十四の三）とあるから、瀬川丑松は被差別民の村全体を代表する象徴的存在として設定されている。お頭の跡目が息子によってそっくり継がれないとすれば、慣習的にも筆頭家の断絶によってその家系は社会的に断絶することになる。しかも、この場合、父を殺したのは牛（丑）という愛児のような存在であるから、父の呪いは子孫に受け継がれていくことはない。それどころか、その血は視覚的にもすでに草を濡らして大地に還元してしまっている。

では丑松は父殺しの象徴的な罪を犯した不肖の子として設定されているのであろうか。牛が丑に通ずる比喩が意図的に使われているのは明らかである以上、凛然としてわるびれない牡牛の流血の、丑松の代償的贖罪行為を象徴すると見ることもできる。父の葬式の後、屠殺の場に丑松を立ち合わせ、一部始終を観察させている藤村の執拗な描写ぶりはこの見方を裏付けてあまりあると言える。同時に群中唯一の種牛の死は血統の断絶をも意味する。父は自らが与えた二つの相反する戒（『隠せ』）と（『行け、戦へ、身を立てよ』）の逆説を子に解決させるためには、死なねばならなかった。そして子は種牛と共に象徴的に死ぬことによって、父を乗り越えて自我を確立し、呪いの血を流し尽くした新しい個人として、人生を開いてゆくことになる。

蓮太郎の死にも強い象徴性がみられる。襲撃されて死に至るより前に、演説中すでに彼が血を吐きながら喋っていることは重要である。その時、彼は高柳の醜業を暴露していた。その内容をみると、つまるところ、蓮太郎自身には同族に当たる女性と高柳が結婚したことを弾劾しているのである。これは我が素性を懺悔に値するほど罪深いものと認識している蓮太郎の人物設定からすると、ごく自然に我が身をえぐって血を流すが如き自己犠牲的行為によって、社会に受け容れられた彼の人生そのものの象徴へとつながってゆく。

蓮太郎は丑松の叔父にも危険な人物と映った。丑松の留守中、訪ねて来た蓮太郎のことを告げる叔父の言葉は、重量感を帯びている。《ちょっと親指を出して見せて、「あの人はこれだって言うじゃねえか——気を注けろよ」》（八の二）と叔父は言う。これは英訳者のケネス・ストロングも解釈をつけずに字面だけの訳に止めているくらいで、難しい箇所である。しかし流血の象徴性に即して見た場合、「これ」とは「裏切者」、つまり虐待者側についてしまった、いわば敵方協力者と見ることは出来ないだろうか。しかも

叔父の言葉に対して、丑松自身決して蓮太郎が「これ」であることを否定してはいないのだ。ただ快活らしく笑って、《叔父さん、そんなことは大丈夫です》と言ったのみである。

それに蓮太郎の死の原因は投石によるショックらしい、となっている。「石もて打たれて死ぬ」に価する罪とは何であろうか。キリスト教の戒律によれば、それは夫や同志や同族への裏切りの罪となる。壮絶な死を遂げた蓮太郎について、《威厳を帯びたその容貌のうちには、どこなく暗い苦痛の影もあって》（二十の三）という死体の描写にはふくみがある。それは傷の痛みや悲劇的事件のムードを高める為のみのものではないことは確かであろう。この時、丑松は何かを蓮太郎の死に見ている。蓮太郎の容貌が暗いのは、それが理想の追求と自我解放のために同族を売るにも似た極端な手段しか取れない段階にあった、先駆者の必然的な自己矛盾と自我解放のために同族を売るにも似た極端な手段しか取れない段階にあった、

我が身にやましいことのない者だけが石を投げる資格があるからではないだろうか。キリストは言ったことになっている。踏みつけられるにもほどがある》（二十の三）という理由で、高政治における腐敗や道徳意識の退廃もさることながら、《しきりに高柳の心を卑しんで……いくらわれわれが無智な卑しいものだからと言って、事実上は新しく同族となった者を売ったことになる。我身の血をしぼり出すような行為だからこそ、演説を終った時には手のハンカチが赤く染まっていたのである。その彼に石を柳の秘密を蓮太郎は暴露した。投げた者は誰かと言えば、彼のいわゆる《無智な卑しい》血をわが子孫に享ける覚悟で、新平民の娘と結婚した高柳の側近である。船中で丑松が目撃した高柳夫妻の仲むつまじい様子からして、美しい妻を高柳程度の男が金銭ずくで娶ったとは思えないように描写されている点も見逃せない。丑松自身、美しい同族の女が高柳の新妻によって秘密を洩らされてしまい、高柳はその秘密をたてにとりひきをしようとたくらむ。この柳の新妻と結婚しなければならなかった血統の呪いに同情の念を表明している。しかし、その丑松も高

111

05 — 島崎藤村『破戒』から学ぶ

小説では秘密の暴露は同族によって行なわれている。蓮太郎がその門前で襲われた寺の名が法副寺であるのも、因果応報の死をもたらす報復寺に通じていると考えられなくもない。

藤村が意図的に構成した配置がここに表われている。被差別人種の劣等感が実はユダヤ系青年であることが判って、ショックがユダヤ人絶滅を唱えるネオ・ナチス団のシカゴ本部長が実はユダヤ系青年であることのある者にとっては、見落とせない共通パターンがここに表われている。ユダヤ人絶滅を唱えるネオ・ナチス団のシカゴ本部長が実はユダヤ系青年であることが判って、ショックがアメリカ全土をゆさぶったことが十数年前にあった。また、黒人市民権運動たけなわだった一九六〇年代のアメリカでは、異人種交婚に対する敵意をむき出しにしたのは白人だけでなく、恋人である黒人の家族の猛反対にあって苦悩した白人女性の恋物語などがベストセラーになっていた。高柳の秘密結婚を蓮太郎に告げたのは、新平民の大尽六左衛門の従弟であり、丑松の素性を洩らすのは高柳の妻となっている。いずれの場合も決定的証言はユダ的内部告発の形で出ているのだ。

こうしてみると、蓮太郎は丑松にとって父的存在であり、生き方のモデルでもあるにかかわらず、丑松が遂に我が素性を彼に告げることが出来なかったという事実が大きな意味を持ってくる。父と同様、蓮太郎もまた丑松にとって乗り越えてゆくべき過渡期の先達でしかあり得ない。新しい世代を担う丑松は、父のとった隠遁や蓮太郎の選んだ自己処罰的贖罪という、究極的には自己破滅に通じる方法以外に、自我確立を成就し、なお生きられる道を見つけなければならない。だからこそ、丑松に蓮太郎の後を継がせる形で、この小説は終る訳にはいかないのだ。

ここで注目したいのは、この血縁で結集した人物グループにおける共通した血では父と蓮太郎に関する血統と流血の象徴は、敬之進――お志保の血縁及び住職の血の呪いと、どう結びついているのだろうか。

の意味である。つまり性に密接した血である。丑松と父の血統は子を生むことによって継続していく、社会的かつ遺伝的な「呪い」と言える。現代のような避妊法の知識もなく、封建時代のような「間引き」も非合法というパターンが出てくる。敬之進の場合、もっと赤裸々に「性欲―子沢山―貧窮―自己崩壊」となった明治期を背景に、人間として自然な夫婦の情愛さえもが家庭分散をもたらすという皮肉な悲劇が浮彫にされている。現実逃避以外には闘争も解決も見出しえない敬之進自身の性格設定にみられるように、人間にとって生における必須要素とも言える本能としての性が、ここではキリスト教の原罪的な意味を帯びて使われている。それは道徳的判断や享楽抑圧などの説教的な姿勢とはかけはなれて、もっと本質的絶望的な人間の悲哀を訴える声にも聞こえる。同じく愛欲の怒濤に苦しんだ藤村自身の伝記と照らし合わせてみれば、この丑松の物語中で敬之進の描写に不当なほどのスペースが割かれている理由が明らかになる。蓮華寺の住職の場合、理性も常識も越えた行動に彼をかり立てるのは、血の騒ぎとしか言いようがない。血統や血縁などという因果関係さえもなく、単に人間であるが故の原罪的な血の呪いである。住職の過去の相手が二人とも悪女などではなく、むしろ立派な女性のように描写されていることからも、住職の「病い」が一時の気の迷いや遊びなどではなく、彼自身にもコントロールの利かない本性の一部と見なされていることが判る。しかもその結果生まれた子は乳不足の為二ヵ月で夭折という結果までつけ加えてあるのだから、親の「血」の為に犠牲になるのは子というパターンが、副筋中の副筋にまで生きている。
丑松の父のように後妻も娶らず性欲を昇華して生き抜いた場合でも、また敬之進のように性を断念しようと努力した場合でも、住職のように愛欲の波に流されるがまま生きる場合でも、彼自身にも苦悩を子にもたらすという設定になっている。実際、血の呪いは強烈である。理想的な「異族交婚」をして結果としては極端な苦悩を子にもたらすという設定になっている蓮太郎の場合も、死の直接原因は結核ではなく、彼が他人の結婚を非難したことである。但し彼の場

合、文字通り我が胸をえぐって血を吐く病いに象徴されるように、呪いが内向する形をとっている。彼には子供がなく、また丑松によって後を継がれることもない。血の呪いに我身のみを苦しめ痛めつけて終る求心円的な存在が蓮太郎である。そしてまた、それはそれなりに、呪いの血を継続させないための手段として、効果があると言わねばならない。それ故、象徴的に呪いのサイクルを断つ蓮太郎の死によって、丑松に新しい人生が開けることになる。

[注]

1 ソフォクレス『オイディプス王』高津春繁訳 ギリシャ悲劇全集 第二巻（人文書院、一九七五年）二六七－二六八頁。
 オイディプスは自ら目を突いて盲目となった後、アンティゴネとイスメネの二人の子供を前にして次のように言う。
 オイディプス・おん身に幸多からんことを、またよこしてくれた報いとして神がおれよりも親切にあなたをお守り下されんことを。子供たち、どこへ来い、このお前たちの同胞のおれの手に来い。この手はな、お前たちの生みの父のかつては輝いていた両の眼をこんなふうにしてしまうたのだ。このおれは、何も見えず、何も知らずに、自分が生まれたその腹から、子供らよ、お前たちのためにもおれは涙を流している。お前たちを見ることはかなわぬが、浮世の浪のまにまに、生きてゆかねばならぬこれからのお前たちの痛い暮しを思うてだ。どのように町人の集りに行って、見物する代りに、泣いて帰って来ぬことがあろうか。また嫁ぐにふさわしい花の盛りとなった時にも、子供たち、このような誇りを身に引き受けてくれる者があろうか。凶事には、欠けるまたお前たちにも禍いとなる。お前たちの父は父親を殺した。自分の種がそこに播かれた生みの母親の腹を耕し、われとわがことってない。お前たちの父は父親を殺した。自分の種がそこに播かれた生みの母親の腹を耕し、われとわが誕生の同じところからお前たちを得た。こう非難されるであろう。さすれば、誰がめとってくれようぞ。子供たちよ、誰もあるまい。疑いもなく、うまずめの未通女として、お前たちは朽ちゆかねばならぬのだ。

2 シェイクスピア『リア王』斎藤勇訳（岩波文庫、一九九三年）一一一－一一二頁。
 リア王は、自らが生み育てた長女ゴネリルと次女リーガンに裏切られ、見捨てられる。

リア王：どうかわしを気にしてくれるな。わが子ながらお前にはもう面倒をかけない。さようなら、もう二度と会うまい、もう二度とお互いにたずねまい。とはいえ、お前はわしの肉を分け血を分けたわしの娘だ。あるいはわしの体に喰い入った病いというべきか、それをわしのものと呼ばなければならないのも是が非がない。お前はわしの腐った血でできた腫物だ、瘡だ、疫病で膨れ上がったただれだ。けれどもわしはお前を咎めまい。汚名はいつかふりかかるだろうが、わしはそれを呼び求めない。

3　シェイクスピア『ハムレット』　市川三喜　松浦嘉一訳（岩波文庫、一九七二年）

ハムレットは母のガートルードを前にして、肉親関係の自覚の中で、堕落の内実を暴き立てる。

妃‥ハムレット、もう何も言わないでおくれ。お前のおかげで、わたしは自分の魂の奥底を見せつけられ、そこに、いくら洗っても落ちない真っ黒なしみがついているのが分った。

（第三幕　第四場）

4　『家』『新生』『桜の実の熟する時』といった作品はもちろんのこと、晩年の作品である『夜明け前』に至るまで、『血』は一貫して藤村の主要なテーマである。こうした藤村文学の傾向を知るには、習作地代の短編を分析することも興味深い。

［付記］

本稿は二〇〇二年二月発行『日本大学国際関係学部研究年報』第二十三集に掲載された、「文学的意匠としての遺伝要素—島崎藤村の『破戒』を中心に—」を改題し、若干の補訂を加えたものである。

06 ツルゲーネフと石川啄木

その比較研究

藤澤 全

[1] 緒言──明治期のツルゲーネフ移入概観

日本の近代文学史には、ツルゲーネフ受容という重い課題領域が存在する。周知のように彼(イワン・セルゲーヴィッチ・ツルゲーネフ、一八一八-八三)は、わが国の文学がいまだ江戸戯作的作風から脱皮できずにいる時期に、まったく独自に己の文業を終えて天界の巨星となった。この十九世紀ロシアの写実作家はまた、その六十五年の境涯のかなりの期間をフランスやドイツで過ごし、祖国はもとより世界各国との文化的交流にも多大の貢献をなした。わが国の場合、それはロシア文学の普及・近代リアリズム文学の成立にと、強く働きかけてくるものであったことは論をまたない。

いま明治期における受容史にわけ入るとして、最初期にツルゲーネフを本邦に移入したのはお雇いロシア人教師たちで、彼等は東京外国語学校露語部の教科書として、本国から取り寄せたツルゲーネフの諸作品を使用するかたちをとった。かくして同校に学ぶ学生たちの間で当該の受容が始まったわけであるが、なかでも飛びぬけた存在であったのが長谷川辰之助という青年であった。彼はたちまちそこから切実なテーマを見出し、学制改革により露語部が東京商業に合併されたのを機に学窓を退き、『小説神髄』の著書である坪内雄蔵（逍遥）を訪ねて翻訳と創作の志を立て、明治十九年（一八八六）に〈冷々亭杏雨〉の号を得、「父と子」を「虚無党形気」と題して訳出したが、これは活字化するに至らなかった（現在はその原稿も散逸）。

そしてこのあと筆名を二葉亭四迷と改め、逍遥のすすめで新時代の文学論「小説総論」を「中央学術雑誌」に掲げ、明治二十年（一八八七）六月に『浮雲』を刊行して、本邦におけるリアリズム小説の先駆をなした。また彼は明治二十一年（一八八八）に「あひびき」と『めぐりあひ』（のち「奇遇」と改題）を、明治二十九年十一月に単行本『片恋』を、明治三十年（一八九七）に『うき草』（『ルージン』）と「夢がたり」（「夢」）を、明治三十一年（一八九八）に「猶太人」（「ペッシコーフ」）、「けふり」（「スモーク」未完）を、明治三十八年（一九〇五）に「わからずや」（「貴族団長家の朝食」）を翻訳・翻案して活字化するとともに、求められて東京外国語学校露語部の教授をつとめた三年間（明治三十二～三十五）、ツルゲーネフを主にロシア語版作品を教材にして、若者たちにロシア文学を説いた。

ほかにも特記すべき事柄が少なくない。その先蹤部にいる森鷗外は、ドイツ留学中にレクラム文庫でツルゲーネフ作品を読み、帰国して直ぐに書いた『舞姫』に受容のあとをにじませる一方、「該撒」（「まぼ

ろし」・「馬鹿な男」・「罵馬」（幻影）などをもって初期の訳業・翻案物とした。これに続いて、五七居士・佐藤武雄の「あらしの花美さほ草紙」（明治二十二・「その前夜」）らの文業があり、明治三十年代では上田敏による散文詩「老嫗」「犬」「わが敵」（明治三十年（一九〇七）から大正始めにかけてでは吉江孤雁の『ツルゲーネフ短編集』（明治四十）、戸川秋骨・蔽戸会同人『猟人日記』（明治四十二）、相馬御風の「その前夜」（明治四十二）、大貫晶川の「煙」（大正二）、松本苦味の「春の水」（大正四）、などの翻訳が出て枢要なる役割を果たした。彼等のうち二葉亭四迷はロシア語版を、森鷗外はドイツ語版を用いたが、あとの者は、最初はアメリカのアスター版を、続いてイギリスのコンスタンス・ガーネットの訳本を原本とした。

当然のことながら、このようにして導入されたツルゲーネフの文学は、たえず時代に先駆する若者たちを刺激した。ちなみに受容者の文業のうちには、嵯峨の屋御室の「初恋」（明治二十二）、国木田独歩の「女難」（明治三十五）・「運命論者」（明治三十六）・「正直者」（明治三十六）、田山花袋の「重右衛門の最後」（明治三十五）、島崎藤村の「千曲川スケッチ」（明治四十五）など、著しく影響の後をとどめるものが存在する。さらに名前のみ挙げるならば、永井荷風・有島武郎・夏目漱石・森田草平・谷崎潤一郎・志賀直哉・芥川龍之介らにも受容が認められた。なお、前記当該作品の作者のうちには、新たに創作上の方法を得るとか、作家・作品論へと文業を拡大させる者が輩出した。〈第一人称小説〉の実践者の独歩はその前者に属し、後者の典型として、相馬御風による「ツルゲーネフ・態度・人」（明治四十二）・「ツルゲーネフ評伝」（明治四十三）などの執筆があった。

[2]『猟人日記』の受容

さて啄木であるが、彼は本邦におけるツルゲーネフ熱の最高潮時期に自然主義文学を志向したことから、自ずと熱っぽく受容の姿勢を示した。それは前記上田敏訳の散文詩十篇、及びそれとも重なる、梧堂という筆名の人（盛岡中学校の教師らしいが不詳）の訳四篇との出会いを最初とする（『岩手県師範学校校友会雑誌を読む』参照）。この十九歳の体験に続いて啄木は『猟人日記』の一部を読み、それを北海道に渡ってから再度咀嚼していた。このことは札幌の「北門新報」明治四十年（一九〇七）九月十八日の紙上に掲げた「秋風記」に、

銭函駅を過ぐれば限界忽ち変じて、秋雲雨を含める石狩の大平原を眺めぬ。赤楊の木立を交へたる蘆荻の間より名知らぬ鳥の飛び立ちたるを見て、何とはなく露西亜の田園を行く思ひしぬ。ツルゲーネフが「猟夫日記」[ママ]さてはト翁が「コサック」中の銃猟の章など心に残れる為めなるべし。

とあること、および「釧路新聞」明治四十一年（一九〇八）一月二十四日の紙上に載る「雪中行」（第一信）に、

所々に枯木や茅舎を点綴した冬の大原野は、漫ろにまだ見ぬ露西亜の曠野を偲ばしめる。鉄の

如き人生の苦痛と、熱火の如き革命の思想とを育て上げた、荒涼とも壮大とも云ひ様なき北欧の大自然は、幻の如く自分の目に浮かんだ。不図したら、猟銃を肩にしたツルゲーネフが、人の好ささうな、髯の長い、巨人の如く背の高い露西亜の百姓と共に、此処いらを彷徨(うろつ)いて居はせぬかといふ様な心地がする。

などとあることによって判然とする。

ここで留意しておかなければならないのは、ひとくちに「猟人日記」を受容したといっても、啄木はこの長編のうちのいずれの翻訳テクストに出会っていたのであろうかということである。むろんロシア語版では読めず、またガーネット英訳版を手にしてもいないので、自ずと二葉亭四迷のものに依存したことは言うまでもない。したがって、

① 「あひゞき」(「国民之友」明治二十一・七~八)
② 単行本『片恋』(明治二十九・十一、春陽堂。ここには改訳「あひゞき」・「奇遇」(初題「めぐりあひ」)・「片恋」(「アーシャ」)の三篇収録)

のいずれかであることは明らかだが、この場合、さらに一つに絞り込む直接の証明材料は存在しない。そこで原話の一場面を判断材料にするとして、〈語り手〉でもある〈自分〉が野原に寝転んでいるとき、眼前に現れた少女(アクリーナ)がしきりに野花を摘み、それを遅れて現れた若者(ビクトル・アレクサンドルイチ)に手渡すあたりの場面は――、

① では〈「……お前さんにあげやうと思って摘んで来たのですよ」、と云ひながら、黄ろな野菊の花の下にあった、青々とした blue bottle の、細い草で束ねたのを取り出して「入りませんか」〉

②では〈……お前さんに呈げやうと思って摘んで来たの〉、と云ひながら、黄ろいリャビンカの下に青々としたワシリョーク（草の名）を細い草で結へた大きな花束のあったのを取り出して、「入りませんか？」

とある。②が再訳形態であるが、両者の著しい違いは野草の表記で、①では〈blue bottle〉とあって〈矢車菊〉の英語綴りのまま、②は〈ワシリョーク〉という〈矢車菊〉のロシア語発音の片仮名表記となっている。この〈ワシリョーク〉が〈矢車菊〉となるのは、米川正夫訳『猟人日記』（昭和十二）からであるから、啄木は原作の訳本からは〈矢車菊〉という植物名に出会うことはなかった。一方、〈blue bottle〉なる単語は、三省堂版『新訳英語辞典』（初版は明治三十五・六・一で、以後版を重ねている）中に「blue bottle n（植）矢車菊」とある。この英語辞典は広く普及していたので、啄木がこれにより当該語の意味をつかむことは十分に可能であった。（啄木の遺品の中に右の辞書〈二十七版〉があった）。

いまここまで押えておくとして、次の「小樽日報」明治四十年（一九〇七）十一月一日に載った〈緑衣生〉なる匿名者の一首に注目してみよう。

ふためきて君が跡追ひ野路走り野菊がなかに寝て空を見る。

これは「心の花」明治四十一年（一九〇八）七月号に〈工藤甫〉の名で載った「緑の旗」五十八首中にも収められており、〈工藤甫〉が啄木であることが明らかなので、掲出の〈緑衣生〉の歌は啄木の作品であることに疑問の余地がない。してみると、先述の「秋風記」及び「雪中行」に取り上げられている『猟人日記』との関わりを無視できない。それも翻訳事情により「あひゞき」に限定される。ちなみに同短編

122

には冒頭部に、〈語り手〉である〈私〉が白樺を背に野草の中に寝転んで空を見上げている場面があり、やがて男女の別れがあって、冷たく立ち去った〈ビクトル〉のあとを追うように、一旦は彼が捨てた花束を拾い上げた〈アクリーナ〉が、慰めようと思って現れた〈私〉に驚き、その花束を捨てて駆け去るという一連の場面が続く。物語の最大の山場にして、リリシズムの美しさが極まるところであるが、実はこのシチュエーションゆえに、前掲歌のうちの〈君〉と〈ビクトル〉、〈跡追ひ野路走り〉去る人と〈アクリーナ〉、〈野菊がなかに寝て空を見る〉人と〈自分〉といった具合に相関関係をなす。また野趣豊かな大自然のもとでの慌ただしい退去といった点でも対応し合っている。この事実を勘案するに、啄木は当該の一首の題材を「あひゞき」から得ていたと判断して差し支えなかろう。

あらためて確認するまでもないことだが、「ふためきて君……」の歌の詠出時、啄木が出会い得るツルゲーネフ原作「Свидание」は、二葉亭四迷訳の「あひゞき」だけで、それも初訳初出形態、もしくは再訳単行本所収形態のいずれかに限られた。先の掲出例示でいえば①か②のいずれかということであるが、ここで先に押えておいたところの、啄木に〈ワシリョーク〉＝〈矢車菊〉という形での把握障害事情があったことを想起するならば、答えは自ずから透けて見えてくるのだ。すなわち、啄木は初訳初出形態（だから①）の「あひゞき」と向き合い、そのことでわざわざ目立つように配置されている北海道の原野を眼前にしての着目（他にこのような英語表記箇所はない、いまだ開拓のいきわたっていない北海道の原野を詩語としての印象も昂じて、「あひゞき」のプロットを借用し、かつ〈blue-bottle〉に対応する〈野菊〉を詩語とした短歌フォルムを形成したものらしい。といっても、このとき啄木は〈歌人〉として生きてはいなかったのであるから、若きジャーナリストの余技として、新紙「小樽日報」の文化欄の一たる歌壇を軌道に乗せるため、実名でも筆名でもない、全く己を覆った〈緑衣生〉を署名としたのであった。この〈緑衣

生〉なる筆名には、だから「あひゞき」中の〈猟人〉はもとより、作者ツルゲーネフのイメージが投影していると言い得るのである。

次に歌集に収められた作品に注目してみたい。まず『一握の砂』の「忘れがたき人人一」の章に配置されているところの、

　　函館の青柳こそかなしけれ
　　友の恋歌
　　矢ぐるまの花

であるが、この一首はどのような歌柄をなすのか。あまりにも人口に膾炙しているので諸家の解釈も出尽くした感があるが、私見ではそこに問題があるように思う。従来のそれはおおむね定説化しているのだが、〈かなし〉を〈愛し〉の意味でとり、作者の伝記要件を重ねて"函館時代をことさら懐かしく回顧した歌"とみなされてきた。この歌の初出する「スバル」明治四十三年（一九一〇）十一月号の「秋のなかばに歌へる」百十首の冒頭に、「以下北海道の曽遊を思ふの歌より」とあるのを根拠とする。しかし「曽遊を思ふ」とはどういうことか。周知のように啄木の函館青柳町時代は、志を得ぬ若者たち――宮崎郁雨・岩崎白鯨・松岡蕗堂・並木翡翠・大島流人・沢田天峰などとの交遊が進み、彼等の恋愛意識や蹉跌の青春に立ち会い（大島流人は結婚破綻）、その一方で、一家離散した己の落魄と流離のかなしみをかこつという状態にあった。したがって「曽遊を思ふ」の主和音は、古語的含みの〈愛し〉（愛する・愛でる・いとおしむ）の意味に限定するのはかまわないとしても、もう一方の意味――〈悲し・哀し〉（切ない・悲哀）と

いった情緒ととれなくはない。
そこで、筆者はその後者を支持主張するものである。この選択には理由がある。それは終句の「矢ぐるまの花」に関してであって、おそらくこれも在函時に視野に入ったところの、北方自生植物〈矢車草＝Rodgersia podophylla〉の属目経験が素材をなし、またそこに既述の受容をもって、「あひゞき」が描く"悲恋の象徴花"たる欧州原産の〈blue-bottle〉、すなわち〈矢車菊＝Centaurea Cyanus〉の切ない悲哀感がシンボライズし、むしろそこに含みの多い青春の感情の凝縮があり、この一首の抒情空間をより広めていると言えるからである。終句の〈矢ぐるまの花〉は、作者にこの認識と情感とレトリックがなければ歌中の具象とはなり得なかった、ということもしっかりと確認しておきたい。
なお作中の〈友〉のモデルは不明で、その人数も単数とは限らないが、それとしてこの一首を味わう際、所見の帰結として、〈「函館の青柳町時代がとりわけもの悲しい。友人たちの恋の諸事情よ、そして花をつけた矢車草の、悲恋の趣きの切実さよ。」と筆者は解釈したいと考える。

　　みぞれ降る
　　石狩の野の汽車に読みし
　　ツルゲエネフの物語かな

右の一首も『一握の砂』の「わすれがたき人人一」に所載する。初出は「東京朝日新聞」明治四十三年(一九一〇)五月七日で、「手帳の中より」五首中の一首であるから、創作も「北海道曽遊」体験からかなり日を経ていたことが判る。それだけ回想性が強いということであるが、啄木に「みぞれ降る巷々の街燈

のひかり薄れて夜はふけてゆく」)「小樽日報」明治四十・十・五、「心の花」明治四十一・七)があるので、初行の「みぞれ降る」は、すでに作者のなかで咀嚼された詩句となす。二行目の「石狩の野の汽車」の旅とは、これが実体験であるならば、それはいつか。この場合、エッセイ「秋風記」の旅ならば「みぞれ」は結びつかず(単なる秋雨)、まして「雪中行」の旅にあっては、それはあり得ない(真冬の北海道では「みぞれ」は雪となる)。したがって晩秋の旅路として設定されていることが明らかで、もしこれを創作上の虚構とすると、三行目の「ツルゲーネフの物語かな」も創意のイメージということで、ぐっと現実離れの状態となる。いずれにしてもこの一首は、北へと流れた作者の漂泊の実体験をモチーフに、既述の〈ツルゲーネフ受容〉をキーワードとした歌柄なのだ。

ではなぜこの時期にツルゲーネフが題材化したのか。またしても謎とするところであるが、これに関しては容易に解(solution)が得られる。次のように—。勤務先の東京朝日新聞社が『二葉亭四迷全集』全四巻を企画し、その編集校訂の実務者として啄木が抜擢された結果、彼は明治四十二年(一九〇九)十一月からこれに携わり、まもなく責任者となって、明治四十三年(一九一〇)五月十日、その第一巻の刊行を果たした。当該の新聞紙上に「みぞれ降る石狩……」の歌が載った三日後のことである。この事実が全てを物語るというべく、啄木は『二葉亭四迷全集』の仕事を通じて着想し、前掲の一首を詠出したのであった。

筆者は「みぞれ降る石狩……」の歌を以上のように読み解く。そして、当該の旅路が意図的に心象化していようとも、その時に作中の〈われ〉が手にしていたとする「ツルゲーネフの物語」は、先に述べた「あひびき」の初訳初出形態であったとなる。自ずとその時、〈われ〉はこれを所載する「国民之友」明治二十一年(一八八八)八月号を携えていたことになり、これはこれでドラマチックなつくりのイメージを

なす、ということも指摘しておきたい。

[3]『その前夜』の受容

ツルゲーネフの長編『その前夜』も、啄木にとっては格別に重い意味をなした。この作品は「あひゞき」が世に出た二年後、五七居士・佐藤武雄の「あらしの花美さほ草紙」題下の翻案として入り、その十九年後に、コンスタンス・ガーネットの英訳『ON THE EVE』からの重訳のかたちで本格的な訳出をみた。相馬御風訳『その前夜』〈近代傑作集第一編〉（明治四十一・四）がそれである。湯浅芳子訳『その前夜』〈岩波文庫〉（昭和二十六・十一）が出るまでというもの、この御風訳本が巷間にいきわたったことはいうまでもない。しかも受容者のうち、例えば土岐哀果（善麿）は己の第二詩集『黄昏に』（明治四十五）を編むに際し、当該の書名にちなむ「その前後」を章題として第二章の柱とした。また島村抱月は大正五年（一九一六）四月、この作品（楠山正雄脚色）を帝国劇場における芸術座第五回公演のだしものとした。啄木が御風訳『その前夜』を手にすることになった経緯は定かでない。上京して赤心館の住人となり、直ちに書き出した小説『菊池君』を六十一枚で中断し、あらためて「病院の窓」を起稿したことと因果関係があるとしたら、その自室への持ち込みは明治四十一年五月十八日頃なのだが……いずれにしても啄木はその二日後、就寝前に同書を半ばまで読み進んだ。当日の日記に「どの人物も、どの人物も、生きた人を見る如くハッキリとして居る書振り！予は巻を擲つて頭を掻むしつた。心悪きは才人の筆なる哉」とある。もしこの時、小説の執筆に取り組んでいなかったら、これほどの衝撃感が生じなかったに相違ない。啄木はツルゲーネフのリアリズム小説に自らの作物、もしくはこれから書こうとするものを反照させ、

その高邁な志とはうらはらに、力量の不安をかこちつつ、受けた刺激をしかと身の内にとどめ、それを自作の創出に反映させずにはいられなかった。以後の彼は、『その前夜』の後半の読みと「病院の窓」の書き継ぎとを交互に平行させていく。そして原稿が六十二枚まで達したところで漸く読みおえ、その三日後（五月二三日）の午後三時過ぎをもって九十一枚の完結をなした。

その間、啄木はこの物語──トルコの支配下にあるブルガリアの祖国解放運動に加わっている青年インサロフと、この人物を恋する娘エレネを中心とした物語のうち、とりわけ「インサロフとエレネの熱き恋」（「日記」五月二十二日）に着目、キャラクター論を超えた人生の奥行きを小説論的に思索し、葛藤にともなう競争心理から批判意識へと転じたあげく、

ツルゲーネフは矢張十九世紀の文豪で（略）予の競争者としては、彼はあまりに古い、話上手だ、少し怠けた考を持って居る。予は予の小説を書くべしだ。（「日記」五月二三日）

との考えに立った。つまりツルゲーネフは小説に現われる人の一生を、

生誕─恋─熱烈な恋
　　　　　├─失恋─涙─意気地なし─死。
　　　　　└─結婚
　　　　　　　├─善良なる良人─父─死。
　　　　　　　└─夫婦喧嘩─意気地なし─死。

のかたちで抽出するタイプの文豪であるが、彼の時代との推移の差を考えると、いまは

```
                          生誕
                        ／││＼
                       恋 恋 恋 恋
                              │
                             暴風
                           ／  │  ＼
                         結婚  苦悶  「わが心君を忘るゝ、
                        ／│    │    天地に家するしらぬ浪
                      不安 父  第二の恋  人といへ」と歌ふ人
                      ／  │    －       －コスモポリタン－死。
                  生殖の機関  平凡なる悲劇の主人公  第三第四－死。
                   －死。     －死。
```

失恋―第二の恋―第三の恋――死。

といったかたちで複雑化していることゆえ、ツルゲーネフの古さを乗りこえて、自分なりに現代の小説を目指すというわけだ。掲出の展開図を記述した当日の日記に、「彼と競争しようと思った事を茲に改めて取消す」ともある。

かくして「病院の窓」は、作者の認識と技量が向上した分だけ完成度が上がった。同宿の先輩たる金田一京助が、さっそく「中央公論」と掛け合った理由でもある。もしこれが掲載されていれば、啄木の文壇への夢はふくらんだはずで、埋もれたことは惜しまれよう。すさまじい受容の顚末である。ここに至って、受容の事実が判らなかったときには思いもつかなかったような表現の中に、もしかしたら無縁とは言えぬものがあることも予想される。そのような可能性のあるものとして、次の二点に注目してみたい。まず一点目は、エッセイ「汗に濡れつゝ」（九）（「函館日日新聞」明治四十二・八・五）の第一段落

大森浜の浪穏かな、六月（一昨年）の或る日であつた。予は岩崎君―友人―と二人、とある砂山の上に寝転んでみた。空霽れて日の光華やかに、砂は心地よく温まつてゐた。何の話をしたかは忘れたが、然うして寝転んでゐたのは三時間か四時間の長い間であつた。

とある箇所で、これは啄木が函館へと渡つた明治四十年（一九〇七）六月の晴れた日、友人の岩崎白鯨と二人で大森浜の砂上に寝転び、心安く「三時間か四時間の長い間」談笑にふけつたというもの。この体験の掘り起こしはむろん表現意図に即し、爾後の展開に必要なシチュエーションとしてごく自然に発想されたかのごとくであるが、あるいは着想の淵源における、心象のレベルでの、もうひとつのイメージ体験といつたものが絡んでいたとしたらどうであろうか。

千八百五十三年の夏のあつい盛りであつた。コーントソフから程遠からぬ莫斯科河（モスコー河）の河岸、菩提樹の陰を枕に偃臥つてゐる二人の青年がある。（略）アンドレイ・ペトロキッチ・ベルセネフというのがその名で、もう一人の髪の柔かな青年は、パウル・ヤコウリッチ・シュービンといふのである。（略）

右は相馬御風訳『その前夜』の冒頭（一頁）である。掲出文のあとに、この両者による会話が続くが、親しい間柄ということでその内容は青春期特有の身辺的もしくは哲学味を帯びたものとなっている。いま割愛部を若干補つて整理してみよう。季節は夏、天候は晴、場所はモスクワ川の河岸（菩提樹の前）、人物は若い青年二人、様態はベルセネフがあお向きでシュービンは腹這い、行為は単なる会話、経過時間は

数時間といったところ。一方、啄木の「汗に濡れつゝ」(九) は、季節は、初夏、天候は晴、場所は函館の大森浜の砂丘、人物は若い青年二人、様態は共に寝転んでいる、掲出部における行為は談笑、経過時間は三時間か四時間となっている。かくして「汗に濡れつゝ」(九) は、「その前夜」の時代設定から約半世紀を隔つといえども、その季節・場所のとり方・青年二人の登場のさせ方・その容態や行為、経過時間帯などとことごとく近似の関係にあるといってよい。しかも当該の一文が冒頭に位置しているところまで同じである。

このようにみてくると、如上の近似は単に偶然のことというだけではすまぬ、やはり『その前夜』を享受した啄木の側に、受容・影響の痕跡をとどめた可能性があることが指摘できるのである。

次に注目しておきたいのは、「明治四十一年作家ノート」の九月二十三日の条に「森ゆけば遠きひゞき す木のうろに臼ひく侏儒の国に来けんかも」とあり、『暇ナ時』の十月十日千駄ヶ谷徹夜会での作として「森ゆけば遠き響す木のうろに臼ひく侏儒の国に来しかも」とあり、「明星」明治四十一年 (一九〇八) 十一月号所載「謎」中に「森の奥遠きひゞきす木のうろに臼ひく侏儒の国にかも来し」とあって、約二年後、歌集『一握の砂』の「秋風のこころよさに」の章に、

　　森の奥
　　遠きひびきす
　　木のうろに臼ひく侏儒(しゅじゅ)の国にかも来(こ)し

とある一首についてである。「侏儒」は小人もしくは一寸法師の意であるから、歌意からいって、これは

啄木の独創に相違はないのだが、さりとて詠出の背後に想を導いたイメージが皆無だったかというと、必ずしもそうとは言えないような気がする。と言うのは、

　「例へば秋の日、森の中にさすらへて、森の神のいみじき歌ごゑに耳をすますとき」…

との御風訳『その前夜』の一節（十八頁）に啄木は確実に出会い、読んでいたからである。ちなみにこれは長身のベルセネフのセリフの一節で、「あまり仰山な文句を持ち出したのできまりが悪くなった様子」との語り手によるコメントがついている。

この場合、会話の流れとしての部分から、「秋の日、森の中にさすらへて、森の神のいみじき歌ごゑに耳をすます」までの、これをひとつの表現体とみたとき、あながちそれと無関係とは言えないのではないか。このことは、先掲歌に収まる啄木の詠嘆のプロットもまた、「森の神のいみじき歌ごゑに耳をすます」―「森の中」―「森の奥」、「さすらへ」る―「来し」、「遠きひびきす」などといった語句の対応関係をなすことによっても判然とする。

したがって、かくなる語句上の相関性をふまえたとき、「森の奥」の一首は独自性を印象づけていると言えども、その背後に『その前夜』が擁す諸要素の存在があるであろうことを、然るべき読者に予感せずにはおかないのだ。これも啄木がツルゲーネフの訳本『その前夜』を繙いていたがゆえに、それからの影響があったと思料し得るに足る、透析結果として導き得る、結論となさしめるものなのである。

[4] 『散文詩』の受容

啄木はツルゲーネフの『散文詩』（原題『セニリヤ』）にも出会っていた。明治期にこれを訳出したものとしては、上田敏訳の「散文詩」十篇――「田舎者」「山霊」「祈禱」「老嫗(ろうばば)」「犬」「わが敵」「物乞」「満足」「処世法」「戦はむ哉」（所収『みをつくし』明治三十四・十二、文友館）と、仲田勝之助訳『セニリヤ』（明治四十三・十一）などがあった。啄木が確実に手元に置いたことがあるのは、

「……『みをつくし』中に輯(をさ)められたる上田敏氏の同文の訳と比しても……」（「岩手県師範学校校友会雑誌」を読む）

とあることをふまえるならば、次の二作品との関わりが問題となる。すなわち一つ目は、散文詩「曠野」（「明星」明治四十一・七）で、これは曠野に踏み込んだ〈旅人〉が、やがて飢えた一匹の〈赤犬〉に出会って同病相憐む仲となるものの、戯謔的にマッチを擦って同犬を死に至らしめ、そのあと帰る道が判らなくなって泣き出すというもの。一方、これに関わるツルゲーネフの作品は「老嫗」である。これは、ひとり曠野をゆく「われ」が後ろに続く人の気配に気づき、立ちどまって問うが目は動かず言葉も発せぬ「瞽(ご)女(ぜ)」だったので驚いたが、やがて先に歩く彼女の姿にいつしか「人の免るに由なき運命」を感ずるのであ

った、という仕立てをなす。

叙事詩としてのプロットでいうと両者の差異性は明らかだが、それでいて共通もしくは対応の関係を看過しうるものではない。いまそれをみておくと、まず冒頭の一行が「路に迷ったのだ！」と「孤り曠野をゆく」(後者が「老媼」、以下同様)、場所が「曠野」と「曠野」、登場者が「旅人」と「われ」・「赤犬」と「瞽女」、出会いによる双互関係が〈誰かの助けがなければ前途多難な「瞽女」と絶対に優位な「われ」〉、趣意に内在するものが〈旅路・出会い・哀れみ・別れ・孤独〉と〈旅路・出会い・哀れみ・同行・運命凝視〉といった対応関係をしている。また生活上の逼迫感、共同体からの亀裂感、生存の危機感などといった面でも両者の近似性を見逃し得ない。これらのことを勘案すると、啄木の散文詩「曠野」の叙事結構のモチーフが、多分に「老媼」に依拠するものであったというふうに推断できるのである。

もう一つの作品は、『一握の砂』の第一章「我を愛する歌」に収められている次の一首(「明星」明治四十一・七)

　燈影(ほかげ)なき室に我あり
　父と母
　壁のなかより杖つきて出づ

で、これは歌稿ノート「暇ナ時」に、明治四十一年(一九〇八)六月二十五日夜二時までの作歌欄にあるから、前記散文詩「曠野」より三日後に成ったことがわかる。同じ夜に「父母は老いていませりあはれ蚊よ皆来て我の瘦脛(やせすね)を螫(さ)せ」の一首も作られているので、離散して長男の責務を果たし得ない作者の、両親

に対する孝養不能の負い目が平素心をよぎっていて、それが詠嘆のモチーフをなしたことはいうまでもない。

それにしても"自分の両親が燈影ない部屋の壁のなかから杖をついて出てきた"というプロットは、一作の歌柄の美的な趣きとはうらはらに戦慄的で、ライフ・イリュージョン（生活幻像）のきわみとなすが、この方は、上田敏訳の散文詩「わが敵」に拠るところがあるといえそうだ。ちなみに同作品は、"かつての論敵はいま墓の中にいるが、その彼が生前の言葉通りにひと夜、自分が寝つかれずにいるところに現れたので、再び論争の継続を挑むが、彼は黙したままやがて消え失せた"という内容で、その亡霊が現れる幻覚のくだりは、

　ひと夜、床にありて、いねられず。げに眼は襲はざりけり。室(へや)はにび色の、覚束なき薄明り、みいりつゝ、忽ち窓前に、わが仇のたてるを見る。頭静に振りてうなづくも、あはれや。

となっている（『上田敏全集』第二巻　昭和五十四・二、八十二頁）。この部分と掲出歌を対照させると、非在の「わが仇」（かつての論敵の亡霊）と不在の「父と母」、「薄明」の「室」と「燈影なき室」、「夜」と〈夜〉の刻、〈「わが仇」〉が「窓前」に現れたこと〉と〈「父と母」が「壁の中より杖つきて出づ」〉といった具合に、構成要素としての人物素・環境（舞台）素・時間素・行動素などがきわめて具体化して対応関係をなし、また、無意識の下層──潜在意識の顕現現象としてのライフ・イリュージョンという面でも、両作品は共通項を具有しあっている。

如上の要件が出揃ってくると、もはや偶然のしからしめるところと言い捨てにするわけにはいかない。

したがって「燈影なき…」の一首は、ツルゲーネフの「わが敵」を受容した体験が生かされての詠出であったろうというふうに裁断できる。ちなみに当該歌の初出冒頭は「灯なき」。一晩に百四十二首作ったうちの一首であることを考慮するまでもなく、啄木は歌興がおこると既に読んだ書物の中からイメージや題材を得ることがしばしばあった。この一首はその一典型をなすものといえるのである。

[5] 『うき草』（『ルージン』）に及んで

二葉亭四迷訳の『うき草』（原題『ルージン』明治三十）との関係も特記を要す。この作品は、一八四〇年代のロシアにかなり多く見かけられた知識人の一典型——すぐれた頭脳を有しながらも、現実を直視して適応する能力を欠いた空想児を主人公として、そのみじめな人生惨敗の姿を描き、十九世紀中葉のロシア文壇に作者ツルゲーネフの名を強烈にアピールした傑作として知られる。わが国では明治三十年（一八九七）に二葉亭四迷によって翻訳紹介されたが、これに刺激された読者は数しれず、たとえば国木田独歩の場合、短編の「正直者」や「女難」の構成にあたって、『うき草』（『ルージン』）から技法上のヒントを得たとされる。

啄木がこの二葉亭四迷訳『うき草』を読んだであろうことは容易に察せられるが、その時期は現存する彼自身の日記類の欠落との兼ね合いで、これを直かに把握することはできない。しかし、仮に『猟人日記』の耽読よりも後だとしても、上京後に金田一京助の世話で身を置いた赤心館および転宿後の蓋平館には、大学等に通う意気盛んな徒輩が頻繁に出入りし、また啄木自身も人脈を開拓するところがあって、直接もしくは間接的にさまざまな情報に出会うことができた。それと共に貸本屋の出入りもあり、たとえば、直

136

吉江孤雁訳の『ツルゲーネフ短篇集』(明治四十一)は、東京朝日新聞社に入社後の四月七日夜、枕の上で読んだ。同日の「ローマ字日記」の末尾に「Makura no ue de "Turgenev Tanpen Syū" wo yomu.」とある。あるいはこの日記の記述をふまえてのことと思われるが、金田一京助は後日、『ルージン』や『貴族の家』や『ふさぎ虫』などを借りた時には、面白いから是非読めということで、到頭私まで読まされた」(『石川啄木』)との回顧譚をのこしている。

こうしたことを勘案するに、啄木は『うき草』(『ルージン』)と出会っていたことは間違いないとして、その時期であるが、もし上京直後の六月二十五日までのことであるならば、次の一首との関係が生じてこよう。

若しも我露西亜に入りて反乱に死なむといふも誰か咎めむ

いま六月二十五日までと言ったのは、同日の「暇ナ時」当該欄の「百四十一首」と明記された歌群の中に、これが記されているからにほかならない。他に類似の歌柄が見当たらないので、ここではこの一首に限られるが、提示の前提条件にて比較文学的考究の視点を据えるならば、二葉亭の訳した『うき草』が投影している可能性をなしとはしない。短歌という様式上の制約により説明に欠けるが、一首中の「我」が「露西亜に入りて反乱に死なむ」と志向するあたりは、『うき草』の主人公ルージンが、フランス国内の反乱(民衆の抵抗運動)に加わって壮烈な死を遂げる結末部に絞っても、あるいはそこへと至る彼の〈ヴ・ナロード〉志向との兼ね合いにおいても、かなりの近似性を認め得るのである。

しかし、それでも当該の一首は、如上の把握では十分なる分析とは言い難い。それと言うのも、ロシア

で起った近時の大事件が、情報に機敏なる啄木の関知するところであったとしたらどうであろうか。ちなみに当該の事件に言及しておくとしよう。一九〇五年一月二十二日(ロシア暦では九日の日曜日)、首都のペテルブルグで十数万の民衆が、ガポン主教の指導のもとに労働者の窮状を訴え、憲法制度を請願するため、皇帝ニコライ二世のいる冬宮へと向かって行進したのに対して、警官隊と軍隊が発砲し、一〇〇〇名以上の死者と二〇〇〇名以上の負傷者を出し、第一次ロシア革命の発端をなした。世に言うところの〈血の日曜日事件〉がこれである。

むろんこの事件は、本邦においては報道が遮断されたが、もし啄木が明治四十一年(一九〇八)六月二十五日の時点でそれに気づいていたならば、「若しも我露西亜に入りて反乱に死なむといふも誰か咎めむ」には、もうひとつの解釈を成り立たせる可能性のなしとはしない。すなわち、創作の題材に及んでの二重の契機といったもので、これを具体的に述べると、その一は、さきに可能性として指摘した『うき草』(『ルージン』)の受容であり、その二は、いま述べた〈血の日曜日事件〉をふまえるものであった……。むしろ、この二重の受容による投影とみる方がよいようにも思うが、目下のところ前提条件の確定をみない。

以上、十九世紀ロシアの作家イワン・セルゲーウィチ・ツルゲーネフの作品が、明治日本へと移入したことによる同時代青年の敏感な反応として、もしくは文業促進の契機として石川啄木に深く関わるところを、受容および影響の問題として考察してみた。むろん、如上の結果をなすからといって彼の文業が少しも誇りの対象となるはずもなく、否、そんな受容を背景に宿すことに構うことなく、やはり彼なりの作品世界の構築として確固たる存在を主張しているのだ。

厳しく他者の眼を遮断した啄木の創作現場を垣間見たいま、その〝天才輩出〟の苦闘のさまに、いささ

かの感慨を禁じ得ない。

[注]

1 啄木の遺品とされる、函館図書館所蔵の三省堂版『新訳英語辞典』中の当該項目についても当った。同図書館の渡辺美樹子氏のご協力に感謝したい。

2 哀果の筆名で編まれた善麿の第二歌集『黄昏に』は、その二章目を「その前後」と銘うち、合計六十六首の三行歌を収めている。すべて啄木の善麿との交遊歌ということであるが、この場合の章題は二重の使用契機を擁していた。すなわち一は、善麿と啄木両者における「われらの事業」＝共同で企画実行しながらも最後に頓挫したところの、文芸雑誌「樹木と果実」の発刊事業にまつわる思いの情感。そして二は、これより数年前、つまり二十二歳前後の善麿がロシア文学、とりわけツルゲーネフの作品に心を傾け、『ON THE EVE』に関しては相馬御風訳の『その前夜』（明治四十一・四）を読み、自らの青春の哀傷感との重ね合わせで、未だ定めやらぬ感動を持続していたこと。したがって、『黄昏に』中の「その前後」には、啄木との提携事業計画に関わる「その前後」と、これと響きの近いツルゲーネフ作品の邦題「その前夜」をふまえた謂の重なり、もしくは近似を認め得るのである。

3 当該公演の際、松井須磨子によって「ゴンドラの歌」が歌われた。この劇中歌は吉井勇の作で、その歌詞は——

いのち短し恋せよ乙女／朱き唇(あかくちびる)あせぬ間に
熱き血潮の冷えぬ間に／明日の月日のないものを

いのち短し恋せよ乙女／いざ手を取りてかの舟に
いざ燃ゆる頬を君が頬に／ここには誰も来ぬものを

いのち短し恋せよ乙女／波に漂う舟のように
君が柔手(やわて)をわが肩に／ここには人目のないものを

となっている。作曲は中山晋平。十七世紀のイギリスの詩人ロバート・ヘリックの詩「Hesperides」の中に、

「乙女たちよ、若いうちに恋の花を摘みなさい……きょう美しく咲き誇る花も明日の命は知れないのだから」との語句があるが、ここは吉井勇の独創であろう。

4 『比較文学辞典』（一九七八年）中の「国木田独歩」の項（八十四頁）参照。

5 十九世紀ロシアの七〇年から八〇年代、農民に土地を解放することを主張して立ち上がった知識階級の革命家（ナロードニキ［人民主義者］）たちによるスローガン、すなわち「ヴ・ナロード」（V narod［民衆の中へ］）のこと。この言葉は広がって、日本でも幸徳秋水の『平民主義』（明治四十）が取り上げ、当時の青年たちに知られて語彙としても定着した。

6 啄木は幸徳秋水の「平民主義」を継いで「ヴ・ナロード」に出会っていた。彼はロシアの青年の思想的行動ビジョンに共感すると共に、おりからの時代閉塞の現状に対処する知恵の発露の場を詩作にもとめ、その内なる思いをモチーフに詩「はてしなき議論の後」を創作した。四連から成るこの詩の各連末には、「されど、誰一人、握りしめたる拳をたたきて、／'V NARODﾞ と叫び出づるものなし。」との句行が措えられ（リフレーン）、詩想と思想の融合が美しくはかられている。なお、同世代の土岐善麿もこの「ヴ・ナロード」に共鳴していた。彼の随筆「南窓記」（『冬凪』所収）中に、「ロシアの『人民の中へ』ゆく運動と青年達の運命は、ツルゲーネフの『ルージン』（二葉亭の訳した『うき草』）などにも示唆されていた」（一五一頁）とある。

［付記］
本文中に提出した啄木作品は、『石川啄木全集』全八巻（筑摩書房、一九七八〜七九年）に依る。なお、本稿は「日本大学短期大学部（三島）研究年報」第十集（一九九七年）に掲載の「ツルゲーネフの『猟人日記』他移入―石川啄木における受容―」に加筆し、改題したものである。

07 虎の書跡

ボルヘスと中島 敦

諸坂成利

はじめに

ボルヘスの一九七二年の詩集 *El oro de los tigres* に、"Tankas"（「短歌」）という作品（短歌六首）がある。その四首目、

Bajo la luna
El tigre de oro y sombra
Mira sus garras.

No sabe que en el alba
Han destrozado un hombre

を読んだ時、私は愕然とした、と同時に非常に興奮を覚えた、と同時に、これを何とか「五七五七七」の日本語に（翻訳嫌いの私としては珍しく）訳したいと考えた。スペイン語では、「母音＋母音」は一音と数えるので、ボルヘスの短歌は一応「五七五七七」の形態をとっている。当時私は学部の四年、スペイン語を始めて四年目、今から考えると恐ろしく未熟であり、未熟さゆえの大胆さから、その頃私が感心した幾つかのボルヘス的と思われる詩も含めて八篇の詩を翻訳し、早稲田大学文学部文芸科の機関誌に発表してしまった。今では多少後悔しているが、その時これを、

しらずして人殺めたる暁月の爪みる黄金の虎と其の影

と訳した。「暁月」は私の造語であるが、「暁月夜」という言葉もあるし、また「暁＝el alba」と「月＝la luna」を表現しなければならなかったのでこのように無理にまとめてしまわざるを得なかった。この翻訳から十六年後、ラテンアメリカ文学を中心に数多くの作品を翻訳・紹介されている鼓先生はこれを次のように訳す。

月の下の／黄金と影の虎は、／爪に眼を凝らす。／しらしら明けに、人を／裂いたとは知らずに。2

鼓先生の訳はほぼ直訳であるが、この二つの翻訳からすでにボルヘスの世界は明らかであろう。これは中島敦の「山月記」である。月光の下で、今一頭の虎が自分の爪を見ている。その爪には人間を殺した時の血がついており、おそらくその口にも血はついているだろう。虎は、何故自分がこのような行動をとってしまったのか、爪を見ながら自責の念にかられているようである。まるで「山月記」の、「人間の心で、虎としての己の残虐な行のあとを見、己の運命をふりかへる時」のようである。しかも爪を見ているのは、月の光で黄金に輝いている虎ともうひとつ、ある仕方での《分裂》までもが描かれている。人を殺したのは、虎の影の部分で、今虎は人間の心で爪を見ているのではないか。この虎はもとは人間であったのだろうか、それとも虎が人間になりつつあるのであろうか。夜明けにまた人を殺めてしまうのではないかという恐怖に怯えながら爪を見ているのであろうか。いずれにせよ、この作品は、「山月記」のどこかに挿入されても全く違和感のない〈短歌〉である。しかもそれを、「山月記」を知るはずのなかったボルヘスが書いているのである。私が最初にこれを読んだ時に、興奮を覚え、愕然とした所以である。

この問題に関しては、昭和六十二年六月二十一日、日本比較文学会第四九回全国大会（於：同志社大学）において「ボルヘスの短歌と中島敦の「山月記」？」というタイトルで発表し、日本比較文学会の学会誌『比較文学』第三十号（一九八八年三月）に研究ノートとして発表した。しかしその時私が中心にしたものは、この両者の文学的同質性から出発して、影響とは何かを考えること、影響と独自性の関係を考えることであり、中島やボルヘスの文学を考えるものではむしろなかった。この「短歌」を知るはるか以前に、私はシュタイナーの『脱領域の知性』（河出書房新社、一九七二）によりボルヘスとナボコフの存在を知り、ほぼ同時に中島敦も知り、ボルヘスと中島敦の文学的同質性には気がついていた。ボルヘスが

143

07 ─ 虎の書跡

偏愛するのは《虎》であり、シュタイナーのボルヘス論のタイトルも「鏡のなかの虎」であり、その頃私は教科書で「山月記」の《虎》に触れたからである。それにしても、なぜ《虎》なのであろう。ボルヘスの場合の虎は、幼少時に見たベンガルの虎の絵が記憶に残り、そのイメージがある仕方で決定的なものとなって、様々な作品の中に登場するようになったとも考えられるが、中島の場合にはそのような幼少時の体験はおそらくない。ボルヘスは作中の虎に喋らせたことはないが、中島の場合は森鷗外の博学に憧れた。共にブッキッシュな作家であった両者が、おそらく知識や書物との対極にある存在としての虎に憧れたことはひとつの反動として理解できる。しかし一体《虎》とは何なのか。本稿では、この問いを整えるべく、ボルヘスと中島敦の同質性を観察しながら、この問題圏の輪郭を描ければ、と考える。

[Ⅰ]

ボルヘスと中島敦の同質性に気付いたのは、無論私だけではない。池澤夏樹は中島敦の作品集の解説で次のように書く。

もしも『文字禍』がボルヘスの作品集のどれかに入っていたとしたら、人は異物が混じっていることに気付くだろうか。主題、長さ、話の展開、結末……どこをとってもこの短編はアルゼンチンの図書館長の作に似ている。たまたま似ているのではなく、知識人としてある手法で書くことに徹底すれば、これくらいの偶然は文学史には珍しくないのだ。しかし、日本でこんなことをし

た作家はいなかった。[引用A]3

ほとんど全くその通りで、「これくらいの偶然は文学史には珍しくない」以外は異論はない。この箇所への異論の理由は、中島敦以外に、これほどボルヘスに似た作品を、模倣、あるいは影響関係無しに書いた作家が世界にいないのではないかと推察されるからである。ナボコフ以上に、「文字禍」の中島敦はボルヘスに似ている。通常の手続きとしては、両テクストの分析作業の結果、類似性が浮かび上がるものであるが、ボルヘスと中島敦の場合にはその作業は不要である。もちろんボルヘスとの比較で言えば、「文字禍」、あるいは「狐憑」や「木乃伊」は特別似ていて、「ボルヘスの作品集のどれかに入っていたとし」ても分からないだろうが、素朴に、なぜこのようなことが起こったのだろうか、と先ず考えざるを得ない。「文字禍」については拙論「文字禍、あるいは書者/読者の不在」4の中で、ボルヘスと中島敦とエクリチュールに関する問題を中心に論じたが、両者の問題意識はほぼ同一のもので、今私が発した疑問には、エクリチュールの分析からは答えようにない。なぜなら、全く同じだからである。この「なぜ同じか」という疑問（本稿もそれに答える性質のものではないが）の答えとしては、一九四二年に亡くなった中島敦の魂が、アルゼンチンの作家ボルヘスに乗り移り、ボルヘスをして、夭折した中島がまだ書き残したものを書かしめた、ということを私は夢想する。ある仕方で凡庸な作家であったボルヘスが、突如彗星のごとく世界文学のマーケットに乗るきっかけとなったのが、一九四四年の *Ficciones* であり、時間的には今日〈ボルヘス的〉と言われる境地に達したのは実は中島敦の方が早く、両者に重なる部分は時間的にないからである。したがってそのようなことも夢想すらできないわけであるが、中島存命中のボルヘスは〈ボルヘス的〉ではなかった。このようなことを夢想すること自体、ボルヘスや中島敦の世界、あるいはその罠に入り込

んでしまっているわけで、この危険を研究者としては一応回避しなければならない。

[II]

しかし両者の類似性の分析は、ある意味で非常に困難である。流星群の如くそれらは流れ去って行き、説明や分析のために、どこを捉えれば良いのかが困難からである。例えば次の箇所はどうであろうか。ボルヘスの「タデオ・イシドロ・クルスの生涯（一八二九-一八七四）」からの引用である。

（彼を、未来に秘された、根本的な、明瞭なある一夜が待っていた。ついに自分自身の顔を見る夜、ついに自分の名を聞く夜が。真の意味を理解すれば、その夜は彼の全生涯を尽くすのである。より正確に言えば、その夜の一瞬、その夜の一行為が、である。なぜなら、行為が私達の象徴だからである。）人生はすべて、それが長く複雑であろうと、実際には「ただ一瞬で」成り立っている。その一瞬に、人は、自分が誰であるかを永遠に知るのである。マケドニアのアレキサンダー大王は、アキレスの伝説の物語に反映された己の鉄の未来を見、スウェーデンのカール十二世は、アレキサンダー大王の伝説の物語にそれを見たと言われている。その知識を、読むことを知らなかったタデオ・イシドロ・クルスに与えたのは書物ではない。彼は乱闘の中で、そして一人の男の中に、自分自身を見たのである。［引用B］

ここには様々な、中島敦の要素が含まれている。まず文体的に非常に特徴的なのが、「人は、自分が誰で

あるかを永遠に知るのである」と書いて、その後にアレキサンダー大王やカール十二世の例を挙げている点である。例えば「名人伝」では、紀昌が師である飛衞殺害を企て、それが未遂に、というよりも引き分けに終わった後、中島敦もこう書き加えなければ気がすまない。

二人は互ひに駈寄ると、野原の眞中に相抱いて、暫し美しい師弟愛の涙にかきくれた。(斯うした事を今日の道義觀を以て見るのは當らない。美食家の齊の桓公が己の未だ味はつたことのない珍味を求めた時、廚宰の易牙は己が息子を蒸燒にして之をすすめた。十六歳の少年、秦の始皇帝は父が死んだ其の晩に、父の愛妾を三度襲うた。凡てそのやうな時代の話である。)

易牙や始皇帝のエピソードは「名人伝」の物語とは無関係でありながら、このように挿入されると物語とのある種の関係性を帯びてくる。それはボルヘスの場合も同じで、ボルヘス批評においては、これは《入れ子構造》と呼ばれ、かつてはジョン・バースらアメリカの批評家によってかなり指摘され、ボルヘスやナボコフの文学が「枯渇の文学 literature of exhaustion」(「名人伝」はまさにそうであるが)などと喧伝されたことがあったが、入れ子同士はテクストの中で無関係では存在し得ず、互いに作用する関係性を所持してしまう。短編でありながら、それがひとつの小宇宙化してしまうのである。中島敦の批評に《入れ子構造》が登場したことはおそらくないのではないかと判断するが、この文体、文の運びはボルヘス同様中島敦の得意とするところである。

晋の魏楡の地で石がものを言つたといふ。民の怨嗟の聲が石を假りて發したのであらうと、或る

賢者が解した。既に衰微した周室は更に二つに分れて争つてゐる。十に餘る大國はそれぞれ相結び相鬪つて干戈の止む時が無い。齊侯の一人は臣下の妻に通じて夜毎その邸に忍んで來る中に遂に其の夫に弑せられて了ふ。楚では王族の一人が病臥中の王の頸をしめて位を奪ふ。呉では足頸を斬取られた罪人共が王を襲ひ、晉では二人の臣が互ひに妻を交換し合ふ。この様な世の中であつた。[引用C][8]

「弟子」からの引用であるが、ここでも「民の怨嗟」の説明に、複数の国の乱れが紹介されている。これを《博学》とだけ述べて済ませることはできない。また[引用A]にある〈知識人〉、あるいは知識人の作家だからという言い方も不充分である。この〈博学〉はそれ自体一種の魔術であり、これこそ両者の文学世界の本質にかかわる問題なのである。また[引用B]はボルヘスと中島敦に共通の重要なテーマであるidentityについても問題を開いている。「乱闘の中で、そして一人の男の中に、自分自身を見た」ということは、本当の《自分》が外部にあるということを示している。事実この引用の後、物語は自分が捕えようとした男マルティン・フィエロと共に、イシドロ・クルスが自分の部下たちと戦うところで終わっている。彼はマルティン・フィエロだったことを理解したのである。これは中島敦の「木乃伊」である。ペルシャ王カンビュセスのエジプト侵攻の時、その軍人パリスカスの様子がおかしくなる。王の、アメシス王の屍を発見して自分に持ってこいという命令を受けて、パリスカスも他の者たちとともに墓所の探索にのりだす。ある日気がつくと、彼は一人である墓所の中にいた。

パリスカスは殆ど無意識に足を運ばせて奥へ進んだ。……見ると、足許に木乃伊がころがってゐる。……彼は、その儘、行過ぎようとしてともつかぬものが、彼の背筋を走った。木乃伊の顔に注いだ視線を、最早外らすことが出來なくなった。彼は、磁石に吸寄せられたやうに、凝乎と身動きもせず、その顔に見入つた。

どれ程の長い間、彼は其處に、さうしてゐたらう。その間に、彼の中に非常な變化が起つたやうな氣がした。彼の身體を作上げてゐる、あらゆる元素どもが、彼の皮膚の下で、物凄く（丁度、後世の化學者が、試験管の中で試みる實驗のやうに）泡立ち、煮えかへり、其の沸騰が暫くして静まつた後は、すつかり以前の性質と變つて了つたやうに思はれた。

彼は大變やすらかな氣持ちになつた。……なんだ。こんな事だつたのか。彼は思はず聲に出して言つた。「俺は、もと、此の木乃伊だつたんだよ。たしかに。」
パリスカスが此の言葉を口にした時、木乃伊が、心持、唇の隅をゆがめたやうに思はれた。[10]

そしてパリスカスの脳裏に、この木乃伊が人間だつた頃の記憶が一瞬に転移する。そして前世の自分もまた、薄暗い小室で、ひとつの木乃伊と向かい合つているのを思い出し、愕然とするのである。

彼はぞつとした。一體どうしたことだ。この恐ろしい一致は。怯れずに尚仔細に觀るならば、前世に喚起した、その前々世の記憶の中に、恐らくは、前々々世の己の同じ姿を見るのではなからうか。合せ鏡のやうに、無限に内に疊まれて行く不氣味な記憶の連續が、無限に――目くるめ

くばかり無限に續いてゐるのではないか？」[11]

パリスカスは逃げ出そうとするが、体は動かず、木乃伊の顔から目をそらすことは出来ない。翌日、他の部隊が彼を発見した時、パリスカスは木乃伊を抱いたまま倒れており、エジプト語で譫言を喋り出す。これが「文字禍」の結末である。パリスカスは〔引用B〕のボルヘスの言葉を使えば、「自分が誰であるかを永遠に知」ったのである。両者に共通している問題は、identityが外部にあるという問題、内なるidentityの《「同じもの」=same》による破壊に他ならない。中島が述べる「合せ鏡」、前世も、そのまた前世も自分が木乃伊と向かい合っていた、それが無限に続くというイメージは、両輪で走っていた車の片輪が奪われ、永久に一軌道を廻り続ける運動にも似て、identityが破壊された時の現象と考えるべきであろう。この「合せ鏡」は、極めてボルヘス的なイメージなのである。このidentityの分裂・増殖は、「山月記」をはじめ中島敦の様々なテクスト中に散見されるが、それよりもここでは、比較的見落とされ易い次の箇所を引用する。「李陵」の司馬遷に関する引用である。

此の世に生きることをやめた彼は書中の人物としてのみ活きてゐた。現實の生活では再び開かれることのなくなつた彼の口が魯仲連の舌端を借りて始めて烈々と火を噴くのである。或ひは伍子胥となつて己が眼を抉らしめ、或ひは藺相如となつて秦王を叱し、或ひは太子丹となつて泣いて荊軻を送つた。楚の屈原の憂憤を叙して、その正に汨羅に身投ぜんとして作る所の懐沙之賦を長々と引用した時、司馬遷にはその賦がどうしても己自身の作品の如き氣がして仕方が無かった。[12]

ここは司馬遷が、魯仲連や伍子胥に「なる」場面である。ボルヘスは「トレーン、ウクバル、オルビス・テルティウス」の註で、トーレンのある教会の主張として、性交の絶頂をむかえる男は皆同一の男である。シェイクスピアの一行を繰り返す男は皆、ウィリアム・シェイクスピアその人である。[13]

を挙げている。司馬遷はここで様々な人間に「なる」のであるが、更に中島は、司馬遷にとって「懷沙之賦」が「どうしても己自身の作品」であるような気がしたと書かざるを得ない。これは《自己》が外部にある「木乃伊」の変奏である。またこの司馬遷の描写は、バフチンのポリフォニー、あるいは人は一人で書くことはあり得ず、テクストは必ず複数の書き手の作品となるというボルヘス的、比較文学的テーゼをも喚起する性質のものである。「どうしても己自身の作品の如き気がして仕方が無かった」と書かなければ、ここは司馬遷が懸命に『史記』を執筆しているようすが活写されているに過ぎない。しかし中島はここでも《自己》の問題に触れてくるのである。

それにしても、中島敦の《自己》とは何なのか？

俺といふものは、俺が考へてゐる程、俺ではない。……

[III]

俺といふものは、俺を組み立てゝゐる物質的な要素（諸道具立）と、それをあやつるあるものとで出來上がつてゐる器械人形のやうに考へられて仕方がない。[引用D]14

と、中島は、カメレオンがほとんど出てこない「かめれおん日記」に書いている。

全くの所、私のものゝ見方といつたつて、どれだけ自分のほんものがあらうか。いそつぷの話に出て來るお洒落鴉。レヲパルディの羽を少し。ショペンハウエルの羽を少し。ルクレティウスの羽を少し。荘子や列子の羽を少し。モンテエニュの羽を少し。何といふ醜怪な鳥だ。15

これは先の司馬遷の引用と呼応している。と同時に、これはボルヘスの「カフカとその先駆者たち」といふエッセーを想起させる。ボルヘスにとってこの認識は、醜怪でも何でもない、ごく当然のことである。おそらくこの點が、両者の重要な差異ではないかと考えられるが、中島にとって《自己》＝ identity とは、そのようなものであり、何故そのようになるかと言えば、

私といふ人間の肉體を組立てゝゐる各部分に注意が行き互るにつれ、次第に、私といふ人間の所在が判らなくなつて來た。[引用E]16

という見方をするからである。私は、この意識作用、あるいは意識の轉換、自己を見るもうひとつの自己という在り方が、「ボルヘスと私」を書いたボルヘスに極めて近いと考える。しかも、これは、結局のと

ころ「文字禍」の《文字》の変奏である。

博士は書物を離れ、唯一つの文字を前に、終日それと睨めっこをして過した。卜者は羊の肝臓を凝視することによって凡ての事象を直観する。彼も之に倣って凝視と靜觀とによって眞實を見出さうとしたのである。一つの文字を長く見詰めてゐる中に、何時しか其の文字が解體して、意味の無い一つ一つの線の交錯としか見えなくなって来る。單なる線の集りが、何故、さういふ音とさういふ意味とを有つことが出來るのか、どうしても解らなくなって来る。[17]

この引用の「羊の肝臓を凝視することによって凡ての事象を直観する」は、先の [引用B] と [引用C] で述べられた〈博学〉に関するボルヘスと中島の文体の共通性の好例ともなるが、この「肝臓」と「凡ての事象」の繋がり（カバラ的だが）は、ボルヘスにも当然ある。

私は考えた。人間の言語においてさえ、全宇宙を包含しないものはない。《虎》と言うことは、それを生み出した複数の虎を、それがむさぼり食った鹿と亀を、鹿を養った牧草を、牧草の母である大地を、大地に光を与えた空を意味する、と。また私は考えた。神の言語においては、あらゆる言葉が事物のこの無限の連鎖を表明するのだろう、暗にではなく明白に、徐々にではなく即座に表明するのだろう、と。時が経つにつれて、神聖な文という概念が、馬鹿げた、冒瀆的なものに思われて来た。神は、と私は考えた、一語を語らねばならず、その語の中にはすべてが満ち

153

ていなければならない。[18]

ボルヘスの「神の書跡」からの引用であるが、その「一語」が卜者にとっての「肝臓」であり、ボルヘスの「アレフ」であり、中島もボルヘスも、分裂や分身を描きながら、そういった《一なるもの》に惹かれていく。

《文字》を見ているうちに、それが判らなくなる、すなわち文字の意味は判るが、じっと見ていると判らなくなる、そういった瞬間がある、自分は自分だと判っているが、それが判らなくなる瞬間があるということである。とすれば、これは再び「山月記」の《虎》の状況に他ならない。従って、中島にとって《虎》とは、《文字》であり、《自己》であり、identityであり、《迷路》であり、《文字》である。「神の書跡」において《虎》に書かれた《文字》は十四語、四十音節であり、主人公は、その法悦の瞬間にそれを読むのである。

〈判らなさ〉とは、判るのに判らないといった状況である。

すべてを理解し、虎の書跡をも理解するに至った。[19]

作家としての「ボルヘス」と、生活者としての「私」の乖離をテーマとする（それ程単純ではないが）「ボルヘスと私」というテクストは、自己の分裂を描いている点で「山月記」と重なる。「今この文を書いているのが、私なのかボルヘスなのか私は知らない」という一文をもって終わるこのテクストが示す状況は、虎なのか人間なのか判らないという状況に重なるのである。中島は「中島と私」を書く程、自分を客

154

知の新視界

体化し、対象とすることはなかった。それが可能であったならば、「かめれおん日記」の苦悩は存在しなかった。中島はボルヘスほど、identityというものを自由に考えてはいなかった。おそらく美意識その他の微妙な違いが両者にはある。しかし把握していた問題圏は、見事に重なるのである。

[IV]

この《虎》＝《文字》＝《自己》＝identityの図式は、究極的にどこに達するのか。紙数の関係で両者のその軌跡を追うことは避けるが、この問題に関しては、中島の「名人伝」とボルヘスの「鏡と仮面」をその到達点と認識している。弓の名人を目指した紀昌は物語の最後で、弓矢を持たず鳥を射落とす甘蠅老師のもとで九年間修行をして都に帰ってくる。紀昌は表情のない、愚者のような顔つきになっている。飛衛はこれを見て、これぞ天下の名人と賞賛する。ところが紀昌は弓をとらない。その理由を訊ねた者に、

紀昌は懶げに言った。至爲は爲す無く、至言は言を去り、至射は射るなしと。成程と、至極物分りのいい邯鄲の都人士は直ぐに合點した。[20]

名人紀昌と一般人との認識の距離を意識させる書き方がここではなされている。かつて小林秀雄は、「分かる」ということが「苦労する」と同じことだ、と述べたことが想起されるが、名人芸を期待する大衆＝読者は紀昌の言葉を誤読したのである。ここでは大衆の程度、およびそれとの対比で、名人の到達した境地が計り知れないものであることが読み取れる。さらに年老いた紀昌は晩年次のように述べたとされる。

既に、我と彼との別、是と非との分を知らぬ。眼は耳の如く、耳は鼻の如く、鼻は口の如く思はれる。[21]

ここには先の［引用D］や［引用E］における自己不安はない。identityの自由が獲得されている。「名人伝」の最後は、更に紀昌が、己の存在の一部とも言える弓矢を忘却していることが明らかになって終わる。これは初めから弓矢を知らない人間が弓矢の名人だ、というのでは勿論ない。弓矢を、その意味が費消されるまで使い尽くしたがゆえの名人、ということであろう。一方、ボルヘスは「ザーヒル」の最後をこう結ぶ。

神の中で自らを失うために、スーフィー教徒は、自分自身の名前か九十九の神の名を、名がもはや意味をなさなくなるまで繰り返す。私もその道を辿ることを切望する。おそらく私は、《ザーヒル》を考えて考えて考えることによって、これを費消し終えるだろう。おそらくその貨幣の背後に、神がいるのだろう。[22]

《ザーヒル》は貨幣であり、これを見た瞬間、それ以外のことが考えられなくなってしまうというのがボルヘスの物語内容で、文学的テクストとして「名人伝」との短絡的な比較はできないが、意味がなくなるまで費消し尽くし、その果てに何かがあるというテーマは同じであろう。そして文学的テクストとしては、この「ザーヒル」よりも「鏡と仮面」を引用すべきであろう。「鏡と仮面」の物語はアイルランドの王がこの詩人に自分の武勲を讃える詩を作らせる物語である。最初王は詩人に一年の時間を与え、一年後詩人は見

事に仕事を果たすが、王は更に彫琢せよと命じる。しかし出来は見事であったので、詩人は銀の鏡を褒美にもらい、作品は三十人の書記に十二度筆写される。一年後、再び詩を携えて詩人はあらわれるが、詩人は作品を読むことを躊躇し、またその詩はより短くなっており、単数名詞の動詞が複数形になっていたり、前置詞の用法も通常ではないという奇妙なものに仕上がっている。しかし王は、これを前作よりも優れているとし、無知な者には分らないが、博識の者にはふさわしいとし、これを筆写させず象牙の箱に安置させ、詩人には黄金の仮面を褒美として与える。そして更にその一年後、再び詩人は宮廷に姿を現わす。

宮殿の歩哨たちは、詩人が原稿を持って来ていないことに気がついた。王は彼を見て驚いた。ほとんど別人のようであった。時ではない何ものかが、彼の顔に皺を刻み、彼の特徴を変貌させたのだ。両眼は、遥か遠くを見ているか、あるいは盲目となったかのように思われた。23

この詩人の描写は、紀昌のそれに酷似している。詩人も、中島敦の《名人》の境地に達したのである。作品は出来ていた。しかしそれはたった一行からなる詩であった。詩人はそれを誦することに躊躇する。しかし王はそれを命じる。詩は朗読された。

それを声高に誦して元気づくこともなく、詩人とその王とは、あたかも秘密の祈りか冒瀆であるかのようにそれを味わった。王も、詩人と同様驚異にうたれ、怯えていた。二人は青ざめて、見詰め合っていた。

若い頃、と王は言った、私は日没をめざして航海した。ある島で、金色の猪を殺す銀色の猟犬

を見た。ある島で、我々は魔法の林檎の芳香を食べて生きた。最も遠い島では、河が弧を描いて天にかかり、その水に魚や舟が走っていた。これらは驚異ではあるが、お前の詩には比ぶべくもない。この詩はある仕方で、これらすべてを内包している。[24]

王はこの詩句、この美を知ってしまったことは罪であり、われわれは贖わねばならないと考え、第三の褒美として詩人に短剣を与える。詩人は宮殿を出るや否やこれで命をたち、王は放浪の身となり、二度とあの詩句を繰り返すことはなかった、というのが「鏡と仮面」の物語内容である。この一行からなる「すべてを内包している」詩句とは、音楽的比喩をもって語れば、複数の音から成る旋律ではなく、一音から成っているかのようで、実際には複数の音を所持し、すべての音を含んでいるかに聴こえる日本の名鐘の音のようなものであろう。それは、「至言は言を去り」のまさに一歩手前、その臨界点を示すもの、中島敦にとっての《虎》＝《文字》＝ identity への問いが消滅する臨界点であろう。と同時に、これは宇宙を内包する「アレフ」であり、一切の書物を所有する「バベルの図書館」であり、「文字禍」の〈文字の靈〉であり、「俺を組み立てゝゐる物質的な要素」を「あやつるあるもの」の元にあるもの、ある仕方での根源であり、詩人の顔を変貌させた「時ではない何ものか」であり、悟浄が求め続けたものであり、作家が《オリジナル》なものを書くこと、その独自性の否定の根源である。ボルヘスはこの視点をやすやすと受け入れ、作者の否定、作者の identity の複数性まで述べているが、あの時代、日本人であった中島敦にその視点を受け入れることはおそらくできなかったのであろう。それゆえ中島は「山月記」（これは思想的にはボルヘス的ではない）を書くことになり、「アレフ」や「バベルの図書館」の存在に気付きながらそれを信じられなかったがゆえに、老荘的な「名人伝」を書いた、というのが私の目下の結論で

ある。「わしらこそ彼等文字の精霊にこき使はれる下僕ぢや」とまで書いた中島も、「一切はすでに書かれている」とは言わなかった。しかしこれは中島の限界を示すものではない。そうであるがゆえに逆にその文学は豊かなものになっていると考える。いずれにせよ、《虎の書跡》を読み解くために、中島敦が問い続けたもの、そしてボルヘスとの類似性の、少なくとも輪郭は明らかであると考える。

[注]

1 ホルヘ・ルイス・ボルヘス、諸坂成利訳、「ボルヘス詩抄」、『文芸早稲田』第六号［早稲田大学創立百周年記念号］（早稲田大学文学部文芸研究室、一九八二年）八二頁。

2 鼓直訳『ボルヘス詩集』（思潮社、一九九八年）七八頁。

3 池澤夏樹、「知性と南風」、『中島敦〈ちくま日本文学全集〉』、（筑摩書房、一九九二年）四五七-四五八頁。

4 「交錯する言語」新谷敬三郎教授古稀記念論文集』所収、（名著普及会、一九九二年［平成四］年三月二〇日

5 中島の「木乃伊」、そしてボルヘスの「タデオ・イシドロ・クルスの生涯（一八二九-一八七四）」、「円環の廃虚」、そして「コールリッジの夢」などはまさにこのテーマ、identity や夢、欲望の転移を扱っている。

6 Jorge Luis Borges, Obras completas, Buenos Aires : Emecé, 1974, 562.
(Lo esperaba, secreta en el porvenir, una lúcida noche fundamental : la noche en que por fin vio su propia cara, la noche en que por fin oyó su nombre. Bien entendida, esa noche agota su historia ; mejor dicho, un instante de esa noche, un acto de esa noche, porque los actos son nuestro símbolo.) Cualquier destino, por largo y complicado que sea, consta en realidad de un solo momento : el momento en que el hombre sabe para siempre quién es. Cuéntase que Alejandro de Macedonia vio reflejado su futuro de hierro en la fabulosa historia de Aquiles ; Carlos XII de Suecia, en la de Alejandro. A Tadeo Isidoro Cruz, que no sabía leer, ese conocimiento no le fue revelado en un libro ; se vio a sí mismo en un entrevero y un hombre. ("Biografía de Tadeo Isidoro Cruz (1829-1874)")

7 中島敦、『中島敦全集一』（筑摩書房、二〇〇一年）四四二頁。

8 中島敦、四五八-四五九頁。

9 シュタイナーはこの問題を正確に把握していると考えられる。George Steiner, *Extraterritorial: Papers on Literature and the Language Revolution*, 1971 (Atheneum, New York: Peregrine Books, 1975).

10 中島敦、一八‐一九頁。

11 中島敦、二一頁。

12 中島敦、五二四頁。

13 Borges, *OC*, 438 "Todos los hombres, en el vertiginoso instante del coito, son el mismo hombre. Todos los hombres que repiten una línea de Shakespeare, *son* William Shakespeare.

14 中島敦、三八八‐三八九頁。

15 中島敦、三九二‐三九三頁。

16 中島敦、三八九頁。

17 中島敦、三二頁。

18 Borges, *OC*, 597-598, "Consideré que aun en los lenguajes humanos no hay proposición que no implique el universo entero ; decir el tigre es decir los tigres que lo engendraron, los ciervos y tortugas que devoró, el pasto de que se alimentaron los ciervos, la tierra que fue madre del pasto, el cielo que dio luz a la tierra. Consideré que en el lenguaje de un dios toda palabra enunciaría esa infinita concatenación de los hechos, y no de un modo implícito, sino explícito, y no de un modo progresivo, sino inmediato. Con el tiempo, la noción de una sentencia divina parecióme pueril o blasfematoria. Un dios, reflexioné ; sólo debe decir una palabra y en esa palabra la plenitud."

19 Borges, *OC*, 599, "...entendiéndolo todo, alcancé también a entender la escritura del tigre."

20 中島敦、四四四頁。

21 中島敦、四四五頁。

22 Borges, *OC*, 595, "Para perderse en Dios, los sufíes repiten su propio nombre o los noventa y nueve nombres divinos hasta que éstos ya nada quieren decir. Yo anhelo recorrer esa senda. Quizá yo acabe por gastar el Zahir a fuerza de pensarlo y de repensarlo ; quizá detrás de la moneda esté Dios."

23 Jorge Luis Borges, *Obras completas II*, Buenos Aires : Emecé, 1989, 47, "Los centinelas del palacio advirtieron que el poeta no traía un manuscrito. No sin estupor el Rey lo miró ; casi era otro. Algo, que no era el tiempo, había surcado y transformado sus rasgos. Los ojos parecían mirar muy lejos o haber quedado ciegos."

24 Borges, *OC II*, 47, "Sin animarse a pronunciarla en voz alta, el poeta y su Rey la paladearon, como si fuera una plegaria secreta o una blasfemia. El Rey no estaba menos maravillado y menos maltrecho que el otro. Ambos se miraron, muy pálidos. /—En los años de mi juventud—dijo el Rey—navegué hacia el ocaso. En una isla vi lebreles de plata que daban muerte a jabalíes de oro. En otra nos alimentamos con la fragancia de las manzanas mágicas. En otra vi murallas de fuego. En la más lejana de todas nos abovedado y pendiente surcaba el cielo y por sus aguas iban peces y barcos. Éstas son maravillas, pero no se comparan con tu poema, que de algún modo las encierra."

＊中島敦の引用に関しては新版の全集に拠ったが、ワープロにない正字に関してはこれを変更せざるを得なかったことを付記する。

08 河野多恵子と『嵐が丘』

人間存在の不思議

榎本義子

河野多恵子（一九二六- ）は女性の心の深奥を描くために、超自然的、神秘的要素をしばしば用いている。作品中に巧みに組み込まれた亡霊や他の超自然現象は、現実と想像、客観と主観の微妙で危うい関係や、平穏に見える日常生活の中に潜む不気味さを浮き彫りにする。彼女の作りだす不思議な世界は、多大な影響を受けたという泉鏡花と共にエミリ・ブロンテ（一八一八-一八四八）を思い出させる。実際、谷崎潤一郎、泉鏡花、エミリ・ブロンテの三人以上に「鮮烈な印象を与えた作家はちょっと思い浮かばない」と彼女自身が述べている。

河野がエミリ・ブロンテの作品を知ったのは、大阪府女子専門学校の英詩の授業であったという。戦時

中爆弾の降下音が響く中で、日々生命の危険にさらされるという切迫した状況に置かれていたときに出会った、エミリの力強く「不滅の生」をうたった詩「私の魂は臆病ではない」("No coward soul is mine")は、彼女に強い感銘を与えた。死に直面して感覚が研ぎ澄まされ、超自然的なものと感応して霊魂の存在を感じた河野は、この詩と「特殊な交わり」をもったというが、彼女はその時の気持ちを『嵐が丘』の超自然性」の中で次のように述べている。

死にたくない、と全身が力む。爆死させられる一瞬に、その力みきった死にたくなさは、肉体から咄嗟に飛びだしそうであったばかりか、確かに何かが飛びだしかけたのを感じたこともある。今もって、恐怖のあまりの妄想だったとは思えない。その何かこそ霊魂というものにちがいなく、私は超自然なるものを信じずにはいられない。…そういう経験を繰り返し、死の公算が大きくなってくるにつれ、二、三篇ずつ教わった彼女たち三姉妹の詩のなかにあった、エミリの詩のひとつをしきりに思いだすようになったのだった。彼女の最後の詩"No coward soul is mine"（私の魂は臆病ではない）である。私はもし死なずに平和に会うことができたら、彼女の人と作品を存分に知りたいと思った。…その詩の一種の神秘思想と激しい精神、そこに射し込んでいる眩しいほどの輝かしい安らぎは、当時の私をどれほど励まし、慰め、救ってくれたかしれない。

さらに、エミリの『嵐が丘』(*Wuthering Heights*, 1847)は河野多恵子がものを書き始めるうえで、決定的な影響を与えた。終戦後、焼け残った古本屋でエミリの人と作品を熱心に求めたが、『嵐が丘』の訳本は手に入らず、彼女がその「全貌に接したのは」、一九四九年、三宅幾三郎訳の新刊書によってであっ

た。『嵐が丘』は彼女をエミリ・ブロンテの「精神的種族」にし、この作品を読んだことが、小説を書きはじめる「二段階目の動機」（三四〇）になったという。また、一九七一年に書かれたエッセイ「半年だけの恩師」では、『嵐が丘』は彼女の文学に「実に多くの影響を与えているようだし、今なお与え続けている」と語っている。いったいこの作品は彼女にどのような影響を与えているのだろうか。彼女が『嵐が丘』を翻案・脚色した一九七〇年までの作品、特に彼女の処女作ともいうべき「女形遣い」を中心に考えてみたい。

『嵐が丘』は読み手の心に応じて、さまざまな解釈を可能にする不思議な小説であるが、河野多恵子はこの作品をどのように読んでいるだろうか。彼女自身はこの小説の特色のひとつとして、まず「超自然性」を挙げている。「不滅の生」をうたったエミリの詩と「特殊な交わり」をもったためか、小説を読んでいる時は勿論その後もずっと、霊魂の不滅を表すキャサリンやヒースクリフの亡霊の出現といった超自然現象に魅力を感じてきたという。だが、『嵐が丘』を何度も読み返すうちに、本当の「超自然性」は、怪奇現象ではなく、ヒースクリフとキャサリンの存在そのものである、と思うようになったという。

私に対する、ヒースクリフとキャサリンの訴えかけは、彼等は絶対的に結ばれ得ない、超自然的な宿命をもった人間同士ということである。彼等は、同じ時代に同じ場所で、男と女として、所謂めぐり合ったのではない。彼等の結ばれ難さと執着ぶり自体が、私にはこの小説の本当の超自然性を感じさせる。…彼等は時によって距てられているばかりか、実は男でもなく、女でもないような気がする。勿論、中性同士なのではない。無性別、つまり性を越えた人間そのもの同士なのである。彼等の繋がり、彼等の同一性は、そういう宇宙にまたとない一組の人間同

士という点にある。(三四二)

　また、作品中最も好きなものとして、エドガーとの結婚を決めたキャサリンが、召使のネリーにヒースクリフに対する愛を告白する場面の「おまえにしろ誰にしろ、自分以上の『自分の命』がある。またあらねばならぬ、という考えはみんな持っているでしょう。もしあたしというものが、ここにあるだけのものが全部だったなら、神があたしをお造りになった甲斐がどこにあるの?」という言葉を挙げ、この言葉は「人間の存在の底知れなさを訴えているように思われる」(三四三)、と彼女は述べている。「自分以上の『自分の生命』」は原文では、"an existence of yours beyond you"(自分を越えた、自分の外にある自分の存在)となっている。それはキャサリンにとってはヒースクリフの存在であり、この後に「ヒースクリフは私なのよ」という有名な言葉が続く。つまり、河野多惠子は『嵐が丘』を単なる恋愛小説ではなく、人間存在の不思議さを解釈し、超自然現象は「人間の存在の底知れなさ」に付随して生じるものだと考えている、と言ってよいだろう。

　一九七〇年に河野の手によって戯曲化された『嵐が丘』はこうした彼女の作品解釈を反映しているが、ここには、もう一つ彼女のこの小説の興味深い読み方が表れている。この戯曲においては、子供の頃自分を虐待したキャサリンの兄ヒンドリー・アーンショウとキャサリンと結婚したエドガー・リントンに対するヒースクリフの憎しみと執念は髪の毛によって表されている。原作には髪の毛に関する場面は三つある。髪の毛はまず三章で吹雪のために「嵐が丘」に泊まった物語の第一の語り手であるロックウッドが見つけたキャサリンの古い日記の中に現れる。そこでは、ヒンドリーが指を鳴らしたと言ってヒースクリフを罵り、彼の指示で妻のフランシスがヒースクリフの髪を思いっきり引っ張る。二つめは七章のリントン家の

子供たちがアーンショウ家に遊びに来る場面である。ネリーの手でこざっぱりした姿になって居間に入ってきたヒースクリフを見て、ヒンドリーが「出ていけ、宿なしめ。お前は良い男になる気か？その上品な髪の毛をつかんでやるから待っていろ──その毛をもう少し長く引っ張ってやる」と怒鳴る。「今でも長すぎる」（五八）とこれに同調してからかうエドガーに、腹を立てたヒースクリフは、手近にあったアップル・ソースの入った深皿を投げつける。もう一つ髪の毛が登場するのは、二巻二章の最後のキャサリンの葬儀の場面である。キャサリンの首にかけたロケットから、ヒースクリフは中に入っているエドガーの「銀糸で結んだ明るい巻き毛」を床に捨て、かわりに自分の「黒い巻き毛」（一六八）を入れる。

戯曲『嵐が丘』においては、こうした場面を基にしてはいるが、髪の毛と怨念が原作とは異なる形で結び付けられている。第一幕四場でリントンの子供たちを招いたパーティーでヒンドリーがヒースクリフの髪の毛を引っ張る。ヒースクリフのこの行為は、子供の頃髪の毛を引っ張って虐めたヒンドリーに対する恨みと復讐心を表していると言えるだろう。また、第二幕一三場では、ヒースクリフはキャサリンとエドガーのエドガー・リントンに対する憎しみの激しさも髪の毛によって表されている。彼はキャサリンとエドガーの娘キャシーから父の形見のロケットを奪い取り、中に入っているキャサリンの髪の毛はしまい、「おれはこの一八年間、身を切り刻まれるような思いをしてきたのだ。エドガー、おまえも同じように切り刻んでやる！」と言ってエドガーの髪を包丁で切り刻み、キャシーにそれを食べさせようとする。髪の毛と怨念が結び付けられる

ことにより、この二つの場面は、日本的な手法で人間の情念の不気味さを際立たせている。

河野多恵子が『嵐が丘』の中に感じ取った「絶対に結ばれ得ない宿命をもった人間同士」の「執着ぶり」、「人間の存在の底知れなさ」とそれに付随する超自然現象、そして人間の激しい執念の不気味さなどは、彼女自身の作品ではどのような形で見られるであろうか。

『嵐が丘』の影響が生の形で見いだされるのは、一九六〇年に『文学者』に発表された「女形遣い」である。この作品は彼女の言わば処女作ともいうべきものであろう。彼女はそれ以前に同じ雑誌に三つの短編を発表しているが、彼女自身の手による年譜によると、それらは「習作」とされている。[6] 人形浄瑠璃の世界を描いたこの作品は、大阪という風土に根ざし、一見非常に日本的に見える。しかし、この作品はさまざまな点で河野の『嵐が丘』の読みを反映し、また、後の彼女の作品に見られる特徴も示している。

「女形遣い」の粗筋は次のようなものである。堀江座の女形遣い吉田幸六は、役に恵まれず、主遣いする兄弟子の吉田玉枝に嫉妬し、人形遣いの命とも言うべき玉枝の左手の指を妻の品に切らせる。その後、主遣いとなった幸六は役を得て、彼の人気は高まる。一方、指を切られ、一人前の人形遣いとして役に立たなくなった玉枝は、堀江座が近松二百年祭を機に近松座と名を改めた際に、幸六の差し金もあって、解雇されてしまう。せめて主遣いを補佐する左遣いに生きようとした最後の望みを断たれて、玉枝は楽屋で首をつって自殺してしまう。その事件の後も玉枝の人気は衰えず、近松座もライバルの文楽座を凌ぐ勢いがあったが、やがて、人気のなくなった楽屋の幸六の女形人形の後ろに、黒衣の人形遣いが添うように黒い影が立つという噂が立ち始める。その後競争相手の文楽座では興行が大当たりし、近松座は傾き始め、やがて閉鎖されてしまう。主だった人形遣いは文楽座に移り、幸六も文楽座に入ることを望むが、果たされず、黒衣姿で女形人形を抱いて入水してしまう。

このように物語の筋を追っていくと、まず目につくのは、『嵐が丘』のキャサリンやヒースクリフの亡霊に見られるような怪奇現象であろう。人形遣いの命である左手の指二本を切り落とされて二度と主遣いにはなれず、仕事まで奪われて「生きながら埋められたような」思いをして自ら命を断った玉枝の「霊魂の力の作用」で、人びとは幸六の女形人形の後ろに立つ影を見たとも考えられる。そしてこの作品は、玉枝の怨念が近松座を没落させ、幸六を死に至らしめた復讐怪談物語と読むこともできるであろう。河野多恵子は「わかれ」（一九六三年）の中では、「亡霊や夢見というようなもの」は「霊魂の力」によると主人公に言わせている。「女形遣い」の中では、「幸六から楽屋の人形の後ろに黒い影が立つ」という作り話を聞いた後に、妻品の夢枕に頭巾を被った黒衣の人形遣いが立つ。品が幸六は何も知らない、と訴えると、その姿はさっと消えてしまう。そしてその後、本当にこの噂が楽屋に広まる。

『嵐が丘』において何度か用いられている夢は、人間の心の奥深い部分、意識下の世界をさらけ出す。キャサリンはエドガー・リントンと結婚する前に、天国に行った夢についてネリーに語る。天国に安住できず、怒った天使たちにヒースの茂みに突き落とされて嬉し泣きしたという夢は、エドガーとはまったく異質であるキャサリンの本質を明らかにし、彼女の未来を予告する。また、ヒースクリフの夢に見た、眠っているキャサリンに身を寄せ覚めることのない眠りに入っている自分自身の姿も、彼の願望と未来を告げている。第一の語り手の都会から来た青年ロックウッドは、雪に降りこめられて泊まった嵐が丘荘でキャサリンの古い手記を見つける。見知らぬ女性に興味をもった青年は、手記を読みながら寝入ってしまうが、夢うつつに、窓辺にキャサリンの亡霊を見る。

河野多恵子の作品においても、夢は人間の深層心理を描くために数多く使われているが、「女形遣い」の中の品の夢は、ロックウッドの夢に似ており、また夢に見たことが実際に起こるという点で『嵐が丘』

の他の夢も思い出させる。彼女は幸六から話を聞いて、玉枝の左手の指を切り落としたことを後悔し、夫の身に何か起こるのではないかと案じていた矢先に黒衣の人形遣いの夢を見る。そして、夫の左手の指を二本失ったという嘘の夢の話を信じ、彼の求めに応じて自分の指を切り落とし、玉枝の墓前に備えるが、その後本当に玉枝の亡霊が楽屋に現れるという噂が広まるのである。

このように、「女形遣い」は人間の深層心理と結びついた復讐怪奇小説とも読めるが、この物語の中心となるのは、玉枝の復讐ではなく、人形遣い吉田幸六の女形人形にかける執念と夫との一体感を求める妻の激しい思いである。

一つの執念にとりつかれた荒々しい悪魔的な人物として描かれている幸六は、キャサリンを失った後手段を選ばず復讐に全エネルギーを注ぐヒースクリフを思い出させる。彼は下の者には、煙管の詰め替えが気に入らないといって煙管で手を打ったり、火のついた吸殻を背筋にはたき込むなど乱暴な態度を取り、贔屓の客の言葉も気に入らないと取り合わない横柄な男で、全盛時代から「終わりを完うできそうな人柄ではなかった」と言われていた。「女形人形の至上の美しさ」を極めるという執念に憑かれた幸六は、年はそれほど違わないのに美しい女形人形の主遣いをする玉枝に、激しい屈辱感と憎悪を感じる。彼にとって黒衣に閉じ込められて左遣いに終わることは、「生きながら埋められたような」生涯であるが、人形遣いをやめることもまた「生きながら埋められますも同じ、暗い、冷たい生涯」(一五六) である。役不足の根深い不満から、彼は妻の品を玉枝の指を切るように仕向ける。

玉枝の役を得て一途に進む幸六は、左遣いに指のない兄弟子を従えて「残忍な張り切り方」で、「この上ない美しさに濡れ」(一六四) た浅香姫を遣う。玉枝を落とし入れた心の咎めに乱れるどころか、一層磨きのかかった芸に生きる人形遣いを導くのは、女形人形の美しさを思う「わが心」ばかりとなる。彼は

女形人形の「至上の姿態」、「生ま身の女のうちに息づきながら、しかも生ま身の女の肉體には決して現われようのない女の色香」（一六七）を求めるようになり、妻に人形のふりをさせ、責め具を使って彼女に残忍な振る舞いをし続ける。「女形人形の至上の美しさに焦がれて貪欲の虜となり果て」（一八二）た幸六は、さらになお一層の残忍さを求めて、楽屋に置いた人形の後ろに黒い影が立つという噂話を作り上げ、妻の指を切って玉枝の墓前に備える。その翌日、彼の遣う「妹背山」のお三輪は、名女形遣いと言われた幸六の芸のうちでも、一世一代の華麗なものであった、と妻品は娘に語る。

前に述べたように、河野多恵子は『嵐が丘』の中で最も好きな言葉として、「おまえにしろ誰にしろ、自分以上の『自分の生命』がある。またあらねばならぬ、という考えはみんな持っているでしょう。もしあたしというものが、ここにあるだけのものが全部だったなら、神があたしをお造りになった甲斐がどこにあるの？」というキャサリンの言葉を挙げているが、「女形遣い」において、「自分以上の『自分の生命』」という言葉は幸六と女形人形の関係に当てはめることができるのではないだろうか。「自分以上の『至上の美しさ』」を極めた自分の遣う人形が、幸六にとっての「自分以上の『自分の生命』」なのだ。「自分以上の『自分の生命』」を失った者は生きていくことはできない。近松座の閉鎖後、人形を遣うことができなくなった幸六は、急に気力が衰え、「黒衣を死衣装に黒い頭巾までつけ」、中将姫の人形を抱いて川に身を投げる。道連れにした中将姫の人形が「花櫛を朝日にきらきらせながら、洗われたすがすがしい頬」（一八八）の幸六の傍らに、道連れにした中将姫の人形が「花櫛を朝日にきらきらせながら、洗われたすがすがしい頬」（一八八）を親しげに寄せていた、と妻は娘に語る。

物語は幸六の墓を訪れた第一の語り手の「私」の次のような思いで終わる。

静まり返った夏の真昼の墓地では激しい日照りに灼き尽された数知れない墓石が、皆一斉に白

く輝き、燃え立つような熱気をめらめらと吐き淀ませているのである。——私はもう一度幸六の墓の前まで戻って行ったが、それを眺めているうちに、暗い地底で、幸六の肉體が冷たい溶液と化したその中に、腐り果てた、彼の黒衣と女形人形のかしらと衣裳とが、ひとつになってどろどろと浸っているさまを想像した。(一九〇)

墓の中で幸六と人形が溶けてひとつになるという「私」の想像は、『嵐が丘』のヒースクリフの言葉を思い出させる。エドガー・リントンが亡くなったときに、ヒースクリフは墓を堀る寺男にキャサリンの棺の上の土をのけさせて蓋を開け、昔のままの彼女の顔を見る。そして、棺の蓋を少しずらして土をかけ、寺男に金を与えてエドガーの棺の脇にどけさせ、自分が死んだときにはこれも蓋を少しずらした自分の棺をキャサリンの隣に置かせる手筈を整え、二人がひとつに溶け合うようにする。そして、「リントンが自分たち二人のところに来る頃には、どちらがどちらかわからなくなっているだろう」と彼はネリーに語る。ヒースクリフはまた、眠っているキャサリンに寄り添って「永遠の眠りに入っている」夢を見たことも彼女に告げる。「そしてもしキャサリンが朽ちて土になってしまっていたら、それとももっと無残な姿になっていたら、あなたはどんな夢をごらんになったでしょうか」というネリーの言葉に、ヒースクリフは「彼女と一緒に溶けて、もっと幸せになっている夢だ」(二八六)と答える。キャサリンにとってヒースクリフは「自分以上の『自分の生命』」であるが、ヒースクリフにとってもキャサリンは彼の「生命」であり、「魂」である。キャサリンが死んだとき、ヒースクリフは「俺は自分の生命なしに生きることはできない!自分の魂なしに生きることはできない!」(一六七)と叫び、その後心の平安を得ることがない。「女形遣死後キャサリンと一緒に溶けて合体する手筈を整えた後に、彼のかき乱れた心はやっと静まる。

い」の結末の「私」の想像は、墓の中で幸六が彼の「生命」であり、「魂」である女形人形と溶け合ってひとつになることによって心の安らぎを得ることを願う、語り手の思いを表していると言えるであろう。「自分を越えた自分の存在」と一体感を求める激しい執念は、幸六の妻品にも見られる。後年幸六の話をするときは「再び若い女に還ったよう」に「一途な様子」（一五二）を示すお品は、彼の遣う女形人形に魅せられ、押しかけ女房となったのである。彼女は人形の「至上の美しさ」を求める夫のためにどんなことでも行う。役不足の根深い不満をかかえた幸六の「玉枝を殺すことができるか」という言葉と「手摺りの生命はこれやろな」（一五八）と言って左手を広げる動作に、彼女は玉枝の左手を傷つける以外に夫の生きる道はないような気になり、酒に酔った玉枝の指を切り落とすということまでする。品は日頃から舞台で夫の遣う女形人形を「自分の影とも片身」とも思ってきたが、指を失った玉枝を左遣いに従えた幸六の遣う浅香姫を見て、無性に気が引き立ったと娘に語る。

悪事の絆に結ばれました幸六が、これまでのどないな慰めようの折りにも増して、ひしと親しう、慕わしう、幸六の腕の女形人形が一際わが身と血も濃う思えますと、母の胸には、姫の姿態も色香もまるでわが身にじかに迫られ、絞り出されてゆきますような生々しい幸せが漲るのでございました。（一六五）

女形人形の「無上の美しさ」に思い焦がれ、「生ま身の女の血を啜るばかりの思いを籠めて」殴り責める幸六の残忍な行為にも、品は耐え、「ああ苦しい、早う殺して下され、そしたら私の霊魂はきっとあんさんの人形に寄ります、あんさんにあんないに美しう創ってもらいます」（一七七）と訴え、念じる。自分

の霊魂が夫の人形に宿るという彼女の言葉は、人形、さらにそれを遣う夫との同一化を願う彼女の気持ちを表していると言える。彼女はさらにまた夫の求めに応じて、自分の指さえ切り落とさせる。幸六とお品の関係に見られるのは、河野多恵子の作品の特色のひとつと言われるサディズム、マゾヒズムである。多恵子は「谷崎文学と肯定の欲望」の中でこの異常な愛について次のように述べている。

人はサディズム、マゾヒズムの性愛時においては（心理的な場合でも）、その心理に在る時は）、相手との現状や未来に対して相手と一体であり得、一体であり続け得る意識を強烈に意識的に成り立たしめてこそ、その快楽が成り立つのであり、彼等はその快楽に臨んでいるうちは、相手との現状や未来に対する不安や疑惑が絶無であるからこそ一体になろうとする異性愛は欠落して、性的無性別同士という間柄に陥り、真向から描くには、ただされ肉体づくりに労を要する世界となる。

お品と幸六は、ここに述べられた性別上の特性を失った「性的無性別同士」と言えるだろう。幸六のお品に対する残虐な行為は、人形の「至上の美しさ」を求めるという思いで二人を結び付け、「相手と一体であり得、一体であり続ける意識を強烈に意識的に成り立たしめ」る。「性的無性別同士」の一体化を求める執着心というこの概念は、多恵子の『嵐が丘』の読み方にも見られる。前述したように、彼女はこの作品を単なる恋愛小説と読むのはおもしろくないと考える。彼女に対する「ヒースクリフとキャサリンの存在の訴えかけ」は、「絶対に結ばれ得ない、超自然的な宿命をもった人間同士」「無性別、つまり性を超えた人間そのもの同士」であり、「彼らの関わり合いには、日常的な如

亡霊といった怪奇現象ではなく二人の人間の「結ばれがたさと執着ぶり自体」がこの作品の本当の超自然性であるという。『嵐が丘』の読み方は、「女形遣い」の中にも反映していると言えるだろう。玉枝の亡霊は、幸六の人形に対する「執着」が作り出したとも考えられる。実際、人形の後ろに立つ影の噂話は、最初は「女形人形の至上の美しさに焦がれて貪欲の虜となり果てた」幸六が、「なお一層の残忍さが欲しうて」選んだ「手段」（一八二）である。この噂が本当に広まるようになった理由については、玉枝と同じように左手の指二本をなくしたお品を見て、誰かが気のせいでそんなものを見たか、それとも本当にそんなことがあったのか、わからないものがもっともらしい怪談話を作りだしたか、あるいは幸六に恨みを持つものがもっともらしい怪談話を作りだしたか、と作者は幸六の娘にあいまいに語らせている。いずれにしても、この作品の中心となるものは、女形人形に対する異常とも言える幸六の「執着ぶり」と、夫とそして夫が遣う人形との一体化を望む妻のお品の激しさであり、玉枝の亡霊という怪奇現象は、それに付随するものに過ぎないであろう。

「女形遣い」は人間の執念の不気味さ、「性的無性別同士」の「関わり合い」が示す「人間の存在の底知れなさ」など、河野多恵子の『嵐が丘』読みを反映しているが、二人の語り手を使用するというこの作品の構成そのものが、『嵐が丘』の影響を感じさせる。『嵐が丘』においては、ロンドンという外の世界から来た青年ロックウッドに、アーンショウ家、リントン家の両家に仕えたネリー・ディーンがヒースクリフとキャサリンの物語を語るという形式が取られていて、善良で温和な「普通の人間」であるネリーが二人

の「異常な」世界を浮き立たせている。「女形遣い」は、英国人の恩師の送別に文楽人形を贈った「私」に、その人形の所有者であった吉田幸六と妻品について、彼らの娘の堀井すがが語るという構成をとっている。第二の語り手堀井すがには、母親から譲り受けた美しい目以外には、「横柄だったという父の幸六や、当時としてはなかなかおはね娘であったらしいその母親を偲ばせるようなところは、こちらにはみじんもな」い。すがは「如何にも内気そうな様子で」(一四九)、「私」の前で話ながら絶えず襟元を整える。すがについてはあまり書き込まれていないが、彼女を語り手にしたことには、幸六やお品とは異なる「普通の」人間に彼らの「異常な」物語を語らせるという書き手の意図が込められているのではないだろうか。

また、第一の語り手が物語の中心人物の墓を訪れ、死者を思うという二つの作品の結末も類似している。『嵐が丘』においては、ロックウッドが旅の途中に嵐が丘荘に立ち寄り、ネリーからヒースクリフの死について、またヒースクリフとキャサリンの亡霊が「歩いている」という村人たちの噂話を聞く。彼らが葬られている所を探し、穏やかな空の下、夏草の間に三つの墓石を見つけたロックウッドは、「この静かな大地に眠る者たちの眠りが安らかでないと誰が想像できるだろうか」(三三四)と思う。「女形遣い」は前に述べたように、「私」が堀井すがの話を聞いた後、吉田幸六の埋葬されている墓地を訪れ、幸六と人形が溶けてひとつになる様を想像することで終わっている。

これまで述べてきたように、「女形遣い」の中には『嵐が丘』の影響が直接的な形で読み取れるが、これ以後一九七〇年までの河野の作品にも、彼女が『嵐が丘』から感じ取ったものが見られる。特に怪異、超自然性は日常性の中で混然となって河野独自の世界を形作り、女の心のさまざまな面を、「人間の存在の不思議さ」を読者に見せてくれる。

「女形遣い」と同じ短編集『幼児狩り』(一九六二)に収められた「雪」においても、超自然現象を生み

出すほどの激しい人間の情念や緊迫した人間関係が描かれている。この物語の中心となるのは、主人公早子と継母の執着しあう心であろう。精神異常の発作から我が子を雪に埋めてしまった母と、その母に我が子として育てられた妾腹の娘の間には、奇妙な激しい感情がかよいあっている。

兄は母と肉親に違いないが、自分もまた母と肉親であるような気が、早子は屡々した。濃密な血が豊かに、率直に流れ込んでいるのではないか、互に爪立ててしがみついている相手の傷口から血を啜り合っているような肉親。彼女は無性に母に執着したし、母の方でもそうだった。自分の娘を殺し、殺した娘の名で呼びかけながら妾腹の娘を育てるようになった母の気持ちの捌け口は兎角早子に向く。しかし、最初は憎しみの眼だけで眺めていたその対象が、永年一緒に住み、同じ不幸の一角を持ち、自分の苦悩の噴出に耐えさせられているのを見るうちに、母は一種の快さを覚え、親しさ、愛着を感じるようになっていたのだろうか。[10]

人間の心の奥底を、意識下の世界まで映し出す夢は、「女形遣い」に始まり、その後河野の多くの作品で用いられているが、「雪」においても、夢は死者の霊魂と結びついている。そしてここでは、執着しあう母と娘の深い内部を照らしだす。母の死を知らせる電話を受け取る直前に、早子は夢の中で母から起こされるが、眠りから覚めかねている。「お前はそういう娘だったのね。判りました。起きないのね、私が死ねという時でも平気なんだね」(九二)という母の言葉に身を起こすと、母は優しく微笑して、二度頷いて消える。闇の中で起き上がった早子は、母を見たのは自分の「脳裏」ではなく、「眼」であるような気がする。夢うつつに死者を見るという設定は、前述した『嵐が丘』のロックウッドの夢を思いださせる。

キャサリンの古い手記を読み、彼女のベッドに寝たロックウッドは、格子窓を叩き「中に入れて」と叫ぶキャサリンの姿を見るが、彼はそれを「脳裏」で見たのか、「眼」で見たのかは定かではない。異常な執着心で結ばれた母のほうでも娘に怪異な「印」を見せる。東京から到着した早子の前で、母の遺体は鼻から「夥しい鮮血」を滴らせる。この現象について、年配の家政婦は、一番会いたく思っていた人を前にすると死体はよくこのような「印」を見せると語る。

この作品の中に見られるもう一つの怪異現象は、雪によって起こる病である。我が子を雪に埋め、妾腹の子を我が子として育てる母と、殺した実子の名で呼ばれる娘は、持病まで共有する。子供のころある雪の日に雪が好きだと言って母から強く折檻されて以来、雪は「忌むべきもの、疎ましいもの」「魔性をもった何かの化身」のように感じられる早子は、母の持病と雪との符合に気づき、雪という障害はどこまでも自分につき纏い、雪のような頼りない存在こそ自分に適ったものであろうと考える。激しい頭痛の持病の暗示にかかって自分も同じ症状を起こすようになったのかもしれない、と考える。激しい頭痛が起こり始めると、彼女は一緒に暮らす木崎との生活よりも、大阪にいる母親のことを「一途に」思う。

雪によって起こる早子の持病は、母親との関係に起因する彼女の存在感、アイデンティティーの不確かさと結びついている。早子は一緒に暮らす木崎に執着しながら、結婚することをためらう。それは、「生まれた時からの自分の存在を考えると、確固としたものは結局自分の柄ではないのだと思い、雪という障害すぎてきた自分に、もういい加減別れなくてはならない」（一一〇）と、早子はあえて雪の仙石原に木崎と共に向かう。頭に激しい痛みを感じながら、彼女は木崎に自分を雪の中に埋めるように頼む。「死ん

じまうよ」という彼の言葉に、早子は「そう、それでいいんだわ、一遍死ねばいいんだわ」(一一二) と答えるが、その言葉には「雪のように頼りない存在」をいったん殺し、生き直したいという彼女の思いが込められている。

このように「雪」においては、夢うつつに見た母の亡霊、母の見せた鮮血の「印」、母と娘の共有する雪によって起こる持病という不思議な現象は、主人公の女性の日常生活の中に組み込まれ、継母との特異な関係と彼女の自己意識と分かちがたく結びついている。

一九六五年以降の作品のでは、さらに超自然性は日常性と渾然一体となって、「人間存在の底知れなさ」を訴えかける。こうした作品の中で超自然現象は、「いまここに実際にあるだけのものではない」、「もう一つの世界」を描くために用いられている。一九六八年に書かれたエッセイ「もう一つの世界」で、河野は子供の頃のエピソードを例に挙げて、この技法について語っている。子供の頃彼女が二階でぐっすり眠っている間に階下に泥棒が入り、女中が襲われたが、大声を出したために賊は逃走したという話を聞いて、怖くなって泣きだした。それは、二階で眠っている自分と階下の賊が同時間に存在したことから生じた恐怖であり、その時の恐怖を表現するためには、「その時一瞬生きた、非現実的なもう一つの世界をぴったり表現できる手段に依らなければならなくなる」という。そして、日常的な細部は「非現実的なもう一つの世界に適わしく移植されるならば、いよいよ輝きを増し、もう一つの世界」に対する河野の関心は、前述した彼女の好きな存在に思える」とも述べている。こうした「もう一つの世界」に対する河野の関心は、前述した彼女の好きな『嵐が丘』の中の「人間の存在はここにあるだけのものが全部ではない」というキャサリンの言葉を思い出させる。河野自身この言葉について、「この言葉は、人間と、普通に言われるところの超自然との繋がりに当てはめて考えても通用する」(三四三)と『嵐が丘』の超自然性」の中で述べている。

一九六〇年代後半に書かれた二つの作品「邂逅」(一九六七)「不意の声」(一九七八)において、超自然現象は、「ここにあるだけのもの」ではない「もう一つの世界」を表現するための「手段」として巧みに用いられ、女性の内奥を、「人間存在の底知れなさ」を、読者に見せる。

「邂逅」では、妹の亡霊という怪奇現象は、主人公に彼女の生きたかもしれない「もう一つの世界」を見せ、これまでの生き方を考えさせる「手段」となっている。終戦の時の解放感と感動に応え、「最も甲斐ある人生」をおくりたいと思いながら、「自分を託すべき仕事」を見いだせないまま、結婚しようとしている俊子のもとに、十数年前に仲違いして、疎遠になってしまった妹の道子が、ある冬の夜に不意に訪ねてくる。道子は姉の代わりに父のすすめる男と結婚した後、離婚、再婚、病気を経験したという身の上話をする。そして、帰り際に彼女はガラス障子に映っている自分たち二人の姿を、「道ちゃん、あなた一体何しに来たの！」と問う姉に指し示し、「わたしの話したこと、あなたのもうひとつの人生よ、ほら、あんなに似ているわ。ひとつあれば、片方は要らないくらい」と言って消えてしまう。そのあと、俊子は読みかけていた手元の同窓会会誌を見て、妹がすでに死亡していたことを知る。

俊子は郷里の「女専」を卒業して以来、父のすすめる縁談を断り、上京して、「執拗く」「不器用に」「最も甲斐ある人生」を歩もうとしてきた。だが、近頃送られてくる会報にのっている同窓生の消息を読むたびに、失敗続きの自分の人生を悔やみ、「この十数年間をもう一度生き直してみたい」という思いに駆られ、「あり得たかもしれない、自分のもう一つの人生」を考えていた。しかし、「さらりと器用な生き方」をしているように見えた妹が語った「自分のもう一つの人生」(五五)を眺めて見ると、そこで特に「最も甲斐ある人生」を歩もうとしてきた。「生まれ育った家で、人並に生活できるお金をもち、のんびりと一時のひとり暮しを楽しめたであろうことだけ」(七四)であることに気づく。そして、亡くなった父親が自分を励ま

ために、妹を差し向けたような気がしてくる。この作品における亡霊は、妹の霊魂が俊子の「脳裏に及んで生じた美しい映像[13]」であるかもしれないし、「自分は一体これまで何をしてきたのだろう」と、自分の生き方に疑念と後悔の念をいだく彼女の心が生み出した幻影かもしれない。いずれにしても、妹の亡霊は、主人公に「もう一つの世界[14]」「もう一つの人生」を示す手段であり、それにより、彼女の「経た人生（の特徴とその源）を浮き立たせ」ることに、作者の意図はある。

翌年に書かれた「不意の声」においては、亡霊はさらにリアリティーをもって現れ、「ここにあるだけのもの」ではない「もう一つの世界」、主人公の女性の心の深層の世界を照らしだす。この小説は、夫との関係が破綻した吁希子が亡父の「不意の声」の暗示で三人の人を殺すという物語であるが、父親は彼女にとって子供のころは怖い存在であったが、戦時中の軍需工場での体験で、自分たちが親の庇護の手の届かないところに置かれて、親でさえ頼りにならないことを知ったため、父への怖れは消える。そして、実家を遠く離れて暮らすようになると、一抹の怖れの残る母親よりも、父親は親しい存在となる。父親の亡霊が彼女の前に初めて姿を現すのは、父の危篤を知らせる電報を受け取った直後、電話を借りに入った鮨屋においてである。父親は「優しい眼つきで」「笑顔になりながら」、「そうか来てくれるのか」と言って、彼女に対して「頷いてみせ[15]」る。

吁希子は「亡父の訪れを請う」ようになり、彼の現れる回数も多くなる。亡霊は全く表情のない死顔を見せることもあるが、そのあとには必ず優しい笑顔を浮かべて彼女に対して頷いてみせる。年々少しずつ若くなっていく父の亡霊は、「あまりに素早く、適切で、大きいので、さしあたり言うべきことはもう何もなくなってしまったような気持ちさせられる」「慰安」（一四六）を彼

女に与えてくれる。

夫婦喧嘩の末に家を追い出された吁希子は、「やってみるがいい。大丈夫だとも、三人までは……」（一五〇）という「亡父の不意の声」を聞き、「みずからを励ますような力が身内に湧きはじめた」。三つの殺人を犯した彼女の前に現れた亡父は、「どうだ、楽になったか？――今夜はゆっくり寝ればいい」と「優しく頷いて」（二〇〇）言う。

父親の亡霊も三つの殺人も、吁希子の細々とした日常生活の描写の中に巧みに組み込まれているために、彼女が本当に亡霊を見、「亡父の不意の声」の暗示で実際に殺人を犯したような現実感を読者に与える。『不意の声』あとがきの中で河野は、「この小説の主人公にとっては、非現実なもうひとつの世界は、現実生活と全く変らぬリアリティをもっている。その両者をそなえた世界こそ、彼女にとっての本当の現実なのだ」と述べている。この言葉も、河野が『嵐が丘』の中でも、神があたしをお造りになった甲斐がどこにあるの」というキャサリンの言葉を思いださせる。「不意の声」の中で、河野が『嵐が丘』から感じ取った超自然現象を生み出す「人間の存在の底知れなさ」が中心となっている。主人公の気持は、「非現実的なもうひとつの世界」をもたざるをえないほど差し迫っていたと言えるだろう。優しく笑顔で自分を受け入れてくる亡父の姿を見、その声の暗示によって殺意を抱くほど捩じれ歪んだ、夫との不仲に悩む吁希子の心こそ、作者の描こうとしたものであろう。

河野はブロンテ姉妹について、彼女たちは「自分ひとりの心のみ」に「異常に勁く、深く、そして熱」く根ざして作品を創作しているので、読者もそこに「自分自身のみの心を感じはじめる」と述べている。

この言葉どおりに、『嵐が丘』は読む者の心に応じて様々な姿を見せるが、河野がこの作品から感じ取った最も大きなものは、超自然性と「人間の存在の底知れなさ」の結びつきであると言えよう。「女形遣い」に見られるような『嵐が丘』の直接的な影響は、彼女の他の作品には感じられない。だが、人間の心の奥底にある「もうひとつの世界の現実」を表す超自然性は、「胸さわぎ」（一九七一）、「妖術記」（一九七八）など、一九六〇年代以降の作品にも見られる。

エッセイ「歌舞伎に思う」（一九九二）の中で河野は、「女も男に劣らず、情熱・欲望・深く鋭く複雑な思念をそなえて」おり、「女の深い内部を表現するために、日常生活にはめったにあり得ない女や超自然の女をどこまでも創造することも、文学では可能である」と述べている。ヒースクリフとキャサリンの存在そのものが生み出す『嵐が丘』の超自然性は、「女の深い内部を表現するため」の、「人間の存在の不思議さ」を鮮やかに照らしだす手がかりを、彼女に与えたのであろう。『嵐が丘』を読んだことが小説を書きはじめる「二段階目の動機」となったと彼女自身が言うように、『嵐が丘』は河野多恵子の原点であり、また、創造力をかき立てる原動力となったのではないだろうか。

[注]

1 河野多恵子「読書遍歴」『河野多恵子全集第十巻』（新潮社、一九九五年）九九頁。
2 河野「『嵐が丘』の超自然性」『全集第九巻』（新潮社、一九九五年）三三九-三四〇頁。
3 河野「半年だけの恩師」『全集第十巻』二六三頁。
4 Emily Jane Brontë, *Wuthering Heights* (London: Penguin Books, 1995) 81.
5 河野「戯曲『嵐が丘』」『全集第九巻』三三一頁。
6 河野多恵子「年譜」『全集第十巻』三七七頁。
7 河野多恵子「わかれ」『全集第一巻』（新潮社、一九九四年）二〇八頁。

8 河野多恵子「女形遣い」『幼児狩り』(新潮社、一九六二年) 一四二頁。
9 河野「谷崎文学と肯定の欲望」『全集第九巻』一二四頁。
10 河野「雪」『全集第一巻』一〇六頁。
11 河野「もう一つの世界」『全集第十巻』一二五頁。
12 河野「邂逅」『全集第三巻』(新潮社、一九九五年) 七三頁。
13 河野「わかれ」『全集第一巻』二〇八頁。
14 河野「妖術記」に呪われて」『全集第十巻』八五頁。
15 河野「不意の声」『全集第五巻』(新潮社、一九九五年) 一二二頁。
16 河野「不意の声」あとがき」『全集第十巻』二六頁。
17 河野「ブロンテ全集」刊行にあたって」『全集第十巻』一九九頁。
18 河野「歌舞伎に思う」『全集第十巻』三三六頁。

[引用・参考文献]

Brontë, Emily Jane. *Wuthering Heights*. London : Penguin Books, 1995.
河野多恵子『河野多恵子全集』全十巻 新潮社、一九九四-一九九五年。
――「女形遣い」『幼児狩り』新潮社、一九六二年。

09 『嵐が丘』を如何に読み替え、如何に書き換えるか

Heathcliffの「悔しさ」を動機として

安藤重和

[I]

　Heathcliff の死による *Wuthering Heights* の結末は、彼に奪われた家屋敷やこの舞台の時空間を巡る支配権が正当な継承者である Hareton Earnshaw と Catherine Linton (Cathy) の所有に回帰することで終わる。二人は結婚後 Thrushcross Grange に住むことになり、閉鎖される *Wuthering Heights* は Catherine Earnshaw と Heathcliff の亡霊が徘徊する館となるであろう。その場合二人の霊魂はこの世界と舞台の守護神＝土地の霊 (the genius loci or pâtron sáint) として啓示され agape のごとく君臨することになる。しかしそうであっても、彼の内には一抹の悔しさが、無念の思いが残りはしないか。(果たして Heathcliff

はあの a single wish に達し、Catherine の that glorious world に真の意味で首尾よく合一・合体しえたであろうか？）

つまり、新しい愛を育む二人の若い男女が Wuthering Heights を捨てて、Linton 家の Thrushcross Grange に移住するということは、この作品の中であの激しく対立し残酷なまでの葛藤を繰り返した理性と野性、文明と自然の戦いが前者の勝利に帰し、後者は敗者で Wuthering Heights は彷徨える亡霊たちの棲む幽霊館と化す、という説を成立させることになる。

その場合には、Heathcliff の過酷なまでの生への戦いも、全て結局は彼を拾ってくれた老アーンショウへの恩返し、恩に報いた道徳物語という前近代的な説話、訓話物語という陳腐な俗説の論理をも成立させてしまいかねない。また、彼は恋人を奪われた腹いせに復讐をする悪漢、野蛮で暴力的で幼い者たちを虐げる冷酷無比な悪魔の化身に成り果てて空しい最後を遂げる非道な男 anti-hero であり、Catherine Earnshaw は物質的富・社会的地位という誘惑に負け、真実の愛を捨てた為に気が狂って死ななければならなかった heroïne、という勧善懲悪小説ということになる。

果たしてそうか、それでは Heathcliff も浮かばれないだろう。彼の葛藤と飢餓、苦行にも似た生の営みは、全て無意味で何にも成らなかったことになる。救いは無いとしても、それは倫理、教訓物語ではありえず、また理性と文明の価値を意味付けるものというのも納得のいかないものである。また、彼は単なる ressentiment ではあり得ない。

従って、この主人公には如何しても無念の思い、今回はこの事後に尚も残る想いの問題を動機付けとしながら、Heathcliff は何処から来て、何をしたのか、彼とは一体誰なのか、そこには the incarnation of nature（自然の化身）という以外にも語られてはい

ない何かがありはしないか、を考察してみたい。

なお、この作品は、Londonから隠遁生活をするために逃れて来たMr. Lockwoodとこの土地で生まれ育ったNelly Deanという二人の語り手を設定し、複雑な語りの重層構造を要しながらも物語の進行につれて語り手たちが次第に後方に退いて行き、主要な登場人物たちが直接読者に彼らの内部情念を詩的表現を用いて語りかけてくるという様相を呈してゆく。かかる意味においてWuthering Heightsという作品世界は極めてpolyphonicな人物たちが棲息する舞台であることを前提として、この架空の文学世界の時空間（Mikhail M. Bakhtinの言うクロノトポス）を存在論的に捉えようとするものである。

[II]

Wuthering Heightsの主題が前半は愛と憎しみで後半は復讐と死だというひどい俗説がある。この読み誤りの観点は、商業的映画化などにおいて前半の物語の部分で終わってしまう、というところなどに端的に表れている。

この愛の悲劇は、後半の部分における前半の悲劇の実存的な意味付け、とりわけCatherine Earnshawの愛と死を巡る意味と無意味の追求、そして結末におけるHeathcliffの告白と真実の暴露を抜きにしては何ものも語れないであろう。彼の告白は作品全体のテーマを意味付けしている。我々が求めるのはこの作品の持つ現代的意味である。

Wuthering Heightsにおける十八世紀的な家族・人間関係、前近代的な社会・環境、そして原始的な自然・風物の設定は、一つの装置として近代英国の市民制社会の制度・機構と激しく衝突しながらも、なお

その上にこの体制を揺るがし、ずれたり擦り抜けたりしながら現代小説に等しいものへと変貌している。そこでは前近代的封建的なものが近代的なものを取込みながら現代的なものと折り重なるように重層構造をなし、高度に発展した現代文明社会の複雑な人間心理などの相対的な関係性や内部構造と対応するような文学の時空間を織り成して一つの世界が存在している。

俗説の成立する最大の根拠は Catherine Earnshaw の愛の裏切りという把握の仕方である。しかし作品の本文中には何処にも彼女がお金や地位身分のために Heathcliff を捨てて Edgar Linton のもとに走った等とは書かれてはいない。Catherine の側から言えば、彼女の真実の愛の告白を途中までしか聴くことなく逃亡、誤解してこの地を立ち去った彼の方が彼女を見捨てたのであり、それゆえ Catherine は孤立し行き場がなくなった、という具合に書かれ展開されている。

He had listened till he heard Catherine say it would degrade her to marry him, and then he stayed to hear no further.

―

Nelly に語る彼女の愛の真実の姿の告白に続いて、Heathcliff の失踪を知って一晩中嵐の中をずぶ濡れになりながら彼を探し求めて熱病に倒れる Catherine の行為の内に、彼女の激しく熱い思いは余す所なく語り尽されている。人はこの彼女の愛の情念と生への飢餓を読み込みながら、何故に Catherine の心変りという理性の保持・社会常識への転化を行うのか。

この見事な伏線と、Hindley の腐敗と堕落の内に荒れ果ててゆく嵐が丘の館に自分の存在すべき場所を無くした Catherine が、さらにに彼女の熱病の看護をしためにそれに感染した Linton 夫妻を共に死に至らしめてしまったという負い目と負債を考えるならば、すべてを失い居るべき場も無い生ける屍も同然な彼女が喪があけた三年の歳月の後に Edgar の救いの手に縋ろうとするのも至極当然の話では無いのか。

（彼女には Earnshaw 家の相続権は一切なかった。）

Catherine が Heathcliff を裏切ったという事実は何処にも書かれていない、その根拠は不在である。そして嵐が丘の大地と原始的荒野に抱かれてふたりが幼きものの無垢の王国を創造し合体しつつも、なおひとりひとりが個体としての宿命として、原始的回帰の果てに再び文明と遭遇せざるを得ないのは人類の宿命であり、悲劇の成立する根拠でもある。Heathcliff は Liverpool の路地において文明の何たるかを、資本制生産社会の地獄をその幼児体験として体得していたが、Catherine にとってそれは未知のものに等しく、しかもそれは人権無視の矛盾に満ちた精神地獄ではなく豊かな文明のもたらす天国として Linton 家の洗練された文化の様式の姿を纏って現れたのである。

We saw-ah! it was beautiful-a splended place carpeted with crimson, and crimson-covered chairs and tables, and a pure white ceiling bordered by gold, a shower of glass drops hanging in silver chains from the centre, and shimering with little soft tapers.[2]

物質的生活の豊かさ美しさ、文化の香りのする近代市民生活の時空間は、自然を始源とする文明のもたらした果実、positive な面であり、例えそれが多くの人々の犠牲=支配と搾取という社会構造の上に成り立っているにせよ、何人も文化・文明のもたらす良質な面の成果は受け入れざるを得ず、また例え近代文明それ自体が自然を侵すもの、自然破壊という側面を持たざるを得ないにせよ、文明と自然という相容れないものの共存と葛藤は不可避なものである。（それは観念としては理性と本能の相克、相対立し葛藤するものと相克＝共有と葛藤は不可避なものとして表されるが、本来文明は自然が生み出したもの、原始から生み出されたものであり、自然回帰・原始回帰はその逆行ゆえの irony という形であれ必ず文明とふたたび遭遇せざるを得ないのである。）それこそ彼等二人が原始化した自然児のままであり得なかったことの意味＝宿命であり、悲

劇のironyである。

しかし物質文明の精神地獄を幼児体験に持つHeathcliffにとって、その豊かさが何によって成り立っているか、誰の犠牲によるものであるかはこの地域の原始的自然に抱かれて育ったCatherineにそれを知り見抜けというのはとても無理な話であり、そのまま受け入れるのが自然な姿なのだが、その自然さが自然さゆえに異質なもの・相入れないものの共有・共存ということによって摩擦と葛藤を生み出し、彼女の内部に自己矛盾・自己分裂を引き起こすのである。それは左右の両極にEdgarとHeathcliffを置き彼女が引き裂かれるという具体的な現実の姿で突き付けられる。

Catherine Earnshawの選択は、Edgar Lintonと結婚し夫の財産でHeathcliffを救い出し、自分を媒体として二人を一体化・統一する、ということであった。

--if Heathcliff and I married, we should be beggars ? whereas, if I marry Linton, I can aid Heathcliff to rise, and place him out of my brother's power.

このような考えは市民社会の社会常識から見れば詭弁と取られるであろうが、彼女は本気であり苦肉の策ではあるかも知れないが、その論理的根拠の正当性は成立しているし、彼女にそれ以外の選択の道・方法は与えられていないのである。

このこと以外の事柄においても彼女の論理的正当性は一貫して貫かれ、巧に構成されている。また逆にHeathcliffが彼女を追い詰め狂気と死に至らしめる彼の論拠・正当性も正確に論理付けられている。かかる意味においてCatherineの裏切りという観点は近代市民社会の道徳、Victoria朝的価値観をもってWuthering Heightsの文学空間に描かれた世界を圧殺しようとする批評である。

[Ⅲ]

では、Edgar Linton の愛はどうであろうか？ 語り手である Nelly Dean は Edgar Linton, as multitudes have been before and will be after him, was infatuated ; and believed himself the happiest man alive on the day he led her to Gimmerton Chapel, three years subsequent to his father's death.[4]

と言っているが、果たしてそうか？ Nelly の見解は社会常識以上のものではありえない。

彼が Catherine に惹かれるのはその野性・自然児の魅力である。また妹の Isabella Linton が Heathcliff に惹かれるのも外面の紳士の風貌にだけ在るのではなく、その内部に秘められたエキゾチックな悪魔的野性である。つまり、彼等は Linton 家の人々に決定的に欠けているもの、自然と野性に魅了されるのである。文化の香り高き理性の王国に棲む存在としての彼等は労働や生産活動という自然への働きかけ、自然と一体と成りながらも相見えてそれを人間化するという行為＝生の営みから疎外されている。存在としての有閑階級は人間的自然・自然的人間という関係性を根源的なものとして欠如しているがゆえに野性・原始を希求する。Edgar の Catherine への愛は本質的なものである。しかし彼の愛は現実においては″報われることのない愛″と言う悲しい宿命を背負っている。

そして、文明のもたらす物質的生活の保護は危険な要因を当初から抱え込んでいた。それは、Edgar の愛と心遣いによって小康を保っていたが、針の筵に座らされたような不安定で危険に満ちた彼女のもので、腫れ物に触るようなものであり、平和に見える生活の裏には爆弾を抱え込むような内部矛盾という危機が潜んでいた。

the gunpowder lay as harmless as sand, because no fire came near to explode it. Catherine は Wuthering Heights の自然と Heathcliff との関係において創造した that glorious world を欠いては生きてゆけない存在である。彼女は exile ──根無し草と成り果てており、そのような Catherine に注ぐ Edgar の優しい愛はその物質生活の豊かさに頼るものであるがゆえに心の人間疎外を抱え込んでいて、彼の愛が物静かで優しく真摯なものであればある程彼女を精神的な苦境に追いやるという irony を生み出す。(Heathcliff が怒り、暴力的になるのはこのことに対してである。) つまり、真綿で首を絞めるような残酷さと痛ましさを秘めているという意味で Edgar Linton の愛の irony は哀切なものである。

Nelly は次のように言っている。

They (Edgar and Isabella) were both very attentive to her comfort, certainly. It was not the thorn bending to the honeysuckles, but the honeysuckles embracing the thorn. There were no mutual concessions ; one stood erect, and the others yielded : and who can be ill-natured and bad-tempered when they encounter neither opposition nor indifference? I observed that Mr Edgar had a deep-rooted fear of ruffling her humour.

彼はこのような哀切な愛のために、まず最初に彼女の熱病の看護をした自分の両親を失い、幸福なはずの新婚生活も Heathcliff の再登場によって破壊されたあげくむき出しの暴力的な葛藤の末に最愛の妻を死にいたらしめてしまう。また、たったひとりの妹 Isabella も彼に奪われる。さらに、亡き妻の忘れ形見、娘 Cathy との静かな隠遁生活も許されず誘拐・監禁・強制結婚の上に家屋敷・財産もすべて略奪される。Edgar Linton はこの愛のためにすべてを失い、自らも亡き妻を思慕しつつ死ななければならない。脆弱で無抵抗にも見える彼のその理性の愛に殉ずる姿に偽りは無いとすべきであろう。文化・教養という衣装を纏った知と理を identity として生きる彼にとって Catherine の持つ自然・野生は無くてはならぬも

の、それを欠いては生きてはゆけないものであり、Heathcliff にとっての、I cannot live without my life! I cannot live without my soul! と同等・同質のものである。(彼の生き方には孤高の精神性が、文化の蓄積による知の結晶が啓示されている。)

Edgar の愛は、この地上に於いては Catherine の原始・野生を文化・文明化することもしなければ、自らの持つ文化・教養を野生・自然化することもできずに、終わる。(それは近代文明の持つ人間疎外と市民社会における自己疎外ゆえに生じる自己疎外の相対的な関係から必然化せざるを得ないものである。) しかし彼の死後、娘の Catherine Linton を通して彼の生前の営為は蘇る。Edgar の愛は聖書のヨブ記におけるヨブのように報われる。死んだ後に彼は救われるのである。あえて言えば、娘の Cathy と Hareton の結婚、そして彼らの Thrushcross Grange への移住によって、それは最終的に、彼は死んで勝利する。これが、Edgar の文化・理性に基づく"愛の殉死"の意味であるが、それは ironical な悲劇──不毛という名の逆説的な意味に於いてのみ成り立つ愛でしかない。元々、文化、物質生活は自然の改変とその活用抜きにしては成り立たないものであるが、この物語では反対に物質文明を代表する Linton 家とその時空間が Catherine という自然を抱え込み、そして自然の化身としての Heathcliff によって暴力的に破壊され、逆に Edgar の死と娘 Cathy の成長という、その改変を通して転生へと引き継がれる。それが Edgar の愛の殉教の意味であろう。

作者は、Edgar Linton の愛を通して近代文明を生んだ市民社会の精髄、文化や教養の成熟がもたらす人間性──pathos 溢れる English humour を彼の人格の中に取込みながら、充分に堪能しながらも、それを砂上の楼閣のようなものの中に押し留めることを、求めている。近代市民社会の生活と人生そのものを存在論的に捉え、それを体制・制度というひとつの枠の中に押し込めようとしている。そこには存在論

193

09 ─ 『嵐が丘』を如何に読み替え、如何に書き換えるか

的宇宙論的な文学の時空間における自立と孤立を通して亀裂 or abyss が啓示されている。つまり、この作品世界では Heathcliff という装置が作動し、Linton 家の、Edgar の、Isabella の、Thrushcross Grange の館のすべてが＝現実の制度・社会の体制が撃ち破られ、破壊されて解体させられて消滅する。そして彼らの世界は転換、転生という姿をとって改変させられるのである。Cathy と新生 Hareton の移り棲む Thrushcross Grange での結婚生活は Edgar Linton と母 Catherine Earnshaw のそれとは全く別世界のものとなるであろう。根底的なものを欠き大地に根を張ることのない、文化・教養という衣装を纏った擬制の精神生活、文明の名の基に構築される虚偽の制度は全て破壊され、全く別のもに改変され再生されるのである。しかし、それが何かは語られていない。

Nelly さんは、The crown of all my wishes will be the union of those two. I shall envy no one on their wedding day : there won't be a happier woman than myself in England![7]
と喜んでいるが、それも単に浪漫の蒸し返しを願っているに過ぎない。この作品はそのように読み、また読み替えていくことを要求している。

――――――――

【IV】

そして、そうであるがゆえにこの嵐が丘の物語は Edgar Linton の愛の物語ではあり得ない。依然として、Wuthering Heights は Catherine Earnshaw を巡る Heathcliff の物語なのだ。ならば、Heathcliff の Catherine への愛についてはどういうことが言えるのか？ それは愛とはいえないものである。

二人の愛の伝説＝that glorious world という神話ができあがっている。幼きものたちの純粋無垢の王国＝自然児たちの穢れ無き世界、それは果たしてそのようなものとして成立し得ていたであろうか？否である。作中にはそれがどのようなものでどういう具合に形成されたかが、具体的に描かれているわけではない。あくまで理念として、浪漫として語られているだけである。この作品をそのように理念化しないで、浪漫を作中より消し去り追放する方法で読み替えてゆくとどうなるか？ Heathcliff と Catherine は最初から違っている。Catherine は文字どおり Wuthering Heights の落し子であり、この大地が育んだ自然児であったが、Heathcliff はそのような意味では自然児とは言えない。孤児として Liverpool の路地における幼児体験を内部に抱えてこの地にやってきた Heathcliff と、何世代にも渡って引き継がれてきたこの大地の旧家の一人娘 Catherine との間には当初から亀裂が準備されていた。それは簡単には越えられない、大きくて深い abyss である。そのような近代都市の矛盾の坩堝、物質的欲望と egoism の精神地獄を深いこころの傷として抱え込む彼にとって、Wuthering Heights の自然と大地はこの傷を癒してくれるもの、"癒しの大地" であり、Catherine の trauma（精神的外傷）を治してくれる angel 天使の存在であったが、一方彼女とは全く相容れない、異質の存在であった。つまり、彼女にとって Heathcliff はあくまで他者、外部なのである。(there is or should be an existence of yours beyond you) そして、彼は外部からこの閉ざされた地域社会に侵入した異邦人であることの宿命から逃れるすべは持ち得ないのである。二人の純粋無垢の王国は最初から壊れている。つまり Catherine にとって自然化・原始化の向こうには文明による豊かな文化の世界とその生活が控えていたが、それは Heathcliff にとっては軽蔑すべき人間疎外と自己疎外の世界でしかない人間の根源性を欠落した、主体性や identity を持ち得ない人々の世界であった。そして、Catherine もまた兄 Hindely の近代都市生活における挫折による堕落と頽廃に示されるように、地

方の旧家の子供らが機械文明と物質生活の近代市民社会においてどう生きてゆくのかという問題から自由ではあり得なかったのである。兄の破滅は彼女にとって決定的要因であった。つまり、産業革命と近代化が進むこの時代にあって前近代的な地方の農家の＝yeomanの息子の典型的な挫折と破滅を目の当たりにして、CatherineはHeathcliffを必要とするのである。そのように読み替えてゆくことが、roman的なものをrealなものへ書き換えてゆくことが、求められている。

Cathrine EarnshowのHeathcliffに対する愛の正当性とは何を意味するのか？ また、逆にHeathcliffのCatherineの背信行為に対する批判と責任追求の正当性が論理的に成立するとしても、それはこの作品の主題であろうか？ 確かに二人はこの正当性の根拠に立ち激しく対立し罵り合い、彼女の方を窮地に追い込み、死にいたらしめることになる。そこで葛藤しているのは、自立することで孤立を招いたそれぞれの自我である。この自我の対立によってCatherineは自己の存在を引き裂かれて死ななければならず、Heathcliffは自己の存在を貫こうとして"my life", "my soul"であるCatherineを失うのである。無論、二人の悲劇は予め前提されてはいるのだが、私が言いたいのはこの激しく厳しい葛藤の中に見られる倫理・秩序の不在であり、道徳律などの不成立＝解体状況なのである。

[注]
1　Emily Brontë, *Wuthering Heights* (Everyman's Library, 1966) 68.
2　Brontë 39.　3　Brontë 69.　4　Brontë 75.　5　Brontë 78.　6　Brontë 77.　7　Brontë 271.　8　Brontë 69.

[参考文献]
Brontë Emily: *Wuthering Heights*, Everyman's Library, 1966.

10 「魔女の厨」のメタモルフォーゼを巡る独と伊

長谷川勉

ゲーテが、二十四歳の時に執筆したと推定され、没後三十九年後にその複写が発見された『初稿ファウスト』〈Urfaust〉では、「アウエルバッハの酒場」から「グレートヒェン悲劇」への橋渡しの役割をするものとして、「往還」〈Land Strase〉と呼ばれる次の場面がある。

Ein Kreuz am Weege, rechts auf dem Hügel ein altes Schloss, in der Ferne ein Bauerhüttgen Faust

Meph：
Ich weis es wohl es ist ein Vorurtheil,
Was giebts Mephisto hast du Eil?
Was schlägst vorm Kreuz die Augen nieder?
Allein genung mir ists einmal zuwieder.

このト書き、ファウスト並びにメフィストーフェレスの台詞、各二行という極めて短い場が、一七九〇年のファウスト第二稿ともいうべき『ファウスト断片』〈Faust, Ein Fragment〉では、除去されて、「魔女の厨」〈Hexenküche〉という長大な場が置かれ、一八〇八年に刊行された決定稿である『ファウスト第一部』に引き継がれる事となる。

Th・フリートリヒとL・J・シャイトハウエルが共同で編じた〈Kommentar zu Goethes Faust〉には、この「魔女の厨」は、一七八八年の春ローマ郊外のボルゲーゼ公園〈Garten Borghese〉で執筆された、と場所と時期が明記されている。

ところで、実は執筆の場所も、時期もゲーテ本人が、それを示しているのである。まず場所については、一八二九年四月十日、ゲーテが、朝食後テーブルにローマの地図を拡げてファルネーゼ公園を示した処、エッカーマンが、「魔女の厨が書かれた処ですね」と言った。するとゲーテは、それをボルゲーゼ公園だ、と秘書の誤謬を指摘しているのである。

次に時期を示すものは、彼の『第二次ローマ滞在』〈Zweiter Romischer Aufenthalt〉の一七八八年三月一日の項目である。つまり、その一週間は、普段の一か月分位の値打ちがあると思える程極めて充実して、

何よりも『ファウスト』の腹案が出来た。その中で新たな一場を書き上げた、というものである。周知の如く、ゲーテのイタリア旅行の動機は、暗く狭く重い北国のヴァイマル公国の公務からの離脱と、明るい南国への抑え難い憧憬の念の充足、並びに古典美の探求にあった筈である。

その後、遥かな時と処を替えて、東洋の医学志望の青年・片山敏彦をドイツ文学へと転向せしめた『タウリスのイフィゲーニエ』〈Iphiegenie auf Tauris〉や『エグモント』〈Egmont〉、『トルクヴァート・タッソー』〈Torquato Tasso〉といった典型的な古典主義作品群が、このイタリア旅行の成果として誕生したのは、納得がゆくとして、南の太陽の下で、元来北の妖怪である魔女を主要人物とする「魔女の厨」が書かれたのは、如何なる訳があるのだろうか。

この場の執筆の場所と時期を明らかにしながら、動機というか、執筆の必然性を明らかにしない作者に代って、エミール・シュタイガーが、〈目は、明るく照らされた事物にむけられる時、同時に目の中に補色を造る。従って、イタリアの明るい空に魅了されたゲーテは、己の中に反対の形象・つまり陰気で不気味な、煙と煤でいぶされてくすんだ北方的な話を形成した〉という見事な説明をする。巧みな説明ではある。しかし、筆者は大碩学シュタイガーの説明の中に、比喩の乱用を感ぜずにはいられない。

第一に、彼のこの説明を受け入れるならば、『タウリスのイフィゲーニエ』をはじめとする南欧的諸作品の書かれた理由は、如何に説明されるべきであろうか。もし、南国で南方的な作品が生み出されるのは当然で、その反対の作品の誕生も前述のような理由で説明可能とするならば、作品とそれを生み出す環境は無関係という事になりはせぬか。

第二に、イタリア旅行中の作者の次の三か所の発言と、シュタイガーの前述の解釈の余りにも大きな落

差をここに指摘したい。

X、この土地と世界史とは、常に切っても切れない関係がある。私の第二の新生、真の意味における再生は、ローマに入るときに始まるのだ。[6]

Y、私は、生まれ変われないぐらいなら、帰国せぬほうがましだ。[7]

Z、北欧からの旅人は、己の生活の補充を見出だし、己に欠けているものを補うためにローマに来たのだと信ずる。だが、やがて彼は全くなんともやり切れぬ思いで、己の考えを根本的に変えて新たな出発をせねばならぬことに気がつくのだ。[9]

XYZのいずれも、ゲーテのイタリア旅行の目的が、外的事情よりも内的理由に重点が置かれている事を物語る。つまり、彼がこの「世界史と結びついている」土地に足を踏み入れたのは、単なる閉鎖的な祖国から開放的な異国への逃走ではなく、自己自身の閉鎖性からの脱却、つまり彼の心を覆っている北方の熊の毛皮との訣別にあったのである。

Xは、旅に出てから三か月後の一七八六年の十二月三日、Yは、一七八七年三月二十二日、一七八七年十月（日は不詳）、と日を追ってその意志は強固なものになってゆくのである。

こうした彼が、シュタイガーの言う「陰気で不気味なしかも煙と煤でいぶされて黒くくすんだ北国的な話」などとする必要があろうとは、どうしても思えない。

ここで、仮に一歩譲ってシュタイガーの補色云々という比喩が、一般の文学作品に適応され得るとしよう。そしてまた古典的統一美を誇る作品群の中にひとつだけ変異ともいうべきものを書く可能性が作家に

はあるものだと仮定しよう。

しかし仮にそうだとしても、前述のような信条の貪欲な自己教養者が、小品ならまだしも、ほとんど生涯をかけて関わった大作の中に、彼がそれからの離脱を懸命に計った「煙と煤で黒くくすんだ北国的な」要素を、わざわざ導入する理由にはなるまい。

結論を急ぐ前に、「魔女の厨」のハンドルングを辿ってみたい。

メフィストーフェレスは、ファウストを誘惑すべくアウエルバッハの地下酒場にいざなったが、相手を不快にするのみで、成功はしなかった。彼は、書斎で霊や鼠達の力を借りたように、今度は魔女の助力を仰ぐことにする。

壁や天井が奇怪な道具でごてごてと飾られた魔女の厨が舞台。主の魔女は、どうやら留守のようである。低いかまどの上に大鍋がかかっていて、その鍋から立ちのぼる湯気の中にいろいろな姿のものが現れる。こう見てみると、シュタイガーの言う「煙と煤で黒くくすんだ北国的な」舞台のように見えるが、ト書きを良く見ると、この鍋の番をして煮こぼれせぬよう泡を掬っているのは、雌の尾長猿で、雄の尾長猿と子猿が火にあたって待っている。なんと家庭的な猿達だろう。囲炉裏を囲んで母親が食事の支度をし、野良仕事を終えた父親が子供を見守り暖をとりつつ待つという、平和な農村家庭の夕餉の前のひとときを連想するのは、筆者ひとりであろうか。

ここにファウストとメフィストーフェレスが、登場する。ファウストは、こんな処は自分の性に合わないと一応不平は言ってみるものの（二三三七—四六）、アウエルバッハの地下酒場ほどの嫌悪感は示していない。こんな汚らしい料理が、私を三十も若返らせてくれるのかい、と言った後に、「お前に、もっと気

のきいた才覚がないなら、もう御免だよ」(二三四三)という台詞を続けるところは、表面上は非難しつつも、実は乗り気十分で次の出し物を催促している様子を示唆しているのだ。

すると悪魔は、魔女の秘薬によらぬ若返り法、金も医者も魔法いらない(二三六〇-一)を教える。まず適度の労働と運動をし、自然に親しむ事(二三五二)、八十歳まで若くていられる最も良い方法(二三五三-四、二三五八-九)、暴飲暴食をしない事(二三五七)、余計な心配をしない事(二三五五-六)、要約すると以上のようになるが、中世世界に君臨する北の魔物の台詞とは信じがたいほどの健全さである。二一世紀のホウム・ドクターの言葉とまごうばかりである。

ところが、ファウストは、こうした常識的な若返り法を断り、魔法による若返り、つまり根本的なメタモルホーゼを望むのである。

はじめ、ファウストは、魔女ではなく、メフィストーフェレスにその薬の調合が出来ぬか、と問う(二三六六-七)が、メフィストーフェレスは、そうした時間と忍耐を要する仕事はあくまでも魔女の担当だ、と答える。

ここではじめて、メフィストーフェレスと猿達との間に話が交わされるが、猿達の答えは、いちいち風変わりである。まず女主の行く先については、「宴会にいますよ。家からね。煙突を通ったんでさ」と順序が逆であるし、外出時間の長さに関しては、「手を暖めている間」などと思わせぶりな答えである。

それからメフィストーフェレスと猿との間に賽の目をめぐる問答(二三九四-二四〇一)、ガラス玉(二四〇二-一五)、篩(二四一六-二二)、鍋(二四二三-二六)、塵払い(二四二七-八)、「書斎(一)」でファウストを眠らせ、「書斎(二)」で新入生を翻弄し、「アウエルバッハの地下酒場」で様々な学生達を手玉にとった海千山千の悪魔が猿達に振り回されて

いるのは注目すべき事である。しかも猿達は妖術を使っている訳でも何でもない。彼等の武器は、臆せぬ無類の率直さ（二三九四-九九、二四一七-二一、二四二三-二五）に過ぎないのである。

この間、ファウストは「魔の鏡」の前に立って近付いたり、離れたてみたりしている。この中に天女とまごうばかりの美しい女性の姿を見たからである。彼は、メフィストフェレスとの出会い以来初めて感動的な台詞を述べる。

彼は、この美しい女体の中に「万天の霊」（二四三九）を感じ、「愛の神よ、願わくば最も速く飛べる翼をわれに与え給え」（二四三一-二）と切に祈る。これは、若返りの薬を飲むための重要なモティベイションとなる。

この言葉をメフィストフェレスが聞き逃す筈がない。悪魔は猿達との会話を一時中止し、神が六日間努力して、最後にブラボーと叫んだ位だから当たり前で、もうじきああした美女を世話しよう、と申し出る。

この、神が六日かかって努力し、その成果に自ら喝采したというのは、勿論旧約聖書創世記第一章第二十七、二十八、三十一節と第二章二十一、二十二節によるのであるが、ゲーテ自身にもエバ誕生に関する次のような詩がある。これは、『西東詩篇』の「比喩の書」に収められている「よきかな」の第一節である。

Bei Mondenschein im Paradies
Fand Jehovah im Schlafe tief
Adam versunken, legte leis

Zur Seit ein Evchen,das auch entschief.
Da lagen nun in Erdesschranken
Gottes zwei liebliche Gedanken.—
〈Gut!!〉 rief er sich zum Meisterlohn,
Er ging sogar nicht gern davon.

創造した女性を〈Meisterlohn〉と自賛し、神自身が、〈Gut!!〉と叫んで、その場を立ち去り難かったと、この詩でゲーテは歌っている。ファウストは、この「よきかな」の神の如く、その場を立ち去り難い風情である。

そうこうしている間に、雌猿が、ほうっておいた鍋が煮えこぼれ、火炎が生じたかと思うと、魔女が恐ろしい叫び声をあげながら姿を現し、怠慢な猿に毒づき（二四六六―六八）、二人の侵入者を罵りながら（二四六九―七四）、炎を浴びせる。しかし、メフィストーフェレスは、塵払いを逆に持ち、柄のほうを使って魔女の小道具である土器やガラス器を叩き、お前の師匠を見忘れたのか、と怒鳴り返す（二四七五―八八）。魔女は、「馬の足」を隠していらっしゃるから、ついお見それいたしました。久しく会わなかったのだから、致し方ない。今回だけは、勘弁してやろうとメフィストーフェレスは言い、何故蹄を隠すのか説明する。それによると、世界中を席巻している文化とやらの影響が悪魔界にも及んで、今や角とか尻尾とか爪を生やした北国のスタイルは流行らなくなったので本人も「ふくらはぎの紛い物」[12]をつけている由である。

ところで、ヴィルヘルム・ケーニヒスは、当時の足の細い青年達は、足にパットを入れたのだ、との説

明をしている。[13]

すっかり南国かぶれになっている魔物は、魔女の世辞にも御機嫌斜めである。お出で下さったので嬉しくて気が狂いそうだなどと煽てても、「サタンの若者」〈Junker Satan〉[14]は禁句だ、「男爵様」〈Herr Baron〉[16]と呼べというのだ。

それから、第二五一九行に於いて初めてメフィストーフェレスの来意が、魔女に告げられ、相手の返事は「お安いご用ですとも！」[17]である。彼女愛用の最上等の薬をくれるとの事である。しかし、まじないなしに飲むと、一時間と生きていられないというので、第二五三一行と第二五三二行の間にある五六語からなる比較的長いト書きに示されたようなまじないの準備がなされ、呪文が唱えられる。

第一回目の呪文は、魔女自身第二五二三行で「魔女の九九」〈das Hexen—Einmaleins〉と称しているものだが、一八二七年三月二十八日ゲーテは、ハレ大学の哲学の教授ヘルムート・フリートリヒ・ヴィルヘルム・ヒンリヒスの著作にからませて、この魔女の九九について述べている。

言うまでもないことだが、この場合は何としても彼は事実に忠実でなければならなかったのだ。ところが彼の著作の中では思想が停滞しており、曖昧模糊とした言葉が同じ部分を同じ振幅で右往左往している所がかなり見られる。これは全く私の書いた『ファウスト』の「魔女の九九」と同じようなものだ。[18]

つまり、「魔女の九九」は、無意味なものがロンド形式で何度も何度も繰り返される一典型だ、という

のがゲーテ自身の説明なのである。

Th・フリートリヒ、L・J・シャイトハウエル両氏は、この数字による奇妙な呪文のヒントを作者が一七五六年フランクフルトで発行された小冊子『不思議な北斗七星』〈Alchimistisches Siebengestirn〉から得ている、と説明をしている。[19]

第二回目の「学術の力云々」の呪文、これまた第二五七三行のファウストの指摘を待つまでもなく、ただ尤もらしい言葉を述べただけで、意味はない。こうした呪文の連続にファウストは耐えられず悲鳴を(二五七四-七六)あげる。いやファウストのみならず、メフィストーフェレスまでも、うんざりしたのか、魔女を「優れた巫女」と持ち上げながらも、呪文はその辺りで止めて、薬を注ぐようにと注文する。

ここで遂にこの場のクライマックスとも言うべき秘薬服用のシーンとなる。この情景は、第二五八二行の次のト書き、並びに第二五八三-八六行のメフィストーフェレスの台詞で説明される。さらに第二五八六行の次のト書きは「魔女が輪を解き、ファウストがそこから出る」と記されているのみだが、ここで主人公のメイクアップは、徹底的に変える事が必要である事は言うまでもない。

秘薬の服用で若返ったからには、以前の書斎人のように静止していたのでは意味がない。そこで悪魔は二度(一度目は二五八七行、二度目は二五九三-九八)運動するように勧告する。その運動の効能は、「キュウピッドが身内で躍動し」(第二五九八行)、「高尚な悦楽の味」(第二五九六行)を味わえる事であると、説明され、「あの薬が身体に入っているから、いまにどんな女性もヘーレナに見えてくるのさ」(第二六〇三-四行)という主人公とマルガレーテとの出会いを予知するよう悪魔の独白で、この場は終わる。

以上「魔女の厨」のハンドルングを瞥見してみたが、前場の「アウエルバッハの地下酒場」との大きな

相違は、主人公が多弁・明朗になり、メフィストーフェレスに連れて来られた場所に強い関心を示した事にある。「魔女の九九」には不快感をあらわしたものの、秘薬を大胆に飲み干すし、「魔女の鏡」に映し出された美女に魅了され、メフィストーフェレスに宥められて、ようやくその場を去るという、いままでのファウストには見られなかった熱烈な執着ぶりであった。

こうした視点に立つ時、もはやこの場を「煙と煤でいぶされ黒くなった北国特有の陰気な話」とのエミール・シュタイガーの意見にくみする訳にはゆかない。

「アウエルバッハの地下酒場」との相違は、主人公の心情のみにとどまらない。「地下酒場」の脇役の学生達は、来訪者に必要以上の好奇心を抱き、当てはずれの批評をしてみたり、執拗に絡んだりしたのに対し、「厨」の脇役である猿達は、ファウストに対し、なんら特別の関心を示さない。従って、少なくとも旅人に対する態度に関する限り、自分達を垢抜けた小パリの市民と自惚れている（第二一七一-二行）ライプツィヒの学生達のほうが遥かに野暮ったくて泥臭く、魔女の配下の猿達のほうが国際都市の住人と呼ばれるのに相応しいではないか。

こうした都会的な他人に対する無関心な態度というのは、ゲーテはドイツでは経験しなかった。従って、イタリアの市民達のそうした態度に接し、彼は大いに驚き次のような感想をもらしている

この土地の人達は、他の人のことを全く気にしない。彼等はたがいに並んで走り廻っていることに気付いていないのだ。[21]

私は、ヴィチェンツァ市民を讃えずにはいられない。この町では大都会と同様の特権を享受出

こうしてみてくると、「魔女の厨」では、主役も脇役もともに明るいイタリアの太陽を浴びて、見事な南国の色に染め上げられている、という事が出来る。なるほど冒頭のト書きでは、この厨の天井や壁が奇怪な道具で飾られていると説明してはいるが、作者がこの場を「煙と煤でいぶされ黒くすんだ北国的な話」にする意図があるのであれば、明るい猿達とは異なる脇役を配すべきであった筈である。

以下、「厨」に於けるイタリア的側面を摘出してみよう。
まず第一にあげられるのは、この場の主題である「主人公の若返り」つまりメタモルフォーゼである。このメタモルフォーゼの構想は、『ウァ・ファウスト』にはなかったことで、ヴァイマルの狭さ暗さから開放され、イタリアの空気に触れて初めて誕生したという事が出来る。さらに、この変容は、メフィストーフェレスでさえも、田園生活の奨励という北方の悪魔の本来の性格を忘れたような意見を述べた事と関連させて見る必要がある。
つまり、これは「サタンの若様」と呼ばれるのを嫌った事と併せて、悪魔でさえも、南国の影響を受けずにはいられなかった事をしめす証左である。
次に注目したいのは、第二三五八行の猿達の、「わたし達が、前足を暖めている間ですよ」という台詞である。これはメフィストーフェレスの魔女の留守期間の質問に対する答えなのだが、この答えが、一七八七年三月十二日雨上がりの朝、鍛冶屋が火を使って余熱のある方石に円陣を作って手をかざしている少

22

208

知の新視界

年グループの光景が下敷きになっている事が容易に推測出来よう。ゲーテが、この少年の一団を「この小猿達」〈diese Affchen〉と愛情をこめて呼んでことも、われわれにふたつの場面の近しい関係にあることをしめしてくれる。ヴァイマルの顕職を嫌った北方からの旅人は、この行為を「活気と機知のある行動」と褒めているのである。

第三は、第二四〇二行から第二四二八行にかけて展開される小道具を媒体とするメフィストーフェレスと猿達とのやりとりである。

この小道具をガラス玉、篩、塵払い、鍋と列挙してみると、如何にもガラクタの道具類という感じがするのだが、ここで一七八七年二月二十二日ゲーテが、ヴェレトリの騎士ボルジャの作った博物館からの帰途のちょっとした出来事と考え合わせる必要を感ずるのだ。

ホテルに戻る途中、二―三人のかみさん達が門前に座って、骨董品をお求めになりませんかと私達を呼び止めた。私が是非買いたいと言うと、彼女達は古い釜とか火箸とかその他ガラクタを持ち出してみせ、担ぐのに成功したと笑いころげるのであった。

美術品を観賞してきて多少目が肥えたと自惚れているゲーテを全ての事に通暁している積もりのメフィストーフェレスに、やんちゃな猿達を茶目気たっぷりのヴェレトリのかみさん達に、擬する事が可能だと考えるのは、筆者だけではあるまい。

元来、弱者と思われて者が、強者とおぼしきものを頓知頓才で笑いのめす図式を、筆者はかつてベルクソンが『ル・リール』で指摘する笑いの一事象「逆転」〈l'inversion〉から拝借し「逆転の道化」なる呼

称を与え、シェイクスピア劇のリアと道化、狂言の大名と太郎冠者などと並べ、メフィストフェレスと猿達を論じた事がある。[28]

ゲーテは、ヴェレトリのかみさん達に担がれている、言うなればの道化達にしてやられている自分をたのしんでいる様子が充分にみてとれる。ここで彼は、イタリア旅行の本来の目的であった北方の熊の衣からの脱皮、つまり精神の華麗な変容が、成し遂げられたのである。『ウァ・ファウスト』では見られなかった観念的な老学者から、行動性のある青年へのメタモルフォーゼは、かかるゲーテにして初めて成就し得たのだ、と筆者は考える。

[注]

1 J. W. Goethe, *Synoptisch-Goethes Faust*, Verlag Neues Leben Berlin, (synoptisch von Dr. Hans Lebede herausgegeben und eingeleitet.)
2 Th.Friedrich u. L. J. Scheithauer: *Kommentar zu Goethes Faust*, Phillip Reclam Jun., Stuttgart, 1959, S. 203, L. 7-8.
3 Johann Peter Eckermann: *Gespräch mit Goethe in den letzten Jahren seines Lebens*, J. W. Goethe Gedenkenausgabe der Werke, Briefe und Gespräche Bd. 24 Artemis Verlag, Zürich, S. 361, L. 11-15.
4 J. W. Goethe: *Zweiter Römischer Aufenthalt*, Goethes Werke Bd. XI, Christian Wegner Verlag, Hamburg S.525, L. 14-22.
5 Emil Staiger: *Goethe Bd. II*, Atlantis Verlag, 1958, S. 51, L. 18-23.
6 J. W. Goethe: *Italienische Reise*, Goethes Werke Bd. XI, S. 147, L. 27-30.
7 Ders: *a.a.O.* S. 217, L. 33-35.
8 Ders: *a.a.O.* S. 430, L. 37-S. 431, L. 3.
9 J. W. Goethe: *Faust I.Teil*, L. 2381-83.
10 Ders: *a.a.O.* L. 2385.

11 J. W. Goethe: Epen, *West-Östliche Divan*, Theatergedichte, Goethe, Bd. 3, Artemis Verlag, Zürich, S. 384, L. 1-8.
12 *Faust I,Teil* L.2502.
13 Wilhelm Königs: *Erläuterungen Goethes Faust Teil L*, C.Bange Verlag, S. 44, L. 32-33.
14 *Faust I Teil*, L. 2503-4.
15 Ders: *a.a.O.* L. 2504.
16 Ders: *a.a.O.* L. 2510.
17 Ders: *a.a.O.* L. 2522.
18 J. P. Eckermann: *Gespräch mit Goethe*, Bd. 24, Artemis S. 602, L. 18-23.
19 Th. Friedrich u. L. J. Scheithauer: *Kommentar zu Goethes Faust*, S. 204, L. 25-7.
20 *Faust I Teil*, L. 2601.
21 J. W. Goethe: *Italienische Reise*, Goethes Werke Bd. XI, Hamburg, s. 211, L. 4-5.
22 Ders: *a.a.O.* S. 58, L. 11-15.
23 Ders: *a.a.O.* S. 200, L. 1-13.
24 Ders: *a.a.O.* S. 200, L. 11.
25 Ders: *a.a.O.* S. 200, L. 26-27.
26 Ders: *a.a.O.* S. 179, L. 16-21.
27 Henri Bergson: *Le Rire*, Presses Universitaires de France 1967, p. 79, L. 28.
28 長谷川勉『ファウストの比較文学的研究序説』（東洋出版、一九七九年）三七-四六頁。

ブレヒトにおける回り舞台と旅の使用法

田中德一

はじめに

ベルトルト・ブレヒト（一八九八―一九五六）は亡命先のアメリカから戻って間もない一九四九年一月、ベルリンのドイツ劇場で、ベルリーナー・アンサンブルの旗揚げ興行として自作『肝っ玉おっ母とその子供たち』（一九三九）（以下『肝っ玉おっ母』と略称）を演出上演したが、その時に採用した「回り舞台」（Drehbühne）が作品の意味を引き出す独特の作用を発揮した。マルセル・マルソーもブレヒトにおける回り舞台のドラマチックな使用法を指摘している。ブレヒトは能の翻案劇『イエスマン』『ノーマン』を書いた直後、日本から訪れた巡業一座の歌舞伎劇と出会っていることがわかっている。それから二年後に

長い亡命生活に入ることを余儀なくされるが、再びベルリンに戻って彼の叙事演劇を自らの手で上演し始めた第一作に、運命的にも日本生まれの回り舞台を使用したわけである。しかし、この回り舞台という舞台機構を用いて大きな効果を上げ得たのは、西洋における一九世紀末からの東洋演劇の受容と演劇改革運動の大きな潮流の中で、ブレヒト独自の工夫があったからである。そこで本稿では、彼の叙事演劇の代表作『肝っ玉おっ母』における回り舞台の使用法について考察し、ブレヒトと歌舞伎との関係を探ることにしたい。

[I]

ブレヒトが能の翻案劇を書いて日本演劇に対する関心を強めていた最中、筒井徳二郎一座が一九三〇年十月と翌年一月の二回にわたってベルリンを訪れており、ブレヒトが一座の芝居を見ていたという当時の資料がある。[2] 現在ではほとんど知る人もいないが、筆者のこれまでの調査により、筒井徳二郎は大阪出身の新派・剣劇役者で、関西劇壇ではどんな芝居も器用にこなす芸達者で通っていたこと、またアメリカの興行会社の招きで一九三〇年から翌年にかけて一年三ヶ月、欧米二十二ヵ国、七十以上の都市を巡って公演し、多大の反響を呼んでいたことが明らかになりつつある。筒井一座の芝居を見た直後に書かれたと思われるエッセイ「日本の演劇術について」[3] の中で、ブレヒトは日本演劇の若干の手法を西洋演劇改革、つまり叙事演劇の推進に応用する方途を研究すべきであると述べている。一九三一年二月、ブレヒトは自作『男は男だ』を改作の上、自ら演出上演したが、そこに筒井一座の歌舞伎的手法から刺激を取り入れている可能性が高い。[4] 一座は欧米で、西洋人のためにわかりやすくアレンジした歌舞伎劇と本業の剣劇を上演

したが、歌舞伎の本格的な舞台機構である回り舞台や花道は使用していない。しかし本稿との関係で言えば、ブレヒトがベルリンで見た一座の演目の中に、歌舞伎の『鞘当』と『勧進帳』が含まれており、両方共に舞台の上を歩く演技、いわゆる「歩く芸」が見られるのであり、歩行や旅をしばしば作品のモチーフとした作家であるブレヒトの関心を引いたことは十分考えられる。

ところで、現在使われているのと同じ原理の回り舞台は、一八世紀に日本で中村傳七や並木正三等によって考案、改良、完成されるに至った。ヨーロッパで最初に回り舞台が使用されたのは一八九六年、ミュンヘンのレジデンツ劇場においてであり、舞台装置家のカール・ラウテンシュレーガーがモーツァルトの『ドン・ジョヴァンニ』演出のために導入したが、その際、やはり日本の手本に従ったのではないかと言われている。回り舞台が西洋演劇界に大きな影響を及ぼすことになったのは、何といっても、マックス・ラインハルトが、一九〇五年、ベルリン新劇場においてシェークスピアの『真夏の夜の夢』の上演にこの歌舞伎の舞台機構を取り入れて大成功を収めてからである。以後、ヨーロッパでは比較的規模の大きな劇場では回り舞台が常設されることになる。しかし回り舞台は、舞台装置の速やかな転換によって時間を節約するという、もっぱら実用的目的に使われることが多かった。

さてベルリーナー・アンサンブルによる『肝っ玉おっ母』ベルリン初演において回り舞台が採用されたが、それは主人公の酒保商人、肝っ玉おっ母ことアンナ・フィーアリングとその子供たちが幌車を引いて旅する際に使われた。しかしブレヒトがこの時、回り舞台を使用したといっても、日本の歌舞伎やラインハルト（ブレヒトは最初、ラインハルトのドイツ劇場で文芸部員を勤めていた）の実験から直接の刺激を受けたというより、むしろエルヴィーン・ピスカートアの「ベルト舞台」(Laufband, laufendes Band) からヒントを得た可能性が強いように思われる。ピスカートアはチェコの作家ヤロスラフ・ハシェクの小説

『実直な兵卒シュヴェイクの冒険』（以下『兵卒シュヴェイク』と略称）を脚色し、一九二八年一月二十三日、ベルリンのピスカートア劇場において初演した際、ベルト舞台を導入して大きな反響を呼んだが、この脚色・演出にブレヒト、フェリックス・ガスバラ、レオ・ラニアが協力していた。ブレヒトは後にピスカートアの演劇実験を回顧しながら、次のように述べている。

　彼は舞台において大々的に進取の試みを行った。彼はモーター仕掛けで走行する二本のベルトを舞台に設置することによって、舞台の床を可動的にしたが、その結果、俳優はその場を去らずに行進することが可能となった。こうして彼は作品全体を動かすことが可能となった。

ブレヒトがこのようにピスカートアのベルト舞台に繰り返し触れているように、ピスカートアの方も再三再四この実験的試みに言及し、ブレヒトの回り舞台は自分のアイディアに恩恵を被っていると添えることを忘れなかった。

またブレヒトは『肝っ玉おっ母』を動かすのに、再び回り舞台というずっと重くて扱いにくい代物を採用したが、着想は私のベルト舞台から得ている。

しかしながら、このピスカートアのセンセーショナルな実験もラインハルトによる回り舞台の導入とその成功を抜きにしては考えられないように思われる。というのも、ベルト舞台をヨーロッパで最初に使用したのはピスカートアその人ではなく、ラインハルトが『真夏の夜の夢』の演出に回り舞台を使用したそ

216

の翌年に、すでにベルト舞台が使用されているからである。すなわち、一九〇六年にベルリンのウンター・デン・リンデン国立オペラ座でグルックのオペラ『オルペウスとエウリュディケー』が新しい演出のもとに上演されたが、その際、夫婦の冥界への道行に移動背景画と組み合わせてベルト舞台が使用されたことがわかっている。回り舞台が着目されるまで、ヨーロッパでは長い間、床の動かない固定舞台が支配し、それがまったく自明のことであった。ところがこの日本生まれの舞台機構が導入されることにより、そういう因襲的な舞台を改革して、可動性と変化に富むものに転換させるきっかけをつくったわけである。一九〇六年十月のある雑誌の「演劇制作者としての回り舞台」という記事には「私たちは回り舞台がまだまだこれから予測のつかない発展を遂げるのを体験することでしょう」と述べられている。回り舞台とベルト舞台の共通性は、舞台の床が可動的なことである。それゆえに、まず回り舞台からベルト舞台の発想が生まれたと考えるのが自然であろう。そしてその延長線上にブレヒトの回り舞台があると考えられるだろう。現にピスカートアがベルト舞台を導入する前に、「どっこい、おいらは生きている」の階層舞台（一九二七）や『ラスプーチン』の地球儀舞台（一九二七）等において、回り舞台を使用して演劇的表現の可能性を追求していたのである。西洋演劇の中に溶け込んだ日本演劇の要素はどのように変化を遂げたのだろうか。

[Ⅱ]

ピスカートアがベルリン・ノレンドルフプラッツの自分の劇場で、ハシェクの『兵卒シュヴェイク』をブレヒト等の協力のもとに上演した際に使った「ベルト舞台」とはどのようなものだったのか。それは舞

台の上手から下手へ横に張り渡された、前方、後方二本のベルトであり、それぞれ幅一・八メートル、長さ十七メートル、電気仕掛けで左右に移動した。重量は九トンであった。それは人物、マリオネットのほか、道具や舞台装置を載せて運び、背景のスクリーン（軍隊・教会・警察等、周囲の世界を風刺したゲオルゲ・グロス作の漫画、それに風景映画も映し出された）と組み合わせて、主人公の兵卒シュヴェイクの前線への行進等、人物の移動や旅を叙事的に、象徴的に表現することに成功したようである。例えば第二部第二場。ブドワイスへの行進の場。前方のベルトが右から左へ動くとすると、シュヴェイクがそれに乗って歌を歌いながら左から右へ行進する。その場合、彼は歩いているのに、客席からは舞台に静止しているように見える。そこに同じベルトに乗って老婆が立ったまま現われ、両者が出会うと、そのベルトが止まり、二人は会話を始める。会話が終わると、ベルトはまた動き出し、老婆の姿が視界から消え、シュヴェイクは先へ行進して行く。やがて前方のベルトに乗って里程標、木々、町の標識が現われ、同じく右から左へ行進する後方のベルトには酒場が運ばれてくると、両方のベルトが止まる、というような具合であった。初演の翌日、一九二八年一月二十四日の新聞には、ベルト舞台に乗った俳優（シュヴェイクを演じたマックス・パレンベルク）が

十歩あるく距離が人生全体の行路となる。もう一本のベルト舞台にはこの世の様々な現象が運ばれて彼に向かって来て、空からは雪が舞い降り、まるで舞台が時間と空間を克服したかのようである。[13]

と評されているのを見ると、ベルト舞台の象徴的作用は明らかであろう。

ピスカートアがマックス・ブロートとハンス・ライマンの原脚色を棄却して、ブレヒト等と新たに脚色し直した意図は、原作の小説の核心を、つまり受動的な主人公の人生をめぐる絶え間ない動きや変化を、舞台用のドラマに作り変えることにあった。

シュヴェイクは移送される──監獄へ、監獄から別の所へ──シュヴェイクはミサに行く助任司祭の道中を御供する、シュヴェイクは検査のために車椅子で運ばれる、彼は鉄道で前線へ向けて輸送され、彼の連隊を探し求めて、何日も何日も行進し続ける、彼の周りには絶え間ない動きがある。すべては絶えず流れ動いている。[14]

このように自ら原作の特徴を捉えたピスカートアが、その叙事的内容を効果的に引き出し、表現する手段として採用したのがベルト舞台であった。彼のベルト舞台は上記のように、主に人物の移動や旅に使われ、すなわち道として使われたわけである。彼はこの可動的な機構の使用によって、「場所・時間・空間の古典的統一を廃止し」[15]、舞台のあらゆる秘められた魅力を引き出すことに成功したという。そして演劇芸術に新しい次元を切り開くことになった。だから確かに彼の演出の独創性と芸術的な表現力は十分に評価しなくてはならない。しかし上で触れたように、少なくともグルックのオペラの演出にすでに先行例が見られるのであり、まったくの無から生み出されたわけではないだろう。ピスカートアも度々使用したように、そもそも回り舞台がその有力な発想源ではなかろうかと思われる。いずれにしても、舞台装置やスクリーンと組み合わせて、人物の移動や旅に使われたピスカートアのベルト舞台というのは、日本の歌舞伎の回り舞台と花道（花道もラインハルトが導入して成功している）の機能を融合したようなものだと考

11 — ブレヒトにおける回り舞台と旅の使用法

えられないだろうか。ピスカートアは一九二九年、『ベルリンの商人』の演出にもベルト舞台を使用した。

[Ⅲ]

ブレヒトはピスカートアの『兵卒シュヴェイク』演出に協力して以来、ベルト舞台や回り舞台の効果に心引かれてきた。回り舞台は『コーカサスの白墨の輪』(一九四五) の演出において、グルシェが山間を移動するのにも使用された。ブレヒトが『肝っ玉おっ母』の演出に回り舞台を使用した方法は、すでに引用したピスカートアの指摘にある通り、やはり彼のベルト舞台にヒントを得たものであろうと思われる (ピスカートアはブレヒトの成功を嫉妬していたようである)。それではブレヒトにおける回り舞台の使用とはどんなものだったのだろう。一九四九年に作られた『肝っ玉おっ母』の上演モデル (Couragenmodell 1949) によって、回り舞台が使われたと思われる場面を見てみたい。

まずプロローグであるが、ここでは肝っ玉おっ母と彼女の家族が「戦場に向かう長い旅路」にあることが示される。幕が開くと二人の息子、アイリフとシュワイツェルカスが幌車を引いて登場し、車の上にはおっ母と唖娘カトリンが乗っている。舞台装置はなにもない。彼等は移動しながら

隊長さん、いくらあんたの家来でも
腸詰くわずにゃ、死なされねえ。
そこは、肝っ玉おっ母の才覚さ
肉のなやみも、霊のなやみも、酒しだい。

とおっ母の商売歌を歌い、娘はそれに合わせてハーモニカを吹く。彼等の登場について「肝っ玉の幌車が逆向きに回転する回り舞台の上を前方に向かって来る」とモデルブックに記されている。ここから察するに、客席から見ると、幌車は回り舞台の回転に比べて非常にゆっくり進むか、あるいは舞台の上にほとんど止まっているように見えたに違いない。ここには記されていないが、その際、彼等は回り舞台の縁に沿って移動したはずである。舞台装置のない、いわゆる「何もない空間」の中で、回り舞台の回転に合わせた幌車の前進は、肝っ玉おっ母の限りない旅を象徴しており、この回り舞台の使用法は以後、特に第七場と第十二場において明瞭な形で繰り返される。プロローグはすぐそのまま次の第一場に移行する。

さらに上演モデルを見ていくと、第七場で唖娘カトリンと従軍牧師が幌車を引いて後方から登場し、客席に平行に舞台前縁を進んで行く。この時、肝っ玉おっ母の戦争商売は絶頂期にあって、幌車には新しい商品がぶら下げてあり、おっ母は指にリングをはめ、首には銀貨のネックレスを巻き、誇らしげに戦争賛歌を歌いながら幌車と並んで闊歩する。戦争のために息子達が行方不明になったり射殺されており、前の第六場では娘が兵士達に顔に致命的な傷を負わされたばかりで、包帯姿も痛々しいにもかかわらずなのにである。

第八場ではスウェーデン王が戦死して束の間の平和が訪れた後、再び戦争が始まるが、その時、従軍料理人とカトリンが幌車を引いて、肝っ玉おっ母は「ウルムからメッツ、メッツからマーレン！／肝っ玉おっ母はどこまでもついていく／戦争させるにゃ食わさにゃならぬ」と歌いながら、戦地へ旅立って行く。

第九場では、落ちぶれた肝っ玉おっ母は従軍料理人にウトレヒトへ行って商売しようと誘われるが、彼を置き去りにして、カトリンと再び幌車を引いて出発する。

第十場では、肝っ玉おっ母とカトリンが幌車を引いて農家の前までやって来て立ち止まり、しばらく家の中から漏れてくる定住者の幸福の歌に聞き入り、ま

たもや車を引いて立ち去る。（次の第一一場では、肝っ玉おっ母が町に買い出しに行っている間に、唖のカトリンが農家の家畜小屋に上り、太鼓を叩いて町の人々に敵の来襲を知らせようとして、兵士達に射殺されてしまう。）

そして最終場、第十二場において肝っ玉おっ母は、死んだ娘に子守歌を歌って幌布を掛けてやり、埋葬費を農夫達に渡すと、連隊を追って去って行く。その幕切れ、おっ母の商売歌が聞こえ出すと、回り舞台が回転し始め、おっ母がただ一人幌車を引いて回り舞台を一周し、次に上手後方に向かって幕となる。第十二場は前場の舞台装置（農家と家畜小屋）を取り去り、まったく何もない舞台の上を幌車が移動したので、第一場（したがってプロローグも）を想起させたようである。この幕切れの効果について、かってブレヒトの演出に参加したマンフレット・ヴェークヴェルトが演出現場のエピソードを紹介している[18]。ブレヒトは最初、おっ母に幌車を引かせて後方に向かわせ、本当に果てしない戦争へ向かって消えて行く様を表現したくて、舞台上から消え去らせたが、平凡な退場であった。ところが偶然にも、おっ母役のヘレーネ・ヴァイゲルが演出家達の意見を聞きに、再び前方に戻って来たとき、驚くほどの効果があり、彼女はまさに限りない旅を続けるかのように見えた。そこでブレヒトはヴァイゲルに、幌車を回し舞台の縁に沿って次のように引かせることにした。

まず後方に向かい、それから幅十二メートルのホリゾントに沿って移動した後、再び前方に向きを変え、そのまま客席の方へ向かって進んだ。その後再度、後方へ方向転換し、幕が閉じた[19]。

つまりこの作品全体を通じて、おっ母の幌車が回り舞台の縁をぐるぐる巡るときは、各地を経巡り歩いて

いるのだという諒解ができているので、幕切れで幌車が一周して客席の方に近づいて来たのに、それは遠ざかって行く意味に受け取れたといわけである。このようにヴェークヴェルトは回り舞台の上での幌車の動きを記号として捉え、演劇における記号の二重の意味作用に論及している。

ブレヒトの『肝っ玉おっ母』における回り舞台の使用法は以下のように考えられよう。第一に、彼の目的は従来の基本的な用い方、場面転換のために装置を速やかに取り換える技術的使用にはなく、ほとんど「何もない空間」で、登場人物を幌車と共に回り舞台の盆に載せて、盆をぐるぐる回転させたということ。ピスカートアの場合のように背景のスクリーンや舞台装置と組み合わせて舞台を回すとか、歌舞伎でよく見られる盆と一緒に舞台装置を回して視覚的効果を狙うというようなことはしなかった（もちろん、野営テントその他の簡単な舞台装置は使われたが）。さらに、幌車が回り舞台の回転とは反対の方へ移動する場合、同じ所に止まって見えるか、ゆっくり動いているようにしか見えなかったということ、そして幌車が回り舞台の周縁をぐるぐる回ることで長い旅路が表されたということである。要するに肝っ玉おっ母やその子供たちが、商売道具の幌車を引く、戦場を追って果てしない旅をするため、もっぱらそのために回り舞台が使用された。だからブレヒトの場合も人物の移動に回り舞台が使われたわけであり、この意図に関してはピスカートアのベルト舞台と共通しており、はっきりした影響の跡がうかがわれよう。

特に肝っ玉おっ母たちが幌車を引いて回り舞台の回転とは逆方向に進んで行く際、車輪は回り、足は動いているのに、彼等と幌車は一つ所に静止しているような印象を与えるので、この使い方と効果は上述したピスカートアのベルト舞台の場合とよく似ているように見える。しかし両者の相違も明らかである。ピスカートアのベルト舞台は、人物の歩行に合わせて背景の舞台装置やスクリーンを動かし、人物の移動を視覚的によりリアルに表現しようとするが、ブレヒトの場合は、背景の装置やスクリーンを使わないで、むしろ観客の

想像力に訴えようとする。また回り舞台の周囲をぐるぐる巡ることが、果てしない旅を意味すると述べたが、これも同様の効果を発揮する。このように回り舞台が独特な方法で使用されたので、人物の移動、すなわち旅について、さらに人生そのものについて、動の中にも不動、変化の中にも不変の印象を強める結果になったように思われる。野戦酒保商人である肝っ玉おっ母は、戦争（三十年戦争）を相手に商売をし続け、戦争によって子供たちを次々に失っていく。けれども彼女の生き方、人生は一向に変わらない。そこで、幌車が筋の展開の重要な節目に舞台に現れ、回り舞台の回転に合わせて移動するが、その車輪の回転と回り舞台の回転は、彼女のいつ果てるとも知れない長い長い戦争人生を、生の変転における不変の側面を象徴的に描いて見せることになったと言えるだろう。その回り舞台は、いわばおっ母の子供たちを次々に振り落としながら、変わることなく回転し続けたのである。

ブレヒトの他の作品では十八世紀の作家、ヤーコップ・ミヒャエル・ラインホルト・レンツのドラマを翻案した『家庭教師』が、『肝っ玉おっ母』初演の翌年、一九五〇年四月にやはりドイツ劇場で初演された時も、回り舞台が独特の方法で使用された。第六場と第九場の、フリッツたち学生がいる二つのハレの場面が、フリッツの故郷であるプロイセンのインステルブルクから遠く離れていて、しかも両地で起きる事件が相互に関連していることを表わすために、幕を明けたまま回り舞台を回転させた。さらに第十四場と第一五場の間の幕間に、「登場人物が市民家庭の居間にあるインテリアの機械仕掛けの人形のように、無意味にぐるぐる回転する」21 印象を与えたという。人物と人物の行為を戯画化しようとするブレヒトの意図は明らかである。『家庭教師』における回り舞台の使用は、このように叙事的手法として

非常に効果的であったが、『肝っ玉おっ母』の場合のように、作品全体のテーマに関係して、登場人物の人生そのものを雄大に、象徴的に表現することに役立つようなものではなかった。

[Ⅳ]

本家の日本の歌舞伎では、普通、ブレヒトの場合のように空の盆を回すことをしない。絢爛豪華な、あるいは大掛かりな舞台装置を場面ごとに取り換えて使う必要から、回り舞台は装置の速やかな転換に利用されている。しかし技術面の効果や時間的経済のためだけではない。舞台と共に飾りつけた装置の観覧に供することによって、その場面を別の角度から見せたり、場面の移り変わりや、局面の展開そのものを観覧に供する。いわば生の変化と多様性を万華鏡のようにぐるっと回して見せるのである。例えば歌舞伎の『佐倉宗吾』や『野崎村』の旅立ちの場面では、舞台を半回し（九〇度）とか本回し（一八〇度）にし、人物が舞台の回転とは逆の方へ歩み、屋敷の脇を通ったり、裏側に回る様まで見せる。ブレヒトとは舞台の回転と人物の歩き方は同じであるが、その舞台面の何という違いであろう。特に『佐倉宗吾』の雪の子別れ場面は、舞台が半回しになりつつ、父の宗吾と子供たちが舞台の上をその回転とは反対方向に歩いて行くが、この場面は親子の永久の別れの瞬間をその回転に引き伸ばして印象づけているわけである。やはりブレヒトとは違って、生の移りゆく局面を印象的に描いていると言うことができる。それに対してピスカートアのベルト舞台の方は、平面的で、人物の移動をそのまま移動カメラで追った映画のようであるが、人物・マリオネット・道具・装置・スクリーンと組み合わせて、生の変化と多様性を表現している点で、むしろ歌舞伎の回り舞台の作用に近いように思える。このようにブレヒトの回り舞台は、歌舞伎の方法を受

225

け継いではいないのである。

さらに旅立ちの舞台的表現自体にブレヒトと歌舞伎との間に差が出てくる。ブレヒトでは、前述のように、人物に回り舞台の上を旋回させて遠くへ旅立つことを表現させているが、歌舞伎では、いわば道をかたどったもう一つの舞台、花道を使ってそれが表現される。『佐倉宗吾』の雪の子別れ場面で舞台を回して子供たちが宗吾にしがみつき、行かせまいとする様を見せた後、宗吾はそれを振りきって花道に立ち、足速に去って行って幕となる。また『野崎村』の幕切れでは、舞台を本回しにして土手の場面に切り替え後、両花道を使い、お染は母お常と共に船で本花道を、久松は駕籠で仮花道を、それぞれ旅立って行く。河竹登志夫氏は「花道論」[22]において、花道は日本文化（歌舞伎の世界）にしか生まれなかった特異の舞台機構であることを論じておられるように、回り舞台とは反対に西洋演劇に根付くことなく今日に至っている。

しかしそれでもなおブレヒトにおいては、既述のように、回り舞台の独自な使用法で時間と空間が処理されているのであり、そこに一種の「道行」といえるようなものが表出されているのではないだろうか。すなわち、肝っ玉おっ母たちが幌車を引いて舞台に現れ、回り舞台の上を旋回しながら旅を続けるのは、三十年戦争の中、人生の無常を果てしなく旅して歩く母子道行と見えてこないだろうか。郡司正勝氏は「道行の発想」の中で、日本演劇における道行の特色について

〈舞台〉の時空は、むしろ「流れる」ことを封じる性格をもつ。いや、もっというそういう力を発揮するところだといったほうがよい。……時間を空間のなかに封じこめるのが、道行の場合の舞台の意義であり、舞の本儀だといったほうがいいのではないか。[23]

と述べておられる。つまり、日本演劇の道行は、ある地点からある地点への移動を表現するのではなく、一つの舞台をあちこちさまようことを特色としているということになる。人形浄瑠璃や歌舞伎の道行物が舞の形をとるのはそのためである。そうであるとすれば、ブレヒトの回り舞台における幌車と母子の行進も、時間を巧みに空間に変換しており、道行の理念に近いものを感じさせるのではないかと思われる。そして、日本演劇の道行が現世での特定の目的地への旅行というより、浄土への永遠の旅路を意味するとすれば、ブレヒトの回り舞台の回転も、やはり永遠の(ただし救いのない)旅を象徴しているのではないだろうか。

能の翻案劇『イエスマン』『ノーマン』、またこれに続く『例外と原則』もそうであるように、ブレヒトの作品ではしばしば旅がモチーフとして使われる。例えば『例外と原則』では目的地への道中そのものが作品の主要な出来事となっており、商人と苦力の旅の途上における対話と一歩一歩の歩行によって、二人の立場、目的、生き方の相違が如実に表わされる。情感の漂うような内容では全くないにもかかわらず、ここでは日本演劇の道行に通じるような、まさに「歩く芸」が俳優に要求されるのではないだろうか。ブレヒトが亡命地のアメリカで、既述のハシェクの小説『兵卒シュヴェイク』を翻案した『第二次大戦のシュヴェイク』(一九四三)は、後半がスターリングラードへの主人公の行進が主な内容である。ヒトラーに忠誠を誓う彼は、冬のロシアの草原を、自分の部隊に追い付くために、人に尋ねながらスターリングラードへ向けて行進するが、どこまで行っても目的地に辿り着かない。このいくら歩いても目的地から等距離だけ離れている様を表わすために、主人公は舞台の上をぐるぐる巡るのである。『肝っ玉おっ母』においてはこの果てのない、救いのない旅路を回り舞台の巧みな使用によって表現することに成功した。やはりブレヒトがかつてピスカートアの『兵卒シュヴェイク』演出に協力したことが、人間の生き方としての

旅をいかに舞台的に表現するかを腐心するきっかけになったのであろう。いま一つ、回り舞台の上を幌車を引いていく行進は、同時に、旅芸人の移動と芸能の場への道程を思わせずにはおかないだろう。幌車は旅役者の車、芝居を持って町に現れ、しばらく滞在してはまた去って行く、あの「テスピスの車」[24]と二重写しになる。またさらに、肝っ玉おっ母とその子供たちが幌車と共に現れ、回り舞台の上を巡るのは、歌舞伎で言えば、役者が花道を歩むのに似て、役者の登場と退場を演劇的に印象づけているかのように見える。現にその際、おっ母たちは商売歌を歌うが、そうなったのはおっ母役のヴァイゲルが望んだからで、ブレヒト等演出陣は元々、元気がよくて「舞台効果のある登場歌」を予定していたという。[25] 否、このことを持ち出すまでもないだろう。商売歌による登場もメタシアトリカルな構造を十分証明している。したがって幌車は、作品の中で『肝っ玉おっ母』というドラマを運んで回り、また客席の我々観客にもドラマを運んでくるという、二重の意味で「テスピスの車」なのではないだろうか。ブレヒトはこのドラマをデンマーク亡命中に制作したが、一九五三年のコペンハーゲン公演のために書いた小論の中で、ベルリン初演について次のような表現を使った。

　肝っ玉の幌車が一九四九年、ごろごろ音を立ててドイツの舞台に登場したとき、このドラマは、ヒットラーの戦争が引き起こした計り知れない荒廃を解き明かすことになったのです。[26]

おわりに

ブレヒトの回り舞台には、ピスカートアのベルト舞台を経て、間接的に日本演劇の手法が流れ込んでいる。ブレヒトはこのドラマに「三十年戦争の一記録」と副題を添えたが、肝っ玉おっ母の人生と戦争の関係を叙事的に表現する重要な手段として回り舞台を採用した。舞台の演技平面を動かして人物の移動や道行を叙事的に表現する。ブレヒトの回り舞台にはベルト舞台から流れ込んでいる花道の機能と意味が生きているように思われる。しかしピスカートアの舞台は、多様な表現手段を投入しながら、動く絵画に留まり、映画的手法に接近しすぎた嫌いがある。それに対してブレヒトの回り舞台は、歌舞伎の方法をとらなかったにもかかわらず、観客の想像力に訴え、演劇空間の表現の可能性を拡大することに成功しており、別の次元で日本演劇の道行の理念に近づいているように思える。

[注]

1 マルソー、イェーリンク対談『パントマイム藝術』尾崎宏次訳(てすぴす双書)六三、未来社、一九七六年、一〇三頁。「ブレヒトが回り舞台を利用したとき、新しい次元が生まれています。回り舞台をドラマティックにつかった最初ですね。」

2 ベルリン初日についての新聞記事に、ブレヒトが客席にいたことが記されている。この資料については稿を改めて触れたい。

3 Bertolt Brecht: *Werke. Band 21. Schriften I.* Aufbau-Verlag Berlin und Weimar und Suhrkamp Verlag Frankfurt am Main 1992, S. 391-392.

4 拙稿「『男は男だ』に見るブレヒトと歌舞伎の関係」、日本比較文学会『比較文学』第三十九巻、一九九六年、

5 二二一-二一六頁。

6 東洋と西洋の回り舞台の創始者については、杉野橘太郎「東西廻り舞台とその創始者」、『早稲田商学』一二六号、一九五七年、七三一～七六六頁が詳しい。

7 実際は一九四一年四月のチューリッヒ初演において、すでに回り舞台が使われており、この時の舞台美術は基本的にベルリン初演にも踏襲されたが、フィンランド亡命中のブレヒトはこの上演に直接関与していたわけではなかった。ベルリンで回り舞台を採用した際、彼の念頭にあったのは、自ら体験のあるピスカートアのベルト舞台の効果だったはずである。

8 Bertolt Brecht: *Gesammelte Werke 16. Schriften zum Theater*. Frankfurt am Main 1967, S. 594.

9 Erwin Piscator: *Theater der Auseinandersetzung. Ausgewählte Schriften und Reden* (= edition suhrkamp 883). Frankfurt am Main 1977, S. 96. またピスカートアはブレヒトが自分に言ったとして「私の芝居でベルト舞台を使いたい」という言葉を記している。Erwin Piscator: *Zeittheater. Das Politische Theater' und weitere Schriften von 1915 bis 1966* (= rowohlts enzyklopädie 429). Reinbek bei Hamburg 1986, S. 330.

10 Friedrich Kranich: *Bühnentechnik der Gegenwart*. I.Band. München und Berlin 1929, S. 268.

11 Karl = Ludwig Schröder: Die Drehbühne als Dramaturg. In: *Die Schaubühne*, 4. Oktober 1906, II.Jahrgang, Nummer 40, S. 332.

12 Erwin Piscator: *Das politische Theater*. Berlin 1929, S. 187-203.

13 このシュヴェイクが歩いているのに静止して見える様子は、映画『天井桟敷の人々』の中で、バローが扮するパントマイム役者バチストが背後の風景を表す舞台道具の移動に合わせて足を動かし、移動しているかのように見せるが、実際は舞台の真ん中に留まったままなのを、さながら想起させる。

14 Günther Rühle: *Theater für die Republik 1917-1933. Im Spiegel der Kritik*. Frankfurt am Main 1967, S. 845.

15 Erwin Piscator: *Das politische Theater*, a.a.O., S. 189.

16 Ebd., S. 190.

17 Klaus-Detlef Müller (Hg.): *Brechts Mutter Courage und ihre Kinder* (= suhrkamp taschenbuch materialien. st 2016). Frankfurt am Main 1982, S.124-193. この回り舞台の使い方は一九五四年一〇月の『コーカサスの白墨の輪』の東ベルリン初演においても採用された。「子供を背負って、孤独に、何もない回り舞台の上を、そのグルシェが山間を逃亡する際にも回転とは逆向きに歩いてきた。」*Die Zeit*, Hamburg, 14.10.1954. In: *Brecht in der Kritik. Rezensionen aller*

230

18 Brecht-Uraufführungen sowie ausgewählter Premieren. Eine Dokumentation von Monika Wyss mit einfuhrenden und verbindenden Texten von Helmut Kindler. München 1977, S. 263. Manfred Wekwerth: Der Zeichencharakter des Theaters. Ein Experiment. In: Klaus-Detlef Müller (Hg.), a.a.O., S.220-222.

19 Ebd. S. 221.

20 ベルリーナー・アンサンブルは「回り舞台のない舞台で、酒保商人の幌車が限りなく前進していく様を表すにはどうしたらよいか」という質問に対して、一つの解決策として注12に例を挙げたような、パントマイムによる方法を勧めている。二輪だけ見せて車の中からひもで回し、実際には車を移動させないで、車を引いて歩いているようにパントマイムで見せる方法である。Ebd. S.207.

21 Jan Knopf: *Brecht-Handbuch*. Theater. Eine Ästhetik der Widersprüche. Stuttgart 1980, S. 302.

22 河竹登志夫『歌舞伎美論』（東京大学出版会、一九八九年）、一四一-一六五頁。

23 郡司正勝『かぶきの美学』（演劇出版社、一九七五年、四版）一五八頁。郡司氏はまたジャン・コクトーの映画『オルフェの遺言』に触れ、この西洋人の芸術の中にも「結局のところ、人間はひとつところをうろついているだけだという」「永劫の人生の旅」に似たものがあり、道行の発想があると指摘しておられる。同書、一五四-一五五頁。

24 ホーラティウスが『詩法』の中で述べているギリシャの悲劇詩人「テスピスの車」は、「現実の根拠をもたない空想の産物」（小苅米『テスピスの車』、panoramic mag. is. vol. 9、ポーラ文化研究所、一九八〇年、六〇頁）とされているが、ここではその「空想の産物」を、所々を遍歴する役者の車に当てはめて比喩的に使っているに過ぎない。

25 Klaus-Detlef Müller (Hg.), a.a.O., S. 132.

26 Ebd. S. 247.

〔付記〕
本稿は一九九五年八月発行、『国際関係研究』国際文化編第十六巻一号に掲載された「ブレヒトにおける回り舞台の象徴的使用」に加筆訂正したものである。なお、「肝っ玉おっ母とその子供たち」からの引用は、『ブレヒト戯曲選集』第二巻（白水社）の千田是也氏の訳を使わせて頂いた。

アフリカン・アメリカン・エグゾティシズム
一九二〇年代パリの黒人表象への一考察

宗形賢二

[序] 一九二〇年代のニューヨークとパリ

一九二五年の秋、黒人といえば多くの人々がアフリカ系アメリカ人の一団が到着した。シャンゼリゼ劇場の呼び物『ラ・レヴュ・ネグル』(*La Revue Nègre* =黒人レビュー)に出演するためにアメリカからやって来たジョセフィン・ベイカー(Josephine Baker)やサキソフォンのシドニー・ベシェイたちである。当時のパリはアフリカ人・アフリカ文化を待っていた。"négrophilie"という黒人趣味を表す言葉がパリのアバンギャルドの間で積極的な意味で使われた時代でもある(Archer-Straw 9)。同年、パリではいわゆる「アールデコ」という言葉を生

み出した現代装飾・工業美術国際展が開催されており、多くのアバンギャルドたちがアフリカ文化、黒人文化にある種の期待と興奮を感じていた時代ともいえる。

彼等の渡ってきた大西洋の反対側の国アメリカでも、第一次世界大戦を契機に、同じく一九二〇年代の繁栄を享受した文化が花開き、自動車、映画、ジャズ、チャールストンなどこれまでにない新しい都会的な風俗や文化が流行した。F・L・アレンの『オンリー・イェスタデイ』(一九三一)はこの時代を描いた古典のひとつであるが、再三引用されるようにこの時代は「スピードと興奮と情熱」(Allen 94)の時代であった。特に「フラッパー」呼ばれる若い女性たちの新しい風俗は、この時代を象徴する文化として欠かせない。コルセットを脱ぎ去り膝下までのミニスカートをはき、化粧しタバコを吸い、禁酒法の中でカクテルを飲む断髪の女性たち。リンド夫妻の『ミドルタウン』の中の判事が嘆いた「移動する個室」としての自動車の普及は当然ながら若者たちの恋愛にも影響を与え、彼等の性道徳は大きく変化する。すなわち、大戦中の社会進出で弾みをつけた女性たちは、母親の世代までの豊かな成熟や優雅さではなく(これは身体的にも同じ)、「反対に、ほっそりすること、薄い胸、短いスカート(短いスカートは少女のように見せるからである)」、若さを強調するロー・ウェスト」、すなわち「成熟していない若さだけを賛美」したのである。彼女たちはヴィクトリア朝の理想や道徳を否定し、何より「解放」と「自由」(Allen 107)を求めた。白人女性の解放と自由を。このような解放と享楽の時代は「狂乱の二十年代」、あるいは「ジャズ・エイジ」と呼ばれる。

一九二〇年代は同時に「ハーレム・ルネッサンス」の時代でもあった。ジョセフィンが一九二〇年代前半住んでいたニューヨークのハーレムは、L・ヒューズやZ・N・ハーストン等の黒人作家、D・エリントンなどを始めとする黒人音楽家といった芸術・文化の花盛り、「ハーレム・ルネッサンス」のまさに

中心地であった。当時の映画スターや著名人たちが、「ジャングル・ミュージック」と呼ばれたデューク・エリントン・バンドを始めさまざまなアフリカ趣味の歌や踊りを見に、「コットン・クラブ」始めハーレムの主要なクラブに足しげく通った。むろん観客にはアフリカ系アメリカ人は許されず白人のみではあった。当時のアメリカ社会でそれまでにないプリミティブな芸術・アフリカン・アートが花開いた背景としては、当然ながらピカソやモディリアニ等ヨーロッパの芸術家によるアフリカ系アメリカ人の芸術・文化運動が花開いた背景があったからだが、さらにF・L・アレンを引き合いに出すまでもなく、フロイトによる深層心理の発見による、近代文明の不健康さとリビドー抑圧からの解放手段としての原始的本能の回復、そして、ベネディクトやM・ミードを輩出したフランツ・ボアズの文化人類学理論など (Stewart)、西洋文明自体の疲弊と脆弱化の一種の治癒を目指した精神活動が、ちょうどこの時代の精神となりつつあったからでもある。

それは一九二二年T・S・エリオットが『荒地』で回復を試みようとした衝動と似ている。アングロ・サクソン系を中心とするヨーロッパ系アメリカ人にとって、第一次世界大戦への幻滅と戦争への嫌悪、そして西洋文明の行き詰まりを感じていたこの時代、異文化の原始的生命力は確かに大きな魅力であった。ジャズやチャールストンというアメリカの娯楽がパリで流行り出した二十世紀初頭はアメリカの時代の始まりでもあった。

そのようなアメリカでは、クー・クラックス・クランが再び台頭し始めた時でもある。このような時代背景の中で、アメリカを捨てパリに生きたジョセフィン・ベイカーというアフリカ系アメリカ女性の持つ意味はどのようなものであったか。アフリカ系アメリカ人の成功譚に必ずと言えるほど登場するこの時代の偶像的「黒人スター」を、一九二〇年代のヨーロッパ、少なくともパリではどのように受け止めたのか、その

黒人愛好(ネグロフォビア)や異国趣味(エクゾティシズム)を支えた黒人表象を、当時流布していた擬似自然人類学的言説を検討しながら再考してみたい。

[2]「フォリー・ベルジェール」への道

現在では、映画初出演の『熱帯の妖精(セイレーン)』(*Siren of the Tropics*, 1927)こそ見られないものの、一九三〇年代の映画『ズー・ズー』(*Zou Zou*, 1934)や『プリンセス・タムタム』(*Princess Tam Tam*, 1935)ばかりか、ジョセフィンを一躍有名にしたバナナ・ダンスの一場面(後年の映像)まで見ることができるが、その衝撃は、この時代ならではのものだろう。何よりベイカーをベイカーたらしめているのは、一九二〇年代のアフリカ系アメリカ人としての身体でありダンスであり若さであった。ジョセフィンという虚実織り交ぜたイコンの中にこそ一九二〇年代の光が凝縮されていたと言いたくなるようなこの時代の個性を抱えている。近年では第二次大戦中の仏軍諜報機関での活躍と叙勲、十二人の孤児を養子として夢の国を作ろうとした「虹の一族(レインボートライブ)」、一九六三年のワシントン大行進への参加、そしてFBIのファイル(No.62-95834)などを取り上げ、後年の人種差別への抗議や人権擁護といった政治的活動が注目されることが多いが、それらの言動が意味を持ったのは、一九二〇年代パリのミュージック・ホールの伝説的スターという燦然と輝く経歴があったからに他ならない。

ジョセフィンは一九〇六年六月三日セントルイスで、洗濯女として働くキャリー・マクドナルド(Carrie Mcdonald)を母として生まれた。ジャズ・ドラマーのエディ・カーソン(Eddie Carson)が父親と言われている。エディはスペイン人の血を引くといわれ、母親は黒人とインディアンの混血である。当時セ

ントルイスは中西部の主要都市として大きく発展しつつあり、音楽ではラグタイム、ダンスではケークウオークが流行する音楽の町でもあった。片や音楽家、他方は素人ながらダンスが上手な上に素人芝居にも出たりする芸能好きな母親。エディが本当の父親だとすれば、まさに両親からダンスから芸能の血をジョセフィンは受け継いだという表現になろう。その少女は幼いころから機会があればボードビル劇場に出入りをし、黒人音楽に親しんでいた。そこにはブルースの女王といわれたベッシー・スミスなどが出ていたのだった。

一九一七年七月イースト・セントルイスで黒人迫害暴動を経験。解放されて新天地を求めた黒人たちが南部から北上し始め、仕事を求め都市に集まり低賃金の労働力を提供することで労働者階級の白人から結果的に仕事を奪い、その憎悪に古くからの人種差別が加わり暴動の引き金を引いたのだった。父親に捨てられた寂しさと貧しさと人種差別の中で、洗濯仕事の手伝いなどをさせながらお決まりの黒人女性の道を辿るよう躾ける母への反発と退屈な毎日にも嫌気が差す。近くの安酒場のウェイトレスになったジョセフィンは、その直後十三歳で最初の結婚。以後公にされたものでも計五回の結婚を経験する。生活苦と舞台への興味から家出同然のように、地元にたまたま来ていた三人のジョーンズ・ファミリー・バンドや歌や踊りの舞台生活が始まる。さらに旅回りのボードビル劇団ディキシー・ステッパー一座に飛び込み、途中のフィラデルフィアでポーターの仕事をしていたベイカー（William Howard Baker）に出会い、一九二一年九月十五歳で二度目の結婚。堅実な生活を一時は夢見たジョセフィンだったが、二人の関係は長くは続かなかった。しかしこの夫の姓だけは生涯使うことになる。そして当時話題の黒人ミュージカル『シャッフル・アロング』のオーディションを再度受けるため一人ニューヨークへと旅立つ。周知のようにこの作品は、一九二七年の『ショー・ボート』、一九四三年の『オクラホマ』と並ぶアメリカミュージカル史の金字塔と言えるひとつである。痩せて色も黒く歳も若すぎ、結局衣装係としてしか採用されなかった

黒人少女が、ある日、一人のコーラスガールの病気で代役として出演したのがきっかけで、一躍スポットライトを浴びることになる。生来のショーマンシップを持つジョセフィンは、子供時代に自分を守るために身につけたといわれるユーモラスな寄り目で観客を惹きつけて離さなかったのだ。続く『チョコレート・ダンディーズ』ではさらに高い評価を得、ついに当時ニューヨークで最も格式の高いといわれた「プランテーション・クラブ」へも出演するようになる。このクラブの当時のスターはエセル・ウォータース。もともとそれほど歌が得意なジョセフィンではなかったが、ウォータースの歌を手本として練習を重ね、その後のスターの道を歩むことになる。

ちょうどこの時期、パリのミュージック・ホールで企画した黒人レビュー(ニグロ)の出演者を探していたキャロリン・ダドリー (Caroline Dudley) は、このニューヨークでジョセフィンを発見する。ジョセフィンにとっても、憧れのパリへの誘いが空からでも降るようにいきなりやって来たことになる。彼女にとって大都市ニューヨークでさえも人種差別の重い空気に満ちていたのだった。この時期のアメリカでの黒人を取り巻く環境は、エッフェル塔と自由の女神を比較した彼女自身の次の言葉にも良く表れている。

「それ（昔見たエッフェル塔の写真）は自由の女神とはとても違って見えたわ。でもそれが何だって言うの。自由のない女神像なんて、肌の色で好きなところにも行けない自由なんて何の役に立つの。そうよ、私はエッフェル塔の方が良いと思ったわ、何の保証もなかったけど。いつかこの目で見てやろうと心に誓ったのよ。」(*Josephine* 42、カッコ内及び訳は筆者、以下同)

238

知 の 新 視 界

こうして一九二五年フランス行きの船に乗る。九月パリで彼女を待っていたのは新進気鋭の絵描き、後にジョセフィン等の黒人レビューのポスターで有名になるポール・コリン(Paul Colin)である。この若い絵描きは十月から始まる「ダンス・ソバージュ」(Dance Sauvage＝野生のダンス)のポスターを劇場から依頼されていたのである。彼の描いたポスターは、当時のパリのアフリカ趣味を十分反映した独特の色と形の組み合わせで、瞬く間にパリの人々の注目を引いた。ジョセフィンも、初めてその黒い身体の美しさを認めて自信を与えてくれたコリンに心を許し、何度もモデルになっている。現在ではその作品を *Josephine Baker and La Revue Nègre: Paul Colin's Lithographs of Le Tumulte Noir in Paris, 1927* に見ることができる。『ラ・レヴュ・ネグル』のポスターのアイデアは、実は当時"local Piccaso"と呼ばれていたメキシコ人画家ミゲル・コバルビアス (Miguel Covarrubias) の作品から来ているという説も出されているが (Baker and Chase 113)、いずれにしてもコリンの残した作品では、黒と赤、白などの原色を鮮明に利用しながら、素朴で単純化されたダイナミックな線で黒人パフォーマーたちの野性的な身体と生命力を強調し、ジョセフィンを始めショーに登場するアフリカ系アメリカ人たちを、見事にいわば「アフリカナイズ」したのであった。

　一九二〇年代のパリはジョセフィンの異国趣味(エキゾティシズム)の舞台をすでに準備していたとも言えよう。エコール・ド・パリと呼ばれる外国人芸術家たちがモンマルトルに集い、古いヨーロッパ芸術の行き詰まりを打破しようとしていたのだ。ピカソはすでに『アヴィニョンの娘たち』で大胆にアフリカの面を利用していたし、むろんマチスやレジェ等によるアフリカ芸術の発見があり、ディアギレフの「バレー・リュッス」やストラビンスキー等の音楽のエキゾティシズムが流行し、ダダからシュールレアリスムへ至る潜在意識下の欲望への関心が高まり、大戦後アメリカから来た黒人兵たちによるジャズやチャールストンの導入、あるい

はヘミングウェイ等国籍離脱者のモダニストとしての作家活動、戦争への失望、嫌悪、その反動としての快楽への逃避。また同時に二〇年代は、世界各国の芸術家、観光客、第一次大戦後の帰還兵らが入り混じり、いわばベルエポックのタブーを帳消しにしようとするお祭り騒ぎ、いわゆるアプレ・ゲールの時代でもあった。そのお祭り騒ぎの中心であったパリのミュージック・ホールの最盛期が一九一九年から一九三五年で、「フォリー・ベルジェール」「カジノ・ド・パリ」「ムーラン・ルージュ」など錚々たる老舗がしのぎを削っていた。莫大な費用、人手、物資等を費やすこの時代のレビューは、一九三〇年代から四〇年代にかけてのアメリカ映画産業に似て、一種の「夢工場」あるいは「娯楽の殿堂」として人々に夢と美と笑いを与える機能も持っていたのだった（Haney 96）。時代が反ヨーロッパ的な原始的で本能的な文化を求めていた。黒人愛好は反体制の香りもしたのだった。

[3]「ダンス・ソバージュ」と黒い身体の衝撃

「黒い美神ェボニービーナス」、「アフリカのエロス」、「黒い真珠」、「琥珀の美女アンバービューティ」と様々な形容をされたジョセフィンのデビューは、まさに伝説的である。一九二五年九月、アメリカの人種差別の息苦しさから一気に解放されるようにパリに向かったジョセフィンは、シャンゼリゼ劇場で「黒人ニグロレビュー」に出演、当時パリで最も才能のある振付師、舞台監督ジャック・シャルル（Jacques Charles）の創った「ダンス・ソバージュ」を踊ることになる。

パリ公演の第一夜、日本の曲芸師などを前座として幕が開く。観客が、呼び物の「黒人ニグロレビュー」の一団に驚いていると、おどけた格好のジョセフィンがいる。まるで何かから開放されたようにチャールスト

ンを踊り始める。それはまさに西洋の型にはまったダンス形式とはまったく異なった自由なダンスであった。そして最後の場面が来る。始めのコミカルな格好から一転、黒く光る滑らかな肌を惜しげもなく露わにしたジョセフィンが、黒人ジョー・アレックス（Joe Alex）を相手に、それまでパリの人々が見たこともないような野性的かつ官能的なダンスを披露する。「ダンス・ソバージュ」と呼ばれるものだ。ヘイニーの臨場感あふれる再現描写はこの時の雰囲気を生々しく伝えてくれる。「観客は息を呑んだ。黒い肉体の見事さに圧倒されたのだ。肌は内側から引き締まり滑らかでランプでも点灯しているかのように輝いている。胸は小さくて丸い、ふたつのリンゴのようだ。尻は堅く引き締まり滑らかで、極端なほど突き出ていた」（Haney 60）。一晩でパリ中が大騒ぎになった。わずかばかりの羽飾りを付けたトップレスの黒人女性のダンスが、新しい美意識を生み出した瞬間であった。できるだけ音を立てず、爪先立ち、絶えず上昇しようとする西洋のダンスとは逆に、ジョセフィンのダンスの特徴は、音とリズムを強調し、重心を下げ、腹や腰、臀部の動きを強調した即興性の強い伝統的アフリカン・ダンスに似ていた。ポール・コリンはこの時の人間離れし且つ官能的なジョセフィンを次のように回顧している。

ぼろきれを纏った彼女の姿は、ボクシングをしているカンガルーか、ゴムでできた女、あるいは女ターザンのようにも見えた。手足をひねり胴体をよじり、四つんばいでステージを横切る、その風変わりな身体運動の中心は躍動する臀部であった。そして、腰の緑の羽飾りの他は何も着けず、頭を真っ黒に固めたベイカーは、反感と熱狂という両極端な反応を引き起こした。小刻みに動く腹部や太腿は何か淫らなものを呼び起こし、まるで魔法で原始時代の生活にでも戻ったかのようだった。（Dalton and Gates 921）

この時の衝撃を一人の女性雑誌記者がジャネット・フラナー(Jannet Flanner)である。「彼女の見事な褐色の身体、フランス人に初めて黒の美しさを証明した新しいモデル」(Flanner xx)この記事は、いわば世界で始めて黒人女性の美しさを英語で紹介した文章かもしれない。

翌二六年、遂にパリ最古のミュージック・ホール、フォリー・ベルジェール劇場で『ラ・フォリ・デュ・ジュール』(La Folie du Jour)に出演する。巨大な卵形の黄金の鳥かごが天井から降りてくると、三本の金のブレスレッドと、ビキニパンツにラインストーンをちりばめた一六本のバナナをミニスカートに見立てただけの裸のジョセフィンがいる。チャールストンを踊りだすと、その身体の激しい動きにあわせてバナナも勢い良く躍動する。その衝撃に観客が言葉を失っている間に、再び黄金の鳥かごと共にゆっくりと天上へ帰ってゆく。十二回のアンコール。又一晩で当時のミンゲットの人気を凌いでしまうほどの興奮を巻き起こした。演出家のポール・デルバル(Paul Derval)は、このショーの前半で、肌もあらわな女性たちをパリのアメリカ人に見立て、徐々に衣服を身に着けていくという演出で、ヌードへの男性客の期待を満たし、同時に裸から衣服という過程で一種の文明的なイメージ "human cultural evolution" (Dalton and Gates 917) を与え、後半のジョセフィンのバナナ・ダンスの野生性と対比させたのである。これは進化vs.退化という構図でもあった。

e.e. カミングズもこのショーの目撃者の一人であった。「人間以下であり人間以上、非原始的であり非文明的な生き物」(Haney 99) だったと、ジョセフィンの衝撃を物語っている。官能的でありグロテスク、動物的であり美的でもある。当時の人々にとってこれほどアンビバレントな表象は他になかったに違いないし、そこに当時の人々が魅了されたのであった。

このバナナ・ダンスでジョセフィンはスターの座を確立したといわれる。フロイトの深層心理学が人口に膾炙し始めた時代、バナナの持つキゾティシズム、植民地主義が、ショー・ビジネスとして見事にジョセフィンのプリミティブなセクシャリティと融合し、家父長的男性社会パリで商品化されたのであった。黒人が、植民地支配と奴隷制度、その延長線上にある擬似優生学による人種差別の対象であった時、それまでの女性の裸体の持つ静謐なイメージを一変させるかのように、これまで聞いたことも見たこともない野性的な音楽とダンスで、褐色の身体の美しさを臆面もなく堂々と披露してしまったのだ。いわば恥知らずな黒人女でもあった。しかし、パリの女たちは「黒い美神」になりたくてオイルを塗り日焼けを始めた。化粧品や水着、カクテル、人形などさまざまなジョセフィン・グッズが出始める。ポール・コランを始め、ピカソやフジタ、マン・レイが競って彼女をモデルにした。大戦により社会進出した女性達が地位の向上を求め、ビクトリア朝的な女性像が瓦解していく時代、髪は短く長身で手足が長く、胸は小さく腰はあくまで若々しく、裸を恐れず自由で活動的、男性に支配されない生き方を求める新しい女性像、すなわちパリの「フラッパー」のシンボルがジョセフィンであった。

しかし、ジョセフィンのパリでのデビューは当時の市民感覚から見て、少なくとも三つの「恥知らず」な要素を含んでいた。黒人、裸、プリミティブ・ダンスだ。特にそのダンスは、気難しい舞踏評論家アンドレ・レビンソン（André Levinson）をも驚嘆させるアフリカの野生とエロスが凝縮されていた。レビンソンによれば、それまでの西洋のダンスの伝統では、たとえばバレーのつま先立ちとジャンプを見ればわかるように、身体の音はできるだけ控えながら、感情が極まると身体を空中に舞い上げるように、音も重さも感じさせないダンスを目指した。逆に、黒人ダンスでは、たとえば足で地面を蹴りながら音とリズムを強調し、ジャズのドラムと同じ原始的なリズムの力強いエネルギーを感じさせる（Levinson 72）。さら

に、身体の各部をそれぞれのリズムに合わせて別々に対応させるのが特徴だが、西洋のダンスではリズムに合わせて身体の統一を重視するという。また、ヨーロッパの伝統では、アフリカン・ダンスの伝統の正面、胸部を見せ、何か高いもの（"above"）を求めるような姿勢になるが、特に女性はできるだけ身体の正面、胸部を見せ、男女とも膝を曲げ尻を突き出しながら地面に近づくような姿勢（"get down"）で踊る（Rose 25-27）。すなわち、西洋では胸で踊り、アフリカでは腰で踊ると言えるのだ。

レビンソンはジョセフィンの動物のような身体の柔軟さとすばやい動き、特にその運動のリズムに感銘し、まるで「ダンスからジャズの音楽が生まれてくるようだ」という。そして『ラ・レヴュ・ネグル』のフィナーレには確かに「野生の輝きとすばらしい獣性」があり、「彫刻家の持つ造型感覚が甦り、アフリカの熱情的エロスが観客を席巻した。彼等の眼前に立っている者はこれまでの単なるグロテスクなダンサーではない、ボードレーヌをも虜にしたあの黒いヴィーナスであった。」（Levinson 74）とボードレールを引き合いに出してまでそのアフリカ性の魅力を賞賛する。

フラナーの短い記事によると、ジョセフィンの『ラ・レヴュ・ネグル』でのダンスは "a stomach dance" だったという（Flanner 3）が、現存する短い映像からも、ジョセフィンのバナナ・ダンスが当時流行のチャールストンとジョセフィン独自の速いビートのベリーダンスを合わせたようなダンスであったことが分かる（Intimate Portrait）。おそらく、当時一九二〇年代ニューヨークの黒人ジャズ・ダンサーの間で流行っていたチャールストンに加え、「シェイク」や「シミー」ダンス、それにバンプやグラインドが混ぜ合わさった、一種のベリーダンスの変形であったと思われる（Rose 21, Baker and Chase 135）。

シェイクやシミーダンスの源流はナイジェリアの Shika に遡るとも言われるが（Jazz Dance 105）、エジプトのベリー・ダンスが国民的な注目を集めたのは、一八九三年のシカゴ万国博覧会でのリトル・エジプ

244

ト(Little Egypt)によるパフォーマンスの"Hootchy-Kootchy"であった。さらに本来女性のダンスであったシェイクダンスを南部生まれの男性たちが、二十世紀初期から一九二〇年代までに"Snake Dance"と呼ばれるグラインド中心のダンスに改良したのだった。このダンスは「リトル・エジプトをしても顔を紅くさせる」(*Jazz Dance* 235)ほどのさらに腰の動きを激しくしたダンスであったというが、仮にこのダンスをジョセフィンがパリでのデビューショー「ダンス・ソバージュ」に取り入れたとしたらどうなるか。むろん演出家はいた。当時パリで最も才能のある演出家といわれたジャック・シャルル(当時はムーラン・ルージュ所属)は、始め予定されていた黒人レビューショーが騒々しいだけで余りにも平凡で退屈なものであったのを、アフリカ色を強調し、あの衝撃的な衣装と「ダンス・ソバージュ」といわれる野性的なダンスを演出したのであった(Rose 5–6)。しかし当時のジョセフィンのダンスは、映像で見るだけでも、演出だけで踊れるタイプのダンスではないのは明らかだ。ポール・コリンやカミングズも驚嘆の声を漏らしたように、まさに人間離れしたある種動物的なもの連想をさせる、と同時に軽快で洗練されたダンスでもあった。手足で踊るチャールストンとは異なり、腰や腹、臀部の動きを強調した、即興性の強いこの「ダンス・ソバージュ」は、当然ながら猥褻にも受け取られたのだった。

[4] ジョセフィンとホッテントットの尻

"Quel cul elle a!"、これこそジョセフィンのステージを見たパリジャン正直な感想であった(Baker and Chase 3)。これについては、ジョセフィン自身のおもしろい言葉が残っている。「お尻は元々付いているのよ。それを恥ずかしいと思うなんて訳が分からないわ。それはあんまり間抜けで見栄っ張りでつまらな

いヤツだから尻に敷かれるくらいしか役に立たないのは確かだけどね。」(Rose 24) ベイカーの臀部へのユーモラスなコメントは、一見恥知らずなアメリカの黒人ダンサーの開き直りに取れるが、ヨーロッパにおける黒人表象の歴史の中ではいささか異なった意味合いを持ってくる。すなわち、当時のヨーロッパにおける黒人（アフリカ系アメリカ人以前のアフリカ黒人）の身体、特に臀部には特別な意味があった。

十九世紀ヨーロッパにおける黒人表象の特徴については、近年ではサンダー・L・ギルマン (Sander L. Gilman) が周知のように「黒い身体・白い身体：十九世紀後期の芸術、医学、文学における女性性の図像学にむけて」において驚くべき内容を報告している。いわゆる「ホッテントットのビーナス」ことSaartjie Baartman またの名を Sarah Bartmann/Saat-Jee が、一八一〇年ロンドンの見世物になり、ヨーロッパ各地で「展示」され、その間わずか五年、二十五歳でパリで亡くなるまでの間に、極端な臀部の大きさや野生性を中心に黒人女性の身体への植民地主義的言説が数多く生産された。さらにその直後身体の隅々の器官まで解剖され、この最も下等とされる人類と最も高等な類人猿であるオラウータンが比較されたりしている。こうして極端に突き出た臀部といわゆる「ホッテントットのエプロン」とが一九世紀ヨーロッパにおけるアフリカ人女性の支配的表象となっていく (Gilman 235)。この原始的な黒人女性の突き出た臀部（脂臀＝steatopygia＝ステアトピギー）は、野性的な性的放縦さをも連想させ、それが当時のヨーロッパの娼婦たちの豊かな腰周りの描写になっていく。いずれの場合も、黒人表象が、退化や原始性、『ナナ』(一八七七) の娼婦たちのイメージに重なり、マネの『オリンピア』(一八六三) における娼婦と黒人女らい病や梅毒などの当時の不治の病、堕落や性的放縦など、当時のヨーロッパ社会においてきわめて否定的な意味を負わされていたことは周知のとおりである。

その後の黒人表象の歴史は、ダーウィニズムの圧倒的な影響の下に、たとえば一八七六年の『犯罪人論』(*Criminal Man*) で有名なイタリアのロンブローゾ (Cesare Lombroso) が、一八九三年に義理の息子ギヨーム・フェレロ (Guillaume Ferrero) と共に書いた *The Prostitute and the Normal Woman* で、パロン゠デュシャテレ (Parent-Duchatelet) の娼婦研究をそのまま受け継ぎ、太った娼婦゠精神施設の女性゠ホッテントットの女性という論を展開し、結論として「売春婦は白人のホッテントット」となったし (Gilman 245)、一八七八年、一八八九年、一九〇〇年などのフランスにおける主要な万国博覧会における人種別展示などに顕著に見られる植民地主義的思考と感覚、あるいは一八九〇年初頭日本に長期滞在したC・H・シュトラット (C. H. Stratz) の身体特徴に基づく人種分類（結局のところシュトラットの研究では、ゲルマン種を頂点とし、白人─支那人（黄色人）─ネグロ（黒人）─ホッテントットという人種のヒエラルキーを確認したにすぎない)、一九一六年のマディソン・グラント (Madison Grant) による『偉大な人種の消滅』(*The Passing of the Great Race*) の「黒」の劣性遺伝説や、ハーバード大学の碩学ロスロップ・ストダード (Lothrop Stoddard) が有色人種の脅威を色分けした世界地図付きで説いた一九二〇年の迷著『有色人種の勃興』(*The Rising Tide of Color*、直後仏訳)、さらにジョセフィンから黒人レビューの一行がパリへ到着した一九二五年には、モリス・ミュレ (Maurice Muret) の *Le Crepuscule des nations blanches* がパリで出版（英訳 *The Twilight of the White Races* は一九二六年、Rose 35) と、この時代はドイツ皇帝ウィルヘルム二世に始まる黄禍論を含め、擬似科学に基づくさまざまな優生学的人種論による人種差別的言説が登場し、それらがアメリカのみでなくヨーロッパでも広く読者を得たことはストダートの著書が英仏両国でもすぐ出ていることからも想像に難くない。[3]

フィッツジェラルドの『グレート・ギャツビー』にストダートがスタートするのは有名だが、ここではむしろこの『有色人種の勃興』に序文を書いたマディソン・グラントの『偉大な人種の消滅』における"darkness"の解釈を当時流布していた人種的言説の一例に取り上げたい。ニューヨーク動物協会の会長であり、またアメリカ自然史博物館の理事でもあったグラントは、ダーウィンとメンデルの理論の中途半端な知識を自分の人種論に応用し、「二十世紀初頭の人種差別主義」の典型的人物となっている (Rose 34)。[4]

グラントによれば人種を特徴づける主な要素として、頭の形（長頭か短頭か）、目の色、髪の色、肌の色、身長、鼻の形、唇の形などがあり、結論として北欧人が最も進化した優れた人種であるとみなす。北欧人の頭蓋骨は長頭型で、髪はほとんどブロンド、目はブルー、グレー、グリーンなどの明るい色である。この色はヨーロッパ人種以外どこにも見られない特徴であるという。黒い (Dark) 目は野生の哺乳類にほぼ例外なく見られる特徴であり、人類に最も近い霊長目の動物に至っては完全に当てはまる。従って、人類の祖先はすべて黒い目をしていたと絶対の確信を持って言えるのである。」(Grant 21-22) となる。すなわち黒い目の色は世界中に見られ、さらに動物にも見られることから、肌は進化の遅れた段階の色であり、北欧人の明るい色こそ最も進化した人種を示す証拠となるというのだ。肌の色に関しては、黒、褐色、赤、黄そしてアイボリー・ホワイトとはっきりと分類できる場合は人種分類に効果的だが、ヨーロッパ人だけを、地中海型、アルプス型、北欧型と三種に分類する場合にはあまり役立たないとしながらも、一般的には北欧人が極めて肌が白く、結果的に"Homo albus" (white man) が他の人種より優れていると結論する。さらに身長は北欧人ほど高く、鼻は、新生児を見ても分かるように、未発達段階では低く横に広がっているとして以下のように結論付ける。「鼻孔が大きく

広がり鼻梁のない鼻は極めて原始的な特徴であり、依然として世界各地のさまざまな人種にかなり見受けられる。それは時にはヨーロッパ起源の人々にも表れるが、どこでも原始的で、平凡で、卑しい特徴である。」(Grant 27) 鼻の低い人間のものであり、鼻の定義に進む。これも北欧人を基準とした同様の論理で、厚く外にめくれ突き出た唇は大昔の迷いもなく次の唇の定義に進む。これも北欧人を基準とした同様の論理で、厚く外にめくれ突欧だけでなくアフリカの黒人も入るのだが、このような場合「必ずしも関係性を示唆する訳ではなく」、単に類似した別々の特徴であると断りを入れる。

グラントの人種分類における"dark"な特徴は、必ず原始的で動物的なイメージでなければならないのであり、人類の原始段階が"dark"であったのであれば、現在の黒人はまさにその原始段階が先祖がえりの法則で甦ったものであると、メンデルの隔世遺伝を応用しながら独自の理論を開陳する。さらに目、髪、肌の色だけでなく鼻や唇の形までもが徹底して黒人と原始性、後進性を結びつける対象とされ、擬似優生学的言説を繰り返すことで、北欧人および白人の優越性を実証しようとしたのであった。

まさに牽強付会のグラントの説は、しかしながら素人科学者ならではの単純化された理論から生まれる小気味良い奇妙な説得力を持っている。一九二〇年代のアメリカで、一時はハーレム・ルネッサンスで花開いたかに見えるアフリカ系アメリカ人の文化も、実はその背景に白人優越主義と黒人蔑視の思想を盛り込んだ擬似自然人類学的書物が広く流通していたことを考え合わせれば、このハーレム文化はむしろ白人による黒人文化の商品化と消費の一過程に過ぎず、本質的な意味でのアフリカ系アメリカ人の理解は、一九六〇年代の公民権運動まで待たなければならなかったといえよう。そしてそのような人種差別の空気を

249

嫌ってジョセフィンを始め多くのアフリカ系アメリカ人が大西洋を渡ったのであった。むろんフランスが手放しの人種的平等の国であった訳ではない。たとえば前述のポスター画家ポール・コリン、ジョセフィンの最大の理解者の一人であるアメリカの彼にしても、描かれるポスターの多くは、真っ赤な厚い唇、大きな口に真っ白な歯、黒い肌、野性的な身体の構図、時には凶暴な目と、まず黒人女性の野性的エロティシズムを強調し、ジョセフィンの黒人男性は、ある意味でアメリカのミンストレルショー同様、戯画化され「他者性」を希薄にすることで、白人男性のセクシャリティと白人男女双方の植民地主義的支配欲を満たしたのである。それはすなわち、黒人の極端な「アフリカナイゼイション」であり、それが一般の人々の集合的無意識あるいは共同幻想を満たし多くの支持を得たと言っても過言ではあるまい。コリンの描くジョセフィンのポスターが、他の黒人女性のセクシャリティのイメージ形成にどの程度影響したかは正確に知る由もないが、一九二〇年代から三〇年代にかけてのジョセフィンのイコンとしての存在の大きさから見れば、ホッテントットのサラ・バートマンを除き、他に比肩すべき強力なイメージを持つ人物がいない限り、その影響力は計り知れまい。

舞踏批評家レビンソンもこの時代の制約を逃れていない。彼は一九二五年の「黒人レビュー」におけるジョセフィン・ベイカーのダンスを見て驚嘆の声を漏らした一人だが、彼のアフリカ文化に対する反応を見ればその人種的偏見は一目瞭然である。レビンソンはこの時代で最も見識のある、同時に最も厳しい批評家であったと言われるが（Archer-Straw 113, Rose 299）、その彼をして、アフリカ系アメリカ人の持ち込んだジャズとそれに伴うジャズダンス（ここでは、主にアフリカ系アメリカ人がアフリカのダンスをもとに生み出した、チャールストンやタップダンスなど腰の動きを中心として踊るダンスで、ジョセフィンのダンスを含むものとする）、彼の評論"The Negro Dance"中の言葉を使えば"Negro music"と"Negro

dancing"とは、ヨーロッパ文明に「(人類以前の)」(pre-human)「黒いウィルス」(black virus)を持ち込む危険があると言わしめた (Levinson 70)。その理論はこうだ。すなわち黒人ダンサーやミュージシャン、ここではジャズやチャールストンなどをフランスへ伝えたアフリカ系アメリカ人のダンスや音楽は、前にも述べたように、西洋の、上昇と静寂を旨とするダンスと異なり、腰を屈め地面を踏み鳴らし強いリズムをとることが基本となる。タップダンスもこの一例である。このリズムは人間の原始的本能にはきわめて強烈な効果を及ぼし、始めは単調なリズムの繰り返しも次第に麻薬的な効果をもたらし、徐々に速度を上げ気分を高揚し最終的には恍惚状態へと導くものだという。これは明らかに後年バタイユが「死へ至る生の高揚」と定義したエロティシズム論と共通した考え方であり、ジョセフィンのダンスの特徴とそれを問題視した理由をも明らかにしてくれるものであろう。レビンソンはなぜリズムがそれだけでは芸術になり得ないかを説く。何よりリズムを重視するジャズの例でも明らかなように、確かにリズムのビートは音楽のメロディーやハーモニーには欠かせないし、ダンサーにとっても基本となるものだが、それがまったく束縛のない状態で一人歩きし、ある芸術様式を支配してしまうと、必ず原始的で下等な ("rudimentary and inferior") ものになる。リズムとは、原初的自然の力であるがゆえに、美的な実体になる前に手を加え再吸収されるべきものであるという (Levinson 72-73)。リズムに堕することで人間的にも堕すると考えたレビンソンの、音楽や舞踏に対する成熟し且つ洗練された美意識が基本にはあるといえようが、同時に、一九二七年に書かれたこのエッセイの深層には、先に述べた「退化」や「劣性」「犯罪」「堕落」を有色人種、特に黒人と結び付ける植民地主義的人種差別の言説に基づく「黒への恐怖」が見え隠れしている。レビンソンは最後には黒人ダンサーを認めるのだが、それはあくまでも当時のヨーロッパ人への皮肉と警告を込めた黒人(ニグロ)文化の認識でしかなかった。

251

12 ― アフリカン・アメリカン・エクゾティシズム

今日の黒人(ニグロ)ダンサーはもはや悪魔に取り付かれた連中ではなく、単にプロのダンサーたちである。今本当に悪魔に支配されているのはヨーロッパのごくつぶしどもだ。原始回帰的かつ背徳的魔力を手放しで受け入れ、黒人(ニグロ)ダンスという快楽に無抵抗に身をゆだねている。この論考では道徳の問題は無関係だが、ひとつだけ興味深い事実は述べておきたい。きわめて皮肉なことに、白人の黒人愛好家たちが自ら原始へと退化している間に、当の黒人(ニグロ)たち自身は文字通り進化していると思われることだ。(Levinson 75)

ポール・コリンを始めさまざまな「野生のダンス」の目撃者が、ベイカーの特に腰部の動きに衝撃を受けたという証言は偶然ではないだろう。ホッテントットの尻を連想させた黒人女性の身体イメージを、まさにその腰部の運動の官能性で百八十度転換させた褐色の身体の登場が、当時のグラントやレビンソンらと同類の因習的美意識を持つ人々にとっていかに衝撃的であったかを物語る証左である。

結び

ジョセフィン・ベーカーの一九二〇年代パリでのデビューとその後の活躍は、その類いまれなダンスの才能とアフリカ系・アメリカ人としての身体表象で、いわゆる黒人(ニグロ)文化を主体的にパリに花咲かせたかのような印象を与えがちだ。あるいは、ヨーロッパの白人男性社会に一矢報いた感がある。しかしこういった言説や商業イメージの再生産をそのまま受け取ることはできない。社会史的視点から見れば実情はむし

252

その正反対であったとみなした方がより正確なジョセフィン像、あるいは黒人表象史になるだろう。すなわち、一九二〇年パリに流れ込んだアフリカ系アメリカ人の多くは、人種差別の著しいアメリカを逃れ、表面的には差別のない、あるいは植民地の「他者」との付き合いに慣れているパリで、主に歌や音楽、ダンサーという芸能の世界に出口を求めた。そして当時のパリのアバンギャルドやそれに追随する人々は、それまでのアフリカ文化の延長線上にアメリカ系アメリカ人からやって来た「アフリカ人」たちを位置づけ、いわゆる「異国趣味（エキゾティシズム）」を享受した。むろん黒人（ネグロ）（文化）愛好家は多く存在した。しかし異国趣味（エキゾティシズム）はあくまでも当事者の蜃気楼にすぎないのであれば、パリのあるいは当時のヨーロッパの人々は、変形誇張された虚構のアフリカ黒人像を創り出し、アフリカ系アメリカ人の上に重ね合わせ楽しんでいたと言わなければならない。その典型がジョセフィン・ベイカーであった。実はジョセフィンを始め多くのパリの黒人たちは、肌を脱色し、髪をストレートにし、話し方も着こなしも白人の生活様式を真似ようとしていたのである。たとえばジョセフィン自身も、自分の肌を少しでも白く撮ってくれるマリ・コーマン（Murray Korman）のような写真家を好んで使ったのだった。それゆえ実際のジョセフィンは、現在残されている写真や映像より確実に幾らかは色が黒かったはずである。このような模倣と自己否定による生存方法は、「長い間の奴隷制度の経験から生まれた重要な生きる術」（Archer-Straw 97）であった。つまり、「他者」性をできる限り消し、白人の恐怖心を希薄にすることで自己保存を図ったと見ることができるのである。

パリでの成功の後一九二八年から世界巡業に出たジョセフィンは、一〇年ぶりに母国アメリカに帰り一九三六年にニューヨークで『ジーグフェルド・フォリー』（Ziegfeld Follies）に参加するが不評、『タイム』が"Negro wench"という蔑称を使って酷評したのはこの公演である（Baker and Chase 204）。その翌年フランス市民権を獲得、人種的な偏見の中で前述の政治的活動を経て、一九七五年パリでレビュー「ジ

12 ─ アフリカン・アメリカン・エキゾティシズム

「ヨセフィーヌ」公演中倒れる。晩年のヨセフィーヌは、借金を抱え仕事もなく、孤児たちの夢の国「虹の一族」の住処レ・ミランド(Les Milandes)城も追われ暗い影を投げかけたが、一度ステージに立てば別人のように往年の魅力が甦ったという。カーネギー・ホールでの公演が実現しアメリカが名実共にジョセフィンを認めたのは、その死のわずか二年前、一九七三年であった。その年の六月、"Black Legend"としてカーネギー・ホールに登場したジョセフィンを、アメリカの観客たちは心から惜しまない拍手で迎えたのであった。むろん往時の歌声ではなかったが、『ラ・レヴュ・ネグル』時代のパリを甦らせるには十分のステージであった。黒人の存在などほとんど認められていない時代に、"Isn't is beautiful to be kissed by the sun in that way?" (Schroeder 116)とパリジャンに言わせたジョセフィンの魅力と役割は、アフリカ系アメリカ人の歴史だけでなく、世界のさまざまな人々に看過できない影響を与えたと言えよう。貧困と人種差別と戦いながら、ショー・ビジネスの世界で頂点を極め、大戦を経て公民権運動、破産、幾度かの結婚と奔放に自分の生き方を貫きながら激動の二十世紀に歴史的人物が、カーネギー・ホールでのショーの最後で、自分の人種差別との闘いに触れ、"I did take the blows, but I took them with my chin up, indignity, because I so profoundly love and respect humanity." (Schroeder, 116)と観客に語った時、誰一人としてその「ヒューマニティ」の意味の脆弱さなど問題にしなかったに違いない。社会史的に見れば、一九二〇年代のジョセフィンの活躍は、彼女が演出家の指示の下、白人男性の思い描くアフリカン・ファンタジーを見せていたとも解釈できる。しかし「琥珀の美女(アンバービューティ)」「黒い美神(エボニービーナス)」としてパリのミュージックホールに君臨した、少なくとも二五年から三〇年代にかけての彼女のスターとしての磁力とそこから発するパワーは、今ではとても想像できないほど強力なものであったはずだ。時代と人種的制約の中で、アフリカン・アメリカン・セクシャリティという表象を最大限に利用しながら、野

放図に且つ強かに舞い踊り、結果的に世界中の人々に"black is beautiful"といういわば美の脱構築的認識を流布させた功績は、ある意味政治的無意識的解釈を超越するものであったと言えよう。レビンソンのジレンマに陥ったようなジョセフィン評に明らかなように彼女の魅力はきわめてアンビバレントであった。野性的で動物的、同時に力強く官能的でもあった。原始的で下品であると同時にきわめて新しく洗練されてもいた。グロテスクであると同時に美しくもあった。黒を嫌悪し恐れながら同時に黒の魅力に深く引かれていくアフリカ系アメリカ人女性のミュージック・ホールのスターとしての表象は、一方で黒人の美しさを世界に認知させながらも、他方ではフランス、さらにはヨーロッパのアフリカン・ファンタジーを再生産し、それはアフリカの「土人」が都会の淑女になったという物語でフランスの植民地主義の成功をも意味するのだが、黒人女性の性的社会的ステレオタイプを固定し流通させてしまったとも付け加えなければならない。ジョセフィンは歴史的にもきわめてアンビバレントな存在である。

［注］

1　FBIの資料No.六二‐九五八三四‐七における人種差別と第二次世界大戦時の日系人の扱いについてのジョセフィンの発言。ジョセフィンの人種差別撤廃に対するさまざまな言動がFBIに注目される火種になった。「真珠湾の後、日本人は強制収容所へ入るか、さもなければアメリカを出るかしなければならなかった。店や事務所は没収された。狼狽の余りただ同然で売り払う者もいた。一生かけて築いた努力と労働の結晶をだ。みんな二、三時間の間に跡形もなくなった。中には、自分たちの店や家具を黒人の仲間にやってしまう日本人もいた。白人よりも黒人がする方がいいと思ったからだ。」(Regester 69、訳は筆者)

2　以下はジョセフィンのパリでのデビューを目撃したジャネット・フラナーが後年その記憶を再現したものである。

"She made her entry entirely nude except for a pink flamingo feather between her limbs ; she was being carried upside down and doing the split on the shoulder of a black giant. Midstage he paused, and with his long fingers holding her basket-wise around the waist, swung her in a slow cartwheel to the stage floor, where she stood, like his magnificent discarded burden, in an instant of complete silence. She was an unforgettable female ebony statue. A scream of salutation spread through the theater. Whatever happened next was unimportant. The two specific elements had been established and were unforgettable—her magnificent dark body, a new model that to the French proved for the first time that black was beautiful, and the acute response of the white masculine public in the capital of hedonism of all Europe—Paris. Within a half hour of the final curtain on opening night, the news and meaning of her arrival had spread by the grapevine up to the cafes on the Champs-Élysées, where the witnesses of her triumph sat over their drinks excitedly repeating their report of what they had just seen—themselves unsatiated in the retelling, the listeners hungry for further fantastic truths (Flanner xx-xxi)."

3　実は、H. W. Debrunner の一九八六年のセミナーでの報告"Blacks in the Mediterranean before 1700"によると、日本人もポルトガルのイエズス会宣教師 Francisco Cabral（一五七〇—八一日本滞在）にとって黒人だったという。"After all, they are Niggers, and their customs are barbarous" (Pieterse 212).

4　一八六九年に設立されたこの自然史博物館は、当時のアメリカ人の「人種」に対する概念を知る上でも興味深い内容の展示をしている。一階がアメリカの動植物および鉱物などに並び、エスキモーや北西部インディアンの展示、二階が世界の鳥類やアフリカの哺乳類に並び、南アメリカの人類、アフリカの人類、そしてアジアの人類と分類され、ここには中国、韓国、日本人などの模型が展示してある。三階には爬虫類、両生類、鳥類、哺乳類、霊長類と並び、ポリネシア地域の人々と東部インディアンが展示され、四階は主に恐竜に関する展示となる。アングロ・サクソンを中心とした太平洋地域の人々やヨーロッパ人やヨーロッパ系アメリカ人として分類された部屋はなく、「人間の生物学と進化」という人類一般に「普遍化」された扱いとなっている。アメリカ自然史博物館では現在でもエスキモーやアイヌの人々と並び中国、日本、韓国人などが博物学的展示の対象となっているのは、やはり注目に値する事実であろう。

[引証文献]
Allen, Frederick Lewis. *Only Yesterday: An Informational History of the Nineteen Twenties*. New York: Harper &

Archer-Straw, Petrine. *Negrophilia: Avant-Garde Paris and Black Culture in the 1920s*. New York: Thames & Hudson Inc., 2000.

Baker, Jean-Claude and Chris Chase. *Josephine: The Hungry Heart*. 1993. New York: Cooper Square Press, 2001.

Baker, Josephine and Jo Bouillon. *Josephine*. Trans. Mariana Fitzpatrick. New York: Marlowe & Company, 1988.

Colin, Paul. *Josephine Baker and La Revue Nègre*. New York: H.N. Abrams, 1998.

Dalton, Karen C. C. and Henry Louis Gates, Jr. "Josephine Baker and Paul Colin: African American Dance Seen through Parisian Eyes." *Critical Inquiry* 24.4 (1998): 903-934.

Flanner, Janet. *Paris Was Yesterday: 1925-1939*. Ed. Irving Drutman. New York: The Viking Press, 1972.

Grant, Madison. *The Passing of the Great Race or the Racial Basis of European History*. New York: Charles Scribner's Sons, 1916.

Gilman, Sander L. "Black Bodies, White Bodies: Toward an Iconography if Female Sexuality in Late Nineteenth-Century Art, Medicine, and Literature." "Race," Writing, and Difference. Ed. Henry Louis Gates, Jr. Chicago: U of Chicago P, 1985.

Haney, Lynn. *Naked at the Feast: A Bibliography of Josephine Baker*. London: Robinson Books, 1986.

Intimate Portrait: Josephine Baker. Videocassette. Lifetime Productions Inc. 1998.

Levinson, André. *André Levinson on Dance: Writings from Paris in the Twenties*. Ed. Joan Acocella and Lynn Garafola. Hanover: Wesleyan UP, 1991.

Pieterse, Jan Nederveen. *White on Black: Images of African and Blacks in Western Popular Culture*. New Haven: Yale UP, 1992.

Regester, Charlene. "The Construction of an Image and the Deconstruction of a Star—Josephine Baker Racialized, Sexualized, and Politicized in the African-American Press, the Mainstream Press, and FBI Files." *Popular Music and Society* 24.1 (2000): 31-84.

Rose, Phyllis. *Jazz Cleopatra: Josephine Baker in Her Time*. New York: Vintage Books, 1989.

Schroeder, Alan. *Josephine Baker. Black Americans of Achievement*. Philadelphia: Chelsea House Publishers, 1991.

Stewart, Jeffrey. "Online News Hour Forum: Harlem Renaissance." 20 Feb. 1998. 12 Dec 2001 〈http://www.pbs.

Brothers Publishers, 1931.（F・L・アレン『オンリー・イェスタディ―一九二〇年代・アメリカ』藤久ミネ訳、筑摩書房、一九八六年）

org / newshour / forum / february98 / harlem1.html〉

Stearns, Marshall and Jean Sterns. *Jazz Dance*. 1968. Da Capo Press: New York, 1994.

Whechel, Harriet, ed. *Josephine Baker and La Revue Negre: Paul Colin's Lithographs of Le Tumulte Noir in Paris, 1927*. New York: Harry N. Abrams, Inc., 1998.

13 アメリカ社会におけるジャポニズム小説
オノト・ワタンナを中心に

羽田美也子

はじめに

　十九世紀後半から二十世紀初頭にかけてのジャポニズムの広がりのなかで、あまたのジャポニズム小説が欧米各国で生み出された。その多くは自らの滞日経験をもとにした創作であり、最も有名なものはピエール・ロティの『お菊さん』であろう。この作品に顕著なように、概してヨーロッパのジャポニズム小説には濃厚なコロニアリズムとオリエンタリズムが密接に絡み合いながら内在している。一方アメリカのジャポニズム小説は、少々趣を異にしている。親日的で日本紹介的な意味合いが強いのである。アメリカにおける女性作家の伝統が、ヨーロッパのジャポニズム小説にみられるような男性的な視点を和らげている

のが、その大きな要因であろうと思われる。メアリー・フェノロサ（Mary Fenollosa, 1865-1954）やフランセス・リトル（Frances Little, 1863-1941）、エドワード・ハウス（Edward Howard House, 1836-1901）、ウィリアム・グリフィス（William Elliot Griffis, 1843-1928）などは、滞日経験もあり、美しい日本を伝えたい、誤った日本人像を訂正したい、という「日本に対する愛着」が作品の底流をなしているかの感さえある。

ところが本稿で扱うオノト・ワタンナ（Onoto Watanna, 1875-1954）は、そんなアメリカのジャポニズム作家のなかにあって特殊な作家である。彼女は滞日経験もなく、日本ものを書くということに使命感といったものも感じられない。それでは、ワタンナという作家の創作意欲を支えたものは何だったのであろうか。ここには、アメリカにおける大衆文化の確立と、市場資本主義経済の拡大が大いに係わっている。出版されたワタンナの作品は生涯に十七冊にものぼり、若い時に雑誌、新聞などに発表した作品の数は更に数えきれないほど多い。しかもその作品のほとんどが、日本を舞台にしたものである。代表作である『日本の鶯』A Japanese Nightingale（一九〇一）は、二〇〇版二十万部以上を売り尽くし、フランス、ドイツ、スウェーデン、イタリアの各語に訳されると共にアメリカ、イギリス、フランスで劇化されている。その後に続く作品も好調な売れ行きを示し、当時の売れっ子作家の一人であった。人気を得ながら、ワタンナという作家はその後十分に研究されてこなかった。本稿では、オノト・ワタンナという一人の女性作家の内面に光をあて、その軌跡を追うことによって、彼女にとって日本は何を意味したのか、結果的に彼女の作品はアメリカ社会においてどういう意義をもっていたのかを考察してみたい。

[1] ジャポニズム作家としての出発

オノト・ワタンナの文筆活動への動機はまさにこの時代の女性作家の典型である。父親の投機の失敗で財産の大部分を失い、ニューヨークからモントリオールに引っ込んだ子だくさんの家族が暮らしていけるかを考えるのが子どもたちの義務でもあった。どうすれば収入を得始めたのをみて、自分にもできるとワタンナは考えた。この動機は、姉のエディスが中国ものを書いて収入を得始めたのをみて、自分にもできるとワタンナは考えた。この動機は、多くの一九世紀女性作家に共通したものである。経済的な動機から書きはじめた作家は、どのような本が売れるかに敏感である。彼女は、大衆の心をつかむべく家庭小説の定石に則って作品をつくりあげた。つまり、突然の不幸が女性を襲い、苦境に陥れられる。彼女は困難に立ち向かい、紆余曲折の末についには乗り越えて幸せを手に入れるというものである。しかし、第一世代の家庭小説作家たちが信仰の力なくしては乗り越えられなかったことを、ワタンナたち第二世代の作家たちは自己の力だけで乗り越えていく。もはや宗教の力は自分の道を切り開いていく上では頼りにならず、頼りとするのは自分自身というセルフ・メイド・マンの発想が浸透している。

オノト・ワタンナが作家活動を始める背景に、姉のエディスの存在があったことは明らかであるが、最初から日本ものを扱おうと思っていたわけではないことは、最初に発表した作品が、日本とは何の関係もない題材を扱っていることでもわかる。[7] だが、たまたま日本がブームになっていた時でもあり、幼い頃から日本の様子を両親から何かにつけて聞いていたこともあって、[8] 日本を舞台にした「古い人力車」"Old Jinrickshaw"（一八九五）を書いてみたのであろう。この作品の力量が認められて、ジャマイカで新聞記

者の職を得ることができたが、当地での暑さに閉口したこともさることながら、こんなことで自分の人生を終わらせたくないという野心が彼女を駆り立てた。弁護士として成功した姉を頼って後に移ったシカゴでは、昼間は速記者としての仕事をしながら、夜は専ら執筆に時間をあてている。日本に関する資料ならば何でも読み漁り、ありとあらゆる新聞、雑誌に投稿したといっても過言ではないほど、精力的に行動している。自らの才能を信ずる者のみがとり得る行動であろう。この間には創作上様々な試行錯誤をしており、ペンネームも題材に応じて使い分けていたようで、その全てを把握することは難しい。しかし、オノト・ワタンナというペンネームを一挙に有名にし、彼女のその後の人生を決定づける画期的な作品、『日本のヌメさん』 *Miss Nume of Japan* （一八九九）がこの頃生まれている。この作品によって彼女はその後の作品の方向性を獲得したといえる。

　十九世紀中葉、多くの女性作家が台頭してきた頃には、決められた社会の枠組のなかでのみ女性たちも書いており、女性たち自身もその枠からはみ出すつもりもなかった。おのずとテーマも家庭の中の事柄と宗教に限定されていたが、ワタンナの時代になると、女性が自分の力で働き、自分の経験を生かし、社会において自己実現していくことが可能になっていた。テーマも多様になり、社会性をおびていった代わりに、宗教性は薄れていった。ワタンナが自己実現を求めて創作活動を行ったとき、日本というタイムリーなテーマに出会い、それが大衆の要求を満たしたと同時に彼女自身の野望をも満足させたのである。

　売れる本を書くということは、経済的な動機から書きはじめた作家にとっては特に重要な点であり、ワタンナは常に大衆の好みというものを意識していた。後にハリウッド映画のプロデューサーの眼で創作にあたって、れた経歴からもわかるように、彼女は常に観客（読者）を意識するプロデューサーの眼で創作にあたっていたと言える。事実、彼女の作品の売れ行きは良好で、出版社は彼女に対して非常に好意的な条件で契約

を結んでいた。前渡し金として一万五千ドル、売り上げの五十％を出版社と折半という条件である。本の装丁も豪華で、表紙に金箔を使い、至る所に日本の事物が挿絵として描かれている。透かし絵を各ページに施したものもある。作家としての地位が高まるにつれ、文壇からも好意的に迎えられるようになり、エディス・ウォートンやマーガレット・ディランド、ジーン・ウェブスター、アニタ・ルース、マーク・トウェイン、ルー・ウォレスなどニューヨークの脚本家や俳優たちとも親交を結んだ。『日本の鶯』の大成功以来、一九一二年まで毎年一作出版していたワタンナであるが、直接の日本体験のない彼女であるからその作品も知識として仕入れた情報を駆使するわけで、勢いステレオタイプなものになり易い。徐々に日本ものを書くことに苦痛を覚え始めた彼女は、一九一一年に『デリアの日記』 The Diary of Delia: Being a Veracious Chronicle of the Kitchen with Some Sidelights on the Parlour を発表した。この作品はメイドとして働くアイリッシュ系アメリカ人女性の日記として書かれたもので、この作品によって新機軸を展開させたかったワタンナは、ウィニフレッド・ムーニー（Winnifred Mooney）というペンネームでサタデー・イブニング・ポスト紙に持ち込んだ。すぐに受け入れてもらえたが、掲載された時には作者名はオノト・ワタンナに変更されていた。

作品の路線に行き詰まりを感じていたこの頃のワタンナは、私生活においても夫との間がぎくしゃくしてきていた。原因は夫のアルコール中毒である。悩んだ末、彼女は一九一二年頃に別居にふみきる。この一作のペースは破られている。だがまた、この期間に自分のことを見直すこともでき、一九一五年には、ジャマイカ時代とシカゴ時代の一年間を振り返って描いた自叙伝的作品、『思い出の記』 Me, a Book of Remembrance を出版した。彼女の親友ジーン・ウェブスター（『足ながおじさん』の作者であり、マー

ク・トウェインの姪）が序文を書き、ニューヨークでは「誰が『思い出の記』の作者？」（"Who is the author of ME?"）「あなたはもう『思い出の記』を買いましたか？」（"Have you bought your copy of ME?"）という宣伝が至る所でみられた。ニューヨーク・タイムズは作者のヒントを匂わせる文章を掲載したり、センセーショナルな方法で売り出した結果、大変な話題を呼び起こした。翌一九一六年には『マリアン』*Marian : A Story of an Artist's Model by Herself and the Author of Me* を出すが、この作品は彼女の姉サラの画家として自立するまでの葛藤を描いたものである。

[2] 作家としての苦悩

一九一七年には、タグボート会社の支配人をしていたフランシス・リーブ（Francis F. Reeve）と再婚するが、この年末息子を事故で失うという不幸な体験をし、以後六年間筆をとれなくなる。彼女の精神休養も考えて、一家はカナダのアルバータ州カルガリー市から北西に四〇マイルほど離れたモーレーに移り、牧場経営をする。この地でのワタンナは、牧場経営者の妻としてまた母として、朝から晩まで全ての雑事を精力的にこなしていた。ニューヨーク時代とはまるで違う生活のなかで、過去の華やかさを思い出すのは、昔の作家仲間あるいは脚本家や俳優といった人たちが、夏になるとバンフに行く途中に立ち寄る時であった。そのような生活のなかで、精神的にも肉体的にも健康を取り戻したワタンナではあったが、次第に牧場での生活に息苦しさを覚え、フラストレーションを感じるようになっていく。後に、当時を振り返って回想した草稿のなかで彼女は、

The approach of winter, and the departure of the children for school brought me each year to a state of despairing melancholy. My duties were so many on the ranch ; there was always so much doing and so many distractions that even if I had wanted to I could not have found the time to write.[11]

（冬が近づき子供たちが学校へ戻る時がくると毎年どうしようもない憂鬱が私をおそった。牧場には私のやるべき仕事が山ほどあり、いつでもやらなければならないことや、気が散ることが沢山あるので、たとえ私が望んでも書く時間をみつけることは不可能だった。）

と述べている。バージニア・ウルフが「女性が小説を書こうと思えば、お金と専用の部屋が必要」[12]と宣言した時より十年も前に、彼女は創作のための時間と空間を求めてストライキに入った。即ち、カルガリーに家を持ち、翌年の冬はここに籠もって小説を再び書きはじめたのである。

as if I had turned on a mental faucet. ... I had so much to write—so much to tell the words ran over each other—they jostled for room and space.[13]

（まるで精神の蛇口をひねったかのように…私には書くべきことが沢山あった。言わなくてはいけないことが山ほどあった。言葉がほとばしりでてきて、納まるべき場所をみつけようとひしめきあっていた。）

この時、彼女は五週間で一気に『サニーさん』Sunny-San（一九二二）を書き上げている。もうだいぶ以前から日本ものを書くことに抵抗を覚えていたワタンナではあったが、永いブランクの後に書く作品については友人のアーサー・ストリンジャーに相談したところ、再び文壇に返り咲くことができるまでは日本ものでいくべきだとのアドバイスを受け、それに従ったのである。この作品がかなり好意的に受け入れられたこともあって、彼女は次の作品で新機軸を展開する。今までの作風とはがらっと変わった作品『牛』Cattle（一九二四）を発表するのである。

I made up my mind that I would not go back to Japanese stories. I would start all over again with a new pseudonym and a new type of writing. I would write of the great ranching country—the "last of the big lands" where I had sojourned now for so long. I had a passionate desire to send out into the world a living picture of Alberta. My former work had been chiefly noted for its delicate and even poetic quality… But I was not going to write with a delicate pen now!

（私はもう二度と日本ものには戻らないと決心した。新しいペンネームで新しいタイプの小説で、すっかり一から出直すのだ。広大な牧場の国について書こう。──私が長い間とどまっている「広大な土地の逞しさ」について書こう。私はアルバータの生きた姿を世の中に送り出すことに情熱的な願望をもっていた。私のこれまでの作品は、主に繊細で詩的でさえあるという評判を得てきた…だが、これからはもう弱々しいものは書かない！）

こうして出来上がった『牛』は、今までの美しいおとぎの国のロマンスといった作風とはすっぱり縁をきっていた。登場人物は、牧場経営者と彼に強姦され妊娠してしまう逞しい中年のイギリス人女性…。カナダの雄大な自然をふんだんに取り混ぜ、地方主義作家へとワタンナは転身を図った。しかも自然主義作家が扱うようなモチーフも織りまぜていた。

［3］オノト・ワタンナにとっての日本

一体オノト・ワタンナという作家にとって、日本とは何だったのであろうか。彼女が日本を舞台として小説を書いていた全盛時代、日本は一八九四年の日清戦争、一九〇四年の日露戦争に勝利を収め、列強の仲間入りをしようとしていた。一九〇四年には、プッチーニの歌劇『蝶々夫人』の成功もあり、同じ東洋の国ではあっても、中国に比べて日本はかなり話題性に富む国であった。中国をとりあげた小説を書いていた姉のエディスに優越感を感じていたこともあった。だが、姉のエディス没後、彼女は終始中国人として行動した姉と、日本人としての仮面をかぶった自分に思いを馳せる。

What then I ardently believed to be the divine sparks of genius, I now perceived to be nothing but a mediocre talent that could never carry me far. My success was founded upon a cheap and popular device, and that jumble of sentimental moonshine that they called my play seemed to me the pathetic stamp of my inefficiency. Oh, I had sold my birthright for a mess of potage [sic].[16]

（あれほど情熱的に天才の神聖なるひらめきだと信じてきたものが、私をちっとも成長させることもない取るに足りない二流の才能以外の何物でもなかったということが、今わかった。私の成功などというものは、安っぽい通俗的な趣向の何かの上に打ちたてられたもので、感傷的な月光の寄せ集めと人が私の芝居を呼ぶのが、哀れなほどの無能の印と私には思えてきた。おお！私は一碗の糞のために私の生得権を売り渡してきたのだ。）

I thought of other sisters…the eldest, a girl with more real talent than I—who had been a pitiful invalid all her days. She is dead now, that dear big sister of mine, and a monument marks her grave in commemoration of work she did for my mother's country.

It seemed our heritage had been all struggle. None of us had yet attained what the world calls success….

It seemed a great pity that I was not, after all, to be the savior of my family, and that my dreams of the fame and fortune that not alone should lift me up, but all my people, were built upon a substance as shifting as sand and as shadowy as mist.

（私は他の姉のことを考えてみた。——長姉は、私なんかよりもずっと本物の才能をもっていたが、可哀相なことに生涯ずっと病身であった。その敬愛する姉も今ではもう亡くなってしまったが、彼女が母の国である中国に対してなしてきた働きを記念して、お墓に記念碑が建てられている。

私たちが祖先から継承してきたものは、ずっと奮闘を続けてきた。家族の誰もが、世間が成功と呼ぶものにまだ到達していない。私が結局のところ家族の救済者たりえなかったのはとても残念である。名声や富という私の夢は、それだけでは私自身も同胞の人たちも向上させることはできないのだが、その夢も砂のように漂い、霧のように実態のないものの上に建てられたものだった。)

　エディスは中国人である母が、英国で教育を受け、西洋の身繕いをしていても、幼い自分が混血ということで好奇心、哀れみ、嫌悪のない混ざった感情にいつも囲まれていた体験をまざまざと回想している。一方ワタンナは、混血であることの苦しさ、哀しさを活字にしたことは一度もない。それどころか、彼女の描く作品のなかではいつも混血の登場人物が、美しく魅力的で最後には幸せを摑んでいる。混血であることの現実を直視して、その哀しさを作品に描いた姉のエディスと、それに完璧に背を向けて美しい虚構の世界をつくり上げたワタンナは、実は表裏一体である。姉の死後、モントリオールとボストンの中国人協会によって、記念碑が建てられたことに彼女は羨望の思いを抱いたのではないだろうか。それと共に、姉の成しえたことに対して、自分の歩んできた道が薄っぺらな欺瞞にしか思えなくなったのだろうか。自分の出生を偽り、一時は日本人として作品を売り出したこともあった。六年のブランクの後で書き上げた作品には、また文壇にもどるための方便で、仕方なく再び日本ものを選んだ。けれども、復帰第二作は、まるで違ったペンネーム、まるで違った作風で新しく出直したいという強い意気込みがみられる。彼女は生まれ変わって出直したかったのである。日本という仮面から逃げ出したかったのである。エディスにとっての中国は切ろうと思っても切り離せない国であっ

18

19

たが、ワタンナにとっての日本は切ろうと思えば切り離せる国だった。あくまで彼女は、観客の反応を常に意識するシナリオライターだった。今日のハリウッド映画が、観客の反応を事前にチェックし、その結果如何では結末さえも変更してしまうように、彼女は読者に何が受けるかを敏感に感じとった作家であった。大衆が望むものを書き上げた作家であった。そういう意味では芸術家というよりは、ビジネスウーマンである。それゆえに、日米開戦時のインタビューに、「私は今まで日本人について書いてきたことを恥じています。彼らを憎んでさえいます。」と答えている。彼女に滞日経験もあり、日本は若き日の自己欺瞞と結びついた、苦々しい思い出でしかないのだろうか。ラフカディオ・ハーンのように日本ものを書く上で本人の心理をもう少し掘り下げることができたなら、彼女の日本に対する思いが、ある意味で表面的で上すべりなものであったがために、マス・メディアと組んで大衆の望むものを書くという姿勢に徹することができたのだろう。そして、その野心が大きければ大きいほど揺り返しも大きかったのである。ワタンナは自分自身の内面の葛藤に苦しめられることになる。

ところが、それにもかかわらず、彼女の作品によって、多くのアメリカの女性が日本についてイメージをふくらませ、日本女性の暮らしぶりを知り、彼女たちの愛と結婚について考えさせられたという事実は否めない。遠いオリエントの小国における恋愛ではあっても、アメリカの女性たちはそこに自分たち自身を投影し、恋愛のバリエーションとして疑似恋愛を積んだのである。アメリカ女性たちがそこに生きる上での指針を教会に求めなくなってからは、指針を与えてくれていたのは小説であった。「自分の人生は自分でつくり上げるもの」というセルフ・メイド・マンの教えは、若い女性の間にも徹底していた。お互いの信頼に基づいた上での結婚という理想をあくまで追求するため、彼女たちは熱心に小説を読み、そこから人生

を学びとる訓練をしていたのである。オノト・ワタンナの小説によって、多くの女性たちは空想のなかで人生経験を積み、世界を広げることができたのである。

[4] アメリカ社会におけるジャポニズム小説の意義

アメリカにおいては、南北戦争後、二〇～三〇年間の高尚な文学体制が、帝国主義的社会機構として機能し、一般大衆にまでエリートの文明の価値観を共有するよう強要してきたという事実があるが、一方ではこれに対抗する大衆文化が育ってきていたのも事実である。雑誌を例とするならば、一八八〇年代中頃には『ハーパー』や『センチュリー』のような高級雑誌の発行部数が十万部から二十万部であった時、一八八〇年代後期から一八九〇年代初期にかけて誕生した新しい種類の大衆向け雑誌――『レィディーズ・ホーム・ジャーナル』、『マンシーズ』、『マクルーアーズ』、『コスモポリタン』――はこの三～四倍の発行部数を獲得していた。高級雑誌に比べて廉価であったこれらの雑誌は、広告によって財源を確保することで発行部数を伸ばしていったのである。また、発行部数を競うために、各雑誌社ともに売れる作家と契約を結ぶことにしのぎをけずり、文学が相対的価値観のなかにおかれた。つまり、マス・メディアと著述家との結びつきが新しい文学体制を生み出し、のみならず、より広汎な意味において文学の可能性のある世界を生み出していったのである。

ジャポニズム小説が生み出されたのは、まさにこのような時代であった。ジャポニズムの流行を捉えて日本を舞台にした小説を書き、商業ベースにのせるということは、マス・メディアと結びつくことを意味し、それはすなわち名前を売ることであったし、社会における自己実現であった。この時代、大衆文学は

万人に対して知的な満足を与えるものとして機能していた。ニーナ・ベイムはその著『女性の文学』のなかで、「(一八二〇-一八七〇の) 女性作家たちは、ものを書くことを天職というよりは職業、芸術ではなく仕事と捉えていた。一八七〇年代かそれ以降になるまで、彼女たちは自分たちを芸術家や、芸術の言語で自己の正当化を図るなどということはなかった」と論証している。第一世代の家庭小説作家たちは、自分は芸術家の仲間ではないと意図的にしかも誇らしげに表明したが、ワタンナたち第二世代の作家たちは、もう控えめな態度で「自分たちは芸術家ではない」とは言わない。堂々と胸をはって、「自分たちは働くことによって自己達成を図っているのだ。それを人が芸術家と呼ぼうと呼ぶまいと」と声高らかに宣言する。

女性に限って考察してみれば、二十世紀初めの四十年間には都会の人口のかなりの部分を女性が占めていた。一八八〇年には女性就労者のわずか四％が事務職であり、それ以外の女性は農業に従事していたものが、一八九〇年までには事務職に携わる女性の比率は二十％以上になっていた。三十年後には、簿記や会計係の約五〇％は女性が占め、タイピストや速記者といった職種では九十％以上を占めるようになっていた。23 だが、男女の賃金格差はまだ大きく、女性の大半は依然として賃金を稼いでくる夫に依存している状態であった。シャーロット・パーキンス・ギルマンが『女性と経済』のなかでみじくも述べているように、「女性が手に入れたい全てのものはたったひとつの小さな金の指輪からやってくる」24 のである。そしてこの状況は、その後何十年もの間アメリカ社会において続いたのである。女性の一生を左右していたものが結婚であった以上、多くの女性の関心はロマンス小説に注がれる。

遠い異国日本での恋愛を、ワタンナは様々なバリエーションで描き、多くの読者を獲得した。彼女はその作品のなかで、日本人あるいは英米人かユーレシアン（日欧混血）の男女を主人公とし、甘ったるい夢物語ではあったが、紆余曲折を交えてロマンスを描いた。しかし、登場人物の多くは本質的にはアメリカ

人男女と出会った時自己信頼（セルフ・リライアンス）の力によって乗り越え、自分の道を自分で切り開いていく、実に積極的なアメリカ人像であった。それがために、読者は登場人物にたやすく感情移入することができ、彼らとの一体感を味わい、作中で新しいロマンスの可能性を探ることができた。読者は、「不思議の国ニッポン」の風俗や習慣、景色や生活様式、大和魂などについて、知識として得ることができると同時に、エキゾチックな香りのするロマンスに心踊らせ、恋愛を疑似体験することによって、想像のなかで体験の幅を広げることができたのである。

ワタンナの作品も含めて、ジャポニズム小説は、アメリカ社会に日本という異質な文化を伝えることで、新しい発見や、未知の世界に入っていく経験を提供した。と同時に、異質な文化を知りえたことによって比較の視点が生まれ、アメリカ人に自国の文化について外側から眺めるという機会をも与えることになった。更に言えば、当時のアメリカ社会に対する警鐘としての意味合いも帯びていた。世紀の転換期、アメリカではセンセーショナルでけばけばしい物語が巷にあふれていた。ダイム・ノヴェルに描かれた西部は、血なまぐさい暴力に彩られ、喧嘩や殺し合い、そしてスリリングな冒険のオンパレードであった。舞台の上では常に、殺人、強盗、強姦といったきわどい出来事が扱われ、世紀末的様相を呈していた。このような社会に対して、ジャポニズム作家たちが描いてみせた日本社会は、センセーショナルでアメリカ社会で暴力的な出来事とは無縁の、静かに時が流れる、素朴で精神性豊かな社会であった。日本社会とアメリカ社会を対比させることで、アメリカ社会の問題点を浮かび上がらせ、彼ら自身の愛国心に今一度語りかけることになったのだ。一七八二年に、「アメリカ人とは一体何者なのか？」という問いを投げかけたのは、ヘクター・セイント・ジョン・ド・クレヴクールであった。この問いは、その後も事あるごとに問いかけ続けられたが、

おわりに

以上述べたように、ジャポニズム小説の出現も「日本人とは何者か」という問いに対する合わせ鏡として、「アメリカ人とは何者か」という問いをアメリカ社会に投げかけるきっかけとなったのである。

以上述べたように、ジャポニズム小説のアメリカ社会における意義としては、アメリカ社会における文化的多様性の幅を広げたということと、当時のアメリカ社会の不安定な状況に対する警鐘としての役割との二点をあげることができる。ところが、二十世紀に入るとモダニズムの出現によって過去の価値観が否定されるようになった。全ての作家が葛藤し、失望を味わうことになったが、ジャポニズム作家にとってはそれに加えて、アメリカ社会におけるジャポニズムの衰退という打撃が伴った。いった原因としては、日本が日清、日露の両戦争において勝利を収めて後、満州での勢力を拡大、韓国を併合、第一次世界対戦に参戦し、山東半島やドイツ領南洋諸島を占領するなどの侵略行為が続いたため、アメリカ社会において日本に対する嫌悪感とでもいうものが芽生えたことが考えられる。これは更に、日本の軍事力に対する警戒心や恐怖心となって根づいていった。常に大衆の嗜好を読み取りながら出版される大衆文学の宿命として、ジャポニズム小説は急速に人気を失っていった。

更に、ワタンナのような女性作家にとっては、一九二〇年代を境に別の大きな問題もあった。女性の理想像の急激な変化である。フラッパーと呼ばれる「近代」の女性たちは、フロイトを読み、性的抑圧からの解放を求めて闘い、ショート・ヘアにショート・スカート、密造酒を飲み、誰とでもキスをした。女性の一生を結婚が左右する社会でありながら、恋愛、結婚、母性という伝統的な女性性に若い女性が関心を

示さなくなったのであった。彼女たちにとって、ロマンティシズムに彩られた遠い異国の恋愛などは、もう時代遅れなのであった。

こうしてみると、アメリカ社会においてジャポニズム小説が栄えた期間は、一八八〇年代から一九二〇年代頃までと云うことができる。それは日本に対するイメージのなかに戦争に纏わる警戒心や恐怖感、威圧的ともいえるような感情が、微かに萌芽としては認められるが、まだはっきりと表面には出ていなかった頃の産物である。ジャポニズム小説が誕生する以前のアメリカにおける日本イメージは、'flowering king-dom'としての楽園、ゲイシャやサムライ、それにミカドが住む異国情緒あふれたおとぎの国であった。ジャポニズム作家たちは、その漠然とした日本イメージに具体性をもたせ、そこに住む日本人の生活をあたかも眼前にあるかのようにアメリカ社会に紹介した。彼らの大半は、日本独特の事物、言葉、風俗、習慣などを、愛情と時には郷愁さえこめて描きだしたのである。その創作動機がどうであれ、また例えば日本に対する愛情が具体的な息吹をふきかけ、オノト・ワタンナという一人の作家が、ミカドが住む異国情緒あふれたおとぎの国に具体的な息吹をふきかけ、オノト・ワタンナという新しいロマンスを探る可能性をアメリカの大衆に次々と提供し、大いにもてはやされたということは疑いのない事実である。そしてこの事実の裏には、一九世紀後半に生まれた文学とマス・メディアとの結びつきが抜きがたく介在している。オノト・ワタンナの成功は、このことを裏付ける一つの例証となるであろう。

[注]

1 本論文では扱う題材がアメリカに限定されることから、「ジャポニズム」ではなく、「ジャポニズム」という言葉を用いることとする。また、外国人作家によって書かれ、日本を舞台とし、日本人を主要登場人物に扱った

2 小説を「ジャポニズム小説」と定義して使うこととする。

3 本名をウィニフレッド・バブコック・リーブ（Winnifred Eaton Babcock Reeve）という。カナダ生まれでアメリカで活躍した作家。一八七九年生まれと称していた時期もあるが、早熟な天才を装いたかったか、あるいは再婚した夫より年上と思われるのを嫌がったためであろう。

4 ハウエルズ（D. H. Howells）は、『ノース・アメリカン・レヴュー』紙のなかで、『日本の鶯』を"a quite indescribable freshness like no other art in the simplicity which is native to the best art everywhere."（最高の芸術にのみ備わっている純粋さ以外には比べるべくもないほどの、筆舌に尽くしがたい清々しさ）と絶賛している。"A Psychological Counter-Current in Recent Fiction" 173, North American Review 881, 1901.

5 オノト・ワタンナに関しては、カナダ、アルバータ州において郷土の作家という視点からの紹介、およびフェミニズムの視点からの言及が見受けられる。また代表作『日本の鶯』の作品紹介が児玉実英著『アメリカのジャポニズム』（中公新書、一九九五年）のなかでなされている。最も親切な作品紹介および作品紹介したものとして、安藤義郎氏の論文を挙げることができる。（日本大学経済学集志第四十巻別冊、四十二巻別号別冊）。なお最近、ワタンナの孫によって『オノト・ワタンナ伝』が出版された（Diana Birchall, Onoto Watanna—The Story of Winnifred Eaton—. Urbana & Chicago: U of Illinois P, 2001）。

6 Edith Maude Eaton (1865-1914)、ペンネームをSui Sin Farといい、代表作はMrs. Spring Fragrance (1912).

7 十九世紀中葉に俄に出現してきたスーザン・ウォーナーやマリア・カミンズなどの家庭小説作家たちを、十九世紀後半に活躍したオノト・ワタンナたちと区別して、第一世代の家庭小説作家と呼ぶこととする。

8 最初の作品A Poor Devilは、ウィニー・イートンというペンネームで書かれており、内容も十四歳のイギリス系カナダ少年の成功物語というホレイシオ・アルジャーのディック少年物語のようなものであった。

9 父親は英国のかなりの家柄の出身で、イートン家は絹を扱う貿易会社を経営し、一時は日本と中国における「最も富裕な英国人」であった。母親は中国人であるが、英国人宣教師夫妻の養子となって英国で教育を受けた。両親は共に訪日経験があり、日本や中国の様子を子供たちに語って聞かせたようである。

10 Doris Rooney, "Souvenir from the Past" 46.

11 Rooney, "Souvenir from the Past" 46.

12 Winnifred Eaton Reeve Papers (Calgary, Alberta: University of Calgary Special Collections, 1982).

13 Virginia Woolf, A Room of One's Own (Harmondsworth: Penguin Books Ltd, 1928) 6. Winnifred Eaton Reeve, "You Can't Run Away From Yourself" [manuscript] n.d., Winnifred Eaton Reeve

14 Papers.
15 Linda Popp Di Biase, "The Alberta Years of Winnifred Eaton" 3.
16 Reeve, "You Can't Run Away from Yourself."
17 Onoto Watanna, *Me, a Book of Remembrance* (New York: The Century Co., 1915) 153-154.
18 Watanna, *Me, a Book of Remembrance*, 194.
19 Di Biase, "The Alberta Years of Winnifred Eaton" 2.
20 Di Biase, "The Alberta Years of Winnifred Eaton" 8. オノト・ワタンナの作品が売れだした頃、彼女は本名を Kitishima Kata Hasche という日本人であると名乗っていた。
21 Naomi Lang, "Alberta Women Who Make News Include Noted Novelist, Scenalist," 6 September 1941, Calgary Public Library.
22 Emory Elliot, ed., *Columbia Literary History of the United States* (New York: Columbia UP, 1988) 475-476.
23 Nina Baym, *Woman's Fiction: A Guide to Novels by and about Women in America, 1820-1870* (Ithaca: Cornell UP, 1978) 32.
24 Elliot, *Columbia Literary History of the United States*, 724.
Charlotte Perkins Gilman, *Women and Economics* (Berkeley: U of California P, 1998) 71.

14 『ドラ・ソーン』と日本の家庭小説

松井洋子

[1] まえがき

人間の道徳的な成長が富より重要である事を主題にした Louisa May Alcott の『若草物語』(Little Women)(一八六八-九)と、奴隷制を問題とし、人間の平等を訴えている Harriet Beecher Stowe の『アンクルトムの小屋』(Uncle Tom's Cabin)(一八五二)は一世紀以上に渡って、これらの作品を生み出したアメリカばかりではなく日本においても広く親しまれている家庭小説である。

本稿で取り上げる『ドラ・ソーン』(Dora Thorne)(一八八三)も当時は多くの読者を獲得した。しかし現在では、他の多くの十九世紀女流作家が書いた家庭小説と同様、忘れ去られ、文学史にもその作品も、

作者バーサ・クレイ（Bertha Clay）の名も見ることはない。

しかし、『ドラ・ソーン』は明治中期には翻訳小説『谷間の姫百合』として、また明治後期には翻案小説『乳姉妹』として日本の読者の前に登場する。本稿では『ドラ・ソーン』の明治期における受容について考察し、日本の家庭小説への影響についても述べたいと思う。

［2］『ドラ・ソーン』と『谷間の姫百合』

『ドラ・ソーン』の舞台は英国の上流社会にあり、英国貴族や貴婦人が多く登場する。しかし、Lord Earl の恋愛相手となるのは、タイトルの Dora というその貴族の屋敷の使用人の娘であった。周囲の反対を押し切って二人はイタリアへ逃げ結ばれるが、二人の価値観の違いは年を重ねるごとに大きくなり、Lord Earl は二人の間に生まれた二人の娘達を残し、英国に戻ってしまう。Dora は二人の娘達がレディになる年代になるまで、田舎町で二人を育てたが、やがて Lord Earl に引きとられ、その後二人の娘達の数奇な運命が語られていく。ベアトリス（一人の娘の名）の死後、Lord Earl と Dora は再会し、再び心を通わせる事になる。作品の後半部分は、『乳姉妹』の筋とともに次の3。『ドラ・ソーン』と『乳姉妹』で詳しく述べる事にしたい。

末松謙澄の『谷間の姫百合』は、前述したあらすじを持つ『ドラ・ソーン』の翻訳小説として、明治二十一年から二十四年にわたって、金港堂から出版された。その後、青木崇山堂が版権を得て大正期に再発行した。この青木崇山堂版の巻頭に侍従の藤波言忠が皇后（のちの照憲皇太后）に金港堂出版の『谷間の姫百合』を献上し、皇后から「面白いので後がみたい」と催促があったと書かれた手紙が紹介されている。

皇后はこの作品を勧善懲悪の書として高く評価されたと思われる。

皇后は、明治期の西欧化を積極的に支持した。明治八年に東京に出来た女子師範学校の開校式に近代日本史上はじめて行啓する。またその折、皇后の眼には舶来の品々が珍しく映り、皇后はその感動を和歌にしたためた。写真や蒸気機関車を見た時の感動や、西洋服で盛装した様子も、和歌に残されている。

また日頃、女子教育に関心をもっていた皇后は華族女学校の節目の行事には必ず出席され授業参観も積極的に行われた。当時は小説を読む事が道徳的に罪悪視され、女学校においては絶対禁止であった。そのような状況の中で皇后がこの作品を読まれた事は、大変意味を持つと考える。

明治期前半の翻訳は、今日でいう翻訳とは遠い翻案的な要素が濃い。当時は西洋とは風俗習慣が違い過ぎていたため、日本人の理解に応ずるように内容表現に手をくわえ、表現に日本的色彩を盛りこんだからである。

謙澄は『ドラ・ソーン』を翻訳するにあたり注意した点は次の通りであると説明している。

本中の地名人名は多くは原語の音に近くするか、またはその一部分の音に当るものを入れて和名にしたことである。但し重要な地名や歴史的に有名な人名は原名を用いている。草木の名称も同様に和名にし、日本において珍しい草木については、西洋人がその草木について語る時の感覚と同様の感覚を表わす和名の草木に置きかえた。

文章は普通の言葉を用い、漢語を省き読んでも聞いても理解出来る通俗文にした。緑と瑠璃との間には原文と同じくその言葉使いに姉妹の差を置かずに表現した。「ラーブ」(love)に翻訳にあたっては、「好く」と「好いて居る」と二つの訳語を用いている。

本文、注は訳者が風俗習慣の違いの説明に使われている。その中で婚姻に関する説明が多くみられる。二人の姉妹が同日同時に秘かに結婚式をあげる計画を立てている場面は次の様な註をつけている。

西洋にては婚姻の儀式は新婦の家にて引受るを通例とす又姉妹凡そ同時に婚姻の約成るときは同日同時に其式を行ふことも多しこれを二對婚姻と傳ふ

夫婦の蜜月（ハネムーン）については「西洋にて新婚の當座を蜜月と言ふ」と説明している。祝いの朝餉については「西洋にては婚姻の式は大概朝の間に之を行ひ引続き手軽き食事あり之を婚姻の朝食と言ふ」と説明し、また結婚の際に「飾りなしの金の指輪を嵌めて上げるから夫れまでは之を嵌めておいでなさい。」という本文の注として、「飾りなしの指輪は結婚の證據として婦人の嵌めるものなり」と記している。

以上のように、女性の読者が多いということもあって、女性の最大の関心事である結婚に関する習慣の違いを説明した事は、この作品への読者の関心を高める上で、非常に重要な役割を果たしたのではないかと思われる。

また明治十六年には、条約改正を悲願とする外国人接待所として「鹿鳴館」が開館し、ほとんど毎夜のようにきらびやかに着飾った紳士淑女達を集め晩餐会や舞踏会が開かれた。特に明治二十一年は「鹿鳴館時代」がピークを迎えた時期であった事もあり、夜会や舞踏会の場面に訳者が説明を加えている。「シャペロン」は淑女達が夜会または舞踏会に出る時連れ立って世話をする年嵩の婦人であると註をつけている。また「自邸にて夜会を催す時には家に引受けの婦人なくして夜会を開く事は西洋人の忌むことに

て斯る家には近親の人杯を補助の名義を假るを例とす」と夜会開催についての常識が記されている。また貴族階級の社交の場でもあった歌劇の観賞については「西洋にて歌劇の期節中は富豪の大家は桟敷を常に買って置き折々之へを知音の人杯に假すこともある。」と説明している。貴族の屋敷内には養花室（はなざしき）があり、「西洋にては座敷續に室中に花卉など植付舞踏などの時には其處に椅子を置き涼を取る便にすることあり。」と註をつけ、西洋の室内の様子も説明している。社交界についてのこうした注は、西洋の女性の置かれた環境を知る上で有益であった。当時鹿鳴館に通っていた女性読者がこのことに注目していた事もこの翻訳作品が好評を博した一因ではなかったのだろうか。

宝石に関して言えば、ある夜会にてdiamonds（金剛石）、feiry rubiie、pretty pale pearl（紅寶石）、purple amethysts（紫寶石）は華やかな性格のベアトリス（緑）が身につけ、pretty pale pearl（唯眞珠）やbright emeralds（玉）は愛らしい性格のリリアン（流璃）が身につけるという場面があり、女性が宝石を身につける習慣が描写されている事も女性読者には興味深いところであったろう。

当時楽器に関しては漢字では表記されていたが、洋琴がピアノと、立琴がハープとルビがふられていた。以上をみるとこの翻訳作品を通して謙澄が西洋文化を積極的に受け入れようとしている態度がみられる。宗教上の行事に関しての謙澄の説明はクリスマスに関してのみである。「十二月二十五日の耶蘇鬼角すする日なり」と記しており、当時はまだキリストを耶蘇としていた事がわかる。

また、「Heaven（天国）」は極楽浄土、「Angel（天使）」は天女、「Bible（聖書）」は経文、「Chapel（礼拝堂）」は本堂、「Church（教会）」は寺、「Minister（牧師）」を和尚と訳している。じっとしている様子を「まるで石仏の様だ」と訳をつけている。

このように明治初期の翻訳作品の特徴といえるだろう。
ろも明治初期のキリスト教の用語が深く日本の風土に根ざした仏教の用語に換えられて用いられているとこ
外国文化を積極的に受けいれようとした時代にあって、一気に近代文学への関心を高めつつあった時に
も拘らず女性読者の多くのは、西洋の風俗習慣の訳者の解説を参考にしながらこの翻訳作品を楽しみ、貴
族階級の人々の恋愛に自分を投影していたのであろう。

[3]『ドラ・ソーン』と『乳姉妹』

次に翻案小説『乳姉妹』について考察したい。
『乳姉妹』は明治三十六年八月から約四ヵ月間、大阪毎日新聞に連載され、特に女性の読者に大変支持さ
れた。この作品は『己が罪』と並ぶ菊池幽芳の代表的な家庭小説となり、明治三十七年に単行本として、
前後編が春陽堂から出版された。その序文として

　今の一般の小説よりは通俗に、気取らない、そして趣味のある、上品なものを載せてみたい。
　誰にも解り易く、また顔を赤らめ合うというような事もなく、家庭の和楽に資し、趣味を助長し
　得るようなものを作りたい。[2]

と述べている。
また、この作品を創作するにあたり、「外国の小説の中にベルサ・クレー（バーサ・クレー）の短かい

小説で面白い筋があり、講談に代用するようなものを書くには、こんな趣向を土台として、少し複雑なものを書けばきっと成功するだろうと考えてこの小説を書いた」という小説執筆の経緯が序文に書かれている。ただし幽芳はバーサ・クレイのどの作品を翻案しているのかを明らかにしてはいない。しかし、当時翻訳作品としても有名であった『ドラ・ソーン』の後半の双子の姉妹の筋立が類似していることで、春陽堂版の後編に収められている批評集の中に幽芳の語った「バーサ・クレーの小説」とは『ドラ・ソーン』（翻訳本名『谷間の姫百合』）である事が指摘されている。

ここで『乳姉妹』の内容を考察してみよう。姉妹として育てられた好江と房江には本人達も知り得ない秘密があった。房江の実の母は好江の母が昔乳母をしていた裕福な家庭の娘であった。ある日、生まれたばかりの房江を連れて、房江の実の母は好江の母を訪問し、台湾の病院に入院している夫（房江の父）の看病に行っている間、房江を預かってほしいとたのんだ。好江の母はそれを快く受け入れ、房江の母は安心して房江を置いて旅立った。しかし、台湾に向う途中、船は台風にあい沈没し、房江を残して亡くなってしまう。

好江と房江は、実の双子の姉妹として育てられた。華かな美しさを持つ好江、心静かな温かさを持つ房江、性格は異なるが、ともに立派に成人する。

時が過ぎ、死の床にある好江の母は、その秘密を房江に伝える様にと好江に話した。富や高貴な身分を、いずれ自分の美貌と、結婚によって獲得しようと考えていた好江は、この秘密を利用して、自分が、房江になりすます事を考える。房江の実家の侯爵家の娘として、好江は幸福な日々を過ごす。やがて房江も引きとられ、二人は、社交界の花となる。侯爵家の後取りとして入った昭信は房江の妖艶な美しさと、房江の清純な愛らしさに、魅かれているが、結局好江と結婚することに決めた。その二人の婚礼も間近になっ

た時、好江が侯爵家の娘になりすまし以前に婚約し、アメリカに行って行方のわからなくなっていた高濱が突然現れ、好江に結婚を迫った。高濱は、自分と結婚をしなければ、好江の秘密を公表すると脅迫する。あくまでも自分の現在の地位と昭信への愛を捨てられないと主張した好江は婚礼の日、高濱に殺され秘密もあばかれてしまった。しかし昭信と房江の思慮深い、寛容な取り計らいで好江は侯爵家の娘として葬られたのである。

この筋立は『ドラ・ソーン』の後半の部分から受容されたと考えられる。ドラの二人の双子の娘達、ベアトリスとリリーが父の実家（父、アールはドラの先夫）に引きとられ、社交界に出て、それぞれ恋愛をする。ベアトリスは侯爵と結婚することになったが、彼女には、父の実家に引きとられる以前、ドラの田舎町の実家で暮らしていた頃、婚約者がいた。彼は外国へ行き行方不明になっていたのだった。彼女と侯爵との結婚を目前にして、以前の婚約者ヒューが彼女の前に突然現れて彼女に結婚を迫るのであった。ベアトリスはヒューとの結婚の意志がない事を伝えるが、それに激昂したヒューは、ベアトリスと湖水近くでもみ合い、ベアトリスは湖水に落ち溺死する。

この二作品の筋立はきわめて類似しており、そのことによって『乳姉妹』は、『ドラ・ソーン』を受容した作品であることが明らかになった。

文学辞典には、バーサ・クレーは十九世紀の女流作家で、主として家庭小説を書いていると数行紹介されているに過ぎない。彼女の作品は、当時の家庭小説の性格を表わしており、感傷的で、教訓的である。そして他の家庭小説と同様に、彼女の作品も人々にとって「教会」としての役割を果たしているという事に注目したい。それは数々の人間ドラマの後に物語の最後に作られる神の国の具現としての「家庭」を提示しているのである。

アメリカ社会にあって、ピューリタニズムの支配が弱くなるとそのあまりに厳しい教育に対する批判も強くなり、キリスト教は、愛と自由と救済の信仰へと変身をとげた。農業社会から工業社会への脱皮により、女性は家庭にという状況の中で、自己充足の手段がフロンティアが消滅し、また社会もフロンティアが消滅し、自己充足の手段を求めた。そこで書き手と読み手の女性が現われ、ピューリタニズムの教訓的な次元を越えたドラマを「家庭」に認識するようになったのである。

『ドラ・ソーン』においても「教会としての家庭が、ベアトリスの死後のストーリーの中で展開される。ベアトリスの死は確かに、彼女の犯した過去の罪への戒めではあるが、彼女の死は、離婚したベアトリスの両親ドラとアールの復縁につながり、姉の死に心を痛めたリリアンが、自分の持つ誠実な性格ゆえに、再び立ち上り、女性の権利を求めて幸福になる事を願い、結婚を決意する。この作品の最後の章はベアトリスに関わった人々の幸福と彼らの子孫達の明るい表情が描かれている。正に登場人物は皆、神に祝福され、神の国にいるような様相を呈しており、この作品は、ハッピーエンディングとなっている。

さて、筋立や二姉妹のそれぞれの人物造型においては、『乳姉妹』は『ドラ・ソーン』と類似している点が見受けられる。しかし『乳姉妹』のほうは、君江の悲劇的な死を教訓に残して終わっており、この結末の部分が『ドラ・ソーン』と異なっていると言えよう。昭信と房江との結婚は暗示されているが、作者は、

その間の経路については、更にまた一編の物語をなすべき事が沢山ありますけれども、私はここに蛇足を添へる事を避けて、まづはこのお話の終局を告ぐる事といたします。[3]

と、『乳姉妹』を結んで、『ドラ・ソーン』に表わされたハッピーエンディングを拒否している。この作品の発表は、「家庭」を視点にしているのではなく、「女性」に視点が向けられている事が、序文にも明らかである。

　房江の方は日本の女子といふ立場から見ても最も高潔な観念と、最も深厚の同情を有して居る、一個の理想の女として仕舞ひましたので、私は今日の日本の社会が要求する最も切実な婦人、理性と情熱とを併せ有し、天然と人事に対する趣味を持ち、そして淑女としてのたしなみに欠くる所のない、まづこれならば、完璧であろうと思はれる女性にこしらえあげたのでございます。

　明治初期には良家の子女達はキリスト教、特にプロテスタント系のミッション・スクールに通うものが多く外国人による外国の教育を受けていたが、明治中期あたりから、文明開化に溺れることなく、良い面を摂取しながら伝統的な日本の女性を創り上げようとする理想のもとに良妻賢母の女子教育が盛んに行われるようになった。実際にそのような教育を受けた女性の読者がこの作品に登場する房江を自分の理想像としたり、自分を投影出来る人物と考えて、彼女の人気を高めた事も確かであろう。また君江からは女性のプライドや富や高貴な身分へのあこがれや、愛情ある結婚などを読みとり、新しい価値観を持つ君江にも読者が理解を示している点が次の作者の序文からうかがえる。

　ただ私の気づかいましたのは、房江に引かへて一方の君江の方は、あまりに大胆であまりに非凡ですから、或は女天一といふような悪口を受ける事かとも思われたに拘はらず、今までもって

そんな批難も聞きませんのは、私のひそかに喜ぶ所でございます。

君江は新しい価値観をもってはいるが、女性の権利を主張する現在のフェミニズム運動に関わる女性とはかなりのへだたりがあるようだ。『金色夜叉』の宮と君江の価値観の同一性を論ずる批評家もいたが、女性の読者は、宮への反応とは違い君江に対しては寛容な態度をとっている。

『乳姉妹』は、新しい女性像と理想の女性像を『ドラ・ソーン』から受容し、恋愛物語から一歩進んでスペンス風の物語に仕立てたところにその特徴がある。女性読者が関心を示したのもこの点であった。また、二人の男性と婚約し、房江の身分を我が物としたという二重の罪の重さは、房江の寛容な姉に対する思いに最後の場面で消されてしまい、読者達が、一つの教訓物語であるという認識をしていない事もうかがえる。筋立の面白さと通俗的なサスペンス性が、この作品の成功につながったといえよう。

[4] あとがき

文学辞典には、日本の家庭小説は、単に道徳的で通俗的な要素を持った作品と定義されている。アメリカの家庭小説のように、信仰心や宗教に根ざした発達をしたかどうかはさだかではない。家庭が教会となってこの地の天国になり、人間が成長する場であるという認識は、当時の日本の家庭にあったとは思われない。また、日本には男女が平等な立場で家庭を支えるという観念はなく、男性と女性は別々の位置を家庭内で与えられていたと思われる。

『ドラ・ソーン』は明治二十年代においては翻訳小説として全編紹介され、訳者の風俗習慣の違いの解説

が加わって完全なかたちで日本の読者に伝えられた。女性を中心とした読者は、社会の西欧化の波と共にそこに描かれた上流社会に興味を持ち、『谷間の姫百合』の人気を支えた。

一方明治三十年代になると『ドラ・ソーン』は翻案され、家庭小説として再登場した。筋立ての面白さと、二人のヒロインの運命の対比に読者の関心が移り、通俗小説としての評価は得たが、西洋の「家庭小説」の核となる「家庭」の重要性を作品の中に訴える事は出来なかったのである。

[注]
1 『谷間の姫百合』（金港堂、一八八九年）
2 『乳姉妹』（春陽堂、一九〇三年）二頁。
3 『乳姉妹』（春陽堂、一九〇四年）二六一頁。
4 『乳姉妹』（春陽堂、一九〇三年）三頁（序文）。
5 『乳姉妹』（春陽堂、一九〇三年）三-四頁（序文）。

[引証文献]
Clay, Bertha. *Dora Thorne*. Hurst & Company, 1883.
菊池幽芳『乳姉妹』春陽堂、一九〇四年。
末松謙澄『谷間の姫百合』金港堂、一八八六年-一八八九年。

[参考文献]
ベーコン、アリス（久野明子訳）『華族女学校教師の見た明治日本の内側』中央公論社、一九九四年。
芳賀登『日本生活文化史序論』つくばね舎、一九九四年。
久野明子『鹿鳴館の貴婦人 大山捨松』中央公論社、一九八八年。
中島建蔵他『比較文学—目的と意義』清水弘文堂、一九七一年。
小河織衣『女子教育事始』丸善ブックス、一九九五年。

佐藤宏子　『アメリカの家庭小説』　研究社出版、一九八八年。
渡邊洋　『比較文学研究入門』　世界思想社、一九九七年。

ブラントとゲルトナーの旅行日記の比較

A・H・バウマン

[1] はじめに

　マックス・アウグスト・スツィーピオ・フォン・ブラントは、一八三五年十月八日ベルリンに生まれた。プロシアのハインリヒ・フォン・ブラント将軍を父に持つことから、身分相応の教育を受けた。ベルリンにあるフランス系ギムナジウム（九年制の中・高等学校）に通った彼は、子供時代にすでにある程度のマルチカルチャー的教育を受け、少なくとも二か国語を習得した。やがて父に習い、軍務の分野でのキャリアをめざした。しかし彼はあまり乗馬を好まず、日本の英語雑誌「パンチ」に「帽子をかぶったストローク」というニックネームまで付けられた。そこから推察するに、彼はやせっぽちで軍事に

おいて必要な肉体的活動性に欠けていたと考えられる。いずれにせよ、彼は数年後、特別任務を待つ間に外交における定職につき、オイレンブルク伯爵の東アジア遠征（一八六〇―一八六二）に参加した。オイレンブルク伯爵は、彼をその知力と勤勉さで高く評価した。彼は、その遠征からの帰国の年である一八六二年五月八日に、二十六歳の若さですでに駐日領事に任命された。その後彼は、プロシア代理公使という外交上は最下位である階級にたどりつくまでに五年ほどかかったが、その職についた翌年、総領事へと昇進し、一八七一年には弁理公使にまでなった。

ブラントは一八六二年十二月二十八日に神奈川に到着した。二回の帰国を除き、日本には一八七五年の春まで滞在した。日本滞在に引き続いて彼は、一八九三年四月一日に清国駐在公使を引退するまで活躍し、一九二〇年三月、引退先のワイマールで亡くなった。

彼の旅行の同伴者であるライツェハルト・ゲルトナーに関する資料は、残念ながら極めて乏しい。おそらくベルリンの北に位置するプレンツラウ地方で、来日以前に農業に携わっており、一八六六年十一月一日に横浜に到着した。彼の弟のC・ゲルトナーはすでにこの時函館に滞在し、副領事という地位にあり、プロシアの代理だけでなく商人としてクニフラー・カンパニーの擁護にあたっていた。R・ゲルトナーは彼の日記の中に弟の言葉を引用し、「弟は、（私が日本で）農業には従事できないであろうが、自分の商社か他の商売で役に立ち、故郷にいる時以上に稼げるであろうと確信していた。」と記している。それゆえR・ゲルトナーが金儲けを狙って弟の呼びかけに応じ、函館へ赴いたことは充分考えられる。

上記の略歴から明白であるように、両者は全く正反対の人物といえる。ブラントは貴族の家系で、軍事や外交上の経歴を持ち、プロシア政府の委託を受け日本に渡り、自信を持って行動し、命令する立場にある自分の社会的地位を自覚していた。一方ゲルトナーは、農民階級もしくは農民階級と接触のあった人物

で、ドイツでは出世や収入を増やす可能性がほとんどなかったが、それを国外に出てまでも求める程の自発性を持っていた。つまり、彼は金儲け狙いの冒険者であった。

本論は、社会的背景の全く異なる二人のプロシア人による一八七六年夏の北海道旅行日記を紹介する。彼らのそれぞれの社会的身分、階級意識、財政上の資力の差、政治面に対する配慮、旅行の個人的動機を考慮に入れ、両者の日記を比較する。

[2] 日記の出版

・ブラントは引退した後、死が訪れるまで文筆家としての活動に専念し、この間に東アジアをテーマとする作品が生まれた。その内容は彼の豊富な体験と知識を反映しており、彼はこの作品によって、ドイツで唯一公認された東アジア専門家としての評判を築いた。彼の主な著作として、おそらく一九〇一年に出版された回想録『東アジアにおける三三年間』を挙げることができるだろう。その第二巻、二四三ページから二五九ページの間に、彼の日記に基づく北海道旅行の体験報告が記されている。

ゲルトナーの日記の一部である一八六六年十一月中旬から一八六七年九月初旬までの分は、『キリスト教的ドイツのための保守的月刊総合雑誌』の中で、前半と後半の二回に分けて出版された。その前半部分（四六〇－四八〇頁）は一八八五年五月に、そして後半部分の北海道旅行の報告については、同年七月号（六八三－七〇二頁）に掲載されている。もし、ゲルトナーが一八六六年十一月から一八七一年の初め頃までの日本滞在の間、日記を書いていたとすると、彼の日記の約四分の一だけが発表されたことになる。また、新聞研究所の情報によると、一八八五年におけるこの月刊誌の発行部数は二〇〇〇－三〇〇〇部程度

であった。したがって、彼の日記の内容が当時の世論の形成やメディアに影響を与えたということは、ほとんどなかったと思われる。

上記のことから分かるように、両者の日記の発行手段の質的差は非常に大きかった。つまり、一方は、三十年以上もの年月から得た知識と経験が三巻にまとめられた重みのある作品のなかに収められ、他方は、日記のほんの一部分のみが三流の月刊誌に掲載されただけである。

さらに前者は、十九世紀における日独関係についての代表的著作として高く評価され、二十世紀初頭の東アジア政策のマニュアルとして扱われ、今日においても重要な文献として引用されている。また、著者自身も東アジア問題の政府相談役として起用され、政府筋は特に、アジアに関わる状況判断の際、ブラントの知識を信頼していた。しかし、彼に疑わしい点がないわけでもなかったことは考慮すべきだろう。たとえば、東京帝国大学医学部の教授であったE・ベルツは、ブラントに対する痛烈な批判家の一人で、ドイツのアジア政治におけるブラントの働きが、一八九五年以降のドイツと日本の外交関係を悪化させたと彼を非難した。しかしこれに加えて、ベルツが日本国家強化のための近代化に貢献することで日本政府から給料をもらっていた一方、ブラントは、当時の外交官として完全にドイツの利益を代表していた点にも注意を払わなければならない。

一方、後者の読者層は、保守的キリスト教徒に限られ、中央党、または中央党よりも右寄りの党を選ぶほど保守的な人びとであった。しかしゲルトナーの記事は、プチブル的生活をする読者に、東洋の異国情緒を味わわせると共に、遠く離れた日本の北海道という地域にすむ住民に農業のやり方を教える働き者のドイツ人は偉くなれるというメッセージを潜在的に伝えた。

[3] 日記

3・1 旅仕度

旅仕度についてゲルトナーは、ブラントがこの企てに必要なすべてのものを用意したと報告している。またブラントは、ヨーロッパ人の使用人のほかに、横浜の自分のもとで働いている三人の日本人(小使い、別当、コック)までも同行させ、その他、折畳式ベッド、食料品、それにとりわけ大きな日本製の特別な蝦夷地図も持っていたと報告している。

当時、日本に居を構えていた数人の外国人が、多数の使用人を雇い入れることができる経済力と地位を有していたことは、この当時の資料からも証明できるが、ブラントの「ヨーロッパ人の使用人」の存在は、彼に関する別の資料からは何の証明もされない。しかしブラントは、オイレンブルク伯爵の東アジア遠征の随行員としてシンガポールに一八六〇年八月初めに到着した後、アチュンという名前の中国人を使用人として雇い入れている。その中国人についてブラントは、「一八六八まで自分の使用人としていたひどく醜いハイナンタオ人(海南島)[7]」と書いている[8]。とすると、ヨーロッパ人の使用人という記述は疑わしく思われる。

ゲルトナーの「ほとんど信じられないような日本人による測量技術によって描き上げられ、数え切れないほど多くの土地、川、山の名称が詳細にしかも小さな字で書き込まれた蝦夷の大きな日本製の特別な地図」に関する発言は興味を引く。彼は、この地図の大きさを、長さ四m、幅二mと述べている。地図がこの地図の大きさだとすると、それは伊能忠敬(一七四五-一八一八)の土地測量によってつくられた地図に関わ

ってくる。伊能によって作成された多数の北海道地図のなかには、並べるとゲルトナーが挙げている地図の大きさに合致すると思われる二つの版、東北海道（二七〇cm×一四九cm）および西北海道（二二三四cm×一五〇cm）が存在する。ゲルトナーは、「ブラント氏が持ってきたのと同じ大きさの蝦夷の地図を（北海道旅行への）出発前に函館で入手した」とはっきり書きとめている。したがって、彼が伊能の地図を所有していたことは、ありえないことではない。そしてゲルトナーの記述の正当性は、彼らが北海道旅行をおこなった一八六七年に、初めて公に入手可能となったという事実から証明できるだろう。

さらに、一九七〇年、フランスで北海道地図を含む伊能の地図が発見されていることが、幕末期に外国人による地図の入手が可能であったことを証明している。しかし不思議なことに、ブラントは自らの記録の中で、シーボルトの地図についてのみ言及している。これは『江戸の天文学者、高橋作左衛門の原本地図に基づく蝦夷と日本の千島列島』というタイトルで、一八五〇年頃ライデンで発行された四八cm×二八大のシーボルトによる写本地図のことかもしれない。[11][12]

ゲルトナーは、自分自身の荷物について次のように書き記している。ウール毛布、枕、防水ゴムシート、下着、衣類、缶詰め、いろいろな種類の飲み物、標本のためのアルコール瓶、スケッチブック等々。さらに、猟銃、ピストル、薬莢、そして銃剣で武装していた。

二人のプロシア人が目前の旅の苦労をできる限り緩らげ、あらゆる事態に備えたこれらの贅沢な装備の運搬には、五頭もの駄馬を必要とした。

この旅仕度には、ブラントらしい発想が見られる。彼は、水路を探し、利用する予定であったので、自分の馬は使用せず途中で駄馬を借りることにしていた。それにより、自分と自分の使用人（ブラントは単数形で記述）、それとゲルトナーの荷物を最小限に絞らざるを得なくなり不足も生じたが、旅の行程を容

298

易にこなせる結果となった。この結果からブラントは、自分自身の先見の明を自負した。ゲルトナーが旅行に「必要なすべてのもの」と述べているのに対し、ブラントは、残念そうな語り口で、「ただ最小限の荷物しか持って行けなかった」と言っている。この観点の相違は、社会的地位と財政上の資力における違いから起こったのだろう。また、両者が後の回想録執筆の際、日記を基にしたのであれば、蝦夷の地図やブラントの使用人数における食い違いをどのように説明づけることができるだろうか。両者の旅仕度の記述を比較し、どちらの方がより信憑性が高いかを判断することはかなり困難である。

3・2 旅 行

ブラントの北海道旅行についての記述は、随筆的であり、『回想録』全体にも報告内容がむりなく溶け込んでいるのに対し、ゲルトナーの『蝦夷内地旅行に関するまとめ』は、素雑な日記形態であり、毎日の出発および到着場所、その間にある村々や小村落、その都度の距離、毎日の総旅行時間や総距離、旅行手段（馬、舟）、並びに入念に書き留めた天候状況が個々に記載されている。例えば、「函館から鷲ノ木までは馬で総計一三里、八時間四五分、曇り、しかし雨は降らず、遠望不可」とある。

旅行の二日目（八月十二日）、ブラントは、シラリカ川と宿泊地との間の四本の川を渡らなければならなかったが、かなり水位が高くとも、最低限いかだを利用することで通行できるだろう」という推測によって潜在的有用性を指摘している。この発言には、ブラントの北海道植民地化に対する異議を唱えるような内容は何も書かれておらず、障害を軽視しがちである。ブラントは、「幅広い渓谷を持つ丘陵は密生した木々に覆われ、水辺の

砂丘との間には、たいへん美しい花々が咲き乱れる牧草地があった」と見ている。一方ゲルトナーは、その丘を「草木で覆い隠されているだけ」そして「川は、浅く石塊だらけで流れは速かった」と捉えた。翌日八月十三日の記録でブラントは、森の植物や野生動物の種類の豊富さと自然の美しさを強調しており、アイヌ民族の雨具についての描写では、民俗学的見解すらうかがえる。ゲルトナーはそれに反して「農耕と畜産を営むのに非常に適している」と記している。つまり、彼は北海道の土地を、利益を期待できる生産手段としての土地と判断しており、この見方は日記全体に示されている。

八月十四日にブラントは、食糧不足を心配している。彼は、「二日前から米と乾燥きのこ以外に食べていない」と書いているが、この旅は三日前に始まったばかりで、その上ゲルトナーは携帯品の中に缶詰めがあることを記述しているので、なぜブラントが食糧不足の心配をしたのか不明である。それに加えてブラントは、借りた駄馬と濃い霧で視界が全く閉ざされてしまった有珠岳(うすたけ)の麓にある道の質の悪さに不満をもらしている。一方ゲルトナーの記述からは、農業的有益性がどの程度のものであるかという視点から、「深く穏やかに流れる川」や「広大で緑豊かな草原」を見ていた印象をうける。ここで注目すべき点は、ゲルトナーが「二つの噴火口をもつ有珠岳(うずたけ)」を実際に見たかのように書いているが、ブラントの上記の発言からするとそれは有り得ないこと、さらに、ブラントが、真偽は自分の地図を見るだけで充分明らかになるはずであるにもかかわらず、「火を吐く山、尻別岳(羊蹄山と見間違えたと思われる)」が北海道の中心にあると書いていることである。

八月十五日付の内容からは、室蘭へ向かったブラントの目的が良くわかる。彼は絵鞆(えども)湾とそこにある防衛施設に興味を抱いた。前者を「優れた停泊地」とする一方、後者を「高さ六フィートの土塀

と板垣、二、三のお粗末な砲台があるだけの砦」と見下した評価をしている。彼は、この砦へ「日本人作家により取り上げられ、その後外国人が繰り返して発表した情報」の確認のため訪れた。一方、ゲルトナーはこの日の日記で、南部陣屋という砦の名を挙げている。シーボルトの地図には二ヵ所の砦が記されており、一ヵ所の南部陣屋は絵鞆湾の陸側に、もう一ヵ所は向かい側にある半島の先端に位置している。ゲルトナーは、小船で湾内を巡ることで（決して暇つぶしとは思われない）、この港の入り口が地元に詳しい人間にしか見つけられず、その地元の人々でさえも嵐や高波の際、岩礁や浅瀬のため航行は困難であろうという判断を下した。ゲルトナーのこれらの見解は、事実に促したもので、植民地化的プロパガンダを目的としたものではない。

室蘭から勇払（ゆふつ）へ進んだ八月十六日のゲルトナーの注意は、地質（軽く、しばしば砂を含んでいる）と土地（丘陵状、木がなく、畜産に最適）に向けられている。記述によると、樽前山から上がる煙がはっきり見え、川の水は豊かであった。同じ道のりの中でブラントは、矮小性のオークが密生している丘とその界隈を「よく手入れされたイギリスの庭園に匹敵する」と見ている。さらに彼の記述には、勇払の渓谷で何百頭もの馬の群れと出会ったとあり、ゲルトナーの畜産への評価を裏付けている。ここで注目すべき点は、元将校であったブラントの視点が再び、単なる「低い土塀で囲まれた官舎」であった勇払の「シーボルトの地図に示された砦」に向けられていることである。その規模から推察すると、砦は本来、ブラントが述べたように印象に残るほどのものではなかったのではないだろうか。そして彼は、植民地化の機会を逃した無念さを読者に呼び起こすために、意図的にそうした記述をおこなったのではないだろうか。

八月十七日、両者の記述は、細部において大きな相違を示している。ブラントが勇払川を「深く幅広い

川に橋が架けられている」と書いているのに対し、ゲルトナーは「幅広く、浅瀬をたよりに渡った」としている。ブラントにとって丘は、オーク、シラカバなどですばらしく生い茂っていた。ゲルトナーは、それを小さくみすぼらしいオーク、シラカバなどが生い茂った土地と述べている。勇払川の岸にシャクナゲの一種をみた彼は、農民としての専門知識に基づき、その「導入は、ドイツの庭園にとってりっぱな装飾となるだろう」と思った。さらに彼は、「とても残念なことに、このシャクナゲはまだ全然熟しておらず、掘り出して持っていくことには無理があった。そして残念ながら、ゲルトナーが常に新しい収入源を開拓しようと目を光らせていたという印象を受けるとともに、逃がしてしまったビジネスチャンスに対する彼の無念さを感じることができる。

さらにこの日、彼らは馬に乗り、「手入れが行き届いている」道を流れの激しい「千歳川」まで進み、この川を船で長都（おさつ）湖まで下った。ブラントにはその湖が「浅い入り江」に見え、ゲルトナーは「浅い入り江の多い、見渡す限り葦が生息する湖」と描写している。

翌日、八月十八日の早朝おこなわれた鹿狩りは徒労に終わり、旅は続けられた。ブラントの記録には、「長都を八時間かけて下った後、我々は、かなり深くて力強く流れる石狩川へ到着した。私は、四十フィートの深さには底をみつけることができなかった。」、そしてさらに、「我々が石狩へ到着するまで六時間かかった」とある。ここでブラントによって述べられた十四時間というこの日の総旅行時間は、ゲルトナーの日記では、「船で十一時間」とある。それに加えて、ゲルトナーは石狩川へのの川筋に関する詳細な地理に関する記述では、長都湖はカマカ川と合流し江別川へと注ぎ、石狩川へと流れ込んでいるとある。そして彼は、勇払から石長さ四十フィートの自分の紐で石狩川の深さを突き止めることができなかった。

狩への平野は「大規模な畜産や農耕に最も適した地帯である」と評価し、その日の記録を終えている。八月十九日にゲルトナーは、石狩庁舎の役人から弟のことを知っているかと話しかけられた。弟は「あかばにさん」と呼ばれていた。ゲルトナーは聞き覚えたままを書いており、どのような意味があったのかは確認できない。「あかばな」から、赤い鼻または酒飲みの鼻を意味して名付けられた可能性が有力ではあるが、埴輪をつくるための赤い色合いをした赤埴に由来するとも考えられる。いずれにしても、ヨーロッパ人の肌の色や顔色をほのめかすことから生じた呼び名で、おそらく尊敬というよりむしろ嘲笑がとれる言葉を記載したという事実は、彼の日本語の知識不足を露わにした。また、R・ゲルトナー本人は、七重近郊で地元の人々から、「あかふと（赤人）」とよばれていた。

ゲルトナーは、「函館と同規模の石狩から、かなり良い馬に乗って小樽経由で余市へ向かった。十時間で十五里もの道のりを進み、夜十一時に松明とランタンの光を手がかりにして到着した。」と書いており、「最もすばらしい遠望」と「実に美しい景色」に感動した。さらに彼にはその日に通った村は、東海岸より裕福で手入れが行き届いているように思われた。一方ブラントも、東海岸と西海岸の相違を書き留めている。西海岸は木が乏しく、蚊や貧しくぼろをまとった人が多い。さらに彼は、「農耕や畜産、馬の飼育を見かけることもなく、手に入れた馬の質は悪かった。」と記し、道のとてもひどい状態については、再び不平を言っている。また、この日の両執筆者の記述は、馬の質の評価だけではなく、距離や時間の記述においても異なっている。ブラントの記述には、その旅行は小樽から余市だけで「距離十里、十一時間三十分」もかかり、夜が訪れると明るさは「二つの提灯のぼやけた光」しかなかったとある。これまでの旅の疲れを癒すため、八月二十日に二人のプロシア人は、余市で休憩を取ることにした。こ

この日の両者の日記で目立っているのは、町にいる「多くのアイヌ人」（ゲルトナー記）についてである。この「強制労働者として容赦なく搾取されている弱い部族」（ブラント記）は、二人に深い印象をうえつけたに違いない。ゲルトナーは、ここのアイヌ人は、姿は落ちぶれているようだが、東海岸のアイヌのように媚び諂うことはないと言っている。ブラントはそれと異なり、「この地のアイヌ人たちは、東海岸の同部族の者より意気消沈した様子をしている」と印象を述べた。さらにブラントは、「彼らは労働者として利用されており、その報酬は、綿布、ナイフの刃、米、タバコによって現品支給されていたが、すべては最悪の品質であった。」と記し、ゲルトナーは、「アイヌ人が、それらの品を持ち帰るために自分たちの上っぱりを用いたが、その行為は文化的レベルの低さを表していた。」と記している。

八月二十日に余市から同名の川の渓谷を上って行った。道の状態の悪さについて両者の見方は一致しているが、渓谷の林業利用に対する判断は分かれた。ブラントは、「渓谷をのぼっていく道沿いには、途方もない伐採によって一平方ルーテ（二・八七ｍ×四・六七ｍ）の良木すら見当たらない。」と記している。

一方、ゲルトナーはそれとは異なり、「周辺の山は非常に上質のオークとトネリコで覆われている。」と述べている。この部分を比較すると、（中略）部分的に野蛮におこなわれた伐採は、悲しい印象を与える」と述べている。ゲルトナーはブラントに比べ、環境を否定的にとらえる思考はない。また彼は、何事につけても有用な面を見出し、偏見をもたず、物事に対し断然拒否の姿勢を示すことはない。

八月二十二日、ブラントは、「長崎のイギリス領事の兄弟であるイギリス人鉱山技術者ゴワーが私を訪ねてきた。」彼は、二〇〇人の労働者を引き連れ岩内から茅沼（かやぬま）の炭坑への道を建設した。」と書いている。（中略）一方ゲルトナーは、ゴワーは岩内から二・五里のカサノマ山（茅沼の書き間違えかと思われる）から海へ向け、急勾配を利用したトロッコの路線を建設した、と述べており、この出来事の

異なった一面を照らし出している。彼もまたゴワーの訪問に触れたが、「彼（ゴワー）は、自分が待っていた副地方長官である山村が函館からやって来たと信じ、誤ってブラントを訪問した。」と書いている。ブラントの出版物の言葉の選択や内容を考察すると、彼にはもったいぶった方法で読者に彼という人物の重要性を意識させようとする意図があったと思われる。（その尊大さは当時の時代精神の反映ではあるが、許されるものではなかっただろう。）ゴワーの訪問先は、実は（ブラントはその印象を残そうと思ったにもかかわらず）ブラントではなく、単なる勘違いであった。

ブラントとゲルトナーの食い違いはさらにみられる。ブラントは、「ユナイ」と名をあげている硫黄泉の湯を「温かい」としているが、ゲルトナーは、「摂氏五十一・五度もある熱さ」と述べている。この温泉についての描写の詳しさを見るだけでも、ゲルトナーの観察の注意深さが良くわかる。そして、この日の彼の日記も、尻別川の西方にある広大な地域での畜産や農耕の可能性が有力であるとしめくくっている。

平船で寿都（すっつ）湾を渡り、同名の地へ向かった。ブラントは、そこから「小屋つきの津軽藩主公式船を自由に使用した」と豪語している。一方ゲルトナーは、ただの「日本式の船」の船との造りの違いを示し、それには日光を遮るための覆いが掛けられていたと記している。

この日彼らは、一時間半の航海の後、新たに船を乗り換えなければならなかった。その船の船乗りが短時間の航海の後、それ以上先へ進むことを拒否したことから、ブラントは、「非常に怠惰である。」と記した。「シロゼ」での休憩の後、二十一時半には船乗りが、「また疲れた。」と記した。

出した。ブラントは、「二十三時まで甲板に残り、風と波が穏やかになったので眠りに就いた。」と記している。一方ゲルトナーの視点からは異なった状況がうかがえる。彼は、「ひどい荒波、暴れ狂う磯波、おそろしく聳え立つ岩礁」という表現を使い、さらに「ブラント氏は旅行を続行するため、この素晴らしい

15 ── ブラントとゲルトナーの旅行日記の比較

夜を利用するよう断固として主張し譲らなかったので、私達は何が何でも船乗りを働き続けさせるほかなかった。」と述べている。その際、風や波に対向する航行は遅々として進まず、彼にとってその状況はかなり危険だと思われた。ゲルトナーの日記には、「二十四時にブラントと夜番を交代し甲板の下へ」とあり、危険や寒さから逃れ得た安堵感のようなものが行間に滲み出ている。夜番となったブラントの全く軍人らしくない振る舞いへの批判的な気持ちが、ゲルトナーの八月二十四日の「ブラント氏は自分でその番をしていたのではなく、毛布にくるまって眠りこんでいた。」という記述にくみとれる。

ゲルトナーは、肘掛椅子に座ってくつろいでいるブラントに「とても怠惰である」と記された船乗りたちは、その地域によく通じているその土地の住民によって構成されていたので、暗闇で激しい向かい風の岩礁を進む危険性を充分に判断できたはずで、無分別さから生命を失いかねない冒険は拒否せざるを得なかった。しかし面と向かって否定することは海に対する恐怖感と解釈され、船乗りとしての面目を失うことを意味することから、軽率な行動により外国人外交官に万が一の事があれば、乗客の安全性に全責任が課せられている船長が処罰を受けたのは明らかである。いずれにせよ、いつの間にか船を安全な場所に停泊させ、船乗りたちも眠りについていることに両者が気づいたのは八月二十四日の朝になってからだった。その朝は向かい風のために労働を削減してくれるはずの「帆を張ることができなかった（ゲルトナー）」。

ゲルトナーに「とても怠惰である」と記された船乗りたちは、その地域によく通じているその土地の住民によって構成されていたので、暗闇で激しい向かい風の岩礁を進む危険性を充分に判断できたはずで、無分別さから生命を失いかねない冒険は拒否せざるを得なかった。しかし面と向かって否定することは海に対する恐怖感と解釈され、船乗りとしての面目を失うことを意味することから、軽率な行動により外国人外交官に万が一の事があれば、乗客の安全性に全責任が課せられている船長が処罰を受けたのは明らかである。

ので、「喧騒と叱責の後（ブラント）」、「いやいやながら（ゲルトナー）」舵を取らざるを得なかったのは不思議ではない。そのため「非常にゆっくりと（ゲルトナー）」しか進まなかった。ブラントは、「瀬棚の二里手前で上陸し、アイヌ人の案内で徒歩で先に進んだが、十四時にはすでに瀬棚に到着し、シーボルトの地図を待たねばならなかった。」と記している。早く到着しても仕方がない状況ではあるが、彼らは船を瀬棚で乗り換え、新たに十二人の漕ぎ手を乗せ日没までに太櫓（ふとろ）へ向かった。

おそらく長い船旅の単調さに原因があったのだろうが、両執筆者は、八月二十五日の記録を徒歩でまるまる一時間進み（ゲルトナー）と立ち寄り先に留めている。八時に太櫓を出発し、日中戸（にちべ）を経て十二時半に太田へ到着。久遠（くどう）に午後三時半、関内に夜の十一時に着き、熊石までは「真夜中すぎに到着（ブラント）」した。「風は昨日より激しい向かい風（ゲルトナー）」で、その上「滝のような雨（ブラント）」であった。彼らは、「日中戸にて蝦夷でいちばん歯ごたえのあるにわとりを、また、久遠で固ゆで卵と新鮮なサケ（ブラント）」を食している。またブラントは、この日の旅を「十六時間の旅」であったと書いている。それは、上記の一日の経過にちょうど当てはまる。一方ゲルトナーは、船で十二時間半、歩いて一時間半進んだとしている。しかし、ゲルトナー自身、出発時刻を八時と述べ、その上「私達がやっと就寝できたのは、夜一時であった。」と書いているので、十二時間半というのは明らかな誤りである。

八月二十六日、「旅が続けられない程の集中豪雨（ゲルトナー）」のため、やむを得ず熊石での休憩となった。そこは、際立って整然とし、清潔感があり、風光明媚な土地であった。

その翌日の八月二十七日から、ようやくブラントにとって「文明化しているといえる地域」に再び踏み

込んだ。それはおそらく、松前藩藩主の護衛が随行し、彼のために道が「特別に修復され、砂が振りまかれており、儀仗兵が村落ごとに彼を待ちうけ敬礼し、また、住民が静粛に正座し、深々と頭を下げ、謙虚さを示す姿勢をとったこと（ブラント）」からきた感覚であろう。いずれにせよ、「最高位の者だけに与えられる敬意（ゲルトナー）」を受けたこととは、ブラントのエゴに絶大な効果を発揮したようだ。筆者が他の論文でも明らかにしているように、常にブラントは自分にふさわしい身分相応の評価を得たいという願望があった。[15]

この日は早朝の六時に出発。それから七時間半後のまだ午後も早いうちに、彼らは次の宿泊地である江差に到着した。「宿泊所であるユニソ寺からの三、〇〇〇軒、人口二万人の町の展望は極めて興味深かった。（中略）毎年八〇〇艘ものジャンク船が荷積みされ、南へとむかう。江差は漁業製品の貿易量で函館をはるかに上回っているようだ。（ゲルトナー）」またゲルトナーは、町全体に活発な商業活動、広い倉庫、商社、一列に並んだ売店が見られ、蝦夷内の他の土地では感じられなかったある程度裕福な印象を受けた。このゲルトナーの綿密な叙述から、町を詳しく見て回る機会と時間の余裕を持っていたことが分かる。一方ブラントは、江差の規模を約三〇〇軒と述べ、港の安全性を強調した。

八月二十八日の報告は、江差を出発した際の二つの全く正反対の描写によって始まっている。ゲルトナーは、「昨日同様、大規模な護衛付きで私達は馬に乗り、早朝五時頃、立派な行列をなして江差を出発した。」と書いている。それとは別にブラントは、「次の日の朝（二十八日）私達は馬に乗りさらに進んだ。午後五時少し前に松前付近にまで達することができた。」と記している。ところで、上記の出発と到着時間は、ゲルトナーの「馬に乗って十二時間」という記述と一致している。

宿泊先は、この日もまた寺であった。ゲルトナーによると、それは町で「最も大きく、山の高い所にあり、大名屋敷のすぐ裏手」にあった。記録を読むと、ゲルトナーが例のごとく自然に重点を置いているのは明らかである。寺の門前からの「壮大な眺望」は、山や海、そして町の描写を詳細にさせた。雨模様で夜になると冷え込んだので、床につく前に僧侶たちを囲み、香料入りホットワインを飲んだ。

次の日、朝、寺を巡った際ゲルトナーは、トラが描かれた衝立障子に気づき、ブラントに注意を喚起した。ゲルトナーによると、苦労して交渉した後ブラントは、この絵を一〇〇ターラーで獲得することに成功し、それを安全のため、油紙にきちんとくるまれた絵を鞍の前にのせ二日間運んだ。」と述べているが、それはいくらなんでもそれはありえないことであろう。函館から北海道の奥地までビールやワインを持ってこさせるような人材と資力を持つ者が、収集熱の成果を自ら運ぶ必要はなかっただろう。ブラントは、トラが等身大の竹やぶから姿を見せている絵だとトラが木の幹の周りに忍び寄せるもので、木であれ竹であれ、その絵はブラントが甥に譲るまで函館の領事館に飾られていた。

松前の近くで、ゲルトナーは多くの石英鉱脈を目にし、その岩石に金の含有性を推測した。ゲルトナーは常に金銭的利益を念頭において観察しており、日記の別な箇所でも石油について言及している。ゲルトナーは、山越えをしたあたりで地面や水面を覆っている黒く粘り強い石油を二瓶採取し、分析のためベルリンにまで送った後、灯油やアスファルトの生産が可能であるという情報を得ている。

八月二十九日の出発は激しい雨で午前十一時まで阻まれた。「美しい家並みの漁村」を抜け福島へと向かい、そこにあった寺の「特に美しい」庭で休憩をとった。さらに知内へと進む途中、ゲルトナーはいつもと同じ様に「鬱蒼とした植生」や「大変肥沃な土壌」、「農耕や畜産に適した土地」を何箇所も目にして

いる。

木古内（きこない）、札苅（さっかり）、当別（とべつ）を経て函館へ向かう旅行の最終日（三十日）にゲルトナーは、詳細な土地の描写と有益な耕地の浪費について、「最も肥沃であるにもかかわらず単なる野生の植物が繁茂しているだけだ。」と残念そうに繰り返している。一方ブラントにとっては、この最後の二日間の旅に記録するほどの内容はなかったようで、たった六行の中に道の状態だけが記されている。そして函館への到着は、ゲルトナーによると午後三時頃で、ブラントによると、「大変骨折れであったが興味深くとても楽しめる旅が終わったのは午後四時頃」となっている。

[4] **おわりに**

ブラントとゲルトナーの日記を比較検討してみた結果、数多くの相違点が出てきた。それらは、二人が視点を置く位置や両者の観察能力の違いによって部分的には説明づけられるだろう。また、自然の美しさ、身体的疲労の度合いといった主観的感情を基準とした判断による相違は、当然領けるものである。しかしながら、距離や時間、同伴者の数または村落の規模といった客観的な判断が下せる部分における相違となると、執筆者の単なる勘違い、あるいは、何らかの目的を持った故意によるものではないかという疑いが否応なく生じる。どちらもありえないことではない。

執筆者の誤謬は、旅行の体験と活字になった時期との間の何年という隔たりからすれば不思議ではない。その間に記憶の多くが不鮮明になり、思い込みから生じた事物が確信のある事実へと変化した可能性もある。また、それらの記述に何らかの目的を持っていたとすれば、それはある事

柄のなかで自分がいかに冒険的で注目に値するより重要な役割を持った人物であったかを誇張し、そのことを出版物に表したいがためであろう。その上、記憶が記録された当時、彼らは、外国にいるドイツ人からの影響力と国民からのそうした人物への尊敬が求められる時代精神の影響を受けていた。したがって、ヨーロッパ人の指導権がここでもまた浸透したという印象を伝えるために、真実を多少とも曲げたと考えられる。例えば、ブラントが八月二八日にすべての同行を拒否したことについて、まるで本当にそれをできたかのような、彼の貫徹力が北海道での単独旅行を許可するよう幕府の代表者に主張している。さらにブラントは日記の中で、自分の勧めに従い、北海道の植民地化がまだ実行可能であった時代に事を起こしていれば、ドイツは、東アジアの政治的・経済的舞台で重要な役割を果たしていただろうと示唆している。そこには、絶好の機会を逃してしまった彼の無念さと失望が反映されている。つまり、後の時代にはとても考えられなかった多くの可能性が、一八六〇、七〇年代の東アジアには残されていた。[16]そして北海道の植民地化は、他国（たとえば、ロシアに対して）との政治的摩擦を起こすことなく遂行でき、また軍事上での優位性を見ても同じ結論が得られた。さらに、かつて将校であったブラントは軍備について、室蘭の港を守っている大砲は粗末であり、防衛施設はポンメルンの歩兵が蹴るだけで倒せるような「板塀」に他ならないなどと例をあげ、プロシアの軍事的優位性を読者に訴えかけている。

ゲルトナーの日記の中に読者は、自然と強い絆を持った男の姿を目にするだろう。彼は景色や風物の記述にかなりの領域を費やしており、自然の美しさに対する感動や喜びがいかほどであったかを推測させられる。しかしその一方で、彼が標本用のアルコール瓶やスケッチブックを携帯していたのは研究意欲や知識欲からではなく、切なる利潤追求を動機としていたと解釈できる。つまり、金銭的な目的のためであれば、いかに愛してやまない自然であろうとも、その自然から言うならば搾取することも厭わなかったはず

である。またゲルトナーは、おそらくこの旅行の際に、北海道のまとまった土地を手に入れ農業に利用しようという考えを思いついたのだろう。その件に関し、ブラントの支援を得たように思えるが、それは、今後の研究課題としていきたい。

[注]

1 *Deutsche Botschafter in Japan, 1860-1973*, OAG, Tokyo 1974, S. 20.
2 筆者はプレンツラウ市の住民登録簿を調べたが、R・ゲルトナーの足跡を辿ることはできなかった。
3 *Allgemeine Konservative Monatsschrift für das christliche Deutschland*. XLII Jahrgang, Leipzig, Verlag Georg Böhme, Juli 1885, S. 467.
4 *Allgemeine Konservative Monatsschrift für das christliche Deutschland*. XLII Jahrgang, Leipzig, Verlag Georg Böhme.
5 Erwin Bälz, *Das Leben eines deutschen Arztes im erwachenden Japan*. J. Engelhorns Nachf, Stuttgart, 1931, S. 256.
6 中央党(一八七〇年から一九三三年までのドイツのカトリック派政党)で、現在のドイツのキリスト教民主同盟CDUの前身。
7 以下、ブラントおよびゲルトナーの記述を直接引用した箇所には、かぎ括弧を用いることとする。
8 Brandt, Max von, Bd. I, S. 78.
9 伊能の地図がどのようにしてフランスへもたらされたのかについては、いまだ明らかになっていない。しかし、例えば函館紛争の間、北海道の反乱軍側で活動したフランス軍事顧問の存在が仮定できるだろう。
10 高橋作左衛門（別称、高橋景保）の父は伊能の師匠であったらしく、父の死後、作左衛門は伊能の師匠になった。そしてさらに、作左衛門は伊能の死後、彼の測量を引き継いだ。
11 別のリトグラフでは、同じタイトルで四十九・五cm×六十七cmの大きさのものがある。そして、シーボルト事件の発端となった日本地図は、もともと伊能によって作成された一三〇cm×一一四cm大の地図であり、高橋からシーボルトに譲渡されたものであった。
12 *Japan mit den Augen des Westens gesehen. Gedruckte europäische Landkarten vom frühen 16. bis zum 19.*

13 日本人とは高橋で、外国人とはシーボルトのことと考えられ、前述した地図を示している可能性は充分ある。
14 ゲルトナーはこれらに加えてパイプや酒についても言及している。
15 Baumann, Andreas H.「日本における初滞在プロシア領事マックス・アウグスト・スツィーピオ・フォン・ブラント」、『日独文化交流史研究』一九九五年号、五六頁、五七頁。
16 Brandt, Max von, Bd. II, S. 146.

[参考文献]

ベーバ著、坂井洲二編・訳、『ドイツ商人幕末をゆく』新潟日報事業社、一九九七年。

Bälz, Erwin, Das Leben eines deutschen Arztes im erwachenden Japan, J. Engelhorns Nachf, Stuttgart, 1931.

Becker, Bert, Georg Michaelis, Ein preußischer Jurist im Japan der Meiji-Zeit, Iudicium Verlag 2001.

Blakiston, "Japan in Yezo", reprint from the "Japan Gazette" in: Herbert E. Plutschow, Historical Hakodate, 1991.

Brandt, Max von, Dreiunddreissig Jahre in Ostasien, Erinnerungen eines deutschen Diplomaten, Bd. II, Leipzig, Verlag von Georg Wigand, 1901.

Foreign Pioneers. A Short History of the Contribution of Foreigners to the Development of Hokkaido, ed. Archives Section, Hokkaido Prefectural Government, Sapporo 1968.

"Japan mit den Augen des Westens gesehen". Gedruckte europäische Landkarten vom frühen 16. bis zum 19. Jahrhundert, Prestel Verlag 1993, Kat. 135.

Schwalbe, Hans, Deutsche Botschafter in Japan, 1860–1973, OAG, Tokyo 1974.

Stahncke, Holmer, Die Brüder Schnell und der Bürgerkrieg in Nordjapan, OAG aktuell Nr. 27, 1986.

Wippich, Rolf-Harald, Japan als Kolonie? Max von Brandts Hokkaido-Projekt 1865/67. Übersee Verlag, Hamburg 1997.

[付記]

本稿は二〇〇二年十一月三十日発行の日本独学史学会の機関誌『日独文化交流史研究』(通巻第五号)に掲載された「ブラントとゲルトナーの北海道旅行」に加筆したものである。

16 文化受容の証人、ラフカディオ・ハーン
中国の作品の語り直しを中心に

梅本順子

はじめに

ラフカディオ・ハーンというと、幽霊話の作家というイメージがある。事実、ニューオーリンズ時代から、ハーンは幽霊話を語り直した作品を数多く仕上げてきた。ニューオーリンズ時代に纏め上げた『中国怪談集』(*Some Chinese Ghosts*, 1884) はそのうちの一冊であり、ハーン自身は後になって書き直したい部分があるというようなことを友人のミッチェル・マクドナルドに語ってはいるものの、ハーン作品の原点を見ることも可能ではなかろうか。というのも、その後、作家としてプロットの弱さを自覚させられたハーンは、「語り直し」に徹することになるが、この『中国怪談集』は初期のころの「語り直し」の醍醐

味を十分感じさせてくれる作品だからである。しかも、フランス語訳から得た元話を独自の作品に書き換えたハーンは、同じ中国をルーツとする作品に日本で出会い、それを意識せぬまま日本の話として再び書き換えるのであった。ハーンは、ニューオーリンズではフランス語作品の英訳とその評論で文芸欄の顔となっていたが、当時フランスがヨーロッパ随一の中国研究の牙城となっていたことから、フランス語を通して東洋へと目を向けることになったともいえるだろう。

これを機会に、中国文学の語り直しに邁進したハーンは、後に日本文化のルーツが中国にあることを知らしめるという点で一役買ったばかりか、日本が中国文化を受容する過程で起きた変容の実態を、その作品を通して日本人に突きつけることになったのである。すなわち、日本人が中国文化に接したとき、それをどのように理解し、土着のものとの間でどのように融和を図ったか、あるいは日本人の理解にかなうように、どのように解釈を加えていったのかは、ハーンの語り直しの作品を読むことにより鮮明になるのである。本論では、これに該当する作品をとり上げ、日本が中国文学を受容する際に失われたものと、ハーンによる語り直しの作品の創作過程をたどりたい。

ハーンが日本で出会った中国を原典とする作品の大半は、説話や伝説など多様な要素を含む作品が多い。中国では、年代を経るに連れて民話や伝承自体が変化し、さらにそれが日本に受容され日本の作品として流布するにあたり書き直されていることからして、その変化の様は我々の想像の域を越えるものがある。つまり、中国での変遷に加え、日本人読者の理解に沿った読み物にするための書き換えが加わることによって、ハーンの接した日本版は、ルーツが中国とはとうてい感じさせないものになっていたのかもしれない。よって、ハーン自身は、日本文化が中国文化の影響を受けていることはかなり前から知っていても、自分がかつて中国ものとして書き直した作品と、日本で遭遇した作品が出典を同じくしていたとはおそらく知

らなかったのではなかろうか。その原典を分かち合う作品とは、先に述べた『中国怪談集』の中にある「孟沂の話」("The Story of Ming-Y")と、晩年日本で仕上げた『天の川奇譚』("The Story of Ito Norisuke") (*The Romance of the Milky Way*, 1905) に収められている「伊藤則資の話」("The Story of Ito Norisuke")である。自分の理想である、女性を大切にする男性主人公のいる作品ということで、ハーンは選んだのかもしれないが、一見異なるように見えるこれらの作品のルーツをたどると、奇しくも同じものに行き当たってしまうのである。

本稿では、恋愛に殉死したような純情な男性主人公の物語である「伊藤則資の話」の成立を、「孟沂」と比較しながらみてゆくことにする。また、反対に女が幽霊と知るや逃げ腰になって殺された、ハーンとしては同情の余地がないと思われる男を描いた、「宿世の恋」("A Passional Karma")もまた、中国の古い話(「牡丹燈記」)をもとにしていることから、「伊藤」とは対照的な一例としてとりあげる。出来上がった二つの作品は、男の女に対する態度を見る限り全く逆だが、果たして中国の原典ではどうであったのだろうか。さらに「伊藤」には、男女が一定期間の別離の後再会するという、いわゆる日本版の「七夕」の要素が含まれている。この「七夕」についても後に触れたいと思う。これらの作品が、ハーンの語り直しによりどのように変えられたのかを、中国の原典、日本でそれを受容し普及のために書き直された作品、そしてさらにハーンによる語り直しの作品をそれぞれ比較することにより考察する。

「孟沂の話」と「伊藤則資の話」の語り直し

「孟沂の話」の原典は、中国の古典の『今古奇観』にあったものである。『今古奇観』は、十七世紀に編

纂され、怪談・奇談を五冊（三言二拍）の書物より収集した四十篇からなる短編集であり、「孟沂」にあたるのは、そのうちの一つといわれる。ハーンは、ニューオーリンズで仕上げた第一作の『中国怪談集』の注の部分で、この作品はグスタフ・シュレーゲル（Gustave Schlegel）によって一八七七年に仏訳されたものが原典であることを述べ、次のようなタイトルを与えている。すなわち、*Mai-yu-lang-tou-tchen-hoa-kouei : Le vendeur-d'hule qui seul possède des la reine-de-beauté ou splendeurs et misères des courtisanes chinoies*（『油売郎独占花魁』という中国語とその仏訳）の一部を挙げ、この作品集の"La Bachelière de Pays de Chu"（「陳家の食客」）という部分にあったと述べている。シュレーゲルの作品は、『今古奇観』の一部をフランス語に翻訳したもので、中仏二ヶ国語の対訳の形式をとっている。

ここで、原典に関して少し付け加えておきたい。シュレーゲルのつけたタイトルは、『今古奇観』の第七話にある「油売郎独占花魁」という一作品の訳であり、「孟沂の話」にあたる部分は『今古奇観』でみると第三十四話の「女秀才移花接木」の導入部の数ページにすぎない。しかも、中国の作者の意図は、孟沂という人物よりは薛涛にあったことは明らかである。すなわち、四川省の女性がいかに才女であるかを知らせるために付け加えた序に過ぎないことを、『今古奇観』は述べている。そのうえ、「これが今に伝わる田洙（孟沂の本名、孟沂はあだ名）が薛涛に遇うの一節だ」は、元話が他にあることを物語っている。

『今古奇観』は、前にも述べたとおり、それまでの説話や奇談を収集したものであるから当然だが、「孟沂」にあたる部分の元話は『剪燈余話』（十五世紀初頭に成立）の「田洙遇薛涛聯句記」（田洙が薛涛の霊に遇った話）に依拠しており、こちらのほうは『今古奇観』にある第三十四話より詳しく、主人公の交際を説明するために数多くの詩を取り上げており、これだけで独立した作品を形成しているのである。

一方、「伊藤則資の話」の原話は、『当日奇観』という日本の古い物語を集めた歌物語であり、原題は

「伊藤帯刀中将重衡の姫と冥婚」である。また、この出典はやはり中国の『今古奇観』に遡れる。『当日奇観』は、ハーンの所蔵していた蔵書(現在富山大学所蔵のへるん文庫)にあることからも、この本に従ってハーンが語りなおしたことは明らかである。

まず、「孟沂の話」の概要にふれておきたい。良家の子女の家庭教師として雇われた若い学徒の孟沂は、町に住む両親を尋ねるべく雇い主の許可を得て外出する。桃花が咲き乱れる小道をたどるうちに、花の香に酔いしれた孟沂は意図せずして見知らぬ道に迷い込み、この世のものとも思われない絶世の美女の薛濤(幽霊)に出くわす。彼女は遥か昔、高名な詩人の高駢に寵愛された名妓である。そのようなことは知るよしもなく、薛濤の虜となった孟沂は、両親の家に帰るという口実のもとに、彼女との逢瀬を続けた。やがて雇い主の知るところとなり、別離の日を迎えた孟沂に、薛濤はヒスイでできた獅子と珊瑚の筆立てを渡して餞とした。その後進士に合格して出世した孟沂は、薛濤からの贈り物を机に備えて思い出にふけるものの、その由来については決して他言しなかった。前述したように、原典では孟沂と薛濤が取り交わした幾篇かの詩が紹介されるが、孟沂は彼女の形見としてその詩を書き付けた綴りを最も大切な宝として周囲の人々にみせびらかすが、ハーン作品ではこの部分は切り捨てられている。

一方、「伊藤則資の話」は、『当日奇観』では歌物語であったものが、ハーン作品では純粋なロマンスになっている。やはり学者として若いころから頭角をあらわしていた伊藤は、寂しい山中を急ぐ道すがら、高貴な屋敷の侍女と出会い、送り届けることになる。その屋敷の女主人である、平家の末裔の姫君と出会うや、やはり虜になってしまった伊藤は、二人の出会いが運命付けられていたことを知らされる。相手の姫が幽鬼の人と打ち明けられても、姫の求愛を拒みきれずに一夜を契る。翌朝、形見を取り交わし、十年後の再会を約して姫と別れた伊藤は、死者同様の暮らしを送り、十年の歳月を経て、約束ど

おりに迎えにきた幽霊の姫君とあの世で結ばれる。ともに異類の女と人間の男という組み合わせであるが、相違は、孟沂が別離後二度と出会うことはなく、その後もそれまでどおりの幸せな生活を送ることになるものの、冥界に誘われて再びそこで姫と結ばれるというところにある。さらに孟沂は別れるまで、自分の相手が幽霊であるとは知らされていないが、伊藤は当初から知らされており、背筋が凍りつくほどの驚愕を覚えながらも、純愛がそれに勝って運命に殉じる。このように女に対する愛情は両者決して偽りがないものの、出来上がりはずいぶん異なるものとなっている。

この相違はどうして起きたのであろうか。しかも、中国の『今古奇観』では、男は幽霊と契ったことを自慢にして、その形見を自慢の種にしている話が続くが、ハーンは二人の関係を純粋なものとして、二人だけの思い出にしまっておく形に書き換えている。子供が聞いても、ハーンは二人の関係を純粋なものとして、机上の品々の由来を決して語ることのない孟沂を描き出したハーンは、日本のほうでは、相手が死者とわかっても躊躇することを嬉々として死者の世界に入らしめたのである。

ハーンが伊藤の物語を書くときに下敷きにした、中国の作者の意図は日本においても着実に継承されている。中国の原典には、薛濤が孟沂と取り交わした詩が含まれており、伊藤のほうも原話の『当日奇観』は歌物語であり、伊藤が姫と取り交わした和歌が中心となっているのである。ただ、中国の物語が薛濤という人物と時代背景なくしては十分理解できないために、日本版にするためには、翻訳ではなく翻案として、より日本人になじみが深く、理解しやすい設定が必要とされたのであった。

学者の愛人の魂が、いまだに若い秀才を求めて彷徨するという「孟沂」の設定を見ると、昔の学者と今の孟沂に共通するのは、学問という志をもち、詩歌に優れるということだけである。二人が交わす詩が見事なできばえであり、知的な交際の高さを歌っても、日本の読者には共感がえられない。それゆえ、日本にこの物語が紹介されるや、愛する二人の遭遇により、いっそうの意味を持たせようとする努力がなされ、数百年の時間と空間を隔てた二人のロマンスを正当化することになったのである。すなわち、薛涛にあたる幽鬼の姫を平重盛の息女とし、前世において伊藤に恋したが、主家の不幸で実らぬ恋への思いを抱きつつ、伊藤の生まれ代わりを求めて幾世代も生き続けているとすることにより、一見唐突に思える求愛さえ同情を持って受け取られることになったのである。

しかも、孟沂が進士を夢見て勉学に励む将来のある秀才であるなら、日本の物語で、姫のために世を捨てることを可能にさせたのは、平家の末裔ゆえにその才を発揮できない、伊藤のような人物だったのである。一方姫のほうも、失恋と平家滅亡という失意の中で死んだので、その思いが残らぬはずがない。源氏と平家の抗争という日本人なら誰でも知っている歴史を引き合いに出すことにより、物語が現実味を持つようになることも確かだ。源平の争いは幾多の文学作品に描かれてきたが、ハーン自身、平家の怨霊を主題にした「耳なし芳一」を語りなおしていることからして、なじみのある材料であったことは疑う余地がない。「孟沂」が、当時の中国の人々なら「薛涛」という言葉より得られる理解が背景にあるからこそ成立するように、「伊藤」には、日本人が「平家の姫の一目ぼれ」という設定から感じ取る印象が大きく作用しているのである。

ただ、ハーンが語り直すときには、どちらの作品においても、詩や和歌にあたる部分は省略しなければ

ならなかった。翻訳したときに、作品が十分理解できるような配慮に加えて、純粋な恋愛、至上の愛を短編にこめるには、詩や和歌がなくとも、すなわち登場する男女の学才を強調しなくとも、二人の関係の設定と会話だけで愛は全うされると考えたからであろう。中国のみならず日本でも詩歌の魅力を強調する主旨の『当日奇観』のような作品が書かれたが、ハーンの語り直しにおいては、純粋な恋愛の方に関心がいってしまって挿入された本来の詩歌の果たす役割は消えてしまうのだった。ただし、ハーンが日本の詩歌にまったく興味がないというのではない。その証拠に、「孟沂」や「伊藤」においては、詩歌そのものより筋立ての面白さに固執し、異類の女と人間の男との恋愛を描くことに専念したといえるだろう。

実在する薛濤について

すでに言及したように、「孟沂」を成立させているのは、薛濤という女性の存在である。安息が得られぬまま漂う霊としての薛濤を理解できたように、中国においても「薛濤」が持つ意味合いを考えてみたい。日本人が平家にまつわる話をしたことにより、「伊藤」を理解できたように、中国においても「薛濤」が持つ意味合いを考えてみたい。日本人が平家にまつわる話を理解できたように、中国においても「薛濤」が持つ意味合いを考えてみたい。日本人が平家にまつわる背景には、どのような事情があるのか。日本人が平家にまつわる話をしたことにより、「伊藤」を理解できたように、中国においても「薛濤」が持つ意味合いを考えてみたい。日本人が平家にまつわる背景には、どのような事情があるのか。

『剪燈余話』も『今古奇観』も、薛濤の才能をともに高く評価しており、長々と詩歌にページを割いているのもひとえに彼女の才能を知らしめるためである。孟沂を虜にできたのは、単なる美人でその色香を持って魅了したからというよりは、それにも勝る才能をもって、孟沂の心を話さなかったからと訴えており、孟沂に別れることを強いた父親や雇い主も、孟沂の手にした唐代の珍品(文鎮や筆たて)に驚く、と同時に、原典では書き残した詩歌の断片によってより深く印象づけられている。中国の原典は、薛濤の数奇な

人生を彩るものの一つとして、彼女の詩の才能を高く評価したといえよう。では、薛涛とはどのような人生をたどった人物なのであろうか。ここで簡単に触れておきたい。

薛涛（七八一？－八三二）は、唐代きっての女流詩人で、四川省成都に居住した実在の人物である。生年については異説があるが、「女校書」の異名をとり、高駢のみならず、元稹、杜牧などとの交際があり、多くの詩を残した。また、薛涛箋という赤色の小ぶりの便箋を作り出したことでも世に知られる。この便箋は、多くの人に珍重され続けたと言われている。有名な薛涛箋をすいたのは、成都市郊外の浣花渓といわれ、現在は成都市内の錦紅を臨む望紅楼公園内に、その井戸がもうけられている。明代の職人が薛涛箋の再現を試みたのが、現在の公園のあたりであり、それが望紅楼公園建設の基礎になったとのことである。

薛涛の娼婦像が、幾世代を経ても才能ある男子を求めつづけるというのが作品の主題だが、ハーンはむしろ純情な女性としてその詩才を十分発揮したという見方が強い。彼女が娼婦であったことを否定する書物さえあるが、大方のところは妓女としてその詩才を十分発揮したという見方が強い。薛涛は、もともと裕福な家の子女であったが、官吏として赴任した父親に伴って成都に移り住んだものの、頼りとする父に死なれて長安に帰ることもできず、苦界に身を沈めることになったという。彼女の娼婦説を否定するものでさえ、薛涛が良家の儀式の際に詩を創作して詠唱していたことを伝えており、当時の歌詠みという地位の低さから逸話が誕生したともいわれている。[2]

薛涛の紹介文のみならず、ハーンが使用した中国の原典では、彼女の詩を高く評価している。高名な遊女、妓女を取り扱った『北里誌』などにも「薛涛」の名前が見られることから、薛涛の才知に対する理解なくしては一連の中国の物語を理解することは難しかったであろう。それ以外にも、薛涛の埋葬された地に植えられた桃の木など、一つ一つの小道具が作品の中で持つ意味合いが問われる作品となっているので

ある。それだけに、ハーンの取り扱いの手並みが問われることになるのであった。

「織女の伝説」と「七夕」について

ところで、「伊藤則資の話」にはいってきたのは、「孟沂の話」ばかりではない。すなわち、『当日奇観』の作者は、「七夕」の伝説をも「伊藤」の中に加味したのである。幽鬼の姫と伊藤が十年後の再会を約したというところに、七夕の伝説が存在するといわれる。いうならば伊藤の物語は、中国を起源とする二つの話が混ぜ合わさってできたものなのである。偶然かもしれないが、ハーンは、「孟沂の話」ばかりか「織女の伝説」("The Legend of Tchi-Nieu")と題する物語を同じ『中国怪談集』の中に収録している。これらの作品の原典が日本に紹介されたとき、日本人作家は、別個に入ってきた幾つかの要素を混ぜ合わせることによって、それぞれの物語を日本人好みの作品として仕上げたのであった。「伊藤」もその一つであることから、ハーンの目にとまったのかもしれない。

このようにして、偶然とはいえ、かつてニューオーリンズでハーンを引き付けた中国の物語は、日本の作品となって、再び彼の前に表れたのである。しかも、ハーンは、七夕に関する「天の川奇譚」と題するエッセイを、「伊藤則資の話」が収録されているのと同じ作品集『天の川奇譚』に収めているのである。

また、「天の川奇譚」の中で、ハーンは「七夕の祭」は「織女の祭」であると明言している。「織女」の元になった話は、時代の変遷とともにいくつかのエピソードが加わって、現在の七夕説話になったといわれるが、その経緯はどのようになっているのか。これらの疑問に答えるためにもハーンの使用した原典をみてゆきたい。

では、ハーンはどのようにして「織女の伝説」の元話を入手したのか。

「孟沂」、「織女」いずれの作品にも老子への言及がみられることから、ハーンは道教関係の書物からアイデアを得ていたとも考えられよう。例えば、ハーンのこれらの作品を翻訳した平井呈一氏は『中国怪談集』の末尾の解題で、「織女の伝説」については「この話は、老子の書いた『感応篇』の第三十四章から採った伝説である」と述べて、「織女の伝説」にさらにジュリアン氏訳と称する話（織女が孝行息子を機織で助ける話）を載せている。だが、老子は『感応篇』を書いてはいない。『感応篇』は老子の道徳を理解するために南宋時代に書かれた注釈書であるから、この一節は平井氏の思い違いにしても、ジュリアンの手になる仏訳本の原典はいったい何をさすのであろうか。つまり、ハーンが拠り所にした、ジュリアンの仏訳というのは、いったい何なのか。

このジュリアンとは、コレジド・フランスの権威であったスタニスラス・ジュリアン（Stanislas Julien, 1799-1873）をさすものと考えられよう。彼は、数多くの中国語の作品を仏訳しているが、代表作は『老子道徳経』(Le livre de voie et de la vertu: Par le philosophe Lao-Tseu, 1842) といわれる。富山大学のへるん文庫にはシュレーゲルのみならず、ジュリアンの仏訳の作品もいくつか入っているが、ジュリアンの作品のうちで、『太上感応篇』にあたると考えられるのは、(Le livre des récompenses et des peines, 1835) である。これは、ところどころに中国語をさしはさんだ仏語訳であり、「織女」に該当するものとしては、「福禄隋之」(Le bonheur et les employs l'accompagnent) があげられるのである。

では、どうして「織女の伝説」が「七夕説話」の原典としてみなされるのであろうか。現在の七夕の風習から、再会するものが「七夕」と考えてしまいがちだが、古代のものは決まった日に再会するというような話はついていなかったらしい。実際ハーンが参照した作品「織女の伝説」は、「董永伝」と呼ぶところのものであることが、ハーン作品自体からも、また前述の平井氏の解説にある短い物語からも明らかで

ある。では、「董永伝」とはどのようなものであったのか。

「董永伝」の源は、漢代の劉向篇の「孝子伝」、すなわち孝行息子の物語であるといわれる。この「董永伝」は、それ以降、『法苑珠林』、『捜神記』さらに『霊芝篇』などに収められており、内容は時代を経て大きく変化を遂げている。しかも、「董永伝」そのものが「孝子伝説」と「七夕伝説」の結合と見られるという。ハーンの作品は、天女が孝行息子（父の葬儀を出すために貧困から自分の身を売り奴隷になった）の妻になり、機織をして借金を返済して奴隷の身を自由にすると、孝行息子を奴隷から解放するだけで天女の勤めは終わるものであり、時代を経て、この短い形式の董永伝に一子をもうけるというエピソードがつくことになったが、さらに後代になると著しい変化が生じ、董永の子供の母親探しが加わり、中には羽衣伝説まがいのものまで出現したという。ここまでくると、かなり怪しい雲行きであるが、ハーンのものが、初期の簡潔な「董永伝」ではなく、一子を設けるエピソードが付いた作品、つまり前述した『太上感応篇』を下敷きにしたことが確認されるのである。しかし、時代を隔てたどの版でも共通して使用されているのが、「天帝の命により地上に降りた織女が、任務を全うしたあかつきには再び天に帰る」という部分であるる。それゆえ、織女は天女（仙女）であり、天への帰還は運命付けられていたと考えられよう。任務を遂行したあかつきには必ず天に帰るという期限付きの中での愛であるからこそ、決まった日にしか遇うことを許されない七夕に匹敵すると考えられるのかもしれない。

語りなおしの手法について

すでに「孟沂」、「伊藤」とハーンが施した語りなおしの特徴については言及してきたが、ここでもう一度その特徴を整理したい。独自の物語をあたかも小説を書くかのように創りあげることをねらいとしたハーンは、好みの作品に語り直すことに余念がなかった。語りなおすといっても、結末をひっくり返すようなことは決してなかったが、彼独自の理想の愛、至上の愛を成立させる小道具として、要素を加えたり、省いたりするのだった。

たとえば、恋するものたちの出会いと別れに関しては、ハーンは原典に忠実であった。それゆえ、孟沂の愛欲生活は半年あまり続き、伊藤はわずか一夜のこととなってしまった。しかし、伊藤の出会いの期間に関しては、原典に従わずに秋としてしまったのである。それというのも、恋人たちの再会のための期間が十年でなければならないと考えたからだった。日本文学における秋の意味を理解していたハーンは、冒頭部分から物語に一貫性を持たせるべく、この物語の舞台にふさわしい秋の光景を作りだそうとしてページを費やすのであった。時には、伏線を張りすぎたという印象さえ与えるほどの念の入れようである。例では、より説得力のあるものにしようとして、ハーンは他にはどのように手を加えたのであろうか。例えば、孟沂については、「もし孟沂がこの忠告に耳を傾けなくても、それは若さと、もともと楽観的な思慮の無さによる[6]」という老子の言葉を入れたりもした。また、孟沂が辿る光景には原典にない描写を事細かに付加えた。[7] 爛漫の桃花の馥郁とした春の光景は、人を夢心地にさせるのもしかたないと感じさせるかのようだ。このような設定を施すことにより、孟沂を霊界にいざなうには十分すぎるものを用意した。

16 ― 文化受容の証人、ラフカディオ・ハーン

伊藤にあっては、自らの解釈で秋と季節を設定しただけでなく、周囲の環境の静寂さと日本の村の暗さを繰り返し強調するのだった。日本の村落についての冗長的な説明も、その意味では読者を幻想的な世界にいざなうプレリュードであった。そして、ここでいう幻想の国とは、死者の国に他ならない。

序論や序章で主人公がこれから訪れようとしている幻想の国の印象を強く植え付けようという手法は、それまでのハーン作品でもよく使用された。例えば、「黄金の泉」("The Fountain of Gold")、「熱帯間奏曲」("The Tropical Intermezzo")、「夏の日の夢」("The Dream of a Summer Day")など、枚挙に暇が無い。これらの主人公は、時には徒歩で、時には船に乗ってでかけるが、図らずしてこの世とあの世の境を越えてしまうのである。まさに、期せずして桃源郷に足を踏み入れてしまう感覚である。そこに住む美女に請われて、異郷の民となるものの、人間界への望郷の念捨てがたく、一時帰国を請う。人間界にもどるや死が待ち受けるか、あるいは死に相当する「苦」を経験する。たいていは、異郷の乙女との再会を願いつつ死んで行くというものである。つまり、死ぬことにより再び乙女との絆を結ぶことを願うのである。

伊藤にしても、一度迷い込んで死者と交わったからには、彼に残された道は、あの世に出向いて再会するしかないのである。伊藤の場合、再会のための迎えがくるのが十年後という、いわば執行猶予が与えられていることで、他の物語とは多少異なるが、この猶予期間をおいた再会の約束が「七夕」を連想させ、よりロマンティックである。ただし、この十年の猶予はハーンが作ったものではなく、『当日奇観』にある元話に忠実に従っただけだが、この十年間の伊藤の変化については、ハーンらしい工夫が見られるのである。

伊藤は不思議な体験については何も語らなかった。だが、家族や友人たちはたちどころに容貌やしぐさに表れた変化を見逃さなかった。医師はどこも悪いところはないといったが、日毎に顔は青ざめ、やせ細り、まるで幽霊のようになり、動くと影のようであった。以前も思索に耽り、孤独がちであったが、今度ばかりは、かつて楽しんだものにも関心を示さない様子だった。例えば、名を挙げようとして取り組んだ文学の研究さえ関心を失っていた。母親は所帯を持たせたらかつて抱いていた大望を蘇らせ、人生への執着を取り戻せるかもしれないと考えたが、生き身の女性とはだれとも結婚しないと誓ったと伊藤は言い放った。歳月はゆっくり過ぎていった。ついに猪の年の秋が巡ってきた。伊藤はかつて楽しんだ一人で散歩することさえできなくなっていた。床から起き上がることさえできなかった。誰にもわけはわからなかったが、伊藤の命運はつきようとしていた。あまりに深く、しかも長く眠ったので、死んでしまったかと間違うほどであった。[8]

たとえば、「生き身の女性とはだれとも結婚しない」とか、「ついに猪の年の秋が巡ってきた」の後に続く変化、「眠りは死んでしまったかと間違えるほどであった」などは、幽霊と結婚したものに起こる変化と考えられる。猶予があったとはいえ、死者と契りを交わした後の伊藤の様子は死者同然である。『当日奇観』の伊藤は迎えがあの世からくる約束の日まで元気であったのみならず、死者である姫の墓を求めて捜し歩き、見つけたあかつきには僧侶に頼んで施餓鬼供養さえしてもらっている。『当日奇観』の伊藤は、死者の埋葬地を確認する意味でも、自分のできることを行い、与えられた猶予期間を有効に過ごした観があるのに対し、ハーンの作品では、伊藤の十年はあってなきがごとしと

でもいえるのである。

ハーンの書き直しは、あの世へと続くトンネルのようなくらい村の印象ばかりでなく、その後の伊藤のおぞましいような変化に凝縮される。仏教的な要素を排除し、純愛に生きる伊藤を強調するあまり、姫に対して精神的に殉死させた。つまり、伊藤の十年をむなしいものにしてしまったのである。姫との再会だけを願う伊藤にとって、十年はあっという間に過ぎることをむうしかなかったのだとでもいいたいように。男の側の任務に執着するハーンは、仏教的なそこにロマンティスとしてのハーンの片鱗をみるのである。考えとか、風習とか一切無視して、たとえ相手が亡者であろうと取り交わした約束の実行に終始させたのである。

しかし、視点を変えると、伊藤の物語をハーン流に変えることを可能にしたのは、日本人の仏教に対する考え方だともいえる。ハーンが参考にした『当日奇観』の伊藤の物語は、幾多の変遷を経てきたかもしれないが、『当日奇観』としてまとめられたとき、この世とあの世の区別が厳密になっている。中国の孟沂の場合は、死者との交わりはその後の生活においてむしろプラスになるものであったし、死者と交わったからといってそれで死者の世界にひきずりこまれるということはなかった。ところが、日本に入ってくるや、死者と生者は住み分けることになった。死者との交わりはタブーとなるが、それだけに、そのタブーを超えるかどうかは、愛情の深さを測る尺度とハーンは考えたのであろう。姫に思いを寄せられた伊藤は、何度生まれ変わろうと、亡者の姫の思いから逃れることはできないことを知らされるが、その思いの強さにむしろ心を動かされ、嬉嬉としてそれに答えている。この伊藤の前向きな思いに感動したハーンは、自分の作品では、伊藤を理想の恋する男に仕立てるために、よりいっそうの工夫を施したのである。

中国の物語である「孟沂」（『今古奇観』）が日本に紹介されて「伊藤」（『当日奇観』）に翻案されたとき、

死者と生きるものの世界が区分されたと書いたが、中国でも死者と交わったために死者の世界に引きずり込まれるという物語がある。これが、最初に挙げた、伊藤とは対照的な男性主人公の登場する、「牡丹燈記」である。ハーンはむしろ、恋愛においては軽蔑すべき男性の典型をこの作品に見出したが、怪奇譚としての日本的な特徴に魅了されて、「宿世の恋」として語りなおした。この作品は「孟沂」以上に日本にもたらされてからの変遷の跡が鮮明である。最後に、この作品の語りなおしの経緯を引き合いに出しながら、本論を締めくくりたいと思う。

「牡丹燈籠」の成立

ハーンが、恋愛においても責任を逃れようする男を、情けない男の代表として語りなおしたと思しき、萩原新三郎こそ、この物語、「宿世の恋」の主人公である。原典は中国の『箭燈新話』の「牡丹燈記」である。この作品の受容と変遷の歴史は、「孟沂」以上に明らかである。ハーン自身、中国に原典があることを理解して語りなおした作品である。では、この作品はどのように受容され、ハーンとしてはさらにどう語りなおしたのか。孟沂同様、その変遷をみてゆきたい。

『箭燈新話』（十四世紀末）の「牡丹燈記」は、孟沂や伊藤の物語と設定のいくつかを共有している。まず、人間の男と幽霊の女の組み合わせである。ただし、「伊藤」の話とは異なって、男と女の間には何一つながりは無い。その点では「孟沂」と似ているが、知的なつながりではなく、ただ愛欲で結びついた関係である。また、伊藤が子供の侍女に導かれたように、牡丹のついた燈火を掲げた侍女が幽霊の女に従うという点でも共通するものがある。

この話を簡単に要約する。男やもめが幽霊とは知らずに美女と見るや恋に落ちるが、隣家の老人の忠告で相手が幽霊と知るや、魔の手から逃れようとして道教の法師に救いを求める。法師にお札をもらい、指示に従って家に引きこもり、ひたすら幽霊の女からの解放を祈る。一定の時が過ぎ去り、もはや悪霊から救われたとして外出するや、女の遺骸が安置されている寺に引きずり込まれて悲惨な結末を迎えるというものである。これだけで終わらず、その死後女とともに悪霊となった男は、女と侍女との三人連れで人間界をうろつき、出会った人々に災いをもたらしたが、より徳の高い僧に罰せられるという勧善懲悪的な結末をもつ。

原典は、江戸時代に日本にもたらされ、『奇異雑談集』、『幽霊の事』、『あやし草』などの中の一作品として翻訳された。女の霊に殺された後から結末までの道教的エピソードは、日本では省略された。文字通りに和訳されただけでは、それほどの普及は見なかったであろうが、上記三冊と前後して出版された、浅井了意による『伽婢子』の「牡丹の燈籠」として人口に膾炙した。さらに明治になって、落語家、三遊亭円朝の高座により「牡丹燈籠」としてさらに広く知られるようになったのであった。

浅井の翻案小説『伽婢子』が目指したのは、これまで述べた「伊藤」同様、日本人に馴染みのある内容にすることであった。まず、舞台を正月十五日から日本では死者の霊が帰るといわれる七月盆へと変えた。そうすることにより、妻を亡くした男やもめにとっては、幽霊の女の訪問は亡き妻の帰還として受け入れられるのだった。もちろん、主人公以下の名称は日本的なものにし、また背景も日本を舞台とするものにした。また懲罰的エピソードを割愛することにより、仏教的「因果」を強調して終わりにした。

これだけでもずいぶん日本的になったのだが、円朝の「牡丹燈籠」は、主人公の名を、『伽婢子』の「荻原新之丞」から「荻原新三郎」へ、幽霊の女を二階堂左衛門尉政宣の息女「弥子」から旗本飯島平左

衛門の息女「お露」へと変えた。円朝は「萩」と「露」という組み合わせを楽しんだとのことである。また、曲亭馬琴の「累解脱物語」や古典落語の「腰抜刀屋」のエピソードも取り入れたといわれる。さらに、本来日本の幽霊は足がないといわれるのに、円朝のお露は「カランコロン」と下駄の音を立てて萩原を訪ねるのである。

このように工夫を凝らした円朝を、ハーンは「宿世の恋」でそのまま踏襲した。日本の幽霊話の最高峰へと押し上げた円朝の功績について自作の中で次のように述べる。

東京の舞台でいつも成功を納めるのは、菊五郎一座による「牡丹燈籠」である。この幽霊劇は、場面が前の世紀の中ごろ（十八世紀中期）で、円朝が話し言葉で書いた恋愛ものの舞台化である。もともと中国の話だが、その特色からは純日本的といえよう。その舞台を見に行ってきた。菊五郎のおかげで、恐怖の世界という新たな楽しみが加わったのである。[9]

ハーンの述べる円朝の高座の舞台化とは、明治二十年（一八八七）七月、春木座で上演されて好評だった「牡丹燈籠」が、これを機についに明治二十五年（一八九二）七月、歌舞伎座で上演されるようになった。読み本としても、明治十七年（一八八四）、速記記者の若林玵蔵が円朝の高座を速記してそれを東京稗史出版社から、十三冊の和装本にして出版したという背景がある。[11] このように円朝も のが、明治中期には一斉を風靡するようになっていた。

では、ハーンはこの作品をどう取り扱ったかに触れたい。実際の「牡丹燈籠」は因果がめぐる長い話だが、ハーンが「宿世の恋」で使用したのは、牡丹の燈籠を持ったお露主従が萩原を訪ね、拒否されると使

用人を買収してついに男を殺して霊界に引きずり込むという圧巻の部分である。この部分だけの簡潔な作品としては、明治二十二年（一八八九）に「牡丹燈」（三頁足らずの小品）という題で、『夜窓奇談』（石川鴻斉篇）に出ている。この作品は円朝の高座を簡略にしたものとのことである。ハーン自身がこの作品については直接言及したものはないが、『夜窓奇談』は現在富山大学のハーン文庫に残っている。

ハーンの作品は、登場人物の性格描写が丁寧に行われており、女から逃れようとした萩原を批判するものの、友人の言動として萩原のような優男を使わないと筋が面白くない旨を述べている。また、現世のみに生きる西洋人ならともかくも、生まれ変わりを信じる仏教徒のくせに、自分を慕ってあの世から舞い戻った女を見捨てようとすることは許しがたいという。そのうえ、身近な時代の物語であることを訴えるかのように、お露主従の墓場探しなどを試みたという。虚実入り混じるエピソードを添えている。また、先ほどの「歌舞伎」での好評を伝えるに加えて、西洋人にこの話を紹介するのは、日本人の怪奇に対する考え方を紹介するためだとして、その意義を説くのだった。

ハーンの語り直しの元話となった作品の中には、翻訳され、さらに翻案を繰り返すうちに、原典の形をとどめないものもある。ハーンはむしろ、宗教とか習慣を超えたところで、彼独自の恋愛ものを創作することに専念したが、あとから付け加えられた部分を剝ぎ取ったために、かえって原典の味がもどったもの、あるいは日本的な雰囲気が増したものにも、中国にその起源をもつものが多々あることを、ハーン自身が自覚していたように、一見日本の伝統的な作品と思われるものにも、様々である。ハーン自身が自覚していたように、一見日本の伝統的な作品と思われるものにも、中国にその起源をもつものが多々あることを、小説の下敷きとなれる作品を模索する過程で見出したに違いない。また、異文化の受容の場面に立ち会うたびに、その研ぎ澄まされた感性により、表面的には異なっていても、その根底にある普遍の要素を感じ取り、作品として結晶させた。とりわけ、早い時期から中国文化に親しんできたハーンは、日本にあっては受容された作

品の様々な形を確認することになった。そんなハーンの作業は日本文化のルーツを明らかにする作業とでもいえるもので、自己の創作を通して、文化的アイデンティティを模索し、葛藤する日本人の姿をも映し出すことになったのである。

[注]

1 Ferris Greenslet, ed. *The Writings of Lafcadio Hearn* (N.Y.: Houghton Mifflin, 1922), 1: 289.
2 Zhang Zheng and Ji Guoping, *Poetess Xue Tao and Park of River Viwing Tower*. (Sichuan Publishes, 1995).
3 平井呈一訳『小泉八雲作品集』第九巻（恒文社、一九七六年）の解題部分、三一九頁。
4 Stanislas Julien, *Le Livre des récompenses et des peines*, (London: Richard Burlington, 1835), 119-20. 中国語による教訓とそのフランス語訳のあとに、それを具体化した物語がついている。次に挙げるのは、その物語である。これが平井氏が言及したものと考えられる。『感応篇』はあくまで老子の教えをわかりやすく説くために南宋時代に作られた書物であり、物語が具体的な教訓となっていることから、ハーンにとっては格好のテキストとなれたのであろう。

Histoires

Tong-yong, qui vivrait sous la dynastie des Han, était réduit à une extrême pauvreté. Ayant perdu son père, il se vendit afin de gagner, par son salaire journalier, de quoi l'élever et lui élever un tombeau. Le maître du ciel eut pitié de lui, et lui envoya la déesse Tchi-niu pour qu'elle devînt sa femme. Elle lui tissa chaque jour une pièce de soie, jusqu'au moment où elle ne put le racheter. Après quoi elle lui donna un fils, et recomonta au ciel. Sous le règne de King-ti, Tong-yong se distingua par sa piété et son désintéressement, et obtint la charge de Tchong-wei. Son fils, Tchong-chou, devint ministre du roi de Kiang-tou.

Ainsi, le bonheur et les emplois ont accompagné Tong-yong, parce qu'il avait rempli les devoirs de la piété filiale.

5 西野貞治「董永伝説について」（『人文研究』、大阪市立大学六-六）
金岡照光「敦煌本「董永伝」試探」（『東洋大学紀要』文学部篇、一九）
中鉢雅量「異類説話の変容――中国恋愛文学史素描の試み」（『中国学会報』、二九）
6 *The Writings* 1 : 224.

7 *The Writings* 1：224-25.
8 *The Writings* 8：327-28.
9 *The Writings* 9：257.
10 永井啓夫『三遊亭円朝』（青蛙社、一九九八年）一一四—一一六頁。
11 矢野誠一『三遊亭円朝の明治』（文春文庫、一九九九年）一一二—一一三頁。
12 *The Writings* 9：257.

17 カール・フローレンツとの関係から見たラフカディオ・ハーン

佐藤マサ子

[1] はじめに──御雇い外国人カール・フローレンツ

　ラフカデイオ・ハーン（一八五〇-一九〇四）については、既に多くの人々による多面的な研究によって、その作品や生涯に関しての解明は非常に進展している様に見受けられる。そこで小稿では、従来考慮されることの無かったドイツ人御雇い外国人、カール・フローレンツ（一八六五-一九三九）との関係を伝える資料を基に、これ迄とは些か異なる角度からハーンが置かれていた当時の社会的な状況や彼が目指したものについて考察したい。

　フローレンツは、帝国大学の雇い外国人教師として初代独文学科教授を務め、第一世代の独文学者を育

成し、ドイツ語ドイツ文学教育を通してドイツの思想や文化を広く文科大学（東京大学文学部の前身）の学生達に伝える一方、ドイツ文献学的方法に基づいて日本古典の研究に力を注ぎ多くの成果を残すと共に、これに拠って、今日で言うところの比較文化・比較文学的研究にも道を開き、現在では殆ど忘れ去られているとはいうものの、この方面からも多くの分野に影響を与えた。一九一四年の帰国後には、ハンブルク大学にドイツに初めて設置された日本学科の初代教授となり、今度はドイツ語圏に現在の日本研究の基礎を築いた。それ故、現在のドイツ語圏の所謂アカデミズムの日本研究は、彼を直接の始祖として現在に至っている。[2]

ハーンは来日当初の一時期と、後には又同僚として、この十五歳年若いドイツ人と交際があった。ハーンと英国人バジル・ホール・チェンバレンとの関係については、書簡資料の研究の成果等によって詳細に知られている。フローレンツは足かけ十年帝国大学でドイツ語ドイツ文学に加えて博言学の教授を兼任し、比較言語学をも講じたが、これはチェンバレンの辞任に伴うものであった。それは一八九一（明治二十四）年十一月からのことであり、この年は丁度ハーン来日の翌年にあたっており、この同じ年の夏にはフローレンツが松江にハーンを訪ねている。[3]

ハーンより二年前に来日したフローレンツは、同時期の雇い外国人教師達が次々日本人に置き換えられていったこの時期に、異例の二十五年余同職にあった。折しも、日本がプロイセンをモデルに新国家経営に邁進していた事情もあって、彼は近代日本の人文科学が構築されていく過程に直接関与した。この点、長く在野にあり、更には同じ東京帝国大学との関係に置いても、御雇い外国人としては不本意な退職をせざるを得なかったハーンとは一種対照的な立場にあったと見られる。

ハーンの日本論の中でも、特に『日本——一つの試論——』（*Japan, an Attempt at Interpretation*）の

成立を考える上では、以上に概観した様なハーンの数多くの作品の中でも、特にアカデミックな作品と言われ、最後の大著でもあり、最晩年迄彼はこれに力を注ぎ続け、一九〇四年の急逝後に出版されたという事情を負っている。

以下に見る様なハーンとフローレンツとの交友関係を、個人のレベルを越えた、いわゆる時代のアカデミズムのトレンドの中での関心事やテーマ化の在り方、或いは学問的な方法の問題等との関わりの中で捉えてその意味を問うならば、ハーンとフローレンツという対照的な二人がそれぞれに追求した物の意味や特色が、より顕著に浮び上がってくるのではないだろうか。

[2] フローレンツの日本古典研究とその史的意義

フローレンツはライプチッヒ大学でサンスクリットの文献学的研究により博士号を得て間もなく、一八八八年に二十三歳で来日した。翌年には帝国大学独語講師となり、二年後の一八九一年十月からは教授待遇となって学生を育てる一方で、彼本来の目的であった日本研究を継続した。ライプチッヒでの学生時代、当時人文科学の先端分野でもあった比較言語学を、現在ではフェルディナンド・ソシュール（一八五七 - 一九一三）への影響をもが指摘されているゲオルク・V・d・ガベレンツ（一八四〇-一八九三）に学び、更にガベレンツの下で、彼が研究中であった漢字や中国語文法に関する当時のドイツでは全く新しい知見をも習得していた。[4]

この様な複合的で先鋭性を帯びた学問修行が、後に彼が日本研究を志す上に大きく貢献し、且つ方向を

決定することになる。斯かる背景に加えて、程なく新日本の学界を担うことになる井上哲次郎（一八五五-一九四四）や有賀長雄（一八六〇-一九二一）との遭遇が、フローレンツに日本を対象に文献学的研究をその手で実際に行う為の直接の契機を与えた。この様にして実現した彼の日本への旅は、インドから中国、更に尚東漸を続けるヨーロッパ比較言語学の対象範囲拡大の道筋と、当に軌を一にしていた。5

フローレンツは来日後直ちにドイツ東洋研究協会（OAG）や日本アジア学協会に所属し、主にOAGでの口頭研究発表や研究紀要への寄稿を基盤に次々と研究成果を蓄積していく。6 やがて日本書紀の注釈翻訳として結実する彼のテーマの一つの中心は、有賀長雄が明治憲法施行に伴う啓蒙活動の一環として皇典講究所で行った講演内容と、チェンバレン（一八五〇-一九三五）の英訳古事記（初版一八八二年、特に訳者の序文）とに触発され、社会構造に対する関心に端を発した日本古代文献史料の研究であった。記紀は当時国家体制を思想的に保証する神道の「バイブル」の役割を果たし、明治国家の主権の正当性を歴史的に証明する拠り所でもあったから、厳格なテキスト批判のトレーニングを積んできた若き文献学徒の目には、古代研究が即、現代研究そのものとなる千載一遇の状況が眼前に展開しているかの如くに映ったものと思われる。7

現在では、このフローレンツの翻訳注釈よりもよく知られているウイリアム・G・アストン（一八四一-一九一一）の英訳（初版一八九六年）に先駆けて、一八九二年から推古紀以後の注釈翻訳を逐次発表していったが、更にそれより以前、一八八九年六月には「中国文化流入以前の日本社会の状況」と題する報告を行い、古代史料翻訳注釈の前提ともいうべき、日本古代の政治や社会の基本的組織構造に対する本格的解明を行おうとしている。8

その方法は、現在の研究史に於いては津田左右吉に起源が措定されている文献史学の方法、即ち文献史

料を批判的に突き合わせて解釈を加える事を通して歴史的な事実を掘り起こす手法に拠っており、古代社会の基本構造である氏組織と氏相互の関係、一氏族としての天皇家の支配形態、良民賤民の区別、土地所有の形態、そして更には、その様な社会組織下にあって何故に天皇権のみが唯一伸張拡大したのかが論じられている。ここでは、今日の日本古代史の基本的問題設定そのものが、殆ど全て網羅的に考慮されている。[10]

史料の基礎的解読や解釈に於いては、本居宣長等の言語研究を基にした研究成果を受容する一方で、単一言語資料だけを基に行う場合の、求め得る知見の限界を指摘し、グリムやボップの研究以来、ヨーロッパで関心を集めていた印欧比較言語学の成果が齎した方法を取入れるべきであると主張し、就中アルタイ諸語との比較の必要性を熱心に説いている。つまり、印欧比較言語学の方法に立脚して「語」の形成諸要素や語素としての音韻の構造分析等を行い、語源に遡って意味を確定していく方法に基づくならば、アルタイ諸語との比較を通して広範な言語資料を基礎に語義判断をする道が開けるのみならず、更にはそれを基に、史料解釈にも新たな可能性が拓かれるとする。チェンバレンも同様の主張をしているが、学問的な厳密性に於いてフローレンツが指摘した方向が、その後比較言語学や国語学の課題として開拓されていった。彼自身もそれを記紀解釈上で試みているが、この方法は現在に至る迄記紀を始めとする日本古代文献の解読の基本的方法として定着している。[11]

フローレンツは更に、比較神話学や民族学・民俗学等の方法論をも駆使して伝説や器物・習俗の収集調査をも行い、特にアーネスト・サトウ(一八四三—一九二九)の祝詞英訳の継承の意味を持ってもいた「大祓祝詞」研究の為には、佃島住吉神社の祭式の実際と歴史料との詳細な対比を行っており、今日の民俗学のフィールド・ワークによる調査と文献研究との総合を図ってもいる。[12]

この様に、フローレンツは終始、記紀などの古代文献史料を多角的な実証研究によって解読しようとしてこれに務めており、その為に主観を抑えて翻訳注釈の形式で原資料を提示する事に努力を傾注した。彼は、自分が提供する原テキストの翻訳注釈によって、日本人の精神世界に関する一次資料がヨーロッパの広範な学識、即ち多くの学問分野の知見の前に提供される事になり、それによって、テキストが含み持つ内容の解釈や判断が得られて、更にそれがより広範な可能性を開く事ができるようになり、それこそが何にもまして重要だと考えたからである。そしてこの方法と実践の在り方こそが、彼が訓練を受けた十九世紀のフィロロギー（Philologie）の理想に外ならなかった。[13]

通常「文献学」と訳されるフィロロギーは、「言語とそこに込められている精神への愛」を原義とすると解され、紀元前三世紀に既に「古典」であったホメロスを学ぼうとした詩人達が、異なる方言によるテキスト理解の為に、テキストを形態的・内容的に分析して、そこから、(1)テキスト中の真偽を見分け、(2)異なる言語の特質を把握し、(3)テキスト理解上の困難な点を解明する、という三点をその課題とした事に起源があるとされる。フローレンツが学んだ十九世紀のフィロロギーは、この考えを「広い世界の多くの言語と、そこに込められている精神」を対象とし、その為に、研究主体が既成の価値観を廃して厳密に対象そのものに相対する事を基礎とした。対象を尊重するそうした立場から、多様なそれぞれに持っている精神の歴史が重視され、歴史主義的で厳密な批判を基調とする学風が形成された。[14]

フローレンツの、この様にフィロロギーに忠実な日本の歴史資料の翻訳注釈は、先述の如くドイツの学術世界に向けて行われたのであり、ドイツのみならず当時ヨーロッパ諸国一般に於ける日本人の内面（思想・宗教）を知る為の基礎資料の不足の解消への貢献が目的であった。彼の精度の高い基礎研究が信頼を得て、やがて、当時ドイツで盛んであった、ユニバーサルな「各国別」文学史や宗教研究シリーズものの

一巻に、「日本文学史」や「日本宗教史・宗教史料」が加えられることになった。更にそこから、文学のジャポニズム現象とも言い得る日本趣味の詩歌等が二十世紀紀初頭のドイツに出現する事態も生ずる。[15,16]以上の様なフローレンツの志向した学問とその背景となった教育や広い意味の文化と、今や人口に膾炙しているの観のあるハーンの著作内容や背景としての諸事情とを比較した時、両者の間に大きな立脚点の相違があった点については多言を要さない事が明らかであろうかと思われる。

［3］フローレンツの松江訪問とハーンとフローレンツの交友

一八九〇年、ハーンが「漂白の一旅人として」[17]横浜に到着し、その年の九月には島根県尋常中学校雇英語教師となった翌一八九一年の七月、先述の如く、フローレンツが松江を訪れて数日ハーン宅に滞在した。この年に、ハーンは松江藩士族小泉セツと結婚し、彼女の献身によって日本や日本人に対しての関心を深めていったことはよく知られている。[18]ハーンはこれから程なく（同年十一月）熊本第五中学校（一八九四年には第五高等学校となる）に転じ、一八九四年一月にこれを辞してから文科大学英文科講師となった。二人は今紙の記者として働き、この時に東京帝国大学からの招聘によって文科大学英文科講師となった。二人は今度は帝大の同僚となったのである。この間の二人の交友を語る記録に拠って、暫くその様子を見ておこう。

『山陰新聞』「明治二十四年七月九日（木）」には、「独逸人来る。」と題する以下の記事が掲載された。

　大学御雇教師独逸人フロレンツ氏は、昨八日伯耆国米子より汽船米子丸に乗り込み正午着松、直ちに北堀に居住せし当尋常中学校教師ヘルン氏方へ投宿せり。[19]

続いて同紙「七月十五日（水）」には「賞与と紀念附たり参観」と題する記事が掲載された。中学校英語教師ヘルン氏は受持の生徒中最も勉励せしもの、即ち五年、四年、三年、二年生の内、各二人、二年生四人へ書籍を賞与せり。又滞松中のフローレンツ氏は一昨日師範学校女子部を参観せし紀念として、生徒一同へ日本文典、仮名遣枕詞字典、国文学読本、能勢学校管理等の書籍一冊宛を贈与せる由。而して氏は本日市内の各小学校を参観すると云へり。[20]

ハーンの助力者として知られる西田千太郎の日記からも、簡潔な文体乍ら、諸事情が良く分かる明晰な記述によって、フローレンツの松江訪問の様子が伺える。その七月八日の記述によれば、「ヘルン氏方ニ今日来松の大学教師独人フローレンツ氏ト会談ス。午後ヘルン氏方ニ同博士ヲ訪ヒ、晩餐会食快談時ヲ移ス」とあり、また十日には「フローレンツ博士ト中学校ニ会談ス。ヘルン氏方ニ伴ヒ、フローレンツがハーン方に止宿し、英語をよくした西田が二人に加わって話が弾んだ様子や、また西田の案内でフローレンツが松江市中を見学散策した様子（「十六日（晴、時々雨）ヘルン氏ヲ訪ヒ、フローレンツ氏ト伴ヒ天守閣ニ登り、市中散歩、望湖楼ニ同氏ノ饗ヲ受ク。」）等が伺える。[21]

『山陰新聞』七月十五日の記事に相当する内容については、同内容のことが知られる。ハーンはフローレンツが松江滞在中、市内の全教育機関を訪問し、特に師範学校の程度の高さに感嘆したこと、教育会で演説してその後夕食会が設定されたこと等と共に、師範学校の女子卒業生各自が手芸作品を彼に贈り、これに対してフローレンツが松江を去る前に各に立派な書物を返礼として贈り一同を驚かせたことなどを記している。[22] 西田の日記の以下の記述も、またこの間の事情を裏付ける形になっている。

344

知の新視界

（七月）十一日ヘルン氏方ニ至リフロレンツ氏ト伴ヒ、教育会ニ出デ同氏ノ演説ヲ通訳ス。師範女子部ニ至リテ数時間ヲ費ヤシ、ソレヨリ中原倶楽部ニ至リテ教育会ヨリ饗応ヲ受ク。賓客ハフロレンツ氏、ヘルン氏、中山氏、及予ニシテ主人ハ斉藤会長、羽左田理事。十一時帰宅ス

（同月）十三日フロレンツ氏、女子師範卒業生ニ書籍ヲ贈与シ度トノ事ニ付協議ヲ受ケ、書籍商ヲ伴ヒ夜間同氏ヲ訪ヒ、夜半帰ル。シャンペーン酒ヲ饗セラル。[23]

『山陰新聞』七月十五日の記事が伝えているハーンが「受持の生徒中最も勉励せしもの」を賞して書籍を贈ったという、良く知られているこのハーンの教育努力の背景には、以上の記述からするに、西田を交えたフローレンツとの歓談のあった事情が伺い知られる。尚、この時フローレンツが松江を訪れた理由が、公務であったのか、全くの私的旅行であったのか、現在迄に知り得た資料から確かなことは言えないが、末松謙澄がほぼ同時期に松江を訪問していることや、同年十月からフローレンツが雇い外国人教師として、事実上の独文主任教授になったことなどから推測すると、教育行政に関わる何らかの公務の性格を帯びていた可能性を全く否定することはできない。

以上に見てきたようなハーンとフローレンツの関係からは、この時に突然生起したのではない親密さを感じとることができる。こうした関係が生起する背景を語ったものとして、晩年のフローレンツを知り得る立場にあった由良哲次（東京高等師範教授で哲学者）によるフローレンツに対する追悼文（一九三九年）の中にある次の記述が注目される。

由良は一九二八–三一（昭和三–六）年にハンブルク大学に留学し、晩年のフローレンツと時折対談する

機会があったというが、以下の引用は、フローレンツがハーン来日当初のことについて聞いた事を語っている一節である。

ヘルン即ち小泉八雲氏が最初日本に来たのは、米国のある新聞誌と関係ある通信員としてであって、それも正式の派遣記者としてではなく、事実は落莫とした漂白の一旅人であった。そして最初から決して日本に対する魅力を含んだ熱情を感じていた理ではなかった。ヘルンは初め当時既に裕富な生活をしていた某外人（中略）に身を寄せていた。所がその家の夫人が、どうしてもヘルンの風格、性格と相容れず、ひそかに嫌悪されていた。（中略）しかし明からさまに断わることも出来ないので、フローレンツ氏が話をして、一時自分の家に寄食せしめたこともあった。当時尚一部には極端な外人嫌悪と、しかし一部には甚だしい外人崇拝との交錯し、毫も尚落ち着きのなかった時代に、縷々として日本人の魂の真味とその性状の潤いのあることを語り、ヘルンの心を次第に日本に向わしめたとの事であった。そしてヘルンの松江に職を定めることにも助言し、かつ勧奨したそうである。ヘルンが真に日本に好意を持ち始めたのは、やはり固有の落着いた地方の気風に接し、これに入り込んだ以後のことであり、殊に次第に深く日本を理解し始めたのは、日本人を夫人に迎え、その助力によって、いろいろの書物を読み取る様になってからのことであった由である。[24]

以下は、ドイツ東洋研究協会の一九一一（明治四十四）年活動報告中の三月一日の記録である。それによれば、この日東京のOAG例会においてヴェンテイッヒ教授（Prof. Dr. Waentig）による「民族心理学

者としてのラフカディオ・ハーン（Lafcadio Hearn als Völkerpsychologe）」と題する講演が行われた。その時の様子が次のように伝えられている。

> …討論ではE・ユンカー氏が個人的見解に基づくハーンの生涯に関して報告をした。長年に亘って友人として暮らしたフローレンツが、今後別の機会に於ける更に詳しいハーンの生涯についての報告を約束した。議長（フローレンツ）がヴェンティッヒ教授に対してその興味深い発表に感謝の意を表し、多くの拍手の内に閉会した。[25]

この記述からも、二人の交友関係は当時良く知られていたことが伺われる。

ところで、このOAG例会での約束に従ってその後フローレンツがハーンの生涯に関する報告を行った形跡はなく、一九一四年に彼は帰国し、彼の帰国途中に第一次世界大戦が勃発した。[26] 戦争当事国、敗戦国という道を辿ることになったドイツの命運の影響を受け、OAGの活動はフローレンツが彼の業績を蓄積していった当時の充実と華やかさを失い、定期的に発行されていた大部であった年報や報告書類の出版も影響を受け、数年分合冊の形態をとることによって辛うじて年報の刊行だけはし続けるという状態となった。[27]

フローレンツ自身もまた、第一次大戦時下と戦後の故国で、誕生間もない日本学講座を維持していく為に多大な労力を必要とした。またフローレンツの性格は、彼が生涯志向し続けた Philologie の精神と相似していた様子で、印象批判的なものに対しては禁欲的であり、手紙を書くことも、日記雑録の類を残すことも少なかった。[28] 彼の没後、第二次大戦下でのハンブルク空爆（一九四三年七月）によって、万葉集注釈の

遺稿を始めとする多くの資料が焼失したが、以上のような諸点からして、焼失した遺稿の中に、フローレンツがハーンの生涯について現在知られている以上の回想を書き残した物があった可能性は低いように思われる。

以上の様に、一九一一年三月のOAG例会での約束が実現された形跡は認められないが、フローレンツは、彼の学問が依拠したフィロロギーに極めて忠実な方法で、ハーンの業績を紹介している。即ち、ドイツの宗教史教科書の一節に日本の宗教を担当執筆した際(Die Japaner, in: Lehrbuch der Religionsgeschichte Bd.I, Tubingen 1925)に、アストンの翻訳(W.G.Aston, Nihongi, Chronicles of Japan from the Earliest Times to A.D. 697, 1896)や神道論(Shinto, The Way of the Gods, 1905)等、或いはグリフィスの『日本の宗教』(W.E.Griffis, The Religions of Japan, 1895)等と共に、ハーンの著作をも参考文献として掲載したのがそれである。これによって、ハーンの『日本瞥見記』『日本——一つの試論——』の二著はそれぞれ、独訳紹介されていた(L. Hearn, Glimpses of Unfamiliar Japan. 2Bd., Boston 1895 は"Idzumo"und "Lotus", Blicke in das unbekannte Japan. Frankfurt a.M. 1906/7として、又 Japan, an Attempt at Interpretation. New York 1905 は、Japan, ein Deutungsversuch. Frankfurt a.M. 1912として)事が知られる。

西田の日記には、この訪問中にフローレンツは杵築(出雲大社)を訪れると共に、西田から方言資料を入手した事も知られる。西田は「出雲音図写、出雲言葉ノかきよせ及ビ其註補及ビ正誤書(予ガ特ニ同氏ノ為ニ一編セルモノ)ヲ贈ル」と謙遜簡潔に記述している。フローレンツは博言学の授業で南東諸語の比較文法等をも講じ、ガベレンツ門下生として、当時の印欧比較言語学の版図に日本語を加え位置づける事に一種の使命をも感じていた節もあるから、篤実で向学心に溢れる西田が、彼の依頼に対して応えたのだと

解し得よう。フローレンツの日本書紀の翻訳（推古、舒明、皇極）が最初に刊行されたのはこの一年後にあたる。日本書紀翻訳は、その後時代を下る形で継続刊行された後、神代の巻が『日本の神話』として刊行されたから[33]、何らかの形でこれら資料や経験が生かされていったであろう事が想像に難くない（日本書紀翻訳はその後、孝徳紀・斉明紀（一八九四年）、天智紀・天武紀（一八九五年）、持統紀（一八九六年）と続き、更に一八九八（明治三十一）年十一月には「神代の巻」に関する翻訳を『日本の神話』として纏め、博士論文として提出し、翌年六月には文学博士号を授与された）。

これ迄に見てきた経緯からして、フローレンツが杵築の出雲大社を訪れた事と、『日本瞥見記』に記されている杵築大社訪問の記述に語られているハーンの感動との間に影響が無かった事は寧ろ考え難い。一方、西田の日記によれば、フローレンツは杵築から帰って直ちに米子に向けて出発し（七月二十五日）、その翌日からハーンは西田と共に杵築へ向かったという。前後の記述からして、前もって計画されていた様ではないから、学問的な訓練を積んだフローレンツの観察がハーンに何らかのインスピレーションや示唆を与え、杵築再訪を促した可能性も否定できない[34]。

二人の日本への関心やそれを基にした両者の著述には、二人の極めて異なった個性が反映しているばかりではなく、双方の記述内容からは、人間が事物を把握する時のその仕方に影響を与えているそれぞれの個人の背景にある教養の傾向や文化の相違性が浮かび上がってくる。その相違性故に相互に影響し合ったであろう可能性を、以上に見てきた諸記録の行間から読み取る事ができるのではあるまいか。

[4] おわりに――ハーンとフローレンツのそれぞれの出雲

フローレンツはこの松江訪問に際しての、極めて印象深かったと想像される杵築の出雲大社訪問について、その経験を想起させる記述を全く残していない。ハーンが語る杵築の大社との遭遇に纏わる印象深い詩的な記述[36]とは全く正反対と言い得る程の対し方である。出雲の旅の経験を想起させる記述を彼の注釈書中に敢えて探すとすれば、出雲の幾つかの地名の解説以外では「スサノヲ」の名義と神格についての概略以下の様な内容の詳細な注解かと思われる。

アストンが出雲風土記の郷名「須佐」に根拠を求め、「須佐の男」と解すのにフローレンツは「すさまじ」の例等を引いて「荒れ狂う」「荒ぶる男」の意だと反論し、神格に関する記述（イザナキの鼻からの出生や激しい涕泣等）が語義と照合するとして、比較神話学の研究報告をも引用し、此の神が東アジアに広範に分布するする嵐の神の一例であると証明した。

この注釈末尾に特に「杵築大社（出雲大社と呼ばれる）の宮司の血統はスサノヲノミコトに由来すると され、現当主（千家氏、男爵位）は、スサノヲから数えて三十二代目だとされる。人々はこの宮司を「生き神」と称している」と付記して居る。[37]ここから僅かに実地見聞の経験が背景にある事が憶測される。

このように研究者（主体）の体験や想念は一度論証過程の実証で濾過し、主観性を極力排除して、客観に近づけようとする所に彼の思考や記述の特色がある。これは彼が依拠した十九世紀人文科学の傾向を反

映し、其の学問の「文法」に立脚して研究対象（客体）を記述したからに他ならず、この点に於いて同時代の日本研究者サトウ、アストン、チェンバレンの中でも彼は最も徹底していた。[38] 従って自身の経験と感性、特に鋭敏な直感による記述に生命があったハーンとは極めて対照的だったと言わざるをえない。

ハーンは、その出雲で初めて日本の伝統社会の美風を知り、出雲の神々を介して民俗に関心を傾けるようにもなった。しかし強く心惹かれて理想化した日本を、その後のより深い日本体験に基づき掘り下げて分析した『日本──一つの試論──』で、陰影を加えた日本観が形成展開される迄の最終過程で、二人は今度は帝大文科大学の同僚として過ごす事となった。一八九六年九月から、一九〇三年一月にハーン宛に井上哲次郎名の解雇通知が届き、同年三月に退職する迄である。彼はこの間、次第に同僚達の中で孤立感を深めていった。[39]

ハーンは退職後、アメリカのコーネル及びスタンフォード等の大学での日本に関する講演の可能性を期して準備を始めた。何れも実現せずじまいであったが、この草稿を著述し刊行しようと試みたのが『日本──一つの試論──』であった。[40] 上述のような経緯から、学術的な内容である事に務め、二十二項目からなる構成に基づき、日本を解明しようとしている。祭りや家族及び家庭生活、神道、仏教、武士の忠義等の項目と共に「社会組織」が取り上げられている。世界の代表的古代社会の組織から説き起こし、日本の伝統社会の構造を、主に西洋社会と比較する観点にたって解説している。ここでハーンはフローレンツの前掲「中国文化流入以前の日本社会の状況」の報告を基礎とした論文「日本古代における国家と社会の組織」を紹介し、特に古代社会組織については殆どこれに依拠し、これを噛み砕いた形で解説している。[41] これをハーンのフローレンツ、特に古代社会組織についての研究成果への信頼の現れと見るばかりでは充分ではなく、寧ろ当時の内外アカデミズムに於けるフローレンツ評価に則ったものと見るべきであろう。[42]

ハーンの帝国大学に於ける孤立とは相反して、フローレンツは一八九九年前掲のように、研究成果の蓄積が評価されて外国人初の文学博士号を授与された。彼が修得し指向していたものが当時の日本には喫緊のヨーロッパ最新学術そのものを具現しており、実際の教育活動のみならず、日本研究の成果の実例を通しても方向と方法を明示し、それに拠って次第に周辺の新世代の学究に刺激と影響を与えていたからである。[43]

日本社会に於ける幾つもの困難な経験を経て、ハーンは時が経つと共に日本社会の陰影深い霊的世界への関心を更に強めていく。彼の直感が捉えた印象を読者の心中に再現する効果的描出は、今尚其の世界へと我々を誘うが、それは亦フローレンツが理性に依拠して解明提示しようとした対象でもあった。往時から百年を隔てた今、彼等を魅了し探求に駆り立てずにおかなかった顕現する事象の数々も、或いは其の背後に見え隠れした魂の在り処も、既に多くは我々の周辺から姿を消し去ってしまっている。

一方、今日におけるハーン研究の盛況に対して、フローレンツが殆ど忘れ去られてしまった観すらある現今の状況自体からは、過去への関心は現代を映すものであり、事物を秩序付ける研究という行為、或いは過去を把握する行為としての歴史記述そのものが、現代の枠組みの反映によって成立しているという事実[44]が自ずと浮かび上がってくる。嘗ての理性尊重を標榜する規範が過去の物となり、個人の感性を重視して共感を媒介に理解を拡げる傾向へとパラダイムそのものが変化した二十世紀後半のトレンドを、二人に対する関心や評価の背景に読み取る事が或いは可能かもしれない。

少なくとも、フローレンツの研究成果を手本に、日本人の内的世界の意味付けが標榜された時代とは、日本がプロイセンを手本に近代国家を形成しようとしていた時代であり、その影響が社会的枠組みのみならず精神世界のシェーマをも外郭から方向付けていた一九四五年以前の事であった。

[注]

1 ハーンの著作と年譜は平井程一全訳『小泉八雲作品集1-12』、『ラフカディオ・ハーン著作集1-15』(恒文社一九八八年)、伝記と日本観は築島謙三『ラフカディオ・ハーンの日本観』(増補版)(葦草書房一九八四年。初版一九六四年)、平川祐弘『小泉八雲 西洋脱出の夢』(新潮社、一九八一年)、チェンバレンとの関係は河島弘美「ラフカディオ・ハーンとバジル・ホール・チェンバレン」(『比較文学研究』三五、一九七九年。一二六-一五三頁)、遠田勝「神国日本」考—チェンバレンとの対立をめぐって—」(『比較文学研究』四七、一九八五年。二四-五三頁)、小泉凡「小泉八雲 参考文献目録」(№四三-八、一九九八年、所収の諸論文及び小泉凡「小泉八雲年譜」(一三四-七)「小泉八雲参考文献目録」(一三八-一四〇)を参照した。尚、本稿はこの『国文学』特集号所収の拙稿「ハーンとカール・フローレンツ—日本の神々との対峙をめぐって—」を、一次資料を補って大幅に改稿したものである。

2 フローレンツの生涯に関する諸資料、著作目録と日本研究の概要、就中文学史、万葉集、神話や神道、古代史の研究が当時の日本の研究者にとって規範的意味を持って受容されたことは、更にはこれ等の研究が基礎となって比較文化や比較文学的研究が多方面に拡がっていったことに関しては、拙著『カール・フローレンツの日本研究』(春秋社、一九九五年)を参照されたい。尚、フローレンツと日本に於ける比較文化・比較文学的研究の誕生との関係については、千葉宣一「最初の比較文学論争」(『現代文学の比較文学的研究—モダーニズムの史的動態』八木書店一九七八年所収」を参照されたい。

3 前掲(注1)平井程一年譜及び(注2)同書二一二頁参照。

4 ガベレンツの言語学史上に於ける意義についてはE. Coseriu, Georg von der Gabelentz el la linguistique synchronique. in: Günter Narr, Uwe Petersen (Hg.), Die Sprachwissenschaft, ihre Aufgaben, Methoden und bisherigen Ergebnisse von Georg von der Gabelentz (Tübingen 1972)と前掲拙著一七一、一九八一-二〇三頁参照。ガベレンツの中国文法研究(Georg von der Gabelentz, Chinesische Gramatik, Leipzig 1881 (Ndr. 1953))は、少なくとも一九七〇年代において「尚有効である」と評価されている(Günter Narr, Uwe Petersen, Vorwort der Herausgeber, 前掲書一-二頁参照)

5 (注2)拙著所収のフローレンツがライプチッヒ大学時代の恩師エルンスト・ヴィンデイッシュに宛てた一連の手紙(三〇八-三一九頁)参照。

6 (注2)同書二〇六-二四二頁参照。

7 Nihongi oder japanische Annalen, übersetzt und erklärt. Teil III, Supplement-Heft v.OAG, Tokio 1892-97,

8 B. H. Chamberlain, *The Kojiki, Record of Ancient Matters.* 1882, Tokyo 1981 (repr.), 有賀長雄「日本上世の政体」(『皇典講究所講演』第一巻一所収)及びこの間の事情については前掲拙著一二六―一三五頁参照。

9 William G. Aston, *Nihongi, Chronicles of Japan from the Earliest Times to A.D. 697*, 1896, (repr.) Tokyo 1982. フローレンツのこの報告はその後論文 Die staatliche und gesellschaftliche Organisation im alten Japan として Mitteilungen der Deutsche Gesellschaft für Natur-und Völkerkunde Ostasiens (以下MOAGと略記する) 44 (1890) Bd.V, 一六四―一八二頁に掲載された。

10 (注7) *Japanische Mythologie* 序文III-V頁参照。この研究は安藤正次等に継承された(『安藤正次著作集四』)参照。安藤はフローレンツの著作目録を作成してもいる(「カール・フローレンツ先生の東亜研究」『愛書』六、八、九、一九三六年)。

11 フローレンツの古代史研究がモデルとなっていた事については前掲拙著一三六―一四七頁参照。

12 Ancient Japanese Rituals, Part IV, Transactions of the Asiatic Society, Vol. XXVII (1899), 1-112頁参照。この様な彼の研究が当時のアカデミズムの世界での注目の的であったことや、フローレンツが柳田国男の民俗学研究に影響を与えていた点については、前掲拙著一一七―一二五頁参照。

13 フローレンツの研究が一貫してフィロロギーの方法と精神に則って行われた点、或いは又、同時代の日本人によるフローレンツの「所謂新しい日本古典研究」が、実際に彼が行った西洋フィロロギーの方法による日本古典研究を手本に、彼と同じ方法(殆どフローレンツの著述の翻訳に近い場合のある点をも含めて)によって行われた点、そしてそれら多くの研究書がその点について明記していない点等については、先掲拙著四六―六〇、一四八―一六四頁参照。

14 Ernst Bratuscheck (Hg.), *August Böckh, Enzyklopädie und Methodologie der philologischen Wissenschaften*, Leipzig 1877, Gerhard Jäger, *Einführung in die Klassische Philologie* (3.überarbeitete Auflage), München 1990, 214-233頁参照。

15 フローレンツの著書がどのようにドイツのアカデミズムの世界に紹介されていったか(新聞などの書評掲載等を含めて)、或いはまた世界文学史叢書(各国別)の一巻として刊行された彼の『日本文学史』に依拠して八

ンス・ベトケやアントン・ライザー等の日本趣味の詩集が出版されたかの諸点、ベトケの詩にG・V・フォン・アイネムが曲を付けて歌曲集が生まれた経緯等については、前掲拙著二三〇、二三九、一〇〇-一〇九頁参照。

16 フイロロギーが西洋中心主義による知的支配としての異文化評価の思考様式であり、植民地主義を構造的に支える知的支配の様式であったとするエドワード・サイード『オリエンタリズム』(大橋洋一訳、一九九〇年平凡社、原著一九七八年)等の主張とは一様に論じ難い問題が日本に於けるフイロロギーの受容についてはあり、考慮される必要がある。就中フイロロギーが自国文化の把握の方法として受容された点、即ちフイロロギー内在化の諸相に関する事例は概念的にではなく、実体に即して考慮される必要がある。

17 由良哲次「晩年のフローレンツ教授」『科学ペン』四号、一九三九年、一三〇-一頁参照。

18 前掲(注1)同書参照。

19 広瀬朝光『小泉八雲論――研究と資料』笠間書院一九七六年、一五八頁参照。

20 前掲(注19)同書一五八-一五九参照。

21 島根県郷土資料刊行会編・発行『西田千太郎日記』所収年譜(六三頁)と考えられる。尚、一九三〇年前後に由良が聞いている「フローレンツのハーンに関する消息」については、従来の論議の対象である良く知られている資料との対照が為されていないだけに注目される必要があろう。特に、一八九六-七年のハーンの西田やヘンドリック宛書簡と対照すべき資料であると思われる。

22 前掲(注1)『小泉八雲作品集一五』所載の翻訳「島根・九州便り」四九七頁。

23 前掲(注1)同書一一五頁参照。

24 前掲(注17)同書一三〇頁参照。

25 前掲拙著二四六-二五三三頁参照。

26 前掲(注1)同書参照。尚、翻訳は佐藤。

27 MOAG Bd. XIV, XVI, XIII 頁参照。

28 Carl Wegmann u. Robert Schinzinger, *Die Geschichte der OAG—1873 bis1980*—Tokyo1982 参照。

29 前掲拙著二五四-二六〇、三〇八-三〇九頁参照。

30 前掲拙著二六九頁参照。

Die Japaner. *in*: A. Bertholet u. E.Lehmann (Hg.), *Lehrbuch der Religionsgeschichte* 4. Aufl., Bd.I, Tübingen 1925, 264-5 頁参照。

31 前掲（注21）同書一一五-一一六頁参照。

32 前掲拙著二一二頁参照。

33 前掲 *Japanische Mythologie*.

34 前掲『小泉八雲作品集五』所収の「日本瞥見記」に記されている「杵築」（一二五-二八一頁）、「杵築雑記」（三二六-三六一頁）、「日ノ岬」（三六二-三七五頁）参照。

35 前掲西田の日記の同年七月十二日条には「目下滞松中ナル千家氏ヨリ車ヲ以テ迎ヒヲレ旅館皆美方ニ饗応ヲ受ク。同客八岡本、山内、毛利諸氏。夜半ヲ過帰ル」とあり、その後の同月二十二日には、「フロレンツ杵築ニ往キテ未ダ帰ラズ」とある事からして、ハーンの出雲大社訪問と同様、フロレンツも西田を介して出雲大社宮司千家氏に大社訪問の許しを得て訪問した可能性が極めて高い。ハーンは大社訪問が千家氏と昵懇の西田の紹介に拠ったと記している（前掲『小泉八雲作品集五』二三六頁）。
（注34）西田の日記の一節「フロレンツ氏杵築ニ往キテ未ダ帰ラズ」がこれを物語っている。同日記、七月二十五日条には「昨夜杵築ヨリ帰着ノフローレンツ氏ニ逢ヒ、ヘルン氏ト共ニ同氏ノ饗応ヲ松勢水亭ニ受ク。午後五時同氏ノ米子ニ向テ出発スルヲ見送リ」とあり、恐らくは松江滞在予定の限界近く迄を杵築で過ごす事になった物と見られる。

36 前掲（注34）のハーンの出雲大社訪問の記述参照。

37 前掲 *Japanische Mythologie*,二一九-二三〇頁参照。

38 前掲拙著二二三-二三六、二一〇-一二三五頁参照。

39 前掲（注1）のハーンの年譜七五〇頁。この背景については井上側の回想「小泉八雲氏（ラフカデイオ・ハーン）と旧日本」が詳しい。帝大講師招聘から在職中における学生や同僚との関係、性格や日本観、或いは退職に至る事情の詳細迄が『懐旧録』に収載されている（春秋社、一九四三年、二三二-二五八頁）。雇外国人を日本人に置き換える当時の方針の中で、夏目漱石帰朝に伴い、ハーンの講義時間数の調整が必要となり、拗れた事が、哲学教授ケーベルの皮肉な一面とは相容れなかった経緯などが、事実を追って記されている。管見によれば、ハーン研究ではこの資料に注目していない様に思われる。ハーンの書簡に記された当時の背景を対照把握する上に興味深い。

40 前掲（注1）『小泉八雲作品集十一』所収「日本―一つの試論―」及び訳者による解説（四六九-四七四頁参照）。*Japan, an Attempt at Interpretation* の書名の日本語訳は複数あるが、平井呈一の一九六四年の同翻訳に従った。

41 前掲（注40）同書二二七-二五四頁参照。訳者による解説にチェンバレンやアストン等の研究・著作の影響が解説されているが、ハーンが明記しているフローレンツ説の影響には触れられていない。尚、同書についてのハーバート・スペンサーの歴史観の影響等については築島謙三（注1）前掲書一六六-二四七頁参照。

42 一八九六（明治二十九）年七月の『史学雑誌』はこの論文を紹介している。その後も同誌をはじめ『早稲田文学』『國學院雑誌』等が彼の古代史・古代史料研究、研究動向についても紹介を続けている（前掲拙著一三九-一四〇頁参照）。

43 前掲拙著二二六-二二七頁参照。

44 ミッシェル・フーコー『言葉と物―人文科学の考古学―』（渡辺一民・佐々木明訳、新潮社、一九七四年）。

中国白話翻訳小説管見

『通俗大明女仙伝』をめぐって

小田切文洋

はじめに

　江戸時代の中期、荻生徂徠やその門下の護園学派の人たちを中心として、漢文訓読の弊害を正すための唐話研究の機運や、黄檗宗の伝来などによる中国趣味の流行を背景にして、白話で書かれた中国の通俗小説類が流行したことは、諸家によって説かれている。明から清初にかけて書かれたこれらの小説は、初めは唐話の学習教材や研究資料であったが、やがて個々の作品自体の面白さに目を開かされ、小説そのものとして読まれるようになる（中村幸彦「近世初期の小説観」『近世文芸思潮攷』岩波書店一九七五年）。従来の日本の小説や物語にはない面白さを伝え聞いて愛読者が広がるとともに、白話文にあまり通じていな

い読者のためにも通読の便宜を与えるため、初めは原文に訓点や訳解（白話語彙である「在下」や「注定」に、それぞれ「ソレガシ」「サダマル」と施訓して意味を取らせるもの）を施したものが、やがては原文から直接の翻訳が行われるようになる。白話小説の翻訳は、頭に「通俗」と銘打って刊行され、かなりの数になる。その主なものは、『近世白話小説翻訳集』全十三冊に収められている。白話小説とその翻訳である通俗物は、読本作者に素材や構想にわたって大きな影響を与えている（麻生磯次『江戸文學と中國文學』三省堂一九四六年）。こうした文学作品への影響ばかりでなく、江戸中期から明治期にかけて、さまざまな性格の文献中にかなりの数をもって認められる（小島憲之『日本文学における漢語表現』岩波書店一九八八年）。白話小説を構成する語彙そのものが、その訓訳とともに、白話小説の翻訳は、原作の理解や受容、また白話語彙（近世中国語）と日本語との交渉という点でいろいろと興味深い材料を提供するだろう。小稿ではそうした通俗物の一つである『通俗大明女仙伝』を択び、基礎的な問題を整理したい。

［I］

和漢雅俗に通ずる三宅嘯山を訳者とする『通俗大明女仙伝』は、寛政元年（一七八九）の刊行である。滄浪居主人の号による自序には、安永九年（一七八〇）と記されている。嘯山七十三歳の時である。蕪村一門とも近い関係にあった三宅嘯山の俳人としての名声を高めたのは、宝暦十三年（一七六三）四十六歳の時に刊行した『俳諧古選』である。元禄期の俳風への復帰を提唱し、発句を選評したこの撰集には、嘯山の漢文による「惣論」が付され、松尾芭蕉を始め有力作者達が活躍した元禄期を頂点として、前後二時期に分けて俳風の変遷が説かれている。その一節に、

厳羽卿曰。詩有別材。非関書也。詩有別趣。非関理也。然非多読書多窮理則不能極其至。豈惟詩哉。（俳諧叢書本に拠る、一三九頁）

と、漢詩の本質を説く南宋の厳羽の言葉を引いて、和歌や連俳も同じだとする。詩の才能は書物の知識とは関係しないし、またその面白さは真理の探求とも関係しないと述べた一節である。この引用に続いて、厳羽の『滄浪詩話』「詩弁」には、

所謂不渉理路、不落言筌者、上也。詩者、吟詠情性也。盛唐諸人惟在興趣、羚羊掛角、無趾可求。故其妙処徹玲瓏、不可湊泊、如空中之音、相中之色、水中之月、鏡中之象、言有尽而意無窮。

（郭紹虞『滄浪詩話校釈』人民文学出版社一九六一年二六頁）

と、詩の本質論が展開されている。虚空に響く音響や、水に映る月のように捉えがたく、しかも残像が持続するのが詩の妙趣だと述べたものである。唐詩を範とする点や詩の鑑賞眼において、嘯山が『詩話』に学んだ点は大きいという（田中道雄『俳諧古選』の成立」『近世文学作家と作品』中央公論社一九七三年二〇八−二二〇頁）。このような正当な詩文への素養も豊富にもつ嘯山が、白話で書かれた通俗小説に関心を持ったのはかなり早い時期のことと思われる。宝暦九年（一七五九）四十二歳の時には、奇行の禅僧道済を描いた『酔菩提全伝』全二十回の翻訳をしている。

こうした通俗小説類への関心は、伊藤東涯門の儒者である芥川丹邱との交流から来ていると思われる。丹邱は、同門で『忠義水滸伝解』の著者でもある陶山南寿とともに、白話を田中大観から学んだ。大観は

「小説詞曲に於てはほとんど天才的性分を有してゐたが、可惜哉僅か廿六歳の青年を以て膝風を病んで没した。…大観にして之れに仮すに尚ほ数年を以てしてしたならば、必ずや冠山・白駒以上に小説戯曲の荒野を開拓したに違ひない」(石崎又造『近世日本に於ける支那通俗語文学史』清水弘文堂一九六七年一五九頁)と、その白話への天分が高く評価されている。この大観に学んだ南寿の『忠義水滸伝解』は、白話小説読解の現代を通じても最高の水準を示しているとされている(高島俊男『水滸伝と日本人』大修館書店一九九一年七七頁)。丹邱の周辺のこうした中国の通俗小説への熱心な探求心が、嘯山を刺激して翻訳の作業へ向かわせたものと思われる。俳人としても大成した嘯山晩年の翻訳である『通俗大明女仙伝』の性格を次に検討していきたい。本文は、『近世白話小説翻訳集』所収の影印本に拠る。『通俗大明女仙伝』の性格を次に検討していきたい。本文は、『近世白話小説翻訳集』所収の影印本に拠る。原作は、康熙五十年(一七一一)の自序跋のある呂熊の『女仙外史』である。百回二十冊本で、釣璜軒貯板、大塚秀高氏の『増補中国通俗小説書目』(汲古書院一九八七年二四二頁)によれば異本はない。原作の本文は、釣璜軒貯板を底本に排印した文衡標点の岳麓書社のものによる。翻訳は、原作の三十回までであるが、刊記に「後編嗣出」とあるので、意図的に三十回までとしたのではないだろう。原作の『女仙外史』の我が国における影響は、清初の白話小説である『好逑伝』などとともに、曲亭馬琴『開巻驚奇侠客伝』の趣向に生かされていることが、麻生磯次氏の前掲書(『開巻驚奇侠客伝と支那文学』)により跡づけられている。しかし、『好逑伝』が早くに西欧に紹介され、我が国でも国学者の萩原広道が翻訳の手を染め、近代の佐藤春夫が完訳(下訳は伊藤弥太郎)しているのと比べて、『女仙外史』は従来あまり注目されてきた作品ではない。

[II]

『女仙外史』は、建文帝と叔父の燕王（後の永楽帝）とが争った靖難の変と永楽十八年に山島省で起こった唐賽兒の乱を素材に取っている。明初に起きた靖難の変は、当時の世の中を動かした大きな政変であるとともに、建文帝の死が不明なため、中国では伝説の世界に好個の話題を提供している。この一連の事件を素材にして、人間の命運を見つめた近代小説に生まれ変わらせたのは幸田露伴である。その名作『運命』の冒頭のところで、『女仙外史』への言及がある。数少ないこの小説への言及であるとともに、作品の本質をよく突いたものとなっている。

其の書の体たるや、水滸平妖伝等に同じと雖も、立言の旨は、綱常を扶植し、忠烈を顕揚するに在りといふを以て、南安の郡守陳香泉の序、広西の廉使劉在園の評、河西の学使楊念亭の論、広州の大守葉南田の跋を得て世に行はる。幻詭猥雑の談に、干戈弓馬の事を挿み、慷慨節義の譚に、神仙縹渺の趣を交ゆ。西遊記に似て、而も其の誇誕は少しく遜り、水滸伝に近くして、而も其の豪快は及ばず、三国志の如くして、而も其の殺伐はやゝ少し。たゞ其の三者の佳致を併有して、一編の奇話を構成するところは、女仙外史の西遊水滸三国諸書に勝る所以にして、その大体の風度は平妖伝に似たりといふべし。憾むらくは通篇儒生の口吻多くして、説話は硬固勁率、談笑に流暢尖新のところ少きのみ。

18 ― 中国白話翻訳小説管見

露伴は、『西遊記』や『平妖伝』の神仙譚的な性格、『三国志演義』の軍記的な性格、『水滸伝』の慷慨節義的な性格をそれぞれ取り混ぜた小説として『女仙外史』を評価しているのである。歐陽健『中国神怪小説通史』(江蘇教育出版社一九九七年二九四頁)をみても、神怪という虚構成分に歴史的事件を流し込んだものとして、この作品を評価している。

「答秋斎」と題する七言古詩によれば、嘯山もこの小説の多彩な内容を高く評価していた(田中道雄「解題」『近世白話小説翻訳集 第三巻』汲古書院一九八五年六三三頁)。また、これから検討していく『通俗大明女仙伝』の序文中でも、

其行文、波乱照応、鏡花水月、有順有逆…

と、文章の変化や結構の妙味を賞賛している。ところで、この一節の前で、嘯山は表現や話柄といった面ばかりでなく主題の上からもこの作品に一定の評価を与えている。それは、正史類が憚って書かなかった燕王の簒奪の罪を描いていることである。

簒弑之罪、欲蓋弥彰。外史用力排之。一閲則使人揮臂於案上。於是乎建文之朝、忠臣孝子名姓、炳然于千載之後。而誅奸諛於地下、発鮫直於世上。何等感慨也。(九頁)

とあるその一節は、原作者の自序に、

と、「燕賊反」の三字を史官が削ったことへの公憤を述べるものがあるだろう。
『女仙外史』の大凡の内容を、嘯山自身の評価を通して確認したところで、次に訳風の検討をしていきたい。前掲の田中氏の解題には、量的に多い削除箇所の指摘とともに、全体を評して「翻訳態度については、緩急自在な、その多様さが注意される。短いながら原文を存して訓点を施す部分、忠実な逐語訳の部分、原文脈に添いつつ自由に直訳する部分、また十行を一行に縮約する部分があったりする」とされている。
今、任意の箇所を原文と対照させながら挙げてみる。

已而于燕王則曰 "受天之命"、夫燕王既為天子矣、為其臣者諱之亦所宜然、乃并諸大忠臣探舌血而書 "燕賊反" 之三字而俱泯滅之時何哉。武王、聖人也、夷、斉斥之曰 "以臣弑君"、煌煌然至今猶載史冊。是則皆聖人之所不得泯滅者而毅然敢泯滅之、彼史官也果何心哉。然此三字辰之麗乎天、恐其終不泯也、遂并帝之年号而尽削之、帝之遜国以後事迹而尽滅之。高皇崩于三十一年、乃称至三十五年、下接永楽元年、若謂并無此建文一帝者。(七頁)

今_{イマ}カノ家_{イェウ}乳母_{ウバ}ヲ尋_{タツヌ}。你往テ事ナラバ造化アラン。故ハ此姑娘後大ニ貴カルベシ。我コノ故ニ参リ。尭挙信_{シンジ}難_{サタク}ハ思へドモ賽兒ト乳母ガ様奇ナレバ、重曰。コノ兒甚_{コハナハダソチ}你ト縁アリ。心ヲ添_{ソヘテ}撫育バ。先荊モ亦地下ニ感激ウレシガルベシ。乳母曰。不_レ消説得_{ズヲヨバアセニ}。(五三頁)

他家正要尋箇乳母、你造化、這姑娘他日大貴哩。老身是這箇縁由的。考廉聴了這些話、欲待信他、恐無是理、欲待不信、賽兒這箇情景却又奇怪。因向乳母道、"如今賽兒也就是你的親兒了、望你撫育長成、先荊在地下也是感激的"。乳母道、"不消説得。……"(一五頁)

傍線部分は、原文の「信じようにも…だし、信じまいとしても…だし」というところを、巧み織り込んで訳している。原文の「不消説得」の箇所は訓点を付けているが、「消」はここでは白話語彙としての用法で、必要とするの意で使われている。それに否定の「不」が付くので全体として適切な訳解になっている。「造化」も同じく白話語彙としての用法で、二一七頁などの例がある。原文の「哩」は、白話小説に用いられる助詞で、確認強調の語気を表わす。訳文では「ベシ」でその語気を表わしている。「地下」を「コケノシタ」と和語の添え仮名で読ませたりして、一工夫を加えた平明で分かりやすい訳文になっている。もう一箇所例を挙げてみよう。

老君又賽兒ニ丹ヲ服シメ。尚コヽニ在テ真気ヲ運ジ。半月ヲ過テ後回去ベシト。青牛ニ乗テ出玉ヘバ。一片ノ紫雲脚下ニ生ジ。童子前ニ引テ去給ケレバ。賽兒頂礼シテ。雲影ノ隠ル迄見送テ後。端坐シテ心ヲ静ツメ。神ヲ煉ルコト又半月。今ハ帰ベキ時ナリト。先身ヲ空中ニ踊シ見ニ（一六二頁）

老君又囑嫦娥、服丹須在此間運行真気、過半月後回去。随倒跨着青牛、一片紫雲忽生四足、道童在前引導、賽兒跪着頂礼。直待雲影没了、然後起来、如前端坐冥心煉神。足勾半月、自想已是可帰時候、便飛身于空中。（五四頁）

右に引用したのは、太上老君から丹薬を与えられるという一節である。訳文は原文にない尊敬語を用いて、重々しく、さらに太上老君から丹薬の生まれ変わりであるこの物語の女主人公唐賽兒が、九天玄女から天書を授か

い感じを出している。原作は、世俗の世界と神仙の世界とを交互に描き分けていくが、訳文では、比較的平明な訳文と固い文語調の訳文とでこれを訳し分けようとしているようである。

[Ⅲ]

前掲箇所中にも見えていたが、嘯山が白話語彙をどのように理解していたのか、添え仮名を中心に、次に幾つか例を挙げて検討していきたい。

這廝何ゾ無礼ナル(カレナン)（三四頁）

這廝直恁無礼（五頁）

「這廝」は、大東文化大学中国語大辞典編纂室編著『中国語大辞典』角川書店一九九四年には、白話語彙とした上で、「(人を軽蔑して)こやつ。こいつ」の意とし、『金瓶梅』や『水滸伝』などの例を挙げる。唐話辞書の流れをくむ、藤井理伯撰の『俗語訓解支那小説辞彙』にも「這廝死を恐ザルヤ」（四一二八頁）と訳した例が見える。石川雅望訳『通俗醒世恒言』巻三には、「這廝コイツメ、人ヲ罵ル辞ナリ」とある。なお、近称の「這」でなく遠称の「那」を用いた「那廝(キャツ)」の例もある（二一二頁・二四一頁・三一五頁）。原文にある副詞の「直恁」は、陸澹安編著『小説詞語匯釈』中華書局一九六四年には、「竟然如此。元曲中有之。」とあり、『漢宮秋』の例を挙げる。以外にも、何ととという意である。角川『大辞典』も白話語彙として認めている。訳文は二つの白話語彙を的確に訳し分けたものとなっている。

一定也コレ皇帝ナラン。（四二頁）

一定也是皇帝了。（九頁）

「一定」は、名詞ではなく副詞としての用法で、現代中国語でもよく使われる。「ある根拠を基に下した判断・推定に対する話し手自身の確信を示し」きっと、必ず、絶対に。」（伊地智善継編『中国語辞典』白水社二〇〇二年）の意である。

海上ノ観音ト申ストモ。這様標緻 候ジト云ケレバ。

海上観音也没有這様標緻。（二二頁）

「標緻」は、前掲『匯釋』に「美貌。（呉語）元、明戯曲中亦有之」とある。通俗物の用例では、西田維則訳『通俗赤縄奇縁』巻一「已ニ標致アリテ」（四 二三頁）などがある。

誰可主張。…柏姨夫是箇有名的正経人、有何料理不来呢。（二四頁）

内ニハ誰カ之ヲ主張セン。…青菴モトヨリ老実ノ人。此コト定メテヨキニ料理セラルベシ。（八二頁）

「主張」はここでは白話語彙としての用法で、前掲角川『大辞典』には、取り決める、主となって決めるの意とする。西田維則訳の『通俗赤縄奇縁』には「主張」とある（二 六二頁）。「正経」は、真面目の

意であるが、「老実」の訳語が与えられている。清田儋叟施訓の『照世盃』には「正経」に「マタキ」と添え仮名をする（ゆまに書房刊影印本四五頁）。「老実」の語も、白話小説に用例が見られる。先の『通俗赤縄奇縁』巻三には、「老実(ヲトナシク)」（四　九四頁）と添え仮名をした例がある。

吾兒的舅舅常到京(キヨウ)都生理(ナリハヒ)、(二五頁)

舅氏近日京ニ往テ生理スレバ、(八四頁)

商売の意としての「生理」は、角川『大辞典』で白話語彙として認めている。用例には凌濛初の二拍を挙げる。通俗物の用例では、淡斎主人訳『通俗古今奇観』巻五「生(シヤウ)理(パイ)日々繁昌シテ」（五　七〇六頁）などがある。また、前掲『小説辞彙』には「生理、生活、生計、生産(ワイナリ)以上皆スギ」とあり、柴野栗山の『雑字類編』にも「営生。過活。生計。活計。養口」（巻七人事門）とある。

兩位哥哥説話甚是有理。我的親事(エングミ)一切雑費都算在里(イリメ)面、(三〇頁)

兩位(フタリノ)哥々ノ説(ヲフセ)甚(ハナハダ)理アリ。我親事ニ用タル雑費イカニモ算シ玉へ。(九四頁)

兄弟三人で財産を等分に分ける時、縁談で使った雑費をその中＝「里面」から引いても構わないと同意している場面である。「哥々」は読本類に散見され、例えば曲亭馬琴『南総里見八犬伝』第三十三回に「哥々が今までかへり来ざるは、のがれがたきよしあればならん」などとある。婚事の意としての「親事」の用例に、羅竹風主編『漢語大詞典』漢語大詞典出版社一九九五年は、関漢卿の『四春園』を始めとして

呉敬梓の『儒林外史』などを挙げる。前掲『小説辞彙』には「親事　エンクミ」とある。

多謝県父母指教、俟与長親商酌来候審。
県父母ノ指教有難シ。長親トモ商酌シ侍リテ報ジ奉ラント（一一三頁）

「商酌」は、前掲『大詞典』に「商量斟酌」と釈義し、『夜譚随録』（清代の志怪小説集）や劉鶚の『老残游記』などの例を挙げる。原文の「俟」は、…するのを待っての意であるが、「…シ侍リテ」とその意を含ませた訳文になっている。ただし、「候審」は訳されていない。

「斗胆」は、角川『大辞典』に主に謙譲語として使うとある。こうして厚かましくも…のような気持ちを添えて使われている。

故此斗胆、不嫌自媒。（四一頁）
斗胆　自媒シ侍ル（一二五頁）

夫人如何一往七日。家中都放心不下。
夫人去玉ヒテヨリ七日ヲ過ヌレバ。家内ミナ放心不下侍キ。（一三六頁）

「放心」はここでは安心するの意で、「不下」が下接するとそれを否定して、気が休まらないの意になる。

前掲『小説辞彙』には、「放心 アンドスルコト」とある。安心の意の「放心」の日本語の用例としては、「一身の内を緩和し、人類の放心を求めしむるに忙しければ」（福沢諭吉『文明論之概略』三）などがある。

一人白面（イロジロ）ノ書生（ワカモノ）。外ヨリ来テ。心肝妹子ソコニヤト云ツヽ。立寄テ（一九八頁）

一箇白面文人端端正正站在面前、叫声、"心肝妹子、為何今夜不在床上安臥。"（六六頁）

「心肝」は、前掲『大詞典』には「喩最親切、心愛的人」とあり、また角川『大辞典』は、「古今小説」第三十八巻から「正是我的心肝情人（＝恋人の意）」という例を挙げる。

我モト雨ノ為ニシテ来ル。先雨ヲ降シテ後再汝ト法ヲ闘シメン。本事（ヲボエ）アラバ逃（ニグル）コトナカレ（二一二頁）

看我此刻就求雨来、然後再与他闘法、有本事不要逃走。（七一頁）

「本事」は、日本国語大辞典編集委員会編『日本国語大辞典 第二版』小学館二〇〇一年に「《中国の近世語から》本来の価値。また、本来持っている能力。また、身につけた技倆や日ごろの心がけ。」とあり、寺門静軒の『江戸繁昌記』の例などを挙げる。前述の唐話辞書の一つ『忠義水滸伝解』二回には「本事 テナト云フコト此方ニテ、得手何芸ニテモ、我会得シタル本芸ナリ」とあり、前掲『辞彙』にも「本事 テナト云フコト此方ニテ、得手モノト云ナリ、十分本事、ナドト云ハ、十分ノ芸ト云フコト」とある。なお、一八三頁にも「本事（ヲボエ）」の例がある。

「公差」は、前掲『大詞典』に「臨時派遣去做的公務」の意とし、李漁の伝奇『奈何天』の例を挙げる。『兒女英雄伝』にも、『警世通言』や呉敬梓の『儒林外史』など白話小説の用例を挙げる。角川『大辞典』にも、『警世通言』や呉敬梓の『儒林外史』など白話小説の用例を挙げる。「公差」(オヤクニン)と添え仮名をした例がある。原文にある「官衙」は、官職名の意である。

忽報有両名公差到来、伝進官衙名束。（七三頁）

時ニ二人ノ公差(ツカヒ)来テ名(ナフダ)ヲ伝。（二二五頁）

下級の役人という意もあり、西田維則訳『通俗金翹伝』に「公差」(オヤクニン)と添え仮名をした例がある。原文にある「官衙」は、官職名の意である。

「眼花繚乱」は前掲『大詞典』に「形容看見美色或繁複新奇的事物而感到謎乱」の意とし、『西廂記』や『兒女英雄伝』の例を挙げる。

軍士皆眼花繚乱、賛嘆不迭。（一六三頁）

見人ミナ眼花乱(メボシミダレチツ)散テ賛美ス。（五一三頁）

以上、『通俗大明女仙伝』における白話語彙への理解の仕方を幾つかの訳例を挙げることで示してみた。

なお、軍談や軍記類にみられる慣用句的な表現の訳例が指摘できるので、最後に付言しておきたい。

瞿能仰天大歎、退向城外。（一〇六頁）

瞿能天ヲ仰テ歎息シ牙ヲ噛デ城外ヘ退ヌ(シリゾキ)。（三三七頁）

原文にない「牙ヲ嚙デ」は、歯ぎしりをするの意で、『太平記』などに散見する。一例を挙げれば、「後より続く御方無し。安からぬものかなと牙をかみて本陣へと引き返さる」(巻三十一「武蔵合戦」新潮古典集成本 四 四四一頁)である。全体として強調表現になっている。

兵士皆紛々ト馬ヨリ落、三軍総崩ト成テ右往左往ニ乱散ヲ。炳文大敗虧輸、士卒皆乱竄逃命。(一〇四頁)

「三軍」は、大軍の意で、他の二語とともに、軍談類に見られる語である。原文にある「虧輸」は、前掲『大詞典』には「指戦敗」とあり、「…就棄了密雲県、大敗虧輸、奔檀州来。」『水滸伝』第八三回などの例を挙げている。また、「乱竄逃命」は、命からがら逃げまわるの意で、訳文はそれを具体的に描き出したものとなっている。

おわりに

稿者は、現在江戸期の白話翻訳小説を対象とした近世における中国語と日本語との交渉を付け仮名に着目して調査をしているが、その手始めに先ず『通俗大明女仙伝』を選び出し、その訳語の選択や訳風、また付け仮名を手がかりにして、白話語彙受容のあり方を粗々と検討してみた。

19 場所、華厳思想、道元

高橋綾子

The vast wild
    the house, alone.
The little house in the wild,
    the wild in the house.
Both forgotten.

No nature (*No Nature*, 381)

詩集 No Nature の最後に収められた"Ripples on the surface"は西洋的であるとか東洋的などとは言い切れない独自の象徴空間を我々の前に提示している。カリフォルニアの「荒野の中に建つ家一軒」、「荒野の中の小さな家」、「家の中にある小さな荒野」と読めば、"nature"は自然または本質であり、性質がなくなって家と荒野が溶け込んでいくかのようなイメージを与える。また、"nature"を仏教思想でいう「自性」と読むこともできる。つまり、"No nature"とは、「自性」をもたないこと、「無自性」であり、「空」であるということになる。このように、"Ripples on the surface"は、スナイダーの詩的文化的可能性を示し、また西洋と東洋の融合的姿勢に、彼自身の「越境性」があるのではないかと考えられる。私は、このようなスナイダーの西洋と東洋の融合的姿勢を表しているのではないかと考える。本稿は私の博士論文の主たるテーマである「スナイダーにおける越境性」に迫るための一考である。

この詩を華厳思想的に解釈すると、「原野の中の小さな家」と「家の中の原野」は、「原野」=「多」、「小さな家」=「一」となり、「一即多、多即一」の関係であると言え得るのではないかと考える。「空」に達することができれば、「原野」のなかに「小さな家」を見、「小さな家」に「原野」を見ることは可能だと考えるのが華厳の教えである。二極と定義した「家」（内）と「ウィルダネス」（外）も自己を滅却して（"Both Forgotten"）「空」に達することができれば二元論を超えた「一軒の大きな空の家」となれると解釈できるのである。また、「一軒の大きな空の家」とは、道元の言うように、「自己が真の無になることは、自己をわするること、自己をわするるとは万法に証せらるるなり」の境地に近づくのではあるまいか。

スナイダーの詩人としての立場は明確である。先達エズラ・パウンドからの引用である、"artists are the antennae of the race"という一文によって詩人としての自己の使命を述べている。モダニストたちの東

376

洋への関心は、詩的技法においてのみ現れていたが、スナイダーは詩的技法に留まらず、その関心は極めて実践的である。パウンドの「民族のアンテナ」を、"How that probably functions in practice is that some people's sensibilities, as well as maybe their lifestyles,"と解釈していることからもそれが現れているのである。

Poetry effects change by fiddling with the archetypes and getting at people's dreams about a century before it actually effects historical change. A poet would be, in terms of the ecology of symbols, noting the main structural connections and seeing which parts of the symbol system are no longer useful or applicable, though everyone is giving them credence.

スナイダーは、人々の心理的原型や無意識の世界に確かな指針を与えるような詩人であろうとしているのだ。また、スナイダーは詩人の役割に、象徴的なエコロジー、つまり構造的な連関を重ね合わせているが、それは詩作と場所に根づく実践が一体であることを言明していることに他ならない。スナイダーの詩作における指針は、スナイダーが "So it does complete a circle." と述べているように、広く東洋思想から学び、一つのサイクルを終えて、再びカリフォルニアの生活に戻った現在、カリフォルニアでの生活に密着した東洋思想の実践を通して花開こうとしているのである。スナイダーのこの詩作の指針こそが、パウンドの「民族のアンテナ」を継承した態度ではなかろうか。

さて、唯識思想の『中正と両極端との弁別』(中辺分別論)の第一章、「相」の冒頭に掲げられている二偈頌に、「虚妄なる分別は存在する そこに二つのものは存在しない しかし そこに 空性が存在し

そのなかにまた あれが存在する…」という一節がある。簡潔な短い詩の中に有から無、無から有の論理があらわされている。ここで「虚妄なる分別」とは、知られるものと知るものを分別することであるが、八識の働きによる迷いの世界を指している。さらに言うと、「虚妄なる分別」は、知られるものと知るものを分別することができれば悟りに通じることができるのだ。「原野の中の小さな家」と「家の中の原野」を認識論的迷いの世界と解釈するならば、「原野」と「家」という認識を両方忘れるとき、つまり「空」に達すれば、悟りである無自性を見出すことができると解釈することもできる。このようにして、唯識思想との関連の可能性も考えてみると、スナイダーの目指す「民族のアンテナ」は益々豊かな融合性を提示しているのではなかろうか。

本稿では、華厳思想や唯識思想、さらには道元の思想がスナイダーの場所の感覚にいかに関わっているかを考察する試みでもある。スナイダーは華厳思想と道元の思想とどのように関わり、詩作に、そしてエッセーの中にどのように反映させてきたのであろうか。スナイダーの詩的原則、"the jeweled net of Indra"が彼のエコロジー感覚に大きく関わってきていることは、「ひとつの生態系における関係性の網目は、華厳仏教のエコロジーが教えるインドラ網を連想させる」と書いていることからも明らかであるし、環境倫理学の観点からもアプローチが試みられている。本稿では、スナイダーのエコロジー形成に限定せず、スナイダーの場所の感覚に華厳思想がいかに関わってきたかに絞って考えていきたい。スナイダーの華厳思想と道元の場所に対する理解はかなり深いものがある。しかしながら、なぜ、場所の感覚がスナイダーの中心的課題となり、詩作の『正法眼蔵』へ理解を跡づけることにより、スナイダーの場所の感覚が多面的な側面を持っているという全体の指針となってきたのかに迫ることは、スナイダーの場所の感覚が多面的な側面を持っていることを解する一助となるのではなかろうか。

また、スナイダーの場所の感覚と道元の「山水経」の関連から、スナイダーがいかにして「流域の思想」を生み出す原動力になったかを論じていきたい。

[Ⅰ]

スナイダーの特徴は「華厳的＝生態学的＝空的＝相互依存の宝石網」というように、華厳経とエコロジー意識と道元の「空」を融合的に扱うところにある。華厳経とエコロジー意識の関係については別稿で扱い、本節では主にスナイダーと華厳経について考えていきたい。

まず、華厳思想の概略に触れてみたい。華厳思想は、「ほとけ」の生命を解き明かそうとしているものである。日本では、奈良の東大寺の大仏、鎌倉時代においては明恵上人、道元の思想の中に生きてきた。華厳がめざすのは、無限の宝を見出すことである。清らかな生命そのものの動きを見出すことを主張する。

華厳思想と明恵上人、道元の関係を述べることは仏教学者の間でさえ、難解なことである。ただし、明恵上人は華厳の実践者であり、華厳禅の確立者として位置付けられている。「阿留辺幾夜宇和」において、「人間には、それぞれもっている性があり、それを本当に生かしきっていかなかればならない。」とある。

ここにも華厳思想の目指すものが垣間見られるのだ。

スナイダーも華厳思想と禅との関係を日本での仏教修行時に以下のように書いている。

...one begins to see the connecting truths hidden in Zen, Avatamsaka and Tantra. The giving of a love relationship is a Bodhisattva relaxation of personal fearful defenses and self-interest strivings—which communicates unverbal to the other and leaves them do the same....
Tantra, Avatamsaka and Zen really closely historically related : and these aspects of philosophy and practice were done all at once, years ago, up on Hiei-zan. Knit old dharma-trails. (*Earth House Hold*, 34-35)

スナイダーは「禅、華厳経、タントラが相互に関連していることを挙げている。

華厳経の中心思想は「性起品」である。「性起品」とは「ほとけ」の生命の現れであり、本来「ほとけ」であるところのわれわれ衆生が無限向上の修行を続けていくことを説く。鎌田茂雄氏は道元の『正法眼蔵』に「性起品」が現れていると述べている。また、「即身是仏」の「一心一切法、一切法一心」に華厳思想が描かれている。

しかあればすなはち、即心是仏とは、発心・修行・菩提・涅槃の諸仏なり。いまだ発心・修行・菩提・涅槃せざるは、即心是仏にあらず。たとひ、一刹那に発心修証するも即心是仏なり、たとひ、一極微中に発心修証するも即心是仏なり、たとひ無量劫に発心修証するも即心是仏なり、た

とひ、一念中に発心修証するも即心是仏なり、たとひ半拳裏に発心修証するも即心是仏なり。[10]

「一心一切法、一切法一心」とは一切の法（存在）に即して一心があるのであり、一心に即して一切の法があるという意味である。存在を離れて独存する一心は存在しないと解釈される。[11]つまり、華厳思想の中心、十玄縁起のひとつである一多相容不同門の、一は多に入り、多は一に入って無礙自在であることを描いているのだ。さらに、極めて短い時間の単位である「刹那」（「クシャーナ」の音写）、分割しつくされた最小の物質である「微塵」（「パラマーヌ」の意訳）は、無量の年月である「無量劫」に対比され、[12]つまり時間的な立場から無礙を論じている十玄縁起のひとつ、十世隔法異成門が現れているのだ。

ところで、華厳思想を貫いているのは「一即多、多即一」という考えである。この考えは空間的に捉えられている。「ほとけ」の光明はどんな小さなものにも貫徹するとされている。小さなものも、無限の世界を包むことができるとも考えられる。小さな世界が多なる世界となり、多なる世界は小さな世界となり、さらに、広大なる世界は、狭小なる世界となり、一つの世界は無辺なる世界であるのである。

また、華厳思想において、時間的にも「一即多、多即一」であると説く。それは菩薩心を発するとき、永遠の時間が一瞬におさまり、一瞬が永遠の時間を包むのである。そのため、一瞬を知ることによって、無限の過去、現在、未来を知ることができるとのである。

詩集 *Mountains and Rivers without Ends* における華厳思想の描かれ方を検討したい。"Bubbs Creek Haircut"の冒頭に、"High ceilinged and the double mirrors, the / Calendar a splendid alpine scene—scab barber—"と書かれている。スナイダーは次のように Ekbert Fass に対するインタヴューにおいて答えている。

…'Double mirror waver' is a structure point. Mutually reflected mirrors. Like, you see yourself many times reflected in a barber's shop. You look and you see yourself going that way and you see yourself going that way. It's a key image in *Avatamsaka philosophy*, Buddhist interdependence philosophy. Multiple reflections in multiple mirrors, that's what the universe is like.[13]

このように、"double mirror waver"は床屋の鏡という意味だけではなく、"in the fixity of time and space"で、時間と空間を固定化しているのである。興味深いのは、鎌田氏も「一即多・多即一」を空間的と時間的に分けて考えている点であり、空間的には一点のなかに全世界が映し出されているという。スナイダーは空間にも時間にも「一即多、多即一」を描いた詩"For Nothing"を書いている。

Earth a flower
A phlox on the steep
slopes of light
hanging over the vast
solid spaces
small rotten crystals,
salts.

"Earth a flower"においては、地球と崖に咲くフロックス一輪が同列に並べられている。空間的な広がりと焦点化された対象は、さらに硬質な物質へと移っていく。"hanging over the vast / solid spaces / small rotten crystals;/ salts."という表現においては、広大な空間と地の塩の結晶が同列に並べられている。これらは、「一輪の花」に地球全体を見ており、さらに、わずかな塩の結晶に空間的な広がりを見ているのだ。つまり、カリフォルニアの自然を題材に空間的な「一即多、多即一」を描いていると言えるのである。

Earth a flower
by a gulf where a raven
flaps by once
a glimmer, a color
forgotten as all
falls away.

第二スタンザにおいて、"Earth a flower"の余韻を残しつつも、時間的な「一即多、多即一」が描かれている。"a raven / flaps by once"(ワタリガラスが一回羽ばたく)一瞬と"a glimmer, a color / forgotten as all / falls away."(一寸の光や一瞬の彩りがすべて忘れ去られていく)不可逆的な時間の流れが対比されている。第二スタンザの終わりの、"forgotten as all falls away."「消えていくように忘れ去られて」とあるように、一瞬が無限の空間的広がりのなかに浸透していくのである。

A flower
for nothing;
an offer;
no taker;

Snow-trickle, feldspar, dirt (*Turtle Island*, 69)

　第三スタンザにおける、"A flower for nothing;/ an offer; no taker;"とは、「一輪の花」は「無のために咲く花」であり、「与えられても」、「受け取る者とていない」花なのである。このようにスナイダーは、「一即多、多即一」という華厳の中心的思想をカリフォルニアという場所において自分の生活に即して描きつづけている。しかしながら、華厳思想において存在しない「無」が「一輪の花」に結びつけられている。それでは、無の境地を象徴する花とは一体何なのであろうか。
　さて、この詩は、「無に捧げる」というタイトルである。一貫して華厳的なテーマでありながら、このタイトルは華厳思想で説かれる「空」("emptiness")ではなく、「無」が用いられていることから、スナイダーは意図的に禅の言葉を用いたのではないかと考えられるのである。禅について、スナイダーは、"Zen is a practice that is concerning with liberation"と述べていることから、この考えると、禅は、修行を通して悟りに到達するが、悟りによって真なる自己（True Self）を見出すのであるが、一般的には自我対無我などのように、自己と「無」は対立概念である。自己と「無」の二元的対立を悟りによって超えたところに、「真なる自己」が現れるのである。

384

知の新視界

スナイダーにおいては、実践における最高点が禅の「無」であり、概念上の最高点が華厳の「空」という捉え方がされているのではなかろうか。

スナイダーが、"The Avatamsaka ("Flower Wreath") jeweled-net-interpenetration-ecological-systems-emptiness-consciousness"と述べていたことから、早くからインドラ網とエコロジー意識と「空」の概念を結びつけた解釈をしていた。これは、概念上であるので、禅の「無」は含まれていない。しかしながら、スナイダー流の「空」の概念は修行を通して得られるもので、禅の「無」に極めて近い。そのため、「空」の行方を考えていきたい。

> The first
> Water poet
> Stayed down six years.
> He was covered with seaweed.
> The life in his poem
> Left millions of tiny
> Different tracks
> Criss-crossing through the mud.

"As For Poets" (*Turtle Island*, 174) は、詩人を"The Earth Poets"、"The Air poets"、"The Fire Poets"、"Water poets"、"The Space poets"、"A Mind Poet"というテーマに分けて詠ったものである。

これらのテーマは「地」、「風」、「火」、「水」、「虚空」、「識」を六界とする原始仏教の分類に一致するものである。上記の引用は四番目の「水詩人」である。「水詩人」の詩における生命については、"left millions of tiny different tracks criss-crossing through the mud."と表現しており、無限の生命の連鎖のなかで生きていく姿が描かれ、華厳思想でいうところの「因陀羅網」相当するのである。"six years"は六界と掛けているとも言え、時間的な広がりが描かれている。六番目の「心詩人」は次のようである。[16]

A Mind poet
Stays in the house.
The house is empty
And it has no walls.
The poem
Is seen from all sides,
Everywhere,
At once.

「心詩人」は空っぽの家にいる。しかしその家は、外部空間と隔たりがないのである。そのため「心詩人」の詩はどこからでも「見られる」("Is seen from all sides")のである。「心詩人」の心は「空」である。「空」は「見る」、「見られる」という対立を超えたところにあるからだ。スナイダーにとって、「空」や「無」は華厳と禅の意識的融合によって用いられていながらも、曖昧な

点がある。スナイダーの「空」にはどのような特徴があるのであろうか。

he carried
"emptiness"
he carried
"mind only"
vijñaptimātra (*Mountains and Rivers without Ends*, 79)

スナイダーの言う「空」とは唯識思想における「空」であり、"mind only"とは「唯識」である。唯識思想における「空」はあらゆる存在に自性はないことを示す。唯識思想は、「空」の真理を心の側面から、つまり主体の側から明らかにしていこうという性格を持っている。そして、すべてのものに固定的な本性があるかのように錯覚する常識的立場やそれを理論的に基礎づける学説を否定しようとする。そして、この否定によって開示される真理を「最高実在」として捉えているのである。

ここでの"he"は Kokopilau (ココペリ)で「背中にこぶのある笛吹き」である。伝説上の人物である Kokopilau は、「空」を背負い、そして、「唯識」を背負ってアメリカにやってくる。

The hump-backed flute player
walks all over.
Sits on the boulders around the Great Basin

his hump　　　is a pack.

「背中にこぶのある笛吹き」は現在のアメリカを歩き回り、過去と現在が彼の存在そのものによって交わっている。この詩を通して、歴史や神話が織り込められており、西洋と東洋が、さらには、過去と現在が遭遇するのである。玄奘は、「六二九年にインドに行き、六五七年の経典（『成唯識論』）、仏画、曼荼羅、そして五十の遺宝を携えて中国に戻ってきた。」という唯識に関わる重要な歴史を述べながら、「背中にこぶのある笛吹き」の伝説を活気付けていく。Anthony Hunt氏はスナイダーの「空」を人間の時間と場所の限界を超えることのできる癒しの知恵（"The doctrine of emptiness is a healing wisdom that 'goes beyond' the limits of human time and place."）として述べている。氏はさらに、「空」の知恵は、場所に生きることにあり、我々が通常考える「歴史的」、「地理学的」コンテクストによって限定されるべきではない（"Snyder ultimately suggests that the wisdom of emptiness may be rooted in, but not limited by, any 'historical' or 'geographical' context that we normally think of."）として、「空」と場所に根づくことを結びつけている。[18]

氏の見解をさらに発展させれば、日本における禅の修業を終えてカリフォルニアに帰国したスナイダーはあたかも"Hump-Backed Flute Player"であるかのように日本で学んだ「空」をもたらす使命を持っていたのではないかと考えられる。氏の強調するのは、スナイダーの「空」が場所に根づくことと切り離せないという点である。これはまさしくスナイダーがウィルダネスを「空であり真」と定義したことに一致する。

スナイダーは、詩集 *Turtle Island* で、"wilderness is the state of complete awareness. That's I need it."[19]

と述べているように、悟り、つまり「空」の概念をウィルダネスと結びつけている。スナイダーは修行を通して「複雑に相互浸透するこの世界に存在する苦痛と美の両方を認識し得る視点」が与えられると考え、この「より広い視点」に立脚することがインドラ網の実践（「インドラ網に参加しよう」）であると言明している。したがって、精神的な理想である「空」の概念や生態学的な理想であるインドラ網はウィルダネスを舞台として実践化されていくのだ。

スナイダーが繰り返し述べる華厳のインドラ網は、「空」の概念とともに、カリフォルニアの自然、ウィルダネスに培われたものである。華厳のインドラ網を空の概念と結びつけている点はスナイダーの思想的な特徴である。このような、「空」の概念とインドラ網の実践的な解釈が、スナイダーの「場所の感覚」を導く原動力となっているのだ。それでは、スナイダーの「場所の感覚」[20]の到達点である「流域の思想」に道元の思想がいかにして関わっているのかを次節で考えていきたい。

[II]

スナイダーは、一九六八年に日本を去り、カリフォルニアに永住することを決意して、一九七〇年に、"Kitkitdizze"というアメリカ原住民の言葉に由来する名の家を建てた。"Kitkitdizze"は、スナイダーの場所に根づく本拠地として、また、修行の場として重要である。山里氏は、"Kitkitdizze house shows how humans and their homes can be self-sufficient and integrated with the bioregion in which they are placed."[21]と述べており、さらに、"Kitkitdizze"は、スナイダーの「流域の思想」を育む根拠地であることはもちろんのこと、ホームレスや没場所性が生んだ二十世紀の疎外感を克服する可能性を秘めたものであるとして

いる。("such shows possibilities of transcending the twentieth-century alienation that arises from home homelessness and placelessness.")また、"Kitkitdizze"を建てることは、カウンター・カルチャーの象徴であるだけでなく、スナイダーの理想である、サンガの形成なのである。("by another important project, that is, building a zendo, a Zen meditation hall, and forming a sangha.") さらに付け加えるならば、"Kitkitdizze"の家はスナイダーの修行、実践の象徴となっているのである。

スナイダーは人間と自然界との関係性を「浸透性」という言葉で表す。エッセー集 *A Place in Space*(一九九五)の序文では、「相互に浸透し合う領域を理解し、私たちがどこにいるか学び、そうすることによって地球全体を視野に入れたエコロジカルなコスモポリタニズムの生き方を確立する」ことがスナイダーの理想であり、流域の思想の実践であると述べている。

「わたしたちがどこにいるかを学び」は、文字通り道元の『正法眼蔵』「現成公案」の"When you find your place where you are, practice occurs."(*The Practice of the Wild*, 25) (「このところをうれば、この行李したがひて現成公案す」)が前提になっていることは言うまでもない。さて、「浸透性の世界」とはいかなる世界なのであろうか。

    There is no use, the water cycle tumbles round—
        Sierra Nevada
    Could lift the heart so high
    Fault block uplift
    Thrust of westward slipping crust—one way

To raise and swing the clouds around—
Thus pine trees leapfrog up on sunlight
Trapped in cells of leaf—nutrient minerals called together
Like a magic song
To lead a cedar long along, that hopes
to get to sea at last and be
a great canoe.

(*Mountains and Rivers without Ends*, 70)

「浸透性の世界」とは、止めることのできない水の流れに広がる山、岩、鉱物の一貫した生命の流れのことである。地霊つまりシエラ・ネヴァダは地殻に圧力を及ぼし、山を隆起させる。それは天候までも動かす力を持ち、森林に雨を降らせる。松は成長し、養分を含んだ鉱物を大地に残し、それは最後まで海へと流れていく。これは生命の連関というよりむしろ、生命が相互に溶け合い浸透的世界を形成した姿なのだ。ここで描いた世界こそ、「浸透性の世界」である。

エッセー *The Practice of the Wild*(一九九〇)には、"Blue Mountains Constanly Walking"[22] という章がある。『正法眼蔵』「山水経」において、あらゆる功徳を備えた山は常に歩く(「青山常運歩」)とされ、その歩く様子は流れると表現されており、それを学ぶことが山を学ぶことだとされている。スナイダーにとって、シエラ・ネヴァダで山、森林、川が相互に浸透しあっていく世界を学ぶことこそ、山を学ぶことであるのだ。

スナイダーは、道元の言う「山水」を総括して、地球の生成過程、また存在そのもの、過程、本質、行為、不足であり、存在も非存在もともに含んだものであるとしている。[23] そして、Wenzi said, "The path of water is such that when it rises to the sky, it becomes raindrops ; when it falls to the ground, it becomes rivers." …The path of the water is not noticed by water, but is realized by water.(文子曰く、「水之道は天に下りて雨露と為り、地に下りて広河と為る」…水の道は水の所知覚にあらざれども、水よく現行す。)の引用から、「山水」が大自然の営みの完全性（"the totality of the progress of nature"）を表すと結んでいる。つまり、場所の感覚に加え、自然の営みの完全性を加えたダイナミクスこそが「流域の思想」なのである。また、スナイダーは、「流域は秩序／無秩序の二分法を超越する。——なぜなら、その姿は自由でありながら、ある程度はまた必然的であるからだ。そのなかで花開く生命が最初の共同体を形成する。[25]」と言っているように、彼の「流域」とは彼の解釈した「山水」に近づいていくのだ。

The Great Mind passes by its own
fine-honed thoughts,
going each way.

"The Great Mind"という表現は言い換えれば、スナイダーの言う「流域の思想」、つまり「山水」となる。そしてスナイダーの場所である、シエラ・ネヴァダの「山水」に見出された「偉大な精神」こそ、パウンドの言う「民族のアンテナ」の進化させた姿なのではないかと考えられる。スナイダーは道元の「山水」を「偉大な精神」として、シエラ・ネヴァダに見出しているのである。

sunk sleepily in

 to the sea.

 The root of me
hardens and lifts to you
thick flowing river,

 my skin shivers. I quit

 making this poem.

　詩人が向き合うのは、あふれる川の流れである。スナイダーはここで詩作を止める。この瞬間読者に残されるのは、「山水」に溶け合い、「山水」と一体になろうとする詩人の姿である。詩人が Great Earth Sangha となった姿である。

　このように、スナイダーが華厳思想、唯識、道元のエッセンスを吸収することにより、場所の感覚から流域の思想を生み出していった過程を跡付けることができたと考えられる。スナイダーは自分の場所に根ざした「空」を見出すために、華厳思想、唯識、道元の力を借りたのではなかろうか。これにより、スナイダーの場所の感覚が普遍化され、文化的な豊饒性を我々に訴えるのだ。スナイダーにとって「空」とは詩作の原動力になっているのと同時にメタファーの中心である。スナイダーの提示する「空」により、詩的イメージがより多層的に、より多文化的な（スナイダーの言葉を借りれば、「コスモポリタン」的視野

に立った)可能性を秘めていったと言える。この「空」こそ、スナイダーの越境する力が秘められているのである。に現れている。この「空」にこそ、スナイダーが詩人として背負う文化的な使命は、この「空」

[注]

1 『仏教の思想』第四巻(角川書店、一九七〇年)一三九頁において、根拠の転換の構造を示す「三種の存在形態」論が論じられている。三種とは、「仮構された存在形態」「他に依存する存在形態」「完成された存在形態」をいう。「存在形態」の訳語をあてた svabhava は、「固有の性質」「本質」を意味する語で、「自性」と漢訳される。ナーガールジュナは「中論」その他の著作の中で、存在要素が不変異の本性をもつという説一切有部の学説を徹底的に批判し、実在は「本性をもたない」こと、「無自性」であり、空であることを明らかにした。

2 Gary Snyder, *The Real Work* (New York: New Directions Books, 1980) 71.

3 Snyder 71.

4 Snyder 71.

5 Snyder 86.

6 『世界の名著』二 大乗仏教(中央公論社、一九七八年)三九九頁。

7 『世界の名著』第二巻の四〇一頁において、眼・耳・鼻・舌・身・意(マナス)とアラーヤ識を総括して識一般を「虚妄なる分別」と述べられている。

8 See Andrew McLaughlin, "Images and Ethics of Nature," *Environmental Ethics* Vol. 7. winter 1985, 293. "Imaging nature as an interconnected network, a view rooted in both ecology and Buddhism, is a more comprehensive and adequate foundation for conceptualizing the practical and ethical dimensions of humanity's relation with nature." Further he argues, "The similarity between the ecological image of a web of nature and some Buddhist metaphors for nature is striking. For example, one Chinese Hua-yen Buddhist metaphor for the total interconnectedness of nature is known as the the Jeweled Net of Indra." (316)

9 『仏教の思想』第六巻(角川書店、一九七〇年)

10 道元『正法眼蔵』第一巻(角川書店、一九七三年)「即身是仏」七三頁。

11 道元 七〇頁。

12 道元 一三八頁。

13 Ekbert Faas, *Toward a New American Poetics : Essays and Interviews* (Santa Barbara : Black Sparrow Press, 1978) 135.

14 禅学大辞典では、「この空には理論的と実践的との両方の意味があり、理論的な空とはすべてのものに固定した実態のないこと、無自性空をさし、それは縁起とか関係性とかいうのとほぼ同義である。実践的な空とは無所得・無執着の態度をさし、無我の実践としての無所得空がそれである。この実践がまたさらに向上して無礙空となるのであり、それはそのまま真空妙有（空と有と二つの対立概念を超越したもの）の境地であり、禅における身心脱落、脱落身心もこの無礙空にほかならない。禅宗ではこの空の概念を無の語で表す場合が少なくない。」（二七〇頁）

15 Gary Snyder, "The East West Interview," *The Real Work* (New York: North Point Press, 1990) 92–137.

16 『世界の名著』二 大乗仏典（中央公論社、一九六七年）二〇三頁「宝積経」の（五四）に、「土の元素（地界）について、恒常でもないとみる観察、無常でもないとみる観察。水の元素（水界）、熱の元素（火界）、風の元素（風界）について、恒常でもないとみる観察、無常でもないとみる観察。空間の元素（空界）、認知の元素（識界）について、恒常でもないとみる観察、無常でもないとみる観察。カーシャパよ、これが中道であり、存在についての真実の観察と言われる。」注としてこれら地界から識界に至る六種を六界あるいは六大という。地・水・火・風の前四者は純粋に物質的な要素、空界は虚空あるいは空間で、物質を成り立たせる原因、最後の識界は心的活動である、と述べられている。

17 この詩の中で、伝説上の人物 Kokopilau について次のように説明している。"In Canyon de Chelly on the north wall up by a cave is the hump-backed flute player lying on his back, playing his flute."

Anthony Hunt. "The Hump-Backed Flute Player: The Structure of Emptiness in Gary Snyder's *Mountains and Rivers without End*," *ISLE*, 1–23.

18 He argues that "The Hump-backed Flute Player" both describes and offers some "understanding of emptiness" by depicting its transmission in mythical and actual time across geographical space from Asia to North America, across the space which stretches from the earth to stars, and across the void that exists between our inner and outer being."

19 Gary Snyder, *The Practice of the Wild* (New York: North Point Press, 1990) 10.

20 スナイダーは、ソローの『森の生活』の中でウォールデン・ポンドについて述べている、「ウォルデン・ポン

ドの向こう側の岸の波はガンジス川の水と混ざり合っている」という言葉に固執している。その理由は、ソローがインド思想に影響されていたことだけでなく、「この惑星における水の循環」という生態学的な見方が現れていることにある。スナイダーも Plane Talk (*Turtle Island*, 222) において同様な疑問を投げかけている。"This is our home country. We dig wells and wonder where the water table comes from."スナイダーは「ウォーターシェッド」という言葉を用いる。この言葉は、ある場所の水質が川全体の水質に影響しているという意味で、ひとつの流域を中心として成立する人間と自然の共同体の全体像を示唆している。流域の思想と同義語で用いられている「生態学的地域主義」は "the true community (sangha) of all beings" を追求してきた結果生まれた概念なのである。"all beings"とは、「自然界に有する深い価値とノン・ヒューマンな存在の主体性を追加する」と述べられているように人間中心主義からの脱却、つまり「パンヒューマニズム」への提案へつながっていく。

21 Katsunori Yamazato, "Kitkitdizze, Zendo, and Place: Gary Snyder as a Reinhabitory Poet," *ISLE*. 53—54. 一九八五年に出版された『正法眼蔵』の抄訳 *Moon in a Dewdrop* では、"The green mountains are always walking."と記述されていることからも、日本語の原文を読み、原文に近づく解釈を行おうとする姿勢がうかがえる。

22 Snyder *Moon in a Dewdrop* 103.

23 Snyder 102.

24 Snyder 102.

25 Snyder 272.

＊本稿は、二〇〇一年十二月一日、日本大学比較文化・比較文学会において「ゲイリー・スナイダーの場所の感覚」として発表した内容を加筆、再校したものである。

20 津軽作家 今 官一

その文学的生涯

高橋 章

　今官一は、一九〇九年(明治四十二年)十二月八日、弘前市西茂森町六五番地槽洞宗蘭庭院で生まれた。父官吾は、南津軽郡藤崎町船場、藤田三次郎の三男で、奥羽線の列車に乗務していた。大館車掌区に勤務し、今晃運の婿養子となり、その娘さだと結婚。(同じ年六月十九日太宰治は金木村で生まれた。)官一が誕生したその日、福士幸次郎は「自由詩社」パンフレットの『自然と印象』に、初めて詩人として詩作品を発表した。

　藤崎町の藤田家は、日本における盲人伝道揺藍期の賢者藤田匡(タダス)の一族である。藤田タダスは、安政六(一八五九)生まれ十五年、昭和召天。年少時、津軽藩兼松塾の秀才。十四歳で失明。メソジスト

教会の本多庸一牧師にキリスト教を学び、一八八二年受洗。伝道者となった人である。黒石、五所川原、青森、藤崎、弘前、能代、秋田の諸教会に奉仕した聖者の風格のある人。『羨まず春花と秋月とを、乾坤別に詩情をうながすあり、固中の妙趣ひと知るやいなや、肉眼盲なりといえども心眼明らかなり』という漢詩にその烈々たる境地を託している。今官一は、その精神的感化と影響を受けている。

父の勤務のため、大正五年岩手県一戸尋常高等小学校に入る。七年一月二十一日、朝陽小学校第二年に入った。二十七日出席しただけで学年修了、学業成績は、修身、国語、算術、図画、唱歌、体操、手工、操行、オール甲であった。同級に行方佐がいた。同年六月三日、青森市新町小学校に転校。同窓に、後のモーツアルト研究家の柴田治三郎がいた。十一年三月、同校卒業。再興第一年目の「東奥義塾」に入学。同期に、新谷武四郎、羽賀与七郎、今井富士雄、奥田啓二、木村繁、鳴海修がいた。四年生の時、詩人福士幸次郎が、国語教師として赴任、文学へ惑溺。『わらはど』同人雑誌を発行し、今官一、今井、奥田、古川英雄、木村、成田三男、行方、蒔苗忠男、三上斎太郎、柳田英二がこれに参加した。昭和三年まで続いたので、太宰治の『細胞文芸』と競い合う形となり、太宰治と今官一が文学の良きライバルとなった。生涯の親友となる奇縁であり、いみじくも忘れられない運命的〈邂逅〉であった。弘前の下白銀町のレストラン「パリスタ」で『わらはど』の前途を祝福して福士幸次郎先生は〈乾杯の歌〉を歌った。

このころ、今官一は、義塾の先輩で、有名な福音説教者、中田重治牧師から、キリスト教徒として洗礼を受けている。(藤田タダス、福士幸次郎など東奥義塾の諸先生の感化は、無視することができない。)

昭和二年、義塾卒業。青森駅のプラット・ホームで、福士幸次郎先生に見送られて上京。早稲田第一高等学院ロシヤ文学科に入学。在学中「プロレタリア映画同盟」に参加。〈青木了介〉のペンネームを用いた。

ある夜、徹夜して『旅人』七枚を書いた。昭和五年、ロシヤ文学科廃止とともに退学、帰郷した。弘前で井上靖らと同人雑誌『文学ABC』を創刊。同年、再度上京、中野区野方町に住む。福士幸次郎先生と隣り合い、文学に没頭。

「二十三歳で、一女児の父となった私は、故里を遂電した天罰てきめんで、己ればかりか、妻子までも飢えにさらさねばならなかった。」（詩人福士幸次郎）とは、この頃の事である。上北沢に住む横光利一に師事し、文学修行と小説製作にひたすら励んだ。

昭和七年八月、「作品」に『船』を発表し、千葉亀雄に推賞されてから、次々と作品を書き、十月に「改造」懸賞小説に応募し、佳作となる。石川達三らの芥川賞作家より一足早く、文壇へのスタートを切ったことになる。

昭和八年、古谷綱武らと同人雑誌『海豹』を創刊し、太宰治を誘い、『魚服記』を載せた。今自身は、『蒸気』を発表。坂爪賢蔵らの「文学祭」には、『妻に語った鬼の話』を書いた。

昭和九年、太宰治、檀一雄らと『青い花』を創刊し、編集責任者となる。

昭和十年、太宰治、檀一雄らと『青い花』を創刊し、編集責任者となる。住所を高円寺四丁目から北沢三丁目に移った。『青い花』が一号で潰れ、日本浪曼派に合流した。

昭和十年、「作品」に書いた『海鷗の章』が好評を得たことなどから、作品社の編集事務に携わった。

昭和十一年九月から「日本浪曼派」に『龍の章』を連載し始め、十二年、その七回目で未完中断。その

後、「文芸汎論」にしばしば短編を書いた。この頃、メトロゴールドウィン社にチェッカーマンとして就職し、同社の上映館を巡回し、入場者数の調査にあたったが、一ヵ月で退職。

昭和十三年から十五年にかけて、「文芸汎論」に、『旅雁（タップカル）の章』、『雷鳥（フミライ）の章』、『朱実（アトニ）の章』の三部作（後に、昭和五十一年九月津軽書房より『巨いなる樹々の落葉』として出版された。）今官一が、暗い冬の時代に、著者の青春をかけて書きつがれた亡びゆく民、北方アイヌ民族によせる限りなき無量の思いをこめた名作である。十三年には、〈芥川賞候補〉となった。アイヌの名門シニオラックの末裔、タップカル、フミライ、アトニたち親子三代にわたる生きざまが、和人（シヤモ）である「私」の深い愛惜のまなざしを通して、哀しいまでに、美しく描きだされている。

少数民族アイヌへの切ない哀りんの調べとアガペー愛に燃える悲愛の一大叙事詩である。幼少にして父母を失い、英国人の養父に引き取られて、ロンドンに遊学した旅雁は、やがて成人し、養父を看取ったのち、サロマ湖（トウ）のコタン（部落）へ帰ってくるが、彼を待っていたのは、雪どけの道を踏んで奥地へ奥地へと進んで行く無数の内地人の群れであり、河を遡る小型蒸気船の群れであった。そして、更に、現実の生活の基礎さえ失った悲惨な同族（ウタリ）たちの悲しみに満ちた姿だった。やがて、旅雁はコタンの若者たちと北方製材を設立し、「私」の父の力添えで、「日の出小学校」が誕生していくのである。新時代の若者たちと北方製材を設立し、「私」の父の力添えで、「日の出小学校」が誕生していくのである。新時代のらしくない日本人として生きようとしつつ、同時にあくまでもアイヌであろうとする旅雁は、父の意思を拒んで帰館しない雷鳥を待ち切れずに、息子の嫁朱実（コタンの姫だった）を孕ませてしまう。アイヌであることを逃れようとし、彫刻家として芸術に生きることを夢みてきた雷鳥は、しかし、旅雁の死を前にコタンへ帰っていく。そして、「私」に心の傾きをみせていた朱実も、イヨマンテ（神送り）の朝、ついにコタンに残ることを告げる。

「アイヌ民族に、いまだ解放なき今日、その解明は、いまだ私の人生につくされてはいない」と著者今官一は記している。だが、四十年近くも原稿紛失状態のため、目にふれることのなかった〈幻の名著〉が、発見され出版されたこの機会にひとりでも多くの人々に読まれることを願うばかりである。

昭和十五年九月、第一小説集『海鷗の章』を竹村書房より刊行。

八月、『現代文学』に『保羅の宿』八十枚、十一月に『氷柱日記』七十枚を発表。『氷柱日記』で、風俗壊乱のかどで、雑誌が発禁になった。稲垣足穂の来訪で、文化学院の『意匠』に『採薇の歌』(のち『女を捜せ』と改題)を書き始め、亀井勝一郎と太宰治の推薦で『文学会』に『子争い』を書いたが、編集者の原稿紛失の厄にあい、実現せず。郷里の『月刊東奥』に随筆を書く。

昭和十六年八月、チクマ書房より『龍の章』を出版。

十二月八日、(カンイチ三十二歳の誕生日)に〈太平洋戦争〉勃発。

昭和十七年、『われ虹をみたり』を『蠟人形』に、『女を捜せ』を『意匠』に連載。しかし、休刊で未完となる。新聞広告を見て、某興信所の私立探偵となったが、中村地平、真杉静枝夫妻の世話で、鉄道省観光局に入り、初出勤には、ロシヤ文学者の中山省三郎の背広を借用した。

昭和十八年、『花もて語れ』を『月刊東奥』新年号より連載。編集後記で、沙和栄一が、「本号より今官一氏の『花もて語れ』連載。同氏の代表作『龍の章』を凌ぐ傑作になるのではないかと思います。どうぞご期待下さい。」と書いている。これが敗戦前の最後の作品となったが、これまでの創作活動を、「日本浪曼派」の圏内にありながら、純芸術派の姿勢を守り、知的な表現に詩情のにじむ特異な作風で、文壇に独自の位置をしめた。」と『現代日本文学大辞典』は評価している。

昭和十九年四月、応召。二等水兵として軍艦「長門」に乗り組む。
「新潮社版の、夜店で買った『展望』を、私はフロシキ包の底へ入れて、一年半に亘り、マニラから、シンガポールへ下って、赤道直下を、うろちょろした。三十五歳の、きわめて不手際な老兵だったが、当直の夜に、戦闘艦橋で、南海の満月に照らしながら、見えもしない『展望』を読むときは、俺だけが、読めるのだという慢心で、たまらなく哀しかった。どの一行も、私には、まひるの太陽の下で読むように一句のまちがいもなくよめた。」（『詩人福士幸次郎』）
レイテ海戦に参加。応召中の体験は、『不沈戦艦長門』（昭和四十六年、R出版）に、極めて綿密、正確、克明に、しかも、淡々と冷静に書かれている。
昭和二十年、終戦。帰国後、日本交通公社となった以前の職場に復帰。職場には作家の北条誠や八木義徳がいた。
昭和二十一年、いままで戦争のために抑圧され、鬱屈していた創作欲が、はけ口を希求しはじめ、筆一本に未来を託して退職。胎動しはじめていた民主主義憲法に基づく新しい日本の歴史の羽ばたきのなかで、今官一の〈青春〉は、新たなる理想と希望に燃えたぎっていた。
「終戦のまぎわ、軍艦は横須賀にいたが、それを追いまわして、南方の海を、経めぐって来た、郵便船は、半年も遅れて、母の手紙を手渡したので、私は昭和二十年七月に、母の励ましの手紙を読んだばかりだったのであるが、新しい墓標〈法信院普 妙貞大姉〉には、その年の『二月十四日没』と刻んであった。
（『不沈戦艦長門』）「青い果実の忍び奏つノクタァン」
死線を越え、九死に一生を得て帰還し、文学と青春への復活を夢見てきたのに、次々と愛する近親との耐え難き死の別離の悲哀が待っていた。今官一は、呆然となった。

昭和二十一年十月十一日、文学と人生の恩師、福士幸次郎先生の召天。「兄さん、ありがとう」の一言を残して静かに息をひきとった。五八歳だった。十月二十六日の葬儀に参列した官一は、焼香するサトウ・ハチローの「顔じゅうがぎらぎらと涙で光っていた」のを見て、涙がでた。「そして、もしも、ほんとうに離れれば、離れるほど、私が、先生に接近できるのだとしたらそれは、今から始まるのだと思った。」(今官一『詩人福士幸次郎』)

昭和二十二年十二月三十日、文学(小説)の師、横光利一先生の逝去。行年四十九歳。「ユルシテクダサイ 後架の詩──無礼トイッテ叱ラズニ 先生カンニンシテ下サイ コレデモイマデハ 洋灯ナノダ タオレルマデノ二分間 ソレデモソレハ人デシタ ササヤク言葉ノ人デシタ 先生 ワタシ モガンバリマス キット Dance 覚エマス 先生 センセイッ!」と横光利一追悼の『後架の詩』をもって惜別している。(土橋治重は昭和三十三年七月号「歴程」に〈この詩を詩集『隅田川のミシシッピィ』の代表作である〉と書いた。)

昭和二十三年六月十三日、人生と文学の親友太宰治が、愛人、山崎富栄と三鷹の玉川上水へ投身心中自殺をしてしまった。三十九歳の惜別だった。相次ぐ、恩師と僚友の死別は、文学に対する決意の契機とはなったが、たゆまず努力を続けた。しかし、今官一は、米軍占領下、制約されるのもやむを得ないことであった。

昭和二十一年五月、交通公社の社内報に『春の設計』、六月『交通新聞』に『郷愁』、八月『芸林間歩』に『柔仏寺』四十枚、九月『交通新聞』に、十月『東北読書新聞』に『善知鳥』、十一月宇野浩二の推ばんで『旅雁の章』三部作の刊行が決定したが、芸林間歩社の不振で原稿紙型ともに紛失という悲運にあった。「文芸」に『長恨歌』を書く。

昭和二十二年一月「芸林間歩」に『続柔仏寺』六十二枚、三月「鱒」に「女の手」、十月「風刺文学」に「金冠」五十五枚、十二月「芸林間歩」に『春泥花』を発表。

昭和二十三年一月「税潮」に『雪をんな』を、「肉体」に『アルス・アマトリア』を、「人間喜劇」に『聖マルコの夜』四十六枚を、六月太宰治追悼文を書き、八月「文芸時代」に「山水蒙」を、「月刊東奥」に『津軽に寄せる』を、「日本未来派」に『晩夏のばら』(太宰治告別式実況)を、「人間喜劇」に『水死人を点景とする建設的な意見』を発表した。

十月には、「文潮」に『幻花行』九十六枚を発表、「九州タイムズ」に『海思』を書いた。

昭和二十四年、「洞窟のヴィーナス」『遠ざかる唄声のクロニクル』『六月十九日』『桜桃忌提唱』など次々と〈太宰治に関するエッセイ〉を発表。

「早稲田文学」六月号に『聖光輪』を発表。六月「文潮社」より『幻花行』を出版。〈『海思』を序に『青い果実の忍び奏つノクタァン』を後書に、『柔仏寺』『続柔仏寺』『柔仏寺後期』を収めたもの〉

亀井勝一郎は『幻花行』を評して「数多い戦争文学の中で、非常にユニークな作品だ。戦争は悪夢にちがいないが、敗けいくさは芸術であった。滅ぶ平家が美しいように、沈みいく軍艦「長門」を描いて、『幻花行』は美しい。」と記している。

『幻花行』は、戦艦「長門」への晩歌であるが、戦争体験を昇華し、母に捧げた〈郷愁〉の書である。今官一は「この書を長門に——母に捧げる」と記す。

コンカン先生が『現代人』同人になった記念に、私に下さった色紙には、

〈 花 幻の世に在らば 世も 幻の花ならむ 〉と、先生特愛のことばを美しい桜の花の絵に書い

てあった。へとらえ得て「幻滅」をいうならば、いかなる瞬間も、幻滅のほかは、在り得まい。不惑を過ぎて、幼童のごとく、いまだに「生」よりも、衰残の「文学」を、いつくしみ得る、所以でもあろうか。〉と、先生は記している。〈母を、横須賀海兵団の営門まで見送って、私の南海遊式のさなかに、倅の戦果を確信しながら、敗戦を知らずに、突如、この世を去ったのである。しかし、倅の勤務の渋滞を虜った、昔気質の父は、一言も、それを報じなかった。私は、敗戦とともに、ふるさとへ帰還して、郷愁の山河の中に、はじめて、母の墓を、発見したのである。〉（今官一）

昭和二十五年三月、「群像」に『日の滴り』を、「交通ペン」に『線路の子』を三回連載したが、休刊で未完となった。

昭和二十六年『華麗なるポロネエズ』を起稿し、五月に一六〇枚を書き終った。十月から十二月にかけて、『日の陰に』を完成。五月童話『幸福の王子』を小峰書店より出版。

昭和二十七年「サンデー毎日」小咄欄など雑文を書く。かたわら、『白鳥の湖』『銀簪』など、新傾向の時代小説に筆を染める。

昭和二十八年九月、「毎日グラフ」の緒方昇編集長の要請を受けて、『文学を見る』の企画に参加、連載をはじめ、三十年末まで、充実したフレッシュな仕事ぶりを示した。

昭和二十九年、『文学のふるさと』として刊行された。私に下さったその本には〈落ち葉 落ち葉 落ち葉の下の落ち葉かな〉と、コンカン先生が筆で記されている。

昭和三十年、「立像」に発表の『銀簪』が、「直木賞候補」となった。

昭和三十一年三月、芸術社より『壁の花』を出版。『暗い砦』（『日の陰に』を改題）『海の百合』『華麗

なるポロネェズ』『星の下のカルテット』を収めたもの]

なお、昭和三十一年（一九五七）十二月二十六日、「木曜書房」より世に出した、今官一の詩集『隅田川のMISSISSIPPI』のなかにある「チンチン電車」の詩が、私には、何故か印象ふかい。

　　くぐっと　危ない急Curveの
　　Chin-Chin-Curveの
　　大曲だ
　　……（略）……
　　牛込の江戸川べりの停車場
　　土地の名前の大曲が
　　そのまま危険な街角の
　　その角店がFlorist
　　いつも清楚な花があり
　　想い出したら　花もて語ろう
　　想い出したら　花もて語ろう
　　……（略）……
　　十年、十五、二十年
　　くぐっと危ない　Curveの人生

昭和三十二年、弥生書房から『詩人福士幸次郎』を刊行した。
昭和三十二年上記「直木賞」を『壁の花』で受賞した。
高見順は『昭和文学盛衰史』(毎日出版文化賞)の第十八章「津軽の作家」でこう書いている。

「今官一が直木賞を受けた。芥川賞の書きまちがいではない。…略…今官一は短編集『壁の花』に対して直木賞が与えられた。この短編集『壁の花』の、あれは見返しというのか、本の題名を印刷したそのページの裏側に、一見アヴァンギャルド画家のような今官一の写真(背景をも含めての印象がそうなのである。)が右上に掲げてあって、その上に、左隅に小さく、これはおそらく今官一の意志ではないだろうと思われる英文が印刷してある。それはこういうのである。"Wallflower by Kanichi Kon"という、おそらく今官一の好みと思われる略歴が出ている。それはこういうのである。

「明治四十二年十二月八日青森県弘前市に生る　昭和四年早稲田大学露西亜文学科中退後は横光利一氏に師事して小説文学に専念す　昭和八年古谷綱武らと雑誌『海豹』を創刊　同九年太宰治らと『青い花』を創刊し後『日本浪漫派』に合流す　戦争中に一等水兵として戦艦長門に配乗され　戦後その体験を通じて『幻花行』を発表す　三十年雑誌『立像』同人となり『銀簪』を発表して直木賞候補にあげられる。

今官一の『幻花行』は昭和二十四年に出版されたものだが、その年の春、彼が郷里の雑誌『月刊東奥』に『林檎と郷愁』という課題で書いた短文をこの『幻花行』のあとがきの冒頭に載せていて、そしてそれについてこう書いている。

「津軽平野の、真只中に、生れ、そこで育った、私にとって、林檎はもとより、郷愁のその白い花の芽生えに始まり、青い葉の茂りと、赤い果の爛熟と、落葉した灰色の幹の沈黙に終る、果樹

園の四季は、そのまま、回想する故郷の、一年三百六十五日を、もっとも効果的に彩る、主調音でさえ、あったのである。

これで見ると、私が今官一の小説からりんごを連想したのは、去年聞いた話からの勝手な思いつきというのでもなかった。

山形の高等学校（旧姓）に学んだ亀井勝一郎は、今官一の今回の受賞を祝う短い文章のなかで「この地（津軽）には平泉以来の古い文化の影響と双方あって東北ではめずらしい独自の『文化圏』を成している。今君の作品に、酒なおもむきのあるものもそのためであろう。津軽的ダンディズムと呼んでいい」（昭和三十一年七月『東京新聞』）と書いている。

私はこれを読んで、インドりんごというものを日本にもたらしたアメリカの宣教師が明治の初年に津軽の町を歩いている姿を想像した。彼がもたらしたものは、インドりんごだけではなく、インドりんごに象徴されるものが津軽にもたらされたのだということが思われるのである。

直木賞受賞作品『壁の花』のなかの『暗い砦』について、『現代小説事典』に、「――日高の国の「カニ」と呼ばれる四十六歳の男が、牧夫としてやとわれていた牧場の娘である十四歳の栗谷ミサキを銃殺した罪で絞首刑になる。「私」は、日高一の無法者であった砂川嘉二の、同名ゆえの心奥の暗い砦をさぐりあてていくのである。」「日皇太子嘉仁親王と同名であった砂川嘉二の、同名ゆえの心奥の暗い砦をさぐりあてていくのである。」「日高の国、新冠郡の山岳地方では、今でも佐原の「カニ」のことを、牧場はじまって以来の大悪人だと云い伝えている。それは、明治政府の新法律が、この地方で適用した、最初の殺人犯だったからである。

カニは、明治三十九年十一月二十日、網走の刑務所で、絞首刑になった。

可憐な十四歳の少女、栗谷ミサキを銃殺した罪によるものである。カニほどの男が、故意に少女（めらし）を射殺する筈はないといって、減刑運動までが企てられたほどであったが、本人が、一も二もなく服罪したので、法廷は、当時には珍しい一回の審理で処決した。官選の弁護人が、躍起となって、過失を論じたにも拘わらず、無駄であった。カニが、牧夫に雇はれていた栗谷牧場の二歳駒が、約半年にわたって、八頭あまりも、野獣の被害をほおむっている事実まで調べあげて、弁論したが、本人は、一向に乗らなかった。」

同じく『壁の花』の中の『海の百合』――「出征したっきり、還らない陸軍将校を、結婚式の三日から、もう六年間も、待ちつづけて、じらされて――あの肉体では、あの若さでは、神経衰弱にも、ならうさョ」と噂されている「憂愁夫人」（ふらう・ぞるげ）の物語である。」

『華麗なるポロネエズ』――三十五歳になってから、突如として海軍に召集された「私」は、「長門」の水兵にふむきな「インテリ野郎」にすぎず、退艦させられ、本部付きの海軍上等水兵として相南逗子町に向かう。そこで、老水兵は終戦をむかえるのである。

『星の下のクワルテッド』――〈三人のマリアと二人のヨゼフに依って編成された典礼曲（オラトリオ）形式の五つの楽章〉という副題が付されていて、「A・村のスピカ・序曲（処女マリアの告知）――Largo (Con Fuoco)」、「B・壁のマリア・（魚夫ヨゼフの抑制と変貌）――Andante Mae-stoso」、「C・裸の街の聖歌隊（聖マリアの合唱「抑制」）――Allegretto Capiccioso (Con Dolce)」、「D・鏡の中のトッカアタ（少女マリアの変貌）――Allegro Vivace」、「E・崖の下のフィナアレ（使徒ヨゼフの系譜）――Allegretto Capiccioso (Con Fuoco)」という小説が、相互に連関してできた物語である。（後に、五木寛之が『日本音楽小説集』のなかに、すぐれた音楽小説として、編入した。）

『壁の花』という題名は、『星の下のクワルテッド』のなかからとられたものであるが、『壁の花』に登場する主人公は、「カニ」「憂愁夫人」「水兵」などを見ても、ある意味で社会から疎外され、落ちこぼれた、「世はづれ者」である。華やかな社会の脚光を浴びることのない孤独な、憂愁の心を抱く哀しい存在である。愛されたい寂しい人たちである。孤独の壁にもたれて空しく誰かを淋しく待っている人たちばかりである。「舞踏会」にたとえれば、誰も声をかけてパートナーになってくれる者はいない。今官一の小説はどちらかというと、「世はづれ者」を書くというよりも、「世はづれ者」の掻き鳴らす「堅琴の歌」を書いているのである。しかし、今官一は、「世はづれ者」の「すじがき」(すとおりい)の面白さを旨とするいわゆる小説らしい小説ではなくて、極めて詩的要素の濃厚なものばかりである。勿論、筋書きや構成や論理がでたらめというのではけっしてなく、みごとな構成や論理や筋書きの面白さがあるのだが……。

『幻花行』のように戦争体験を素材として用いながら、そこに疑問もあり、異色もある。「戦争小説」ではなく、「戦争を装飾模様に織ったやうな、作者としての心理的曲折があって、「詩的心理的幻想小説」とでも呼べそうな作品である」(『日本小説代表作全集一九』解説、昭和二十四)と評されるような、海の百合など極めて詩的心理的幻想の世界である。壁の花の中の作品で、海の百合など極めて詩的心理的幻想の世界である。

昭和三十四年(一九五九)二月二十五日、「荒地出版社」より刊行した『風流博物誌』のなかに、「鉄砲百合〈Easter-Lily〉」を、みてみよう。〈たまには、植物の話もしよう。動物や鉱物のキナくさい匂いに息づまってくると、ひとは窓をあけて、五月ならば、新緑の樹立にたましいのいこいを求めたがる。生からの逃避だというひともいるが、必ずしも私は、そうは思わない。現実の生活が、じつは死なのかもしれないからだ。そうだとすると、その場合は、逃避ではなくて、「復活」乃至は「よみがえり」というべきであろう。…(略)…イースター・リリイというのが、鉄砲百合なのかどうかも、調べたことはない。しか

し、私の生れた津軽では、鉄砲百合の盛りは六月の初旬であった。はちきれるばかりの生命力でふくらみきった蕾が、茎から直角につきでている鋭さが、諸々の危機をはらんだ銃口を思わせたが、それの噴き出すばかりの生命の横溢には、北国の初夏が感ぜられた。

江木高遠の床にころがっていた、花束のなかにも、百合ならば、蕾の一つや二つは混じっていたにちがいない。それが贈り主のエチケットである。

百合は、蕾をクライマックスにして、開花とともに衰える花だからである。

自ら三十二歳の若い生命を絶った青年外交官の異国的な悲劇を彩る花として、百合はきわめて印象的だった。

うるわしの白百合
ささやきぬ むかしを
イエスきみの墓より
生まれししむかしを……

と賛える「復活」の花を、結びつけても、見劣りがしないほど、明治の死は、生命力に溢れていたのかもしれない。萎びかけた鉄砲百合のように、毒々しく雌雄の「シベ」だけがむき出しになって、粘っこく糸をひいているのが「現代の生」なのだとすれば、「明治の死」は、蕾だったのかもしれぬ。〉

鉄砲百合は、あのシーボルトが日本ユリの球根を一八二九年ドイツへ帰国時に持ち帰り、ゲント植物園に植えたが開花せず、一八四〇年再び送られたものから開花したのが、初めてである。（清水基夫『日

本のユリ」参照）

英名は、純白の花が「純潔」を表すことから、キリスト教の行事に使われチャーチ・リリー（Church Lily）イースター・リリー（Easter Lily）その他がある。我が国では、琉球百合、薩摩百合、為朝百合、筒長百合、サガリユリ、ニオイユリ、ジャコウユリ、高砂ユリなどがある。

昭和三十五年（一九六〇）二月二十九日、「弥生書房」から『文学碑めぐり』という本が出たが、その中に、「葛西善藏」について今官一は一文を載せた。

昭和四十年六月十五日、「一水社」より『にっぽん好色美女伝』を刊行。秋田のお百、おさん・茂兵衛、夜嵐おきぬ、安達ヶ原の鬼婆、お岩さま、おはん長右エ門、静御前、おこよ・源三郎、笠森おせん、などを描いた講談である。

昭和四十六年十一月、「県政の歩み」に『鐘の鳴る夜よ来てくれ！』を三十回連載。「東奥日報」の「十枚小説」の選者など、郷里の若き文学志望者たちの誠実な指導を心がけた。

さきに（昭和四十四年十二月三十日）『KONKAN 津軽ぶし』を出版していた「津軽書房」が『今官一全作品集』を企画していた。

そして、『KONKAN 津軽ぶし』は、実に面白くて、抱腹絶倒せざるを得ない場面がおおかった。コンカン先生は、英治氏が心配されたことは、わがコンカン先生に限っては、杞憂であったではないか。コンカン先生は、大衆庶民の心を十分に抱腹絶倒させるスットボケタ極めて高尚なユーモア精神に満ちておられる方だ。わざわざ、「芥川賞の方へ蛙飛びする」必要のないほど、文士として、いかなる文学ジャンルをも、注文に応じて、職人の一徹さで、みごとな芸術作品として、磨き上げる鬼才ある人ではないか。あの長谷川伸氏が、はやくから、その異彩に注目しておられた故に、初めてお目にかかったとき、「ああ、君があの今君

か!」と、喜んで迎えてくださった場面などを、連想するのである。
「あとがきに代えて」とサブタイトルがついた《津軽になんか無いかもしれない津軽に就いてのバラード》とある文章に私は、魅せられてしまった。
昭和五十年二月二十日、「講談社」より『親鸞全集』が刊行されたが、今官一訳、『聖徳太子奉賛』（大日本国粟散王聖徳太子奉賛）を載せた。みごとな和訳である。著名な仏教学者や高僧たちの文章のなかにまじって、堂々の名訳である。
昭和五十四年（一九七九）十月、今官一は、脳卒中で倒れ、代々木病院に入院。
昭和五十五年（一九八〇）一月、故郷「弘前」市に移住。車椅子の生活が始まる。同年八月『今官一作品』上下二巻を「津軽書房」より刊行。
昭和五十七年十二月七日、「東奥日報」の「あすなろ随談」に大きな今官一の顔写真がのり、その下に「故郷弘前で三度目の冬を迎える直木賞作家今官一さん」と書かれていた。トルストイか、ヘミングウェイか、…ほほのあたりまで白髭を蓄え左手で煙草をうまそうに吸っておられる懐かしいコンカン先生のお姿である。
大きなおだやかな微笑をたたえた表情ゆたかなお顔。黒い瞳がこころなしか、ふかい涙に潤んでいるように見える。波乱万丈の人生を、文学ひとすじ、真実一路に生き生きと生き抜いて来られた〈極北の人生と文学の恩師〉の気高くも、実に優しいエイコーン（肖像）が輝いている。遠く遥かな水平線を、見詰めておられるようにも思われる。
昭和五十七年（一九八二）一月二十四日、弘前の詩人葛西三枝子さん主宰の詩誌『波』（第一八号）には、巻頭に『初夢』と題して今官一の詩が載った。

東京駅の近くの船の博物館で志賀直哉先生と会っていた　ふと阿川弘之の話をしようとして軍艦の話をしょうとしてご存知でしょうが……といいかけて眼が覚めた
夢の中の先生は木綿の着物を着ておられきさくな隣組の小父さんのように面倒見のいい小父さんだった

いまにして思えば、この「初夢」の詩が、コンカン先生の最後をかざる〈詩〉ではなかろうか。と、思ったが、どうやらそれはまちがいだった。
今官一（コンカン）先生が、天に召された最後の記憶が、この昭和五十六年暮れの大晦日の日であったからなのだから…。私が先生にお目にかかった最後の記憶が、この昭和五十六年暮れの大晦日の日であったからなのだ
昭和五十八年三月一日、弘前市内白戸病院で昇天。七十三歳。
今官一は二月二十一日流行性感冒にかかり、それを乗り切る体力のないまま、一週間後の三月一日朝、息をひきとった。しかし、死の床につく直前、東奥日報連載中の『思い出す人々』の最終原稿（七十回）を自らすすんで書き終えたことや、久しぶりにトランプに打ち興じた事などを考えると、ひそかにさよならを告げていたのかもしれない。

414

知の新視界

[参献文献]

海老沢有道・大内三郎『日本キリスト教史』日本基督教団出版局、一九七〇年。

『今官一作品上巻・下巻』津軽書房、一九八〇年。

『キリスト教文学事典』教文館、一九九五年。

『日本キリスト教歴史大事典』教文館、一九八八年。

『日本キリスト教教育史』思潮篇　創文社、一九九三年。

小野正文『津軽の文学と風土』北方新社、一九七五年。

21 二十一世紀における国際テロリズムの脅威管理

脅威評価の方法論について

大泉光一

テロ組織のハイテク兵器「ステガノグラフィー」

二〇〇一年九月十一日現地時間の午前九時前後に米国で起きたオサマ・ビン・ラディン氏率いるイスラム過激派国際テロ組織「アル・カイダ」グループによる、同時多発テロ事件は六千人以上の犠牲者を出す史上最悪のテロ事件となった。

同時多発テロ事件は、未然に防ぎきれない自爆テロだったことも確かであるが、直接的な引き金になったのは、民間旅客機のハイジャックである。未然防止が可能なハイジャックさえ止められれば被害は最小限にとどまったと想定される。

このようなテロ行為を未然に防ぐためには、当然のことながら綿密な情報（information）および諜報（intelligence）活動が必要となる。

「アル・カイダ」による日本も含む欧米諸国内外における軍事施設、在外公館などの米国関連施設に対するテロ行為が予測されていて、標的にされる可能性の大きかった軍事施設や公共施設を中心に警備が強化されていた。それも、テロ手段がNBC（核・生物・化学）兵器によるものであろうと予想されて対策が練られていたのである。ところが、誰もが予想しなかった大規模な自爆テロを許す結果となった。米国政府は予想外のテロ手段や標的等に関する的確な脅威評価（threat assessment）や情報収集・分析・評価ができなかった点で、大きな課題を残したといえる。

こうした問題の背景には、事件を引き起こした「アル・カイダ」グループの構成員が仲間同士で連絡をとる際、偽名、合言葉などの使用のほかに、デジタル画像に秘密情報を埋め込む技術を使い、インターネットで連絡を取り合っていたのであるが、誰もが予想しなかった理由がある。ちなみに、この技術は「ステガノグラフィ（電子あぶり出し）」という名称で知られているが、デジタル画像の中に、文書や写真など別の情報を埋め込む暗号技術の一種である。例えば、アダルト系サイトのポルノ写真に極秘指令の画像を隠し、これをEーメールで送るか、ウェブサイトに掲載する。テロリスト仲間が問題の画像を選んでクリックするとパスワード入力画像が現れ、パスワードを入れると極秘指令が表示されるのである。

ところで、世界最高の情報機関だと過度に自賛しているCIA（米中央情報局）がハイジャックと同時テロを予期できなかったのは、自己満足による無能力やFBI（米連邦捜査局）との縄張り意識、それに現地での協力者獲得やアラビア語教育よりも衛星画像に頼るハイテク偏重が主因であると指摘されている。

知の新視界

ちなみに、CIAやFBIのテロリズムに関する情報の入手方法には、

1、マスコミ報道や治安当局の公開資料などの一般情報（Open—Source Information）
2、主としてスパイを活用して入手する人的情報（Human Intelligence Collection (HUMINT)）
3、技術的情報（Technologycal Intelligence Collection）
 (1) 信号情報【Signal Intelligence Collection (SIGINT)】
  ①電話・ファックスなどの傍・盗聴して情報を入手する通信情報（COMMINT）
  ②信号・電波等をとらえて分析して、相手の能力や特性などを調べる電子情報（E. LINT）
 (2) 衛星画像による偵察写真情報【Photographic Intelligence Collection (PHOTINT)】

などがある。

脅威と脅威評価

脅威とは、危機の発生を暗示するメッセージであり、潜在的な可能性を警告する環境である。脅威は、人為的なものであり、概して自然災害や労働争議などとは無関係であるが、それは、環境の悪化が目に見えない形として現れる一つの形態であるといえる。脅威は潜在する危機の前兆であり、日常生活の中では、それは気付かれないことが多い。例えば、テロリストが海外で日本のNGO関係者を標的に選定したとすれば、このことは日本のNGO関係者の側にとってはまったく知る予知がない。しかし、テロリストがその

人物を標的にした時点から、それはその人物にとっての脅威となるのである。誘拐・拉致事件において、それが突然発生する予測できないものであると、考えられているのはこのためである。しかし、先に述べたように、脅威は環境の変化として現れるものであると、テロリストがNGO関係者などを誘拐・拉致する際には、必ず綿密な情報活動を行うのである。その内容は、標的にした人物のパターン化した日常生活、ルーチン化した通勤ルートおよび通勤手段、スケジュール、それらの状況などを調べて、より確実な方法で目的を達成するための準備なのである。そうした兆候を的確に察知することによって回避をはかり、対応策を練ることが可能となるのである。また、危機の発生には、必ず原因と結果が伴い、その原因が危機を誘発するものである。そうした要因も一つの脅威の形態としてとらえることができるのである。したがって、そうした脅威を排除することが、重要となってくるのである。

また、脅威とは可能性である。先に述べたように、テロリストがたとえ標的を選定しても、それが実行に結びつくとは必ずしも断言できない。日本人のNGO関係者やテロリスト側の状況の変化によって、危機として発生するかどうかは変わってくるのである。このことは危機管理によっては、その回避が可能であることを示すものである。テロリズムとは、弱者の手段であり、彼らは基本的に楽な標的を（soft-targets）を偏好するのである。したがって、テロリストは危機管理体制を十分に整えている組織や人物を、標的リストから除外するのである。それゆえに、テロリストに対しても、個人に対しても危機管理の充実が求められるのである。いずれにせよ、危機の発生は、企業や個人の側の要因によって発生することが多いのである。

以上の点を考えると、脅威は、弱点（Vulnerability）＋リスク（Risk）で表わされる。すなわち、ここでいう弱点とは、法の執行状況、警察や軍の能力および状態、外部援助の有無、本質的な標的の可能性、こうした弱点およびリスクを放置しておけば、それが危機に発展する必然性が生じるということである。さま

危機管理体制の不整備・不拡充、などが含まれる。また、リスクは、自然および人間が引き起こす可能性のあるものを含むが、テロリズムによって引き起こされたものは、人的リスクといえる。こうした弱点およびリスクはそれ自体が危機を発生させる要因となる。したがって、それらを認識し、本質的な脅威を見出す必要があるのである。このリスクと弱点の分析こそが、まさに危機管理計画の立案の開始を可能にするのである。言い換えるならば、脅威というものを正確に認識することによってはじめて、そのレベルを順序立てて見ることができ、その成果および脅威に対応するために必要な情報の割り当てを行うことができるのである。そうした分析結果に乗っ取って、予測される事態のために計画された対応策を本来あるべき状態に保ち、不足している情報や人材を順序立てて組み合わせることによって、いかに脅威を排除するかを認識することができるのである。つまり、脅威評価を行うことは、効果的な危機管理活動を実施する前提であるといえるのである。

脅威評価の方法論

危機管理を行ううえで、最も重要な不可欠要素として、危険評価（Risk Assessment）と脅威評価（Threat Assessment）がある。

まず、危険評価（リスク・アセスメント）とは、出張や中・長期滞在する国における犯罪率、テロ組織の活動状況、犯罪の特徴などを把握し、分析・評価して対応策を導き出す作業である。

次に脅威評価（スレット・アセスメント）とは、テロ、革命、戦争、内乱というような誰の目にも明らかな危機状況を分析するのではなく、日常の生活環境の中で、それが目に見えない形でいかに劣化してい

脅威評価とは、環境・脅威・友好状態および標的への衝撃を分析し、脅威の予防あるいはその対応のために方向付けられた計画行動であるといえる。

脅威評価の方法論は、未だにこの問題に対する関心の薄さであるといえる。リスク・マネジメントは大恐慌からの教訓であり、クライシス・マネジメントがキューバ危機に端を発しているならば、脅威評価の必要性を真剣に考えるようになったのは、一九七八年のイラン革命からである。当時、米国は事前にイスラム教シーア派指導者ホメイニ師によって革命が起きることを予知できず、在イラン米国大使館員ら百人以上が人質に捕られるという苦い経験をした。

脅威評価は、最も困難な課題の一つであり、日本政府も企業も最も不得意とする分野である。しかしながら、この脅威評価を怠った危機管理は、万一、事件や事故が発生した時には、常に後手に回って問題に対処せざるを得なくなり、時にそれは政府や企業にとって手に負えないような事態にまで発展することがある。したがって、日本は欧米諸国のように効果的なインテリジェンス（諜報）機関を持たないという特殊事情もあるが、今回の米国における同時多発テロ事件を契機に今後、日本政府や企業は早急に何らかの対策を講じなければならないのである。

完璧な脅威評価分析には、脅威評価の公式《脅威＝リスク＋弱点＋ニーズ》の評価・分析》を認識しなければならない。ここでいうニーズには、使命と必要条件が含まれ、環境および関連する要件、標的の形態を総括的にみる、なども含まれている。脅威評価の方法は多種多様であるが、代表的な手法は次の通りである。

るかを分析し、それが何時、どこで、どのようにして本格的な危機的状況に発展するのか、その可能性を分析し、察知する作業である。したがって、脅威評価とは、

(1) 定量分析

公開されている一般情報の統計的処理による指標を用いて脅威を分析・評価する。カントリーリスク分析によく使用されるが、債務問題と異なり、単に経済的指標だけでなく、社会・政治的要素を評価する必要があり、現実には極めて困難である。

(2) 現地社会に影響力のある人物を通しての情報の入手。

(3) リコネッサンス（reconnaissance：探索（活動））

本国からテロ対策の専門家を派遣し、脅威の現状を専門家の眼と肌を通して評価する。

(4) シナリオを描き、シュミレーション化する。

知見をもとに、考えられる全ての脅威の可能性およびその発展傾向のシナリオを検討する。

(5) 現地専門家の様々な情報を集積して分析・評価する。

(6) 周辺国情報分析

当該国の実情を把握できない場合、国境を出入りする商人や難民からの情報を分析して脅威を評価する。

(7) 危険要素のチェック・リスト分析、などがある。

外交官などの特定の個人または企業（施設等も含む）に対する脅威評価は、前記の方法などを用いて、その地域で活動しているテロリストやマフィアたちの立場に立って実施しなければならない。つまり、彼らがその目的を達成する上で、何が標的として最も有効的か、そしてそれを成功させるための最善の攻撃方法はどのようなものか、革命税や戦争税の支払い強要、爆破、脅迫、エグゼクティブの誘拐、暗殺、製

品汚染、その他のいずれかを分析しなければならない。また、彼らの過去の攻撃パターンはどうであったか。身代金の要求金額および解決額はどうか、誘拐された被害者の解放率と殺害率、あるいはグループ同士の協力または敵対関係はどうか、反政府組織、学生組織、労働組合、ジャーナリズム、国家権力との関係はどうか、などについて慎重に検討しなければならないのである。

図はテロリズムの脅威評価方法を示したものである。これによると、一般的に脅威評価は、①使命分析、②対象国の政治・経済・社会環境の分析、③リスク（危険）の認識、④友好的状態の分析、⑤標的の分析の五つに分類されるが、これらの中で⑤の標的の分析が最も重要となる。なお、標的の分析は、歴史、能力、弱点、価値、成功の可能性の評価されそうな人物や施設の優先順位を知ることができる。

まず歴史は、過去にテログループが標的とした人物や施設、その戦術およびそのテロ行為が（テロリスト側と標的にされた側）成功したかどうかを調査することであり、そうすることによって、特に標的にされそうな人物や施設の優先順位を知ることができる。

能力は、知ることができる範囲で、テロ組織の人材（経歴、性格、カリスマ性、特技など）、軍事訓練、所持している武器（銃器）の種類、NBC（核・生物・化学）兵器の種類および弾薬（プラスチック爆薬、セムテックス爆薬、ニトログリセリンなど）、化学物資（農薬、活動資金源などに関して綿密に調査して認識することである。既成概念にとらわれた見解や固有の弱点についても、再度標的の弱点を十分に認識しなければならない。また、標的への興味、目に見えるものの弱点ばかりではなく、状況的および業務的弱点も知る必要がある。およびの接近などの問題も認識することが重要である。

価値は、象徴的価値と資産的価値の評価である。象徴的価値とは、例えば、日本と関連のある標的の破

テロリズムの脅威評価

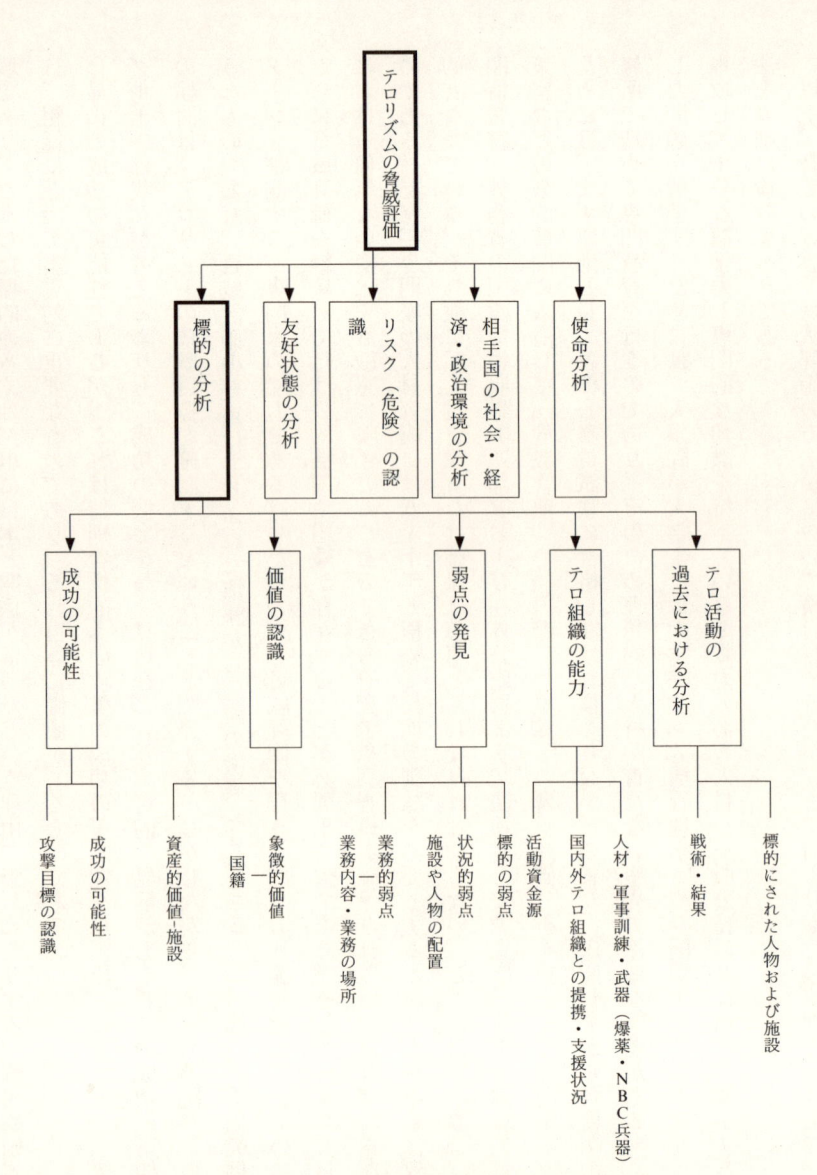

```
テロリズムの脅威評価
├── 標的の分析
│   ├── 成功の可能性
│   │   ├── 成功の可能性
│   │   └── 攻撃目標の認識
│   ├── 価値の認識
│   │   ├── 資産的価値・施設
│   │   ├── 国籍
│   │   └── 象徴的価値
│   ├── 弱点の発見
│   │   ├── 業務内容・業務の場所
│   │   ├── 業務的弱点
│   │   ├── 施設や人物の配置
│   │   ├── 状況的弱点
│   │   └── 標的の弱点
│   ├── テロ組織の能力
│   │   ├── 活動資金源
│   │   ├── 国内外テロ組織との提携・支援状況
│   │   └── 人材・軍事訓練・武器（爆薬・NBC兵器）
│   └── テロ活動の過去における分析
│       ├── 戦術・結果
│       └── 標的にされた人物および施設
├── 友好状態の分析
├── リスク（危険）の認識
├── 相手国の社会・経済・政治環境の分析
└── 使命分析
```

テロリズムの脅威評価方法（大泉光一 作）

壊であり、こうした標的の多くは、単に日本と関係があったという理由で狙われたりする。資産的価値とは、組織にとって本質的に重要なものであり、それ自体に価値があるものである。

最後の成功の可能性であるが、これは特別な標的への攻撃の成功の可能性を見極めることである。テログループは我々が考えるよりも、成功の機会を高く見込むという本質的な見解がある。この成功の可能性の検討は、テロリストの攻撃目標を確認するということと関連する。しかしながら、テロの手段がどのようなものであれ、脅威評価の要点はありふれた情報から危険の徴候（indication）を見出し、その発展パターンを推測する、専門家の能力である。したがって、脅威評価を行う上で、方法論が確立されていて、さらに脅威評価を継続して行う公的機関や組織が存在することが必要不可欠である。そして何よりも日常における何気ない変化をも敏感に嗅ぎとることのできる研究者や調査員が確保されていなければならないのである。ただ、専門家の人材育成には五〜十年と極めて長期の訓練を必要とするため、人材不足は致命的となっている。それ故に、人材育成または確保は急務とされなければならない。とくに日本の場合、内閣情報官、外務省の国際情報収集関連部署および在外公館警備室、法務省公安調査庁、警視庁国際テロ対策室などの公的機関に入所して「危機管理」や「国際テロ組織」の脅威評価分析を担当する専門家になるためには、まず原則として各種公務員試験に合格しなければならない。つまり、入所してから各機関の研修所で初めて専門教育を行うのであり、そのため理想的な人材が育たない極めて深刻な問題がある。こうした問題を解消するためには、人事院が大学または大学院で「危機管理学」や「国際テロリズム研究」を専攻し、十分な語学力と専門的な知識を持っている即戦力のある人材を一般公務員とは別枠で採用する方法を真剣に検討すべきである。

以上、脅威の意義と脅威評価の方法論について検討してみたが、まず何よりも危機管理を行う上で、脅

威評価はなくてはならないものであるということが理解される。そしてそれは、日常的および最新のものでなければならない。正確に指導された脅威評価は、それぞれの計画の主要な構成要素や危機管理計画となる。脅威が正確に理解されれば、適切な対応策や手続きを確立することが出来、要求される情報や援助組織を振り分けることが可能となり、必要な人材をも確保・訓練・準備することができるのである。このような認識なしに予防策や対応策を考えることはできないのである。

[参考文献]

1 大泉光一「二十一世紀における国際テロリズムの脅威管理―脅威評価の方法論について―」『国際経済研究』通巻二三八号、二〇〇一年十二月・二〇〇二年一月、五一・五五頁。

2 大泉光一「クライシス・マネジメントの具体的方法―脅威評価と情報の役割が重要―」『エコノミスト』毎日新聞社、一九九二年四月二十一日号、五二-五九頁。

3 大泉光一『クライシス・マネジメント―危機管理の理論と実践―』(第三訂版) 同文舘、二〇〇二年四月。

4 Morris, Eric and Alan Hoe. Terrorism Threat and Response. New York: St. Martins's Press, 1988.

5 Seger, Karl A. The Anti-Terrorism Handbook. Presidio, 1990. 58-60.

22 許容紛争と訴訟能力を欠く者の上訴

小田 司

[1] はじめに

訴訟能力は、一般的に個々の訴訟行為の有効要件であるとされている。つまり、民事訴訟手続に関与する当事者が自ら単独ですべての訴訟行為を有効に行い、又は裁判所及び相手方の訴訟行為を単独で有効に受けることができるためには、訴訟能力を有していなければならない。訴訟能力を欠く者が自ら単独でした訴訟行為及びこの者に対して行われた訴訟行為は、無効とされる。訴訟能力を欠く者が自ら単独で訴えを提起した場合、あるいは訴訟能力を欠く者に対して訴えが提起された場合には、補正がなければ、訴えは不適法として却下される。この訴えを却下した判決に対して、訴

[2] 訴訟能力の概念

本稿の目的は、このパラドキシカルな問題に関して、わが国及びドイツにおける判例・学説の立場を検証し、理論の深化を試みることである。訴訟能力を欠く者による上訴の問題について検討するにあたり、まず、この問題を検討するうえでの前提となる訴訟能力の概念を明らかにし、さらに、この問題を解明するための論拠となりうる訴訟能力の存否をめぐる紛争（許容紛争）についても検討を加えることとする。

1 訴訟要件

わが国民事訴訟法の母法国であるドイツにおいては、訴訟能力は訴訟要件の一つであり、原告又は被告のいずれかに訴訟能力が備わっていないときは、裁判所は本案について審理することができず、本案判決を下すことができないとされている。[3] そして、訴訟手続に関与する当事者の一方に訴訟能力が欠けているときは、原則として訴えが不適法として却下されることになる。[4]

ドイツ普通法時代には、訴訟能力や当事者能力などの訴訟要件は、「訴訟（訴訟法律関係）の成立要件」

訟能力なしとされた者が単独で上訴を提起した場合、裁判所はこの上訴をいかに処理すべきであるかということが問題とされている。上訴の提起行為は、訴訟行為の一つであるから、訴訟能力が訴訟行為の有効要件であるという一般原則に従えば、訴訟能力を欠く者が自ら単独で提起した上訴は無効として扱われなければならないはずである。しかし、現在の通説は、訴訟能力の欠缺を理由に訴えを却下した判決に対して、訴訟能力なしとされた者が上訴を提起した場合には、この上訴は適法として扱われなければならないとしている。[2]

であると考えられていたが、今日では、訴訟要件の一つとされる訴訟能力が当事者の一方に欠けている場合の不適法な訴えでも、この訴えが却下されるまでは訴訟が係属することから、訴訟要件は訴訟の成立要件であるとは考えられていない。ただ、このような場合には本案判決を下すことができない。したがって、ドイツにおける現在の判例及び通説によれば、訴訟要件は本案判決を下すための要件、すなわち本案判決要件であるとされている。[6]

さらに、近時ドイツにおいては、訴訟能力などの訴訟要件は、本案審理のための要件でもあるという見解が主張されている。[7]このことは、しかしながら裁判所が本案審理の前に必ず訴訟要件の存在について判断しなければならないということを意味するのではないとされている。裁判実務においては、訴訟要件の存在に疑いがなければ、裁判所は訴訟要件について調査することなしに本案の審理を開始する。[8]つまり、訴訟要件が本案審理のための要件であるということの意味は、訴訟要件の存在に疑いがある場合、あるいは訴訟要件が欠けているということが明白な場合に、裁判所は本案について審理することができないということである。[9]したがって、訴訟要件が本案審理のための要件であるという見解に従えば、ある訴えに理由がないということが明らかな場合でも、訴訟要件の存在に疑いがあれば、原則として請求を棄却することは許されないということになる。

これに対してわが国の通説は、訴訟能力はそれじたい訴訟要件ではないが、訴訟能力を欠く者が訴えを提起したり、又は訴状の送達を受領したときは、訴訟係属が適法ではないから、これが補正されないかぎり、裁判所は訴えを却下しなければならないとしている。[10]つまり、訴訟成立過程において当事者の一方に訴訟能力が欠けている場合には、「訴え提起・訴状送達が有効なこと」という訴訟要件が欠けることにな[11]

り、訴えの不適法却下をもたらすことになるから、訴訟の成立過程に限り訴訟能力は訴訟要件となるとされている。[12]

問題は、わが国の通説が主張するように、訴訟能力は訴訟の成立過程においてのみ必要であるのか、あるいは訴訟手続全体を通じて具備すべき要件であるのかということである。

訴訟手続において、当事者双方の訴訟能力が要求されるのは、とりわけ自己の利益を正しく認識しえない当事者、すなわち訴訟能力を欠く者を保護することにある。訴訟能力を欠く者が、適式に代理されていない場合には、自ら自己の利益を十分に主張し、又は防御することができず、この者を自己の利益に反する不適切な訴訟追行から保護しなければならない。それは、訴訟において訴訟能力を欠く者と対等な攻撃防御の機会が保障されなければならないからである。訴訟能力を欠く者の保護は、訴訟の成立過程においてのみ必要なのではなく、訴訟手続全体を通じて認められなければならない。

訴訟係属後、当事者が訴訟能力を失った場合、この者に訴訟代理人がいなければ訴訟手続は中断する（民事訴訟法第一二四条第一項第三号）。このことは、まさに訴訟能力を欠く者に対する本案の審理及び判決がこの者の利益保護に反するという判断によるものである。また、訴訟代理人がいて訴訟手続が中断しない場合でも、法定代理人による能力の補充がなければ、訴訟能力を欠く者に対する本案の審理及び判決は許されない。[13]

わが国においても、訴訟能力は訴訟の成立過程においてのみ必要なのではなく、ドイツの判例・通説の見解と同様に、訴訟手続全体について具備すべき要件、すなわち訴訟要件（本案判決要件）であると解すべきである。[14]

2 訴訟行為の有効要件

ドイツ及びわが国において、訴訟能力は個々の訴訟行為の有効要件であるとされており、この点について一般的に争いがない。したがって、訴訟能力を欠く者は自ら単独で訴訟行為を有効に行うことができず、また訴訟能力を欠く者に対して行われた訴訟行為も無効となる。

訴訟能力が個々の訴訟行為の有効要件であるという一般原則に対して、この原則は本案審理のための訴訟行為についてだけ妥当するという見解が主張されているが、この問題は訴訟能力の存否をめぐる紛争と深く関係することから、ここでは立ち入らず、次章において詳しく検討することにする。

以上、訴訟能力の概念について概説したが、ドイツにおける判例・通説の見解と同様に、わが国においても訴訟能力は、本案判決の要件（訴訟要件）であり、それと同時に個々の訴訟行為の有効要件であるとするのが妥当ではないかと思われる。すなわち、訴訟能力とは、自ら単独ですべての訴訟行為を有効に行い、又はすべての訴訟行為を自ら単独で有効に受けることができる能力であり、訴訟手続全体を通じて具備すべき要件であるということができる。

以上の考察結果を前提とし、訴訟能力の存否をめぐる紛争、すなわち許容紛争における訴訟能力を欠く者の訴訟行為について検討を加えることにする。

[3] 訴訟能力の存否をめぐる紛争

1 許容紛争における訴訟能力を欠く者の取り扱い

訴訟能力は、本案判決の要件であるから、当事者の一方に訴訟能力が欠けている場合には、裁判所は本

案の審理を行うことができず、そして本案判決を下すことができない。したがって、裁判所は訴訟の開始段階だけではなく、訴訟のすべての段階、すなわちすべての審級において、職権により訴訟能力の有無を調査しなければならない。[16] 調査の結果、当事者の一方に訴訟能力が欠けているということが判明した場合、裁判所は補正がなされなければ訴えを不適法として却下することになる。

わが国においては、当事者が訴訟能力を欠く場合の手続処理として、専ら訴訟能力なしとされた者が提起した上訴の有効性を問題としているが、すでに第一審において訴訟能力の存在について当事者間に争いがある場合（許容紛争）、あるいは裁判所が一方当事者の訴訟能力の存在について疑いを抱いた場合には、訴訟能力の存否に疑いがある者の訴訟行為を有効として扱わなければならないのかという問題が生じる。裁判所は、訴訟能力の存否について口頭弁論に基づき審理・判断するまでは、訴訟判決及び本案判決のいずれも下すことはできないが、訴訟能力は訴訟行為の有効要件であり、訴訟能力を欠く者は訴訟行為を有効に行うことはできないとされているから、原則として訴訟能力の存否をめぐる争いにおいても訴訟行為を有効に行うことができないことになる。訴訟能力の存否に疑いがある者の訴訟能力の存否をめぐる争いについて適法に審理・判断に関与させなければならないから、裁判所は訴訟能力についての争いが判決により解決されるまでは、訴訟能力を欠く者であっても、この紛争に限って訴訟行為を有効に行うことができるとしている。[17] そこで、ドイツの判例・学説は、訴訟能力を欠く者でも、訴訟能力の存否についての争いにおいては訴訟行為を有効に行うことができるというドイツの判例・学説に対して、訴訟能力は訴訟行為の有効要件ではないから、このような取り扱いは不要であるという見解が主張されている。[18] これは、Abend、Bernhardt、Groger などによる主張である

が、この中で特に注目されるのはGrogerによって展開された見解である。彼は、本案判決と直接関係する訴訟行為のみが重要であること、訴訟能力が訴訟行為を欠く者により提起された訴えであっても訴訟係属の効果が生じることなどを理由に、訴訟能力が訴訟行為の有効要件であるという一般原則は、本案審理のための訴訟行為についてのみ妥当するもので、たとえば訴えの提起、上訴の提起又は訴訟能力の存否についての争いにおける訴訟行為などには適用されず、したがって、許容紛争において訴訟能力を欠く者の訴訟能力を擬制することは不要であるとしている。

仮に、このような見解が正しいとすれば、許容紛争における通説の取り扱いは不要ということになるが、訴訟能力は訴訟行為の有効要件であるという一般原則を本案審理のための訴訟行為についてだけ制限することが可能であるのかということが問題である。

確かに訴訟能力を欠く者の訴え提起により、訴訟能力者による訴え提起の場合と同様に訴訟は係属するが、このことから訴訟能力を欠く者の訴え提起、すなわち訴訟行為が有効であるということを結論づけることはできないように思われる。訴訟能力を欠く者による訴え、あるいは訴訟能力を欠く者に対する訴えであっても、精神活動に障害がある場合、すなわち意思能力の欠缺が問題である場合には、訴え提起の段階で訴状から訴訟能力の欠缺を知るのは困難であり、また訴訟能力を欠く者の訴えを全く無視することは司法拒否の禁止に反し許されないから、通常の場合、裁判所は当事者に訴訟能力が備わっているか否かにかかわらず訴えを受け入れる。訴えの提起は、裁判所に特定の裁判を求める行為（取効的訴訟行為：Erwirkungshandlung）であるから、裁判所は訴訟能力を欠く者による訴え提起でも無視することはできず、これについて適法か不適法かの判断を下さなければならない。訴訟能力を欠く者の訴えであっても、これが不適法として却下されるまで、訴訟係属の効果が生ずるということは、訴訟能力を欠く者の

欠く者の訴え提起が有効であるということを意味するのではなく、裁判所が無効な訴え提起に対しても必ず適法か不適法かの応答をしなければならないということから生ずる訴訟法上の効果である。したがって、訴訟能力を欠く者の訴え提起により生ずる訴訟係属の効果から、訴訟能力を欠く者の訴え提起も有効であり、訴訟能力が訴訟行為の有効要件であるという一般原則は妥当しないという結論を導き出すことはできない。

また Groger によれば、本案判決と直接関係する訴訟行為のみが重要であり、訴訟能力が訴訟行為の有効要件であるという一般原則は、本案審理のための訴訟行為についてだけ妥当するとしているが、このことは、訴訟要件の審理と本案の審理を厳格に区分していない現在の訴訟手続の構造には妥当しないように思われる。

ドイツ普通法時代には、ローマ法以来の伝統である先行手続 (Verfahren in iure) と本案審理の手続 (Verfahren in iudicio) という二段階の手続構造をとっていたため、訴訟能力などの訴訟要件に関する審理と本案についての審理を分離することは可能であったが、現行の訴訟手続では、訴訟能力などの訴訟要件の審理と本案の審理は厳格に区分されておらず、どちらも同一手続内で平行して行われることになっているから、訴訟能力が訴訟行為の有効要件であるという一般原則を本案審理のための訴訟行為についてだけ制限することはできず、訴訟手続における全ての訴訟行為について適用しなければならない。

さらに、訴訟能力が訴訟行為の有効要件であるという一般原則を本案審理のための訴訟行為に制限することは、追認を認める現行の民事訴訟法の規定に反することになる。[25] 訴訟の最初の段階で当事者に訴訟能力が欠けていたとしても、後にこの者が訴訟能力を取得すれば、過去の訴訟行為を追認することが可能である（ドイツ民事訴訟法第五五一条第一号、第五七九条第一項第四号、日本民事訴訟法第三十四条第二

項)。しかし、訴訟能力は訴訟行為の有効要件であるという一般原則が、本案審理のための訴訟行為についてだけ妥当し、本案審理以外の訴訟行為は、訴訟能力の有無にかかわらず有効であるとするならば、本案の審理以外に行われた訴訟行為は、追認の対象から除外されることになる。したがって、訴訟能力が訴訟行為の有効要件であるという一般原則を本案審理のための訴訟行為に制限することは、訴訟能力が訴訟能力を欠く者が行った訴訟行為を追認することなしに有効として認めなければならないという結果を招き、訴訟能力を欠く者による訴訟行為の追認を認める現行の民事訴訟法の規定、さらに訴訟能力を欠く者を保護しなければならないとする訴訟能力制度の趣旨に適合しない。

結果として、訴訟能力が訴訟行為の有効要件であるという一般原則は、全ての訴訟行為について妥当しなければならないものので、原則として訴訟能力の存否についての争いを審理する場合にも適用されなければならない。したがって、訴訟能力の存否に関する争いにおいて適法に審理を進めるためには、訴訟能力を欠く者の訴訟行為も有効とする手続上の取り扱い、すなわち訴訟能力の擬制が必要である。通説が一般的に承認している訴訟能力の存否をめぐる争い(Zulassungsstreit)というのは、民事訴訟の特殊な形態であり、訴訟能力は訴訟行為の有効要件であるという一般原則の例外を示すものであるということができる。[26]

2 法的審問請求権

裁判所が訴訟能力の存否をめぐる争いについて適法に審理・判断するためには、訴訟能力を欠く者であっても訴訟能力の存否に関する審理に関与させ、この争いの枠内で訴訟行為を有効に行わせることが必要である。[27] こうした取り扱いが許されることの根拠について、わが国では十分な説明がなされていない。わが国では、専ら訴訟能力を欠く者の上訴との関係で、訴訟能力について争っている当事者は、上訴審でも

その点の判断を受けることが保障されなければならないとしている。これに対してドイツでは、ドイツ基本法第一〇三条第一項が規定する法的審問請求権（Anspruch auf rechtliches Gehör）を根拠に、訴訟能力を欠く者でも訴訟手続に関与させ、訴訟行為を有効に行わせることができるとしている。

ドイツ基本法第一〇三条第一項によれば、裁判手続において、すべての人に対して法的審問請求権が認められている。この請求権は、裁判官によるすべての訴訟手続について保障されるものであり、民事訴訟法で特に規定されてはいないが、基本法との関係から民事訴訟においても民事手続上の一般原則として承認されている。法的審問請求権とは、訴訟手続に関与するすべての人に対して、判決の基礎となる事実と法律状況について意見を述べることができるという権利を当事者に保障するというものである。

さらに、この法的審問請求権は、ドイツ基本法第一条第一項に規定されている「侵すことのできない人間の尊厳」との関係において認められるもので、人間、つまり訴訟に関与するすべての者は、訴訟手続の客体にされてはならず、訴訟手続の主体としての役割が保障されなければならないということを意味するものだとされている。したがって、訴訟に関与する者は、訴訟の結果に対して何らかの影響を与え、そして訴訟の結果を受け入れられるように自己の権利に関して判決が下される前に意見を述べることが保障されなければならない。

このように、法的審問請求権は人間であるという「侵すことのできない人間の尊厳」から直接導かれるもので、人間の能力に左右されるものではない。したがって、未成年者、精神活動に障害がある者、又はその他の理由から行為能力、そして訴訟能力が欠けている者に対しても認められる権利だとされている。

しかし、訴訟における法的審問請求権の行使は、これも訴訟行為であるから、その有効性は権利を行使する者の訴訟能力の有無に左右され、通常の場合には法定代理人によって行使されなければならない。このことは、あくまで通常のケースについて妥当することであって、訴訟に関与する者の行為能力、又は訴訟能力の承認・否定が問題となる場合、あるいは訴訟に関与する者の精神状態について裁判上の措置（後見裁判所による世話人の選任等）が講じられなければならないような場合には、訴訟手続への独自の関与が認められなければならない。[36]つまり、訴訟に関与する者の訴訟能力について判断をしなければならないような場合には、その者の法的地位に重大な影響を与えることになるため、訴訟能力の存否について判断を下さなければならない。訴訟能力に疑いのある者でも訴訟手続に関与させることが必要であり、この者を関与させないで訴訟能力について審理・判断することは、基本法が保障する法的審問請求権の侵害であり、再審事由に該当するとされている。[37]

訴訟能力を欠く者でも、訴訟能力についての争いが判決によって解決されるまでは、訴訟能力をもつことを認め、この紛争に限って訴訟行為を有効に行わせるという許容紛争における通説の取り扱いは、ドイツ基本法第一〇三条第一項の法的審問請求権を肯認することが可能である。[38]日本国憲法には、ドイツ基本法第一〇三条第一項に対応する明文規定は置かれていないが、解釈上、民事裁判における法的審問請求権は日本国憲法第一〇三条第一項により根拠づけられるものである。日本国憲法第三十二条は、裁判を受けるすべての者に対して、裁判事項について自己の意見を表明し、聴取される機会が与えられることを要求する権利を保障している。したがって、訴訟手続に関与する者の精神状態について判断を下さなければならないような場合には、その者の法的地位に重大な影響を及ぼすため、わが国においても日本国憲法第三十二

条の「裁判を受ける権利」に基づき、訴訟能力を欠く者の訴訟手続への独自の関与を認めることは可能であろう。

[4] 訴訟能力を欠く者の上訴

1 訴訟能力を欠く者による上訴の適法性

わが国においては、訴訟能力を欠く者による上訴の問題として、通常、訴訟能力の欠缺に対する上訴について論じられているが、ドイツでは訴訟能力を欠く者が提起した上訴の問題を二つのケースに分類している。一つは、すでに第一審において訴訟能力に関する争いがあり、つまり許容紛争が上訴の提起により上訴審で継続される場合であり、もう一つは、訴訟能力の欠缺が上訴の提起により初めて上訴審において問題となる場合、すなわち訴訟能力の欠缺を看過した本案判決に対して上訴が提起された場合である。この二つのケースは、上訴審において訴訟能力の存否についての問題を解明しなければならないという点で共通するが、第二のケースは許容紛争を経由していないことから、第一のケースと分けて取り扱われている。

第一審において、すでに訴訟能力について当事者間に争いがあった場合には、権利保護の理由から、訴訟能力についての争いを上訴の提起により適法かつ有効に上訴審に移審させ、第一審の訴訟能力についての判断を上訴裁判所に審理させることが認められなければならない。したがって、「訴訟能力についての争いが判決によって解決されるまでは、訴訟能力を持つことを認め、この紛争に限って訴訟行為を有効に行うことができる」という許容紛争における原則が上訴審でも適用され、第一審で訴訟能力の欠缺を理由

に訴えを却下した訴訟判決又は本案判決に対して、仮に訴訟能力を欠く者が上訴を提起した場合でも、この者の上訴を適法として取り扱わなければならない。[40]

上訴提起は、訴訟行為であるから、原則として上訴提起者に訴訟能力が備わっていなければならないが、上訴裁判所における訴訟能力存否の問題は、上訴の適法要件であると同時に理由具備性の要件でもあるから、上訴裁判所は理由具備性の要件の枠内で訴訟能力について判断しなければならない。[41] 訴訟能力の欠缺を理由に訴えを却下した訴訟判決に対して上訴が提起された場合で、上訴審において訴訟能力の欠缺が認められるときには、上訴裁判所は上訴を不適法として却下するのではなく、理由なしとして棄却する。[42] また、本案判決に対して上訴が提起された場合で、上訴審において訴訟能力の欠缺が認められるときには、上訴を不適法として認容し、第一審判決を取り消したうえで訴えを却下しなければならない。[43]

第二のケース、つまり第一審が不当に訴訟能力の欠缺を看過して本案判決を下し、これに対して訴訟能力の欠缺を理由に上訴が提起された場合について、ドイツ連邦通常裁判所は、「第一審で不当に訴訟能力者として扱われた者が、本案判決の取り消しを求めて上訴を提起したときには、この者を訴訟能力者として扱わなければならない」としている。[44] 結論として、ドイツ連邦通常裁判所の判断は正当であると思われるが、ただ、第一審において訴訟能力者として扱われたのであるから、上訴についても訴訟能力を認めるというのでは理由として不十分であるように思われる。

本案判決に対して訴訟能力を欠く者が訴訟能力の欠缺を理由に上訴を提起した場合に、この者の上訴を適法としなければならない理由は、まず、上訴審において適法に訴訟能力の欠缺を主張させることを認め、そのことにより第一審の訴訟能力についての判断が正当であったか否かを上訴裁判所に審理させる可能性

を上訴提起者に与えなければならないということにある。先に説明したように、上訴審における訴訟能力の問題は、上訴の適法性の問題であるばかりでなく、理由具備性の問題でもあり、上訴裁判所が第一審から継続して上訴提起者に訴訟能力が欠けていると判断したときには、上訴自体は不適法であるが、同時に上訴には理由がある。このような場合に、上訴を不適法として却下すれば、上訴に理由があるにもかかわらずこれを顧慮することができなくなり、結果として第一審の不当な本案判決が維持されることになる。このような結果を回避するためには、訴訟能力を欠く者の上訴であってもその適法性を認めける訴訟能力についての判断を上訴裁判所に審理させるのが妥当である。

さらに、本案判決に対する訴訟能力を欠く者の上訴を不適法として却下すれば、第一審判決が確定するが、この場合に訴訟能力を欠く者に対して、強制執行が行われる危険が生じる。今日、ドイツ及びわが国の通説によれば、判決手続のみならず強制執行手続においても、両当事者に訴訟能力が備わっていなければならないとされているが、確定判決を債務名義として強制執行を行う場合には、執行機関は訴訟能力について審理することができないとされているから、訴訟能力の欠缺を看過した本案判決の場合には、訴訟能力を欠く者に対して強制執行を行うことが可能となる。したがって、訴訟能力を欠く者を強制執行の危険から保護するためにも、訴訟能力を欠く者の上訴を認め、本案判決の取り消しを可能にすることが必要である。

もっとも、訴訟能力を欠く者に対する本案判決が確定したとしても、再審の訴え（民事訴訟法第三三八条第一項）によりこの判決を取り消すことができるとされているが、再審の訴えは、訴訟能力を欠く者にとって最終的な手段であり、また、上訴による救済と再審の訴えによる救済を比較した場合、証明責任との関係で、上訴による救済が訴訟能力を欠く者にとって有利であるから、上訴の適法性を認め上訴審にお

いて本案判決を取り消させた方が、訴訟能力を欠く者の保護としてより効果的であると思われる。[48]

許容紛争が上訴審において継続される場合と、訴訟能力の欠缺を看過した本案判決に対する上訴の場合では、結局、どちらの場合でも訴訟能力を欠く者の上訴を適法として扱うことで一致するが、訴訟能力に関するその他のケースに分類することは、たとえば訴訟能力を欠く者に対する判決送達の効力など、訴訟能力に関するその他の問題を解決する上で有益である。

わが国の通説は、訴訟能力の欠缺を看過して判決した場合でも、この判決は有効であり、訴訟能力を欠く者本人に対する送達により上訴期間が進行し、その経過により判決は確定するが、判決確定後は再審の訴えによる救済が与えられるとしている。その理由は、訴訟能力を欠く者にも適法に上訴することが認められているのであるから、この者に対する判決の送達も有効として扱われなければならないこと、そして、訴訟能力を欠く者本人に対して判決が送達された場合に、送達が無効で上訴期間が進行しないとすると、訴訟が終局的に終了したか否かにつき未確定の状態が続き、法的安定性が損なわれるからであるとされている。[49]つまり、通説は、許容紛争を経由した場合であるか否かを問わず、一律に訴訟能力を欠く者に対する判決の送達は有効であるとしている。

裁判所が訴訟能力の存否について実際に調査することなしに本案判決を下した場合、すなわち訴訟能力の欠缺を看過して本案判決が下された場合には、許容紛争の場合と同様に扱うことはできず、本来の訴訟能力の問題として取り扱われなければならない。訴訟能力の欠缺を看過した本案判決が、訴訟能力を欠く者に対して送達された場合には、民事訴訟法第一〇二条第一項により送達は無効である。[51]したがって、判決送達により上訴期間は進行せず、上訴期間の経過により判決は確定しないため、上訴により争うことが可能である。上訴の提起により上訴審において許容紛争が開始された場合には、許容紛争の原則が適用さ

れるから、訴訟能力を欠く者が提起した上訴であってもその適法性を認めることにより、訴訟能力欠缺の主張を可能にし、第一審の訴訟能力についての判断が正当か否かを上訴裁判所に審理させることが認められなければならない。上訴裁判所が訴訟能力の存否について審理・判断した後には、許容紛争を経由しているため、訴訟能力を欠く者に対する判決送達は有効であり、上訴期間が進行し、その経過により判決は確定する。このような取り扱いは、訴訟能力を欠く者の保護を目的とする訴訟能力制度の趣旨に適合するばかりでなく、訴訟能力の問題を終局的に解決することができるため、訴訟の相手方の利益にもかない適切である。

許容紛争が上訴審において継続される場合と訴訟能力の欠缺を看過した本案判決に対して上訴が提起された場合を分類することにより、本来の訴訟能力の問題として取り扱われなければならないのか、あるいは許容紛争における原則、すなわち訴訟能力は訴訟行為の有効要件であるという一般原則の例外を認めるべきなのかを明確にする必要がある。許容紛争を経由していない場合には、許容紛争が開始されるまで、訴訟能力は訴訟行為の有効要件であるという一般原則に基づき、問題の解決がなされなければならない。

2 本案判決の内容に対する訴訟能力を欠く者の上訴

訴訟能力の欠缺を看過した第一審判決に対して、本案の審理を求める控訴が提起され、控訴裁判所が控訴提起者の訴訟能力に疑いを持った場合、いかなる取り扱いを要するのかという問題がある。この問題については、わが国において全く論じられていないため、ドイツ連邦通常裁判所の判例に基づき検討を加えることにする。

一九九〇年二月二三日のドイツ連邦通常裁判所判決は、訴訟能力を欠く者が訴訟能力の欠缺を理由と

して本案判決に対して控訴した場合には、この控訴は適法であるが、控訴提起により本案についての審理を求めた場合には、控訴を不適法として却下しなければならないとしていた。これに対して、一九九九年十一月四日のドイツ連邦通常裁判所判決は、控訴審において、控訴提起者にすでに第一審から訴訟能力が欠けていたことが判明した場合には、訴訟能力の欠缺を理由に控訴されたか否かを問わず、この者の控訴を適法として取り扱わなければならないとし、一九九〇年二月二十三日のドイツ連邦通常裁判所判決の判断を修正した。

ドイツでは、訴訟能力は職権調査事項とされているが、訴訟能力の欠缺を主張することが必要であるのか、また、ドイツの判例・学説によれば、訴訟能力は本案判決の要件とされているが、訴訟能力を欠く者の控訴は、訴訟能力を欠く者による訴えの提起と同様に扱われなければならないのかということが論点であるように思われる。

一九九〇年二月二十三日のドイツ連邦通常裁判所判決は、訴訟能力を欠く者の控訴が適法であるためには、訴訟能力の欠缺を理由として本案判決に対して控訴した場合には、この控訴は適法であるが、本案についての審理を求めた場合には、不適法として却下しなければならないとしているが、結論として、一九九九年十一月四日のドイツ連邦通常裁判所判決の判断が正当であると思われる。

裁判所は、ドイツ民事訴訟法第五十六条第一項に従い、訴訟能力の欠缺について第一審のみならず訴訟のすべての段階、すなわち上訴審においても職権により調査しなければならない。すなわち、訴訟能力の存在に疑いがあれば、当事者の主張に左右されることなく訴訟能力の存否について調査する。したがって、上訴により訴訟能力の欠缺を主張せず本案についての審理を求めた場合であっても、上訴裁判所は、訴訟能力の存否について審理・判断しなければならない。

訴訟能力は、本案判決の要件であるとされており、当事者の一方に訴訟能力が欠けている場合には、補正がなければ訴えは不適法として却下される。しかし、この訴訟能力欠缺の際の訴え提起についての取扱いは、そのまま訴訟能力の欠缺を看過した本案判決に対する上訴について当てはめることができない。訴訟能力の欠缺を主張せず、上訴により本案についての審理を求めたとしても、訴訟能力の存在に疑いがあれば、上訴裁判所はこれについて職権で調査しなければならない。調査の結果、上訴提起者に訴訟能力が欠けていることが判明したとしても、この結果を上訴審についてのみ制限すべきではなく、訴え提起の場合の却下と同様に上訴を不適法として却下すべきではない。訴訟能力の欠缺を理由に上訴を却下すれば、第一審での不当な本案判決が維持されることになり、訴訟能力を欠く者に対する適切な保護を欠くことになる。[58] さらに、この判決を取り消すためには再度、訴訟能力の欠缺を理由に争わなければならず、訴訟経済にも反する。したがって、訴訟能力を欠く者が訴訟能力の欠缺を理由として上訴を提起したか否かを問わず、訴訟能力を欠く者の上訴であっても適法として扱い、本案判決を取り消したうえで訴えを却下することが訴訟能力を欠く者を保護する上で必要であり、また訴訟経済の面からも適切である。[59]

付け加えるならば、訴訟能力を欠く者が自己の訴訟能力の欠缺を知らずに上訴を提起して本案についての審理を求めた場合に、この者に訴訟能力欠缺の主張を要求すること自体無理であり、訴訟能力欠缺の主張の有無により上訴の適法性について判断することは適切でない。[60]

[5] おわりに

本稿においては、許容紛争と訴訟能力を欠く者の上訴に関する問題として、訴訟能力の概念、許容紛争

における訴訟能力を欠く者の取り扱い、訴訟能力を欠く者による上訴の適法性及び本案判決の内容に対する訴訟能力を欠く者の上訴について考察してきた。考察の結果をまとめれば、以下のとおりである。

訴訟能力は、本案判決の要件であり、それと同時に個々の訴訟行為の有効要件でもある。したがって、訴訟能力は訴訟手続全体を通じて備わっていなければならず、当事者の一方に訴訟能力が欠けている場合には、本案の審理を行うことができず、本案判決を下すことができない。さらに、訴訟能力を欠く者が自ら単独で行った訴訟行為は、無効である。

訴訟能力が訴訟行為の有効要件であるというこの者に対して行われた訴訟行為は、無効である。

訴訟能力が訴訟行為の有効要件であるという一般原則は、全ての訴訟行為について妥当する。したがって、許容紛争においては訴訟能力の擬制が必要である。許容紛争は、民事訴訟の特殊な形態を示すものであり、訴訟能力を欠く者であってもこの争いが解決されるまでは、訴訟行為を有効に行うことが認められる。

許容紛争における訴訟能力の擬制、すなわち訴訟能力を欠く者であっても訴訟行為を有効に行い、又は有効に受けることができるという取り扱いは、ドイツ基本法第一〇三条第一項の法的審問請求権により根拠づけられる。わが国においては、これに対応する明文規定は存在しないが、日本国憲法第三十二条の「裁判を受ける権利」に基づき、解釈上、法的審問請求権を肯認することができる。

許容紛争が上訴の提起により上訴審において継続される場合には、権利保護の理由から訴訟能力を欠く者の上訴であっても、これを適法として扱わなければならない。訴訟能力の欠缺を看過した本案判決に対する上訴については、訴訟能力を欠く者を保護するため、上訴の適法性を認め、第一審における訴訟能力についての判断を上訴裁判所に審理させなければならない。

訴訟能力を欠く者が控訴の提起により本案の審理を求めたとしても、訴訟能力を欠く者に対する適切な

保護が必要であり、この者の控訴を不適法として却下すべきではない。訴訟能力を欠く者が訴訟能力の欠缺を理由に上訴を提起したか否かを問わず、上訴の適法性を認め、本案判決を取り消したうえで訴えを却下しなければならない。

[注]

1 新堂幸司『新民事訴訟法』（弘文堂・一九九八年）一二六頁、高橋宏志『重点講義民事訴訟法〔新版〕』（有斐閣・二〇〇〇年）一六二頁、松本博之＝上野泰男『民事訴訟法〔第二版〕』（弘文堂・二〇〇一年）一六九頁以下〔松本〕、木川統一郎＝中村英郎編『民事訴訟法〔新版〕』（青林書院・一九九九年）五十七頁〔高地〕、上田徹一郎『民事訴訟法講義〔第二版〕』（法学書院・一九九八年）九十四頁〔本間〕、林屋礼二『新民事訴訟法概要』（有斐閣・二〇〇〇年）三十五頁、林屋礼二＝河野正憲『民事訴訟法〔第二版〕』（青林書院・一九九九年）五十一頁〔松原〕、吉永順作＝奈良次郎編『判例に学ぶ新民事訴訟法』（青林書院・一九九九年）四十頁〔奈良〕、小室直人＝賀集唱＝松本博之＝加藤新太郎編『基本法コンメンタール新民事訴訟法1 第一編総則』（日本評論社・一九九七年）八十六頁〔難波〕、上原敏夫＝池田辰夫＝山本和彦『民事訴訟法〔第三版〕』（有斐閣・二〇〇一年）七十八頁〔山本〕など多数。

2 新堂・前掲注1 一三四頁、高橋・前掲注1 一六六頁、中野＝松浦＝鈴木編・前掲注1 九四頁〔本間〕、中野貞一郎「当事者が訴訟能力を欠く場合の手続処理」『民事訴訟法の論点Ⅰ』（判例タイムズ社・一九九四年）八十七頁以下など参照。

3 Vgl. *Arens* / *Lüke*, Zivilprozeßrecht, 6. Aufl. (1994), § 9 III ; *Baumbach* / *Lauterbach* / *Hartmann*, ZPO, 56. Aufl. (1998), Grundz § 253 Rdnr. 13 ; *Jauernig*, Zivilprozeßrecht, 25. Aufl. (1998), § 33 III ; *Rosenberg* / *Schwab* / *Gottwald*, Zivilprozeßrecht, 15. Aufl. (1993), § 96 I 2 ; *Zöller* / *Greger*, ZPO, 21. Aufl. (1999), Vor § 253 Rdnr. 9.

4 *Jauernig* (Fn. 3), § 33 V 4 ; *Rosenberg* / *Schwab* / *Gottwald* (Fn. 3), § 96 V 6 ; *Thomas* / *Putzo*, ZPO, 20. Aufl. (1997), Vorbem § 253 Rdnr. 10 ; *Zeiss*, Zivilprozeßrecht, 8. Aufl. (1993), § 41 I 1.

5 *Bülow*, Die Lehre von den Prozeßeinreden und die Prozeßvoraussetzungen, Neudruck der Ausgabe Gießen 1868

6 (1969), S. 6, 9 ; *ders.*, ZZP 27 (1900), 236.

7 *Arens / Lüke* (Fn. 3), § 13 I ; *Baumbach / Lauterbach / Hartmann* (Fn. 3), Grundz § 253 Rdnr. 13 ; *Jauernig* (Fn. 3), § 33 III ; *Laubinger*, FS für Ule, S. 164 f. ; *Musielak*, GrundkursZPO, 3. Aufl. (1995), Rdnr. 98 ; *Rosenberg / Schwab / Gottwald* (Fn. 3), § 96 I 2 ; *Schlosser*, Jura 1981, 648 ; *Zöller / Greger* (Fn. 3), Vor § 253 Rdnr. 9.

8 *Jauernig* (Fn. 3), § 33 III ; vgl. auch *Harms*, ZZP 83 (1970), 167 Fn. 1 ; *Schellhammer*, Zivilprozeß, 7. Aufl. (1996), Rdnr. 350 ; *Schilken*, Zivilprozeßrecht, 2. Aufl. (1995), § 7 I ; *Schwab*, JuS 1976, 69 ; *Zeiss* (Fn. 4), § 41 I.

9 *Schwab*, JuS 1976, 69.

10 BAG NJW-RR 1986, 157 ; BGH ZZP 89 (1976), 331 m. Anm. von *Greger*; *Berg*, JR 1968, 257 ff. ; *ders.*, NJW 1955, 235 f. ; *Martin*, Prozeßvoraussetzungen und Revision (1974) S. 29 ff. ; *Sauer*, Die Reihenfolge der Prüfung von Zulässigkeit und Begründtheit einer Klage im Zivilprozeß (1974) S. 10 f. ; *Schwab*, JuS 1976, 69 f. ; *Wieser*, ZZP 86 (1971), 304 ff. ; abl. *Rimmelspacher*, Zur Prüfung von Amts wegen (1966), S. 121 ff. ; *Grunsky*, Grundlagen des Verfahrensrechts, 2. Aufl. (1974), § 34 III 1 ; *ders.*, ZZP 80 (1967), 58 ff. ; *Henckel*, Prozeßrecht und materielles Recht (1970), S. 227 ff. ; *Lindacher*, NJW 1967, 1389 f. ; *ders.*, ZZP 90 (1977), 131 ff.

11 新堂・前掲注1 一三四頁、高橋・前掲注1 一七〇頁注17、上田・前掲注1 一九四頁、林屋・前掲注1

12 新堂・前掲注1 一三四頁、高橋・前掲注1 一七〇頁注17、上田・前掲注1 一九四頁、林屋・前掲注1

13 中野・前掲注1 一三四頁、松本＝上野・前掲注1 八十二頁、松本＝上野・前掲注1 一七一頁〔松本〕、木川＝中村編・前掲注1 一五八頁〔高木〕、中野＝松浦＝鈴木編・前掲注1 三四八頁〔宇野〕など多数。

14 中野・前掲注2 八十二頁、松本＝上野・前掲注1 一七一頁〔松本〕。

15 Vgl. z. B. *Jauernig* (Fn. 3), § 20 IV 1 ; *Rosenberg / Schwab / Gottwald* (Fn. 3), § 44 III 1 b) ; *Stein / Jonas*

一四二頁、林屋・河野編・前掲注1 一四二頁〔宇野〕など多数。

〇〇年〕九十八頁、栂善夫「訴訟能力」法学教室二一五号（二〇〇一年）二十一頁。

〔高木〕、中野＝松浦＝鈴木編・前掲注1 三四八頁〔松本〕、伊藤眞『民事訴訟法〔補訂版〕』（有斐閣二〇

一三四頁。

16　Vgl. *Bork* (Fn. 8), § 51 Rdnr. 8；新堂・前掲注1　一三二頁、高橋・前掲注1　一六五頁、中野＝松浦＝鈴木編・前掲注1　九四頁〔本間〕、小室＝賀集＝松本＝加藤編・前掲注1　八六頁〔難波〕、上原＝池田＝山本・前掲注1　七十八頁〔山本〕。意思能力を欠く者の訴訟行為については、佐ột鉄男「意思能力」『判例講義民事訴訟法』（悠々社・二〇〇一年）八十三頁参照。

17　*Oda*, Die Prozeßfähigkeit als Voraussetzung und Gegenstand des Verfahrens (1997), S. 46 ff.；*ders.*, ZZP 110 (1997), 113；松本＝上野・前掲注1　一七一頁〔松本〕、小室＝賀集＝松本＝加藤編・前掲注1　八十六頁〔難波〕。なお、わが国では、訴訟能力は職権探知事項であるとする見解がある。たとえば、菊井維大＝村松俊夫『全訂民事訴訟法〔Ⅰ〕』（補訂版）』（日本評論社・一九九三年）二六三頁、高橋・前掲注1　一六三頁、上田・前掲注1　一九七頁、林屋・前掲注1　一七〇頁など多数。

18　*Abend*, Prozesse nicht parteifähiger und existenter Parteien, Diss. Erlangen (1953), S. 10 ff.；*Bernhardt*, Der geisteskranke Schuldner in der Zwangsvollstreckung, Diss. Freiburg (1967), S. 23 ff., 81 ff.；*Groger*, Prozeßhandlungsvoraussetzungen im streitigen zivilprozessualen Verfahren, Diss. Göttingen (1964), S. 48, 63, 76.

19　*Groger* (Fn. 18), S. 48, 63, 76.

20　BverfGE 10, 302, 306；BGHZ 18, 184, 189；BGHZ 35, 1, 6；BGH NJW-RR 1986, 157, 158；BGH NJW-RR 1987, 757；BGHZ 110, 294, 295 f.＝NJW 1990, 1735＝ZZP 103 (1990), 465 m. Anm. von *Bork*；BGHZ 143, 127；*Jauernig* (Fn. 3), § 20 IV 3；*Oda* (Fn. 16), S. 14 ff., 37 ff.；*Rosenberg / Schwab / Gottwald* (Fn. 3), § 44 IV 2；*Schellhammer* (Fn. 7), Rdnr. 1195；*Stein / Jonas / Bork* (Fn. 8), § 56 Rdnr. 5；*Zöller / Vollkommer* (Fn. 3), § 56 Rdnr. 13 m. w. N.

21　*Groger* (Fn. 18), S. 48, 63, 76；わが国でも、同様な見解が主張されている。柏木邦良「訴訟要件と訴訟内紛争――単一的訴訟把握に対する１つの反省――」民事訴訟雑誌十九号（一九七三年）七十八頁以下、一〇五頁。

22　*Goldschmidt*, Der Prozeß als Rechtslage, 2. Neudruck der Ausgabe Berlin 1925 (1986), S. 371.

23　*Jauernig* (Fn. 3), § 33 V 1；*Rosenberg / Schwab / Gottwald* (Fn. 3), § 97 I 2 a) (3)；*Stein / Jonas / Leipold*, ZPO, Band 3, 21. Aufl. (1997), § 271 Rdnr. 29.

24　*Goldschmidt* (Fn. 21), S. 364, 371 f.

25　*Wetzell*, System der ordentlichen Zivilprozesses, Neudruck der 3. Aufl. Leipzig 1978 (1969), § 70, S. 941；vgl. auch *Martin* (Fn. 8), S. 20.

　　Baumgärtel, Wesen und Begriff der Prozeßhandlung einer Partei im Zivilprozeß, 2. Aufl. (1972), S. 132 f.；

26 Güntzel, Die Fehlerhaftigkeit von Prozeßhandlungen der Partei im Zivilprozeß und die Möglichkeit ihrer Heilung, Diss. Marburg (1966), S. 92 f.

27 Oda (Fn. 16), S. 36 f.

28 Baumgärtel (Fn. 25), S. 103 ; Güntzel (Fn. 25), S. 91 ; Roth, JZ 1987, 899 ; Reinicke FS für Lukes, S. 766 ; Wieczorek / Schütze / Hausmann, ZPO, Erster Band, 3. Aufl. (1994), § 52 Rdnr. 5 ; vgl. auch Fn. 17. 中野・前掲注1 一三四頁、高橋・前掲注1 一六六頁、中野＝松浦＝鈴木編・前掲注1 九十四頁〔本間〕、新堂・前掲注2 八十七頁など多数。

29 BverfGE 7, 53, 57 = JZ 1957, 542 ; BGHZ 48, 327, 331 f. ; Röhl, NJW 1953, 1531.

30 BGHZ 48, 327, 329 ; Jauernig (Fn. 3), § 29 I ; Rosenberg / Schwab / Gottwald (Fn. 3), § 85 I ; Schilken (Fn. 7), § 8 VIII; Stein / Jonas / Leipold, ZPO, Band 2, 21. Aufl. (1994), vor § 128 Rdnr. 10 m. w. N.

31 Schmidt / Aßmann in Maunz-Dürig, GG, Band IV, Stand 27. Lieferung (1988), Art. 103 Rdnr. 66 ; vgl. auch Kirberger, Rpfleger 1976, 3511 ; Schilken, Gerichtsverfassungsrecht, 2. Aufl. (1994), § 11 II Rdnr. 128 ; Stein / Jonas / Leipold (Fn. 30), vor § 128 Rdnr. 35.

32 BverfGE 7, 53, 58 = JZ 1957, 542 ; BverfGE 9, 89, 95 ; BGHZ 35, 1, 8 ; BGHZ 48, 327, 333 ; Brüggemann, JZ 1969, 362; Eickmann, Rpfleger 1982, 449 ; Röhl, NJW 1958, 1269 ; Rosenberg / Schwab / Gottwald (Fn. 3), § 85 I ; Schilken (Fn. 31), § 11 I ; Stein / Jonas / Leipold (Fn. 30), vor § 128 Rdnr. 11 ; Wintrich, BayVBl 1957, 139.

33 BverfGE 9, 89, 95 ; ebenso BGHZ 48, 327, 333.

34 BGHZ 86, 24, 29 = NJW 1982, 2449, 2451 = LM Nr. 6 zu § 579 ZPO m. Anm. von Blumenröhr; BayVerfGH Rpfleger 1976, 350 m. Anm. von Kirberger; Eickmann, Rpfleger 1982, 450 ; Röhl, NJW 1958, 1268 f. ; Winter, Rpfleger 1984, 220. Jura 1981 656 ; Schmidt / Aßmann in Maunz-Dürig (Fn. 31), Art. 103 Rdnr. 29 ; Winter, Rpfleger 1984, 220.

35 BGHZ 35, 1, 9; BGHZ 84, 24, 29 = NJW 1982, 2449, 2451 = LM Nr. 6 zu § 579 ZPO m. Anm. von Blumenröhr; Bay-VerfGH Rpfleger 1976, 350 m. Anm. von Kirberger; Eickmann, Rpfleger 1982, 450 ; Käck, Der Prozeßpfleger (1991), S. 73; Schmid / Aßmann in Maunz-Dürig (Fn. 31), Art. 103 Rdnr. 29 ; Waldner, Aktuelle Probleme des rechtlichen Gehörs im Zivilprozeß, Diss. Erlangen (1983), S. 217.

36 BGHZ 84, 24, 29 = NJW 1982, 2449, 2451 ; BayVerfGE Rpfleger 1976, 350 m. Anm. von Kirberger; Schmid / Aßmann in Maunz-Dürig (Fn. 31), Art 103 Rdnr. 30 ; Waldner (Fn. 35), S. 218.

37 Vgl. BayVerfGH Rpfleger 1976, 350 m. Anm. von *Kirberger*.

38 たとえば、中野貞一郎「民事裁判と憲法」『講座民事訴訟 ①民事紛争と訴訟』（弘文堂・一九八四年）十四頁。

39 *Stein / Jonas / Bork*; (Fn. 8), § 56 Rdnr. 16 ; vgl. auch BGHZ 110, 294, 297 = NJW 1990, 1734, 1735 = ZZP 103 (1990), 464, 466 m. Anm. von *Bork*; OLG Hamm MDR 1992, 411, 412.

40 BGHZ 18, 184, 189 = FamRZ 1955, 358 = NJW 1955, 1714 ; BGH NJW 1966, 2210 = FamRZ 1966, 571 m. Anm. von *Grunsky* ; BGH FamRZ 1969, 477, 478 ; BGHZ 86, 184, 186 = NJW 1983, 996 ; BGHZ 110, 294, 295 f. = NJW 1990, 1734, 1735 = ZZP 103 (1990), 464, 465 m. Anm. von *Bork*; *Hager*, ZZP 97 (1984), 174, 176 ; *Jauernig* (Fn. 3), § 20 IV 3 ; *Schellhamer* (Fn. 7), Rdnr. 1195 m. w. N. ; *Stein / Jonas / Bork* (Fn. 8), § 56 Rdnr. 16 ; miβverständlich *Abel*, Zur Nichtigkeitsklage wegen Mängel der Vertretung im Zivilprozeß (1995), S. 150.

41 ZZP 103 (1990), 469 f. = NJW 1989, 984 ; *Arens / Lüke* (Fn. 3), § 9 III Rdnr. 118 ; *Bökelmann*, JR 1972, 246 ; *Bork*, *Schellhammer* (Fn. 7), Rdnr. 1195. わが国では、控訴審において訴訟能力の欠缺が認められるときには、第一審判決を取り消したうえで事件を第一審に差し戻さなければならないとしている。とえば、高橋・前掲注1　一六六頁参照。

42 BGHZ 18, 184, 190 = FamRZ 1955, 358, 359 ; BGHZ 24, 91, 94 ; BGHZ 40, 197, 199 ; *Bork*, ZZP 103 (1990), 469 ; *Rosenberg / Schwab / Gottwald* (Fn. 3), § 44 IV 2 ; *Schellhammer* (Fn. 7), Rdnr. 1195. わが国では、訴訟能力の欠缺が認められるときには、第一審判決を取り消したうえで事件を第一審に差し戻さなければならないとしている。新堂・前掲注1　一三五頁、高橋・前掲注1　一六六頁。これに対して、控訴審において補正を命じ、補正がなければ、第一審判決を取り消したうえで訴えを却下しなければならないとする見解がある。

43 小室＝賀集＝松本＝加藤編・前掲注1　八十六頁〔難波〕、新堂幸司＝鈴木正裕＝竹下守夫編『注解民事訴訟法(1)』（有斐閣・一九九一年）四七三頁〔飯倉〕。

44 BGHZ FamRZ 1972, 35 = MDR 1972, 220 = JR 1972, 246 m. Anm. von *Bökelmann*.

45 *Bökelmann*, JR 1972, 246 ; *Bork*, ZZP 103 (1990), 469 f. ; *Hager*, ZZP 97 (1984), 178 f.

46 BGHZ 18, 184, 190 = FamRZ 1955, 358 ; BGHZ 40, 197, 199 ; BGH FamRZ 1972, 35 = MDR 1972, 220, 221 = JR 1972, 246 m. Anm. von *Bökelmann* ; BGH NJW-RR 1986, 1119 ; BGHZ 110, 294, 295 f. = NJW 1990, 1734, 1735 = ZZP 103 (1990), 464, 465 m. Anm. von *Bork* ; OLG Karlsruhe FamRZ 1973, 272, 273 ; OLG Hamm MDR 1992, 411, 412 ; *Baumbach / Lauterbach / Albers* (Fn. 3), Grundz § 511 Rdnr. 9 ; *Hager*, ZZP 97 (1984),

47　178 f.; *Kirberger*, JuS 1976, 643 f.; *Stein / Jonas / Bork* (Fn. 8), § 56 Rdnr. 16; *Zöller / Gummer* (Fn. 3), § 511 Rdnr. 5; kritisch *Abel* (Fn. 40), S. 103 ff.

48　*Hager*, ZZP 97 (1984), 178 f.；小田司「民事執行手続における訴訟能力の諸問題─ドイツにおける議論を参考にして─」日本法学第六六巻第一号（二〇〇〇年）六九頁以下。

49　小田・前掲注47　八十七頁以下。

50　木川＝中村編・前掲注1　五十八頁（高地）、松本＝上野・前掲注1　一七二頁（松本）、上田・前掲注1　一〇〇頁、中野＝松浦＝鈴木編・前掲注1　九十五頁〔本間〕、伊藤・前掲注14　九十八頁、石川明＝小島武司編『新民事訴訟法』（青林書院・一九九七年）六十六頁〔小池〕、佐上善和『民事訴訟法〔第二版〕』（法律文化社・一九九八年）二五五頁、小山昇「訴訟能力について」法学研究第三十四巻第三号（一九九九年）五八一頁。

51　中野・前掲注2　八十八頁、新堂＝鈴木＝竹下編・前掲注43　四七四頁〔飯倉〕。

52　坂原正夫「訴訟能力の欠缺を看過した判決の効力」『慶應義塾大学法学部法律学科開設百年記念論文集法律学科編』（慶應通信・一九九〇年）一四八頁以下、高橋・前掲注1　一七二頁注22、小田・前掲注47　八十二頁以下。

53　*Oda* (Fn. 16), S. 101.

54　BGHZ 110, 294, 296 ＝ NJW 1990, 1734, 1735 ＝ ZZP 103 (1990), 464, 465 m. Anm. von *Bork*.

55　BGHZ 143, 122, 127 f.

56　BGHZ 86, 184, 188 f. ＝ NJW 1983, 996, 997；BGH NJW-RR 1986, 157；BAG NJW 1958, 1699 ＝ AP Nr. 1 zu § 56 ZPO m. Anm. von *Baumgärtel*；BAG AP Nr. 5 zu § 56 ZPO m. Anm. von *Rimmelspacher*; *Stein / Jonas / Bork* (Fn. 8), § 56 Rdnr. 4.

57　本稿〔2〕1参照。

58　*Oda* (Fn. 16), S. 101.

59　BGHZ 143, 122, 127；OLG Hamm MDR 1992, 411, 412；OLG Düsseldorf MDR 1997, 500；*Oda* (Fn. 16), S. 81 ff；*Wieczorek / Schütze / Hausmann* (Fn. 27), § 52 Rdnr. 41；*Zöller / Vollkommer* (Fn. 3), § 56 Rdnr. 14.

60　OLG Düsseldorf MDR 1997, 500.

［付記］
原稿締切との関係上、平成十三年十二月八日以降に公表された文献については、参照できなかったことをお断わりしておく。

二十一世紀社会における「国際政治経済秩序」の理念と構想

「戦争と平和論」を踏まえて

前田利光

[1] 歴史危機の深層構造と地球市民社会の構想

わたくしは、二〇〇二年一月十五日刊行の論文集『歴史認識と国際政治経済危機の深層——情報革命・国際通貨・環境問題——』の〈はしがき〉と〈プロローグ〉（Prologue）において、二十一世紀の「持続的社会経済発展のための人間形成」（Human Formation for Sustainable Social Economic Development）及び「環境要素の持続的発展」（The Environmental Component of Sustainable Development）と人類普遍の原理である恒久の世界平和実現のための諸要素を展望して、次のように論点を開示しておいた。すなわち、アルベルト・アインシュタイン（Albert Einstein、一八七九-一九五五）は、終戦二年目の一九四七年十

月、世界政府論者の立場から、「国連総会への公開状」を発表し、国連改革案を具体的に提案した。この世界政府論者としての彼の提案に対して、ソ連の代表的科学者たちは、批判した。これに対して、アインシュタインは、翌一九四八年二月の返書の中で次のように述べている。

「全体の破壊を避けるという目標は、他のいかなる目標にも優位しなければならぬ。」(The objective of avoiding total destruction must have priority over any other objective.)と。

二十世紀は確かに「戦争と革命」の歴史であった。すなわち、ファッシズムと独裁権力という政治暴力と原子爆弾の投下を促す極限の戦争暴力によって、人々はたえず「全体の破壊」の危機に脅かされてきた。

要するに、資本主義は政治と戦争の暴力を伴って「発展」してきたのみならず、経済恐慌と持続する「市場の暴力」を不可避的に伴いながら発展してきた。

われわれは、いま、これらの歴史的事実を、深く受容して、正しい歴史認識によって、二十一世紀社会の方途に生かさなければならない。

二十世紀末以降、世界資本主義は、「サイバー空間」と情報・通信革命を内部化して「完熟」したが故に「朽ち果て」ざるをえない歴史を形成しているのだろうか。加速化する世界市場化とそれに伴う国民経済及び国民国家の危機が、不可逆的な地球環境の危機と融合化しながら、世界市場の〈Gewalt〉とその肥大化によって深化してきている。これこそ正しく外国為替市場の攪乱を、最大限の利潤実現の絶好のチャンスにしてしまう「二十一世紀の妖怪」といわなければならない。いい換えればこの妖怪は、二十世紀末以降各国の社会経済秩序(「国民経済」)の持続的な発展を急速に不可能にしてきているのみならず、世界政治経済秩序を麻痺させてきている。とりわけ、通貨価値の変動と情報・通信革命を広く、深く、資本蓄積メカニズムの内部に組み込むことによって、最大限の利潤実現をめざす二十世紀末以降の世界の金融

資本の運動は、地球環境を浸食しながら世界市場化を加速させると同時に、諸矛盾の成熟化と特質を顕在化させてきている。にもかかわらず、それに対抗しうる理念も構想も国際システムも未だ確立していない。この現実は、戦争の世紀から平和の世紀への転回、人類普遍の世界平和への不可逆的大転回を詰問している。

実際に、その諸矛盾は、富の生産と分配から、自由と人権などに至るまでの不平等化を、民族及び各国間、諸地域間そして各階層間、企業、産業間さらには、男女間、世代間に連鎖的に波及してきている。しかもなお、アジア諸国からロシア及び中南米諸国へ連鎖した通貨──経済危機が、日米統合的経済構造の実態と諸矛盾を剔抉する形で波及し、国民経済循環と世界経済循環の再生産関係を崩壊させながら「複合危機循環」構造を創出したのがアジア通貨危機であった。

そこで、この二十一世紀初頭の国際政治経済の現実を凝視して、その危機の深層構造と法則を歴史的に認識するならば、何よりもまず、情報・通信革命との融合化を深めながら加速化する国際資本移動のグローバル化が同時に、諸矛盾の構造的深化とグローバル化を促してきていること、したがって、このいわば新しい世界経済の価値価格法則の貫徹形態とそれを超えて暗中飛躍する〈二十一世紀の妖怪〉を、コントロールできる新しい国際政治経済システムを構築しなければならない。

端的に言うならば、この〈二十一世紀の妖怪〉は、覇権主義の拡大と理念化による覇権国家の再構築を、依然として「戦争」を手段に世界戦略を展開しながら実現しようとするアメリカ資本主義の構造危機と再生産諸関係にある。したがって、この二十一世紀の歴史的危機創出のリーディング・ファクターの機能を拡充してきている「軍産複合体国家」の疾走をも、十分にコントロールできる高度な「世界政府」を創設することが緊要な歴史的課題となってきている、と言わなければならない。

なぜならば実際、国際政治経済危機の深層構造を創出し、そこを住処（すみか）として、諸矛盾のグローバル化を促す、この〈二十一世紀の妖怪〉に対抗しうる構想と理念、それらは、国民国家間の外交的努力やそれに基づく「国連」そしてIMFや世界銀行などの、現実に存在する国際機関のそれらを超えたものであることだけは、危機における歴史的現実が明示してきている。

例えば、持続的に増幅する難民創出の、いわゆる紛争と戦争の論理、それと三位一体の諸関係にあるグローバル資本主義とその危機創出の経済法則の貫徹の犠牲を強いられる人々、その期待に対応した新しい創造力となって、歴史的負の遺産を克服する方途を、国際的連帯と実践を通して、提示しているのは、むしろ「NGO・NPO」ではないだろうか。

要するに、この「非政府非営利組織」であるNGO（Non-governmental Organization）やNPO（Nonprofit Organization）を構成し、人道主義の原理と思想の発展を支える、いわば地球市民が二十一世紀社会の主役となりつつある。したがって、このトランスナショナル・シビル・ソサイェティ（Transnational Civil Society）形成の原理とその実現を促し、その創造的発展の諸条件の成熟を保証することのできる「新しい世界政府」と「世界貨幣」を創出できる新時代であることを深く認識したい。

実際、R・N・クーパーは、『将来の通貨制度』（*A Monetary System for the Future.*）において、「プラザ合意」の前年、一九八四年、アメリカ資本主義とドル支配のヘゲモー時代の終焉を踏えて、新しい国際通貨制度に基づく「共通の通貨政策とその通貨政策を決定する加盟国合同発券銀行をもち、すべての民主主義先進工業国に共通する一つの通貨の創設」を強調している。

この、いわゆるクーパー説を、C・F・バーグステン（Bergsten）が、「プラザ合意」二年後の一九八七年段階、すなわちアメリカ資本主義の経済総力と構造的凋落が顕在化する一方、日本資本主義の構造的

バブル化が決定づけられていく一九八七年、「日米エコノミー化」による両頭支配=バイゲモニー(Bigemony)体制の構築の可能性を想定した二十一世紀ヘゲモニー(Hegemony)の形態と方向性を構想した事実に照射してみると、クーパー説の特徴が現実性を高揚しながら、根源的な課題とも関係する世界平和と人間の生存権とも関係してきている。

これは、アジアの動態やアフリカの地域共同体構想へと連動する世界平和と人間の生存権とも関係する。

実際、二〇〇一年九月十一日の「同時多発テロ」を、二十一世紀型の新しい戦争と規定した上での「国益最優先主義」に基づく、いわば〈Aggressive Unilateralism〉(攻撃的で強引な一方主義)の国際権力化と普遍的理念化の戦略を実現したブッシュ政権、そして、それに間髪を入れず同調したイギリスと日本、このシンボリックな政治的軍事的統合化は、C・F・バーグステンの「ドル―円」両頭支配=バイゲモニー(Bigemony)体制のシンボリックな現象を世界に示しえたとしても、これを歴史的に考究するならば、バイゲモニー体制再構築の方途をむしろ閉ざす結果を生み出した。つまり、アジアの中での歴史的位相を喪失した日本は、人類普遍の原理である恒久平和と人権主義の歴史的遺産と不可逆的価値を国際化できない。

実際、テロ発生の夜、ブッシュ大統領は、これはテロではなく、二十一世紀型の新しい戦争である、と規定した上で、「あらゆる国が、あらゆる場所で、決意すべきだ。われわれの側につくか、テロリストの側につくか」と二者択一を迫ると同時に、「これは世界の戦いだ。文明戦争だ。進歩と多元的共存、寛容と自由を信じる者の戦いだ。」と。事実上の「世界戦争宣言」によって、国際テロリストを、国連と国際司法裁判所に委ねて断罪する道を、間髪を入れず断絶したことを看過してはならない。

この事実を、ブッシュ政権が、「京都議定書」からの離脱と「包括的核実験禁止条約」(CTBT)批准拒否宣言という、〈Aggressive Unilateralism〉、すなわち「攻撃的で強引な一方主義」の二十一世紀世界戦

略と重ねて考究してみると、戦争の持続化を手段とする軍産複合体のアメリカ資本主義の「国益最優先主義」と「覇権国家主義」のシナリオの存在が脳裏にひらめくのは、この私だけだろうか。

しかも、このアメリカの意志を受けて後方支援を表明したムシャラフ政権のパキスタンに対する経済制裁を解いたのみならず、国際機関を代表する世界銀行もIMFも、すでにパキスタン向け融資枠増幅を決定したアジア開発銀行に準ずるなど、国際システムの理念も機能も全く擬制化してしまっている。

周知のように、「米・ソ冷戦体制」の拡大再生産による負の遺産創出を象徴する旧ソ連のアフガニスタンへの軍事的介入と、それに対抗して、アメリカによる報復「戦争」勢力の構築という、この少なくとも一九八〇年代末以降の「米・ソの世界戦略史」の総決算との連続性を意図的に断絶して、「同時多発テロ」のひとコマで歴史を語り、今日の戦争と平和を判定する基準を作成するという、擬制の国際的理念は決して許してはならない。実際、「テロ報復戦争」によって、アフガニスタンの領土と人々の生活破壊は増幅され、テロと同じように無実の人間の命を奪う、「報復戦争」によって激増した難民の存在事実とその国際政治経済危機（諸矛盾）の深層構造は、根源的には、「戦後米・ソ冷戦体制史」がしからしめた人類史上の負の遺産である。いわば、二十世紀の偽りの同盟史と擬制的平和主義からの大転回の根拠でもある。

要するに、難民救済支援金やアフガニスタン国家復興のための援助金供出の多寡によって、戦争の罪悪史を免罪するがごとき政治や国際関係だけは、決して許してはならない。

同時にまた、「米・ソ」を核とする戦後冷戦体制史に貫ぬく論理と構造を、歴史的に「断罪」するばかりでなく、いかなる正当化しうる根拠に基づく戦争であっても、世界法に照らして断罪することができる強力かつ高度な「世界政府」構想を実現しなければ、「戦争の非制度化」すなわち、世界平和の制度化を伴う二十一世紀の新しい国際安全保障の理念も構想も現実のものとはならない。

この二十一世紀社会における「平和の思想と戦争の論理」を、根源的に考究することは極めて重要である。そこで、「平和思想史」から批判的に学んでおきたい。

すでに周知のように、エラスムス（Desiderius Erasmus、一四六六／六九-一五三六）は、一五一七年の『平和の訴え』において、「平和の女神」に、「一切の善きものの源泉」である戦争の愚かさを訴えさせている。この近代史上最初の「平和論者」エラスムスに対し、グロティウス（Hugo Grotius、一五八三-一六四六）は、一六二五年すなわち、一六四八年の「ウェストファリア会議」で、ようやくにして終結に至る「三十年戦争」眞っ只中で完成させたが、彼は理性の使命としての自然法に普遍的な原理を定めて、防衛のための、侵害された権利回復のための、そして刑罰の承認を、戦争を正当化しうる法的根拠とすることによって、諸国民の法に基づく最高権力者（＝元首）によって宣言された、いわゆる「正義の戦争」の法的関係（交戦権）及び法的効果を承認している。このグロティウスの思想と法（制）を止揚すること、これは、二十一世紀社会の創造的──持続可能な発展のための歴史的根本課題である。

［２］二十一世紀社会と平和・人権思想──戦争批判の歴史的意義

『平和思想史』の著者田畑忍は、一九六四年に、その序　戦争の論理と平和の論理　をまず次のように規定し、叙述している。すなわち、「戦争にかんする思想あるいは論理には、戦争主義の論理と、それと対立的に戦争を否定する平和の論理とが存在している。戦争主義の論理は遂行の論理であるが、平和の論理は歴史的発展の論理であって将来を志向し、戦争のない未来というヴィジョンを内包している。」と、そ

して「人類の歴史は、かつては戦争の歴史であった。平和主義の論理も十分にその事実を認めなければならない。人類の生活の中に、まず法をとおして、次には道理をとおして実現する時代である。すなわち平和主義の法的実現は、その第一歩にほかならない。すでに、その平和の法は、遠くフランスの革命憲法に始まって、そのような一部戦争放棄の規定にならう諸国家の憲法が、相ついでつくられてきた。また武装はこれを保持しながら、永久平和の政策をとり、あるいは条約によって永久平和主義を続けている国々がある。スイス、スェーデンがそうであり、あるいは新しくオーストリアが憲法法規をつくって永世中立の宣言をした。あるいは社会主義国家のユーゴスラビアがノン・ブロック主義に踏みきった。いわゆる積極的中立主義をとる国も、ふえてきている。いずれも武装をつづけながらの中立主義であり、非軍事同盟主義である。」と。

この一九六〇年代の歴史段階を深く認識した田畑忍の世界平和主義思想の原理は、一九六二年の「キューバ危機」、翌六三年の「部分的核実験停止条約」、六四年の「ベトナム戦争」、六五年の「国連人種差別撤廃条約」を踏えた「国連国際人権規約」、そして六六年に突入した「中国文化大革命」時代と六八年以降の「ヨーロッパ共同体」の発展史と中東戦争史さらには、翌六八年の「ソ連のチェコへの軍事介入」など、歴史認識を踏えて、戦争の論理を否定し、「戦争のない未来というヴィジョンを内包」したいわば、絶対平和主義思想とその原理を創造し、その運動を展望している。

したがって、田畑忍は、「平和主義は必ず戦争主義に勝利する、と私は確信している。そしてそのような国民的自覚を、国内において横溢するようにすることが今日最大の急務であると思うのである。」と結んでいる。しかも、田畑は、「内村鑑三先生は、かつて「日本の天職は世界を平和ならしめることである」

と云った。先生は「使命」と云わずに「天職」という言葉を使っている。彼は世界を平和ならしめる世界的な運動の先頭に立つことが日本の天職である、と云った……」と。実際、内村鑑三の『英文論説』に貫ぬく世界平和思想は、安重根の『東洋平和論』をも受容したいわば二十一世紀社会構想論でもある。

要するに、内村が、「日清戦争」から「日露戦争」へと疾走し、植民地拡大主義に発展の「原理」を求めた日本帝国主義批判の思想と平和主義の理念の構築をめざしたことは、彼が、ロンドンで「日・米同盟条約」（軍事同盟）調印の翌一九〇三年六月三十日の『万朝報』で、「戦争は人を殺すことである。……爾うして戦争廃止論の声の揚がらない国は未開国である、然り、野蛮国である。」と断言している事実からも明らかである。

ところで、米・ソ冷戦体制史が歴史的に内包し、受容しながら拡大再生産してきた諸矛盾の本質と起点を想起しておくことは重要である。

要するに、アメリカは、ソ連に対して、原子爆弾という、すべてを瞬時に破壊し尽くす核兵器の威力を、日本人の大量虐殺の現実を盾に、全世界に凝視せしめることによって、スターリン＝ソ連の戦後世界へ向けての戦略と思惑の機先を、なんとしても制しておくことを、至上命題としていた。そこに、「冷戦体制の構築」とその人類史的負の遺産史を決定づける問題の本質がある。

この事実は米・ソ冷戦体制史の戦後史が論証している。しかも、一九四五年十月には、「戦争を防ぐに足るだけの権力をもった制限的世界連邦政府樹立」を目指した「ダブリン会議」が、そしてアメリカを中心とする「世界連邦主義者連合」が一九四七年二月に成立した。翌年三月には、前文と四十七カ条からなる「世界憲法シカゴ草案（Preliminary Draft of a World Constitution）」が発表された。これは、「世界人権宣言」の制定を基礎づけた思想である。

これらの歴史的事実を踏まえて、一九九六年七月八日、オランダ・ハーグの「国際司法裁判所」が、いわゆる「核兵器の使用や威嚇が国際法に照らして違法かどうか」という国際法的問題を、国連総会から要請されていたのに対する、「勧告的意見」を、歴史的に読み込むならば、自ずと、その事実は、剔抉されるのである。

すなわち、国際司法裁判所は、「核兵器の使用や威嚇は、一般的に国際法に違反する」、との法的判断を明示した。しかも、前年一九九五年十月三十日から十一月十五日までの「口頭陳述」では、二十二カ国のうち十五カ国が、「国際法違反」を主張し、陳述書提出の三十五カ国のうち、「合法説」は、わずか七カ国であった。

この「口頭陳述」に出廷した広島と長崎の市長は、「核兵器使用の違法性を強く訴え」た。これに対し、日本国政府が、「核兵器の使用は実定国際法違反とまではいえない」との考えに執着しつづけたこと、しかも、日本から選出されている小田滋判事が、「唯一人、国連の諮問を受理すること自体に反対」した事実は、戦後の日米関係史の基本的性格を如実に物語っている。この「冷戦体制史」とその中での「日米関係」の史的連続性の事実を踏まえて、世界平和を原理とする二十一世紀社会構築へと、大転回すべきである。

いずれにしても、「国際司法裁判所」に対して、「核兵器の違法性を宣言する『公的良心の宣言』署名が二十五カ国三六九万人分も提出されたこと、そして一九九九年五月、「世界一〇〇カ国以上から一万人の市民が集まった「ハーグ市民平和会議」の最終日、『公正な世界秩序のための十基本原則』が採択され、

……

1、すべての議会は、日本の憲法九条のような政府に戦争の禁止を定めた決議を行うこと

2、国際司法裁判所の決定を無条件に受け入れること
3、地雷禁止条約の批准

などを明文化したことは、二十一世紀社会システム構築の理念と構想を明示しているものである。

要するに、これらの歴史的事実を確認した上で、「世界政府の思想」原案ともいうべき「世界憲法シカゴ草案」を想起すると共に、一九四八年の「平和を守るための世界知識人会議」が、「原子爆弾の禁止」を決議し、二年後の一九五〇年には、「平和擁護世界大会委員会」が、「原子兵器の絶対禁止宣言」、すなわち「ストックホルム・アピール」に五億人が署名した事実、そして、一九五五年、「ラッセル=アインシュタイン宣言」の提唱に、湯川秀樹らノーベル賞受賞の九名が署名した平和運動を受けて、一九五七年、カナダのパグウォッシュで「科学と国際問題に関する会議」、いわゆる「パグウォッシュ会議」の思想と理念の発展を、二十一世紀社会の「世界システム」構築の理念として生かすためには、少なくとも、「国際政治のニュー・パラダイム」の創出と合意が前提となる。

いい換えれば、冷戦体制と社会主義諸国の構造的崩壊と、情報・通信革命の進展に伴う、いわば「二十世紀の政治経済社会システム」からの転回が加速しつつある歴史的現実の中で、「国家権力への志向を明確にする」民族運動――紛争が持続する一方、「一国内において文化的独自性を確認しようとする」エスニシティと、「先住民」の躍動する運動の国際的な共有化と普遍化がある。

このような「エスニシティと先住民と多文化主義」の価値の社会的認識と共有化は、複数の民族及び多様な文化が「共存」しうる国際社会と地域共同体の構築、それは多元的価値の共生と実現を求めている。

このような地球社会における複合的な動態を共有しながら、基本的には「世界平和の制度化」すなわち、

「戦争の非制度化」に基づく「国際安全保障システム」を構築すること。そして、加速するグローバル資本主義の展開と、それに伴う構造危機の論理とメカニズムを剔抉して、戦後史を根底から規定してきた「冷戦体制」の政治経済構造、とりわけ「軍産複合体」存立の経済法則とメカニズムを、根源的に転回せしめながら、新しい二十一世紀社会の理念と「世界システム」の構築を目指さなければならない。

したがって、情報・通信革命の進展に伴う「創造的破壊」の二十一世紀社会と、人間及び自然（地球環境）との共生関係は、NGOやNPOなどの発展を含む、「不確実性の時代」における「新しい可能性」の実現を示す基本的な形態である。

言うまでもなく、「富や資源の配分、また自然環境との闘いや社会環境の改革・整備に至るまで、国境空間の中で日常生活の多くの時間をすごしている私たちがトランスナショナルな国境を越える国際空間を実態としてイメージし、そこでより安全に、より豊かな人生を送るルールや政治の合意の形成の方法および仕組みを人種や民族の壁を越えて考えだしていく思考」様式の成熟、そして、それに基づく政治経済社会哲学、それが二一世紀社会の原理とならなければならない。この視座において、情報・通信革命の進展諸形態及びインターネット社会における地球市民的成熟と、ニューパラダイムとの共生関係は、極めて重要性を帯びてくる。

その場合、人種も言語も宗教も異なる諸民族や国家が、文化や歴史や思考様式の特質を生かしながら、それらを越えて、欧州連合（EU）という、一つの統合体を形成し、発展の方向性を確実にしつつある現実から、何を、どのように学び、自ら直面している歴史的詰問に生かしていくか、という問題でもある。

なぜならば、二十世紀の政治経済社会から二十一世紀への、歴史の一大転回の・・・・・「パラダイム」と、メカニズムの構造再編成―構築のデバイス（device）は、「固有の文化・歴史・言語・宗教などをもとにして、

一つのアイデンティティを共有する共同体的な集団」である「エスニー」が活躍する国際舞台(international arena)の実現を出発点にして、国際政治の理論のなかでこれまで欠落してきたものを逆照射する」。この方法と視座からいわば、動態とグローバル化のアジアやアフリカの現実と未来が創造される。

実際には、「主権国家の権力の掌握を正統化するアイデンティティ集団としての「民族」と呼ばれているエスニー」を、国家形成エスニーと規定したうえで、その他のアイデンティティ集団としてのアジアやアフリカの現実と比較するところから、主権国家＝民族国家＝領域国家のみを構成要素とする西欧型の近代国家システムからいわば「はみだしもの」扱いにされているこれらの集団の役割を確かめ、これらマイノリティ集団を含む現実の国際舞台の実相をいかにとらえるべきか」、という新しい詰問は、歴史認識の創造的破壊の持続によって克服されていくのである。

要するに、情報・通信革命を通じて融合化する現代のInnovationが、開かれた社会への可能性としては、インターネットを通して、世界憲法草案に基づく「電子世界政府」を構築する方途も内包していることとは否定できない。しかし、現実には、世界市場原理主義が、瞬時にして通貨の市場価値価格を破壊するエネルギーを保全・培養すると共に、人間の生活及び社会的生存権と不可逆的な地球の生態及び環境を侵食してきている。この二十一世紀社会の現実としての「誤謬性」と負荷の「相互作用性」を持続的に正しながら、「開かれた社会」秩序の理念とシステム構築をふまえて、それらの国家と人間を内包し尽すことのできる世界政府とその支柱となりうる世界中央銀行及び新しい世界貨幣の創出と連動し、有機化した地域連邦政府構想を論究してきたのである。

[参考文献]

拙著『歴史認識と国際政治経済危機の深層—情報革命・国際通貨・環境問題—』税務経理協会、二〇〇二年、『増補版 世界経済の変動と日本経済—構造分析と市場経済法則の研究—』同、一九九八年。

秋野豊『偽りの同盟』勁草書房、一九九八年。

浅田喬二『増補日本帝国主義と旧植民地主制—台湾・朝鮮・「満州」における日本人大土地所有の史的分析—』龍渓書房、一九八九年。

Bergsten, C. Fred. "Economic Imbalances and World Politics." *Foreign Affairs*, Spring 1987.

Cooper, Richard N. "A Monetary System for the Future." *Foreign Affairs*, Fall 1984.

Eichengreen, Barry. *International Monetary Arrangements for the 21st Century*. Washington, D. C.: Brookings Institution, 1994、藤井良広訳『二一世紀の国際通貨制度—二つの選択』岩波書店、一九九七年。

Eichengreen, Barry. *Towards a New International Financial Architecture: A Practical Post-Asian Agenda*. Wasington, D. C.: Institute for International Economics, 1999.

エラスムス、箕輪三郎訳『平和の訴え』岩波書店、一九六一年。

深瀬忠一『戦争放棄と平和的生存権』同、一九八七年。

Gilpin, Robert G. *The Political Economy of International Relations*. Princeton: Princeton UP, 1987、佐藤誠三郎他訳『世界システムの政治経済学—国際関係の新段階』東洋経済新聞社、一九九〇年、*The Challenge of Global Capitalism: The World Economy in the 21st Century*. Princeton: Princeton UP, 2000、古城佳子訳『グローバル資本主義—危機か繁栄か—』東洋経済新聞社、二〇〇一年。

亀井俊介・道家弘一郎訳『内村鑑三英文論説翻訳篇上・下』岩波書店、一九九六年。

初瀬龍平編著『エスニシティと多文化主義』同文館、一九九六年。

Kapp, William. *Environmental Disruption and Social Costs*, 1975、柴田徳衛・鈴木正俊訳『環境破壊と社会的費用』岩波書店、一九七五年。

鴨武彦『国際安全保障の構想』東京大学出版会、一九九〇年、松井芳郎『国際法から世界を見る』東信堂、二〇〇一年。

コーテン・D、渡辺襲也訳『NGOとボランティアの二十一世紀』学陽書房、一九九四年。

北沢洋子・村井吉敬編著『顔のない国際機関—IMF・世界銀行—』学陽書房、一九九五年。

Krummacher F. A. & H. Lange. "Krig und Friden Geschichte der deutsch-sowjetischen Beziehungen" (1970).

宮崎義一『ドルと円──世界経済の新しい構造──』岩波書店、一九八八、『複合不況──ポスト・バブルの処方箋を求めて──』中央公論社、一九九二年。

日本環境会議・「アジア環境白書」編集委員会『アジア環境白書二〇〇〇/〇一』東洋経済新聞社、二〇〇〇年。

Nathan, Otto and Heinz Norden. *Einstein on Peace.* New York: Simon and Schuster, 1960、金子敏男訳『アインシュタイン平和書簡』、全三巻 みすず書房、一九七四年。

Nussbam, Arthur. *A Concise History of the Law of Nations.* Macmillam Company, 1958、一又正雄訳『戦争と平和の法』、全三巻 巌松堂、一九五〇──一九五一年。

斎藤充功『伊藤博文を撃った男』時事通信社、一九九四年。

鈴木俊郎『内村鑑三伝』岩波書店、一九八六年。

常深康裕『スーパーテクノロジー──世界を変えたネットワークとシステムの興亡』行人社、二〇〇一年。

田畑忍『平和思想史』法律文化社、一九六四年。

田畑忍編著『近現代世界の平和思想』ミネルヴァ書房、一九九六年。

田畑茂二郎『世界政府の思想』岩波書店、一九五〇年、『国際化時代の人権問題』同、一九八八年。

高柳先男『戦争を知るための平和学入門』筑摩書房、二〇〇〇年。

高柳先男『パワー・ポリティクス』有信堂、一九九八年。

Yergin, Daniel, and Joseph Stanislaw. *The Commanding Heights: The Battle between Government and the Marketplace That is Remaking the Modern World.* New York: Simon and Schuster, 1998、山岡洋一訳『市場対国家──世界を作り変える歴史的攻防上・下』日本経済新聞社、一九九八年。

自由貿易主義の理論的根拠

古典派の貿易思想を中心として

小林 通

[1] はじめに

一九七〇年代は先進諸国の経済にとっていくつかの大きな試練に遭遇した時期であった。その一つはドル・ショックであり、もう一つは二度のオイル・ショックであった。これらの出来事は、西側自由主義経済社会内部における戦後の構造的内部遺制を解消させる切っ掛けになるとともに、その経済の構造的変化をもたらす結果にもなった。八五年九月プラザ合意以降急速な円高傾向は、七十年代の経験によって改善された産業構造、貿易構造をさらに大きく変化させてきた。国際的な貿易上の不均衡や摩擦、保護貿易、管理貿易の抬頭といった輸出環境の悪化により、輸出に極

[2] 古典派の自由貿易論

端に存在しない貿易構造が志向され、企業活動の国際化が積極的に展開されてきた。さらに輸入においても、わが国企業の海外事業活動などにより、製品輸入が急増し、輸入構造の変化とともに国内への雇用空洞化現象をもたらした。ボーダーレス・エコノミーは、経済的に国境を薄くさせると同時に、各国家間での新しい形体の国際分業体制や自由貿易体制が求められてきている。特に現在の世界的な不況下においては、特にわが国を中心としたアジア諸国は、通貨危機以来その感が強まってきている。

新しい考え方を模索するには、過去の教訓やよりよい遺産を継続し、考慮することが重要な事柄と思われる。ここでは保護貿易主義が全般的に捉られいてた時代にとって変わった古典派の自由貿易主義に焦点を当て、それが現代の自由貿易主義思想にどのように継承され、影響を与えているのかに関して論じていくことにしたい。[2]

(A) A・スミスの貿易論

十八世紀中葉から後半に至ると、重商主義の経済理論が解体をはじめ、それと同時に今までの重商主義的保護政策論に替わってそれを論破した自由主義的な経済理論が次第に抬頭しはじめ、自由貿易論を提唱する様になってきた。完全に定式化され、また論証されたものは少数であったが、それぞれに重商主義の本質である国富は貨幣（＝金貨・銀貨）であるという考え方に反駁し、また貿易差額説の無意味さを論証することによって、保護主義的な政策論を批判し、自由主義的な貿易論がその中核を形成するようになっていた。[3]

このように自由貿易主義は、例えばD・ノース、N・バーボン、J・タッカー、D・ヒュームなどが、先駆的な主唱者となり、A・スミス、リカードに至って完成されていった。特にこの時期は、産業資本の目覚しい抬頭という新しい波が足元に迫ってきた時代であり、それを現実の問題として捉え、経済の論証のために応用することができたのである。

スミスの時代では、すでに重商主義的国家政策によって、国内商業や外国貿易を発展させ、資本主義生産の発展を促進していた時代ではなく、そういった発展がすでに邪魔になりつつある時代であった。一七〇〇年イギリスの輸出額は、約六四八万ポンドであったが、約一世紀後の一八〇〇年では輸出額は、約三、八一二万ポンド、輸入額は約三、〇五〇万ポンドとなった。フランスでも、十八世紀の初頭と後半では五・四倍もの外国貿易の増加になっていた。しかし、この世紀の両国の貿易の発展は、重商主義者たちの手になるものではなかった。国際収支上の順差額や金銀などの貴金属の流入を、貿易の目的と考えていた重商主義者たちは、輸出の奨励にはつとめたが、それ以上に輸入を禁止したり抑制することに専念し、そのため逆に貿易本来の自由な発展を妨害した。

スミスの経済理論の基調は、自由放任的思想にあり、またその思想の目指す所は、中世的干渉諸制度、ある意味においてその延長線上にある重商主義的諸政策の弊害を指摘し、その存在の根拠を覆し、もって各人の経済的活動をそれらの束縛より解放し、自由な制度の実現を助成することであった。すなわち、ケネーやチュルゴー同様スミスの思想は、このように国内商業、外国貿易そして資本主義生産の発展の障害となってきた重商主義の理論や政策を排除し、それらの発展に新しい方向性を志向することを使命としていた。重商主義者とは異なり、スミスは富を貨幣（すなわち金、銀貨）とは考えずに、人々に役立つ必需品、必需品そのものであると捉え、貨幣は、本来このような必需品などを購買するための手段でしかない

と考えていた。貴金属（金、銀貨を含む）や国際収支の黒字それ自体は、国富を増大させるものではなく、一国の富は、それらが必要品や必需品と交換されてはじめて増大するのであるとした。スミスにおいて、そのような富、すなわち人々に役立つ必要品などを増加させるには、どのような手段によって達成されると考えられたのであろうか。それは、彼の経済理論の中で最も重要でその核心となる分業の理論によってである。その理由は、次のようなことによって理解されることになろう。すなわちスミスが、その大著『諸国民の富』の第一篇第一章に「分業について」という主題を設定したには、次のような理由があったからである。一つは、分業が労働の生産性を改善させ、増大させる最も効果的な手段であり、結果的には一国の富を増加させる大きな要因になるからであった。また二つには、生産要素の構成要因のうち当時としては、人的労働を生産の最も主体的な存在要因として捉え、その属性を有効に活用する方法として考えたこと。そしてそれが第一義的であり、他はその派生関数とみたこと。第三には、見えざる手に導かれて、各経済主体が各人の利己心のおもむくままに経済行動を行なった場合でも、国富を増加させるとするスミスの考えは単なる工場内の作業分業（技術分業）を越えて、それを敷衍した社会分業へ、さらには国際間での国際分業をも、その伏線として彼の考えの中にあったからであると思われる。すなわち、分業は、一工場内でも、社会においても、また広く国際間においても富の源泉であるいは富裕の発展にとって必須の原因であるとしたことである。

スミスは、分業を工場内の「一製造業の技術的分業」を基本的形体として、「種々の産業および職業相互間の分業」へと、また「国家間相互の分業」へと結びつけている。当然のように分業による利益は、これらの諸形態のすべてにおいて享受されることができると考えている。すなわち、スミスによれば本来分業というものは、人間の本性の中にある一定の性向、それ以上説明できない本源的な諸原理の一つ、つま

474

りある物を他の物と取引し、交易し、交換するという性向の非常に緩慢で漸進的ではあるが、必然的な帰結なのである。しかも、この性向は、人間に固有であり、それは、一切の人間に共通した、しかも他のどのような動物類には見られないのである。

このようにして、スミスは、分業が交換に対する人間の本性中にある交換性向から生じるとし、分業の発生原因を人間の交換性に求めた。またスミスは、その発展を交換可能な範疇、換言すれば、市場の広さに依存するとして、「市場がきわめて小さい場合には、誰一人として一つの仕事に献身するための刺激をうけることができない。というのは、自分自身の労働の生産物の中で、自分が必要とするような部分と交換する力が欠如しているからである」とする。これは、国内市場の限界が結果的に国際間の交換を通じての国際分業の可能性を示唆することになっている。

さらに言えば、労働が国富の源泉である以上、各国民は、労働の熟練、器用、および判断、すなわち労働の生産力の程度、労働に従事する人々の数がこれに従事しない人々の数に対して保つ比例の大小によって、その富が決定されている。そして特に国富を増大させるには、第一の労働の生産力を高めてゆかなければならない。スミスによると、このような労働の生産性向上は、分業によってもたらされるとする。分業には工場内のマニュファクチャー的分業と社会的分業とがあるが、どちらの分業も労働の生産性をたかめる点では同じとなる。分業の行なわれる範囲を制限する事情を市場の広さや資本の大きさに求め、分業による労働生産性は、市場を拡大するほど有効に向上する。それ故、国内商業や外国貿易の発展が、労働生産性の向上のためには、どうしても必要となることになる。国内商業や外国貿易を発展させるためには、政府はこれらのものに統制や制限を加えてはならないことになる。もし、ある国が外国からの輸入に制限を加えれば、制限を受けた国は、狭められた市場のために分業の利益を十分に発揮することができなくなり、輸入

国はいつでも高い価格でその商品を輸入することになるだろう。他方、ある国が人為的に輸出を奨励するならば、その産業は、労働生産性が割合に低い状態でも、存続するだろうと考える。しかしながら、スミスはいつまでもこのような労働生産性の低い産業へ資本や労働を集中させることは、その国全体の労働の生産性の向上を遅延させることになるとする。そしてそれぞれの国々が自由に比較的安価に生産することができる商品は、ほかの国から輸入するようにして、国際分業を行なうほうが、すべての商品を自国で生産するよりも有利になると論ずるのである。[11]

スミスの自由貿易主義は、畢竟、国際的分業による資本および労働の自由なる流通を根拠とするものである。思うにかれに従えば、一国内の技術的、社会的分業が、人間性より自然的に発達する結果となると同様に、国際間にも自然的に分業をきたし、経済的交流を生ずることになる。そのため、貿易自由の原則が、一国内に行なわれて社会全般の利益をもに参加し、利益を享受することができるという考え方があったからであろうと思われる。すなわち、英国一国の富の増加を目的としただけではなく、分業によってより多くの国々が、富を増殖することができるとしたものであり、この世界主義が重商主義を論駁することが必要となったからである。『諸国民の富』の第四篇は、商業主義（Commercialism）、重商主義（Mercantilism）の批判で始まっている。スミス以前の欧州諸国の支配的な経済政策であった国家主義的な干渉政策は、スミスの自由経済とは正に反対の考えであった。すなわち、金銀などの貴金属を貨幣として捉え、一国の富の源泉は、金銀などの貨幣の増殖であるとして、それを増加させるための保護貿易政策、例えば工業製品の輸入制限や農産物の輸出制限政策がとられていたからであった。

「富が貨幣または金銀より成るということは、貨幣が商業用具および価値の尺度として、二重の機能をもつことから自然に生じる通俗的見解をもたらすのに対して、それが国際間に行なわれて各国相互の幸福を

もたらさない理由はないのである」。

スミスの国際分業論の基調は、重商主義政策を詳細に論駁することから始められていたと言っても過言ではないであろう。その真意は、彼の『諸国民の富』において見出すことができる。例えば、トーマス・マン（Thomas Mun ; 1571-1641）の一国の富を増加させる目的で書かれたもの（"England's Treasure by Forraign Treasure : or, the ballance of our forraign trade is the rule of our treasure"『外国貿易によるイングランドの財宝』一六六四年）とは体系的に非常に異なっていると述べている。換言すれば、国民経済体系から乖離して、世界主義を根本思想として世界経済に言及し、商業は一国民だけというものではなく、世界各国の国民がそれぞれにそれを享受するという考え方である。「貨幣は商業の用具であるから、貨幣をもってさえいれば、他のどのような商品によるよりも一層容易にわれわれの必要とするどんな物でも手に入れることが可能である」として、その結果重商主義経済政策は、輸入を減少させ、輸出を増加すべく努めたのであると考えた。それはすなわち、「富が金銀より成るということ、そして金銀は、鉱山のない国では、専ら貿易差額によって、すなわちその国の輸入する価値よりも大きな価値を輸出することによって、国内消費用の外国品の輸入をできるだけ減らし、内国産業の生産物の輸出をできるだけ増やすことが、必然に経済政策の大目的となった。その故、経済政策の一国を富ますための二大方法は、輸入に課する制限と輸出に与える奨励とであった」のである。

本来の貨幣の職能としての支配手段と直接の富の源泉とを同義語としてみた所に、重商主義の根本的ドグマが存在したと考えたからであったと言ってよいだろう。スミスの考えた富とは、人々の役に立つ必需

品や必要品そのもののことであり、金銀貨は、このようなものを購買するための手段でしかなかった。

「金銀の輸入は、一国民が外国貿易より収得する主なる利益でもなく、いわんやその唯一の利益でもない。およそどこでも地域間において外国貿易が営まれる場合には、これらの地では、皆外国貿易中自国内において異なる利益を収得する。すなわち外国貿易は、それらの地域間の土地および労働の生産物中自国内において何らの需要をも見ざる剰余部分を海外に輸送し、しかしてこの剰余部分の代りに自国内にて需要のある何か他の物を持ちかえる。さらに言えば、外国貿易はその国の冗物、これをその国民の欲望の一部分を満足させ、そして彼等の享楽を増加しうる他のあるものと交換するに依り、価値を与えるのである。」

またスミスは、「統治がよくゆきとどいた社会では、普遍的な富裕（uniresal opulence）が人民の最下層の階級にまでひろがっているのであって、これこそは、分業の結果あらゆる工芸の生産物のすべてを通じてゆきわたるのである」として、…そこで一般的豊富が社会のすべての階級をつうじて大増殖したためにひきおこされたことなのである。これこそは、分業の結果あらゆる工芸の生産物のすべてが人民の最下層の階級にまでひろがっているのであって、これこそは、分業こそが、富を増加させ、利益をもたらすものであるとして、それを大いに奨励していかねばならないとした。しかし、分業の発展は、市場の拡大によって制限される。

そのため、必然的に狭隘な国内市場に限界がもたらされると、次には広大な海外市場にそれを求めていかなければならない。国際間の自由な交換によって、始めて分業からの利益を享受できるのである。換言すれば、それは国際間における各国の分業を基礎として、当事国で自由貿易を展開して得られるものである。

この点に関して、スミスによれば、「買うよりも、自分で作る方がかえって高くかかるものは、決して自分の所で作ろうとはしないのが、すべての分別ある一家の主人の主義である。また靴屋は自分の衣服を自分で作ろうとはしないで、裁縫師から買う。また靴屋は自分の靴を自分で作ろうとはしないで、裁縫師に作らせる。……もしある一外国が一貨物をわれわれ自ら作るよりも安くわれわれに供給しうるならば、われわ

れは、自分たちが多少ともこの外国に比べて得意とする自国の産業を活動させ、その生産物の一部をもって、この生産物を買った方が得策である」[18]としている。

すなわち、交換が、同一国民でなく異なる国民との間でも、輸出入の自由な状態に従うならば、必ずや利益を得ることができるとする。しかも、従って「分業の諸利益は、スミスの見る所では、一国民の地理的境界以上にもおよんだのである。諸国民は、各個人と同様に種々なる利益を、即ち自然的なものであれ、後天的なものであれ、位置、土壌、気候の諸情勢から得たものであれ、長期の実行に、または遺伝的性質に基くものであれ、諸国民をして特殊な諸商品を生産するに適したところの種々の利益を所有するのである。個々の労働者間の・個々の職業間の・および諸地方間の分業は、熟練の増進、時間の節約をもたらした。そして、同様なる結果が、諸国民間の分業においても生ずるであろう。両当事者は、彼らがその生産に一層適合する諸商品を自由に交換すれば、利益を得るであろう」[19]としている。

このように、スミスは、国際間において分業が行なわれ、自由貿易を実施すれば、それぞれ貿易当事国間にとって利益を享受することができると考思する。そして、それは、例えば大きな自然的諸長所のある国があり、他国がその点で比較し競争するのは無益であるとの見解を示し、「ある一国が特殊の諸商品を生産するうえで他国に対してもつ自然的長所は、時には非常に素晴らしいものであって、これと競争するのは無駄だと全世界に認められる程である。スコットランドでも、温室、温床、温壁等をもってすれば、極く良質のブドウができるし、また少なくとも同質のブドウ酒を外国から輸入する費用の約三十倍をかければ、極く上等のブドウ酒でもこのブドウで、造り得る。スコットランドでボルドウ産の赤ブドウ酒やブウールゴニュウ酒の醸造を奨励するというだけのために、外国産ブドウ酒の輸入を全部禁止する法律は果して合理的な法であろうか。自国で需要される等量の財貨を外国から買うのに要する所よりも三十倍も多い

自国の資本と労働を。ある一事業に向けるということは、明らかに不条理だとするのであれば、自国の資本なり労働なりを、それ程ひどく目立たないにしても、なお正しく同種の不条理が認められるに相違ない。ある一国の他国に優れている長所が、自然的なものであろうと、後天的なものであろうと、いずれにしてもこの点では無関係である。とにかく一国がこれらの長所をもち、他国がそれを欠いている間は、後者にとっては自ら造るよりも、むしろ前者から買う方が得策であろう。けだし、一工匠が他の職業を営む隣人に優るところは自然的な長所ではなく、習得された後天性の長所に過ぎぬ、それでも両者は自分の本職でないものを自ら作るよりも、互に相手から買う方が有利だと思っている。」[20]

このようにして、スミスは対外貿易の原則として自由貿易を基調とする国際分業を主張することになる。各国がその得意で優位な産業に全資本ならびに労働を集中させ、また不得意で不利な産業の生産物を自国にて製造せずして、より廉価なものを外国から購買することが、すべての国々の国民の富を増加させる最善の方策であるとの見解をもったのである。それ故、余剰生産物の交換を自由に行なって、別の形態で富の増殖を行なうことが、外国貿易の使命であり、この点においてこそ重要な意義を有することになるのである。

しかし、スミスの外国貿易論は、J・S・ミルによって余剰物捌口論 (the vent for suplus theory) であるとして批判された。その点をスミスによれば、「ある産業部門の生産物が、その国の需要を越える場合には、その剰余はこれを国外に送り、国内に需要のある何かと交換せねばならぬ。この輸出がないと、その国の生産的労働の一部は体止し、その年々の生産物の価値は減じるにちがいない。イギリスの土地と労働は、概して内国市場の需要にあまるほど穀物や毛織物や金物類を生産する。故に、そのあまる分は外国に送り、国内に需要する何かと交換せねばならぬ。このあまった分が、それを生産する労費を償うにいたる

だけの価値を取得するのは、専らこの輸出のお蔭げである。かくして購入された外国品が、既に内国市場の需要に超過する場合には、この余分は再輸出して、それ以上に内国で需要ある何かほかのものと交換せねばならぬ。……もっとも、一つの社会の如何なる時代においても、原生産物並に製造品の剰余分、即ち国内に需要のない部分は、国内にて若干の需要ある物と交換するために、国外に送らねばならぬ[21]」のであるとする。

さらにスミスにおいては、外国貿易の主たる利益は、金銀の輸入ではなく、国内にて需要なき剰余生産物を国外に持ち出し、需要あるものを国内に持ち込むことによって享受されると示唆する。すなわち、「およそ、どのような地方のあいだに外国貿易が営まれるにせよ、これらの地方のすべては、二つの別個の利益をそれから引き出す。外国貿易は、それら諸者の土地及び労働の生産物の中で、国内に需要のない剰余分を国外に送り、この剰余分の代りに国内で需要ある何か他のものを持ち帰る。すなわち、外国貿易はその国のあり余る物に、これを国民の欲望の一部を満足させ、彼らの享楽を増大しうる他のあるものと交換することによって、価値を与える。外国貿易のおかげで、内国市場が狭隘なために、技術または製造業のどの部門でもその分業が最高度の完全の域まで進むのを妨げられるということがないようになる。一国の労働の所産の如何なる部分でも、その内国消費によれば、これに最も広汎な市場を聞いてくれることによって、外国貿易はそれらの諸国を励してその労働の生産力を改善せしめ、かくしてその社会の真の所得と富を増加させる[22]。」その議論の本質的な帰結は、貿易がなければ余剰生産能力が存在するにいたるということである。それ故、外国貿易を導入すれば、国内生産からなんらの資源をも移転することを要せず、純利益が存在することになる[23]。

スミスの余剰物捌口論に対する批判は、リカード (David. Ricardo ; 1722-1823) によっても展開された。

彼によればスミスは、われわれが、穀物、毛織物製品、および金物類の剰余を生産するというなんらかの必要に迫られていて、それらを生産する資本は他の方法では使用されえない、と結論した。しかしながら、どんな方法で資本を使用するかは、常に選択の問題なのである。それ故、かなりの期間にわたってなんらかの商品の剰余が存在することは決してありえない。仮にそれが存在するとすれば、それはその自然価格以下に下落することは決してありえない。

リカードはさらにスミスから次の点を引用して批判を加えている。「もし一外国が、一商品をわれわれ自身がそれを作るよりも安くわれわれに供給することができるならば、われわれの勤労の生産物の若干部分をもって、それをその国から買うほうがよい。その国の勤労の総体は、常にそれを雇用する資本に比例するから、このことによっては減少せず、ただそれがもっとも有利に雇用されうる方法を見出すべく、放任されるだけであろう」としている。われわれは諸商品を製造し、それでもって海外から財貨を買う。なぜならば、われわれは国内で作製することができるよりも、もっと大なる分量を取得することができるからである。しかしスミスのこの意見は、われわれはただちにふたたび自分たちで製造する。しかしスミスの命題の内容の示すところは、いわゆるリカードの比較生産費説と対比する絶対的生産費説によって外国貿易が営まれることを説明するものである。これがスミスの外国貿易論の特徴となっているものである。

要約すれば、これらの点をすべて考慮してスミスの外国貿易論を論ずれば次のようになろう。すなわち、一国の富の増加は、分業の発展によりもたらされるものであり、その分業の改善、発展は、市場の広さに依存する。狭隘な国内市場は、その範囲がいつかは限定され、事物の自然の成り行きとして生産物が余剰

となる。しかしこの国民の総生産物は富の源泉である。それも、富の形態としては真実であり、余剰物であってもむだな、無価値な物として排除することは回避せねばならないのである。すなわち、その余剰生産物を別の生産物と交換することによって、別の形態で国富の増大を考えることが必要になってくる。そうすることによって、自国内で生産の不可能な生産物や費用のかかりすぎる生産物は、国内の余剰生産物と交換に手に入れることが可能となる。その結果、一国の富は、いままで以上に増大するのである。市場の範囲が広ければ広いほどいいのであって、国内市場で余剰となった生産物は、技術革新を促進し、労働の生産力を高めることによって、外国貿易を通して他の富と交換されることになる。スミスにおける外国貿易の役割は、正にこの点に存在したと考えられる。

(B) リカードの貿易論

国際分業により貿易利益を生み出すことを解いた一理論であるリカードの比較生産費説は、単に古典派の枠に留まらず、今日でもこれほど明解で、重要な、また色々と解釈される理論は他には見当たらないであろう。それだけにまたその問題点を解く魅力も必然的に大きくなる。

リカードの理論それ自体が、多くの仮定に立脚しており、また甚だ抽象的であり必ずしも一義的に明解なものではない。例えば、労働費用の観点からのみ議論をおし進めているが、リカードのそのモデルは、今日厳密に言えばあてはまらない。すなわち「人間は道徳的意味では、国際的単位である」かもしれないが、しかし厳密に経済用語では、人間は国際的単位ではない。異なった国々の人間の個人的属性は、相異しており、どのような場合にも気候・天然資源、技術水準そして知識のうん蓄は、ある国と他の国とでは異なっている。これに関連すると、国家間で一人当たりの産出量の直接的比較は、なんらの

意味がないことになるのである」[26]ことが場合によっては認識されなければならない。

A・スミスにおいて分業は、一工場内の一製造業の技術的分業を基本的形態として、またこの分業の形態を敷衍した上での「種々の産業及び職業相互の分離」、すなわち社会的分業（職業分業）へと、さらには、国際間における分業、すなわち国際分業へと結びつける伏線となっている。当然のように分業の利益は、これらの諸形態における分業において享受されることができると論じている。この点に関して、リカードの理解は、A・スミスのそれと合致していないのだろうか。すなわち、換言すれば、一般的な分業の理論が、国際的な分業の理論とその本質的な意味で、リカードにおいては妥当しないのであろうか。リカードの比較生産費説の法則は、その原理がA・スミスのそれを踏襲し、より上の次元におし進めたとするJ・S・ミルの指摘は正当であったのだろうか。その点に関連しながら、リカードの比較生産費説の解釈を行ってみよう。

リカードの比較生産費説の設例は、その組み合せは完全ではなかったけれども、その後のどの理論よりも国際分業による貿易利益に関して理解が容易である点で、今日でもなお意義あるものである。すなわち、それによれば、「イギリスは、ラシャ（服地）を生産するには一年間一〇〇人の労働を要し、またもしもブドウ酒を醸造しようと試みるなら同一時間に一二〇人の労働を要するかもしれない、そういった事情のもとにあるとしよう。それ故に、イギリスは、ブドウ酒を輸入し、それを服地の輸出によって購買するのがその利益であることを知るのであろう。

ポルトガルでブドウ酒を醸造するには、一年間に八十人の労働を要するにすぎず、また同一国で服地を生産するには、同一時間に九十人の労働を要するかもしれない。それ故に、その国にとっては服地とひきかえに、ブドウ酒を輸出するのが有利であろう。この交換は、ポルトガルによって輸入される商品が、そこではイギリスにおけるよりも少ない労働を用いて生産されうるにもかかわらず、なおおこなわれるであろ

う。ポルトガルは服地を九十人の労働を用いて製造することができるにもかかわらず、それを生産するのに一〇〇人の労働を要する国からそれを輸入することによって生産しうるよりもイギリスからひきかえにより多量の服地を取得するであろうブドウ酒の生産にその資本を使用するほうがむしろ有利だからである。

このようにして、イギリスは、八十人の労働の生産物に対して、一〇〇人の労働の生産物を与えるであろう。このような交換は、同一国の個人間では起こりえないであろう」と論じている。

これを要約すれば、一国が二商品の生産において、他の国に比べて絶対的優位をもち、しかもその一商品が他の商品よりも生産上より大なる優位性をもつ時は、前者を生産し後者を輸入することが有利である。そしてまた、一国が二商品の生産において、他国にくらべて絶対的劣位で、しかもその一商品が他商品よりも生産上より大なる劣性を有する時には、前者を輸入し、後者を生産することが有利である。

それ故、このような場合には、両国はそれぞれの比較的に優位とする商品の生産に特化し、その生産物を相互に交換することになる。一国が他国にくらべてどちらの商品の生産においても絶対的優位性を有する場合にも、ある商品を自国内で生産するよりも外国から輸入したほうが少ない費用でその商品を手に入れることになる限り、この商品を外国から輸入することになり、絶対的劣位である国もいずれかの商品を輸出することになり、これら両国間において貿易の成立を見出すことになる。

しかし、リカードによれば、この点に関して、国内商業と国際間での取引との相違を認識し、これらの交換は、国際間では行われるが、同一国内の個人間では生じないと主張するのである。すなわち、同一国内では、商品の生産にこのような差異が存在する場合には、二商品それぞれの生産は絶対的優位性を有す

るところで生産されるはずである。このような事情が起こるのは、異なった国と国とが存在して可能となる。それは、同一国内においては生産要素、労働と資本の移動が自由であるのに反して、異なった国と国との間ではその移動性が困難であるからである。

それ故、「一国内においては財貨の相対価値を定めるその同一のルールは、二国もしくはそれ以上の国々の間で交換される財貨の相対価値を定めるものではない」ということになる。

リカードの理論は、貿易からの利益が各国内で特産物の生産における比較優位の相違から発生して、国家間での絶対的比較では何も発生するものではないというものであったと思われる。

本来比較生産費説は、貿易の成立を論証すると同時に、貿易利益を明らかにするところの理論でもある。すなわち、リカードは、「外国貿易の拡張は、商品の数量したがって享楽品の総量を増大させるにはきわめて有力に貢献するのであろうが、しかしけっしてただちに一国の価値額を増大させるものではない。すべての外国財貨の価値は、それらとひきかえに与えられるわが国の土地と労働の生産物の分量によって測定されるから、われわれは、仮に新市場の発見によって、わが国の財貨の一定量とひきかえに外国財貨の二倍量を取得するとしても、より増大なる価値を得ないであろう。もしもある商人が、一〇〇〇ポンドの額の外国財貨を購買することによって、イギリス市場で一二〇〇ポンドで売ることができるある分量の外国財貨を取得しうるものとすれば、彼はその資本のこのような使用方法によって、二十パーセントの利潤を取得するであろう。しかしその利得も、輸入商品の価値も、共に取得された外国財貨の分量の多少によって増減することはないであろう。たとえば、彼がブドウ酒二十五樽を輸入しようと五十樽を輸入しようと、ある時には二十五樽が、また他の時には五十樽が等しく一二〇〇ポンドで売れるかぎり、それは彼の利益にはすこしも影響しないのである。いずれの場合にも、彼の利潤は二〇〇ポンドで、すなわち彼

の資本に対する二十パーセントに、限定されるであろう。そしていずれの場合にも、同一の価値がイギリスに輸入されるであろう」と論じている。

リカードにおいては、「すべての取引の目的は、生産物の価値を増加させることによってではなく、その分量を増加させることによって、有利なものになる」のである。

「もしも外国貿易の拡張により、あるいは機械の改良によって、労働者の食物と必需品が低減された価値で市場にもたらされうるならば、利潤は上昇するであろう。もしも、われわれが、自国の穀物を栽培したり、あるいは労働者の衣服およびその他の必需品を製造するのではなく、より安い価格でこれらの商品をわれわれに供給することができる新しい市場を発見するならば、賃銀は低下し利潤は上昇するであろう。しかし、もしも、外国貿易の拡張により、あるいは機械の改良によって、より安い値段で取得される諸商品が、もっぱら金持ちによって消費される諸商品であるならば、利潤率にはなんらの変更も起こらないであろう。たとえブドウ酒、ビロード、絹織物、およびその他の高価な商品が五十パーセント下落るとしても、賃銀率は影響を受けないであろう。またその結果として利潤はひきつづき不変のままであろう。

そうしてみると、外国貿易は、収入が支出される諸物の分量と種類とを増加し、また諸商品の豊富と低廉とによって、貯蓄と資本の蓄積とに刺激を与えるから、一国にとって高度に有利であるとはいえ、輸入される諸商品が労働の賃銀が支出されるその種類のものでない限り、資本の利潤をひき上げる傾向をすこしももたないであろう」ことになる。

[注]

1 小林通『国際経済の新視点』(時潮社、一九九三年)一七頁参照。
2 小林通『現代国際経済システムの原点と構図——重商主義の現代的意義——』(時潮社、二〇〇一年)特に二〇三頁以降参照。「国際化時代と経済摩擦」『国際関係学部開設十周年記念国際シンポジウム——新しい創造の世紀に向けて——』一九九〇年 二三一〜二九頁参照。
3 小林通『現代国際経済システムの原点と構図——重商主義の現代的意義——』(時潮社、二〇〇一年)一四六頁。
4 舞出長五郎『経済学史概要上巻』(岩波書店、一九四一年)二〇三頁参照。
5 スミスは、『諸国民の富』の序論の冒頭において、「すべての国民の年々の労働は、本来その国民が年々消費するすべての生活の必需品と便益品とを供給する資源であって、その必需品と便益品とはこの労働の直接の生産物であるか、あるいはその生産物をもって他の諸国民から購入した物である」と述べている。すなわち、富の源泉を流通過程において捉えることではなく、生産過程においてこそ富本来の源泉が存在するとしたのが、スミス経済学の理論的基調であった。
6 小林通『外国貿易論 (改訂版)』(高文堂出版社、一九九一年)三十八頁。
7 スミスの通称 The Wealth of Nations (『諸国民の富』)の正確な名称は、 An Inquiry into the Nature and Causes of the Wealth of Nations (『諸国民の富の本質と原因に関する研究』) である。本稿では The Wealth of Nations (『諸国民の富』) とする。
8 Cf., Smith 7-10. 竹内謙二訳『国富論』(慶友社) 十二〜十四頁参照。
9 Cf., Smith 17. 邦訳 十七〜十八頁参照。
10 Cf., Smith 19. 邦訳 二十四頁。
11 小林通 前掲書 三十八頁。
12 舞出長五郎 前掲書 二〇六頁参照。
13 A. Toynbee, *Lectures on Industrial Revolution of the Eighteenth Century in England* (1993) 61.
14 Smith 396. 邦訳 第四編四頁。
15 Smith 416. 邦訳 第四編三十〜三十一頁。
16 Smith 413. 邦訳 第四編。
17 Smith, vol. I, 413. 邦訳 第一編十六頁。
18 Smith, vol. III 422. 邦訳 第三編三十八〜三十九頁。

19 L. L. Price, *A Short History of Political Economy in England, from Adam Smith to Arnold Toynbee* (1891).
20 石渡六三郎『英国経済史』(日本評論社、一九三〇年)三三三-三三四頁。
21 Smith, vol. III 423-424. 邦訳　第三編四十一-四十一頁。
22 Smith, BK. II 352-359. 邦訳　第二編二一二-二二〇頁。
23 Smith 413. 邦訳　第二編二二六-二二七頁。
24 Samuel Hollander, *The Economics of Adam Smith* (U of Toronto P, 1973) 269. 小林　昇監修『アダム・スミスの経済学』(東洋経済新報社、一九七六年) 三九〇頁。
25 Smith, BK. IV, chii, 422. 邦訳　第四編三八-三十九頁。
26 D. Ricardo, *The Works and Correspondence of David Ricardo*, ed. P. Sraffa, Vol. I, (1951) 295. 邦訳『デヴィド・リカードドゥ全集』I (雄松堂書店、一九七二年) 三四〇頁。
27 J. Robinson, *Refelctions on the Theory of International Trade* (1974) 4. 小林　通訳『国際貿易理論の省察』(駿河台出版社、一九七七年) 七頁。
28 Ricardo 135. 邦訳　一五七-八頁。
29 Ricardo 134. 邦訳　一五六-一五七頁。
30 Robinson 4-5. 邦訳　七-八頁。
31 Ricardo, vol. I 128.
32 Ricardo 318-9.
33 Ricardo 319-20.
　 Ricardo 132-4.

国際結婚にみる異文化の交流と実践(2)
三島市に生きるフィリピン女性家族の事例から

吉田正紀

はじめに

グローバル化する状況のなかで、異なった文化をもつ人間が最もダイレクトに出会い、生活する場は国際結婚であるといえる。文化の交流の在り方に関心をもつ人類学研究者にとって、極めて注目すべき領域と考えられる。筆者はすでに、「国際結婚にみる異文化の交流と実践(1)―インドネシアに嫁いだ日本女性の事例から」において、インドネシア人と結婚した日本女性が、インドネシアの文化とどのように出会い、また日本の文化をどのようにとらえ直し、そこで生まれる対立や確執をどのように調整し合いながら生活してきたのか、そこにどのような新たな関係が生まれているか検討した。

本稿では、静岡県三島市に居住するフィリピン人女性と結婚した家族を対象に、異なる文化の交流と実践の在り方を考察するものである。平成九年度のゼミ学生の協力を得、九家族にインタビューを試み、二人の出会い、夫の国の印象、日本語の習得、家庭内の使用言語、子供の言語習得と教育、宗教への理解と関わり、食生活、仕事、つきあい、娯楽や大衆文化、生活習慣の比較、日本人の性格や行動様式など、結婚生活の全般について語ってもらった。結婚生活を継続するにあたり、その法的・経済的・情緒的側面の重要性はいうまでもないことであるが、インタビューでは彼らが直面した文化的課題に焦点を絞った。自己の文化に育まれて生きてきた女性が、結婚を契機として、地理的に遙かに遠く、大変異なった文化をもつ男性の祖国で生きて行かなくてはならない状況は、インドネシアに嫁いだ日本女性と同一である。異なった文化を携えて嫁いできた女性たちが、どのように異なった文化・言語・習慣と出会い、かつ異文化の障壁にどのように挑戦しているのか、文化の交流と具体的な実践の事例を検討したい。

本論に入るにあたり、国際結婚に関する出版と研究動向、近年の日本における国際結婚の動向、日本におけるフィリピン女性の国際結婚について、その研究動向を含めレビューすることから始めることにする。

［1］わが国における国際結婚に関する出版と研究の動向

近年、国際結婚に関する出版物が目につくようになった。その多くは国際結婚をしている当事者が自らの結婚生活の体験を綴ったものである。これまでも、例えばヤンソン由実子（一九八一）は、自己の体験を軸に、日本における国際結婚への差別や偏見の歴史を描いた。石川幸子（一九九二）は、国際結婚の現実と問題点を、法律や言語や宗教やアイデンティティなどいくつかの側面から検討したものである。

日本の人文科学の分野で、国際結婚に関する先行研究はそれほど多くはないが、さまざまな専門分野からのアプローチが試みられている。その中でも、社会学における関心は高く、『家族社会学研究』第八号（一九九六）では、特集「わが国における国際結婚とその家族をめぐる諸問題」が収められている。近年の日本の国際化の状況を反映した国際結婚家族の現況や社会化が論じられている。その後も、離婚、ドメステック・バイオレンスなど国際結婚にみられる負の側面が注視されている（宮島喬・長谷川洋子 二〇〇〇、定松文 二〇〇二）。

竹下修子は『国際結婚の社会学』（二〇〇〇）を、嘉本伊都子は『国際結婚の誕生』（二〇〇一）を出版し、国際結婚の歴史的形態に関心を向けている。歴史学の分野では、小山騰（一九九五）が、日本で国際結婚の開始についての歴史的研究を発表している。澤岻悦子（二〇〇〇）、林かおり・田村恵子・高津文美子（二〇〇二）、植木武（二〇〇二）らは、年老いていく戦争花嫁の証言から近代女性史研究に貢献している。法律学の分野では、国際化の進むなかで、国際結婚をめぐる法的問題が注目されている（奥田安弘 一九九六、山田鐐一他 一九九五）。人類学の分野では、ハワイにおけるアメリカ人との国際結婚についての研究は決して多いものではなく、新田文輝（一九九二）が、ハワイにおけるアメリカ人との「二文化家族」とその子供たちの社会化について研究を行なってきたことが目につくに過ぎない。

人類学的な国際結婚研究の近年の成果として、ブレーガーとヒル（一九九八）の編著『異文化結婚（*Cross-Cultural Marriage*）』を上げておく必要がある。世界のさまざまな地域での多様な結婚を、各著者の個人的経験をふまえ、かつアイデンティティ、子供と言語、離婚など通文化的なキーワードを用いながら、既成概念、選択、国家の規制、所属と家族、パーソナリティ、子供と言語、離婚など通文化的なキーワードを用いながら、国際結婚家族の比較研究を行なった。これは、今後の国際結婚の人類学的研究に一つの方向性を与えるものとして特記しておきたい。

[2] 近年の日本における国際結婚の動向

平成一二年度版「在留外国人統計」によれば、「日本人の配偶者等」(日本人の配偶者又は子)の外国人登録者数は、二七万七七五人で、平成十年度末に比べ五九三一人(二・二%)増となっている。国籍別(出身地)別構成比をみると、ブラジルが九七、三三〇人(三五・九%)と最も多く、ついで中国(十八・一%)、フィリピン(十七・一%)、韓国・朝鮮(八%)、タイ(四・一%)の順になっており、以上の五ヶ国で全体の八十三・二%を占めている(表1)。とくに中国およびフィリピンやタイなどの東南アジア諸国が増加していることがわかる。厚生省が発表した人口動態統計によると、外国人との結婚の割合が一九七〇年〇・五%、八〇年〇・九%、九〇年四・一%へと着実に増加している(表2)。

日本の統計では、国際結婚とは「夫婦の一方が外国人」の婚姻を指しているが、近年の著しい傾向は、国際結婚の発生頻度の増大と配偶者の国籍の多様性にあるが、さらに日本の男女の国際結婚の形態に変化がみられることである。一九六五年から一九七五年までは、日本女性の国際結婚の割合が日本男性より多かった。それ以前にも日本女性は第二次世界大戦後のいわゆる戦争花嫁として、アメリカ人を中心に、カナダ人、オーストラリア人の軍人や民間人と結婚したことが知られている(新田文輝 一九九五:竹下修子 二〇〇〇)。しかし一九七五年以降、日本国内における日本人の国際結婚の形態がこれまでとは逆転し、女性より男性の方が外国人の女性と結婚するケースが増加していることである。一九九二年を例にとると、国際結婚数は男性の方が女性のそれの三倍となっている(表2)。その傾向は現在でも続いているという。

河原俊昭(二〇〇〇)は、男女の比率の差から、日本人の国際結婚の型をフィリピン型(外国人女性配偶

者の優位)、アメリカ型(外国人男性配偶者の優位)、韓国・朝鮮型(男女均衡)とに分類している。
このような現象の動機や発生の背景を理論的に詳しく論じる余裕はないが、とくに一九七〇年代以降の著しい日本の経済発展、社会変化、それに伴う人的交流の増大が、日本人の国際結婚の形態や発生率に大きな影響を与えてきたといえる。このような状況を背景として、アジアの諸国にとって、日本は経済的に優位となり、「憧れ」の対象となった。日本の経済が今のように発展する以前は、日本人と結婚し日本に住みたいと希望する外国人は僅かであったが、日本が豊かになるにつれ、日本人と結婚し、日本に居住しようとする外国人が増えたということになる(宿谷京子 一九八八)。とりわけ、これまで国際結婚の実績の少なかった韓国・朝鮮、中国、アメリカ人以外の国の女性たちが、日本人男性と結婚するケースが増えている。日本企業の海外進出により、現地でその国の女性と出会う機会も大幅に増大した。
具体的には次のセクションで述べるように、八十年代から、アジアからとくに性風俗業で働くフィリピン女性たちの来日や、日本の農村地域でのフィリピン女性との集団見合い結婚によって、多数の日本人男性との間に婚姻が成立するようになった。日本女性にとっても、海外留学や海外旅行による経験、ビジネスのグローバル化によって外国人労働者の雇用が増大し、配偶者選択の幅が拡大している。九十年代には、日本社会の日常を拒否した若い日本女性が、神の島バリへ嫁ぐ事例は大きな話題ともなった(山下晋司一九九六：松村章子一九九八)。まさに現在はかってないほどの、「結婚のグローバリゼーション」が起こっているのである(新田 一九九五)。

［3］フィリピン女性との結婚形態と研究動向

外国人が結婚を目的として日本に入国する際、在留資格ビザによって、三つのタイプに分けることができる。一つは日本人が外国へ赴き、現地で外国人と結ばれて、一緒に日本に戻り、そのまま日本で生活するタイプ、次のケースは留学や仕事のために日本に来日した外国人が、日本人と結婚し、そのまま日本に居住するケースである。三つ目は観光ビザで入国した後、資格変更申請して日本に居住する場合である。

近年の国際結婚の傾向はすでに述べたように、日本全体の婚姻数の減少とともに、国際結婚の割合が着実に増加していることである（表2）。とりわけ日本人男性と外国人女性のカップルが急増しており、その外国人妻の国籍は、これまで多かった韓国、朝鮮、中国、アメリカから、フィリピンやタイなどその他の外国人へと移ってきている。その要因として、経済的に豊かな日本人男性との結婚を希望するアジア人女性がふえていることが上げられる。日本人男性の妻として、現在日本に居住する外国人の国籍は、アジアからの「花嫁」の数の多さに、驚かされる。そのうち配偶者としての資格で在留する外国人妻のうち、二十一～二十四歳までの層はフィリピン女性がずば抜けて多い（宿谷 一九八八）。

日本では一般に結婚を見合い結婚と恋愛結婚に分けて考えることが多い。フィリピン女性の日本における国際結婚を考えるときも、このカテゴリーと都市と農村と関連で考えると整理しやすい（新田 一九九五）。一般に農村での結婚は見合い婚が多く、都市の場合は恋愛結婚が多い傾向があることは、日本人同士あるいは私の調査した三島市の場合も当てはまる。実際的には農村にも恋愛による国際結婚もありうるし、都市部でも結婚斡旋業者を通じてまとまる見合い結婚もありうることである。男性の結婚難が農

村と都市の社会問題になると、多くの斡旋業者が出現し、見合い結婚の必要性が生じてくることもあろう。一方、日本国内においても、海外においても、未婚男女が職場や学校やその他の場所で外国人と一緒に仕事をしたり、勉強したり、個人的なレベルでの付合いによる国際交流の機会が増大するにつれ、恋愛や国際結婚へと発展していることは事実である。

[4] 都市におけるフィリピーナの国際結婚

アジアから入国する女性の多くは、結婚して正規に日本に滞在する者より、興業ビザでエンターテイナーとしてやってくる出稼ぎ女性、いわゆる「じゃぱゆきさん」である。かつて日本にも海を渡って出稼ぎにいく女性たち「からゆきさん」から命名されたものである（山谷哲夫 一九八五）。日本に出稼ぎに行くフィリピーナの数が年間一万人を超え、また彼女たちの資格外活動や不法在留が本格的に社会問題化したのは一九七九年である。それゆえその年は出入国管理局の職員の間で「ジャパゆき元年」と呼ばれ（久田恵 一九九二）、それ以降不法な滞在件数は著しく増大した（山谷 一九八五）。

「じゃぱゆきさん」の活動範囲も、東京や大阪の盛場だけでなく、高崎、佐久、和歌山、奈良、富山などの地方都市にも拡大していった。なかにはストリッパー、売春、ポンビキなどヤクザとの深いコネクションを持つ者もいた。山谷（一九八五）はそのような「じゃぱゆきさん」の個人史に焦点をあてて、彼女たちの活動を克明に描いている。出稼ぎの彼女たちのなかには、何度か日本に滞在し、パブやスナックで働くうちに、日本人男性顧客との個人的な付合いを経て恋愛、結婚に結びつくケースはよく知られている。ちなみに一九九三年に興業ビザで新規に入国した外国人のなかで、フィリピン人が四二、六一二人と

全体の約五六％を占めているのが際立っている(新田　一九九五：一〇四)。

このようなフィリピーナと日本人男性とのドラマティックな出会いを描いたノンフィクションに、久田恵の『フィリピーナを愛した男たち』がある。また自らフィリピン人との結婚にのめり込み、フィリピン人との国際結婚に関する情報や支援のネットワークを作って活動している玉垣洋一(一九九五)は、『フィリピーナと結婚すること──笑いと涙！恋愛と生活の秘密』で、自らの体験を明らかにしている。久田や玉垣の事例は、仕事で日本国内にいるが外国人が日本人と恋愛結婚する場合であるが、日本人男性が仕事でフィリピンに滞在しているとき、現地の女性と知り合うケースがある。新田(一九九五)は、これらのタイプを国内派と国外派に区別している。後者の事例は三島に二例みることができるが、大半は前者である。

筆者(二〇〇一)がとりあげた、日本人女性とインドネシア人男性の場合は、留学で日本国内にいる外国人が、日本人女性と恋愛結婚し、インドネシアに日本女性を連れて帰った場合であるが、この場合は新田の区分にはあてはまらず、その中間に位置するカテゴリーといえよう。

[5] フィリピン女性の農村での国際結婚

フィリピン女性との国際結婚は、都市の盛場で働く女性たちとの間で生まれるばかりでなく、むしろ過疎の農村部で初めて行なわれるようになったことである。それは、現代農村の花嫁飢饉の状況を明らかにし、農業後継者の未婚・高齢化の対策として、世間に広く知られるようになった。

それは一九八六年の春、山形県西村山郡朝日村で、嫁不足を解決する手段として、初めて村役場が中心となってフィリピンから数人の花嫁を迎えたことをきっかけとして始まった。さらに同県内だけでなく、

498

他の東北地方や新潟県の同じ問題を抱えた村々でも、東南アジアへ花嫁を求める見合い旅行が実施されるようになった。ここに日本の農村における新しい国際結婚の形態が生まれたのである（新田 一九九五：宿谷 一九八八）。

アジア人花嫁誕生の背景とその実情について、宿谷京子は『アジアから来た花嫁―迎える側の論理』(一九八八)において、人権擁護の立場から過疎化対策として始められた状況を報告している。それは生活苦にあえぐ、アジアの女性の犠牲の上に成り立っているのではないかと指摘している。佐藤隆夫も『農村と国際結婚』(一九八九)において、農村における業者による国際結婚を社会婚、自主的な国際結婚を個人婚と区別し、農村の国際結婚のもつ性格を人権問題としてとらえた法律家の分析を明らかにしている。一方結婚の当時者たち、とくに日本の女性と結婚ができない婚期を逸した農村の後継ぎ男性たちにとってのアジア人との国際結婚はイエの存続だけでなく、村の存続をかけた問題であり、彼らにとっての人権問題であるという相反する視点もある（新田 一九九五：一〇二−一〇三）。

また一九九〇年代はじめより、精神科医として、またNGOの活動家として山形県の外国人花嫁のケアに携わってきた桑山紀彦は、『国際結婚とストレス：アジアからの花嫁と変容するニッポンの家族』(一九九五)において、農村部に移住してきたフィリピンや韓国からの女性たちのカルチャーショックや農村の嫁不足問題、日本の家族の在り方などについて論じながら、日本に住む新しい移民とどのように共生するか、新たなる多民族共生社会の在り方を模索している。しかしながら、桑山(二〇〇一)は、迎える側にも国際結婚そのものを誤解している事が多いが、一方「海を越えて来た女性たち」も自己中心的な性格構造が強く、「自助組織ができにくい」問題点を指摘している。[5]

[6] 三島市のフィリピン家族

国際結婚をした家庭や定住外国人は、日本各地でみられるようになった。静岡県においても、一九九五年の外国人登録数は四五、八七五人で、構成比の三・四％、前年と比較して四・七％の増加となっている（平成八年度版在留外国人統計）。一九九九年末では五八、六二五人となり、四年の間に二十八％という著しい伸びをみせている（平成十二年度版在留外国人統計）。しかしながら、三島市内の外国人登録者数をみると、平成九年十二月末から平成十一年十二月末まで、世帯数で六一三世帯から四九〇世帯へ、人口で一、一二一人から九九四人へと減少している。

出身地別の状況は、平成十一年末ではブラジル 二四四人（二四・五％）、韓国 二四一人（二四・二％）、中国 一一七人（十一・八％）、フィリピン 七十三人（七・三％）、ラオス 五十人（五％）、ペルー 五十人（五％）、インドネシア 四十二人（四・二％）、タイ 二十五人（二・五％）、パラグアイ 二十二人（二・二％）、北朝鮮 二十一人（二・一％）、アルゼンチン 十八人（一・八％）の順で、南米、東アジア、東南アジア諸国出身者が多いことが特徴である。三島市も全国的な外国人登録者の傾向と一致している（三島の統計 二〇〇〇 十三頁、表3）。

筆者は、平成九年十二月から平成十年二月かけ、三島市内での外国人家族二十家族からの聞き取り調査を実施したが、そのうちフィリピン人家族は九家族で、最も多数の事例を提供してくれている。彼女らの家族はすべて「妻外国・夫日本」のカップルからなり、フィリピン人の妻の年齢は三十－四十代で、二十年以上の滞在が二人、他の家族の滞在年数は七－十六年ほどで、欧米系より滞在期間は長い（表4）。本稿

では、このように日本人男性と結婚をしているフィリピン女性を対象にしながら、二つの異なった文化をもった男女が、自己の背負う文化と配偶者の文化をどのように調整し合いながら生活しているのか。そこには配偶者の文化への一方的な同化の傾向がみられるのか（A＋B＝A＋B＋α）。双方の文化だけではもち得なかった新しい共生の文化が生まれるのか（A＋B＝2A）。ここでは言語、子供の教育、仕事、社会的活動、食事・料理、宗教、大衆文化、生活習慣、国際結婚における出会いを中心に考察する。

フィリピン女性と日本人男性の出会いには二つのパターンがみられる。第一は日本人の夫が仕事でフィリピンに滞在しているとき職場で知り合う場合や、夫が留学中に知り合ったケースで、概して女性の学歴は高い。第二は興業ビザで来日したフィリピン女性が、日本のレストランやスナックで働いているときと、夫の両親が口を聞いてくれたとか、同居が認められたケースがいくつかある。しかしどの結婚も斡旋業者を通じての見合い結婚ではなく、恋愛結婚である。

6・1 言語

フィリピンでは、英語とタガログ（フィリピン）語が国語であるが、来日したフィリピン女性は、さらにスペイン語を理解する者も多く、他の東南アジアの国々の人たちのように、多言語の状況のなかに生きてきた。さらに日本で結婚し、生活を継続していくために、日本語の習得を今も継続中で、それが結婚して一番大変だと述べるものが多い。しかしインタビューでは、流暢な日本語を話す者がほとんどである。小学校時代に日本語を学んだ経験があるイダさんを除く八名は、日本に来てから日本語を学んでいる。夫や夫の母などの家族や日本語の教師について学んだ者もいるが、さまざまな方法で日本語を学んできた。

に教えてもらったりした者やボランティア活動のなかで学んだ者がいる。セシルさんは職場での会話やテレビ番組から新しい言葉を学んだという。マリールさんは敬語の使い方、男ことばと女ことばの使い分けに苦労したというが、今はとても上手に話している。在日二十一年になるアグネスさんは、日本語の読み書きが難しく、少しだけしか理解できず、銀行などで困ることがあるという。

アグネスさんは初め家庭で英語を使っていたが、次第にテレビや近所の子供たちと遊んだりしているうちに日本語を覚えている。積極的に話すことで覚えるように努力したという。ブラジル滞在経験のあるステラさんは、ブラジル料理、フィリピン料理、イギリス料理、スペイン料理を教えたりしているうちに、日本語を習得したという。

滞在年数に関係なく、全員英語の重要性は認めているが、日本語の中に英語を混ぜて子供と会話をするよう努力しているステラさんを除いて、家庭でのコミュニケーション言語は日本語である。その理由をアグネスさんは、子供は日本人なので日本語が一番大切であるからという。またマリタさんやマリアンさんの言葉を借りれば、夫たちが次第に日本語しか話さなくなってしまったからという。子供が英語を話すと友人や学校で仲間はずれにされたりするため、幼い頃は日本語を重視したいという。

子供が成長するにつれ、母親が話すことができる英語を、子供たちにもっと英語を学ばせたいと思っている子供も多い。子供にどのように学ばせるか、子供の将来を考えて検討しなければならない課題の一つとなっている。夫も第二の言語としての英語の重要性はよく認識している。

6・2 子供の教育

子供たちは、地元の公立学校に通っている者が多い。エニーさんは「教育は今のままでいい」という。

また滞在十一年目のマリアンさんや二十二年なるアグネスさんは子供が「普通」に育っていくことを望んでいる。イダのお子さんは、理由はわからなかったが、小学校五年生のとき、いじめを受け、二学期登校拒否したそうである。それだからこそ、皆と同じように生きていくことを希望しているのかもしれない。子供たちは、ふだん近所の日本人やフィリピンの子供たちと変わりなく遊んでいるという。家庭教育においては、滞在十六年のステラさんは、日本人の良いところを学ばせ、また忘れつつあるところを回復させたいと願っている。最近日本人の子供は、親を大切にしなくなったので、親を大切にする心を自分の子供に学ばせたいと考えている。他人に何かしてもらったら、有り難く思う気持ちが自然とわくようになってほしいとも付け加えている。

将来子供を留学させたいかという質問に対して、留学したければしてほしいが、あくまでも本人の意思だという。留学先はとくにフィリピンを上げる者はいなかったが、行かせたい国として、イダさんはアメリカをあげ、テッシーさんは住んでいる町がニュージーランドと交流をもっているので、ニュージーランドに行ければよいと考えている。ステラさんは、子供たちをアメリカやイギリスなどの英語圏に留学させたいと考えている。その理由としてアメリカでは、学生は朝から晩まで大学に行き、夜も図書館で勉強し、アルバイトをする時間もないくらい勉強するような環境があり、勉強しやすいシステムがあることをあげている。そこには、筆者の経験からも、日本の大学制度や大学生の勉学・生活態度にはない長所がうかがえることは確かである。

6・3 仕事

八名の職種をみると、家事、フィリピンからの輸入品販売、夫の居酒屋風レストランの手伝い、ホステ

ス、飲食店勤務、薬品会社勤務、英語・料理教室の講師、コンビニ勤務などをしており、家事だけという人は少なく何らかの仕事をしている人たちがほとんどである。一般に働き者で、日本人の夫も彼女の活動を頼りにしている。

輸入品販売のマリアンさんは、家にじっとしているのがいやで、細々と輸入品を売り始めたが、夫の理解もあって今は自分の店をもっている。客との関係もよく、家事もきちんとするし、土建業の夫も「要するに働き者だよ」と誉めていた。会社員の夫の仕事でブラジルにも滞在したことのあるステラさんは、公民館でブラジル料理を中心に、フィリピン、イギリス、スペインの料理を教えたり、自宅で英語を教えている。仕事の選択は、滞在年数に関係なく、彼女たちの学歴、夫の職業、彼女たちを取り囲む家庭環境、妻の仕事に対する考え方や夫の理解度が強く影響している。

6・4 社会活動

彼女たちがボランティアとして参加している国際交流団体「グローバル」は、三島や沼津地区で国際結婚をしている人たちの団体で、彼女たちの主要な社会活動の場となっている。生涯教育のプログラムに参加して、テニスやリズム体操の練習をしている者もいる。ステラさんは、国際交流のイベントを企画したりしている。その活動に一部として始まった活動から「日本語の会」が生まれている。

アグネスさんは元大学講師でもあり、自治会の役員を引き受けたり、マラソンを教えたり、積極的に日本人のグループと交流を重ねている。お茶会に招かれたり、地元のライオンズ・クラブやロータリークラブに頼まれて話したこともあるという。また一緒に温泉に行ったり、誰とも友達となれるので、多くの友人がいる。

カソリック教会の活動にも積極的に参加し、毎週のミサやクリスマス・パーティは、彼女たちにとって大切な社交と楽しみの場となっている。交流団体には時折しか出席できないという。自宅で幼稚園児や小学生に英語を教えているマルタさんは、国際交流団体には時折しか出席できないという。忙しくてなかなか暇がとれないそうだ。マリアンさんは結婚当初はよく参加したが、現在は自営の店が忙しく、それほど熱心ではなくなっている。しかしそのネットワークは商売とも関係するので、打ち合せ会などには出席するようにはしているという。テッシーさんもグローバルの会に入って、フィリピンのことをスピーチしたり、地元の韮山小学校や大仁中学校に、毎年バンブー・ダンスを教えに行っている。フィリピン人とも日本人ともよく付き合っている。このように、学校、自治会、国際交流団体での活動などを通じて、極めて積極的な地域への参加がみてとれる。とくに国際結婚の人たちをつなぐ交流団体は、彼らの間にネットワークを作るだけでなく、地域の活動との結びつきを作る役割を果たしている。

6・5 食事・料理

言語とならび、日本への同化を求められているものに食物と料理がある。日常の食生活は日本食が中心である。結婚当初は日本の料理ができないため、食物の名前や料理法を覚えなければならない苦労があった。テッシーさんは日本に来て初めて刺身などの日本の食物を見て、「何でこんなもの食べるのかな」と思ったが、今は寿司や刺身は大好きだという。ステラさんはフィリピンにも日本料理店があったから、日本料理にはすぐ慣れたが、納豆、鰻、たくわん、寿司が食べられるようになるまでには三年かかったという。アグネスさんも納豆や梅干しや鰻、刺身を日本にきて初めて食べたが、今は刺身を除き食べることができるそうである。マリールさんも初めて食べた物は刺身、鰻、納豆などである。納豆はとくに苦手だったが、

玉葱やトウバンジャンを入れて辛くして、美味しく食べていると述べている。多くのフィリピン女性は寿司、てんぷら、すきやきなど代表的な日本料理は好きで、比較的スムーズに受け入れられているが、刺身は今もアグネスさんやマルタさんのように好きではないという者もいる。しかし箸の使い方など日本的な食習慣は完全に身につけているようだ。魚の料理法もフィリピンではフライが多いが、日本では焼いたり、煮たりするという違いも知るようになった。

食の分野で、自国の料理を家庭で作っているかという点では、フィリピン料理を作る家族も多く、子供たちも好き嫌いなく食べるという家族もある。フィリピンの食材も手に入り、食べたい物を料理できるという。マリールさんは美味しい豚肉を沖縄から送ってもらっているという。

滞日九年になるテッシーさんも、フィリピン料理をよく作り、おじいさんもおばあさんも平気で食べるとのことである。かつては食べなかったが、現在食べるようになった家族もあり、日本人の夫側から妻方への食文化への歩み寄りがみられる。食べれるやつは食べれるよ。前は全然だめだった。でも今は十年もたったからね。結構食べるなと述べているし、味覚の変化をさらに「フィリピンに遊びに行っても、日本料理ばかり、その日本料理もフィリピン料理の味がする。でも今は食べれるよ」と語っている。妻のマリアンさんのように、日本食も好き嫌いなく何でも食べるようになっていることにみられるように、フィリピン女性の日本社会への一方的な同化ばかりではないことがうかがえる。それは三島地区に住むタイやマレーシアの家族とのインタビューで、夫や子供に妻の母国の料理が食卓に出されていることが確認されている。

ファースト・フードは子供と行くときはあるが、家族で行くことは稀である。フィリピンでは家族が多いことや貧しいので、家庭料理が好んで作られたし、日本でも同じような行動をしている。アグネスさん

は自分で料理を作らないと気が済まないと述べている。マリールさんも夫が料理人なので、コンビニなどを利用することはないそうである。マルタさんは一人のときにお弁当やコーヒーをよく買いにいくという。夜も開いていて便利であると指摘する点で日本人と変わらない行動様式がみられる。
フィリピンの料理は、自国の家庭だけでなく、さまざまな機会にも提供されているし、ボランティアとして日本人の女性に教えているフィリピンの女性もいる。これらの行為は、自らのエスニシティを自覚させるよい機会ともなっている。

6・6　宗　教

彼女たちの生活における異質な文化の交流は、宗教信仰の分野でもみることができる。カトリックの信者でもあるフィリピン女性が、毎日曜日に地元の教会に出掛けることは普通のことである。それも家族一緒の場合が多い。

教会でのフィリピンの友人たちとの交流は、母国語を話せる楽しい時間である。同時に日本人や他の国の信者とも出会う機会でもある。ステラさんの日本人の夫のように教会の子供達の役員となって、妻や子供の宗教や交流を積極的に支援している日本人の男性もいる。

日本の宗教習慣との関わりも、文化の相違とその受容を認識させる機会である。彼女たちに日本の宗教との関わりを尋ねてみると、初詣でお寺や神社へ行ったことがあるが、その違いはよく分からないと述べている。行ったとき自分の神に祈ってしまうという者もいる。近所の人の葬式に参列した経験のある者も多いが、儀式の時間の長さや座っている時の足の痺れに苦痛を感じていたと感想を述べている。やはり彼女たちはクリスチャンで、教会には感動を覚えるが、他の宗教施設では何の感情も湧かないというのが正

直のところのようである。日本の神社仏閣へは、家族のお供で行く場合がほとんどといえるし、宗教的関心をもった者はいない。

しかし家族が亡くなった場合、日本式のお葬式をするという者もいるし、ステラさんはフィリピンが土葬なので、火葬が可哀相という感じを抱いているが、やはり日本式に骨にしなければならないのかと感じている。マリアンさんによれば、カトリックの方法で葬式をしたいという者もいる。日本の葬式では人があまり泣かないのに不思議だという感想を述べている。日本人の死に対する風習に戸惑いながらも、いつかそれを受け入れなければならないのかということも感じているようだ。

日本の伝統的な宗教は多くの日本人の習慣ともなっているが、マリアンさんの夫のように創価学会に加入している者もいる。彼は自分がお題目を唱えるとき、妻も一緒に唱和しているという。夫によれば、内容はよくわからないが、夫のすることにただ協力しているのではないかと述べている。「学会がいいからやっているのではなく、お父さんがちゃんとやっているんだから、やってるだけの話」と妻の行動を解釈している。反対にその夫は、通常創価学会は他の宗教に対してあまり寛容でないにも関わらず、クリスチャンである妻の信仰には理解をみせている。「妻が一人のとき、お祈りをしていても、それがいいと思っているんだから」という。異なった宗教信仰をもつ国際結婚の家庭には、異質な信仰への理解がより具体的に求められるようだ。

6・7 大衆文化

彼女たちの最大の楽しみはテレビである。歌、ドラマ(トレンディ、時代劇、サスペンスなど)、バラエティ、アニメ、スポーツ、ニュース、料理番組などさまざまな番組を楽しんでいる。音楽代わりに付け

っ放しという家庭もある。インドネシアで暮らす日本人がニュースを除き、あまり現地のテレビを楽しんでいないのとは対照的である。マリアンさんは店の仕事で忙しく、テレビを見る時間は少ないようだが、アメリカ映画やサムライ映画が好きである。マリールさんは「水戸黄門」や「暴れん坊将軍」などの時代劇が好きという。イダさんは「サザエさん」、「ドラゴンボール」、「ドラえもん」を八歳の子供とよくみるという。アグネスさんも子供と一緒に、歌やバラエティーやドラマの番組をみることが多い。テッシーさんは特にサスペンス・ドラマが好きだという。日本に来たころ、彼女はテレビばかり見ていて、分からないところを夫に聴いて覚えたという。このように、テレビは言葉の学習、夫や子供とのコミュニケーション、気晴らしなどさまざまな効用があるといえよう。

古典歌舞伎や能などの古典芸能についての関心や経験はほとんどない。三島に住むアメリカやカナダなどの欧米人との関心の違いがそこにみられると思う。

音楽については、やはり母国の音楽が好きだという人は多い。言葉がわかるからであるが、日本の歌も聴いている。ステラさんは三人の子供たちがテレビでみる「スマップ」とか日本の歌手の歌を子供と聴く。音楽を一人で聴いているという答えはなかった。テッシーさんは「日本の歌好きです。英語も聴くんですけど、やっぱ、日本の歌好きなんです」と若者言葉で答えている。家庭内のコミュニケーション、話題の共有の源としてのテレビと音楽は、家庭内で重要な位置を占めているようだ。それは日本を知るうえで、格好のメディアとなっている。

6・8 生活習慣

食事、娯楽、買物、付合いに関してはスムーズに受け入れることができたようである。また滞在年数の

長短に関係なく、彼女たちにとって日本人の外国人への対応の仕方や日本の良い習慣に気づき、住みやすいと答えた者がいる。彼女たちは外国人に対して親切で、分からないことはいろいろ教えてくれると回答した人がいる。例えば、日本人は外国人に対して親切で、分からないことはいろいろ教えてくれると回答した人がいる。また人に何かしてもらったら、「ありがとう」という日本人の習慣を良い習慣であるとみなしている者もいる。一方生活していく過程で、困ったことや理解しにくい習慣に遭遇したことも多々あった。十五歳と二十歳になる子供をもつアグネスさんは、子供が幼い頃言葉が不自由なので、子供が病気をすると病院を探すのに苦労したことをよく記憶している。また洗濯機、冷蔵庫などの家電技術の発達で、何でも便利になったが、日本人はあまりに仕事に熱心で、忙しくても病気でも休むことをしないメンタリティをどのように判断してよいか、分からないと述べる人がいた。

エニーさんは、フィリピンでは物をもらったら、すぐお返しをする習慣がないので、どのように対応していいか分からなかったという。お返しの習慣は私が生活したインドネシアにも、アメリカにも無かったので、日本独自の慣習に思える。「葬式が理解できなかった」とか、「座るの慣れるのが大変だった」とか、日常生活の習慣を理解し、それに慣れていくことも時間の要することのようだ。赤ん坊が自動的に煙を吸ってしまうからである。煙草を所かまわず吸うことも、日本人の悪い習慣と映っている。習慣も、フィリピンでは「フォークで押さえ、スプーンで食べる」ため、日本の洋風食習慣も彼らを戸惑わせたようだ。前と思っている「ナイフで切ってフォークで食べる」習慣も、フィリピンでは「フォークで押さえ、スプーンで食べる」ため、日本の洋風食習慣も彼らを戸惑わせたようだ。

彼女たちは、日本人の価値観の変化に対してある種の危惧を抱いている。その例が、ステラさんの、日本人の極端なプライバシー思考が、日本人の良さを失わせていると感じている。その結果、子供たちが要求すれば、親たちは彼らに部屋を分け与えている。その結果、子供たちは共有することに我慢が出来なくなっているように思えるというのである。ステラさんはさらに続けていう。「最近、日本人は

510

知 の 新 視 界

6・9 国際結婚——その出会いの事例

三十九歳になるセシルさんは、二十歳の頃初めて来日した。その後も興業ビザで日本に六ヵ月滞在したあと、二週間フィリピンに帰る生活を続けている。離婚したあと四人の子供はフィリピンで生活しているが、彼らを養うため仕送りを続けている。大学生と高校生になっている子供もいるが、子供は皆大学に入れたいと願っている。彼女は現在御殿場でホステスをしているが、店で知り合った日本人男性と同居中である。いずれ結婚し、フィリピンで挙式をしたいと考えている。本来は同国人と結婚した方がよいと思うが、一度同国人との離婚経験もあり、結婚にあたっては人間性が大切だと指摘する。驚くような明るさで、これまで言葉には苦労したが、日本食にしろあまり取り立てて苦労もなく、違和感なく暮らしているようだ。

三十一歳になるテッシーさんは、来日九年、沼津のスナックで働いているとき夫と知り合って結婚し、現在二人の子供がいる。今もスナックで働いているが、夫は車関係の仕事である。夫の親が彼らの結婚に大反対で、子供ができるまで口を聞くことができなかったほどであった。

三十四歳のマルタさんも日本に来て結婚したが、双方の両親が結婚に反対だったので、結婚式はせず、届けだけで済ませている。「最初は日本に電話しても、"いません"て、電話をつないでくれなかったが、今は仲がいいよ。娘がいないから、本当の娘みたいにかわいがってくれる」と述べている。来月からは夫の両親と一緒に生活を始めるという。

分け合うことができない。このままでは、人を助けることのできない、人の気持ちが分からない人間になってしまうのか」と心配している。

マリアンさんはダンサーとして富士市に来たばかりの頃、現在の夫と知り合った。土建業をしていたので、若い衆の料理も作らなければならないので、夫に教えてもらったという。夫にリーダーシップはあるが、現在では何でも一人前である。彼女は店も持っているし、若い衆にも、フィリピン女性にも慕われているし、恐ろしい旦那とうまくやっているし、近所でも評判の働き者として知られている。

マリールさんも日本では夫とは日本で知り合い、フィリピンの市役所で結婚式をしたあと、市内のレストランでパーティをし、日本に帰ってホテルでパーティを開いたという。結婚するにあたり問題になったことはなく、言葉の違いくらいであった。「国際結婚」は特別のことではなく、ただ配偶者の国が違うだけという。宗教の違いがあっても、結婚式は市役所でするなど、衝突を起こさないようにした。結婚に対して、周りの人達の理解がとてもあったと述べている。

四十六歳のステラさんは、フィリピンに赴任中の夫と同じ職場で知合い、結婚して来日した。結婚にあたり、互いの両親が反対したが、結婚してもおかしくない年ごろだったので、二人でフィリピンの教会に申し込んだ。国際結婚は悪くはないが、お勧めできないという。例えば親子関係や家族内の助け合いについて考えが違うからであるという。夫は子供と意見があうが、彼女とは一致しないことに不満をもっている。日本では子供が親から金をもらうが、フィリピンでは子供が親にお金をあげたいと思っている。また彼女は離れていても、妹の大学の金を出したり、家族が協力しているように家族の助け合いを重視するからである。

四十二歳のアグネスさんは、夫が仕事でフィリピンに来ているときに知り合い、結婚したが、国際結婚については皆すべきであると積極的に賛成している。「日本人の男性は封建的なので、世界を広く見るため、また助け合いの心をもっともてるようになる」のではないかとコメントしている。

おわりに

　フィリピンの女性たちとのインタビューから、彼女たちのバイタリティにあふれた日本での生活ぶりを知ることができる。日本での日常生活をスムーズに遂行させるために、言葉や食物、料理、付合いなどの領域で、これまでの自己の生き方の変革を実践している。言い換えれば、自らが育まれた文化と全く異なる状況におかれ、言語の習得と子供の教育、宗教的習慣の理解、食生活やつきあいなど、多くの領域で同化を求められている。だがそれは必ずしも女性側の一方的なものではなく、夫や子供たちの側も、妻の言語や習慣や食生活に関心を抱き、歩み寄りが見られることである。日本人の夫も日本の文化のなかだけで生きるのと違い、異なる文化への寛容さを発展させたり、理解を深めていかなければならないのである。

　女性たちの同化の努力は、彼女たちを育んだ文化を超えようとするものであるが、それを可能にするのは、他者＝配偶者・家族の存在である。他者の存在は、異なった文化の存在は、二人をこれまでと異なった存在にするようだ。そこに、他者なしでは生きられないような共生の関係が形成されていくように思われる。そういった意味で国際結婚は、異なった文化の共生の実践の場であることは事実である。

　彼女たちはまた、絶えず日本の文化と社会への批判的観察者として登場する。彼女の国では一般的でない埋葬方法、儀式での無駄な出費、盆暮れを初めとする贈答慣行、たてまえと本音の付き合い、親子関係の相互扶助や家族のまとまりの軽視、単身赴任の制度など、生活面で受け入れざるを得なくても、異なる価値観から生じている現象は、なかなか納得がいかないようだ。複数の言葉だけでなく、複数の食文化や異なった習慣との出会いや対立が日常茶飯事に具体的に登場する国際結婚の家庭は、まさに新しい文化が

日々生まれている実験室のようだ。

国際結婚は、異なる文化への関心と寛容、および自文化からの離脱と再認識という二つのプロセスが同時平行的に実践されているプロセスと考えられる。国際結婚にみられる個人レベルでの交流は、互いに他者を必要とする共生の精神によって、対立と確執を超えて新たな関係を作り出す。このような国際結婚のもつポジティブな側面は、グローバル化する現代社会の状況のなかで、学ぶべき生活態度であり、集団の対立と確執を和らげる指針となるといえないだろうか。

[注]

1 吉田正紀『国際関係研究』二十二-一（日本大学国際関係学部・国際関係研究所、二〇〇一年）一三七-一六一頁。

2 筆者の国際結婚に関する研究は、平成九-十一年度日本大学総長指定の総合的研究「国際摩擦の総合的研究」に参加し、国際関係学部の佐藤三武朗教授・植山剛行助教授と「民族の出会いと共生」を担当したことに負うところが多い。

3 例えばアフガン人の妻となり、現在ニューヨーク滞在中の泉久恵の半世紀を描いた『国際結婚 イスラームの花嫁』（二〇〇〇）、ドイツ人と結婚した川口マーン恵美の『国際結婚ナイショ話』（一九九七）、十九歳でインドネシアで結婚し、その生活を明るく描いた今井千香子の『アジアのミラクルパンチ』（一九九九）、アジアを旅し、恋に落ち、結婚した顛末を描いた風海りんねの『アジア恋愛のススメ—七転八倒、ビルマの花嫁日記』（二〇〇一）、韓国から嫁を迎えた一家の『ビビンバ家族—それでも妻は韓国人』（二〇〇〇）、アメリカ人と結婚し国際結婚の手続きに苦労した体験を基にしたパターソン林屋晶子の『レポート国際結婚—涙と笑いのグリーンカード取得』（二〇〇一）など多数ある。涙と笑いに満ちた体験を文庫版で出版するものが多いが、長期滞在者ならではの現地の文化や習慣へ観察と体験が生き生きと描かれていて、単なる旅行記より頗る面白い。しかし海外での国際結婚についての出版物はほとんど女性によるもので、男性によるものは極めて少ない。例外としてバンコクで出版された水野潮の『ドリアンの木の下で』（一九九九）や坂田米夫（一九九九-二〇〇

〇）の作品は、優れたタイの生活誌となっている。また日本人と結婚した人たちによって日本での生活が描かれた出版物を、著者はまだ知らない。世界各地で国際結婚をしている人たちの声を集めたものとして、東京新聞編集局『私たち幸せです』（一九九七）、斎藤弘子・根本厚美編『国際結婚一〇〇家族』（一九九八）、川滝かおり『国際結婚物語』（一九九二）、国際結婚を考える会編『素顔の国際結婚』（一九八六）『楽しくやろう国際結婚』（一九九〇）などがある。

4 新田（一九九五）は、接近と交換理論からこの問題の解釈を試みている。

5 筆者も多民族化する日本において、異なった文化をもつ人間との共生の在り方に関心をもっているが、在日インドネシア人の間には、東京や横浜にインドネシア人の相互扶助組織ができ、日本人とばかりでなく、インドネシア人の間の多民族交流の場を提供していることとは対照的である。

6 調査対象者総数二十人の内訳は、アメリカ四人、カナダ二人、ニュージーランド二人、オーストラリア一人、フィリピン八人、マレーシア二人、タイ一人であった。欧米系は三十代の男性が多く、三島地域の中学・高校の英語教師として滞在している。彼らの滞在期間は短く、一年前後が一番多い。彼らの多くは未婚である。アジア系の家族はすべて「妻外国・夫日本」カップルで、平均して六年から二十三年の滞在である。

[参考文献]

石川幸子『国際結婚』サイマル出版会、一九九二年。

泉久恵『国際結婚―イスラームの花嫁』海象社、二〇〇〇年。

今井千香子『アジア・ミラクル・パンチ』徳間文庫、一九九九年。

植木武編『戦争花嫁 五十年を語る』勉誠出版、二〇〇二年。

奥田安弘『家族と国籍―国際化の進むなかで』有斐閣、一九九六年。

川口マーン恵美『国際結婚ナイショ話』草思社、一九九七年。

川滝かおり『国際結婚物語』廣済堂、一九九二年。

風海りんね『アジア恋愛のススメ』ワニ文庫、二〇〇一年。

河原俊昭「アジアが変える日本文化―国際結婚と多文化共生社会」『異文化理解の座標軸』浅間正通編著 二四三‐二七一頁 日本図書センター、二〇〇〇年。

桑山紀彦『国際結婚とストレス―アジアからの花嫁と変容するニッポンの家族』明石書店、一九九五年。

同右 「国際結婚によって日本の家族は変わるか」『筑紫哲也の現代日本学原論 二』外国人四九‐五四頁 岩波書

国際結婚を考える会　『素顔の国際結婚』　株式会社ジャパン・タイムス、一九八六年。
同右　『楽しくやろう国際結婚』　明石書店、一九九〇年。
小山騰　『国際結婚第一号　明治人たちの雑婚事始め』　講談社、一九九五年。
駒井洋編　『新来・定住外国人がわかる事典』　明石書店、一九九七年。
斎藤弘子・根本厚美編　『国際結婚一〇〇家族』　明石書店、一九九八年。
坂田米夫　『婿殿のチェンマイ日記　死ぬなら今』　四谷グランド、一九九九年。
同右　『婿殿のチェンマイ日記　タイ人になろう』　四谷グランド、二〇〇〇年。
定松文　「国際結婚にみる家旅の問題、フィリピン人女性と日本人男性の結婚・離婚をめぐって」『国際社会2
　　変容する日本社会と文化』宮島喬・加納弘勝編、東大出版会、二〇〇二年。
佐藤隆夫編著　『農村と国際結婚』　日本評論社、一九八九年。
宿谷京子　『アジアから来た花嫁』　明石書店、一九八八年。
東京新聞編集局編　『私たち幸せです・国際結婚一一二話』　東京新聞出版局、一九九七年。
澤岻悦子　『オキナワ　海を渡った米兵花嫁たち』　高文研、二〇〇〇年。
竹下修子　『国際結婚の社会学』　学文社、二〇〇〇年。
玉垣洋一　『フィリピーナと結婚すること——笑いと涙！恋愛と生活の秘密』　乃木坂出版、一九九五年。
財団法人　入管協会　『在留外国人統計　平成八年版』　一九九六年。
同右　『在留外国人統計　平成十二年版』　二〇〇〇年。
日高博　『ビビンバ家族』　海拓舎、二〇〇〇年。
新田文輝　「国際結婚とこどもたち　異文化と共存する家族」　明石書店、一九九二年。
同右　「最近の日本における国際結婚——接近と交換理論を中心とした試論」『吉備国際大学社会学部研究紀要』五、
　　九五-一〇九、一九九五年。
林かおり・田村恵子・高津文美子　『戦争花嫁——国境を超えた女たちの半世紀』　芙蓉書房出版、二〇〇二年。
Breger, R. & Hill, R. *Cross-Cultural Marriage: Identity and Choice* Berg.Oxfrod / New York, 1998.
久田恵　『フィリピーナを愛した男たち』　文春文庫、一九九二年。
フセイン栄子ほか　『アジアン・パートナー』　スリーエーネットワーク、一九九七年。
パターソン林屋晶子　『レポート国際結婚』　知恵の森文庫、二〇〇一年。

松村章子『バリ結婚物語』情報センター出版局、一九九八年。

三島市『三島市の統計 二〇〇〇』二〇〇〇年。

宮島喬・長谷川洋子「在日フィリピン人女性の結婚・家族問題——カウンセリングの事例から」『応用社会学研究』四十二号 立教大学社会学部、二〇〇〇年。

山下普司《南》へ——バリ観光のなかの日本人」岩波講座 文化人類学七 『移動の民族誌』青木保他編 岩波書店 三十二-五十九頁、一九九六年。

水野潮『ドリアンの木の下で』Aree Books、一九九九年。

山田鐐一他『わかりやすい国際結婚と法』有斐閣、一九九五年。

山谷哲夫『じゃぱゆきさん』情報センター出版局、一九八五年。

ヤンソン由実子『国際結婚 愛が国境を越えるとき』PHP研究所、一九八一年。

嘉本伊都子「国際結婚をめぐる諸問題——「境界線上」の家族」『家族社会学研究』八、五十三-六十六、一九九六年。

同上「「国際結婚」の歴史社会学的類型」『社会学評論』四十八(1)、六十二-八十二、一九九七年。

同上『国際結婚の誕生』新曜社、二〇〇一年。

表1 平成12年度版在留外国人統計（p.15）

[第11表]　「日本人の配偶者等」の外国人登録者数の推移　　　　（各年末現在）

国籍(出身地)	平成7年 (1995)	平成8年 (1996)	平成9年 (1997)	平成10年 (1998)	平成11年 (1999)	構成比 (%)	対前年末 増減率(%)
総　　数	244,381	258,847	274,475	264,844	270,775	100.0	2.2
ブラジル	99,803	106,665	113,319	98,823	97,330	35.9	−1.5
中　　国	37,310	39,948	43,714	45,913	48,698	18.0	6.1
フィリピン	39,909	42,521	44,545	45,619	46,152	17.1	1.2
韓国・朝鮮	21,385	21,090	20,738	21,078	21,753	8.0	3.2
タ　　イ	7,004	7,881	8,955	9,878	11,100	4.1	12.4
そ の 他	38,970	40,742	43,204	43,533	45,742	16.9	5.1

[第6図]　「日本人の配偶者等」の外国人登録者数の推移

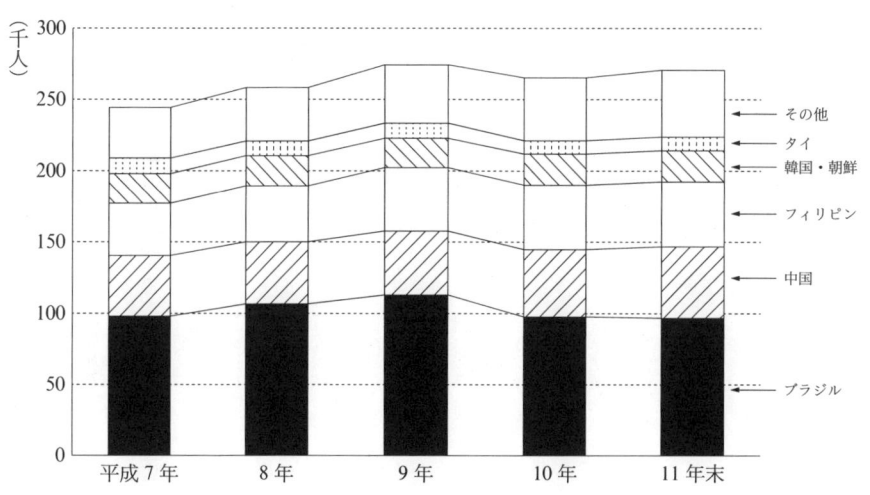

表2 日本人同士および外国人との結婚

	夫妻とも日本人	夫日本人・妻外国人	妻日本人・夫外国人
1965	950,696 (99.6)	1,067 (0.1)	3,089 (0.3)
1996	936,144 (99.6)	1,056 (0.1)	2,920 (0.3)
1967	948,611 (99.5)	1,384 (0.1)	3,137 (0.3)
1968	951,528 (99.5)	1,460 (0.2)	3,324 (0.3)
1969	979,063 (99.5)	1,719 (0.2)	3,360 (0.3)
1970	1,023,859 (99.5)	2,108 (0.2)	3,438 (0.3)
1971	1,085,639 (99.5)	2,350 (0.2)	3,240 (0.3)
1972	1,093,988 (99.5)	2,674 (0.2)	3,322 (0.3)
1973	1,065,730 (99.4)	2,849 (0.3)	3,344 (0.3)
1974	994,096 (99.4)	3,177 (0.3)	3,182 (0.3)
1975	935,583 (99.4)	3,222 (0.3)	2,823 (0.3)
1976	865,221 (99.3)	3,467 (0.4)	2,855 (0.3)
1977	814,958 (99.3)	3,501 (0.4)	2,570 (0.3)
1978	786,977 (99.2)	3,620 (0.5)	2,660 (0.3)
1979	781,774 (99.1)	3,912 (0.5)	2,810 (0.4)
1980	767,441 (99.1)	4,386 (0.6)	2,875 (0.4)
1981	768,774 (99.0)	4,813 (0.6)	2,944 (0.4)
1982	772,296 (98.9)	5,697 (0.7)	3,259 (0.4)
1983	752,101 (98.6)	7,000 (0.9)	3,451 (0.5)
1984	729,483 (98.6)	6,828 (0.9)	3,680 (0.5)
1985	723,669 (98.3)	7,738 (1.1)	4,443 (0.6)
1986	698,433 (98.2)	8,255 (1.2)	4,274 (0.6)
1987	681,589 (97.9)	10,176 (1.5)	4,405 (0.6)
1988	690,844 (97.2)	12,267 (1.7)	4,695 (0.5)
1989	685,473 (96.3)	17,800 (2.5)	5,043 (0.7)
1990	696,512 (95.9)	20,026 (2.6)	5,600 (0.7)
1991	717,105 (96.1)	19,096 (2.6)	6,063 (0.8)
1992	728,579 (96.0)	19,423 (2.6)	6,439 (0.8)

(厚生省大臣官房統計情報部人口動態統計 1994；新田文輝 1995：97)

表4　三島の統計

16．年次別の外国人登録世帯と人口

(各年12月31日現在)

年次	世帯	人口		
		男性	女性	合計
平成9	613	581	540	1,121
10	501	517	480	997
11	490	501	493	994

(資料/市民課)

17．国籍別の外国人登録人口

(平成11年12月31日現在)

国籍	男性	女性	計	国籍	男性	女性	計
アルゼンティン	12	6	18	タイ	10	15	25
オーストラリア	1	2	3	英国	3	1	4
ブラジル	131	113	244	米国	10	8	18
カナダ	4	3	7	ボリヴィア	7	9	16
中国	63	54	117	イラン	1	0	1
フランス	2	0	2	パラグァイ	13	9	22
ドイツ	3	1	4	ロシア連邦	2	2	4
インド	2	2	4	バングラデシュ	1	0	1
インドネシア	37	5	42	モロッコ	1	0	1
韓国	124	117	241	ウズベキスタン	1	0	1
朝鮮	6	15	21	南アフリカ	1	0	1
ラオス	25	25	50				
マレイシア	1	6	7				
オランダ	1	0	1				
ニュー・ジランド	2	1	3				
パキスタン	6	1	7				
ペルー	27	23	50				
フィリピン	2	71	73				
ポーランド	0	1	1				
シンガポール	0	2	2				
スペイン	1	1	2	合計	501	493	994

(資料/市民課)

表4 フィリピン女性の滞在年数と子供の数
(1998年)

	フィリピン女性（仮名）	年齢	子供の数と年齢	滞在年数
1	マルタ	34歳	0	8年
2	セシル	39歳	4人（本国）	8年
3	エニー	30歳	2人	9年
4	テッシー	31歳	2人（2歳、9歳）	9年
5	マリアン	―	1人（7歳）	10年
6	マリール	―	0	11年
7	ステラ	46歳	3人（12・15・17歳）	16年
8	イダ	―	1人（8歳）	21年
9	アグネス	42歳	2人（15歳、20歳）	21年

執筆者紹介（執筆順）

秋山正幸　あきやま・まさゆき
日本大学常務理事。日本大学教授、スペイン国立バリヤドリード大学名誉教授、博士（国際関係）、英語英文学博士（Ph. D）著書に『ヘンリー・ジェイムズ作品研究』、『ヘンリー・ジェイムズの国際小説研究─異文化の遭遇と相剋』、『ヘンリー・ジェイムズの世界─アメリカ・ヨーロッパ、東洋』 *A Study of Narrative Techniques: Comparative Approaches to Works of Henry James and Selected Japanese Authors* など。

川本皓嗣　かわもと・こうじ
帝塚山学院大学教授。東京大学名誉教授、博士（比較文学）。著書に『日本詩歌の伝統─七と五の詩学』（英訳版 *The Poetics of Japanese Verse: Imagery, Structure, Meter*）、『岩波セミナーブックス アメリカの詩を読む』、共著『アメリカ名詩選』、共編著『文学の方法』、『翻訳の方法』、『芭蕉解体新書』など。

亀井俊介　かめい・しゅんすけ
岐阜女子大学教授、東京大学名誉教授。著書に『近代文学におけるホイットマンの運命』、『サーカスが来た！ アメリカ大衆文化覚書』、『日米文化交渉史覚書』、『メリケンからアメリカへ』、『アメリカン・ヒーローの系譜』、『亀井俊介の仕事』（全五巻）、『アメリカ文化と日本』、編著に『近代日本の翻訳文化』（叢書・比較文学比較文化3）など。

富田　仁　とみた・ひとし
日本大学法学部教授。日本仏学史学会長。著書に『作品にみる東西文学の接点』、『日本近代比較文学史』、『フランス小説移入考』、『鹿鳴館擬西洋化の世界』、『フランス語事始─村上英俊とその時代』、『舶来事物起原事典』、『海外交流史事典』、（編）『海外交流史事典』（編）など多数。

佐藤三武朗　さとう・さぶろう
日本大学教授、日本大学副総長、国際関係学部長、博士（国際関係）。著書として『ハムレット』、上下巻、『フランス詩集』、小説『天城恋唄』、『海が消える』など。論文として "Hamlet, Polonius and Ophelia in Meiji Japan"、『文学界』時代における藤村とシェイクスピア』ほか。

藤澤　全　ふじさわ・まさし
日本大学国際関係学部教授。博士（国際関係）。著書に『啄木哀果とその時代』、『日系文学の研究』『若き日の井上靖研究』 *Japanese Immigrant-Emigrant Literature*, *Comparative Studies of Yassushi Inoue and Others* など。

諸坂成利　もろさか・しげとし
日本大学法学部助教授。主要論文に「〈換喩〉としての「虎狩」─中島敦とボルヘス・ナボコフ」、「ギャスケルにおける《母》＝《大地》─ドストエフスキイ、フォークナー、カミュと」、「ポルヘスの比較文学」、「日本におけるギャスケル─過去の受容と将来性」、「翻訳・夢・引用─ボルヘスの翻訳論」、「〈受け入れる〉─非＝自己を *Faulkner* の *Light in August* から」、「フォークナーと福永武彦─影の部分」、「代表作人バートルビー」序論─」など。

榎本義子　えのもと・よし
フェリス女学院大学教授。訳書に『キダー書簡集』。主要論文に「シャーロット・ブロンテの「滅びと異郷の比較文化」所収」、「ベルギー体験」、「E・M・キダーの教育における異文化融合の試み」（異文化交流と近代化』所収）、"A Woman Missionary's Vision: Conflict and Harmony between Two Cultures" (*The Force of Vision 2* 所収）など。

安藤重和　あんどう・しげかず
日本大学法学部教授。著書に、『欧米文学交流の諸様相』（分担執筆）、『欧米文学を読む』、共著、『異文化との出会い』（編著書）、「思考する感覚」（編著書）

長谷川勉　はせがわ・つとむ
日本大学法学部教授。日本大学にて博士号取得（国際関係）。著書に『ファウストの比較文学的研究序説』、『ファウストの変容及び交差と比較に関する研究』、『魔術師ファウストの転生』、『ドイツ語圏の社会と文化』、『比較文学とその周辺』、『手塚治虫氏に関する八つの誤解』など。論文に「『嵐が丘』に提示される思想（I、II、III）、『厭世文学と諷刺の方法』、「E・A・ポーの方法的想像力（I、II、III）」、「D・H・ロレンスの原始回帰と異文体験」、「ポーの終末論と黙示録的世界」など。

田中徳一　たなか・とくいち
日本大学国際関係学部教授。著書に『演劇は異文化の架け橋』、訳書にサン・キョン・リー、論文に「ブレヒトの『肝っ玉おっ母』に見る歌舞伎的要素」、「男は男─東西演劇の出合い」など。

だ」に見るブレヒトと歌舞伎の関係」、「筒井徳二郎一座の欧米巡業旅程」、「筒井徳二郎一座海外巡業のレパートリー」、「アメリカのニュース映画に見る筒井徳二郎一座」、「旅回り役者・筒井徳二郎の足跡」など。

宗形賢二　むなかた・けんじ

日本大学国際関係学部助教授。共著に『比較文学の地平―東西の接触』、分担執筆『思考する感覚―イギリス・アメリカ文学のコンテクストから』（ドライサーの劇場都市―『シスター・キャリー』とショーウインドーの誘惑）、論文「アメリカ世紀末文学の都市と博覧会の眼差し」、「19世紀転換期のオリエンタリズム―Madame Butterfly と J. L. Long について」など。

羽田美也子　はだ・みやこ

日本大学国際関係学部非常勤講師。同校にて博士号（国際関係）取得（ph. D. 2000）。主要論文に「近代女流文学の深層―初期アメリカ小説との比較において」、「明治前半期におけるイデオロギーとしての女性政策」、「ヨーロッパとアメリカのジャポニズム文学」、「アメリカにおけるジャポニズム文学の研究」など。

松井洋子　まつい・ようこ

日本大学短期大学部教授。訳書『人生の皮肉』〈短篇集〉（共訳）、論文『金色夜叉』と『ホワイト・リリース』日米比較文学研究序説」、「黒岩涙香の教養小説、家庭小説における『バーサ・クレイ受容―『妾の罪』を中心に」、「Adapted Stories in the Meiji Era in Japan」など。

A・H・バウマン

日本大学国際関係学部教授（日欧文化交流史）。主要論文に「ハンス・ヴォルフガング・ブラウンの業績とその歴史的背景」、「Petrus Hartsingius Japonensis, A Critical Biography"、"日本における初滞在プロシア領事マックス・フォン・ブラント"、"ゲルトナーの日記"など。

梅本順子　うめもと・じゅんこ

日本大学国際関係学部教授。著書に『浦島コンプレックス―ラフカディオ・ハーンの交友と文学』、共著に『比較文学の地平』、論文に"Lafcadio Hearn and Urashima"、"The Liberation of Women in Works Retold by Lafcadio Hearn"、"ラフカディオ・ハーンとレオナ・ケイロウセ」、「ラフカディオ・ハーンの伝記執筆を巡る問題に関する一考察」など。

佐藤マサ子　さとう・まさこ

日本大学国際関係学部教授。学術博士（お茶の水女子大学）、Ph. D. （ハンブルク大学）。著書に『カール・フローレンツの日本研究』、Karl Florenz in Japan—Auf den Spuren einer vergessenen Quelle der modernen japanischen Geistesgeschichte und Poetik 等。論文に「『虫の声』をめぐる感性の成立―日本的文化規範システム (habitus) の形成をめぐって―」など。

小田切文洋　おだぎり・ふみひろ

日本大学大学院総合社会情報研究科・国際関係学部教授。著書に『渡米した天台僧達』、論文に「『唐鏡』における漢籍受用の一考察」、「物語文学における双子譚的な要素の展開」など。

高橋綾子　たかはし・あやこ

日本大学国際関係学部国際文化学科卒業。現在、新潟大学大学院現代社会研究科博士後期課程在学中。現在「ゲイリー・スナイダーにおける越境性」というテーマで博士論文準備中。論文に「寒山像を巡って―ゲイリー・スナイダーの英訳寒山」、「ゲイリー・スナイダーの場所の感覚」、"Shaping of Ecological Consciousness on Gary Snyder"など。

高橋　章　たかはし・あきら

日本大学国際関係学部国際文化学科教授。著書に「宗教と文学」、共著に「詩人哲学者 吉満義彦」、主要論文に、"Ishikawa Takuboku and Christianity"、"Raphael Koeber and Christianity"、"Arishima Takeo and Christianity"、"The Information Age and Ethics"などがある。

大泉光一　おおいずみ・こういち

日本大学国際関係学部・大学院国際関係研究科教授。主要著書に『クライシス・マネジメント―危機管理の理論と実践』、『危機管理学研究』、『企業危機管理の理論と実践』、『テロリストの世界地図』、『海外ビジネスマンの危機管理術』、『国際テロの標的』、『テロ対策の知識と実際』、『バスク民族の抵抗』、『狙われる日本人』、『グローバル化する国際犯罪と警備対策』、『海外ビジネスにおける危機管理のノウハウ』など。

小田　司　おだ・つかさ

日本大学法学部助教授。法学博士（ドイツ・ヨハネス・グーテンベルク大学）。著書に Die Prozeßfähigkeit als Voraussetzung und Gegenstand des Verfahrens (Carl Heymanns Verlag 1997). 論文に"Beweis der Prozeßfähigkeit"、"Begriff und Funktion der Prozeßfähigkeit bis zur Reichscivilprozeßordnung von 1877"、"ドイ

ツ民事訴訟における訴訟能力の問題点」、「民事執行手続における訴訟能力の諸問題」、「執行機関による訴訟能力についての調査権限と訴訟能力の欠缺を理由とする救済手段」など。

前田利光 まえだ・としみつ

日本大学国際関係学部・大学院教授・経済学博士。著書に『歴史認識と国際政治経済危機の深層』、『資本主義発展における人間と自然』、『世界経済の変動と日本経済』、『経済発展と資本の理論』、『日本資本主義と土地問題』、『世界経済危機と労働者・農民』、『日本経済史』(共著)。主要論文に「融合化する国際通貨価値格変動・情報革命・地球環境問題」(総合政策研究・第8号)ほか。

小林　通 こばやし・とおる

日本大学国際関係学部教授。博士(国際関係)。著書に『現代国際経済システムの原点と構図』、『国際経済の新視点』、『外国貿易論』。翻訳に『M・ジョーンズ国際貿易と国際収支』、『ジョーン・ロビンソン国際貿易論の省察』、『テリー・クックM&A成功戦略』、"Some Aspects for the Reform of the Common Agricultural Policy"など。

吉田正紀 よしだ・まさのり

日本大学国際関係学部教授。イリノイ大学大学院博士号取得(文化人類学・Ph.D. 1990)。著書に『民俗医療の人類学―東南アジアの医療システム』、共著に *Structuralism's Transformation*、『オセアニア 2　伝統に生きる』、『食と健康の文化人類学』など。訳書に『千年王国と未開社会―メラネシアのカーゴカルト運動』、共訳に『文化人類学―人間状況への視角 I、II』。

(職名は二〇〇三年二月現在)